BOARD OF EDUCATION, SOUTH KENSINGTON,
LONDON, S.W.

SCIENCE EXAMINATIONS, 1906.

REPORTS, &c.

REPORTS OF THE EXAMINERS ON THE SCIENCE EXAMINATIONS, AND SUMMARIES OF THE RESULTS. NAMES OF SUCCESSFUL CANDIDATES IN THE COMPETITIONS FOR ROYAL EXHIBITIONS, NATIONAL SCHOLARSHIPS, FREE STUDENTSHIPS, AND WHITWORTH SCHOLARSHIPS AND EXHIBITIONS.

LONDON:
PRINTED FOR HIS MAJESTY'S STATIONERY OFFICE,
BY WYMAN & SONS, LIMITED, FETTER LANE, E.C.

And to be purchased, either directly or through any Bookseller, from
WYMAN AND SONS, LTD., FETTER LANE, E.C.; or
OLIVER AND BOYD, EDINBURGH; or
R. PONSONBY, 116, GRAFTON STREET, DUBLIN.

1906.

Price Sixpence.

CONTENTS.

GROUP I.—PURE AND APPLIED MATHEMATICS.

BOARD OF EXAMINERS.

V.—Pure Mathematics	Rev. J. F. Twisden, M.A., *Chairman*.
VI.—Theoretical Mechanics	A. R. Willis, M.A., D.Sc.
XX.—Navigation	P. T. Wrigley, M.A.
XXI.—Spherical and Nautical Astronomy	Major P. A. Macmahon, F.R.S. H. B. Goodwin, M.A., late R.N.

Report on the Examinations in Pure Mathematics.

EVENING EXAMINATIONS.

STAGE 1.

Results : 1st Class, 632 ; 2nd Class, 1,138 ; Failed, 1,423 ; Total, 3,193.

A.

The questions in ARITHMETIC were, perhaps, a little harder than usual. Those most frequently attempted were Questions 1 and 3. The latter contains two questions on the metrical system of measures, which were often correctly answered.

Q. 2. Find by contracted multiplication the product of 32·5467 and 2·4918 so as to obtain the product true to four decimal places.

Express as a decimal

$$\frac{1}{2^2} + \frac{1}{3^3} + \frac{1}{4^4} + \frac{1}{5^5},$$

and find the square root of the expression true to four decima places.

From this question it would appear that more attention is paid to contracted work than was formerly the case, so that several good answers were sent up to the first part of the question. Very few treated the second part properly.

Q. 4. A rectangular box measures externally (when the lid is down) 4 ft. long, 2½ ft. wide, 1½ ft. high ; it is made of wood an inch thick. Taking account of the wood only, find the ratio of the weight of the lid to the weight of the whole box.

By how much does the ratio exceed $\frac{1}{4}$?

Is an easy question in the mensuration of rectangles ; it requires care and a correct appreciation of the data ; these were often wanting, and so there were many failures, but the right result (81/308) was obtained fairly often.

Q. 6. An alloy of silver is mixed with an alloy of gold in the ratio of 57 to 13 ; the percentage of lead in the silver alloy is 13·75 and that in the gold alloy 16·25 ; what is the percentage of lead in the mixture ?

Was answered correctly in a good many cases ; but only by those who otherwise did well.

On the whole the work in Arithmetic was well done.

9201.   4,000—Wt. 7762.   12/03.   Wy. & S.   4971r.   A

B.

The book work in GEOMETRY was, on the whole, fairly well done. The deductions and problems came in for a good deal of attention and were done well by one and another.

Q. 7. *BC* is the base of an isosceles triangle *ABC*, and *D* is the middle point of *BC*; show that the straight line *AD* is perpendicular to *BC*.

Define a triangle, an isosceles triangle, and a right angle.

Was, of course, very often taken. The work, however, was marked by some very prevalent faults, viz.: (*a*) It was very often said that in the triangles *ABD* and *ACD*, the sides *AB*, *AC* are equal, *AD* common, and the angle *ABD* equal to *ACD*, therefore the triangles are equal in all respects. (*b*) The definitions were often faulty, *e.g.* a triangle was defined as a figure having three sides; an isosceles triangle as a triangle having two equal sides and two equal angles; a right angle as an angle of 90°. It hardly admits of a doubt that the prevalence of such faults as (*a*) and (*b*) proves that the teaching in many schools was not good.

Q. 8. If two straight lines cut one another, show that the vertically opposite angles are equal.

A and *B* being two points on the same side of a straight line *PQ*, from *A* a perpendicular *AC* is drawn to *PQ*, and is produced to *D* so that *CD* is equal to *AC*; show that, if *DB* cuts *PQ* in *E*, the straight lines *AE*, *BE* make equal angles with *PQ*.

The second part of the question is given in most text books; both the first and second parts were very often answered.

Q. 9. Two triangles have equal bases, and the angles at the base of one triangle are equal to the angles at the base of the other triangle, each to each; show that the triangles are equal in all respects.

ABCD is a parallelogram, and in *DC* or *DC* produced a point *E* is taken such that *BE* is equal to *BC*; also *CA*, *EA*, and *BD* are joined; show that the angle *CAE* equals the difference between the angles *DCA* and *DBA*.

In reference to the first part of this question, it is worth noticing that the proof by superposition (in itself, of course, a good proof) did not seem to be as well understood as the proof by a *reductio ad absurdum*.

The second part is, perhaps, harder than it looks; it was very occasionally well answered, *e.g.*, there were four good answers in about 400 consecutive papers.

Q. 10. Define parallelograms about a diagonal of a parallelogram, and the complements of those parallelograms.

Show that the complements of the parallelograms about a diagonal of any parallelogram are equal to one another.

In a given parallelogram construct complements each three-sixteenths of the area of the parallelogram.

Q. 11. Define a square. *E*, *F*, *G*, *H* are the middle points of the sides of a square *ABCD*; show that *EFGH* is a square.

Hence, in the particular case when a right-angled triangle has two equal sides, show that the square on the hypotenuse equals the sum of the squares on the other two sides.

Q. 12. *ADEF* is a rhombus, having the angle at *A* a little greater than a right angle, and *B* and *C* are points in *DE* and *EF* respectively such that *ABC* is an equilateral triangle; if *ADEF* be such that a side of it equals a side of the triangle *ABC*, show that the angle *DEF* is ten-ninths of a right angle.

These three questions elicited a few good answers, particularly the first parts of Q's. 10 and 11. The force of the word "Hence" in Q. 11 was not felt by more than a very few, but most of those few found the required answer easily.

3

C.

In ALGEBRA the questions most frequently attempted were Q's. 13, 15, 16, 17, and on the whole they were well done.

Q. 13. (a) From
$$5x^3 - 6x^2 + 7x - 8$$
take the sum of
$$9x^3 - 7x^2 - 5x + 3 \text{ and } - 10x^3 - 8x^2 + 6x + 4.$$

(b) If
$$x = -\frac{1}{4},$$
find the numerical values of the three given expressions and of the remainder you have obtained, and show that the excess of the first value over the sum of the second and third values equals the fourth value.

There were very many failures in the numerical substitutions. The first part of the question was correct in most cases.

Q. 14. (a) Reduce
$$(x^3 - 7x + 12)(x - 1) - (x^2 - 4x + 3)$$
to its simplest form. Also show that it is the product of three factors.

(b) If we suppose that x stands for a positive whole number, show that the three factors are either three consecutive even numbers or three consecutive odd numbers.

Was commonly avoided.

Q. 16. (a) Resolve the following expressions into their simplest factors :

(i) $x^2 + 9x - 52$.

(ii) $ax^3 - 4a^3x$.

(iii) $(a^2 + b^2 - c^2)^2 - 4a^2b^2$.

(b) Find two consecutive numbers such that the difference of their squares is 49.

(a) (iii). The expression was very seldom put into four factors, and in (b) it was curious to notice in how many cases $(x+1)^2$ was treated as if it were less than x^2.

Q. 18. A man has a certain number of horses, all of the same value ; also he has seven more cows than he has horses, and each cow is worth two-thirds as much as a horse. If he had the same total number of horses and cows but seven more horses than cows, the whole value of the animals would have been 56*l.* more in the latter case than in the former. Find the value of one of the horses.

Why cannot you determine the number of horses, as well as the value of each, from the data ?

Is an easy question, and sometimes the value of one horse was found. The second part of the question proved difficult, *e.g.*, in about four hundred consecutive papers the point was explained only twice.

STAGE 2.

Results : 1st Class, 241 ; 2nd Class, 899 ; Failed, 843 ; Total, 1,983.

Each question was attempted fairly often ; but Q's. 25, 26, 30, 32, 38, and in some schools Q. 36 were attempted markedly less often than the others. Still the work was, on the whole, good or fairly good ; though, if estimated by the number of candidates who get 120 marks and upwards, it is not so good as it was last year. It may be added that several of the questions set this year are quite easy, *e.g.*, Q's. 21, 22, 25, 27, 28, 31, not to mention others.

9291.   A 2

A.

In GEOMETRY the book work was well written out, with the exception
given below :—

Q. 22. Define a sector of a circle, a segment of a circle, and similar
segments of two different circles :—

    (a) C is the middle point of the line joining two given points
A and B ; a circle is drawn whose circumference passes
through A and B ; show that its centre must be on the
line drawn through C at right angles to AB.

    (b) Two unequal circles are in the same plane and their
centres coincide ; show that the one must lie entirely
within the other.

In Q. 22, the reasoning was in many cases given as if the writers had not
made up their minds as to the point that they are required to prove.

Q. 24. Show how to describe a circle about a given triangle.

    Given the diameter of the circle circumscribing a triangle, an
angle of the triangle, and one of the sides containing the angle,
show how to construct the triangle.

    Show also that there is an ambiguity in the construction
exactly resembling that in the ambiguous case of the solution
of triangles.

The "ambiguity" was seldom or never well explained.

Q. 25. $ABCD$ is a parallelogram, and from B a line is drawn to cut CD
or CD produced in E ; from A a line is drawn at right angles
to BE meeting it in F. Show that the area of $ABCD$ equals
that of the rectangle under BE and AF.

Is a very easy question. Thus, if AE is drawn, the rectangle AF, BC
is twice the triangle ABE ; also the parallelogram $ABCD$, is twice the same
triangle ; and therefore the rectangle is equal to the parallelogram. In
fact the whole difficulty consists in drawing the line AE, yet in about 500
consecutive papers there were only 35 answers to the question.

B

In ALGEBRA the following points deserve notice :—

Q. 27. (a) If

$$\frac{a}{b+c} = \frac{b}{c+a}$$

show that either

$$a = b, \text{ or } a + b + c = 0.$$

    (b) If

$$a^3 - b^3 + ab(a - b) = m(a^2 - b^2),$$

show that either

$$a = \pm b, \text{ or } a = m - b.$$

In (a) scarcely anyone put the equation into the form

$$(a-b)(a+b+c)=0,$$

and hence deduced the alternative conclusion, either

$$a=b \text{ or } a+b+c=0.$$

So also in (b).

Q. 28. (a) Extract the square root of

$$15 - 4\sqrt{14}.$$

    (b) Express the quotient of

$$10\sqrt{6} - 2\sqrt{7}$$

divided by

$$3\sqrt{6} + 2\sqrt{7}$$

in its simplest surd form, and find the value of the expression
as a decimal correct to four significant figures.

N.B.— $\sqrt{42}=6{\cdot}4807$.

5

(c) Show that
$$\sqrt{(13 + 3\sqrt{13})} + \sqrt{(13 - 3\sqrt{13})} = \sqrt{(26 + 4\sqrt{13})}.$$
The surds were, on the whole, well handled.

Q. 29. Solve the following equations :—

(a) $3x + 4\sqrt{(169 - x^2)} = 56.$

(b) $\dfrac{(x + a)^2 + (x - b)^2}{(x + a)^2 - (x - b)^2} = \dfrac{a^2 + b^2}{2ab}$.

(c) $\dfrac{x - 1}{x + 1} = \dfrac{2y}{9}$, $\dfrac{y - 1}{y + 1} = \dfrac{x}{10}$.

The equations (a) and (c) were solved fairly often ; in (b) one root was sometimes found ; both roots, seldom or never.

Q. 32. When are quantities said to be in continued proportion ?

If five quantities a, b, c, d, e, are in continued proportion, show that the ratio of the first to the last is the fourth power of the ratio of any two consecutive quantities.

Show also that c is a mean proportional between a and e and that
$$ab + bc + cd + de$$
is a mean proportional between
$$a^2 + b^2 + c^2 + d^2 \quad \text{and} \quad b^2 + c^2 + d^2 + e^2.$$
Was well answered in a few schools, but it was not often taken.

C.

In TRIGONOMETRY the work was on the whole fairly good.

Q. 33. Explain why the logarithm of the product of two numbers is equal to the sum of the logarithms of the numbers.

By means of logarithms given below, find the fifth root, and the fifth power of 0·69889 correct to five decimal places.

If
$$4 \log_{10} x + 7 = 0,$$
find x.

If
$$y \log_{10}0·0424 = \log_{10}0·2165,$$
find y to four places of decimals.

The work requiring logarithms was often well done, and in particular, though there were many failures, x and y were calculated quite as often as could be fairly expected.

Q. 34. Draw an appropriate diagram, and from it find the numerical values of the sine, cosine, and tangent of an angle of 45°.

Find also the true logarithm and the tabular logarithm of sin 45° and of tan 45°.

If A be any angle between 0° and 90°, find tan A in terms of sin A, and also in terms of cos A.

Q. 35. Show, in a carefully drawn diagram, an angle 234°, and explain, with reference to your diagram, why both the sine and the cosine of that angle are negative.

Assuming that sin 36° 56' is 0·6, and that cos 36° 56' is 0·8, find the angle whose sine is −0·6 and whose cosine is + 0·8.

Find from the annexed table the numerical value of sin 326° 42'.

These two questions came in for many good answers, though, of course, there were failures as to one or other of the points involved, and in particular, very few found that the numerical value of sin 326° 42' is −0·54902.

Q. 36. Establish the following identities :—

(a) $\sin^4 A + \cos^2 A = \cos^4 A + \sin^2 A$.

(b) $\sin^2 A \tan^2 A = \tan^2 A - \sin^2 A$.

(c) $\sin A \cos A = \dfrac{\tan A}{1 + \tan^2 A}$.

(d) $\dfrac{\cos^2 A - \sin^2 B}{\sin^2 A \sin^2 B} = \dfrac{1}{\tan^2 A \tan^2 B} - 1$.

Was well answered in some schools.

Q. 37. Two points A and B are 2,000 yards apart on a straight road, and P is a flagstaff off the road ; it is found that the angles PAB and PBA are 33° 18′ and 105° 20′ respectively.

Calculate the distance BP, and the number of square yards in the triangle ABP.

Was often well answered, but the first part more often than the second.

Q. 38. Show that the area of a quadrilateral is equal to the area of a triangle having two sides equal to the diagonals of the quadrilateral, and the included angle equal to either of the angles between the diagonals.

Find the area of the quadrilateral in which the diagonals are 216·5 ft. and 447·5 ft. long respectively, and are inclined to each other at an angle of 116° 30′.

Was answered very occasionally.

STAGE 3.

Results : 1st Class, 154 ; 2nd Class, 461 ; Failed, 253 ; Total, 868.

The results are distinctly better than those of last year. The work on the whole was satisfactory, and in many of the schools the teaching has been good.

A.

Q. 41. If a straight line cut two sides of a triangle proportionally show that it is parallel to the third side.

Show how, through a given point, to draw a straight line such that the part of it intercepted by two given straight lines is divided in a given ratio at the point.

Draw a triangle ABC whose sides AB, BC and CA are respectively 2, 2½ and 3 inches long ; find a point P in AB such that AP is to PB as 4 to 7, and construct a straight line PQ to meet AC produced in Q so that PQ is bisected by BC.

Q. 42. State the conditions under which two rectilineal figures are said to be similar.

Show that these conditions are satisfied in the case of two triangles which have the angles of the one respectively equal to the angles of the other.

Show also that polygons which are equiangular to one another are not necessarily similar, but that polygons which are similar to the same polygon must be similar to each other.

Q. 44. A quadrilateral is inscribed in a circle ; show that the rectangle under the diagonals is equal to the sum of the rectangles under the opposite sides.

A, B, C, D are four points in order on the circumference of a circle, and A and C are fixed, but B and D move in such a way that the sum of the rectangle under AB and CD and that under BC and DA is constant ; find the locus of a point which divides BD into parts having a given ratio to each other.

These three questions were those usually selected ; the propositions were nearly always well written out, and there were a good many solutions of the riders.

Q. 43. If A, B, P are three given lines ; show how, by a geometrical construction, to draw a line Q, such that A^3 may be to B^3 as P to Q.

Q. 45. AB is a chord of a circle, and tangents at A and B intersect at P ; through P a straight line is drawn to cut the circumference at Q, AB at R, and the circumference again at S. If N is the middle point of QS, show that QN is a mean proportional to PN and NR.

Q. 46. If through a fixed point O a straight line be drawn to meet a given straight line in P, and on OP a point Q be taken so that the rectangle $OP.OQ$ is constant, show that the locus of Q is a circle.

In a Peaucellier's cell, OA, OC are two equal rods, and AB, BC, CD, DA four other equal rods, the six rods being hinged together at the points O, A, B, C, D ; show that in all positions of the rods, the rectangle $OD. OB$ is constant. If O be fixed and B move in a straight line, what is the path of D ?

Q. 43 and 45 were well answered several times, and a few of the best candidates answered Q. 46 correctly.

B.

Q. 47. (a) Simplify

$$\frac{x + 2x^{\frac{1}{3}}y^{\frac{1}{3}} + y -}{x^{\frac{1}{2}} + y^{\frac{1}{2}} + z^{\frac{1}{2}}}$$

(b) Find the value of

$$\sqrt{\frac{2}{3}} - \sqrt{\frac{9}{32}},$$

having given

$$\sqrt{6} = 2.4495, \quad \sqrt[3]{18} = 2.6207.$$

(c) Reduce to its simplest form

$$(x - \omega) (x - \omega^2) (x - \omega^3)$$

when

$$2\omega = - 1 + \sqrt{(-3)}.$$

Was frequently well done.

Q. 48. Resolve each of the following expressions into four factors :—

(a) $\frac{1}{3}\{ (a + b + c)^5 - a^5 - b^5 - c^5\}$

(b) $a^4 + b^4 + c^4 - 2b^2c^2 - 2c^2a^2 - 2a^2b^2.$

(c) $(a^2 + 2bc)^3 + (b^2 + 2ca)^3 + (c^2 + 2ab)^3 - 3(a^2 + 2bc) (b^2 + 2ca) (c^2 + 2ab).$

A fair number of candidates used the remainder theorem successfully with (a) ; many made out (b) ; and a few succeeded with (c).

Q. 49. Solve the equations :—

(a) $781x^{\frac{2}{3}} + 32x^{\frac{3}{2}} = 7776x^{-\frac{1}{6}}$

(b) $\dfrac{(a + b - x)^2 - a^2}{4b^2 - (a + b + x)^2} = \left(\dfrac{2a + b - x}{a + 3b + x}\right)^2$

(c) $x^2 - 2xy + 3y^2 = 3 (x - y), 2x^2 + xy - y^2 = 9 (x - y).$

The equations were fairly well solved, but in (b) the root $x = 2a + b$, and in (c) the solution $x = 0$, $y = 0$, were often left unnoticed.

Q. 50. If x_1, x_2 are the roots of the equation

$$(x - b) (x - c) + (x - c) (x - a) + (x - a) (x - b) = 0$$

find the value of

$$(x_1 - a) (x_2 - a) + (x_1 - b) (x_2 - b) + (x_1 - c) (x_2 - c).$$

Q. 51. (*a*) The sum of n terms of the series 1, 2, 3, 4, ... is 500500 ; find n.

   (*b*) Show that the sum of 100 terms of the geometrical progression

$$8, 12, 18, 27, \ldots$$

exceeds the sum of 100 terms of the arithmetical progression

$$8, 12, 16, 20, \ldots$$

   by

$$81 \ (1 \cdot 5)^{99} - 20616.$$

   (*c*) Find the harmonical progression whose third term is 5, and whose fifth term is 9.

These two questions were frequently answered in very good style.

Q. 52. Adopting the usual notation, assume that

$$(x + a)^n = x^n +_n C_1 \, ax^{n-1} +_n C_2 \, a^2 x^{n-2} + \ldots +_n C_n a^n.$$

and show that it follows from the assumption that

$$(x + a)^{n+1}$$
$$= x^{n+1} +_{n+1}C_1 ax^n +_{n+1}C_2 a^2 x^{n-1} + \ldots + \quad C_{n+1} a^{n+1}.$$

   State carefully the reasoning by which it can be shown hence that the Binomial Theorem is true for all positive integral values of n.

   Expand

$$\left(1 + 2x + \frac{x^2}{2}\right)^8$$

in ascending powers of x, as far as x^4 (inclusive).

Was not often well done. A clear statement of the reasoning was rarely made, and in the example numerical mistakes often occurred. More attention ought to be paid to the Binomial Theorem.

C.

Q. 53. (*a*) Show, from a geometrical construction, that

$$\sin 2A = 2 \sin A \cos A,$$

   where $2A$ is less than a right angle.

   (*b*) If A is an angle between one and two right angles, show, without a new diagram, that the formula just given holds good.

   (*c*) Express $\cos^2 2A \sin 2A$ in terms of $\sin 6A$ and $\sin 2A$.

(*a*) and (*c*) were well answered, though few made out (*b*) properly. Theorems on angles greater than a right angle are very difficult to most students, and require much careful teaching before they are clearly understood.

Q. 54. (*a*) Show that

$$\sin\theta = \frac{2t}{1 + t^2}, \text{ and } \cos\theta = \frac{1 - t^2}{1 + t^2} \text{ where } t \text{ denotes } \tan\frac{\theta}{2}.$$

   (*b*) Show that

$$\frac{1 - \cos\theta}{1 + \cos\theta} = \tan^2\frac{\theta}{2}, \text{ and } \frac{1 + \sin\theta}{1 - \sin\theta} = \tan^2\left(\frac{\pi}{4} + \frac{\theta}{2}\right).$$

   (*c*) If

$$\cos\theta = \frac{\cos\alpha - \cos\beta}{1 - \cos\alpha \cos\beta},$$

show that one value of $\tan\dfrac{\theta}{2}$ is $\tan\dfrac{\alpha}{2} \cotan\dfrac{\beta}{2}$.

Q. 55. Establish the formula

$$\sin 3A = 3 \sin A - 4 \sin^3 A.$$

Hence show that

(i) $$\sin x = 3^n \sin \frac{x}{3^n}$$
$$- 4 \left(\sin^3 \frac{x}{3} + 3 \sin^3 \frac{x}{3^2} + \dots + 3^{n-1} \sin^3 \frac{x}{3^n} \right)$$

(ii) $$\sin x - x + \frac{x^3}{6} > 3^n \left[\sin \frac{x}{3^n} - \frac{x}{3^n} + \frac{1}{6} \left(\frac{x}{3^n} \right)^3 \right];$$

where x denotes the measure, in radians, of an acute angle.

These two questions were attempted freely ; Q. 54 was often fully answered, and the first part of Q. 55 was nearly always done correctly, but there were not many answers to parts (i) and (ii) of the question.

Q. 56. In a triangle ABC a line is drawn to bisect the angle A and to meet BC in D ; find the length of AD in terms of a, b, and $\frac{1}{2} A$.

Show that twice the area of ABC equals

$$BC.AD \cos \tfrac{1}{2} (B - C).$$

Was answered a fair number of times.

Q. 57. (a) Show that the ratio of the radii of the inscribed and circumscribed circles of the triangle ABC is

$$4 \sin \frac{A}{2} \sin \frac{B}{2} \sin \frac{C}{2}.$$

(b) If the inscribed circle passes through the orthocentre, show that

$$\cos A \cos B \cos C = 4 \sin^2 \frac{A}{2} \sin^2 \frac{B}{2} \sin^2 \frac{C}{2}.$$

The first part (a) was often made out ; (b) was established now and then.

Q. 58. Find the number of angles in two regular polygons, such that an angle of the one may be six-sevenths of an angle of the other.

Of all pairs of polygons which satisfy this condition find the pair with the largest number of angles.

A good many answered the first part, and several were also successful with the second part.

STAGE 4.

Results : 1st Class, 5 ; 2nd Class, 4 ; Failed, 5 ; Total, 14.

The number of candidates was small, but the work as a whole was decidedly satisfactory.

The questions in Solid Geometry were generally answered rightly. In Descriptive Geometry the diagrams were carefully drawn, and, as a rule, full explanations were given of the methods of construction.

Good work was done by the candidates who took up Geometrical Conics, but only in three or four cases were the questions on Spherical Trigonometry really well answered.

HONOURS IN DIVISION I.

Results : 1st Class, 5 ; 2nd Class, 48 ; Failed, 52 ; Total, 105.

There were 105 Candidates who took the paper, i.e. thirteen more than there were last year.

All the questions were answered once at least, except Q. 84 (b), which was several times attempted in vain.

Q. 84. (a) Show that the sum of the squares of the coefficients in the expansion of $(1 + x)^n$ is

$$\frac{\lfloor 2n}{\lfloor n \, \lfloor n}$$

where n is a positive integer.

(b) Find the coefficient of x^{n+4} in the expansion of

$$(1 + x)^n \log (1 + x)$$

where $x^2 < 1$, and n is a positive integer.

(c) Show that the coefficient of x^n in the expansion of

$$\log (1 + x + x^2 + \ldots + x^{m-1})$$

is either

$$-\frac{m-1}{n} \text{ or } \frac{1}{n}$$

according as n is, or is not, a multiple of m.

Q. 89. (a) If a straight line drawn through S, one of the centres of similitude of two circles whose centres are C and C', cut one circle in P, Q, and the other in P', Q', show that the rectangles $SP . SQ'$ and $SQ . SP'$ are each equal to the rectangle contained by the tangents from S to the circles.

(b) Show how to describe a circle to pass through a given point and touch two given circles.

Q. 90. Given two sides of a quadrilateral inscribed in a circle and the ratio of the other two sides ; show how to construct the quadrilateral, (a) when the given sides are adjacent, (b) when the given sides are opposite.

In Q's. 89 and 90 the first parts were answered fairly often ; but there were very few correct answers to the second parts.

Q. 92. Two given circles have their centres at a distance d apart, one of them with centre I and radius r being entirely within the other, whose centre is O and radius R ; MN is a chord of the outer circle drawn so as to touch the inner circle, and C is the centre of the circle which passes through M, N, and I. Show that the locus of C is a circle of radius

$$\frac{R^2 - d^2}{2r}$$

having its centre at O.

Was answered far less often than might have been expected.

Q. 95. (a) Show that

$$\begin{vmatrix} \sin 2\alpha, & \cos \alpha, & \sin \alpha \\ \sin 2\beta, & \cos \beta, & \sin \beta \\ \sin 2\gamma, & \cos \gamma, & \sin \gamma \end{vmatrix}$$

$$= -4 \sin \frac{\beta - \gamma}{2} \sin \frac{\gamma - \alpha}{2} \sin \frac{\alpha - \beta}{2}$$
$$\times \{ \sin (\beta + \gamma) + \sin (\gamma + \alpha) + \sin (\alpha + \beta) \}$$

(*b*) If

$$\begin{vmatrix} \sin 2\alpha, & \cos\alpha, & \sin\alpha, & 1 \\ \sin 2\beta, & \cos\beta, & \sin\beta, & 1 \\ \sin 2\gamma, & \cos\gamma, & \sin\gamma, & 1 \\ \sin 2\delta, & \cos\delta, & \sin\delta, & 2 \end{vmatrix} = 0,$$

and if a, β, γ, δ, are different positive angles, each less than 2π, show that

$$\alpha + \beta + \gamma + \delta = n\pi,$$

when n is an integer.

(*a*) was well answered six times but (*b*) only once.

Nos. 71400 and 71202 sent up very good answers. It was No. 71400 who answered Q. 95 (*b*), and a very good answer it was.

As usual the candidates showed a distinct tendency to pay more attention to questions in Algebra (81–86) than to the other questions.

Stage 5.

Results : 1st Class, 79 ; 2nd Class, 198 ; Failed, 112 ; Total, 389.

The general results are good, but not quite as good as those of last year. The questions in Descriptive Geometry were taken fairly often, and the drawing was usually good, but the necessary explanations of the methods adopted were in many cases not clearly stated.

The work in the more elementary portions of Analytical Geometry showed a sound knowledge of the principles and methods of the subject, but want of accuracy in the arithmetical calculations frequently marred the results. In the more advanced part of the subject weakness was shown in dealing with the general equation of the second degree. Thus in the first of the two examples in

Q. 7. Interpret the equation

$$12x^2 - 2xy - 2y^2 + 14x + 8y - 6 = 0 ;$$

also show that

$$9x^2 + 24xy + 16y^2 - 170x - 185y + 625 = 0$$

represents a parabola having its vertex at (3, 4). Give a diagram in each case.

Very few candidates discovered that the left hand side of the former equation was the product of two linear factors, and even they were frequently unable to interpret the result.

In the Differential and Integral Calculus most of the work was very satisfactory.

Q. 8. Explain fully what is meant by a differential coefficient, and give an illustration taken from the motion of a point along a straight line.

Find, from first principles, the differential coefficient of x^3, and of $\cos x$.

Find

$$\frac{dy}{dx}$$

in the following cases :—

$$y = \tan 4x, \quad y = \frac{2 + x^3}{1 - x}, \quad y = xe^{-3x}, \quad y = \sin^{-1}\left(\frac{x}{2a}\right).$$

Q. 9. Find the equation of the tangent to the curve

$y = f(x)$ at the point $(x'y')$.

In the catenary

$$y = \frac{c}{2}\left(e^{\frac{x}{c}} + e^{-\frac{x}{c}}\right),$$

show that the length of the perpendicular let fall from N, the foot of the ordinate PN, upon the tangent at the point P, is of constant length.

Also, if the normal at P meet the axis of x at G, show that PG varies at PN^2.

Q. 10. Find the following integrals :—

$$\int 3x^{\frac{3}{2}}dx. \qquad \int a\sin^3 x\,dx. \qquad \int a\sin x\,\cos 2x\,dx.$$

$$\int \frac{9-x}{3-x^2}dx. \qquad \int \frac{x\,dx}{\sqrt{2-3x^2}}. \qquad \int x\log x\,dx.$$

The methods required in these three questions were well understood, and the candidates seemed to have had considerable practice in obtaining numerical results.

Q. 11. The base of an uniform solid cone is a circle of radius a, and the altitude is h.

Apply the integral calculus to obtain

(1) the volume ;

(2) the position of the centre of gravity ;

(3) the moment of inertia about the axis.

Q. 12. The axes of an ellipse are of lengths $6a$, $12a$. Find the area of the segment cut off by a line through one extremity of the major axis, and inclined 45° to that axis.

Show also that the volume generated by the rotation of this ellipse about the major axis is half the volume generated by its rotation about the minor axis.

These two questions, though not quite so often taken, were answered correctly a good many times.

STAGE 6.

Results : 1st Class, 25 ; 2nd Class. 24 ; Failed, 12 ; Total, 61.

The results in this stage are very good. Several excellent papers were sent in, and quite a large proportion of the candidates deserve a First Class.

Q. 21. Obtain the equation of a plane in the form

$$\frac{x}{a} + \frac{y}{b} + \frac{z}{c} = 1.$$

What form does the equation take, (1) when $c = 0$; (2) when $c = \infty$?

A plane

$$3x - y + z + 1 = 0$$

cuts the plane

$$5x + y + 3z = 0$$

in the line PQ. A plane is drawn through the point $(21, 4)$, perpendicular to PQ. Show that this new plane contains the point $(2, 3, 5)$.

Q. 22. Find the equation of a plane which contains a given line, and is also perpendicular to a given plane.

OA, OB, OC are three edges of a cube, and *OD* is the diagonal through *O*. Show that the projections upon a plane perpendicular to *OD* of the six edges *CB′ B′B, BD′ D′A, AA′, A′C*, which do not meet the diagonal *OD*, will form a regular hexagon.

Q. 23. Indicate on a diagram the form of the surface

$$3x^2 + 4y^2 + z^2 = 20.$$

What must be the value of *p* in order that the plane

$$lx + my + nz - p = 0$$

may touch this service ?

Show that there are two tangent planes parallel to the plane

$$3x + 2y + z = 0$$

and give the co-ordinates of their points of contact with the surface.

Show also that the line joining these points of contact passes through the origin.

In Solid Geometry Q.'s 21 and 23 were often well answered ; Q. 22 less often.

Q. 24. When is a function $f(x)$ said to have a maximum value ? Find the condition that $f(x)$ should have a maximum value when $x = a$, when the first of the successive differential coefficients of $f(x)$ which does not vanish when $x = a$ is the *n*th.

A portion of a paraboloid of revolution cut off by a plane perpendicular to the axis has a coaxial right cylinder inscribed in it. Show that the greatest possible volume of this cylinder is ½ the volume of the paraboloid.

Q. 25. Show that the curvature of a circle is measured by the reciprocal of the radius. Established *one* of the two formulæ

$$\rho = \frac{\left\{1 + \overline{\frac{dy}{dx}}\Big|^2\right\}^{\frac{3}{2}}}{\frac{d^2y}{dx^2}}$$

$$\rho = r\frac{dr}{dp}.$$

Find ρ at the points where the axis of *x* meets the curve

$$3y^2(x + c) = x^3(3c - x).$$

Q. 26. In the curve $r = f(\theta)$ find an expression for the angle contained by the radius vector and the tangent at any point *P* on the curve.

Trace the curve $r = a\sec\theta \pm a\tan\theta$ and draw the asymptote.

If a radius vector *OPP′* be drawn cutting the curve in *P* and *P′*, and if the tangents at *P* and *P′* meet at *T*, prove that $PT = P'T$.

In the Differential Calculus Q.'s 24, 25, 26 were all frequently made out quite rightly. Points of weakness were :—In Q. 24 many did not see clearly the essential points that *n* must be an even number, and $f^{(n)}(a)$ negative.

In the latter part of Q. 25 many could not overcome the difficulty involved in finding ρ at a point where $\frac{dy}{dx}$ is infinite, or has more than one value.

Q. 27. In finding an integral between given limits

$$\int_a^b f(x)\,dx$$

it is often convenient to change the variable. Explain how to find the proper limits for the new variable : illustrate the method with

$$\int_0^2 \sqrt{\frac{x^2}{2-x}}\cdot dx,$$

by taking a new variable θ, where
$$x = 2 \sin {}^2\theta.$$

Show also from graphical considerations that

$$\int_a^b f(x)\,dx = \int_0^{b-a} f(x+a)\,dx,$$

$$\int_a^b f(nx)\,dx = \frac{1}{n}\int_{na}^{nb} f(x)\,dx.$$

Q. 29. The co-ordinates of any point on a cycloid being given in the form

$$x = a\,(\theta + \sin \theta)$$
$$y = a\,(1 - \cos \theta),$$

Show that the whole length of a cycloidal arc from cusp to cusp is $8a$; and that the whole area bounded by this arc and the line on which the generating circle rolls is $3\pi a^2$.

Both in the Integral Calculus and in Differential Equations there were many very good answers, though the last part of Q. 27 was rarely established ; and in Q. 29 many failed to see that the origin is at the vertex and the axis of x is the tangent there : thus the limits of θ were not correctly determined, and the wrong area was calculated.

STAGE 7.

Results : 1st Class, — ; 2nd Class, — ; Failed, 1 ; Total, 1.

There was only one candidate ; he answered one question fully and two other questions partially.

HONOURS IN DIVISION II.

Results : 1st Class, — ; 2nd Class, 1 ; Failed, 2 ; Total, 3.

Three candidates took this paper ; the first answered fairly well, the second moderately ; the third was disqualified.

DAY EXAMINATIONS.
STAGE 1.

Results : 1st Class, 398 ; 2nd Class, 542 ; Failed, 208 ; Total, 1,148.

On the whole the work seems to be better than the work sent up in the Evening examination. It is, perhaps, a little better than the work sent up in the Day examination of last year.

In ARITHMETIC the questions most frequently taken were the following :—

Q. 1. Reduce to their simplest forms :—

(a) $2\frac{1}{15} + 1\frac{9}{10} - 3\frac{1}{24}$;

(b) $(9\frac{1}{4} \times \frac{35}{37}) \div (6\frac{1}{4} \times 1\frac{14}{21})$.

Find how many times the excess of the greater over the less of the two expressions (a) and (b) is contained in the greater of them.

Q. 4. A merchant sells goods to a customer at a profit of 44 per cent., but the customer becomes bankrupt, and pays only 14s. 4½d. in the pound. What per cent. does the merchant gain or lose on the whole transaction ?

Q. 6. A man gives by his will one-tenth part of his property to each of his three daughters ; he gives a sixth part to each of his two younger sons ; he makes his eldest son residuary legatee. In consequence, the eldest son comes in for £5,280. Find the sum received by each of the other children.

The other questions were rightly answered, fairly often.

Q. 2. Find by contracted multiplication the product of 3·14159 × 8·7342 so as to obtain the product true to four decimal places.

Divide 1·73205 by 1·41421, by contracted division, so as to obtain the quotient true to four decimal places.

From the answers to this question it appeared that some of the candidates can use contracted methods of multiplying and dividing decimals. In this connection it may be observed that if, for instance, the question is to write down 2·8876173 true to five places of decimals, very many do not seem to understand that the answer is 2·88762, not 2·88761.

GEOMETRY. The questions in this section were fairly well answered. But it may be well to notice that the object of teaching Geometry is to impart correct notions of lines, angles, triangles, &c., and correct ways of reasoning about them. Neatly drawn diagrams are often a great help in these respects, but they are not a substitute for correct reasoning.

Q. 8. At a given point in a straight line show how to make an angle equal to a given angle.

A and B are two points on level ground, and P is a somewhat distant inaccessible point, on the same ground ; you are provided with a few pegs and some rope ; show how you could fix a point Q, such that BQ may be parallel to AP.

The answers to this question would have been better, perhaps, in some cases, if the candidates had realized that the point P is inaccessible. For the most part, however, it seemed plain that if they had gone on to the ground with some rope and a few pegs, they would not have been able to lay down the line BQ.

The following, which requires to be stated at full length, calls for notice. The first part of the question was often answered as follows :—Let the given angle be BAC, and D the point in the line DE ; with centre A and any radius cut AB in P and AC in Q ; also with centre D and the same radius, draw an arc cutting DE in F ; with centre F and radius equal to the distance PQ cut the arc in G ; join GD ; then GDE is the required angle. This, of course, follows from Euclid I—8. The method—which is really the same as Euclid's—is quite satisfactory, provided it is distinctly understood that the reasoning depends on the equality of the chords FG and PQ. Very commonly, however, it happened that the proof broke down because of a confusion between the chords and the arcs.

Q. 11. Show how to describe a square on a given straight line, having only ruler and compasses. Describe a square, one of whose sides (AB) is two inches long.

Show how to cut off from the square a third part of its area by means of a line drawn through A.

The reasoning in the first part was often unsatisfactory, apparently because the students had not distinctly in mind what they meant by the word "square." The teachers ought to keep the definitions distinctly before their class.

In ALGEBRA the questions most commonly attempted were the following :—

Q. 13. (a) Find the sum of $3x + 5y - 6xy$, $7x - 8y + 54xy$, and $- 11x + 4y - 51xy$.

    (b) If $x = -\frac{1}{2}$, and $y = \frac{1}{3}$, find the numerical values of the three expressions and of the sum that you have obtained, and show that the sum of the first three values equals the fourth value.

Q. 16. (a) Simplify the following expression :

$$\frac{a}{(2b-a)\,(a-b)} - \frac{1}{a-b} - \frac{2}{2b-a}.$$

    (b) Find the value of x, for which the following expression equals 0 :—

$$\frac{1}{a-b} + \frac{1}{b-c} + \frac{x}{(a-b)\,(b-c)},$$

where a, b, c denote three different numbers.

Q. 17. Solve the following equations :—

    (a) $\dfrac{5x-2}{3} - \dfrac{x+14}{2} = \dfrac{x-8}{4} - 2.$

    (b) $\dfrac{a}{a^2-x} + \dfrac{b}{b^2-x} = 0.$

    (c) $2x - \dfrac{y+2}{5} = 21, \qquad \dfrac{x-4}{6} - 4y = 29.$

    In (c) verify your result, by substituting the values of x and y, which you have found, in both equations.

Q. 18. An express train, which travels one-third as fast again as an ordinary train, performs a journey of 252 miles in $1\frac{1}{2}$ hours less time than the ordinary train. Find the average speed of each train in miles per hour.

In very many cases the results were correct, but it may be noticed that the substitutions in Q. 13 were often omitted, or wrong.

Q. 14. (a) Divide $(x^3 - 1)^3$ by $x^3 - x^2 - x + 1$.

    (b) Find the value of c that will make $2x^4 - x^3 + 10x^2 - 2x - c$ divisible by $2x^2 + x + 5$ without a remainder.

Q. 15. (a) Write down $x^2 - 7x + 10$ in factors, and, assuming that x stands for a positive number, find under what circumstances the given expression will be negative.

    (b) Verify your result by considering two cases, viz., first when x stands for 4, secondly, when x stands for $\frac{1}{2}$.

These two questions were taken fairly often, but the answers to Q. 14 (b) and Q. 15 (a) illustrate the difficulty of inducing learners to reason about their results. In the former, they would often find the remainder $-c-15$, but could not draw the conclusion, that c must equal -15, if there is to be no remainder. In the second case, they would find that the expression equals $(x-5)\,(x-2)$, but were quite unable to make out that it is negative only when x is less than 5 and greater than 2.

STAGE 2.

Results : 1st Class, 306 ; 2nd Class, 1,167 ; Failed, 487 ; Total, 1,960.

The work is distinctly better than the work sent up in the Evening examination, and also than that sent up in the Day examination of last year.

GEOMETRY. The work was mostly directed to Q.'s 21, 22, 23, but there were a good many answers to Q.'s 24, 25, 26.

Q. 21. Show how to divide a given straight line into two parts, so that the rectangle contained by the whole line and one of the parts may be equal to the square on the other part.

If A, B, C be three given straight lines, show how to construct a line X, such that the square on X shall equal the excess of the square on A above the rectangle contained by B and C.

In the deduction, when the side (P) of a square equal to the rectangle under B and C had been found, there ought to have been no difficulty in finding the side of a square equal to the excess of the square on A over the square on P, by Euclid I—47. In many cases, however, the method was to draw the square on A, to cut out of it a square equal to the square on P, and then to find a square equal to the remainder by Euclid I—45 and II—14. Of course, such a clumsy method was in most cases ill carried out.

Q. 22. If a straight line drawn from the centre of a circle bisects a chord which does not pass through the centre, show that it cuts the chord at right angles.

Also state and prove the converse of the above theorem.

Let O be the centre of a given circle in which a chord AB is drawn and produced to C so that BC is equal to the radius OA ; let CDE be drawn to pass through O and to meet the circumference in D and E. Show that the angle ACO is one-third of the angle AOE.

In the second part the reasoning not unfrequently ran thus :—"In the triangles ADB, ADC the side AB equals the side AC, and the side AD is common, also the angles at D are right angles, therefore the triangles are equal in all respect (Euclid I—26)." The fallacy, whether expressed or implied, that the conclusion follows from Euclid I—26, is one that the teachers ought to be very much alive to.

Q. 23. Two circles touch one another internally, show that the line which joins their centres will, if produced, pass through the point of contact.

Two circles touch one another internally, and the diameter of the smaller circle is greater than the radius of the larger circle. Chords of the larger circle are drawn to touch the smaller circle ; show that the longest of these chords is at right angles to the line which passes through the centres of the two circles.

In several cases candidates tried to prove this easy proposition by means of "limits." It is hardly necessary to say that those who are learning the elementary properties of the circle have not reached a point at which they can be trusted to use limits. The result of introducing learners prematurely to such a method is to muddle, not to enlarge, their minds.

Q. 24. Show how to inscribe a circle in the smaller sector formed by joining the centre C of a given circle with two points, A and B, on its circumference.

If from any point P on the arc of the sector, perpendiculars PM, PN be let fall on the radii CA, CB, show that the diameter of the circle drawn through P, M, N, and the chord MN, are each of constant length.

The first part was answered as often as could be fairly expected ; the second part very seldom.

Q. 25. Two given circles touch each other internally ; show how to draw a chord of the larger circle, which shall touch the smaller circle and be of a given length.

When the diameters of the given circles are 4in. and 2in. respectively, construct a chord of the larger circle, which shall be 2½ in. long and shall touch the smaller circle.

This question was answered oftener than might have been expected.

B

Q. 26. Show that the arcs intercepted between two parallel chords of a circle are equal to one another.

A circle, whose radius is constant, is moved about in its plane so as always to cut two fixed straight lines APR, AQS in points P, Q, R, S whose positions on the lines and on the circumference change as the circle moves.

Show that in all positions the sum of the arcs RPQ and PQS is constant.

As in Q. 24, the first part was answered fairly often; the second part very seldom, though, if taken the right way, the proof is easy.

ALGEBRA. The questions most often attempted were Questions 29, 30, 31 but the others were taken fairly often.

Q. 27. (a) If $(a + b)(a^3 + b^3) = (a^2 + b^2)^2$, and if neither a nor b is zero show that $a = b$.

(b) Show that the product of any three consecutive integers is divisible by 6 without remainder.

(c) Show that if unity be added to the product of any four consecutive integers, the result is a perfect square.

This question is easy, but there were many failures in (a) and (b); in (c), however, the answer was often right, though sometimes ill-expressed.

Q. 28. (a) How does an index of a power differ from a power? The number 2401 is a certain power of 7, what is that power? and what is the index of the power?

(b) Extract the square root of

$$1 + \frac{\sqrt{3}}{2}.$$

(c) Show that four times the quotient of $\sqrt{(4 + \sqrt{7})}$ divided by $\sqrt{(3 + \sqrt{5})}$ can be put into the form

$$\sqrt{35} - \sqrt{7} + \sqrt{5} - 1.$$

This question was not often attempted; the answers to (a) and (b) were right in most cases; that the attempts to answer (c) failed in most cases shows that only a few candidates can handle surds, for the question is easy.

Q. 29. Solve the following equations :—

$$(a)\ x + \frac{1}{x - 3} = \frac{41}{5};$$

$$(b)\ x^2 - 2(b + c)x + b(b + 2c) = 0;$$

$$(c)\ bx + \frac{a}{y} = 2b, \frac{a}{x} + by = 3a.$$

(a) and (b) were often solved correctly. The attempts at (c) mostly failed. Many found $3ax = 2by$, but could get no further.

Q. 30. (a) If a and β are the roots of the equation

$$3x^2 + 2x + 1 = 0,$$

find the sum, difference, and product of a and β, and form the equation whose roots are

$$\frac{a}{\beta^2} \text{ and } \frac{\beta}{a^2}.$$

(b) Find the condition that in the equation

$$ax^2 + bx + c = 0,$$

one root may be double the other.

It should be borne in mind that the values of the sum, product, difference, etc., in fact the values of the symmetrical functions of the roots of a quadratic equation, should be found without solving the equation. As a consequence of not attending to this, the equation asked for in (a), viz. :— $3x^2 - 10x + 9 = 0$ was very seldom found.

Q. 31. The length of a room is 6 feet more than its breadth, and its breadth is 9 feet more than its height. If the area of its four walls be 1,152 square feet, find the dimensions of the room.

This question is easy, and it was often well answered.

Q. 32. (a) Show that the area of a rectangle varies jointly as the sides which contains one of its angles.

(b) Explain carefully under what circumstances you are justified in saying that the area of a rectangle equals ab ; where a and b are the length of the sides.

(c) The area of a circle is 27 times that of a second circle. If the diameter of the latter circle is 5 ft., show that the diameter of the first circle is very nearly 26 feet.

N.B.—Of course, the area of a circle varies as the square of the diameter.

The answers to (a) and (b) were nearly always unsatisfactory. Why they should be so is plain enough. The candidates know that a piece of carpet 5 yards long and 3 yards wide contains 15 square yards, and so do not feel that there is anything to be explained in such questions as (a) and (b). It requires a good teacher to make his pupils feel the difficulty, and to clear it up for them. That questions about units are not the self-evident matters that learners are apt to think, becomes plain when unfamiliar units are in question. As teachers know who have to deal, for instance, with dynamical units.

TRIGONOMETRY. Questions 33, 34, 37 were usually selected. These relate to quite elementary matters, and were often answered well or fairly well.

Q. 33. State what is meant by a table of the logarithms of numbers ; state also some cases in which such tables can be used with advantage.

From the annexed table write down log 772 true to five places of decimals.

By means of logarithms given below, calculate the cube root of

$$\frac{772 \times 9}{5 \times 3 \cdot 2809}$$

Draw to scale (say of 1 in. to 20 ft.) a triangle ABC having a right angle at C, whose sides AB and BC are 77·2 ft. and 42·4 ft. long respectively, and calculate the number of degrees, with the odd minutes and seconds, in the angle BAC. Compare the result with that obtained from the diagram by means of a protractor.

Much of the logarithmic work was good, but in form it was often illogical. Such statements as the following were often made, viz. :

$$\log a - \log b = 2 \cdot 6508 = 447 \cdot 5.$$

Q. 35. (a) Explain, with reference to a diagram, what is meant by the sine, cosine, and tangent of an obtuse angle.

(b) Taking the case in which A denotes an acute angle, show that
$$\cos (90^\circ - A) \cos (180^\circ - A) \tan (180^\circ + A)$$
$$= \sin (90^\circ + A) \sin (180^\circ - A) \tan (180^\circ - A).$$

(c) Assuming that tan 16° 42′ is 0·3, find as decimals, correct to three places, the values of
cos 16° 42′, tan 73° 18′, sin 163° 18′, and cos 196° 42′

The definitions relating to obtuse angles were seldom well given, e.g., the positive and negative signs were forgotten.

Q. 36. (a) Calculate all the values of θ between 0° and 360° which satisfy the equation
$$3 \sin^2 \theta - 5 \sin \theta + 2 = 0.$$

(b) Find the value of x from the two following equations :—
$$3 \sin \theta + 5 \cos \theta = 5, \quad 5 \sin \theta - 3 \cos \theta = x.$$

(a) The actual angles (41° 48′ 37″ etc.) were seldom calculated, even when the values of $\sin \theta$ (1 or ⅔) had been found. (b) Very few found that the value of x is ± 3.

Q. 38. In a triangle ABC the angle A is 60°, and the area of ABC equals that of an equilateral triangle, one of whose sides is p ; show that
$$AB^2 - BC^2 + CA^2 = p^2.$$

It was surprising to notice how few attempted this easy question, and how very few proved the required result, e.g., in a group of nearly 400 candidates, about one in twenty attempted it, and not quite one in sixty succeeded in answering it.

STAGE 3.

Results : 1st Class, 88 ; 2nd Class, 193 ; Failed, 115 ; Total, 396.

The work on the whole did not differ much from that of last year, but there was a perceptible increase in the number of papers gaining more than two-thirds of full marks.

In GEOMETRY all the questions were freely attempted and there were a good many complete answers. But the last parts of Questions 41, 44, and 46 were often left undone.

In Q. 44 many of the answers failed to make out that the triangle found was similarly placed, as well as being similar, to the given triangle.

Q. 41. By means of a geometrical construction, show :—

(a) How to draw a line which is a fourth proportional to three given straight lines.

(b) How to draw a line which is a mean proportional to two given straight lines.

From a point X in the prolongation of AB, a side of a triangle ABC, a straight line is drawn cut BC in P and CA in Q ; show that
$$XP : XQ :: PB. AC : AQ. BC.$$

Q. 44. If the straight lines joining a given point to the vertices of a given triangle are divided, all internally or all externally, in the same ratio, show that the points of division are the vertices of a similar and similarly placed triangle.

Show how to inscribe, in a given triangle ABC, a triangle similar and similarly placed to another given triangle DEF.

Q. 46. A straight stick (AB) has marks P and Q on it which divide its length into three equal parts ; it is held under water, and the depths of A and B are known ; find the depths of P and Q.

P, Q, R divide the circumference of a circle into three equal parts ; the circle is held under water and the depths of P, Q R are known. Find the depth of the centre of the circle.

ALGEBRA :—

Q. 47. (a) Show that the sum of the squares of three consecutive odd integers increased by 1 is a multiple of 12.

(*b*) Show that the sum of any series of consecutive odd integers is the square of an integer or the difference of the squares of two integers.

(*c*) Show that
$$\sqrt[3]{(90 + 34\sqrt{7})} - \sqrt[3]{(90 - 34\sqrt{7})} = 2\sqrt{7}.$$

In (*a*) instead of starting with $2n-1$, $2n+1$, $2n+3$ the weaker candidates assumed n, $n+2$, $n+4$ as the three consecutive integers, thus neglecting the condition that the integers are *odd* ones; this of course led to failure.

Q. 48. (*a*) Find all the values of x and y which satisfy the equations
$$x^3 + y^3 + xy = 25, \qquad x^3 + y^3 - xy = 37.$$

(*b*) If
$$ax^2 + y^2 + z^2 = 0, \qquad ax + y + z = 0,$$
and
$$yz + zx + xy = 0,$$
where neither x, y, nor z equals zero, find the value of a, and hence show that the three equations are not independent of each other.

In (*b*) very few could show that the three equations are not independent of each other.

Q. 49. (*a*) Find the number of permutations of $(p + q)$ things taken all together, when there are p things alike of one sort, and q alike of another sort.

(*b*) In the case of 15 things of 5 different sorts, 3 alike of each sort, find the number of permutations of the things taken 4 at a time.

(*a*) was commonly done; (*b*) came right a few times.

Q. 50. (*a*) Express as a decimal, correct to five places, the coefficient of x^9 in the expansion of $(1+x)^{-\frac{1}{3}}$ by the Binomial Theorem.

(*b*) By means of the Binomial Theorem find to five places of decimals the cube root of 1001.

(*c*) Expand
$$\left(\frac{1 + x}{1 - x}\right)^{\frac{1}{3}}$$
in ascending powers of x as far as x^3 (inclusive).

The work on the Binomial Theorem was somewhat better than last year, but the numerical results sent up still leave much room for improvement.

Q. 51. A vessel contains a mixture of wine and water, the quantity of the wine being to that of the water as 3 to 4; a second vessel contains a mixture of wine and water, but the quantities are in the ratio of 5 to 9. The two mixtures are put into one vessel, and now the quantity of wine is to that of water as 25 to 36. Find the ratio of the quantity of liquid in the first vessel to the quantity of the liquid in the second vessel.

Q. 52. An uneven number of barrow-loads of earth are arranged at equal intervals in a straight line: they have to be taken in a wheelbarrow to a point in the prolongation of the line; show that the man with the barrow goes just as far in moving the heaps one by one, as he would have done if the earth had been dumped down originally into one great heap at the place of the middle one of the small heaps.

The problems in these two questions were made out very frequently, although in Q. 52 there were many cases in which the result was only shown to be true for 5 or 7 heaps, instead of $2n + 1$ heaps, where n is any integer.

In Trigonometry Q.'s 54 and 58 were those most often completely answered.

Q. 53. (a) Show from a geometrical construction that
$$\sin A + \sin B = 2 \sin \tfrac{1}{2}(A+B)\cos \tfrac{1}{2}(A-B)$$
where A and B are each less than a right angle.

(b) Find the positive angles less than 360°, which satisfy the equation
$$10 \cos x + 24 \sin x = 13,$$
by first reducing the equation to the form
$$\sin(\theta + x) = \text{const.}$$

(c) If a and β are two positive angles, each less than 2π, which satisfy the equation
$$a \cos x + b \sin x = 1,$$
show that
$$a = \cos \tfrac{1}{2}(a+\beta)\sec \tfrac{1}{2}(a-\beta),\; b = \sin \tfrac{1}{2}(a+\beta)\sec \tfrac{1}{2}(a-\beta).$$

(a) was usually correctly done, but only comparatively few succeeded with the other parts of the question.

Q. 55. (a) If O be any point in the plane of the triangle ABC, show that
$$\sin BAO \sin CBO \sin ACO = \sin OBA \sin OCB \sin OAC.$$

(b) If P be a point inside a triangle ABC such that the angles APB, PBC, CPA are equal, and if x, y, z are the distances of P from A, B, C respectively, show that
$$\frac{ax}{\sin(120° - A)} = \frac{by}{\sin(120° - B)} = \frac{cz}{\sin(120° - C)} = \frac{2abc}{\sqrt{3}(x+y+z.)}.$$

(a) was often done; (b) is hard and was not often attempted, but there were a few verifications of the first equation in the result.

Q. 56. Let D be the middle point of AB, a side of a triangle ABC, and let ACD be one-third of the angle ACB; AB and BC being given, find a formula by which the angle ACB can be calculated. Also show that AB must be greater than BC and less than $BC\sqrt{5}$.

Show how the triangle ABC might be constructed from the data.

This question was not often taken in hand; a few found the formula asked for, and showed how the triangle might be constructed, but no one made out the limits of AB correctly.

Q. 57. (a) Two circles of radii 3 and 4 inches have their centres 5 inches apart; find the area common to the two.

(b) Six circles, each one inch in diameter, are described with their centres at the angular points of a regular hexagon, and each circle touches two of the others. Find the area of that portion of the hexagon which is not covered by the six circles.

There were many imperfect answers; it was quite an exceptional case to find both parts right.

STAGE 4.

Results: 1st Class, –; 2nd Class, 1; Failed, 2; Total, 2.

There were only two candidates in this stage; one answered fairly well the other was very weak.

23

STAGE 5.

Results : 1st Class, 36 ; 2nd Class, 14 ; Failed, 7 ; Total, 57.

The work in this stage was distinctly good.

In ANALYTICAL GEOMETRY all the questions were well answered, though of course Q.'s 4 and 5 on the more advanced parts of the subject were less often taken than Q.'s 1, 2, and 3.

In DESCRIPTIVE GEOMETRY there were only some half-dozen answers to each of the questions, Q.'s 6 and 7, the bulk of the candidates having evidently confined themselves to Conics and the Calculus.

In the DIFFERENTIAL CALCULUS the discussion of the limit and the use of limiting values in the first part of Q. 8 was not so good as the work in Q.'s 9 and 10.

In the INTEGRAL CALCULUS in Q. 11 four or five of the integrals were often obtained correctly, and occasionally all six were right. In Q. 12 the area and the position of the centre of gravity were made out rightly several times ; the radius of gyration was found two or three times.

STAGE 6.

Results : 1st Class, 3 ; 2nd Class, 4 ; Failed, 3 ; Total, 10.

Of the ten candidates one was excellent, and two others were distinctly good.

In SOLID GEOMETRY Q. 21 was made out five or six times ; Q.'s 22 and 23 only twice.

In the DIFFERENTIAL CALCULUS all the questions were generally well answered ; in Q. 26 some found a difficulty in making out the greatest and least values of the area.

In the INTEGRAL CALCULUS the chief fault was in the answers to Q. 30 where the area of the surface of revolution was several times stated to be

$$\int 2\pi\, y\, dx, \text{ or } \int \pi y^2 dx, \text{ instead of } \int 2\pi y\, ds.$$

In DIFFERENTIAL EQUATIONS the two questions, Q.'s 31 and 32, were well answered several times.

STAGE 7.

There were no candidates.

Report on the Examinations in Theoretical Mechanics.

EVENING EXAMINATIONS.

DIVISION I. (SOLIDS).

STAGE 1.

Results : 1st Class, 142 ; 2nd Class, 226 ; Failed, 150 ; Total, 518.

The work is of much the same character as that of the work of last year, but there are this year hardly as many good papers as there were then. By good papers is meant such as obtain more than 60 marks.

The faults in the work were for the most part such as arise from imperfect knowledge. Thus :—

Q. 3. Explain how to find the resultant of two forces acting along intersecting lines ; and state how the method can be extended to finding the resultant of three forces acting along lines in one plane, and not passing through a common point.

Under what circumstances will three forces acting along lines in one plane not have a single resultant ?

In answer to the last part of this question it was very seldom or never explained that when the resultant of two of the forces has been found, it may turn out to be equal, parallel and unlike to the third force, and that then the reduction can be carried no further.

Q. 4. Explain what is meant by the centre of gravity of a body, that of two or more bodies, and that of a plane area.

An equilateral triangle is hung from a point which trisects one of its sides ; draw a diagram to illustrate the position of equilibrium.

It was seldom shown that the triangle comes to rest with one side vertical.

Q. 6. Explain the principle of the Roman steelyard.

Draw a diagram to show the arms, the graduated scale, the weight and the sliding poise.

How does the weighing capacity of the instrument depend upon the weight of the poise ?

It was too often evident that the candidate was not acquainted with an actual steelyard ; candidates should be made familiar with weighing instruments which depend upon the simple principle of the lever.

Q. 7. Define the tenacity of a material, and illustrate your definition by means of the statement that the tenacity of steel is (about) 120,000 lbs. per square inch.

Assuming that one-tenth of the tenacity is a safe working stress, find the greatest weight that can be carried by a steel chain, each of whose links is made of metal having a cross-section of one-fifth of a square inch.

"Tenacity" was usually defined incorrectly. The answer to the second part would often have been right, if the question had referred to "a steel rod having a cross section of a fifth of a square inch" ; the question, however, has reference to a chain.

Q. 9. Explain precisely the meaning of the symbols in the equation of dynamics

$$v^2 = V^2 + 2fs.$$

Convert it into an equation of energy and then express its meaning in words.

A body is projected vertically upwards with velocity 100 ; what will be its velocity when it is at one half its greatest height ?

The given equation was very seldom converted into an equation of energy.

Q. 10. Two bodies A and B are connected by a fine thread which passes over a smooth fixed pulley ; the mass of A is 15 lbs. and the mass of B is 10 lbs. If A is allowed to fall and to draw up B, find the loss of the potential energy of the system and its kinetic energy, when A has fallen 20 ft. Find also the velocity with which A is falling and B rising at that instant.

Explain the effect it would have on the velocity of A and B, if we suppose that the pulley is made to turn on its axis by the thread which connects A and B.

In the last part of this question it seemed to be seldom or never understood that part of the kinetic energy of the system is taken up by the pulley and consequently that the velocities of A and B are diminished.

Q. 11. Define "centrifugal force."

ABC is a triangle, B being a right angle. A body is at B moving towards C with uniform velocity v ; under what circumstances will its motion have an acceleration in the direction of BA ? Has it any velocity in the direction BA ?

It was fairly often understood that, when a body moves in a circle, the centrifugal force is the reaction of the moving body against the restraints which keep it in the circle ; but otherwise the answers were imperfect and indistinct.

STAGE 2.

Results : 1st Class, 108 ; 2nd Class, 361 ; Failed, 205 ; Total, 674.

A good deal of the work was untidy. This fault is very common in other divisions, but perhaps it was most conspicuous in this division. In many cases the want of neatness is due to imperfect knowledge ; in many other cases it is due to hurry. Teachers should try to train their pupils to do their work deliberately. In the present case it would be easy to write out eight complete answers on 5 or 6 pages of the paper supplied, and to do so in less than three hours. The hurry also would account for the bad writing and bad spelling which occurred in many cases.

Some of the questions set this year in Stage 2, Solids, are perhaps a little harder than usual, and this may be one reason why the work is not so satisfactory as in Stage 2, Fluids. However, the subject of this section is intrinsically the harder, and this is probably the chief reason of the difference in the results.

As might have been expected the questions most seldom attempted were Qs. 21, 25, 26, 28.

In regard to other questions the following points may be noted.

Q. 23. State the conditions of equilibrium when a number of forces act in one plane on a rigid body.

Two uniform ladders are between two smooth parallel vertical walls, in a vertical plane perpendicular to the walls, with their lower extremities in contact upon a smooth horizontal plane and their upper extremities against the walls. Show that if the lengths of the ladders are 18 and 32 feet respectively, and the distance between the walls 33·6 feet, the two ladders will be at right angles to one another when they are in equilibrium, the weight of both ladders per foot being the same.

Q. 24. A smooth hemispherical bowl is held firmly with its rim horizontal. A rod of uniform density rests on the rim, with one end against the inner surface of the bowl. Explain what are the forces that keep the rod at rest, and show them in a diagram.

In the position of equilibrium, if a given length of the rod is within the bowl, find the whole length of the rod.

Were often attempted, and some knowldge of the forces concerned was shown, but the results were seldom worked out.

Q. 26. It is said that a good balance should be true, sensible and stable. Explain the meaning of these words in this connection.

Show that the sensibility of a balance is measured by the expression $\tan \theta \div (P - Q)$, explaining the notation. Hence also explain how a balance should be constructed so as to have a high degree of sensibility.

The requirements of "sensibility" and "stability" were only understood by few. If this subject were taught by a rough model, the student would be more likely to obtain a grasp of the mechanical principles, and to give an intelligent answer. A theory learned by rote is, when written out, difficult both to read and to estimate.

Q. 25. Draw a horizontal straight line ABC, AB being 1 in. and BC 3 in.

Let ABC denote a uniform beam of weight w resting on a rough prop at B and underneath a rough prop at A. Find the direction and magnitude of the least force applied at the end C which will just begin to draw out the beam from between the props.

Q. 27. Enunciate the principle of "virtual work." Utilise the principle to investigate the relation between the power and the weight on a rough inclined plane.

If the angle of friction be 45°, determine completely the least force which will drag a weight of 100 lb. down a plane inclined at 30° to the horizontal.

The answers to these two questions showed that friction is understood by very few. Thus in the latter part of Q. 27, it is necessary to find the *direction* of the least force and then the magnitude follows. In nearly all cases a wrong direction was assumed, and then the resulting magnitude was wrong. A like remark applies to Q. 25. It would seem, to judge by the work submitted, that the subject of the equilibrium of rough bodies has been crammed rather than studied.

STAGE 3.

Results : 1st Class, 19 ; 2nd Class, 45 ; Failed, 25 ; Total, 89.

The answering was better than usual, quite 50 per cent. of the candidates having studied the subject to advantage.

Marks were occasionally dropped through careless reading of questions ; thus in

Q. 43. O is the point of intersection of AD, BE, CF, the medians of a triangle ABC ; forces P, Q, R, act from O to A, B, C respectively ; if the ratio of Q to R equals the ratio of BE to CF, find the resultant of the three forces.

It was often assumed that the force P was given in magnitude as well as in direction.

Q. 44. Take two bars, AB, BC, freely jointed at B, and show, with explanations, how they may be used, with a small roller, to form an Amsler's planimeter.

Show also that a planimeter may be constructed with one bar, an end of which is constrained to move in a fixed straight groove.

About half-a-dozen good replies were given to this question on Amsler's planimeter ; the reply to the second part proved that the principle was understood.

Q. 45. ABC is a given triangle in which AB and AC are equal ; let AC and CB be two rods joined by a smooth hinge at C ; AB is a string joining the ends A and B. The system stands upright with AB horizontal, and C above AB. If a given weight is suspended from C, find the stresses in AB, BC, and CA, putting the weight of the rods out of the question.

Verify your results by considering the case in which ABC is an equilateral triangle.

The subject of jointed frames should be quite familiar to those taking Stage 3 ; some weakness was shewn here.

Q. 46. A body descends vertically, under gravity, in a medium resisting as the square of the velocity. If V be the terminal velocity, show that the distance described in time t is

$$\frac{V^2}{g} \log \cosh \frac{gt}{V}$$

Q. 47. Give a case of motion which gives rise to the differential equation

$$\frac{d^2x}{dt^2} + \mu x + \nu = 0,$$

and show that the solution may be given a circular or exponential form, according as μ is numerically positive or negative.

Q. 50. A right circular cone can oscillate about a horizontal axis passing through its vertex and perpendicular to the axis of the cone.

Find the length of the equivalent simple pendulum ; and, if it be let fall from the position in which its axis is horizontal, show that the square of the angular velocity at the lowest point is

$$\frac{10gh}{4h^2 + r^2}$$

where h is the height and r the radius of the base.

Q. 51. State in a few words the general method of finding the instantaneous change in the reactions of the points of support of a body, when one of the points of support is removed.

AB is a uniform rod and C a point between B and the middle point G ; the rod is held horizontally by two vertical strings attached to A and C. If the string at A is cut, find the instantaneous tension of the string at C.

The best candidates answered these questions well.

Q. 49. A surface rolls with angular velocity ω on a fixed surface ; determine the acceleration of the point of contact along the normal in terms of ω and the curvatures of the surfaces at the point. Show that there is no acceleration of the point along the tangent in the plane of motion.

Was seldom attempted and only once or twice fairly done.

Q. 52. There are four perfectly elastic balls with their centres in a straight line, viz., A, A_1 and B, B_1. The masses of A and A_1 are equal, and so are those of B and B_1, also the mass of A is twice the mass of B. If a velocity (u) is given to A in the direction of A to B, find the velocities with which the bodies are moving at the end of the last impact.

Was often perfectly answered ; some candidates lost marks by not realizing that there are more than three impacts of the balls.

DIVISION II. (FLUIDS).

STAGE 1.

Results : 1st Class, 71 ; 2nd Class, 89 ; Failed, 52 ; Total, 212.

The questions and parts of questions which require calculations produced a good deal of satisfactory work. The questions which require statements of, or easy reasoning from, principles were not so well answered. But, speaking generally, the results were much the same as those obtained last year.

Q. 1. A body, whose mass is $4M$, moves in a straight line under the action of a force equal to the weight of a mass M ; what acceleration does this produce in the velocity of the body ?

If at any instant the velocity of the body were 15 ft. per second, what would be its velocity at the end of three seconds, and what distance would it describe it those three seconds ?

Show in a diagram an instance of a body whose mass is $4M$ moved by a force equal to the weight of M.

The diagram drawn nearly always showed a want of knowledge of mechanical principles.

Q. 2. State any one property of the centre of gravity of a body.

If A is one corner of a square board, and if the square is hung up by A, in what position will it come to rest ? If it were slightly disturbed from that position, how would it move ? And why would it come to rest after a time ?

If it were hung up by means of an iron axle passing through a hole in board near A; and if the board were placed vertically above A, how would it move if left unsupported? And why would it not return to the position from which it started?

The case of the body falling from the highest position was so treated as to show that it was supposed that the body would fall to its lowest position and stay there. That it is only kept from returning to its first position by friction, resistance of the air and the like seemed to be quite outside of the range of the candidates' knowledge.

Q. 5. Illustrate, by considering the case of water at rest in a bent tube, the fact that the surface of still water is level.

Suppose the tube to have two upright legs, but the cross section of the one greater than the cross section of the other, so that the smaller quantity of water in the thinner leg balances the larger quantity in the thicker leg. Explain why it is able to do so.

The reason why the weight of the smaller quantity of water balances the weight of the larger quantity was seldom well given. The explanation, moreover, was often obscured by an attempt to consider the atmospheric pressure.

Q. 6. A liquid measure, of the form of a conical frustum, tapers from the bottom to the brim.

Explain how to estimate—

(1) The fluid pressure at any point of the curved surface;

(2) The whole pressure on the base;

(3) The resultant pressure on the base.

Was not very often attempted.

Q. 7. Define Specific Gravity (or Specific Density).

If two volumes of liquids having given specific gravities are mixed, explain how to find the specific gravity of the mixture. Apply the process to find the specific gravity of a mixture consisting of 3 pints of a liquid whose specific gravity is 0·92 and 7 pints of one whose specific gravity is 0·87.

In answering this question it has been assumed that when the 3 and the 7 pints are put together there are 10 pints of mixture. Mention a case in which the two liquids would mix, but the volume of the mixture would differ from the sum of the volumes of the components.

Q. 8. Describe briefly the method of finding the specific gravity of a solid heavier than water by means of the balance.

State how the method must be modified to meet the case in which the solid is lighter than water.

The specific gravity of a body is 0·7, and its weight in vacuo is 2 oz. If the weight of the sinker in water be 2 oz., what will be the weight of the body and the sinker in water?

Q. 9. Draw a diagram to explain the word "metacentre."

How does stability of flotation depend upon its position? Find its position in the case of a floating sphere.

Were often answered well or fairly well.

Q. 11. In the previous question the mass of air is transferred to a vessel of a cubic yard capacity with the alteration of temperature stated; determine the resulting pressure in lb. per square inch, taking atmospheric pressure as 15 lb. per square inch.

29

Q. 12. Explain the action of the Barometer Gauge of an Air Pump.

The External Barometer stands at 29·5 in. ; at a certain stage in the process of exhaustion the Barometer Gauge stands at 15 in. ; after the next stroke it stands at 16 in. What part of the contents of the receiver were withdrawn by that stroke ?

Were not very often attempted.

STAGE 2.

Results : 1st Class, 76 ; 2nd Class, 159 ; Failed, 68 ; Total, 303.

Several very good papers of answers were sent in, and the results are at first sight much more satisfactory than those obtained in Solids, Stage 2. But the difference is perhaps partly due to a difference in the intrinsic difficulty of the subjects, and partly to a difference in the questions actually set. The difference is illustrated by the answers to Questions 21, 22, which might have been set in Solids, Stage 2.

Q. 21. State what is meant by angular velocity.

A point moves with a constant velocity along the circumference of a circle ; what is its angular velocity with respect to the centre of the circle ?

If AB and CD are two diameters of the circle at right angles to each other, and if O is a point midway between the centre and A, find the angular velocity of the point with respect to O at A, B, C, D, respectively.

Q. 22. You are asked to find the resultant of more than two forces ; state whether it is sufficient to find the magnitude of the resultant. If it be not sufficient, state what more is sufficient.

$ABCD$ is a square, and forces of 9, 12, 5, 5, units act along A to B, B to C, D to C and D to A respectively ; show that the resultant acts through B, and find it.

In Question 21, e.g., very few found the angular velocity of the moving point when at C (or D). Again, Question 22 is an easy question, yet in many cases it was not completely made out.

Q. 23. Investigate a formula for the specific gravity of an alloy of two metals, of specific gravities s, s', whose weights are in the ratio of n to n'.

The specific gravities of tin and lead being 7·4 and 11·4 find the specific gravity of pewter containing 80% of tin and 20% of lead.

Draw a diagram showing how the specific gravity varies with the percentage of lead.

Many failed through not noticing that weights, not volumes are given. In the last part of the question, some of the students plotted a few points, but very few, if any, noticed that the points lie on a hyperbola.

Q. 26. Investigate the position of the centre of pressure of a rectangle immersed vertically with a side horizontal and at a given depth. Mention an instance of the practical importance of the subject of centre of pressure.

The practical importance of the subject of the centre of pressure was seldom illustrated. Hydrostatics should always be studied with an eye to practical and every day applications.

Q. 27. Show by a diagram the meaning of the term " metacentric height."

In a ship of 10,000 tons displacement the moving of 20 tons from amidships a distance of 40 feet across the deck causes the bob of a pendulum 20 feet long to move through one foot. Prove that the metacentric height is 1·6 feet.

The given numerical result (1·6) often appeared at the end of the work when it was doubtful whether the subject of the question was understood Many defined the "metacentric height" as the height of the metacentre above the centre of buoyancy ; but they got the 1·6 all the same.

Q. 28. Two vessels of volumes V, V', have masses M, M', of air in them at absolute temperatures T, T'. Compare the pressures P, P'.

The old difficulty concerning the formula $pv = Rt$ sometimes presented itself, the candidates failing to understand that the formula has reference to a given mass of gas.

Q. 30. Explain the action of surface tension when a capillary tube is immersed vertically in a liquid.

If the section of the tube be an equilateral triangle show that the liquid rises twice as high as in a cylindrical tube whose radius is that of the circle circumscribed to the triangle.

Q. 31. Find the pressure on a plane caused by a jet of water impinging on it, making the assumption that there is no splashing, and that the water flows away on the plane.

Find the pressure in pounds weight, when the plane is horizontal, and when the jet has a section of a square inch, and falls from a height of 10 feet.

Q. 32. Let A be the middle point of BC, an arc of a circle whose centre is O, and suppose that OA is vertical. Let the arc represent a tube of small bore filled with water, and let it be made to turn round OA as an axis ; find the smallest number of turns it must make per minute, if all the water is thrown out of the tube.

A few very good answers were given to Question 30 and the like was true of Questions 31, 32.

STAGE 3.

Results : 1st Class, 27 ; 2nd Class, 28 ; Failed, 11 ; Total, 66.

The work was, on the whole, well done. Thus, while eleven students got fewer than 110 marks, twenty-eight got from 110 marks to 220 marks, as many as twenty-seven got 220 marks or more.

Several of the questions were often well answered ; thus :—

Q. 43. Equal weights of n substances of specific gravities

$$s_1, s_2, \ldots s_n$$

are taken. If an alloy be formed without change of volume, prove that its specific gravity s is given by

$$n.\frac{1}{s} = \frac{1}{s_1} + \frac{1}{s_2} + \ldots + \frac{1}{s_n}.$$

Q. 44. Investigate the position of the centre of pressure of a plane area immersed in homogeneous fluid.

State the analogy with pendulum motion and with the dynamical theory of the axis of spontaneous rotation.

Find the depth of the centre of pressure in the case of a half-penny, 1 inch in diameter, immersed vertically so that its highest point is at a depth of 3 inches.

Q. 47. Describe a differential air thermometer.

Two equal glass bulbs of volume V are connected by a horizontal uniform tube, of cross section a cm.^{2}, in which a small filament of mercury separates the air in the two bulbs ; if the bulbs be originally at the same temperature and the filament in the symmetrical position show that when the temperatures of the bulbs are θ_1, θ_2 degrees absolute centigrade the displacement of the mercury will be

$$\frac{V(\theta_1 - \theta_2)}{a(\theta_1 + \theta_2)}.$$

Q. 52. What is the mechanical equivalent of heat?

In an experiment a horse working for $2\frac{1}{4}$ hours raised the temperature of a mass equivalent in capacity for heat to 26·6 lbs. of water, by 180° F.; what was the horse-power of the horse?

Were answered by the students as if they felt sure of their ground, and this remark applies also to the first part of Question 48.

Q. 48. If we assume the atmosphere to be of uniform temperature, show that the logarithm of the pressure changes uniformly with the height.

If H be the height of the homogeneous atmosphere, prove that at height H the barometer stands at e^{-1} of its height on the ground.

On the other hand several questions, *e.g.* :—

Q. 45. An area, whose plane is vertical, is immersed in water; it is known that the depth of its centre of pressure below the surface of the water equals $k^2 \div z$; assuming this, explain the notation, and show how the formula is modified if the area is turned round a horizontal axis which is in its plane and which passes through its centre of gravity.

Let the area be a rectangle, and at first let one edge be in the surface of the water; show how the centre of pressure will move if the area be turned round an axis bisecting its vertical sides.

Q. 50. State what is meant by the energy of a plane film; and show that the superficial energy per unit of area equals the tension per unit of length.

A light thread with its ends tied together forms the internal boundary of a plane film; explain why it will take a circular form.

Q. 51. Show how the principle of Archimedes may be deduced from the principle of energy.

A sphere, of radius r, is held just immersed in a cylindrica vessel, of radius R, containing water, and is caused to rise gently just out of the water, prove that the loss of potential energy of the water is

$$Wr\left(1 - \frac{2}{3}\frac{r^2}{R^2}\right),$$

where W is the weight of water first displaced by the sphere.

Were answered as if the students were uncertain about the reasoning, and it was often hard to make out whether the answer was right or not. This applies also to the second part of Question 48.

Q. 46. Explain how to find the work done in compressing a given quantity of air at a constant temperature.

A quantity of air has the volume of a cubic yard at a pressure of 15 lbs. per square in.; find the number of foot-pounds of work that must be done to compress it, at a constant temperature, to a cubic foot.

(N.B.—Hyper. Log. 3 = 1·0986.)

Explain carefully under what circumstances PV will represent a certain number of foot-pounds.

This question brought out a very curious point. It appeared from the work that quite a large number of the candidates think that nine cubic feet make a cubic yard. This was not a solitary blunder, like that of the candidate who supposed that 81 cubic feet is the right number, but was the opinion of an imposing minority.

Q. 41. Find the centre of gravity of a portion of a right cylinder terminated obliquely by a plane.

Whatever be the inclination of the plane to the base, show that the centre of gravity can never be at a greater distance from the axis than a quarter of the radius of the base.

Q. 49. A body, floating in stable equilibrium in a homogeneous liquid, receives a small vertical displacement; find the time of an oscillation.

Let the floating body be a paraboloid of revolution, terminated by a plane at right angles to its axis, whose specific gravity is 0·25, and let it be loaded at its vertex by a particle, whose weight equals that of the body; show that the time of a small vertical oscillation is very nearly nine-tenths of what the time would be, if the weight of the particle were doubled.

These questions require a little more in the way of pure mathematics than the other questions; in Question 49 the answer was made out by several of the better candidates. The attempts to answer Question 41 almost invariably failed. Seeing that the answer depends on the moment of mass and the moment of inertia of a circular lamina about a tangent, the question ought not to have presented much difficulty; but instead of assuming or obtaining these determinations, the candidates showed that they could not perform the integrations; in some cases they wandered off into double and even triple integrals, and, of course, arrived at no result.

HONOURS.

Results: 1st Class, 1; 2nd Class, 1; Failed, 1; Total, 3.

Each of the three candidates attempted a fair number of questions; on the whole they were well prepared considering the difficulty of the questions. One did rather poorly, but one did a decidedly good paper.

The questions appeared to be of the right order of difficulty.

DAY EXAMINATIONS.

DIVISION I. (SOLIDS.)

STAGE 1.

Results: 1st Class, 20; 2nd Class, 56; Failed, 53; Total, 129.

The number of candidates was 129: a good many came from one weak centre. The work does not compare very unfavourably with that sent up in the Evening Examination, and on the whole the work was perhaps better than that of last year.

Q. 1. Define "momentum" and "energy."

If a mass of 100 lb. move in a straight line from rest under the action of a force equal to its own weight, find its momentum and energy at the end of a minute.

Was well done by 25 candidates; others failed owing to confused ideas about units.

Q. 2. Mention the four points which go to the complete specification of a force.

Illustrate your answer by the reaction of a horizontal table which supports a ball of uniform density resting on it.

Was fairly well done.

Q. 3. *ABC* is a triangle having a right angle at *C*, and the side *AC* is twice as long as the side *BC*. A force of 20 units acts from *B* to *A*, one of 10 units from *B* to *C*, and one of 15 units from *A* to *C*. By means of a construction drawn to a fairly large scale, find the resultant completely.

The triangle and the force *BC* being as above, how must the forces along *CA* and *AB* be chosen so that the three forces may not have a single resultant?

A usual mistake was to assume that the forces act at a point.

Q. 4. Define the centre of gravity of a body, and state what is the position of the centre of gravity of a triangular board—putting the thickness of the board out of the question.

Draw a triangle *ABC* to a fairly large scale, and construct the position of its centre of gravity.

In the diagram, which you have drawn, take a point *P* in *BC* such that *PC* is one-fourth of *BC*; find the position of the centre of gravity of *ACP*, and show that its distance from the centre of gravity of *ABC* is one-fourth of *BC*.

Many omitted to give a proof in the last part of the question.

Q. 5. Define the moment of a force with reference to a point. If two forces act along intersecting lines, show how to find any one of the points about which the moments of the forces are equal but of opposite signs.

Two lines *AB* and *AC* are inclined at an angle *BAC* of 60°; a force of 7 units acts from *A* to *B*, and one of 10 units from *A* to *C*; show how to draw the straight line in which are situated all the points such that the moments of the forces about them may be equal and of opposite signs.

In most instances an insufficient explanation was given.

Q. 6. Sketch the beam of an equal-arm balance showing how it is itself supported and how it supports the pans for the goods and weights. Explain what the sensibility depends upon.

How can stability of equilibrium be ensured?

An article is found to weigh 438 grains, but on weighing again with the article in the weight-pan the weight is found to be 437 grains; what is the true weight of the article?

Explanations as to "stability" were in general not well given. In the rider it was a frequent assumption that the result must be the arithmetic mean.

Q. 7. *AB* is a rod loaded at *A* so that the distance of the centre of gravity (*G*) from *A* is one-tenth of *AB*; the rod can turn freely round an axis at *C*, which is halfway between *A* and *G*; the weight of the rod is 4 lbs. A weight of 10 lbs. is hung from *A*, and a weight (*P*) of 1 lb. is placed so as to balance the weight at *A*; find *AP* as a fraction of *AB*.

Q. 10. State what is meant by "acceleration" and by "constant acceleration."

The units of distance and time being feet and seconds, illustrate your statement by explaining what is meant by an acceleration of 10.

Using the same units, two points *A* and *B* begin to move at the same instant in straight lines; *A* has an initial velocity of 100 feet per second, and the acceleration of its velocity is 10; *B* has no initial velocity, and its acceleration is 20. Find (*a*) how many seconds elapse before they are moving with equal velocities, (*b*) the distances that they describe respectively in that time.

These two questions were often well done.

C

Q. 12. A simple pendulum 40·5 inches long was observed to make 59 beats in a minute, at a certain place ; show that $g = 32\cdot209$ at that place.

If the pendulum were lengthened by half an inch, how many fewer beats would it make in an hour?

Was seldom attempted, and not once with complete success. Arithmetical calculation by contracted methods is imperfectly understood.

STAGE 2.

Results : 1st Class, 22 ; 2nd Class, 62 ; Failed, 89 ; Total, 173.

The number of candidates was 173, and there were fewer good papers than usual. The work compares unfavourably with that sent up in the Evening Examination.

Q. 21. State Newton's second law of motion, and show that, with a proper choice of units, it can be expressed by the equation $F = Mf$.

If the units of length and time are a furlong and a minute, find the number of pounds in the unit of mass, when the unit of force equals the weight of 11 lbs. ($g = 32$).

Was generally attempted, but the majority did not understand how to change units.

Q. 23. A uniform rod AB rests on a rough horizontal table ; state how the reaction of the table acts, and explain whether the roughness of the table affects your answer.

A thread AP is fastened to the end A and pulled by a force P in a direction inclined to the vertical. The force P is not sufficient to cause motion. Find the line along which the reaction now acts, and show that the rod will not slide, so long as $P \sin (\theta + \phi) < W \sin \phi$; where ϕ denotes the angle of friction, and θ the inclination of the thread to the vertical.

A common fault was to take the reaction as acting at the centre of the rod.

Q. 24. A uniform beam, of length $2a$, is placed in a fixed smooth hemispherical bowl of radius r, $r < a$; show that in the position of equilibrium the angle θ which the beam makes with the vertical is given by

$$\sin^2 \theta - \tfrac{1}{4}\frac{a}{r} \sin \theta - \tfrac{1}{2} = 0.$$

Several candidates ignored the fact that having drawn the diagram so that the three forces acted through one point, the result could be found by elementary geometry.

Q. 27. A weight rests on the lowest point of a fixed smooth vertical ring, and is pushed uniformly up the ring till it is level with the centre.

Draw a diagram of the work done, and show from it how the rate at which the force increases depends upon the angular distance traversed by the weight.

The subject of the diagrammatic representation of work when variable seems to have been neglected by teachers, as only one or two candidates understood what was required.

Q. 29. Prove that the free path of a projectile under gravity is a parabola.

Find equations for the determination of the initial conditions that the projectile may pass through a given point.

The answers were usually restricted to bookwork and that was frequently cumbrous.

Q. 32. Prove that the centrifugal force at the equator due to the Earth's rotation is nearly the 289th part of the Earth's attraction at the same place.

Very well done by those candidates, few in number, who attempted it.

DIVISION II. (FLUIDS.)

STAGE 1.

Results : 1st Class, 11 ; 2nd Class, 43 ; Failed, 14 ; Total, 68.

There were several good sets of answers sent up, but on the whole the results are not nearly so good as those of the Evening Examination. Most of the faults and errors were such as are due to imperfect knowledge ; but in some cases they arose from the inability of the writer to express his meaning clearly.

There are two prevalent faults to which attention may be drawn.

Q. 8. Explain the distinction between stable and unstable equilibrium.

If part of a wooden sphere be cut off by a plane, explain why the remainder will float with the flat surface upward.

Very few understood that in the case of a floating sphere, or segment of a sphere, the fluid pressure at each point acts at right angles to the surface, and consequently the resultant fluid pressure must act through the centre of the sphere.

Q. 10. The formula for a perfect gas is $PV = RT$; explain carefully the meaning of the letters, and state the two laws or properties of a perfect gas which are embodied in the formula.

If the temperature of a gas were 25° C., what would be the numerical value of T (in the formula) ?

A certain quantity of gas is at a temperature of 17° C. under a certain pressure ; another quantity which is twice the former is under the same pressure at a temperature of 27° C. ; find the ratio of their volumes.

Very few realize that Boyle's Law applies to some definite quantity of a gas. The statement "The volume of a gas varies inversely as the pressure" is inadequate, and in most cases implies a misconception. It should run thus : "The volume of *any given quantity* of a gas, &c."

STAGE 2.

Results : 1st Class, 5 : 2nd Class, 13 ; Failed, 20 ; Total, 38.

The general remarks on the work in Stage 1 are applicable to the work in Stage 2. Several good papers were sent up.

Q. 23. A pair of opposite vertical faces (or sides) of a cubical vessel are kept from rotating outwards about their lowest edges, which are hinged, by a taut string connecting their middle points.

Find the tension of the string when the cube is filled with water.

Evaluate the tension when the capacity of the vessel is 6·23 gallons.

Q. 24. A side, of length a, of a vertically immersed quadrilateral is in the surface of a fluid ; the opposite side, of length b, is parallel to it at a depth h : prove that the depth of the centre of pressure is

$$\frac{1}{2}\frac{a + 3b}{a + 2b}h$$

These two questions were often well answered, but a good many mistakes were made in applying statical principles.

Q. 26. Suppose that a rectangle $ABCD$ represents a vertical face of a rectangular solid floating in stable equilibrium, and that AB is under water; let E and F be the middle points of BC and CD. Suppose that E is fastened to one end of a thread, the other end of which is fastened to a fixed point at the bottom of the water; suppose also that the body comes to rest with ADF above the surface of the water. If s denote the specific gravity of the solid, show that

$$12s = 7 + \frac{2b^2}{a^2}$$

where AB and BC are denoted by a and b.

Q. 27. A cylinder formed of a thin flexible substance is subjected to an internal fluid pressure; explain how the tension at any point is measured.

In the case of an upright cylinder filled with water, find the tension at any assigned point of the curved surface. Find also the whole resultant force which tends to tear the curved surface asunder along any vertical line.

Q. 28. Define the metacentre of a floating body. Assuming the general formula for its position $(HM.V = Ak^2)$, find its position in the case of a right cylinder whose axis is vertical.

A cylinder, whose specific gravity is 0.4, floats in a liquid whose specific gravity is 0.6; if the radius of the base is given, find under what circumstances it will float with its axis horizontal.

These three questions are rather hard, and the attempts to answer them were not worth much. Rather better results might have been fairly expected, at least in regard to Questions 27 and 28.

Q. 30. When is a vapour
    (i) superheated,
    (ii) saturated,
    (iii) at its critical temperature?
Under what circumstances does a vapour obey very closely the Gaseous Laws?

Was tried by most of the candidates. The answers in very many cases illustrated the remark made above as to the want of ability on the part of the writers to express their meaning clearly. Attention had been very generally given to the subject of the question, but in few if in any cases were all three points clearly and briefly defined. Sometimes one or two points came out clearly, but in most cases the result of many words was to leave the matter obscure.

Report on the Examinations in Navigation and in Spherical and Nautical Astronomy.

NAVIGATION.

STAGE 1.

Results : 1st Class, 2 ; 2nd Class, 7 ; Failed 8 ; Total 17.

Only seventeen papers were sent in for this Stage, and the work was not good. Two candidates only succeeded in reaching 60 per cent. of the total, and eight were below 40 per cent. Very few had any real grasp of the subject, and the logarithmic calculations were unusually erratic.

STAGE 2.

Results : 1st Class, 11 ; 2nd Class, 24 ; Failed, 11 ; Total, 46.

In this Stage there were forty-six candidates, whose work was of an average character. Eight obtained 70 per cent. of the marks and upwards, 27 from 40 to 69 per cent., and 11 fell below 40 per cent. of the total.

A few remarks as to the answering of particular questions are appended.

Q. 21. Two ships sail from the same point. The first sails NE *a* miles, and then SE *a* miles. The second sails SE *a* miles, and then NE *a* miles. Will they reach the same position ? Give a reason for your answer.

There were few satisfactory answers, and a very general tendency was noticeable to solve the question by simply drawing a parallelogram.

Q. 23. Explain the method of finding deviation of compass by reciprocal bearings taken on board and ashore.

If the bearings observed on board are S. 85° E. and N. 87° 40′ E., and the corresponding bearings observed ashore N. 82° 40′ W. and N. 84° 20′ W., find the respective deviations.

As on former occasions many mistakes were made in the work of the practical example. These are to a great extent due to the failure to construct a satisfactory diagram shewing simply a single line of bearing upon which the compass ashore is situated and the directions of correct magnetic and compass meridians. In several cases also, in reversing bearing, N. 84° 20′ E. was given as the reverse bearing to N. 84° 20′ W. instead of S. 84° 20′ E.

Q. 27. Find the compass course and distance from Jamaica (Lat. 17° 56′ N., Long. 76° 11′ W.) to the Lizard (Lat. 49° 58′ N., Long. 5° 12′ W.) ; Variation 3° 40′ E., Deviation 2° 50′ E.

Great want of accuracy was shewn in the work of this simple straightforward question.

Q. 31. A ship sails from Cape Finisterre (Lat. 42° 53′ N., Long. 9° 15′ W. to Cape Race (Lat. 46° 40′ N., Long. 53° 5′ W.). Find the distance and the latitude of the vertex.

Considerable improvement was exhibited in the logarithmic work involved in this question, as compared with former examinations.

Q. 32. Day's Work. The necessary calculations were well and accurately done.

SPHERICAL AND NAUTICAL ASTRONOMY.

STAGE 1.

Results : 1st Class, 8 ; 2nd Class, 5 ; Failed, — ; Total, 13.

The results in this Stage, for which thirteen papers were sent in, were unusually good, more particularly in the case of the group of candidates indicated by Numbers 69687-69696.

STAGE 2.

Results : 1st Class, 1 ; 2nd Class, 11 ; Failed, 3 ; Total, 15.

Fifteen papers were sent in for this Stage, and the results were distinctly below the average. One candidate gained 80 per cent. of total marks, but no other succeeded in reaching 65 per cent. The practical work was inaccurate, and there was but little knowledge of theory.

The Sumner Double-Chronometer question was fairly well done, but hardly any candidates attempted Question 25, which deals with the combination of a line of position with the bearing of a known point of land.

NAVIGATION AND ASTRONOMY.

STAGE 3.

Results : 1st Class, — ; 2nd Class, 2 ; Failed, 3 ; Total, 5.

Of five candidates examined, one took Spherical Astronomy, the remainder confining their attention to Section A, which deals with Navigation and Nautical Astronomy. One candidate gained 53 per cent. of total marks, and a second 38 per cent. The other papers were failures. The candidate who answered questions in Stage 3, Spherical Astronomy, sent up one good answer, and attempted two other questions not wholly without success.

HONOURS.

Results : 1st Class, — ; 2nd Class, 1 ; Failed, 1 ; Total, 2.

Two papers were sent in, one of which obtained 65 per cent. of the maximum. The other was a failure. Neither candidate took Spherical Astronomy.

39

GROUP II.—ENGINEERING.

BOARD OF EXAMINERS.

I. Practical Plane and Solid Geometry	Professor John Perry, M.E., D.Sc., LL.D., F.R.S., *Chairman*.
II. Machine Construction and Drawing	J. Harrison, M.I.M.E., Assoc. M. Inst. C.E.
III. Building Construction and Drawing	Professor W. E. Dalby, M.A., M. Inst. C.E.
IV. Naval Architecture	J. Slater, F.R.I.B.A.
VII. Applied Mechanics	Professor Henry Adams, M. Inst. C.E.
XXII. Steam	C. E. Goodyear.
V.*p.* Practical Mathematics	Professor T. H. Beare, B.Sc., F.R.S.E., M. Inst. C.E.

Report on the Examinations in Practical Plane and Solid Geometry.

EVENING EXAMINATION.

STAGE I.

Results : 1st Class, 649 ; 2nd Class, 518 ; Failed, 658 ; Total, 1,825.

The number of candidates in this stage was 1,825, being five less than in 1905. The high standard of last year was maintained, and there are many schools in which the teaching is extremely efficient. Not only are the principles of the subject well understood, but care and accuracy in drawing is secured, the amount of distinctly careless work in these schools being very small. On the other hand, there are some schools in which the work is almost wholly bad, and these schools account for nearly the whole of the failures.

In all schools there is evidence that some portions of the subject do not receive adequate treatment, and that improvements are possible, more especially with students of less than average ability. The following points may be specially mentioned :—

(a) There is a general lack of exact knowledge of the simpler facts relating to the tangency of lines and circles. See the detailed remarks under Question 3.

(b) In dealing with the important subject of vectors, the teaching often lacks precision. The simple graphical rules for the addition and subtraction of vectors have not been assimilated, and confusion results. In specifying direction, many candidates seem unable to distinguish East from West, and clockwise angles from counter-clockwise. Direction arrows are often omitted, a serious defect in vector work.

(c) The evidence afforded by the answers to Question 10, relating to a line in space, indicates that this branch of the subject is either badly taught or comparatively neglected. In a large number of cases the candidates were evidently quite unable to form any mental picture of the conditions of the problem, and their answers were absurd and worthless. The only successful method of dealing with lengths and angles in space is to provide students with a few simple models, devoid of construction lines, on which these quantities are directly measured, and the results verified by drawing projections of the models, and then determining the same lengths and angles by geometrical construction. Suitable and inexpensive models will be suggested by a study of the questions set in the day and evening examination papers of the last few years.

(*d*) Teachers might, with advantage to themselves and to their students, occasionally ask for written answers to questions on certain parts of the subject which are of fundamental importance. In this way, misconceptions and difficulties could be detected and corrected, and, at the same time, useful practice would be provided for the students.

Q. 1. *In working this question employ a decimal scale of ¼ inch to 1 unit.*

> *Draw a circular arc, radius 10 units, centre O. Mark a chord AB of this arc, 3·47 units long, and draw the radii OA, OB. Measure the angle AOB in degrees.*
>
> *From B draw a perpendicular BM on OA, and at A draw a tangent to meet OB produced in N. Measure carefully BM and AN (on the above unit scale), and calculate the sine and the tangent of the angle AOB.*
>
> *Give the correct values of the angle, the sine and the tangent, taken directly from the examination tables supplied.*

The first two parts were well answered, indicating a widespread knowledge of trigonometrical ratios, but a rather common error was to make the chord 3·47 inches long instead of 3·47 half-inch units. With regard to the last part, comparatively few discovered from the tables that the angle whose chord is 0·347 is exactly 20°, and therefore that the correct values of the other functions were known.

Q. 2. The figure is the plan of a building site to a scale of 1 inch to 10 yards. Determine the area of the site in square yards.

Of the optional questions this was the favourite, and the answers were fairly satisfactory. The most usual though not the best method was division into triangles and calculation of their separate areas by measurements of bases and heights. Errors in scaling and measurements in vulgar fractions were few, and the arithmetic was not so bad as in some previous years. Some, in attempting to reduce the figure to an equivalent triangle, went wrong over the re-entrant angle.

Q. 3. Draw the electric lamp to the dimensions given, which are in millimetres. Mark carefully the points of junction of the several arcs.
> N.B.—A mere copy of the diagram will receive no credit.

Attempted by about 60 per cent. of the candidates. Very few obtained correctly the points of junctions of the circular arcs, or determined properly the centres of the upper and lower arcs. Students seem to have a very scant knowledge of elementary tangential properties of circles. Teachers should give attention to this matter.

Q. 4. In arranging some elementary experiments in statics, cyclist trouser clips are used as spring balances. In order to be able to measure pulls, a series of weights are hung on a clip, and the corresponding openings AA are measured. The results being plotted, give the curve shown. For instance, when the pull is OM ounces, the opening is ON inches. On SS construct a decimal scale of ounces, which, being applied to the spring at AA, shall measure any pull up to 32 ounces.

Rarely attempted, not more than 10 per cent. of the candidates taking the question. There were a few full and complete answers, but the great majority got no marks. A scale of ounces in *equal* parts was generally shown, and even this was seldom sub-divided decimally.

Q. 5. The figure is the plan of a corner of a landing. S is a stone, on which a stove is to rest. Show the corner of the landing carpet folded over along the line LL. On this fold draw the hole which must be cut in the carpet, so that when the latter is turned back into position the hole shall just fit the stone S.

This question was, perhaps, too easy. It was frequently attempted and very well answered.

Q. 6. Two pieces of sheet material are hinged together at A One of them is pinned or hinged to the drawing board at B, and the point P on the other piece is moved in a straight line from L to M. Find the paths described by the points Q and R of the second piece.

Neither a favourite question nor well answered. The results were very inaccurate, and few discovered the geometrical character of the loci. It might, perhaps, have been better to have stated explicitly in the question that AB, AP, AQ, and AR were equal, and that P, A, Q, were in a straight line.

Q. 7. A *and* B *are two points in a body which is moving in a plane. At a certain instant the positions of* A *and* B *are given by the vectors.*

$$OA = 2 \cdot 2'_{\;75°}, \quad OB = 5 \cdot 5'_{\;33°},$$

O *being a fixed point of reference, and angles being measured anti-clockwise from a line drawn along the tee square to the right (eastwards).*

Plot the points O, A, *and* B *to a scale of 1″ to 1′. Measure the magnitude and direction of the vector* AB, *that is, the position of* B *relatively to* A.

This was usually well done, though some gave the vector sum $OA + OB$ instead of the vector difference $OB - OA$. Also occasionally West was substituted for East, and clockwise rotation for counter-clockwise.

Q. 8. The vertices A, B, C of a triangle, referred to a point O as in Q. 7, have the positions defined by the vectors

$$OA = 3''_{\;15°}, \quad OB = 4''_{\;75°}, \quad OC = 2''_{\;115°}.$$

Determine the centre of area, G, of the triangle, having given that

$$OG = \frac{1}{3} \left(3''_{\;15°} + 4''_{\;75°} + 2''_{\;115°} \right) = a_{\;a}, \text{ say.}$$

Measure a and a.

Seldom attempted and rarely well done. Very few obtained G in any way. Some made the vector addition $OA + OB + OC$ but did not plot G from the result. The vector equation given was in fact seldom understood.

Q. 9. A piece of card is pinned temporarily to a drawing board, and forces P and Q are applied to the card as shown. It is desired to balance these two forces by a force of 30 ounces acting as A, so that the card shall remain at rest on removal of the pins. What must be the line of this third force, and what the original magnitudes of P and Q?

Not very frequently attempted. Candidates often failed to see that the line of the required force must pass through the intersection of P and Q. But having assumed an arbitrary line through A, they were generally able to draw a corresponding triangle of forces, and to measure results consistent with their initial error.

Q. 10. A *thin metal plate* ABC, *resting on the ground, is shown in plan A piece of thin wire* AD, 2·5″ *long, with one end soldered to the plate at* A, *is also shown in plan at* Ad.

    (a) *What is the distance of the end* D *of the wire from the plate?*

    (b) *What angle does* AD *make with the plate?*

    (c) *Draw the elevation of the plate and wire on* xy.

There were many good answers, but far too many worthless ones, and, on the whole, the results were disappointing. A frequent mistake was to draw the elevation of AD on xy 2″ long, and to give in answer to (b) the angle between this elevation and *xy*. Sometimes (a) was correctly answered, and the angle just mentioned given in answer to (b). The given *xy* was often incorrectly transferred; and the elevations *a'*, *b'*, *c'* were often shown above the *xy* line.

Q. 11. The roof of a house is rectangular in plan, and two adjacent surfaces are each inclined at 32° to the horizontal. What is the inclination to the horizontal of the "hip," or line where the two surfaces meet?

Not very frequently attempted. The question was not well understood.

Q. 12. The hopper shown in the diagram is required to be lined on its inner surface with sheet metal bent out of one piece. Find the shape of this piece, the joint being along *AA*.

Many good answers. With the poorer candidates, a common mistake was to give the shape of the elevation as the shape of the development. There was some want of accuracy in extending the development, after having obtained the true shape of one face.

Q. 13. Two elevations of a kitchen salt-box are given. Copy the elevation *A*, and from it project a plan. From the plan project an elevation on *x'y'*.

N.B.—The view *B* need not be drawn.

A favourite question and satisfactorily answered. The principal defect was inaccuracy in transferring dimensions.

Q. 14. The figure shows a portion of a timber joint. Represent this in pictorial projection, in a manner similar to that used for the cube, where lines parallel to *oy* and *oz* are drawn horizontally and vertically, and to a scale of full size, and lines parallel to *ox* are drawn by using the 45° set-square, and to a scale of half size.

N.B.—The figure need not be copied, dimensions being taken directly from the diagram.

Fairly often attempted, and with much success. This kind of projection is attractive to students, and they are able to apply it well.

STAGE 2.

Results : 1st Class, 253 ; 2nd Class, 436 ; Failed, 218 ; Total, 907.

In this stage there was an increase of 8 per cent., the numbers of candidates for 1905 and 1906 being respectively 843 and 907. The work was very satisfactory and the proportion of failures unusually small. The previous remarks under (*b*), (*c*) and (*d*) apply in this stage, though not quite to the same extent. Further, more care should be given to the accurate determination of the lengths of curves, as detailed in the special remarks on Questions 21 and 32. And in some schools the use of blunt soft pencils is still permitted.

Q. 21. *In working this question employ a decimal scale of ½ inch to 1 unit.*

Draw a circular arc, radius 10 units, centre O. Mark a chord AB of this arc, 3·47 units long, and draw the radii OA, OB. Measure the angle AOB in degrees.

From B draw a perpendicular BM on OA, and at A draw a tangent to meet OB produced in N. Measure carefully BM, AN, and the arc AB (on the above unit scale) and calculate the sine and tangent of the angle, and the angle in radians.

Give the correct answers for the degrees, sine, tangent, and radians, the numbers being taken directly from the examination tables supplied.

Very well answered in regard to the first two parts. The remarks under Q. 1 apply to the last part of the question. The tracing paper method of finding the length of the arc was often successfully used, and with due care gave the most accurate result.

Q. 22. The figure is the plan of a field in which there is a pond P; scale ¼ inch to 10 yards. Find the total area of the field (including the pond), and the area of the pond in square yards.

A favourite question and very well answered. The measurements were usually made in decimals. A good proportion showed a fair knowledge of some method of obtaining the area of the curved figure.

Q. 23. In arranging some elementary experiments in statics, cyclists' trouser clips are used as spring balances. In order to be able to measure pulls, a series of weights are hung on a clip, and the corresponding openings AA are measured. The results are as tabulated.

Pull = P ounces	0	4	8	12	16	20	24	28	32
Opening $AA = x$ inches	0	0·51	1·15	1·83	2·53	3·24	3·89	4·44	4·96

Plot a curve showing the relation between P and x, the scale for P being ¼" to 1 ounce. Use this curve to graduate a decimal scale of ounces, which being applied to the spring at AA shall measure any pull up to 32 ounces.

A fair number plotted the curve and did so well, but very few understood how to obtain the required scale.

Q. 24. The figure is the plan of a corner of a landing, scale 1" to 1'. S is a stone on which a stove is to rest. Show the corner of the landing carpet folded over along the line LL. On this fold draw the hole which must be cut in the carpet, allowing a margin of 1½" all round for turning under, so that when the carpet is turned back into position, the hole shall just fit the stone S.

The candidates were well able to answer this question, but sometimes the drawing was a little inaccurate.

Q. 25. Four pieces of sheet material are hinged together at A, B, C, D, these points forming the corners of a jointed parallelogram. One of the pieces is pinned or hinged to the drawing board at P, and the hinge point B is moved in a straight line from L to M. Find the locus of Q, that is the path that would be traced by a pencil moving with Q.

Frequently attempted and fairly well done. Owing to slight inaccuracies in working, a large number failed to obtain a straight line locus, and very few appeared to recognize the special properties of the mechanism.

Q. 26. A and B are two points in a body having plane motion. At a certain instant the positions of A and B are given by the vectors

$$OA = 0·44'_{75}, \quad OB = 1·1'_{33},$$

O being a fixed point of reference, and angles being measured anti-clockwise from a line drawn along the tee-square to the right (eastwards). Plot the points O, A, B, to a scale of ½" to 0·1'. What is the position of B relatively to A?

At the instant under consideration the velocity of A is 5_{15}. feet per second, and the angular speed of the body 10 radians per second. To a scale of ¼ inch to 1 foot per second, draw a vector triangle, or velocity image, showing the velocity of A, the velocity of B relatively to A, and the velocity of B. Read off the velocity of B.

Seldom attempted, and good answers were very rare indeed.

Q. 27. If m_1, m_2, m_3 are the masses of three bodies in a plane, and A_1, A_2, A_3 three vectors defining the positions of their centres of mass G_1, G_2, G_3, then the position of the centre of mass G' of the three bodies is given by the vector equation—

$$OG = A = a_a = \frac{m_1 A_1 + m_2 A_2 + m_3 A_3}{m_1 + m_2 + m_3}$$

Plot G_1, G_2, G_3 to a linear scale of one-half, when
$$A_1 = 8''_{30°}, \quad A_2 = 7''_{47°}, \quad A_3 = 6''_{78°},$$
$$m_1 = 1\cdot5, \quad m_2 = 1\cdot0, \quad m_3 = 2\cdot5.$$
Determine G and measure a and a.

Rarely attempted. The plotting of the triangle was fairly satisfactory, but the vector equation was not well understood. A few obtained the answers by the vector method suggested, but the majority employed other and less direct methods.

Q. 28. A cardboard lever is pinned or hinged to a board at the point O Forces P and Q are applied to the lever as shown.

The linear scale of the drawing being $\frac{1}{4}$, and the magnitude of P being 1·85 lbs., what is the moment of P about O? Find the magnitude of Q if the lever is balanced.

Show a force which, being applied to the lever near O, shall relieve the pin from all pressure, and allow of its being removed without disturbing the equilibrium.

A fair number of candidates gave good answers. Some failed to express the moment of P in proper units. In other cases an incorrect balancing force was shown which did not pass through O, or did not pass through the inter-section of P and Q.

Q. 29. *A thin metal plate ABC resting on the ground is shown in plan. A piece of thin wire AD, 2·5″ long, with one end soldered to the plate at A is also shown in plan at Ad.*

(a) *Find the distance of the end D of the wire from the plate, and the angle between wire and plate.*

(b) *Draw the elevation of the wire and plate on xy.*

(c) *From the elevation project a new plan on x_1y_1.*

Generally well done. A considerable number, however, were unable to project the new plan properly.

Q. 30. The roof of a house is rectangular in plan, and two adjacent surfaces are inclined to the horizontal at 30° and 40° respectively. Find the inclination to the horizontal of the "hip," or line in which the two surfaces meet.

What is the magnitude of the dihedral angle between the surfaces?

Answered by about 35 per cent. of the candidates, with, for the most part, satisfactory results.

Q. 31. The figure represents a hanging lamp shade and a tilted mirror. Draw the two elevations of the image of the conical shade in the mirror.

N.B.—If P is any point in space, and P' its image, then the plane of the mirror bisects PP' at right angles.

Not very frequently attempted. A common mistake was to give the *projection* of the shade on the mirror, instead of the image as specified in the question.

Q. 32. The figure shows a funnel made of sheet metal. Draw the developments of the cylindrical and conical portions, showing the shapes of the plates from which the funnel is bent. Omit all allowances for overlap at the joints.

The favourite of the optional questions. The answers were generally right in principle, but there was great inaccuracy in plotting the length of the outer circular arc in the development of the cone. The tracing paper method is not sufficiently practised.

> Q. 33. A timber joint is shown. Represent, in pictorial or metric projection, the two portions of the joint, separated from each other and placed in any suitable positions. The projection is to be similar to that employed for the cube, where lines parallel to *oy* and *oz* are drawn horizontally and vertically, and to a scale of full size, and lines parallel to *ox* are drawn by using the 45° setsquare, and to a scale of half size.

Fairly often attempted, and very well answered. A few did not follow the instructions in regard to angles and scales, but most of the answers were very good.

STAGE 3.

Results : 1st Class, 26 ; 2nd Class, 81 ; Failed, 104 ; Total, 211.

The number of candidates was 211, which, compared with 161 last year, shows the large increase of 31 per cent. The proportion of Failures was about the same as last year, but there was a higher percentage of First-Class passes, and the work of this year was superior. Candidates in this stage have now a good knowledge of vectors, and also of fundamental problems in Descriptive Geometry, as evidenced by the satisfactory answers to Question 48.

> Q. 41. Four pieces of sheet material are hinged together at A, B, C, D, these points forming the corners of a jointed parallelogram. One of the pieces is pinned or hinged to the drawing board at P, and the hinge point B is moved round the quadrant M. Trace the locus of the point Q.

A favourite question. The majority understood "quadrant" as meaning the circular arc, and so omitted the two radii. The drawing was somewhat inaccurate, and few recognised the principle of the mechanism and the nature of the locus.

> Q. 42. In the figure, LL represents a horizontal beam, and the diagram gives the moment of inertia, I, of any cross section about the neutral axis. You are required to divide LL into eight parts, such that the length of each part shall be approximately proportional to the mean moment of inertia of the part. That is $\dfrac{l}{I}$ is to be the same for all the segments. Give the value of this common ratio, l and I being measured on the same scale.

Only ten attempts. Of these, five were worthless, four were poor, and one was very creditable. The method adopted in the latter case was first to draw an $\dfrac{l}{I}$ curve, next to plot an integration curve, and then to use the latter in projecting the required points of division after the manner of Question 4.

> Q. 43. The horizontal scale of the given map, contoured in feet, is six inches to the mile. Find the horizontal area inclosed by the given figure $FFFF$. Find also what the area measures approximately on the actual sloping surface of the ground.

Not often attempted. There were some very good answers. The most frequent error was to take the slope of the arête as the average slope of the ground.

> Q. 44. A and B are two points in a body having plane motion. At a certain instant the positions of A and B are given by the vectors
>
> $$OA = 0{\cdot}44'_{75^{\circ}} \quad OB = 1{\cdot}1'_{33^{\circ}},$$

O being a fixed point of reference, and angles being measured anti-clockwise from the eastward direction.

Plot the points O, A, B to a scale of $1''$ to $0.1'$. What is the position of B relatively to A?

At the instant under consideration the velocity of A is 5.15 feet per second, and the angular speed of the body is 10 radians per second. Draw a vector triangle, or velocity image, showing the velocity of A, the velocity of B relatively to A, and the velocity of B. Read off the velocity of B.

Show the point I of the body which is instantaneously at rest.

Attempted by 25 per cent. of the candidates. There were one or two full answers, but few could proceed beyond the finding of the position B relatively to A.

Q. 45. A card is temporarily pinned to a board. Forces measuring 1.3 and 2.2 lbs. are applied to the card as shown. A clockwise couple of 11 lb. inches is also applied. The linear scale of the diagram being $\frac{1}{4}$, find the line of action and the magnitude of the force which, acting on the card, will produce equilibrium, so that if the pins are removed the card will remain at rest.

Attempted eighty-one times. There were twenty-three absolute failures. Of the remaining answers the majority were good.

Q. 46. The figure indicates how the position of a point P in space may be defined by a vector OP. Here O is an origin, OZ a vertical axis, ZX a reference plane, and ZN a plane containing OP. Then the vector

$$OP = r\theta, \phi \text{ say,}$$

where

$$r = \text{length of } OP,$$
$$\theta = \text{horizontal angle } XON,$$

and

$$\phi = \text{angle of elevation, } NOP.$$

If A_1, A_2, A_3 are vectors defining the positions of the vertices of a triangle in space, then the position of the centre of area G of the triangle is given by the vector equation

$$A = \tfrac{1}{3} (A_1 + A_2 + A_3) = r\theta, \phi, \text{ say.}$$

Draw the plan of the triangle and determine G, having given

$$A_1 = 4''_{\ 20°,\ 40°}, \quad A_2 = 3''_{\ 47°,\ 57°}, \quad A_3 = 2''_{\ 76°,\ 29°}.$$

Measure r, θ and ϕ.

Not a very popular question, but the answers were generally very good. The plan of the triangle was nearly always right. The determination of the centre of gravity was generally found by a method other than that suggested by the vector equation.

Q. 47. The figure shows a braced tie of a large girder. It is loaded with its own weight, and there is also a longitudinal pull of 220 tons. The weight is taken as equivalent to 11 tons acting at each joint, R_1, R_2 being the forces supporting the weight. Write down the magnitudes of R_1, and R_2. Draw the force diagram or reciprocal figure for the tie, and measure the forces in the bars a, b, c, and d, distinguishing pulls from thrusts.

Adopt a force scale of $\frac{1}{4}$ inch to 10 tons.

There were 116 attempts, fairly successful. Many lost time by using a graphical construction to determine R_1 and R_2; from the symmetry of the figure it should have been evident that these were each equal to half the weight of the tie.

Q. 48. *A thin metal plate ABC resting on the ground is shown in plan. A piece of thin wire AD, 2·5″ long, with one end soldered to the plate at A, is also shown in plan at Ad.*

    (a) *Find the distance of the end D of the wire from the plate, and draw the elevation of the wire and plate on xy.*

    (b) *Draw the plan of a sphere which touches the plate, has its centre O on AD, and which passes through D.*

    (c) *Represent by a scale of slope a plane which contains BC and touches the sphere.*

The answers to (a) and (b) were quite satisfactory. Part (c) was badly answered. The scale of slope was often displaced. And when two points on it were correctly found, the decimal sub-divisions were omitted.

Q. 49. The figure represents a hanging lamp shade and a tilted mirror. Draw the two elevations and the plan of the image of the conical shade in the mirror. From the plan project on *x′ y′* the elevation of the mirror, the shade, and as much of the image as would be seen within the boundary of the mirror.

    N.B.—If *P* is any point or space, and *P′* its image, then the plane of the mirror bisects *PP′* at right angles.

Fairly often attempted. As in the answers to Q. 31, the projection of the shade on the mirror was frequently confused with the required image.

Q. 50. The figure represents a sheet metal pipe. Draw the plan of the section of the pipe made by the horizontal plane *SS*.

    Obtain a development of the truncated oblique cone, showing the shape of the piece required to form the middle portion of the pipe. Omit all allowances for seams.

A favourite question, but its popularity was not justified by the results. There are many surfaces which can be approximately built up of portions of oblique cones, and the development of the oblique cone should be better understood.

Q. 51. The circular arc *ABC* rotates about its chord *AC*. Draw the elevation and the plan of the figure generated.

    Determine the shadow cast on the horizontal plane by parallel rays of light, one of which *R* is given. Show the margin of light and shade on the surface of the solid.

Another favourite question, also badly answered. The majority of the attempts got each less than 10 per cent. of the maximum marks. The answers were wrong in principle, indicating superficial knowledge and fallacious reasoning.

Q. 52. A person using a theodolite at a station point *A* observes the angular elevations of two objects *P* and *Q* above the horizon to be 35° and 65° respectively. The horizontal angle (or azimuth) between their directions, that is between vertical planes containing them, measures 75°. Find the angle *PAQ* subtended by the two objects at the place *A*, as would be measured by a sextant.

A very popular question and well answered.

HONOURS.

Results : 1st Class, 7 ; 2nd Class, 14 ; Failed, 21 ; Total, 42.

There were 42 candidates who took Honours, an increase of four over the number last year. There was a marked improvement of the work in comparison with that of recent years, the answers to the vector portion of the subject being exceptionally good. The only unsatisfactory part was the general avoidance of Questions 61 and 62, seeming to indicate a lack of inventiveness and resource in dealing with new problems.

Q. 61. The figure shows a skew pantograph. Four pieces of sheet material are hinged together at A, B, C, D, these points forming the corners of a jointed parallelogram. If one of the pieces is pinned or hinged to the drawing board at P, and if any point Q in an adjacent piece is moved along a curve, there is some point R in the opposite piece which traces a similar curve, but turned through some angle.

Plot the points A, B, C, D, Q, having given
$$AB = CD = 4'', \quad AD = BC = 3'', \quad ABC = 90°,$$
$$AQ = 2·5'', \quad BQ = 2''.$$

Determine P and R so that the curve traced by R shall be a half size (linear) copy of that traced by Q, and be turned through a clockwise angle of 75°.

Only three attempts. Two of these only plotted the five points. The third made a further construction, but did not solve the problem.

Q. 62. The figure represents one half of a symmetrical arch. You are required to divide the curve LLL into eight parts, so that the length of each part shall be approximately proportional to the mean square of the depth of the part. That is $\dfrac{l}{d^2}$ is to be the same for all the segments. Give the value of this common ratio.

Attempted once only and with no success. The answers to Questions 61 and 62 were disappointing. Honours candidates should display more resource in attacking unfamiliar problems.

Q. 63. The slide valve of a steam engine is actuated by a Joy gear. The figure gives eight positions 0, 1, 2 . . . . 7 of the valve, corresponding to the eight crank positions θ of
$$0°, 45°, 90°, \ . \ . \ . \ 315°.$$

Measuring from the point A, the displacement x of the valve for any crank position θ is given approximately by the Fourier equation—
$$x = c + a_1 \cos\theta + a_2 \cos 2\theta + a_3 \cos 3\theta + a_4 \cos 4\theta$$
$$+ b_1 \sin\theta + b_2 \sin 2\theta + b_3 \sin 3\theta.$$

Determine the eight constants in this equation.

If the speed of the crank shaft is 10 radians per second, what is the velocity of the valve when $\theta = 0$?

Harmonic analysis is now becoming well known, and the answers were good. The best results were obtained by the vector or radial method. The accuracy of this graphical process is shown by the enclosed table in which the answers used by the Examiner are for comparison placed above those obtained by candidate No. 3053.

c	a_1	a_2	a_3	a_4	b_1	b_2	b_3
2·58″	1·08″	− 0·28″	0·03″	0·01″	1·97″	− 0·09″	0·000″
2·575″	1·08″	− 0·28″	0·03″	0·01″	1·97″	− 0·0875″	0·000″

Q. 64. A and B are two points in a body having plane motion. At a certain instant .the positions of A and B are given by the vectors
$$OA = 0·44'_{75°}, \, OB = 1·1'_{33°},$$

O being a fixed point of reference, and angles being measured anti-clockwise from the eastward direction. Plot the points O, A, B to a scale of $\frac{1}{4}''$ to $0·1'$. What is the position of B relatively to A?

At the instant under consideration the velocity of A is 5·15 feet per second, and its acceleration 45·60° feet per second per second, the angular speed of the body being 10 radians per second, and the angular acceleration 60 radians per second per second.

Draw vector triangles of velocity and acceleration, or velocity and acceleration images, from which the velocity and acceleration of any point of the body can be found.

Measure the velocity and the acceleration of B relatively to A.

Show the point Z in the body the instantaneous acceleration of which is zero.

Attempted by about 35 per cent. of the candidates. There were some really good answers, but the majority were only partially successful. This is a fundamental problem in plane motion, and is capable of very useful extension to a series of connected links constituting a machine, and to the force and couple actions due to inertia.

Q. 65. A card is pinned to a board at three points A, B, C ; linear scale ¼.

A number of forces (not shown) are then applied to the card in the plane of the board. The pins B and C being now removed, it is found that the moment of the system of forces about A measures 16·8 lb. inches. In a similar manner it is found that the moments of the system about B and C measure 4·6 and —7·9 lb. inches respectively.

Find the force which will balance the system, and show it acting on the card, so that the latter will not move if all three pins are removed.

Of the twenty attempts, ten were worthless, and seven were good. It was generally overlooked that the line of the resultant must pass through the outer or inner centres of similitude of circles with centres at A, B, C, and radii proportional to the given moments, and could thus be very readily found.

Q. 66. The figure indicates how the position of a point P in space may be defined by a vector OP. Here O is an origin, OZ a vertical axis, ZX a reference plane, and ZN a plane containing OP.

Then the vector

$$OP = r\theta, \phi \text{ say,}$$

where

$$r = \text{length of } OP,$$
$$\theta = \text{horizontal angle } \hat{X}ON,$$

and

$$\phi = \text{angle of elevation } NOP.$$

If m_1, m_2, m_3 are the masses of three bodies in space, and A_1, A_2 and A_3 three vectors defining the positions of their centres of mass G_1, G_2, G_3, then the position of the centre of mass G of the three bodies is given by the vector equation

$$OG = A = \frac{m_1 A_1 + m_2 A_2 + m_3 A_3}{m_1 + m_2 + m_3} = r\theta, \phi \text{ say.}$$

Draw the plans of G_1, G_2, G_3 to a scale of 1″ to 1′ when

$$A_1 = 4'20°, 40°, \qquad A_2 = 3'47°, 57°, \qquad A_3 = 2'76°, 26°.$$
$$m_1 = 1·5, \qquad m_2 = 1·0, \qquad m_3 = 2·5.$$

Determine G and measure r, θ and ϕ.

Nineteen attempts, all fairly good except one ; but even amongst Honours men the mistake is sometimes made of taking the magnitude of $\frac{1}{m}(a_\alpha + b_\beta)$ as equal to $\frac{1}{m}(a + b)$ or the direction as $(\alpha + \beta)$.

D

Q. 67. You are given a bowstring truss under the action of wind forces, and supported at the ends A and B. Determine the supporting forces at the ends, that at A acting in a vertical line. Also draw the force diagram or reciprocal figure for the truss, and measure the forces in the bars a, b, c and d, distinguishing pulls from thrusts.

The most popular optional question. The answers were very satisfactory.

Q. 68. *A thin metal plate ABC resting on the ground is shown in plan. A piece of thin wire AD, 2·5″ long, with one end soldered to the plate at A is also shown in plan at Ad :—*

(a) *Find the distance of the end D of the wire from the plate and draw the elevation of the wire and plate on xy.*

(b) *Obtain the projections of a line from B which meets the wire AD at an angle of 70°.*

(c) *Draw the plan and elevation of the projection of the wire AD on the plane through BC and D. What angle does the wire make with this plane ?*

The answers to all the parts of this question were as a rule very good.

Q. 69. The figure represents a hanging lamp shade and a tilted mirror. Draw the two elevations and the plan showing the image of the conical shade in the mirror.

Also draw a perspective view of the shade, the mirror, and so much of the image as is visible in the mirror, the point of sight being on the same horizontal level as the vertex of the conical shade, and at a distance from the picture plane equal to three times MM.

Thirteen candidates selected this question. There were only three bad attempts, but there were few full and complete solutions. As in the other stages, the projection on the mirror was sometimes given instead of the image

Q. 70. The figure represents a pipe made from sheet metal. Draw a development of the pipe showing the shape of the sheet from which it is bent.

Draw the plan of the section of the pipe made by the horizontal plane SS. Find the area of this section, and the area of either end of the pipe, the linear scale of the figure being $\frac{1}{4}$.

There were five good attempts and nine worthless answers. See the remarks under Q. 50.

Q. 71. The line LL rotates about the axis AA. Draw the plan and elevation of figure generated.

Determine the shadow cast on the horizontal plane by parallel rays of light, one of which R is given.

Attempted eighteen times and with very creditable results. There was a pleasing variety in the methods adopted.

Day Examination.

There were more candidates in Stage 1 than last year, but fewer in Stage 2, the numbers for 1905 and 1906 being respectively 120 and 128 in Stage 1, and 144 and 89 in Stage 2.

Stage 1.

Results : 1st Class, 68 ; 2nd Class, 28 ; Failed, 32 ; Total, 128.

In Stage 1 the work was very satisfactory, and the results, as regards the proportion of highly marked papers, compare favourably with those of the evening, or of any previous examination. The general observations in paragraphs (a), (b), (c), and (d) of the report on the Evening Examination apply to this examination, in further illustration of which see the remarks under Questions 3, 8, 10, 27, 28 and 29. Attention may be called to the value of tracing paper in connection with such problems as the determination of the lengths of curves, the plotting of loci, the drawing of rolling curves, the copying of figures in new positions, etc. Questions 4, 5, 14, 23, 26 and 32 afforded opportunities for the application of this expeditious, accurate and pleasing method, of which the candidates did not take sufficient advantage.

> **Q. 1.** *In this example employ a decimal scale of ½ inch to 1 unit. Draw a right-angled triangle ABC, base BC = 7·66 units, hypothenuse BA = 10 units. Measure the altitude CA and the base angle B, and calculate the sine, cosine and tangent of B.*
>
> *Give the correct values of the angle, sine, and tangent taken directly from the examination tables supplied.*

Attempted by all the candidates except five. As a rule the figure was accurately drawn and measured, and the calculated results fell within allowable limits. Many candidates failed to observe that as the lengths of the base and hypothenuse were given the cosine of the angle B was known, and hence the correct value of B could be obtained directly from the tables. Hence also the correct values of sin B and tan B appeared in the tables. Accordingly, in answer to the last part of the question, many gave, as the correct value of the angle B, the value which they themselves had obtained by measurement with the protractor, using the tables to find (by interpolation when necessary) the correct values of the sine and tangent of this same angle.

> **Q. 2.** *The lines AA, BB, if produced, would meet in a point out of reach. What is the distance of this point from the point K? Measure the angle between the lines in degrees and in radians.*

Attempted by about 40 per cent. of the candidates, nearly every one of whom knew how to determine the required angle. A fair proportion also knew how, by means of proportion, to calculate the required distance, but only a comparatively small number were able to draw and measure with that degree of accuracy necessary to determine the numerical result correct within allowable limits.

> **Q. 3.** *One link of a chain is shown. Draw the figure to the given dimensions, which are in millimetres. Show the construction for determining the centre C, and measure the radius r. Mark the joins of the tangential arcs.*
>
> *N.B.—A mere copy of the diagram will receive no credit.*

Although attempted by 41 per cent., probably less than 4 per cent. were able to determine by construction the required centre, and only quite a few knew that the joining points of the arcs were on the lines joining the centres of those arcs. On the whole the answers were distinctly poor.

> **Q. 4.** *There is certain point O about which the triangle ABC could be turned, so as bring A to A', and AB along A'L, as, for example, by the employment of tracing paper, with a pricker inserted at O. Determine the point O, and draw the triangle in its new position.*

Attempted by about one-third of the candidates; the answers were fairly satisfactory. The majority first drew the triangle in its new position and then determined by construction the position of the centre O; while others, by pricking through, first copied the given triangle on tracing paper and then determined, by trial, the centre O, about which the tracing paper should be turned in order to bring the given triangle into its new position.

> **Q. 5.** *A piece of sheet material H has a motion determined by the condition that two pins a and b fixed in it slide in two grooves AA and BB cut in a fixed plate K. Determine the path traced on K by the point P carried by H.*

More than 50 per cent. attempted this question. It was observed that although it was intended to test the candidates' acquaintance with one of the many uses to which tracing paper may be put, probably one-half determined the locus, or, more generally, only a part of it, by means of intersecting arcs, described with the compass. The solutions obtained by this more clumsy method were not only less complete, but more inaccurate than those obtained by the more ready method of using tracing paper.

Q. 6. When a person looks into the angle formed by two perpendicular plane mirrors, he sees himself by a double reflection, and without the customary lateral inversion. Verify this by the following construction :—

A is the object. The image b in the mirror OM of a point a in it is found by drawing a m b perpendicular to OM, and setting off m b equal to m a. Find the images of the other points a, a, and complete the image B. In like manner find the image C of the object A in the mirror ON. Now find the image of B in ON, and the image of C in OM.

About 25 per cent. attempted this. As a rule only three images were drawn, viz., B and C, and either the image of B in ON or the image of C in OM, but few demonstrated the coincidence of the two last images.

Q. 7. A road is formed along the side of a hill, as shown in cross section at RR, by cutting away material A, and depositing it as an embankment B. The scale of the figure being 1 cm. to 1 yard, determine :—

(a) The number of cubic yards of material removed at A per yard length of road.

(b) The point F reached by the foot of the embankment, assuming the material removed at A to expand $\frac{1}{13}$th in bulk.

N.B.—The point F on the diagram is purposely misplaced, and is not to be copied.

Attempted by 30 per cent. As a rule the candidates adopted a correct method of procedure, and there was a good proportion of fairly correct answers.

Q. 8. *A ship sails for two hours with a velocity of* $15_{21}°$ *miles per hour (directions being measured anti-clockwise from the East). The vessel then slows down and changes her course, and goes for* $1\frac{1}{2}$ *hours at* $12_{99}°$ *miles per hour. Finally, she sails for* $\frac{3}{4}$ *hour at* $8_{125}°$ *miles an hour.*

Plot the course of the ship to a scale of 1 inch to 10 miles, and find the magnitude and direction of the straight line from start to finish.

Over 90 per cent. attempted this, but although a quite straightforward problem, there was a large number of incorrect answers. The mistakes were due not so much to ignorance of the rule for vector addition, as to the candidates' ignorance of the directions of the cardinal points of the compass.

Q. 9. Three light ropes are knotted together at a point O. Three boys A, B, C pull at the ropes, and in one position of equilibrium the angles between the ropes are measured, and found to be

$AOB = 105°, BOC = 118°, COA = 137°.$

If the pull exerted by the boy A is 95 lbs., what are the pulls of B and C?

Use a scale of $\frac{1}{2}$ inch to 10 lbs.

Attempted by 70 per cent., the solutions being correct in nearly every case.

Q. 10. *You are given the projections of a piece of wire AB fixed in the horizontal plane at B.*

(a) *Find the true length of the wire, and the angle the wire makes with the horizontal plane.*

(b) *From the plan project a new elevation of the wire on x′ y′.*

All except eight candidates attempted this question, which was fairly
well answered on the whole, although there were too many worthless
attempts. The mistakes made, and the incompleteness of many answers,
showed that in the working of such exercises many students had not
handled, measured, or constructed such models as are, to some students,
essential to a clear understanding of the important part of the subject to
which this problem belongs.

Q. 11. The plan is given of a triangular prism with equilateral ends,
resting with a rectangular face on the ground. Determine the
height of the upper edge *AA*, and draw the elevation of the
prism on *xy*.

The triangle *d e f* is the plan of a section of the prism.
Show this section in the elevation. Also find the true shape of
the section.

Seventy-five per cent. attempted this question. In the majority of cases
the three views were correctly and neatly drawn. Occasionally the height of
the prism was made equal to the length of the plan of an end of the prism, thus
converting the prism into one the ends of which were isosceles triangles
instead of equilateral triangles. The more commonly occurring errors were
those made in determining the true shape of the section.

Q. 12. You are given the scale of slope of a plane and the figured plan of
a line ; unit for heights 0·1". Determine the figured plan of the
point where the line intersects the plane.

This question was the one least often attempted, being selected by less
than 8 per cent. of the candidates; the majority of these gave quite correct
solutions, but there were many poor answers.

Q. 13. The figure shows the size and shape of a rectangular box with the
lid open at right angles, dimensions parallel to *OY* and *OZ*
being set off full size, and parallel to *OX* half size :—

(a) Draw an end elevation of the box and open lid, that is, an
elevation on a plane parallel to *XOZ*.

(b) From the elevation project a plan.

(c) From the plan project a new elevation on a vertical plane
which makes 45° with the vertical faces of the box.

N.B.—The pictorial view is not to be copied, but dimensions
are to be measured from it.

Attempted by 62 per cent. In the main this was well answered. A
considerable proportion, however, neglected to show the inside of the box
by means of dotted lines in the two elevations, while others drew the lid
half the correct height.

Q. 14. You are given a map of a portion of Snowdon to a scale of one
inch to the mile, contoured in feet above sea level, and showing
the line of the railway from Llanberis station to the summit of
the mountain. By means of tracing paper and a pricker, or
otherwise, measure the length of the railway. If the average
slope of the line is 1 foot rise in *x* feet of length, what is *x*?

Where is railway steepest. and what is its inclination to the
horizontal at this place?

Attempted by 25 per cent. There was a satisfactory proportion of good
answers. No part of the question appeared to present any difficulty. In
finding the average slope several candidates went wrong when determining
the total rise. In answer to the last part of the question a few candidates
drew a curve showing the height of each point on the railway. They then
drew the steepest tangent to the curve, measured its actual inclination to
the horizontal, and gave this as the required inclination. It did not occur
to them that as their horizontal and vertical scales were different this
would not give the inclination asked for.

STAGE 2.

Results : 1st Class, 19 ; 2nd Class, 42 ; Failed, 28 ; Total, 89.

In Stage 2 the work was fairly satisfactory, but was not so good as in the Evening Examination, nor as last year. Candidates showed a tendency to relapse into the use of soft and blunt pencils, and the drawing was in many cases inaccurate and slovenly.

Q. 21. *In this example employ a decimal scale of ½ inch to 1 unit. Draw a right-angled triangle ABC, base BC=7·66 units, hypothenuse BA = 10 units. With centre B, radius BA, draw an arc to cut the base BC produced in D and draw the chord AD.*

Measure the base angle B, the altitude CA, the chord AD and the arc AD, and calculate the sine and the chord of the angle B, and the value of the angle in radians.

Give the correct values of the angle B in degrees and in radians, and the values of the sine and chord of the angle, taken directly from the examination tables supplied.

Attempted by every candidate. As a rule the figure was very accurately drawn, there were remarkably few errors of a serious kind, but a considerable number of answers were rendered incomplete by the omission of one or other of the many results asked for, the length of the arc being the result most frequently left out. The last part of the question was, in a number of cases, misunderstood in the manner indicated under Q. 1, Stage 1.

Q. 22. The lines AA, BB if produced would meet in a point P out of reach ; what is the distance of this point from the point K ? Measure the angle between the lines in degrees and in radians. Show two lines making 1·4° with AA and converging to P.

Attempted by 35 per cent. Only one or two candidates worked the latter part of the question accurately ; the other parts were generally well answered.

Q. 23. Determine the point O about which the quadrilateral $ABCD$ can be turned through a clockwise angle of 55°, bringing A to A'. Draw the quadrilateral in its new position.

Attempted by 46 per cent. Very little ingenuity was displayed in using tracing paper to solve this problem. The number of cases in which the centre O was found accurately by construction was scarcely satisfactory. The question was not so well answered as the corresponding one in Stage 1.

Q. 24. The point P' is the image of P in the mirror OM obtained by drawing PMP' perpendicular to OM and setting off MP' equal to MP. The point P'' is the image of P' in the mirror ON, similarly found. Draw this figure when $OM=3''$, $MP=1''$, $MON=40°$.

$PQRS$ shows the path of a ray of light reflected from both mirrors, the construction for which is sufficiently indicated. Draw two such rays through P for which the angle $PQM=70°$ in one and 90° in the other, and in each case measure the angle between the incident and reflected rays, marked θ in the figure. Do you observe any relation between your angles θ and the angle MON ?

Attempted by 53 per cent. There was a very satisfactory proportion of complete and accurate answers.

Q. 25. A road is formed along the side of a hill, as shown in cross-section at RR, by cutting away material A, and depositing it as an embankment B. The scale of the figure being 1 cm. to 1 yard, determine :—

    (a) The number of cubic yards of material removed at A per yard length of road.

(b) The point F reached by the foot of the embankment, assuming the material removed at A to expand $\frac{1}{12}$th in bulk.

N.B.—The point F on the diagram is purposely misplaced, and is not to be copied.

Attempted by 25 per cent. Although a fair proportion appeared to know the general lines on which the problem ought to be solved, there were not many complete answers. Even where attempts were made to find the mean height of the area of the cross section of the material A, an inaccurate rule was often employed.

Q. 26. A piece of sheet material K has a motion determined by the condition that the two grooves AA, BB cut in it slide over two pins a, b secured to a fixed plate H. Determine the path traced on H by the point P carried by K.

About 55 per cent. attempted this question, but, unfortunately, in probably quite half the cases an entirely wrong locus was obtained, namely, the ellipse which would have been traced on K by P, a point on H, if the pins a and b had moved in the slots of K, while the latter remained fixed ; in other words, many students unconsciously altered the conditions of the problem, an indication of careless reading of the question.

Q. 27. A shot having 1·5 units of mass strikes a target with a velocity of $1,200_{10°}$ feet per second, and rebounds with a velocity of $300_{110°}$ feet per second. The duration of the blow being estimated at $\frac{1}{100}$ of a second, the average force F exerted during the impact (that is the rate of change of momentum) is given by the vector equation.

$$F = 1\cdot5\ (1,200_{10°} - 300_{110°}) \div \tfrac{1}{100}$$
$$= (180,000_{10°} - 45,000_{110°})\ \text{pds.}$$

Find F in magnitude and direction.

Attempted by only 20 per cent. It is not easy to determine precisely why this question was not more popular ; teachers are in the best position to do this. Possibly the difficulty lies in interpreting the given vector equation. If so the task of removing the obstacle is surely a simple one. But even some of the candidates, who evidently realised that the difference of two vectors was required, failed to apply the simple rule in order to determine this difference. The subject of vectors is one which teachers must endeavour to deal with in a more efficient manner.

Q. 28. In a laboratory experiment a polygon with five hinged joints is constructed out of strips of sheet metal. This link polygon being placed on a drawing board, forces, which can be measured by the springs S, are applied at the corners. If the figure takes the form shown, and the force A measures 2·08 lbs., what would you expect the forces B, C, D, E to measure.

Show the resultant of the three forces E, A, and B.

Let the force scale be $\frac{1}{4}$ inch to 0·1 lb.

Attempted by nearly 40 per cent. This question was only moderately well answered. The first part is a very easy problem, requiring the application of the principle of the triangle of forces five times over. Of those who attempted it many drew a separate triangle of forces for each joint of the frame. Of those who solved the first part only a small proportion afterwards determined the line of action of the resultant of the three specified forces, and of these, many drew a new link polygon for the purpose instead of using the given one. The properties of link polygons are not sufficiently studied experimentally.

Q. 29. You are given the projections of a piece of wire AB fixed in the horizontal plane at B.
  (a) Find the true length of the wire and the angles the wire makes with the two planes of projection.
  (b) From the elevation project a new plan of the wire on $x_1\ y_1$.

All except three candidates attempted this. There were certainly many most excellent answers; at the same time the number of worthless results was far too large. It is quite clear that owing to unsatisfactory or ineffective methods of presenting the subject, many of the candidates had never realised what they had to determine when working this type of exercise. The matter is one which requires very serious consideration by teachers. This branch of the subject possesses inherent difficulties, which, however, are easily surmounted by even the less able students if proper methods of teaching are adopted. As the complete mastery of this particular problem delights a student, and often alters his attitude to the subject as a whole, besides giving him power to successfully attack a multitude of other problems, the teacher cannot devote too much time and trouble in seeing that it is intelligently dealt with. Suitable models for measurement by the student should be employed, as specified elsewhere.

Q. 30. The figure shows the size and shape of a rectangular box with the lid open at right angles along the hinge OY, dimensions parallel OY and OZ being set off full size, and parallel to OX half size.

    (a) Draw an end elevation of the box with the lid open at 60°, that is an elevation on a vertical plane parallel to ZOX.

    (b) From the elevation project a plan.

    (c) From the plan project a new elevation on a vertical plane which makes 45° with the first vertical plane.

    N.B.—The pictorial view is not to be copied, but dimensions are to be measured from it.

Attempted by about 72 per cent. As the question presented no difficulties, from its very nature, there was a large proportion of satisfactory answers. As in the Stage 1 papers, the thickness and depth of the box were often not shown in the two elevations, while the height of the lid was frequently drawn one-half the correct height.

Q. 31. A coal scuttle (with parts omitted) is shown. Draw a plan projected from AA.
    Draw a development of the cylindrical part AA of the scuttle, omitting the curve where it intersects the conical foot.

Attempted by 50 per cent. The proportion of correct and carefully executed solutions was rather small, though the method of obtaining both plan and development seemed to be generally understood.

Q. 32. You are given a map of a portion of Snowden to a scale of one inch to the mile, contoured in feet above sea level, and showing the line of the railway from Llanberis station to the summit of the mountain. By means of tracing paper and a pricker, or otherwise, measure the length of the railway. If the average slope of the line is 1 foot rise in x feet of length, what is x? Where is the railway steepest, and what is its inclination to the horizontal at this place?
    A curve CC is begun, showing the height MP above sea level of any point P on the railway, distant OM miles from Llanberis station as measured along the railway line on the map. Complete this curve.

About 40 per cent. attempted this question. Some very satisfactory answers were given in response to the first part of the question. In completing the curve CC showing the height of any point on the line, many candidates appeared to consider it sufficient to plot the heights of a few points, e.g., the stations, and then to draw a fair curve through these; curves obtained in this way showed only very inadequately the varying slope of the railway.

Q. 33. A star in the north has an angular elevation of 30° above the horizon, and one in the south-east an elevation of 60°. Determine the plane containing the stars and the spectator, and measure its inclination to the horizontal, and the direction in degrees north of east of the lines of steepest slope up the plane.

About 12 per cent. attempted this, and almost invariably the answers were correct. The candidates choosing this were clearly those who thoroughly understood their work, for as a rule they were successful in attacking the other questions which they selected.

Report on the Examination in Machine Construction and Drawing.

STAGE 1.

Results : 1st Class, 1,718 ; 2nd Class, 1,724 ; Failed, 1,706 ; Total, 5,148.

The number of candidates in this stage was 5,148, being about 4½ per cent. greater than in 1905. The quality of the work was equal to that of recent years, and in many schools was excellent. But there are still far too many instances of schools in which the teaching is evidently of the most slipshod character. In these cases the work is rough and untidy ; the candidates are unable to draw correctly the simplest of machine details such as nuts or keys, they cannot insert dimensions properly, do not understand the meaning of section lines, and sometimes are ignorant of projection. Candidates so taught are quite unfitted to proceed to the higher stages of the subject. To remedy this, copies should be sparingly used in class, the efforts of the students being directed rather to the sketching and drawing of actual machine details, a collection of which should be procurable from manufacturers in the neighbourhood, and the work should be confined to simple fastenings and the like, until these can be neatly and accurately represented. Some detailed criticisms of the work in Stage 1 now follow.

TRACING.

Trace in ink on the tracing paper supplied the eye-bolt shown on Diagram X. Insert the dimensions and print the title as shown.

The lines should be very black, of uniform and moderate width, and as continuous as possible.

On the whole the tracing was well executed, but many candidates used weak ink or drew fine lines, showing that they had not been taught the requirements for printing purposes. Others wasted time by first drawing the copy in pencil and then tracing that instead of the original drawing. A few did the tracing by freehand or in pencil and in consequence received no credit for this portion of their work.

Example 1.

1½-INCH BEARING.

The diagram gives dimensioned hand-sketches of details of a simple bearing. Draw full size, inserting dimensions :—

  (a) An elevation corresponding with A, but in section, adding the cap and one of the ⅝″ studs.

  (b) An elevation, projected from (a), looking on the face indicated by the arrow. In this view the cap, cap screws, and the ⅝″ studs should be shown.

  (c) A plan.

N.B.—Do not draw the pictorial view, nor the parts separated as in the diagram. Dotted lines, representing hidden parts, are not required.

This example was the one generally chosen, and in a large number of schools the work was uniformly good, with very few failures, and more than half the candidates passing in the first class. In many cases, however, and in some schools throughout, bad work was prevalent, the teaching being evidently most faulty. Thus, soft blunt pencils were used ; centre lines were omitted or erased ; dimension lines were too frequently placed close up to the main lines of the drawing, or were crowded together, or the written figures were small and scarcely legible. Again, many candidates have very hazy notions about the use of section lines. It was quite common to find a view, otherwise good, spoiled by being completely covered by such lines, like a flat wash over an elevation. And it was quite as common to find a view ruined by some such muddle of cross hatching as could conceivably be obtained by taking a number of part section planes, one behind the other. But perhaps the most striking evidence of defective teaching was seen in the many grotesque attempts to insert the $\frac{5}{8}''$ stud. Too many candidates lost marks by drawing the plan out of projection, and occasionally the example was cancelled because the views were scattered over the sheet in defiance of the rules of projection. The plotting of dimensions to scale was good throughout.

Alternative Example 2.

END OF A CONNECTING-LINK OF AN AIR COMPRESSOR.

Make full size separate scale drawings of details, with dimensions as follows :—

(a) A longitudinal and an end view of the rod end A. The screw thread may be drawn in the manner shown.

(b) Three views of the nut B.

(c) Three views of the wedge C.

(d) Three views of the head D.

N.B.—No credit will be given for drawing the parts assembled, as in the diagram. Dotted lines, representing hidden parts, are not required.

When this example was selected, which was comparatively seldom, it was generally taken by the better candidates, and so was often well done. What failures occurred were for the most part attributable to the candidates ignoring the very clear instructions and drawing the parts assembled as in the diagram, and not in separate detail, as required.

Questions, only two to be answered.

The Sketches in answer to these questions should be drawn freehand on the squared foolscap paper, the lines on which may be taken as ¼-inch apart.

Good use was made of the squared paper, and it was satisfactory to find that *freehand* sketching was almost universal.

Q. 11. Sketch full size, inserting dimensions, two views of a wheel boss, fixed to a shaft by means of a sunk gib key, as follows :—

Diameter of shaft	2″
Diameter of boss	4″
Length of boss	3″
Width of key	$\frac{5}{8}''$
Depth of key	$\frac{3}{8}''$
Taper of key, ¼″ per foot.	

This question was fairly well answered. The two principal defects were in making the key way extend only part way through the wheel, and in not extending it in the shaft a sufficient distance to allow of the insertion or withdrawal of the key.

Q. 12. Name the materials of which the parts of Example 1, and the several parts A, B, C, D, E and F of Example 2 would be constructed.

This question was also frequently well answered, but occasionally most unsuitable materials were named, such as cast iron for the rod end or for the bolt.

Q. 13. Sketch full size, inserting dimensions, a 1" rag bolt *or* Lewis bolt, suitable for securing the frame of a machine to a stone foundation. Explain how the bolt is fixed in the stone.

Very few really good sketches were received. Bad proportions were the rule. The hole in the stone was often parallel, and when undercut it might be too small at the top to allow of the insertion of the bolt. Moreover, the nut was often shown screwed down on to the top of the lead filling, showing no room for a flange.

Q. 14. Explain briefly, with sketches, how you would set out, drill, and tap the hole marked H in Example 1, on the diagram.

Candidates had not much power of description, though it was evident that many had used a drilling machine. Few, however, employed the holes in the cap for marking out the required tapping holes.

Q. 15. Sketch in section the armature of a small drum wound motor, showing clearly how the stampings are secured.

This question was seldom attempted, indicating that a knowledge of electrical work is not very common.

STAGE 2.

Results : 1st Class, 671 ; 2nd Class, 1,669 ; Failed, 1,474 ; Total, 3,814.

The work sent in showed clearly that the students had not sufficiently sketched from actual machine parts. There has been too much working from copies. Much better work would result if copies were banished altogether from the course of instruction and their place taken by actual machine details, even of the simplest kind. This method of working would improve the freehand sketching, would cultivate the habit of reading a drawing correctly, and would train the student to observe details and machinery of every kind and description.

The quality of the drawing was generally poor. Clumsy lines, the result of a blunt pencil, and the bad joining up of curves to lines were persistent features of the work. The tracing was, however, fairly well done.

Example 3, Diagram Y.
ADJUSTABLE FOOTSTEP BEARING.

Draw to scale and complete the two projections partly shown in Diagram Y. Example 3, and also draw a vertical section through line *E F*, correctly projected, looking in the direction of the arrow marked *G*.

Scale, ½ size.

No dotted lines need be shown and figured dimensions need not be inserted.

A large proportion of candidates who tried this example failed to realize the real arrangement of the footstep bearing from the views given, and did little more than set out to scale the views given on the diagram. There were some notable exceptions, however, in which the views were correctly drawn, sectioned, and lined in neatly.

Alternative Example 4, Diagram Y.
LIFT VALVE.

Draw, full size, an outside view corresponding to the vertical section shown in Example 4, Diagram Y. Draw also a sectional plan through line *C D*, with the spindle *K* removed. Finally draw a sectional elevation taken through the centre line, looking in the direction of the arrow marked *H*.

Also make a plan and the two end elevations of the spindle marked *K*, all the necessary dimensions being shown on it.

Scale, full size.

No dotted lines need be shown and figured dimensions need not be inserted in the three first views.

This simple example was not understood by a number of candidates. The views were not properly projected from one another, and the exact construction of the valve and its seating was evidently unknown to most of the candidates.

Questions, only two to be answered.

The sketches in answer to these questions should be drawn freehand on the squared foolscap paper.

Q. 21. State of what materials you would make the parts marked *M*, *N*, *O*, *P*, in the footstep drawing, Diagram Y, Example 3. Also sketch an arrangement to prevent the rotation of the footstep bearing (*N*) in the casting *O*.

The first part was generally well answered. The answers to the second part were, however, as a rule poor. Many candidates sketched a method which entirely destroyed the vertical freedom of adjustment of the footstep, and some destroyed the horizontal freedom as well.

Q. 22. A wrought iron crank shaft is formed by bending a 2″ round bar as shown in sketch.

How would you proceed to turn the part marked *A*.

Most of the candidates who attempted this question gave a correct method for throwing the crank shaft out of the centre of the lathe, but few indicated how to get the crank pin in the axis, and how to set the work so that the crank pin should be truly parallel with the crank shaft.

Q. 23. A plate girder is made up of a vertical web 2′ deep connected to top and bottom flanges, 1 wide, by two angle irons 3″ × 3″ × ½″. The web and flange plates are ½″ thick. Sketch a section of the above girder, putting in the necessary dimensions. Show also a suitable stiffener.

Not generally attempted, but fairly well answered except with regard to the stiffeners.

Q. 24. Sketch to scale, half size, inserting dimensions, a double-riveted butt joint with two straps, as used in the longitudinal joint of a boiler. Rivets, ⅞″ diameter, pitch, 3″, and thickness of plate, ¾″. What would be the efficiency of this joint?

The answers indicated that few candidates had ever sketched from and measured an actual riveted joint.

Q. 25. Show, by sketches, the method of holding and insulating the bars of a commutator of a continuous current dynamo. The shaft is 3″ diameter, and the outside of the bars 8″ diameter.

Fairly well done by a few candidates.

STAGE 3.

Results : 1st Class, 102 ; 2nd Class, 236 ; Failed, 365 ; Total, 703.

There was an increase in the number of candidates taking this stage. The quality of the work was better than that of last year, though the freehand sketching of mechanical details in connection with the answers to the questions was generally poor. The tracing was, however, exceedingly well done, and a large proportion of the candidates gained full marks for this part of their work.

Generally, the draughtsmanship was poor, the lines being clumsy, and the joining of the curves with the lines inaccurate. There were notable exceptions, however, and there were designs, both of the pulleys and the slide valve, which would do credit to a first class drawing office.

Example 5, Diagram Z.

The main shaft of a machine shop makes 75 revolutions per minute. A countershaft is to be placed between the shaft and a machine the driving pulley of which is 1' diameter and which is to be driven at 300 revolutions per minute. The velocity ratio of the drive from the main shaft to the countershaft on to the fast and loose pulleys is to be equal to the velocity ratio of the drive from the countershaft to the machine pulley.

1. Write down the diameters of the pulleys which must be placed on the main shaft and the countershaft respectively.

2. Work out the width of the belt connecting the main shaft with the fast and loose pulleys on the countershaft, assuming that the belt is ⅛" thick, that the safe working stress is 75 pounds per inch of width, that the ratio of the maximum to the minimum tension is 2·56 to 1, and that the belt transmits 3·9 horse power.

3. Design the fast and loose pulleys, assuming the countershaft to be 2" diameter, drawing—

  (a) A sectional elevation of the pulleys in a plane containing the centre line of the shaft to a scale of 6 inches to 1 foot.

  (b) An end elevation of the fixed pulley to the same scale.

Show clearly the arrangement you make for the lubrication of the loose pulley.

Full marks cannot be obtained unless the drawings are properly dimensioned.

This was the generally selected example, and on the whole it was fairly well done. Many failed to find the proper width of belt, but few failed to find pulleys of the proper size for the main shaft and countershaft. Some simply drew a pair of fast and loose pulleys without any attempt to design them to fulfil the given conditions ; a few others had such faith in their mathematics that pulleys of absurd widths were drawn, notably one 3 feet wide, this being the width of belt found to transmit the given horse power.

Alternative Example 6, Diagram Z.

Figures 1 and 2, Diagram Z, show the ports of a steam engine cylinder. The valve gear consists of a single eccentric sheave connected directly to the valve spindle by an eccentric rod. Cut-off is to take place at 80 per cent. of the stroke, whilst the maximum opening of the steam port is to be 1½" and the lead is to be ⅛". The valve is also to have ⅛" exhaust (inside) lap. Steam pressure, 160 lbs. per square inch.

1. Determine and write down clearly the travel of the valve, the steam (outside) lap, and the angular advance of the eccentric sheave corresponding to the above conditions, neglecting the effect of the obliquity of the connecting rod.

2. Design the valve and as much of the valve spindle as is necessary to show the way it is connected to the valve, drawing—

  (a) A sectional elevation of the valve along the centre line of the valve spindle. The valve spindle is to be 1¼" diameter.

  (b) A cross section of the valve.

  (c) Plan of the valve.

These drawings are to be half size, and each is to show the end of the valve spindle connected to the valve.

Full marks cannot be obtained unless the drawings are properly dimensioned.

Many of the candidates who chose this example made a good design, though only a few succeeded in finding the proper outside lap, travel, and angular advance to fulfil the given conditions. There were some designs in which the valve spindle passed through the valve without any protecting boss so that the steam would simply blow through into the exhaust. Other designs showed the inside lap as a projection over the exhaust port.

On account of the general difficulty which candidates felt in solving the first part of the problem, the following simple method of solution by the Bilgram diagram may be found useful.

From any point O, Figure 1, draw a circle whose radius is equal to the given maximum port opening, viz., 1½".

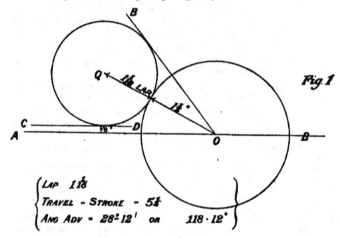

Fig. 1

LAP 1¼
TRAVEL - STROKE - 5½
ANG ADV = 28°·12' OR 118·12°

Draw OB to represent the crank, position corresponding to 80 per cent. cut off, AB being the line of stroke.

Draw CD, parallel to AB, at a distance from it equal to the given lead, viz., ⅛". Then by trial find a circle whose centre is Q, to touch CO, the circle whose centre is O, and the line OB. The radius of this circle is the required lap. The length OQ is half the travel and the angle AOQ is the angular advance.

Questions, only two to be answered.

The sketches in answer to these questions should be drawn freehand, and may be drawn by the side of the written answer on the squared foolscap paper attached to the drawing paper. Additional foolscap may, if required, be obtained on application to the Superintendent of the examination.

Q. 31. Describe, illustrating your answer with sketches, a practical method of setting an eccentric sheave on a crank shaft to a given angular advance. In your answer, assume that the crank is formed on the shaft and that the webs are machined.

Few good answers were given to this question. A typical answer was :— Set the piston on a dead centre and then turn the sheave into the proper position and mark off the keyway.

63

Q. 32. Two tie rods, each 2″ diameter, are to be joined by means of a muff cotter joint. Sketch the joint and write on the chief dimensions. The maximum shearing stress in the cotter is not to exceed 6 tons per square inch, and the maximum bearing stress is not to exceed 10 tons per square inch. The load on the ·tie rods is equivalent to a stress of 4 tons per square inch.

This was generally attempted and in many cases good answers and good sketches were given. Fully two-thirds of those who tried the design failed to grasp that it is necessary to increase the diameter of the rod inside the muff to get a good joint.

Q. 33. Sketch the joint (in section) between two cast-iron pipes of a hydraulic main in which the pressure is 700 lbs. per square inch and explain how the joint is made.

A fair proportion of good sketches were made in answer to this, though the majority of the sketches were badly done, the proportions of the joint were altogether wrong, and the method of packing shown quite inadmissible.

Q. 34. Sketch the arrangement of the brush holder for a dynamo, showing clearly how the pressure of the brush on the commutator may be regulated, and how the lead of the brushes may be varied.

Few attempted this, but the majority of the answers were good.

Q. 35. How would you take the buckle out of a steel plate, say 3′ wide and 8′ long?

The answers to this were disappointing, because so many said that the buckle could be taken out by hitting it on the top with suitable hammers.

HONOURS.

Results : 1st Class, 3 ; 2nd Class, 12 ; Failed, 67 ; Total, 82.

There was a fair proportion of good work, though generally the draughtsmanship was not of a first rate quality. There were some notable exceptions.

Example 7.

Design an eccentric sheave and strap for operating the slide valve of a high-speed engine making 400 revolutions per minute. The diameter of the crank shaft at the place where the sheave is to be keyed is 9 inches. There is no restriction on the width of the sheave. The steam pressure acting on the valve is 140 lbs. per square inch, and the net area on which the steam pressure acts is 80 square inches, and the co-efficient of friction is 0·2. The travel of the valve is 6 inches. The weight of the reciprocating parts, which include the valve, valve spindle and connections, and a portion of the eccentric rod, is 330 pounds. Calculate and state the maximum load along the eccentric rod due respectively to valve friction and inertia of the moving parts, assuming them to move with simple harmonic motion. State also the tensile stress, compressive stress, and bearing pressures which you use in the course of the design.

This was the generally selected question. Many designs were sent up without any calculations at all, and even where calculations of the inertia stress had been attempted the designs were quite unsuitable for the high speed required, and in fact were mere copies of eccentric sheaves designed for low-speed engines.

Alternative Example 8.

Design a small hand-driven portable machine for cutting keyways in a 1¼″ shaft. The machine is to be as light as possible, and arranged so that it can be conveniently and quickly clamped to the shaft. Its size is to be such that a keyway can be cut 8 inches long.

Few selected this question and only a small proportion of these made, or indicated rather, a workable design. Most of the designs were more suitable for power driving, and the method of attaching the machine to the shaft was generally crude and clumsy.

Questions, only two to be answered.

The sketches in answer to these questions should be drawn freehand, and may be drawn by the side of the written answer on the squared foolscap paper attached to the drawing paper. Additional foolscap may, if required, be obtained on application to the Superintendent of the examination.

Q. 41. Describe, illustrating your answer with sketches, the method of moulding a rope pulley with a V groove, so that the groove is chilled.

As a rule well answered.

Q. 42. Sketch a tube expander, and briefly explain the principle of its action.

A few good answers, accompanied by neat sketching, but very few gave any indication of the principle of the action of an expander.

Q. 43. Make a careful sketch of a part of the track of an electric railway in which a separate conductor is used for the return, showing clearly the way the live and the return rails are respectively supported and insulated.

Notwithstanding the many miles of electric track now in operation in this country, one or two candidates only attempted this question, and the answers were poor.

Q. 44. Two spur wheels are required to transmit 50 H.P. between two shafts, with a velocity ratio of 2 to 1, the speed of the smaller being 100 revolutions per minute. The distance between the shafts is 3 feet. Determine the pitch p of the teeth, assuming that the width of the tooth is twice the pitch, that the depth is $0·7p$, that the thickness at the pitch line is $0·48p$, and that the whole of the pressure is considered to be uniformly distributed along the line of contact between one pair of teeth. Take a working stress of 1 ton per square inch in tension.

The generally selected question. The solution was in most cases correctly given.

Q. 45. Sketch the main bearing for a 9-inch shaft, arranged for forced lubrication. Show carefully the oil ways. What pressure would the oil be supplied at?

Attempted by many, but the sketching was poor and the knowledge of detail small.

Q. 46. Draw a short specification for the mild steel plates of a boiler, or for the steel ties for a bridge.

Many good answers but few really complete ones.

HONOURS PRACTICAL EXAMINATION.

There were 17 candidates asked to come to this examination, and of these 15 presented themselves.

There were three alternative designs, relating respectively to a steam engine, hydraulic machinery, and girder work.

Each question was selected by more than one candidate, but the larger number took the question relating to the steam engine.

Three candidates did first-class work, and as it happens each took a different question. These three were passed in the first class.

The remaining 12 candidates did sufficiently good work to justify the award of a second class.

Report on the Examination in Building Construction and Drawing.

STAGE 1.

Results : 1st Class, 918 ; 2nd Class, 1,282 ; Failed, 1,208 ; Total, 3,408.

Speaking generally, the improvement in drawing is undoubted, many of the sketches being excellent and far better than the tracing. The knowledge of elementary construction is very fair, but there is a general lack of practical knowledge of materials, and this could be obviated in the way that has been suggested in the remarks on Questions 3 and 10. The powers of description are bad, and great carelessness is shown in not following the instructions, in misreading the questions, and in selecting the questions to be answered. It is probable that far better results in these examinations would be obtained if, towards the close of the course, teachers were to give an hour's written examination to the whole class as a test. It is clear that in many cases the candidates have no idea of what a written examination is, and consequently waste valuable time at the beginning and are much hurried during the last half-hour.

Q. *1. Make a neat tracing in ink of the drawing given, with the writing : the lines should be firm and solid and should finish accurately at the proper points.

The general average of the tracing has certainly improved since attention was drawn to it two years ago, but many of the tracings are still very bad, some of the worst being done by candidates whose pencil sketches are very fair indeed. This would indicate that more attention should be given to tracing in the Schools. Many marks were lost through candidates' carelessly omitting to trace the printing and writing as well as the drawing. Full marks were gained by 176 students, while 127 were so bad that no marks could be given.

Q. 2. Describe fully what you know of blue lias lime, its origin, manufacture, preparation and the precautions to be taken in its use.

This question was attempted by only 365 candidates, and was badly answered on the whole. Very few of those who tried the question seemed to be aware of the difference between blue lias and common lime. Only two candidates obtained full marks, 55 got none.

Q. 3. What are the essential properties of a good brick ? Distinguish between the following bricks, and state for what purpose they are chiefly used : Fletton, gault, red rubber, blue Staffordshire.

This was attempted by 1,066 candidates ; the first part of the question as to the properties of a good brick was fairly well answered, but the latter part badly. Fletton bricks, though so largely used now, seemed to be unknown to all but a few, and the vaguest notions prevailed as to gaults. This shows the want of practical teaching. It should surely be possible to have in all schools specimens of the various kinds of bricks in ordinary use, so that the students might see and handle them for themselves. Full marks were awarded to 10 candidates, 40 obtained no marks.

Q. 4. Show by a sketch on your squared paper how a pole should be slung by a rope for lifting vertically.

This eminently practical question, although attempted by 1,216 candidates, was answered very indifferently. Many quite misunderstood the question and sketched elaborate pictures of posts with guy ropes, or rough Derrick arrangements, and a very slight amount of consideration should have shown a number of the candidates that by no possibility could a pole be lifted vertically by the methods indicated in their sketches. 117 answers were awarded full marks, while the fact that of those attempting the question, 680, or 56 per cent., obtained no marks speaks for itself.

Q. 5. What is the size of a countess slate? Describe clearly and fully what is meant by "lap," and "gauge" in a slated roof, and illustrate your answer by sketches.

This was attempted by 3,004 candidates, or 90 per cent. of the whole number, and 205 obtained full marks. Attention was called last year to the total ignorance displayed by many candidates as to what "lap" in a tiled or slated roof means, and the same lack of knowledge was very apparent this year. It is extraordinary how many candidates showed both by their descriptions and their sketches that they were under the impression that "lap" is the amount which the tail of one slate projects beyond the head of the course immediately below it, so that over a large portion of a roof there would be only one thickness of slates and never more than two. This ignorance on such a simple practical matter is not creditable to the teachers. As there were three parts to this question, most of the candidates obtained some marks, but 225 failed altogether to get any.

Q. 6. Draw to a scale of $\frac{1}{12}$ (1" to a foot) the plans of two consecutive courses of a square three-and-a-half-brick pier in Flemish bond : the joints may be shown by single lines.

This was the most difficult question in the whole paper, and though it was attempted by 1,905 candidates, the results were very poor. Marks were given for any intelligent attempt to keep a face of Flemish bond and to minimize the number of straight joints. But in a large number of cases no bond whatever was shown in the thickness of the pier and no attempt made to break the vertical joints. Only 77 obtained full marks, and 547 failed to get a mark.

Q. 7. You have the choice of the following stones in building a mansion with stables attached : state in what parts you would use them, giving your reasons : Granite, Whinstone, Hard York, Craigleith, Portland whitbed, Box ground Hopton Wood, Derbyshire marble.

Very little attention seems to be given to the nature and characteristics of building stones, although the subject is distinctly mentioned in the Syllabus. The question was attempted by only 304 candidates, or less than one per cent., and nearly all the answers were poor ; five candidates got full marks, 24 none.

Q. 8. Sketch full size on your squared paper a vertical section through the junction of two 3-inch round cast iron rain-water pipes, and describe the method of jointing.

This was attempted by 2,241 candidates of whom only 35 obtained full marks. The descriptions were generally very meagre and the sketches poor ; also carelessness in reading the question led several candidates to draw the junction between two lead pipes. It is curious that in many cases the pipes were shown with their ends simply butted together and secured by an iron collar. 412 candidates failed to get any marks.

Q. 9. A York stone sill is described as "7" × 4½" rubbed, weathered, and throated." Draw to a scale of ⅓ (1½" to a foot) a cross section of this sill, and describe in their proper order the operations of the mason in preparing it.

2,064 candidates attempted this question, and the drawing of the stone sill was generally good, but the description of the proper order of the mason's operations in preparing it were generally poor and showed a lack of practical knowledge. 33 obtained full marks, 41 none.

Q. 10. If lead weighs 710 lbs. per cubic foot what is the thickness of 6 lb. sheet lead ? What weight lead should be used for flats, dormer cheeks, flashings, hips and valleys, soil pipes ?

1,003 candidates tried this question, and a considerable number worked out the thickness correctly, but the second part of the question was badly answered, many having no idea of the weight of sheet lead for practical purposes. 24 lb. and 30 lb. lead for flats, and 10 lb. for flashings, being instances of what must simply have been wild guessing. If the schools were only provided with a few specimens of 5lb., 6lb. and 7 lb. lead for the students to see and handle such ignorance as is displayed in the answers to this question would be impossible. 112 got full marks, 82 failed to get any.

Q. 11. A window opening 3 feet wide is spanned by a wooden lintel 4″ deep with 6″ bearing at each end. Draw to a scale of $\frac{1}{8}$ (1″ to a foot) an elevation of the opening and the lintel with a segmental discharging arch over it in two half-brick rings.

This was the favourite question, and was attempted by 3,054 candidates, and on the whole was well answered, though the mistake was too frequently made of letting the arch spring from the lintel, instead of forming a proper skewback quite clear of the end of the lintel. This mistake, which is very common in inferior work, ought to have been avoided. 846 answers were given full marks ; 286 failed to gain any marks.

Q. 12. A compound girder is composed of a 12″ × 5″ rolled steel joist with a 9″ × $\frac{1}{2}$″ steel plate top and bottom. Sketch on your squared paper one quarter full size (3″ to a foot) a section through this girder : the rivets need not be shown.

This question, which was intended to test the knowledge of the students as to what a rolled steel joist is, was attempted by 2169 candidates Although some of the sketches were excellent, 100 obtaining full marks, many candidates had no idea of the shape of a R.S.J., and sketched the most preposterous forms. It would have been thought that no ambiguity could possibly exist in this question as to what was required, and yet in a large number of cases two joists were combined either alongside or on top of each other. 513 obtained no marks.

STAGE 2.

Results : 1st Class, 605 ; 2nd Class, 1,437 ; Failed, 655 ; Total, 2,697.

The work, as a whole, in this stage was a decided improvement upon that of last year, but many of the attempts were so bad that the candidates would have failed to pass even in the previous stage. It cannot be too often repeated that a candidate for any of the higher stages should have previously passed first class in the one below. It would also be a great advantage to students if in the course of their instruction they had occasional short test examinations for practice in drawing up intelligible descriptions and preparing drawings to given conditions.

Q. *21. Make a neat tracing in ink of the drawing, Figure 21, with the writing and figures. The lines should be firm and solid and should finish accurately at the proper points.

About three per cent. obtained no marks, and only 1½ per cent. full marks. It was on the whole fairly well done, but the printing and dimensions were, as is usually the case, very weak. This may have arisen in some instances from the position of the candidate with regard to the light in the examination room, but it was probably more often due to want of practice.

Q. 22. Describe fully the preparation of the trench, the mixing and laying of the concrete, and the laying and jointing of the pipes in a straight run of 4-inch glazed stoneware house drain laid at an average depth of 3 feet. Draw, half-full size, a longitudinal section through one of the joints.

Attempted by 1,986, of whom 25 failed to obtain any marks and 4 obtained full marks. Such parts of the question as were covered by text-book knowledge were well answered, but the practical parts, such as boning the trench to a regular fall, driving pegs for the level of the concrete, and leaving a hand-hole under the sockets, were very weak. The drawing of a finished joint in section was disgraceful, not more than half a dozen out of many hundreds being even approximately correct. The majority rounded over the bottom of the socket into the bore of the pipe and showed the socket about four times too deep. Some specified that the joints were to be made with concrete, but nearly all gave neat cement instead of adding a small portion of sand, up to, say, $\frac{1}{3}$, as a provision against expansion. Many assumed 4″ as the *outside* diameter of the pipe.

Q. 23. Draw to a scale of $\frac{1}{12}$ (1″ to a foot) the elevation of 4 feet run of a half-brick honey-combed sleeper wall 8 courses high including footing, and the ends of 4 joists suitable for a span of 6 feet ; also draw a cross section of it showing the sleeper and joist. Show the joints of the brickwork and state under what circumstances a damp proof course would be required.

Attempted by 1,298, of whom 33 failed to obtain any marks and 15 obtained full marks. This was, on the whole, fairly answered but many omitted the wall plate and carried the openings into the top course, giving no stability. The joists proposed for the span of 6 feet varied from 3″ × 1¼″ to 9″ × 3″ the proper size being about 5″ × 2″.

Q. 24. Sketch on your squared paper a hand mortising machine for working timber, and describe how it is used.

Attempted by 676, of whom 18 had no marks and 24 full marks. This question was remarkably well answered ; the sketches were in general not only in fair proportion but showed very clearly the construction and manipulation. The information had evidently been derived at first hand.

Q. *25. The diagram, Fig. 25, shows a three-light opening in a ground floor room : the centre is to have a pair of French casements opening inwards and the side lights double hung sashes. Draw to a scale of $\frac{1}{12}$ (1″ to a foot) a plan through the central and one side opening showing frames, casements, &c., and a vertical section to the same scale through the bottom rail of the French casement.

Attempted by 1,122, of whom 85 got no marks and only 3 obtained full marks. Although attempted by a large number there were very few good answers. The majority were unable to draw a passable section of the bottom rail and sill of the casement, and many designed it in such a way that the door would neither open or shut, nor keep the rain out. The left hand leaf of the casement was in many cases made to open first.

Q. 26. Explain fully what is meant by the terms "render, float and set" on brickwork. Describe the composition of the stuff used for each operation and the mode of executing it.

Attempted by 1,440, of whom 44 did not obtain any marks and 13 were awarded full marks. Fairly well answered but in many cases too briefly. An excess of sand for the lime to carry was frequently given. Portland cement was frequently specified instead of lime, whereas if cement had been intended the question would necessarily have said so.

Q. 27. A cistern is required to hold 1,000 gallons ; what should be its length, breadth and height, and of what material should it be constructed if used for storing drinking water ? What would be the weight of the water in the cistern when full ?

Attempted by 742 ; 47 had no marks and 16 full marks. Some of the answers to this questions were ludicrous, outrageous sizes being given. Very few allowed for a margin above the surface of the water for overflow, etc. No consensus of opinion existed as to the material of the tank ; nearly every material was specified in turn.

Q. *28. The diagram shows a block of stone being lifted by a sling chain and dogs ; with a pull of 5 cwt. in the crane chain show graphically what the stress will be in each part of the sling chain surrounding the letter *A*, assuming free play at the eye of the dogs.

Attempted by 723 ; 112 had no marks and 22 full marks. This was a very elementary example but only a few candidates gave complete answers. They were nearly all wrong with the stress in the horizontal part of the chain which they worked without due regard to the result in passing through the dog. Very few realised that the stress in the horizontal part of the sling equalled that in the other parts. Practically no candidate appeared to have been taught that "lines drawn parallel to the forces acting at the angles of a frame in equilibrium form a closed polygon," and its corollary that "lines drawn from the angles of this polygon parallel to the sides of the frame must meet in a point and determine the magnitude of the stresses in the sides of the frame."

Q. 29. An internal brick wall 12 ft. long has to be removed and replaced by a fir beam which has to carry a distributed load of 4 tons. Calculate the scantling of the beam. If the same load, instead of being distributed, were concentrated at a point 4 ft. from one end, would you consider the beam strong enough ? Give your reasons fully.

Attempted by 412 ; 65 had no marks, 17 full marks. There was, as last year, a general failure to comprehend the principles of the strength of beams. Some most elaborate answers ended with impossible results. Wrong formulæ were frequently used, and feet and inches, tons and cwts. hopelessly mixed. Teachers should explain the general principle by leverage moments and not rely upon formulæ which are as likely as not to be wrongly applied.

Q. 30. Draw to a scale of ⅛ (1½″ to a foot) a section through two consecutive spandril steps with moulded nosings of a hanging stone staircase and describe clearly how such a staircase is constructed.

Attempted by 1,154, of whom 37 failed to obtain any marks and 7 had full marks. This question was well answered by several candidates who knew the practical difficulties of fixing such steps and how they were overcome. Those who relied upon book knowledge indicated it very plainly and failed to give a reasonable description of the fixing, while in very many cases their section of the steps was absurd.

Q. *31. The diagram is an outline plan of a first-floor room which is to have a single-joisted floor : state the number, lengths and scantlings of the timbers which you would require for the plates and joists—including trimmers—for this floor.

Attempted by 1,973 candidates of whom 73 got no marks and 14 full marks. The same want of knowledge in determining the sizes of joists was shown as in last year's papers. The simple practical rule of "take half the span in feet, add two and this gives depth in inches, one-third of depth gives thickness" would in many cases have made the difference between success and failure if it had been applied. Scantlings of different depths were often given.

Q. 32. Explain clearly the various ways in which the water seal of traps of sinks and w.c.'s is lowered and rendered ineffective, and state what precautions you would take to prevent this ; illustrate your answer by sketches.

Attempted by 820, of whom 76 had no marks and 4 full marks. Sketches were not so frequently made use of as they might have been, and, owing to their absence, the descriptions were often not very clear. The position of antisiphonage pipes was generally understood but the explanation of their necessity was generally imperfect. The other causes of unsealing were not very frequently stated.

STAGE 3.

Results : 1st Class, 177 ; 2nd Class, 407 ; Failed, 337 ; Total, 921.

On the whole the average merit of the candidates is higher this year than last, and two candidates stand out prominently by gaining practically full marks on the paper. The lack of practical knowledge, and reliance on text-book descriptions instead of on the results of personal observation are the principal faults noticeable. Several candidates did not attempt a single question in Division II. The subjects of this Division are most important if the students are to keep pace with modern work, and more attention should be paid to them. The want of knowledge of the details of iron construction has already been alluded to. Some of the candidates appear to be too inattentive to read the instructions, and work out all the questions in those Divisions where one only is to be attempted, thus contributing by their own carelessness to almost inevitable failure.

Q. 41. Describe fully the tests which you would apply on the job to ascertain the quality of a sample of Portland cement submitted to you.

This question was attempted by 531 candidates. Many of the answers were practical and good, but a considerable number shewed signs of only a theoretical knowledge of the subject, and the condition that the testing of the cement was to be done "on the job," i.e., by rough and ready methods, was too often ignored. The book tests as to specific gravity, chemical composition, etc., are not such as could be applied by a foreman or clerk of works in ordinary cases. Fourteen obtained full marks and two failed altogether.

Q. 42. Compare the relative advantages of (a) marble, (b) concrete and iron, and (c) solid teak for a staircase from the point of view of resistance to fire. Give your reasons fully.

This question was attempted by 163 candidates, many of whom shewed good practical knowledge and discussed with intelligence the relative advantages and drawbacks of each form of construction, but some of the notions as to the behaviour of marble when exposed to fire were of the wildest description, such as that "Marble being a very cold material would keep the fire down." Two candidates were awarded full marks and only one failed entirely.

Q. 43. Describe the methods in practical use for preserving timber from the effects of moisture. Classify oak, elm, and fir as to their suitability for use in (a) moist ground, (b) ground alternately moist and dry, and (c) dry soil.

219 candidates tried this question, but the majority of the answers were poor and shewed but a vague and superficial acquaintance with the more recent methods of preserving timber. In too many instances the answers to the second part of the question were evidently mere guesses. No candidates obtained full marks, two got none.

Q. *44. The diagram represents, in outline only, a steel truss for a north light roof. Draw to a scale of $\frac{1}{48}$ (4 ft. to an inch) a suitable truss, and construct the stress diagram for a vertical load of $\frac{1}{2}$ cwt. per foot super to a scale of 20 cwt. to an inch. Draw one quarter full size the detail of joint at foot of north side. The trusses are supposed to be 8 feet apart.

This question was attempted by 281 candidates, but only one obtained full marks. Considerable improvement was shown, as compared with last year, in the drawing of the stress diagrams, but the majority of the answers gave a far heavier and stronger truss than was necessary. As the span was only 20 feet, the north side of the roof needed no strut, and two were amply sufficient for the long side ; but in many cases the trussing was so elaborate that the purlins would have been only about 3ft. apart. The details of the joint were very rarely shown correctly, and in many cases the sketches shewed an almost complete ignorance of the very elements of iron roof construction. Attention has previously been called to this lack of of practical knowledge, and more time should be given to the drawing of large scale details of the jointing of iron roof trusses. Seventeen answers failed to obtain any marks.

Q. 45. A beam 20 feet clear span is subject to a distributed load of 10 tons combined with a central load of 5 tons : draw the bending moment diagram and the shear stress diagram : scales, 4 feet to one inch, 20 ton-feet to an inch, and 10 tons to an inch. What is the value of the bending moment in the centre and the reaction at each end ?

This was a simple question, and the bending moment was worked out correctly by a large number of candidates. The method of obtaining the shearing stress was not so well understood, and very few worked it out correctly ; it is, however, of almost equal importance with the bending moment, and should receive more attention from teachers, and the change from positive to negative shear should be noticed and explained. Too frequently the distributed load was treated as a series of concentrated loads, and in many cases a wrongly applied method was shown of producing a parabola. The nature of these mistakes shews evidence of inaccurate teaching. 383 candidates attempted the question, of whom 39 obtained full, and 31 no marks.

Q. 46. A compound girder, composed of two rolled steel joists placed side by side with one $12'' \times \frac{1}{2}''$ top plate riveted on, carries in the centre of its span, which is 16 feet clear, a steel stanchion, the weight of which, with its superincumbent load, is 35 tons : calculate the scantling of the joists, and sketch the base of the stanchion and its connection with the girder.

This was the most difficult question in Division II, and was only attempted by 110 candidates. Very few appreciated the difficulty resulting from the absence of the bottom plate in the compound girder, and scarcely any attempt was made to work out the sectional area of the metal required. The connection of the stanchion with the girder was very badly drawn, showing again the necessity for more careful attention being given to this part of the subject. Only one candidate obtained full marks, and seven received none.

Q. 47. How does a mason's scaffold differ from a bricklayer's scaffold ? Sketch the end view of a mason's scaffold, about 30 feet high, to a scale of $\frac{1}{48}$ (4 feet to an inch) : name the parts and mark the scantlings. What is the particular advantage of bracing in scaffolding ?

546 candidates attempted this question, but in too many cases the supports of the mason's scaffold were both described and shown as running into the wall. Full marks were awarded to six answers, while nine obtained no marks.

Q. 48. Describe clearly, illustrating your answers by sketches, the "cylinder" and "tank" systems of hot water circulation, and state the relative advantages and drawbacks of each system.

This was attempted by 397 candidates and should have been better answered. A few showed careful teaching and a clear practical knowledge of both the cylinder and the tank systems, but in many cases complete ignorance was displayed as to how the circulation of hot water is effected, several sketches showing merely a pipe from the cold water cistern to the boiler, and another pipe rising from the boiler to the roof passing through a cylinder on the way, and without even the primary circulation pipes. Also in the tank system the flow pipe from the boiler was often shown connected with an open cistern in the roof. A number of the answers must be the result of careless and inaccurate teaching. Fourteen obtained full marks, eighteen failed completely.

Q. 49. An 18″ brick wall, with the usual footings and concrete, is to be underpinned to a depth of 6 feet. Describe fully how this should be done, and draw an elevation and section of the first portion of the completed work to a scale of $\frac{1}{48}$ (4 feet to an inch) showing the old footings by dotted lines.

This, again, was a practical question, and although attempted by 546 candidates, the answers were very disappointing; in some cases piles were shown driven vertically under the old concrete in order to support it; iron joists were shown longitudinally under the old concrete, and many other foolish and impractical proposals were made. Generally, the work described was of far too elaborate a character. Three candidates obtained full marks, thirty obtained none.

Q. 50. Draw to a scale of $\frac{1}{48}$ (4 feet to an inch) a "Belfast" roof truss for 40 ft. span with a rise of 6 ft., with detail of joints one-eighth full size = $1\frac{1}{2}$″ to a foot.

Very few candidates seemed to know what a "Belfast" roof truss is, and the question was attempted by only 65 candidates, of whom 16 gained no marks. No one obtained full marks.

Q. 51. A billiard room is to be covered with a lead flat having a lantern light 12 ft. × 6 ft., clear internal dimensions. Draw to a scale of $\frac{1}{12}$ (1″ to a foot) a cross section through the lantern showing 12″ of the lead flat on each side with the trimmers and joists. Describe the precautions which you would take to prevent condensed water falling on the table.

This was the favourite question in this stage, and was attempted by 621 candidates. It is satisfactory to note the great improvement in drawing shown by the sketches for this lantern light, many being really excellent. The great fault was that frequently the sill of the lantern was kept too close down to the lead flat, thus allowing for no firring up which the fall of the flat would necessitate. In some cases a sloping skylight or even a flat light was shown instead of a lantern. Thirteen candidates obtained full marks, while 54 failed altogether.

Q. *52. Trace neatly in ink the drawing Fig. 52. The lines should be firm and unbroken and should finish exactly at the proper points.

It is again satisfactory to be able to report a marked improvement in the tracing. The subject was not an easy one, and on the whole it was very well done. Full marks were obtained by 147 candidates while only four failed to obtain any marks.

HONOURS.

Results: 1st Class, 6; 2nd Class, 24; Failed, 180; Total, 210.

The work in this stage was perhaps a trifle better than last year, but is still very poor. There were 210 papers submitted. Some whole classes did good work, others had a majority of failures. It is useless for teachers to send candidates up in this stage unless they are well prepared; they should have obtained a first class in Stage 3 before attempting Honours.

Q. 61. What are the main points to be attended to in arranging an efficient system of lightning conductors for a large building? Describe clearly the measures which you would adopt for rendering secure from damage by lightning (a) a church; (b) a factory chimney; and (c) a small powder magazine.

This was attempted by 85 candidates, all of whom obtained some marks. The answers were, as a rule, in such general terms that there was little of practical use in them. Many stated that the conductor should be kept away from all ironwork, that it should be properly insulated, and that the earth plate should be buried in coke, all of which is contrary to present practice. With regard to the factory chimney many candidates stated that it would require four or five conductors down the shaft, in mistake for four or five conducting points attached to a band on top and one conductor down the outside of shaft.

Q. 62. A retaining wall with vertical back and battering face is 12 feet high above lower ground level, 1 foot thick at top, and 3 feet thick at bottom ; it supports safely a bank of earth level with the top having a natural slope of 45 degrees. Draw the wall to a scale of $\frac{1}{16}$ ($\frac{1}{4}''$ to a foot) and show the line of thrust when the wall weighs 1 cwt. per cubic foot, and the earth 90 lbs. per cubic foot, and calculate the stress on outer edge of base assuming that the wall has no tensile strength. What thickness must a rectangular wall of the same material be to do the same work with the same maximum stress ?

Although attempted by 79 candidates this question was, as a rule, very badly answered, few knowing even how to find the thrust against the wall, although there were one or two good answers. Eight obtained no marks, while none obtained full marks. Some misread the question, taking the "bank of earth level with the top" to imply a surcharged wall, but these knew still less how to find the thrust. Several gave the thrust of the earth as acting through the line joining the centres of gravity of the earth and the wall, and there is no doubt that the teaching was in fault in this respect. Other whole classes gave the horizontal thrust equal to the weight of the earth wedge. The maximum pressure was frequently given in lbs. per square inch, but the common custom is to give the pressure on building materials and foundations in tons per square foot. The equivalent rectangular wall was in the majority of answers given as equal to the mean thickness of the battered wall.

Q. *63. The diagram shows the plan of a roof covered with slates with lead hips and valleys and ornamental tile ridging. Write a specification for (1) the joiner's work for one of the dormers ; (2) the slating ; and (3) the plumber's work.

This was attempted by 143 candidates, only one of whom failed to get any marks. Many candidates gave a good specification for one of the trades, but very few were equally good in all three trades. Specifications should always be definite, such expressions as "if required," "if necessary," etc., applied to ordinary details of construction show a doubt amounting to ignorance of how the work should be constructed.

Q. 64. Draw to a scale of $\frac{1}{96}$ (8 ft. to an inch) plan of a class room for 40 infants in an elementary school, showing the entrance door, the windows and the seats ; also a cross section passing through one of the windows ; also draw to a scale of $\frac{1}{16}$ ($\frac{1}{4}''$ to a foot) cross section through the seats. No fireplace need be shown.

This was attempted by 153 candidates, all but one obtaining some marks. There were many good answers so far as the planning and the section were concerned, but some gross mistakes in the cross section through the seats. A common height given for the infants' seats was 1 foot 5 inches, one gave 2 feet. One gave the room as 40 feet by 34 feet 9 inches, by 20 feet high to flat ceiling, arm-chair seats 2 feet wide and 15 inches deep, single desks, with flat top, 2 feet 6 inches by 2 feet. Several got over the difficulty of knowing which side the windows should be by putting them on all four sides.

Q. 65. Describe the construction, mode of driving, and advantages of concrete piles.

Attempted by 125 candidates, three of whom obtained no marks and one full marks. There were a few good answers to this question, but the sketching was, as a rule, very poor. The majority of the descriptions were very vague, particularly with regard to the driving of the piles. So many candidates stated that the piles should be driven by forcing a jet of water down a pipe through the centre, instead of mentioning this as a special case ; that there has evidently been imperfect teaching. One said a groove was made down the side of the pile to pass a hose down. Nearly all stated that the driving was done by a monkey, whereas the monkey is the clip hook that runs up and down to raise and release the ram, hammer, or tup that drives the pile. One wrote "the piles are usually driven in with what is called a monkey, which is a huge hammer driven by hydraulic means." Many said concrete piles were formed by steel cylinders sunk in the ground, the core dug out, the concrete filled in and the steel cylinders withdrawn after the concrete had set hard. This again shows either defective teaching or a collective misunderstanding of the "Simplex" and allied systems.

Q. 66. A factory chimney shaft, octagonal on plan, and having an internal diameter of 6 feet, is to be erected 80 feet high above top of footings. Draw to a scale of 8 feet to an inch a section of one wall from top to bottom showing the cap and the footings, and a plan of the shaft taken at a height of 30 feet from top of footings. Also, draw to a scale of $\frac{1}{2}''$ to a foot an enlarged section of one wall for a height of 15 feet above the footings showing the fire-brick lining, and state how high you would carry this.

Attempted by 113 candidates, of whom four obtained no marks. There were many bad failures in the answers to this question. The majority of those attempting it knew that the set-offs occurred at intervals of 20 feet, but they did not know that over 5 feet diameter the top length should be $1\frac{1}{2}$ bricks thick. The common errors were to bond the fire-brick lining to the main wall, to project the concrete inside the base only to the same extent as on the outside instead of right across, and to put air inlets to the space between the chimney wall and lining, which only tends to spoil the draught.

Q. 67. The diagram shows the party-wall between two houses without basements in a terrace of uniform height. One house is to be pulled down and in its place a hotel is to be erected with a basement 12 foot below the original ground-floor level, and the party wall is to be carried up 20 feet above its original height. It is decided not to pull down the old wall but to underpin and thicken it. Draw to a scale of 4 feet to an inch a section from top to bottom of the wall when raised and thickened, including footings, hatching in the old portion, and figuring the total thickness at the various stages. Describe fully the precautions which you would take while doing the under-pinning.

This was the most popular question, being attempted by 155, but the same ignorance of practical work in underpinning was shown in these answers as to Question 49 in Stage 3. Needles through a wall to be underpinned are exceptional, and adjoining property should be interfered with as little as possible. Comparatively few mentioned the bonding of the new portion to the old in the thickened walls, or the erection of flying shores across the site between the existing buildings. Many carried up the new work flush with the old 14 inch wall on the further side, and so encroached $2\frac{1}{2}$ inches on the existing roofs. A large number left in the whole of the footings and concrete, building round them on the inside. The majority of those who mentioned shoring described raking shores on the hotel site and many said they were to be left in until the thickening was completed.

Q. 68. Describe with sketches, the lighting, ventilating and heating of a ward containing 6 beds in a cottage hospital.

Attempted by 87 candidates of whom only one failed to get any marks. Some of the answers to this question showed a practical acquaintance with the subject, and very good plans were given, others showed no knowledge of the ordinary requirements and gave also very rough sketches. Neat sketching is most important.

Q. 69. Show by diagrammatic sketches what difference is produced in the bending moments of a beam continuous over three equal spans (a) when the three spans are uniformly loaded; (b) when one of the end spans is unloaded; and (c) when both the end spans are unloaded.

This was attempted by only 36 candidates, of whom 11 obtained no marks at all. The majority of the answers showed no knowledge whatever of the stresses on continuous beams, and only one candidate was approximately correct. The majority of the sketches were exceedingly rough. Very few candidates seemed to know that there was any difference between bending and bending moments.

Q. 70. What is meant by the term "modulus of elasticity"? Assuming the modulus of elasticity of wrought iron to be 26,000,000 lbs. per square inch, calculate the length of a tie-bar, 2 inch diameter, when loaded tensionally with 30 tons, if its length when unloaded was 20 feet.

Attempted by 49 candidates, of whom five obtained full marks and four none. Many of the answers were distinctly good and, on the whole, the question was fairly well answered by those who attempted it. Some of the answers were spoilt by such fractions as 20 $\frac{10000}{2300000}$ feet, 20 $\frac{394}{1713}$ feet, 20 feet and $\frac{1800}{1197}$ of an inch, instead of 20·0164 feet, or 20 feet 0·197 inches. Several gave the modulus of elasticity as the force that would double the length of a bar *if its cross section remained unaltered*, and several others stated that it was the force that would stretch a bar to double its length *or compress it to half its length*. This shows very defective teaching.

HONOURS PRACTICAL EXAMINATION.

Seventy-three candidates, from among those who sat for the Honours paper this year, were admitted to the Practical Examination in Design, the subject being a lodge and entrance gates for a park. As far as the drawing is concerned, a considerable improvement was shewn as compared with the work sent in last year, and the majority of the elevations were good, but the planning was in many cases very defective. The main faults were : (1) Want of compactness and a failure to appreciate clearly how the building would be roofed. This should always be kept distinctly before the mind of a designer when making the plan of a building. (2) Awkward arrangement of the staircases. Not only were these often shown in a bad position, but they were in many cases far too steep, and insufficient horizontal space was allowed to work in the stairs properly. (3) Bad arrangement of fireplaces. Those on the upper floor were often placed without any reference to those on the ground floor, and in positions where it would be impossible to carry the jambs without elaborate constructive expedients the necessity for which was evidently quite unappreciated. Several designs were really excellent, and showed much taste, but many candidates had too evidently taken the speculating builder's suburban villa as their model. The entrance gates and piers were on the whole satisfactory, and some of the window details were very good. In too many cases the estimate of cost was too low, and the price put down for the gates and piers was occasionally ludicrous.

Report on the Examination in Naval Architecture.

The number of candidates in Stage 1 was 22 less, and in Stage 2 the same as sat at last year's examination. On the whole there was an improvement in the work sent in as compared with last year. A number of candidates answered more than the number of questions permitted, and there was a comparatively large number of failures due to candidates not answering the compulsory questions, or not selecting questions from each of the sections into which the examination paper is divided. It therefore appears that the instructions printed at the head of the examination questions are not sufficiently read, or that the importance of carrying out those instructions is not sufficiently realised. Arithmetical errors were far too common in both stages, and the work should be done with more system.

The rough sketches in connection with the practical questions were well done on the whole. Some of these sketches were exceptionally good, but generally in such cases the number of questions answered was comparatively few, and there may have been some cases where, on account of spending too much time on well-finished sketches, by the use of instruments (a test of which is given by the drawings required to be done to scale), a sufficient time has not remained for those students to attempt the number of questions permitted, and possibly obtain a higher class. What is required in answering the practical questions is clear freehand sketches, approximately to scale, and these should be encouraged. In Stage 2, 39 candidates failed through not answering any of the questions set in the "Laying Off" section of the paper. This is an important branch of the subject, and it should receive more consideration than the results of the examination seem to indicate it has received. Teachers should bring the above points strongly before the notice of the students.

STAGE 1.

Results : 1st Class, 134 ; 2nd Class, 119 ; Failed, 78 ; Total, 331.

PRACTICAL SHIPBUILDING.

Q. 1. Show by sketches, the forms of sections of rolled steel bars commonly used in shipbuilding ; name them, and state for what parts of the vessel they are severally employed.

A favourite question, attempted by about 81 per cent. of the candidates, and the answers were generally very satisfactory.

Q. 2. Sketch a set of building blocks, and show how they are secured in place. What is the spacing and dimensions of the blocks your sketch represents ?

Attempted by about 55 per cent. of the candidates, and the answers were generally satisfactory ; but some of the candidates did not show very clearly how the blocks are secured in place, and others gave sketches of blocks used for "dry-docking," instead of those used on the building slip.

Q. 3. Sketch roughly a stern-frame for a single screw-vessel, showing how it is secured to the keel and shell plating. Of what material is the stern post made ?

Attempted by about 53 per cent. of the candidates. Many of the sketches were very good. A few candidates stated that "cast-iron" was the material the stern post was made of; this should have been "cast-steel," but frequently forged mild steel is used.

Q. 4. What is a deck stringer plate ? What are its uses ? Show by a transverse sectional sketch how you would connect a deck stringer to the beams, framing and shell plating of a ship.

Attempted by about 42 per cent of the candidates. Generally satisfactory, although a number of candidates did not shew the rivets connecting the stringer to the beams and side plating, or did not state the uses of the stringer clearly.

Q. 5. Make a rough sketch showing the cross section of a side-bar keel, and its connections to the garboards and transverse frames. How are the butts of the keel disposed ?

Attempted by about 46 per cent. of the candidates, and the answers were generally satisfactory, except that the disposition of the butts of the keel were frequently omitted ; many of the sketches were very good. A few candidates sketched the bar and flat keel plate instead of the side-bar keel.

Q. 6. Sketch and describe the different kinds of fixed pillars used in shipbuilding. Where are they fitted ? What purposes do they serve, and how should they be arranged for maximum efficiency ?

Attempted by about 36 per cent. of the candidates, and, with a few exceptions, was fairly well answered. A number of candidates described and sketched a "portable pillar," but this was not asked for in the question, "fixed pillars" only being referred to.

Q. 7. Describe the method adopted in the shipyard for bending a beam to its correct curvature. Show by sketches and otherwise how the beam arms are formed in the case of (1) a bracket plate knee, and (2) a slabbed or welded knee. What is the depth of the beam knees?

Attempted by about 37 per cent. of the candidates, and the answers were generally very satisfactory.

Q. 8. Show by sketches the disposition of the rivets in (1) a double riveted lapped joint, and (2) a treble-riveted butt joint. State the distances of the rivets from the edges of the plates and from each other, in terms of their diameters, supposing the joints are to be made watertight.

Attempted by about 53 per cent. of the candidates, and the answers as to the disposition of the rivets were generally satisfactory ; but in some cases the spacing of the rivets was not stated clearly, whether it was intended from edge to edge, or centre to centre of the rivet holes. Some of the candidates shewed a disposition of rivets suitable for "non-watertight" work.

Q. 9. What is a side keelson ? Sketch one, showing its connection to the other parts of the vessel, and state what useful purpose it serves.

Attempted by about 28 per cent. of the candidates, and the answers were generally poor and incomplete. The useful purposes served by such keelsons were frequently not stated. A few candidates gave sketches of side stringers or bilge keels.

Q. 10. Describe by sketches and otherwise, how a large transverse water tight bulkhead is constructed and secured to the ship.

Attempted by 26 per cent. of the candidates; about one-half of the answers were satisfactory, the sketches of the remainder were poor and incomplete.

DRAWING.

Q. 11. Enlarge, in pencil, the given drawing, to a scale of twice that upon which it is drawn.

Only three candidates failed to attempt this question, which was generally well answered. Some candidates traced the sketch on the tracing paper attached to the examination sheets and then placed working lines on the tracing. There is no need for this, and the working lines should be placed on the sketch sheet supplied.

CALCULATIONS.

Q. 12. What are the weights of a cubic foot of wrought iron, mild steel, yellow metal or gun-metal, teak, English elm, and yellow pine ?

A mild steel plate $\frac{13}{16}''$ thick is 18' long, 5' wide at one end, tapering to 3' 6" wide at the other end, and has two circular lightening holes cut in it 2' and 1' 6" in diameter respectively. What is its weight in lbs ?

Attempted by about 52 per cent. of the candidates, and the answers to the first part of the question were very satisfactory, but some of the answers to the second part were full of arithmetical errors, and shew a want of system in setting out the work clearly. There was frequently a mixing up of units, and multiplying feet by inches.

Q. 13. What is meant by "displacement" and "centre of buoyancy"?

The water-planes of a vessel floating in sea water are 3' 6" apart, and their areas, commencing with the load water-plane, are :— 13540, 11755, 8520, 3875, and 0 square feet respectively. Calculate the displacement of the vessel in tons.

The favourite question of this Section of the examination paper, and attempted by about 67 per cent. of the candidates. Some very good solutions were given, but arithmetical errors were frequent. The "centre of buoyancy" was not clearly defined by a large number of candidates, and some stated that the "centre of buoyancy" was the "centre of gravity" of the immersed portion of the ship, instead of "centre of gravity" of the volume of displacement.

Q. 14. What are the fundamental conditions which must be fulfilled, in order that a vessel may float freely, and at rest, in still water?

Attempted by about 25 per cent. of the candidates, and was very well answered. A few stated as one condition that "centre of gravity" and "centre of buoyancy" must be in the same vertical "*plane*," instead of same vertical "*line*."

Q. 15. Define the terms "draught" and "trim."
Describe the method adopted for marking the draught marks correctly on a ship, and state where, and how they are fixed on the hull. Select any type of ship with which you are acquainted, naming the type chosen.

Attempted by about 21 per cent. of the candidates, and the answers were disappointing. There were only a small number of fair papers, the others were very poor.

STAGE 2.

Results : 1st Class, 79 ; 2nd Class, 175 ; Failed, 76 ; Total, 330.

PRACTICAL SHIPBUILDING.

Q. 21. Sketch the lower portion of the midship section of any vessel, extending from the middle line, to the margin-plate in a Mercantile vessel, *or* to the 3rd longitudinal in a War vessel ; showing inner and outer bottom plating, framing, &c. Indicate which parts are continuous and which intercostal ; give scantlings and state sizes and spacing of rivets.

A favourite question, attempted by about 59 per cent. of the candidates, and generally very good answers were given.

Q. 22. Why are stealers worked in the shell plating?
Show by sketches how a stealer is worked, in either an inner or outer strake of plating, and show the disposition of the rivets.

Attempted by about 34 per cent. of the candidates, and generally satisfactory answers were given, except that the chasing of the plates in the vicinity of the lap was only referred to by a few.

Q. 23. Show a good shift of butts of the flat keel and gutter plates, with reference to those of the vertical keel, and angles connecting them ; also with reference to the butts of the garboard strakes of plating.

Only 6 per cent. of the candidates attempted this question. About one-half of the answers were fairly well done, but the others were poor and incomplete.

Q. 24. Where, how, and for what reasons are zinc protectors fitted to the hulls of ships?
What precautions are taken to prevent deterioration of the underwater portion of the shell plating?
What portions of the internal parts of the hull of a steel vessel are most liable to corrosion on service?

A favourite question, attempted by about 51 per cent. of the candidates, and very satisfactory answers were generally given, although the first part of the question was seldom fully answered.

Q. 25. Show, by rough sketches, the general arrangement of the equipment necessary around the building slip for a large vessel ; also show the arrangement of staging neccessary. Give a rough plan, without details, of the means of conveying the materials from the machine shops to the ship.

Attempted by about 32 per cent. of the candidates, and some very good answers were given ; the others were generally satisfactory.

Q. 26. How would you take account of, prepare, get in place and secure a shell plate in wake of the boss where a shaft leaves the ship ?

Attempted by about 17 per cent. of the candidates ; about one-third of the answers were good, but the others were poor. The question was described too much in general terms without explaining in detail ; the sighting battens for setting cradle and adjusting the plate were only mentioned by a comparatively small number.

Q. 27. How are the entrances into double-bottom compartments, or ballast tanks, made watertight ?

Show how such compartments may be sounded, and what provision is made for the escape of air, when the compartments are being filled with water.

A popular question, attempted by about 61 per cent. of the candidates, and generally very well answered. Some did not make a very clear sketch of the watertight manhole cover.

Q. 28. Sketch a rudder for any type of vessel with which you are acquainted, naming the type selected. State the sizes and disposition of rivets, pintles and bolts.

Explain.—(1) How such a rudder may be readily unshipped.

(2) How water is prevented from finding its way through the rudder trunk into the ship.

(3) How the rudder is prevented from turning beyond a certain angle.

(4) What means are taken to prevent the rudder from being accidentally unshipped at sea.

Attempted by about 36 per cent. of the candidates, and generally well answered ; some very good answers were given. A few did not show the centre line of pintles and rudder head in the same straight line.

LAYING OFF.

Q. 29. What lines are usually employed for fairing the form of a vessel ? Where are each specially valuable as tests of fairness ? What is a diagonal ? How would you proceed to obtain the form of a diagonal, in the sheer and half breadth plans?

The favourite question of this section of the examination paper, about 52 per cent. of the candidates attempting it. About three-fourths of the answers were satisfactory, with the exception that a diagonal was only correctly described by a small number ; the remainder of the answers were poor,

Q. 30. What is a ribband ? Where are they placed, and how are they secured ? Describe, with sketches, how you would proceed to obtain the necessary information to prepare a ribband for the ship, and state what distinguishing marks, etc., are placed upon it.

Attempted by about 38 per cent. of the candidates. The answers were generally incomplete, and only about one-third of those who attempted it obtained fair marks.

Q. 31. What information is given to the frame bender for bevelling **the** frames ? State the position on the frames at which bevellings are given, and explain clearly how the information is obtained. In what form is this information given to the workman ? Illustrate your answer by taking three or four frames nearest the sternpost.

Attempted by 17 per cent. of the candidates, and about one-third of the answers were fairly satisfactory, the others were poor. Very few candidates correctly illustrated the answer by taking three or four frames nearest the stern post.

DRAWING.

Q. 32. What does the given sketch represent. It is drawn on a scale of $\frac{1}{4}''$ to 1 foot ; draw it neatly in pencil on a scale of 1" to 1 foot, and show the number of rivets you consider necessary in the frame and bracket angle bars, &c.

Six candidates did not attempt this *compulsory* question. The drawing was generally well done, but some of the candidates appeared not to have any ship curves with them at the examination. A number of candidates did not describe what the sketch represented, and in some cases the rivets were drawn by hand instead of by compasses, and the spacing of the rivets was stated but not shewn to scale.

CALCULATIONS.

Q. 33. State the rule known as "Simpson's first rule."

The semi-ordinates of the deck boundary of a ship, commencing forward, are :—0, 14·6, 23·0, 28·1, 31·0, 32·2, 32·5, 32·4, 31·9, 30·5, 24·7, 19·3, and 0 feet respectively. The length of the deck is 384 feet. Find the area of the whole deck, and the longitudinal position of its centre of gravity.

Twelve candidates did not attempt this *compulsory* question. The answers were generally satisfactory, but arithmetical errors were far too frequent. A number of the candidates, in stating Simpson's first rule, omitted to state that the ordinates must be an odd number. Many used a wrong common interval, obtained by dividing the length of the deck by the number of ordinates, instead of the correct interval obtained by dividing by the number of spaces. Some candidates stated the rule incorrectly, but worked the question correctly.

Q. 34. Describe, in detail, how you would proceed to obtain the curve of displacement of a vessel, having given the curve of tons per inch immersion. Show by rough sketches the usual shapes of these curves, and also show how to deduce from the curve of tons per inch immersion, a curve representing the heights of the centre of buoyancy above the keel.

Attempted by 15 per cent. of the candidates. About one-third of the answers were satisfactory ; the remainder were poor. Many explained how to deduce the heights of the "centre of buoyancy" above the keel from the displacement curve instead of from the curve of "tons per inch."

Q. 35. A middle line keelson, 400' long, is made up of mild steel plates 36" deep. The plates of the middle half of the length are $\frac{14}{16}''$ thick, and the plates at the ends are $\frac{13}{16}''$ thick. The keelson continuous angles—two at the bottom and two at the top—are $6\frac{1}{4}'' \times 4\frac{1}{4}'' \times \frac{18}{16}''$. Calculate the weight of the keelson including rivets, &c.

Attempted by 27 per cent. of the candidates. About one-half of the answers were good, but the others were very poor. A frequent mistake in dealing with this question was to mix up feet and inches, and in many cases the work was laid out in a slovenly manner, resulting in muddle.

Q. 36. Define the terms "centre of buoyancy," "centre of gravity," "centre of flotation," "metacentre" and "metacentric height."

The centre of gravity of a ship is 12′ from the bottom of keel. In this condition her displacement is 2,500 tons. She is then loaded in the following manner :—

95 tons are added 8′ 6″ above the bottom of keel.

270 „ „ „ 12′ 6″ „ „ „

and 435 „ „ „ 10′ 9″ „ „ „

Find the new position of the centre of gravity from the bottom of the keel.

Attempted by about 35 per cent. of the candidates, and generally well answered. Several candidates stated that the "metacentre" is the point of intersection of the line joining the "centre of buoyancy" and "centre of gravity" in the upright condition, with the line joining those points when the vessel is slightly inclined. The "metacentric height" was often described as the distance between the "centre of buoyancy" and the "metacentre."

STAGE 3.

Results : 1st Class, 27 ; 2nd Class, 65 ; Failed, 98 ; Total, 190.

There was a decrease of about 5 per cent. in the number of candidates who sat at the examination in this stage, as compared with last year.

The standard of the answers was not so good as last year, and a large number of papers had to be cancelled owing chiefly to candidates' not complying with the instructions printed at the head of the examination questions.

A conspicuous and disappointing feature of the worked papers in this stage was :—(1) the failure of 37 candidates (nearly 20 per cent. of the total) to attempt either of the questions set in the "Laying Off" Section of the examination paper, and (2) the generally poor answers of those who did attempt one or both of those questions. In some cases candidates wrote on their worked papers—"No laying off ever learned," and other similar remarks. This is very unsatisfactory ; so much of the work of the preparation of materials is carried out on the mould loft floor, that it is absolutely essential candidates should possess a knowledge of the general problems in laying off. The two questions set this year merely involved finding the intersection of a plane at right angles to one of the planes of projection, with the lines of a ship or a cylindrical surface, and all the candidates in this stage should be sufficiently well acquainted with the theory of laying off to be able to obtain at least some marks.

It appears that, generally, more attention should be given to the printed syllabus which is now prepared in much detail and is considered sufficiently comprehensive.

The practical questions were, on the whole, well answered, and it is satisfactory to note that there was an improvement in the quality of the sketches, and sketching is much to be encouraged.

The *compulsory* question, No. 52, which requires candidates to place their own lines for calculating purposes, and measuring the ordinates by means of a scale, was generally well answered, but 4 candidates made no attempt to answer the question.

A few candidates attempted all the questions set in the "Calculations" section of the paper although the instructions clearly stated that candidates must not attempt more than three questions, including No. 52, from that section. Arithmetical errors were far too common, and many of the answers contained an unfortunate mixing up of units, feet and inches, or pounds and tons, in the same formula.

F

PRACTICAL SHIPBUILDING.

Q. 41. Describe, with sketches, giving scantlings, how a large machinery or cargo hatchway is framed out in a deck, and point out the means adopted to compensate for the loss of transverse strength due to cutting the beams.

A popular question, about 120 candidates attempting it, and about 25 per cent. of the answers were very good. The sketches were, on the whole, well done, and in several cases they were very clear indeed. Where difficulty was experienced, it was generally only in the second part of the question.

Q. 42. A crew space of a vessel is approximately 50' × 28'. Show by sketches, giving details and approximate dimensions of fittings, a good arrangement for messing and sleeping as many as possible of the crew, allowing for a suitable width of gangway.

Attempted by about 67 candidates. It was generally well answered, except as regards the details that were asked for.

Q. 43. Describe, with sketches, how the cast steel shaft brackets of a twin screw ship are secured in place. What tests are made before these brackets are accepted as fit for the service intended ?

This was also a favourite question, about 114 candidates attempting it, and about 25 per cent. of the answers were very good. The sketches were generally fairly well drawn, but the tests stated for such castings were, in many cases, insufficient for the purpose of determining the fitness of the brackets for service.

Q. 44. Sketch roughly the midship section, and briefly describe the construction of a large lifeboat forming part of the equipment of a ship. Indicate the materials used and the fastenings.

Attempted by 36 candidates. About six of the answers were satisfactory, but the remainder were generally poor and incomplete. Many candidates gave an outline of a lifeboat such as is used for rescue purposes round the coast.

Q. 45. Describe generally, with sketches, any system of refrigeration used on board a steamer arranged for carrying cargoes of frozen meat, showing how the pipes conveying the freezing medium are arranged, and state what arrangements are made for observing and regulating the temperature from outside the chamber. What insulating material is used in the holds, and how is it arranged ? Give detail sketches.

About 34 candidates attempted this question, and about nine of the answers were very good, but the remainder only answered parts of the question. One or two of the candidates stated that liquid air is used as the freezing medium ; another stated that a brine preparation of water mixed with a certain proportion of calcium carbide is used. The arrangements for observing and regulating the temperature of the chamber were generally omitted.

Q. 46. Roughly sketch, in plan, a good arrangement of engine bearers for a large twin-screw steamer, naming the type of vessel selected. Give sections of the bearers at a crank pit, and at a transverse bearer.

Only 30 candidates attempted this question, but it was generally well answered. There were about 8 very good answers.

Q. 47. Sketch and describe, in detail, how cabins are built. Describe briefly how cabins are ventilated, with hot or cold air, in any modern type of vessel with which you are acquainted, naming the type selected.

Attempted by about 90 candidates. It was generally fairly well done, but the answers generally lacked details. The latter part of the question was frequently unanswered, and one candidate in answering it stated, "sidelight when opened catches the air and it rushes in and causes a vacuum, causing the bad air to rush out."

Q. 48. Sketch and describe the construction of a davit, with all its fittings, for carrying a large lifeboat. State how the positions of the davits are fixed in relation to the boat, and how the boat is secured in the davits and lowered overboard. How would you determine the suitable overhang of the davits?

About 108 candidates attempted this question, and about 25 per cent. of the answers were very good. Many of the sketches were very good, but some were very poor indeed. On the whole it was fairly well answered. One candidate stated that davits were forged of cast steel to the required form and dimensions.

Q. 49. Describe, with detail sketches, the arrangements made, in either (a) a large passenger steamer fitted with bulwarks, or (b) a warship fitted with bulwarks, to free the upper deck of the vessel from both large and small quantities of water, which may be shipped in rough weather at sea.

The most popular question, about 132 candidates attempting it, and it was generally very well answered, with the exception that details asked for were frequently omitted. A few gave sketches of scuttles opening inwards, or hinged on the lower edge of the scuttle.

LAYING OFF.

Q. 50. How would you fix the position of the centre line of a hawse pipe?
Having given the projection of the centre line of a hawse pipe in the sheer and half breadth plans, and the diameter of the pipe, show how to obtain the development of the line in which the surface of the hawse pipe meets the outer surface of the shell plating.

Attempted by about 104 candidates, but only about six satisfactory answers were given; and generally the answers were poor. In the majority of cases the shape of the hole in the shell plating was described as obtained by the practical method of putting a rod through holes representing the centre of the hawse pipe in the deck and side of a ship, instead of working geometrically. The question involves merely finding the intersection of single cant planes, parallel to the centre line of the hawse pipe, with the given cylindrical hawse pipe and the form of the ship.

Q. 51. Show how to lay off, and obtain the necessary bevellings, of a stern cant frame, stepping on to the transom of a steel ship.
How would you obtain the true expanded form of the stern plating above the knuckle of a steamer with a tumble-home stern, such as is generally fitted in a tug-boat?

About 70 candidates attempted this question, and about 20 per cent. of the answers were good; the remainder were poor and incomplete. In building steel ships of ordinary form, it is generally only necessary to cant the stern frames which step on the transom, but the fact that the frame ended off the middle line of the vessel seemed to cause great difficulty. Many obtained the true form, etc., of a cant in the fore body.

The second part of the question was badly done, only about 10 fairly good answers were given. The true shape of the intersection of a plane, at right angles to the tumble home of the stern in the sheer of the vessel, with the form of the vessel, is the key to obtaining the true expanded form of the stern plating.

84

CALCULATIONS.

Q. *52. The given sketch represents half of the fore body of a small vessel. Calculate the displacement in tons, and the vertical position of the centre of buoyancy of the form represented by the sketch, between waterlines *A* and *B*, 6 feet apart, and between the sections *C* and *D*. The sketch given is on a scale of ¾″ to 1 foot, and three waterlines spaced 1′ 6″ apart should be introduced between waterlines *A* and *B*. The sections are spaced 15′ apart.

Ordinates to be measured to the nearest decimal place.

This was a *compulsory* question, but four candidates made no attempt to answer it. The answers were generally very satisfactory, and about 120 obtained good marks. There were, however, far too many arithmetical mistakes. In the fore body given, five stations were shown and two waterlines, the candidates being instructed to insert three additional equally spaced waterlines, making five in all. Several of the candidates, however, took only four stations, and in one case the ordinates for twelve water-lines were worked to. Although the question only required ordinates measured to the nearest decimal place, several candidates worked to two and three places of decimals. Many of the answers for displacement were twice as much as they should be on account of multiplying by two for both sides, instead of what was asked for, viz. :—the displacement of the form represented by the drawing given.

Q. 53. Explain why ships passing from salt water into fresh water usually change trim.

A vessel of rectangular section 200′ long and 40′ broad floats at a draught of 14′ forward and 18′ feet aft when in sea water, the centre of gravity being then 4′ above the centre of buoyancy. Find the draught at each end at which she will float when in fresh water.

About one-half of the candidates attempted this question. About a dozen answers were fairly good and the rest were poor. A few stated that fresh water is heavier than salt, and generally it was stated that as the vessel is of rectangular form, there would be no change of trim, but that the vessel would sink bodily. It seemed to be overlooked that the centre of buoyancy in salt water is abaft the centre of length on account of the difference in draught forward and aft, and that the additional volume of displacement in river water produces a change in the longitudinal position of the centre of buoyancy and a consequent change of trim. This comparatively easy question should have been better answered.

Q. 54. Distinguish between "Gross" and "Register" tonnage. Describe, briefly, how each is obtained for a vessel of known type and particulars.

State clearly in what respects Gross Tonnage differs from displacement.

In what class of vessel is a negative register tonnage possible, and why ?

Attempted by about 50 candidates, and generally well answered. About 20 per cent. of those who attempted it obtained good marks, but the remainder of the answers were poor and incomplete.

Q. 55. A lifeboat, with outfit, weighs 30 cwt., and is capable of carrying 50 persons. It is to be carried in a pair of forged steel davits, having an overhang of 5′ 9″. Calculate the necessary sizes at the collar and heel of the davits. How would you determine the size at any other part of the davits ?

Only nineteen candidates attempted this simple question, and the answers were generally disappointing. About seven of the answers were fairly good. In many cases the weight of the passengers was omitted altogether. In applying the ordinary bending formula, the mixing up of units was very common and led to absurd answers being given, one diameter being given as ·258 of an inch.

Q. 56. Describe fully how the metacentric diagram for a ship is constructed, and state to what uses it is put. Sketch the metacentric diagram for any type of ship with which you are acquainted, and figure on it the metacentric heights for the light and load conditions. Name the type of vessel chosen, and state the leading particulars of the vessel.

About 75 candidates attempted this question, and about one-third of those gave satisfactory answers. The remainder of the answers were generally incomplete. The first part of the question was generally well answered, except that many candidates referred to BM as representing metacentric height. The second part of the question was badly done generally. Candidates in this stage should have a clearer knowledge of metacentric height, and should be familiar with approximate values of the metacentric heights of typical vessels.

HONOURS.
Results : 1st Class, 4 ; 2nd Class, 9 ; Failed, 66 ; Total, 79.

There was an increase of about 15 per cent. in the number of candidates who sat at the examination in this stage, as compared with last year. The standard of the answers was not so good as last year, and it is suggested that more attention should be given to the syllabus, which is now prepared in considerable detail.

It is again necessary to point out the great lack of neatness in the working of many of the papers, which often resulted in confusion and failure, especially in calculations. Arithmetical errors were far too common, and often from slips in cancelling. Students should be directed to pay more attention to the dimensional units to be employed in a calculation. A very large proportion of incorrect answers were due to carelessness in mixing up feet and inches or pounds and tons in the same formula.

The stability questions were fairly well answered, but the students in this stage ought to shew a more complete knowledge of the properties of the metacentre, and the geometry of the metacentric diagram.

The subject of rolling seems not to be treated as well as is desired ; the questions set were of a very elementary character and should have been treated much better than they were.

The answers to the questions on resistance were generally satisfactory, but the strength questions were poorly done.

The questions relating to the elements of design were, on the whole, well answered, and it is satisfactory to note that several of the candidates had a fair knowledge of the current literature on this branch of the subject.

Q. 61. Having given three equidistant ordinates of a plane curve, and the common interval between them, deduce a rule for calculating the area included between the curve, base line, and two consecutive ordinates. Deduce also a rule for calculating the moment of such an area about one of the end ordinates.

Illustrate your answers by means of a simple numerical example.

Attempted by about 60 per cent. of the candidates, and generally well answered. The question refers to Simpson's third, or five-eight rule. In several cases Simpson's first rule was quoted and proved.

Q. 62. Prove that for angles of heel for which the sides of a vessel, with ordinary waterlines, are wall-sided, the righting lever $GZ = (GM + \frac{1}{2} BM \tan^2 \theta) \sin \theta$, G representing the centre of gravity of the vessel, M the metacentre and B the centre of buoyancy.

A prismatic vessel of rectangular section 30′ broad, draws 10′ of water, and has a metacentric height of 1′. If weights be shifted so as to raise the centre of gravity 15″, find the angle to which the vessel will loll over.

Only nineteen candidates attempted this question, and there were about seven good answers. The formula quoted is a very useful one, as the majority of ships may be regarded as wall-sided for small angles of heel. In attempting the second part of the question, it was generally overlooked that the vessel would loll over until GZ becomes zero, which value substituted in the formula stated, enables θ to be found.

Q. 63. What are the effects of a large sea breaking over, say, a well-deck steamer, or a vessel with bulwarks, the freeing ports being assumed set up with rust, due to neglect?

A vessel of 700 tons displacement has a freeboard to upper deck of 6'. The centre of gravity is 1' 6" above water, and its metacentric locus is horizontal. A sea breaking over the bulwarks causes a rectangular area 50' long and 20' broad, on the upper deck of the vessel, to be covered with water to a depth of 1'. Calculate the loss of metacentric height.

A popular question, and generally well answered. Several candidates took the centre of gravity of the vessel as 1' 6" above the water on the upper deck, instead of 1' 6" above the water line of the vessel.

Q. 64. Show how a curve of statical stability may be practically constructed from a curve of dynamical stability.

In a particular vessel the dynamical stability

$$= W. \, GM. \, (1 - \cos \theta),$$

θ being the angle of heel from the upright. Deduce the equation of the curve of statical stability, and the form of the section of the vessel, supposing it to be of constant section throughout.

Attempted by 18 candidates, and only about four satisfactory answers were given. Many of the investigations were very laborious, and made without success. It was often stated that the integration of a curve of statical stability up to any angle is the dynamical stability at that angle, but it seemed to be quite overlooked that the question asked for the reverse of this process, and that by differentiating the expression given for the dynamical stability, the equation to the curve of statical stability is readily obtained, and the form of the section seen to be circular, unless she be wholly submerged.

Q. 65. Obtain an expression for the slope of the tangent to the curve of metacentres, at any draught, in the metacentric diagram.

A log, of which the section is 2' square, floats with one diagonal vertical. Sketch the curve of metacentres, and calculate the draughts at which it is horizontal.

Only six candidates attempted this question, and the answers were disappointing. The first part of the question is an easy example on the geometry of the metacentric diagram, and the second part should be simple for Honours students.

Q. 66. Define "surface of buoyancy," "surface of flotation," and "curve of pro-metacentres."

Prove that the surface of buoyancy is closed, and wholly concave, to some interior point, and find the limits to its size, as the displacement of a given ship is varied.

Attempted by 28 per cent. of the candidates, but only about five obtained good marks. Many stated that the surfaces of buoyancy and flotation were the surfaces of imaginary cylinders extending throughout the vessel's length.

Q. 67. Find the expression which gives the height of the longitudinal metacentre above the centre of buoyancy, in a floating body, and explain what use is made of this information.

Calculate the longitudinal metacentric height for a square log of fir of specific gravity ·5, 18' long and 2' 6" side, when it is floating in a position of equilibrium.

This was also a popular question, 83 per cent. of the candidates attempting it. About one-third of the answers were very good ; but it is surprising how many went wrong in one or both of the parts of this comparatively simple question. Many candidates treated the question as referring to transverse inclinations instead of longitudinal, and some jointly considered both transverse and longitudinal. A large percentage of the answers to the second part of the question were based on the assumption that the sides of the log would be vertical when floating in a position of equilibrium, instead of with one diagonal vertical and the other horizontal.

Q. 68. Investigate the rolling motion of a vessel in still water, on the supposition that there is no resistance, and obtain a formula, giving the angle of inclination at any instant. Deduce the time of a single swing.

Calculate, and state in seconds, the time of a single swing of an empty steel circular pontoon, 10' in diameter, floating at mid-depth. The centre of gravity is 6" below the centre of figure.

Twenty candidates attempted this question, and only about three satisfactory answers were given. The answers were generally incomplete. Most of the candidates who attempted the first part of the question simply quoted the formula, instead of deducing it from the equation of motion. The attempts to answer the calculation were generally laborious and unsatisfactory. Many tried to deduce the radius of gyration of the circular pontoon by working from the moment of inertia of a rectangular figure, whereas by noting that all the material of the steel plating forming the pontoon is distant the radius of the section from the axis, it is at once seen that the radius of gyration is the radius of the section, viz. :—5 feet.

Q. 69. State why the ordinary, or short-period, pendulum observations are untrustworthy, for giving the inclination of a ship in a sea-way. Investigate the error of a short-period pendulum in giving the inclination of a ship rolling in still water.

Show how, by means of two such pendulums placed at different heights on the middle line, the axis of still water oscillations may be ascertained.

Attempted by eleven candidates ; one or two of the answers were very good, but the others were very poor, shewing that the effects of rolling were little understood.

Q. 70. Give a brief outline of Mr. W. Froude's surface friction experiments, and state the chief results reached with reference to the variation of resistance due to—(1) variation in character of surface, (2) varying dimensions of the same character of surface, and (3) change of velocity, the dimensions and character of the surface remaining unchanged.

Find the resistance in pounds per ton of displacement, and the horse-power necessary to overcome frictional resistance in the case of a ship 330' long, 58' beam, 23' 6" draught and 6,882 tons displacement, when going at 18 knots. Assume that the surface friction of one square foot of the bottom, moving at a speed of one foot per sec. = ·0034 lbs.

Another favourite question, 65 candidates attempting it. About one-third of the answers were very good. The failures in the calculation were due mainly to the use of wrong units, or to bad arithmetic. One candidate stated that the resistance amounted to 264727497·46 lbs., and that the resistance per ton of displacement is 38321 lbs.

Q. 71. State Froude's law of comparison, as applied to the relative resistance of models and ships. How would you sub-divide the total resistance, offered by the water, to the motion of a ship ? To what parts of the resistance does the law not apply ?

Two ships of unequal size are made from the same model. Prove that at the speed where the resistance varies as the 6th power of the speed, the same effective horse-power is required to drive both ships at the same speed.

Attempted by 61 candidates. The first part of the question was, in most cases, well done, but the second part was rarely attempted, and generally answered unsatisfactorily. It is an example illustrating the general principle of the economical propulsion of large vessels.

Q. 72. A box-shaped vessel 100' long, 35' broad and of 1,000 tons displacement, is on the crest of a wave of her own length, 5' high, of which the profile is a curve of sines. The weight of the vessel is uniformly distributed along its length. Construct, to scale, the curves of shearing force and bending moment, and state in tons and foot-tons respectively their maximum values.

Nineteen candidates attempted this question, but only about five satisfactory answers were given; the remainder were poor. The majority of the curves were badly drawn, and very little working was shewn.

Q. 73. Find the maximum longitudinal stresses (in lbs. per square inch) upon a section of the vessel referred to in Question 72, assuming the depth of the vessel is 15', and that the plating on the deck, side and bottom is $\frac{7}{20}$" thick. (No allowance need be made for rivet holes.)

If Question 72 has not been worked, assume that over each one-third of the length of the vessel, from each end, two-fifths of the total weight of the vessel and cargo is uniformly distributed, and that the vessel floats in still water.

If the vessel has a continuous bulwark each side, 3' high and $\frac{7}{20}$" thick, what will then be the maximum stresses? Explain the significance of your result as applying to actual ships.

About 28 candidates attempted this question, the first part of which was generally well done. Several of the candidates mixed up the units of the expressions in the formula used to obtain the stresses, and obtained absurd results. The second part of the question was not so well answered, many neglecting the change in the neutral axis of the section, due to the addition of bulwarks. A correct deduction from the difference in the value of the maximum stresses due to the addition of bulwarks was rarely stated.

Q. 74. State generally the present rules as to maximum load-line in merchant ships. Is there any legal enforcement in the case of vessels of foreign nations? What are the leading considerations in determining the freeboard for any particular vessel? What bearing has the reserve of buoyancy on the stability and behaviour of the vessel at sea?

Attempted by about 23 candidates, but only two or three answers were satisfactory. Generally the answers were very poor and incomplete.

Q. 75. Having given the moulded dimensions of a vessel of known type, also the specification and designed speed, how would you determine the weights of hull, outfit and machinery, and the light displacement?

How would you proceed to estimate the weight, and position of the centre of gravity, longitudinally and vertically, of the transverse framing of a vessel?

About one-half of the candidates attempted this question, which was generally very well done; about thirteen obtaining very good marks.

Q. 76. Describe generally the development of turbine machinery from the naval architect's point of view, as applied to marine propulsion.

What do you consider to be the advantages and disadvantages of turbine engines, as compared with reciprocating engines?

State, as far as you can, comparative results of any two similar vessels with which you are acquainted, one vessel being fitted with turbine engines and the other with reciprocating engines.

Twenty-one candidates attempted this question, and the answers were generally satisfactory. About five obtained very good marks.

Nineteen candidates who had done sufficiently well in the written examination were summoned to South Kensington to sit for the practical examination in Design.

The designs were, on the whole, good; three or four candidates did exceptionally good work.

It should be noted that the drawing of border lines is not required. Accuracy and neatness of drawing is insisted on, and the inking in of the drawings, though desirable, should not be proceeded with until it has been ascertained that the lines of the vessel are fair. The fairing lines should be left on the drawing. In two or three cases there were arithmetical errors in working the displacement sheet.

Report on the Examination in Applied Mechanics.

In all stages the answering this year on the whole showed a distinct advance, and there was evidence of careful, and in many cases of successful, teaching. Confusion of units is becoming less and less noticeable, but in the higher stages many candidates still mix up feet and inches, or tons and pounds, in one formula, and it is desirable again to draw attention to the fact that constant drill in the working out of numerical examples is the only way of eradicating this evil. It is perhaps too often the custom to allow students to write down a formula, insert numerical data, and then leave the problem unfinished, otherwise candidates would more quickly realise when they had obtained an absurd result, and would either check their calculations or state that a slip must have been made and that the result was an incorrect one. Undoubtedly the best method to secure greater accuracy in arithmetical work would be to insist on attendance at courses of instruction in Practical Mathematics. As in previous years, it was often impossible to determine where students had gone wrong in their arithmetical calculations owing to the untidy and careless manner in which the various steps in the calculations were written down. It should be impressed upon students that accuracy and tidiness in work nearly always go together. The answers to the questions dealing with the method of carrying out certain experiments showed again conclusively that too little attention is paid by many teachers to the careful preparation beforehand of demonstrations in the laboratory. Even where the candidate gave a reasonably intelligent explanation of the method of carrying out an experiment, he was frequently quite unable to state what results would be obtained and how the results would be recorded, and what physical interpretation would be placed upon the results. Hardly any candidate, even in Honours, showed any acquaintance with the fact that in all experimental work the appliances used should be thoroughly tested for accuracy both before and after the conclusion of the experiment, and though the answers to these questions during the last two or three years have steadily shown an advance, there is still a great deal of leeway to be made up. From the replies to Question 26 it is evident that teachers are somewhat prone to neglect at the present day the teaching of the principles of simple mechanism, and it is desirable that more attention should be given to this branch of the subject. In the elementary classes more time should be given to problems such as that of Question 13. The Examiners would again emphasise the necessity of compelling students always to write down the units in which their answer is expressed. Such statements as "a force of so many foot-pounds" or "a stress of so many inch-tons" are still far too frequent and point to want of care on the part of the teachers.

STAGE 1.

Results : 1st Class, 659 ; 2nd Class, 507 ; Failed, 541 ; Total, 1,707.

Q. 1. Describe, with careful sketches, only *one* of the following (a), (b), (c) or (d) :—

(a) The operation of centering, fixing in the lathe, and turning a shaft or spindle, say about 2 inches diameter and 3 feet long.

(*b*) An hydraulic accumulator.

(*c*) A circular saw and saw bench.

(*d*) The preparation of a sand mould for the casting of a pulley or the like.

This question was answered fairly well, although a certain proportion of the candidates had evidently to rely on books for their knowledge of workshop processes. Sketches, with few exceptions, were extremely poor. It is desirable to draw attention again to the great advantage it is to students to encourage them to make sketches of the various machines and appliances with which they come in contact in the shops. The greatest weakness in the answers to this question was shown in the sketches of the details of the various machines, for example, such a detail as the stuffing-box of a hydraulic accumulator.

(*a*) The question on the lathe was a favourite one, and, as a rule, was well answered.

(*b*) Some curious designs of accumulators were sketched, and one candidate advised that milk should be mixed with the water to keep it (the water) from going bad.

(*c*) Most of the sketches of the circular saw and saw bench were crude and out of proportion, and it was evident that this part of the question was, in some cases, attempted by candidates who were quite unfamiliar with a saw bench.

(*d*) It was clear from the quality of the answers that this division of the question was attempted only by candidates who had had real foundry experience, but there were one or two most remarkable answers, so extraordinarily foolish as almost to force the Examiners to come to the conclusion that the candidate was deliberately writing nonsense.

Q. 2.— Answer only *one* of the following (*a*), (*b*) or (*c*) :—

(*a*) Describe how you would determine experimentally the coefficient of sliding friction between two pieces of metal of any convenient size when the speed of rubbing is low.

(*b*) Describe how you would determine experimentally the modulus of rigidity of *either* a block of indiarubber *or* a steel rod.

(*c*) Describe how you would determine the mechanical efficiency of *either* a Pelton waterwheel, *or* a small turbine ; state carefully what measurements you would make, and what calculations would be needed.

The answers on laboratory work were generally bad, and apparently most of the blame for this must be placed upon teachers.

(*a*) In describing this experiment not one candidate in a hundred, who made use of the plan of sliding one piece of metal over another by means of a weighted string passing over a pulley, referred to the allowance which must be made for the friction of the pulley, though several made the perfectly senseless remark, "take a frictionless pulley and a perfectly flexible cord," as if it were quite possible to find such things in any laboratory or workshop.

(*b*) Very few candidates appeared to have any real knowledge of the modulus of rigidity, and it is evident that the subject of shear, which is the most important factor in the Strength of Materials, is almost neglected by the majority of teachers. Most of the candidates who made any attempt at this division of the question described experiments for finding either the modulus of tension, or the modulus of compression. Many of the answers were quite irrelevant and exceedingly absurd, one candidate stating "the centre of gravity is the modulus of rigidity in other words."

91

(c) Very few candidates attempted this division of the question, and though most of them were able to describe fairly satisfactorily some form of brake or dynamometer for obtaining the power developed by the water-wheel, or turbine wheel, very few appeared to have anything but the most hazy idea as to the method of determining the actual energy supplied to the motor.

Q. 3. In connection with a contract for the supply of cast-iron pipes, certain bending tests were specified on bars (cast at the same time) 40 inches long, 2 inches deep, and 1 inch thick.

The following results were obtained when one of these bars was tested on edge on a 36-inch span :—

Load at centre of beam. Pounds.	100	400	800	1,200	1,600	2,000	2,400
Deflection at centre of beam. Inches.	·012	·048	·098	·150	·204	·256	·314

Plot on squared paper a curve to show the relation between the load at the centre of the beam and the deflection at the centre of the beam.

From your curve determine the load which will be required at the centre of the beam in order to give a deflection of ½ inch.

The plotting was on the whole satisfactory, but some of the candidates went out of their way to choose inconvenient scales, such as 1 inch = 0·06 inch, and a number of candidates were unable to express ½ inch as a decimal, candidates writing ½ = ·102, or ·0125, and so on.

Q. 4. In a direct-acting steam-engine mechanism the stroke of the piston is 2 feet and the crank shaft makes 150 revolutions per minute.

What is the speed of the crank shaft in radians per second? What is the speed of the crank pin in feet per second? What is the mean speed of the piston in feet per minute?

Usually well answered. The most common mistake was to multiply by 60, instead of dividing by 60, in order to convert the speed per minute into speed per second. Very few candidates had the slightest idea that any connection exists between angular and linear velocity, and therefore the bulk of the candidates wasted time in unnecessary arithmetic.

Q. 5. In a shale mine in order to drain one of the pits a treble ram pump, driven by an electric motor, is employed. The rams are 9½ inches in diameter by 12-inch stroke, they each make 34·75 strokes per minute, and the height to which the water is lifted is 393 feet.

Find :—

(a) How many gallons of water this pump can lift per minute.

(b) How many foot-pounds of useful work are done per minute.

(c) The useful horse-power when the pumps are running steadily.

This question was attempted by a very large number of candidates, and arithmetical blunders were extremely common. Actual mistakes in units were not very frequent, most of the blunders being purely arithmetical. A considerable number of candidates, however, are still uncertain as to the proper formula for the determination of the area of the circle.

Q. 6. Hemp ropes are employed to transmit power from the engine shaft to the driving pulleys on the different floors in a spinning factory. The maximum tension in a rope is twice the minimum tension, the breaking strength of one rope is 5,700 lbs., and it is desired to have a factor of safety of 30.

Find the maximum horse-power which can be safely transmitted by one of these hemp ropes at a speed of 70 feet per second.

The maximum allowable tension in the rope in this question was generally correctly found, but a common mistake was then to work out the horse-power transmitted, using the maximum tension, instead of the difference between the maximum and the minimum tensions. A common error was to write 70 feet per second = ⁷⁄₈ of a foot per minute.

Q. 7. A cycle track is approximately elliptical in shape, the maximum radius of curvature being 150 yards and the minimum 50 yards.

Find at each of these two places, the ratio which the centrifugal force bears to the weight, if the speed of the racing cyclist is 25 miles per hour. What would be the two inclinations of the track to the horizontal if the track is laid so as to be perpendicular to the resultant force in each case?

Comparatively few candidates attempted this question ; as a rule the answers showed a sound knowledge of the formula for centrifugal force, but mistakes were made in units, such as obtaining the velocity in miles per hour, and measuring the radius in yards.

Q. 8. The floor of a room, which is 12 feet square, is supported by timber joists 9 inches deep by 3 inches thick.

It is found by testing a piece of timber of the same quality as that of the joists that a beam 2 inches deep by 1 inch thick on a span of 24 inches is broken by a load at the centre of 1,000 lbs. What load, uniformly spread over its length, will each joist carry, the factor of safety being 9?

If the joists are spaced 15 inches apart, centre to centre, what load per square foot will the floor carry?

The factors which govern the strength of a beam seemed to be quite well understood by a large proportion of the candidates, but there are a few here and there who think that the strength depends simply upon the cross sectional area. The question of the factor of safety was not at all satisfactorily dealt with by the bulk of the candidates ; such an extremely nonsensical answer as the following shows this :—" Breaking load = 9,000 lbs. ; factor of safety = 9 ; therefore safe load = 9,009 lbs."

Q. 9. A tie-bar in a roof is made of steel angle bar ; the section of the steel angle is 4 inches by 4 inches by ⅝ inch, and the tie-bar when finished in the workshop is 20 feet in length. When in position in the roof the tie-bar may during a gale have to resist a total pull of 22½ tons ; what is the tensile stress per square inch in the metal of the tie-bar under these conditions, and how much would the tie-bar lengthen under this load?

Young's modulus of elasticity is 12,500 tons per square inch.

Very few of the candidates were able to calculate correctly the area of the cross section of an angle bar. The most common answer was that the area = 2 × 4 × ⅝ = 5 square inches. The rest of the work of the question was satisfactory.

Q. 10. To do the cutting work in a small screw cutting lathe it is found that 0·47 H.P. is required, and that the frictional losses in the gearing, bearings, &c., absorb another 0·21 H.P. How many foot-pounds of work per minute is the driving belt giving to the lathe?

The countershaft is driven by an electric motor, and the countershaft and belts absorb 0·17 H.P. How many watts must the motor give off in order to keep the lathe running?

If the voltage is 220, how many ampères will the motor require, assuming that its own efficiency is 89 per cent.?

1 H.P. = 746 watts, and ampères multiplied by volts = watts.

A favourite question, and usually very well answered.

Q. 11. A railway truck weighing 10 tons starts from rest down an incline ½ a mile long of 1 in 250. If the frictional and other resistances are equivalent to 8 lbs. per ton weight of the truck, with what velocity will the truck be moving when it gets to the end of the incline?

How far would it then run along a level stretch of the line before coming to rest?

Attempted by only a few candidates, most of whom made serious blunders. The idea of friction as a resisting force seemed quite unfamiliar to most of the candidates, and absurd answers were, as a result, frequently obtained. For example, one candidate stated that the velocity of the truck at the foot of the incline would be 500,000,000 feet per second.

Q. 12. The right-angled bell crank lever, centred at A, shown in the sketch, is attached to a spring by one of its arms, and to another lever, centred at B, by the other arm.

If the spring requires a direct pull of 20 lbs. in order to stretch it 2 inches, find what force P, applied as shown, will stretch the spring this amount.

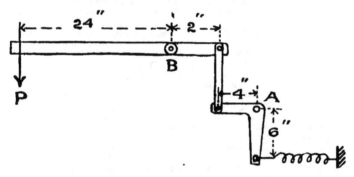

A favourite question, and the answers as a rule were satisfactory.

Q. 13. Two adjacent positions G_1, G_2 of the centre of mass G of a balance weight were obtained by geometrical construction from a skeleton diagram of the mechanism. These positions, measured in feet from two perpendicular axes, were found to be as follows :—

	x	y
G_1 - - - -	0·167	0·073
G_2 - - - -	0·352	0·146

The displacement G_1 G_2 took place in 1/50 second. Find the x and y components of the mean velocity of G for this interval.

Plot the points G_1, G_2 on squared paper.

This question was attempted by only a few candidates, and usually with poor results. Instead of plotting the values of x and y, the candidates, as a rule, plotted G_1 against G_2.

STAGE 2.

Results : 1st Class, 176 ; 2nd Class, 744 ; Failed, 349 ; Total, 1,269.

Q. 21. Describe, with careful sketches, only *one* of the following, (*a*), (*b*), (*c*), or (*d*) :—

    (*a*) The operation of centering, fixing in the lathe and turning a shaft or spindle, say about 2 inches diameter and 12 feet long.

    (*b*) An hydraulic accumulator.

    (*c*) A circular saw and saw bench.

    (*d*) The preparation of a sand mould for the casting of a pulley or the like.

Most of the candidates selected division (*a*) of this question, and showed a good practical knowledge of the operations required in the piece of work they had to describe. The other sections of the question were not so satisfactorily answered.

Q. 22. Answer only *one* of the following, (*a*), (*b*) or (*c*) :—

    (*a*) Describe how you would determine experimentally the coefficient of sliding friction between two pieces of metal of any convenient size when the speed of rubbing is low.

    (*b*) Describe how you would determine experimentally the modulus of rigidity of *either* a block of india-rubber *or* a steel rod.

    (*c*) Describe how you would determine the mechanical efficiency of *either* a Pelton waterwheel, *or* a small turbine ; state fully what measurements you would make, and what calculations would be needed.

Nearly all the candidates selected division (*a*) of this question also, and the answers were good, though very few of the candidates made any reference to making a series of observations in order to obtain the mean value of the coefficient of friction.

In division (*b*) the answers were fairly satisfactory, most of the candidates described a direct experiment in torsion in order to obtain the modulus of rigidity, but a few explained the method of torsional oscillations.

In division (*c*) the answers were not at all satisfactory ; the descriptions of the various measurements that were required were vague and unsatisfactory, and appeared to show that the candidates had never themselves taken part in the carrying out of such an experiment.

Q. 23. In connection with a contract for the supply of cast-iron pipes, certain bending tests were specified on bars (cast at the same time) 40 inches long, 2 inches deep, and 1 inch thick.

The following results were obtained when one of these bars was tested on edge on a 36-inch span :—

Load at centre of beam, pounds	100	400	800	1200	1600	2000	2400
Deflection at centre of beam, inches	·012	·048	·098	·150	·204	·256	·314

Plot on squared paper a curve to show the relation between the load at the centre of the beam and the deflection at the centre of the beam.

95

From your curve determine the load which will be required at the centre of the beam in order to give a deflection of ⅛th of an inch.

Calculate, in lbs. per square inch, Young's modulus of elasticity for this cast-iron. The deflection of a rectangular beam, length l, breadth b, depth d, loaded with W at its centre is

$$\frac{Wl^3}{4Ebd^3}$$

This was probably the question attempted by the largest number of candidates, and on the whole it was well done, though many came to grief over the last part of the question. Many candidates, as in Stage 1, were unable to convert ⅛ inch into a decimal.

Q. 24. In a direct-acting steam-engine mechanism, the stroke of the piston is 2 feet, the length of the connecting rod is 3 feet, and the crank shaft makes 150 revolutions per minute. Find the speed of rotation in radians per second, and the speed of the crank-pin in feet per second.

Draw to scale on the piston path as base, a diagram which will represent in feet per second the speed of the piston at each point in its path during one complete revolution of the crank. The crank shaft is assumed to revolve at a uniform rate.

Determine from your diagram the four positions of the crank in each revolution when the speed of the piston is exactly equal to the speed of the crank-pin.

Use the following scales :—

Linear Scale.—1 inch to 6 inches.

Velocity Scale.—1 inch to 10 feet per second.

This was attempted by comparatively few candidates. The second half of it was on the whole very badly answered! The effect of the connecting rod on the piston speed was generally neglected. It was often stated that the dead centres were two of the positions at which the piston speed was equal to the crank pin speed.

Q. 25. In a shale mine, in order to drain one of the pits, a treble ram pump, driven by an electric motor, is employed. The rams are 9½ inches in diameter by 12-inch stroke, they each make 34·75 strokes per minute, and the height to which the water is lifted is 393 feet. Find :—

(a) How many gallons of water are lifted per minute.

(b) How many foot-pounds of useful work are done per minute.

(c) The useful horse-power when the pumps are running steadily.

(d) The efficiency of the pumps if the B.H.P. of the motor is 50.

This question was attempted by a large majority of the candidates. The arithmetic in many cases was bad. It was extraordinary that students who obtained such absurd figures as 9 per cent., or 914 per cent., for the efficiency of the pump did not at once see that there must be something wrong in their arithmetic.

Q. 26. In the epicyclic train shown in the sketch, the wheel A, which has 30 teeth, is fixed. The rotating arm a, which rotates about the centre A, carries a wheel B, which gears with A, and has 12 teeth, and also a second wheel C, which gears with B, and has 15 teeth. To the wheel C is rigidly fixed an arm b.

If the speed of the arm is n revolutions per minute clockwise, what is the speed of the wheel C about its centre C? Find, for one revolution of the mechanism, the path of a point on the arm b, whose distance from the centre C is equal to the distance between the two centres A and C.

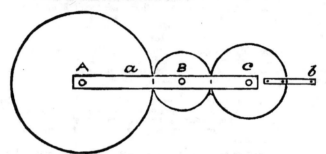

Attempted by very few candidates, and, as a rule, quite incorrectly answered. Most of those trying the question worked out the problem as if it were a simple wheel train. It was quite evident that mechanism is much neglected by teachers.

Q. 27. The speed cone of a small lathe has three steps of diameters 5⅞ inches, 4¼ inches, and 2¾ inches, respectively. On the corresponding cone of the countershaft the diameter of the largest step is 7½ inches. Find the diameters of the other two steps on this cone in order to obtain uniform tightness of the driving belt at all speeds, if the driving belt is crossed.

As a rule very well answered.

Q. 28. A fly-wheel mounted on a horizontal spindle in bearings is rotated by winding a cord on the spindle, attaching a weight to the cord, and allowing the weight to fall to the ground.

In an actual experiment the falling weight was 21 lbs., the total height of fall, 5 feet; the height of fall of the weight for one revolution of the spindle was 5·05 inches ; the time taken by the weight from starting from rest to reach the floor was 7·6 seconds, the whole time of rotation of the fly-wheel starting from rest was 70·25 seconds, and the total number of rotations of the fly-wheel was 109·9. Find :—

    (a) The energy in inch-pounds in the falling weight at the instant of striking the floor.

    (b) The energy in inch-pounds per revolution lost in friction in the bearings of the spindle.

    (c) The moment of inertia of the fly-wheel.

Attempted by only a very small minority, and on the whole very badly answered. Few candidates apparently had ever had an opportunity of carrying out this well-known experiment.

Q. 29. Describe, with sketches, how you would measure the quantity of water flowing down a small stream.

This was badly answered by the few candidates who attempted it. Some were familiar with the weir gauge, and gave correct formulæ for determining the quantity of water passing over the weir, but, in the case of some of the candidates, the weir was used merely as a means of getting an area, and the velocity was then determined independently higher up the stream. Where a cross sectional area and velocity method was adopted, candidates were nearly always satisfied with one experiment for determining the surface velocity.

Q. 30. A rolled steel joist, 12 inches deep, with flanges 4 inches wide, and 1 inch thick, and a web ½ an inch thick, supports a wall over a span of 14 feet, the weight of the wall being equivalent to a distributed load of 1,600 lbs. per foot run. In addition to this load another cross girder rests on the centre of the rolled joist, and transmits to it a load of two tons. Find, neglecting the weight of the joist :—

    (a) The maximum bending moment in this joist in inch-pounds.

    (b) The maximum shearing force in lbs.

    (c) The maximum intensity of the tensile and compressive stresses in the flanges of the joist.

The answers to this question were not at all satisfactory, most of the candidates confusing their arithemtical work owing to the fact that they used the expression $\frac{w\,l^2}{8}$ instead of $\frac{W\,l}{8}$ for the bending moment in the centre of the beam.

Q. 31. A solid steel shaft has to transmit 150 H.P. The number of revolutions of the shaft per minute is 115, and the maximum twisting moment in each revolution exceeds the mean by 25 per cent. If the maximum intensity of the shearing stress is not to exceed 9,000 lbs. per square inch, what must the diameter of this shaft be ?

As a rule well answered, but many candidates came to grief by mixing up foot pounds and inch pounds.

Q. 32. The friction of a thin plate when moved edgewise through water is found by experiment to be ¼ lb. per square foot of surface in contact with the water, when the velocity of rubbing is 600 feet per minute, and that it varies as the square of the velocity of rubbing.

How many foot-pounds of work per minute will be expended in overcoming the skin friction in the case of a ship steaming at 18½ knots, if the immersed surface of the ship when floating at her load line is 27,620 square feet ?

If this skin friction is 70 per cent. of the total resistances encountered by the ship, what is the total horse-power usefully expended in propelling the ship ?

The answers to this question were very unsatisfactory owing to faulty arithmetic. When candidates get beyond 1,000,000 in their calculations, they appear to put in, or leave out, a few ciphers in the most haphazard way, and cancelling is a frequent source of bad blunders.

Q. 33. Draw the profile of a cam to do the following work :—It has to lift vertically with uniform velocity a moving bar, the length of the travel of the bar being 6 inches ; it then has to allow the bar to descend again with uniform velocity, but at one half the speed of the ascent. The two movements occupy one revolution of the uniformly rotating cam. The diameter of the roller working on the cam is ½ inch, and the least thickness of metal round the cam centre must be 2 inches.

The line of stroke of the moving bar passes through the cam centre.

Attempted by very few candidates, but well answered.

Q. 34. Two adjacent positions G_1, G_2 of the centre of mass G of a balance weight were obtained by geometrical construction from a skeleton diagram of the mechanism. These positions, measured in feet from two perpendicular axes, were found to be as follows :—

	x	y
G_1	0·167	0·078
G_2	0·352	0·146

The displacement $G_1 G_2$ took place in $\frac{1}{20}$ second. Find the x and y components of the mean velocity of G for this interval. Find also the magnitude and direction of the resultant velocity.

Plot the points on squared paper, and represent the mean velocity of G as a vector.

Only a small minority attempted this question, and the answers were very poor. It appears that candidates who can plot correctly a long curve from experimental data (such as that given in Question 23) are quite at a loss when the question assumes the usual co-ordinate geometry form.

STAGE 3.

Results : 1st Class, 8 ; 2nd Class, 110 ; Failed, 133 ; Total, 251.

Q. 41. Describe, with careful sketches, only *one* of the following, (a), (b), or (c) :—

(a) A small planing machine for metal ; show in greater detail how the reciprocating motion is given to the table, and how the various feed motions are given to the cutting tool.

(b) An hydraulic accumulator ; show in greater detail the supply and relief valves, and the self-acting mechanism for controlling these valves.

(c) A concrete mixing machine ; show in greater detail how the proportions of sand, ballast, and cement are regulated, and how the necessary amount of water is added.

(a) This division was attempted by the majority of the candidates, and, as a rule, the sketching was satisfactory, and the descriptions were concise and clear, but many of the candidates neglected the feed motions for the tool.

(b) Well answered, the sketching being in many cases exceedingly good.

(c) Attempted by very few candidates, and the answers were very unsatisfactory.

Q. 42. Answer only *one* of the following, (a), (b), or (c) :—

(a) Describe fully, with detailed sketches of the apparatus, how you would determine the co-efficient of friction for a steel shaft running in a gun-metal bearing.

Explain carefully how you would arrange for uniform lubrication, and how you would measure the temperature of the bearing.

(b) Describe fully how you would determine the mechanical efficiency of either a Pelton wheel, or a small turbine ; state in detail all the measurements you would make, and all the calculations which would be required in order to obtain the result.

Show by a curve how the mechanical efficiency of such machines varies as the effective work done is gradually increased from zero to full load.

(c) In a certain contract a large amount of concrete has to be used. It is necessary to determine the proper proportions of sand, broken stone, and cement to employ in making this concrete ; explain fully how you would do this.

(a) The answers to this division of the question were not at all satisfactory, the experimental methods described being in many cases crude in the extreme. One candidate seriously suggested that the temperature of the bearing might be obtained by the melting points of various metals placed in holes drilled in the bearing.

(b) Fairly well answered, though many of the methods described for determining the energy given to the wheel were by no means free from possible causes of serious error.

(c) Only a few candidates attempted this, and the bulk of those who did answer it confined themselves to describing simple tension experiments on briquettes of sand and cement.

Q 43. In connection with a contract for the supply of cast-iron pipes certain bending tests were specified on bars (cast at the same time) 40 inches long, 2 inches deep, and 1 inch thick.

The following results were obtained when one of these bars was tested on edge on a 36-inch span :—

Load at centre of beam, pounds.	100	400	800	1200	1600	2000	2400
Deflection at centre of beam, inches.	·012	·048	·098	·150	·204	·256	·314

(a) Plot on squared paper a curve to show the relation between the load at the centre of the beam and the deflection at the centre of the beam.

(b) Calculate in lbs. per square inch Young's modulus of elasticity for this cast-iron.

(c) Calculate in inch-pounds the total work done in bending this beam up to a load of 2,400 lbs. in the centre of the span.

(d) The beam eventually broke with a load of 3,200 lbs. in the centre. Assuming that the ordinary beam formula holds up to the breaking point in cast-iron beams, what was the maximum intensity of tensile stress in the metal at the instant of rupture?

Very well answered on the whole, but many candidates obtained incorrect results owing to taking the span of the beam as 40 inches instead of 36 inches.

Q. 44. In a direct-acting steam-engine mechanism the stroke of the piston is 2 feet, the length of the connecting rod is 3 feet, and the crank shaft makes 150 revolutions per minute.

(a) Draw to scale on the piston path as base a diagram which will represent in feet per second the linear velocity of the piston at each point in its path during one complete revolution of the crank. The crank-pin is assumed to revolve at a uniform rate.

(b) Draw also to scale on the same base an acceleration diagram for the piston during one complete revolution of the crank.

State clearly the scales to which the two diagrams are drawn.

(c) From the acceleration diagram, determine the two positions of the crank at which the acceleration of the piston is zero.

The first two sections of this question were fairly well answered, but very few candidates obtained the acceleration diagram correctly, and still fewer were able to determine the positions of the crank when the piston acceleration was zero.

Q. 45. In a shale mine in order to drain one of the pits a treble ram pump, driven by an electric motor, is employed. The rams are $9\frac{1}{2}$ inches diameter by 12-inch stroke, they each make 34·75 strokes per minute, the height to which the water is lifted is 393 feet, and the total length of the 6-inch discharge pipe is 700 feet. Find :—

(a) How many gallons of water are lifted per minute.

(b) How many foot-pounds of useful work are done per minute.

(c) How many foot-pounds of work are done per minute in overcoming the friction in the pipe (the coefficient of friction is 0·0075).

(d) The B.H.P. required to lift the water and overcome the pipe friction.

Attempted by the majority of the candidates. The most frequent source of error was the mixing up of feet and inches. For example the volume pumped per minute was calculated in cubic inches, and the result was then multiplied by $6\frac{1}{4}$ in order to convert it into gallons. The methods employed for determining the friction in the pipe were very bad. Very few of the candidates were familiar with the ordinary formula for the frictional losses in a pipe, and a favourite method was simply to multiply the weight of the water pumped per minute by the coefficient of friction.

Q. 46. Find the maximum horse-power which can be transmitted by a hemp rope 1 inch in diameter at a speed of 70 feet per second, if the rope is broken with a pull of 5,700 lbs., and it is desired to have a factor of safety of 30.

The angle of the groove in which the rope runs is 60°, and the coefficient of friction may be taken as 0·25, and it is in contact with the pulley for half the circumference.

Find also the centrifugal tension in the rope if the flywheel is 10 feet in diameter, and the reduction in the horse-power transmitted due to this tension.

Weight of rope for 1 foot of length = 0·28 lbs.

This question was badly answered. Many of the candidates who attempted it neglected the effect of the groove in the rim of the pulley, and worked out the problem as if it had been a flat belt running on a flat pulley. Only a few candidates obtained a correct solution to the second part of the question dealing with the centrifugal tension in the rope.

Q. 47. In the epicyclic train shown in the sketch, the wheel A, which has 30 teeth, is fixed. The rotating arm a, which rotates about the centre A, carries a wheel B, which gears with A, and has 12 teeth, and also a second wheel C, which gears with B, and has 15 teeth. To the wheel C is rigidly fixed an arm b. Find for one revolution of the mechanism :—

 (a) The path of a point on the arm b, whose distance from the centre C is equal to the distance between the two centres A and C.

 (b) The path of a point on the arm b, whose distance from the centre C is one-half that between the two centres A and C.

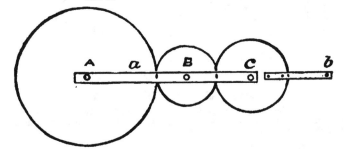

Attempted by only a minority of the candidates, and the work as a rule was unsatisfactory. Most of the candidates seemed to be quite unfamiliar with such a piece of mechanism as an epicyclic train, and most absurd curves were obtained for the path of the point b.

Q. 48. A tripod has the following dimensions :—The apex point is O, and the lengths of the three legs AO, BO, and CO are respectively 18·0 feet, 17·5 feet, and 16 feet. The lengths of the sides of the triangle formed by the feet AB, BC, and CA are 9·0 feet 9·5 feet and 10 feet respectively. Find graphically, or in any other way, the forces which act down each leg of the tripod when a load of 10 tons is suspended from it.

As a rule fairly well answered, but the graphical work was often very rough and incorrect.

Q. 49. A cone clutch has an angle of 50°, and a mean diameter of 10 inches. Find the thrust on the sliding part parallel to the shaft when the clutch transmits 2 horse-power at 120 revolutions per minute, if the coefficient of friction between the two parts of the clutch is 0·35.

A favourite question and well answered.

Q. 50. A steel shaft $2\frac{1}{4}$ inches in diameter is driven by a 20 H.P. gas engine at 100 revolutions per minute. The shaft is supported by three bearings, spaced 15 feet apart between centres, and the centre of the driving pulley is 6 inches beyond the centre of one of the end bearings. Pulleys are arranged, as shown on the sketch, to work certain machines, and the horse-power taken off each of these pulleys is shown on the sketch ; in addition each bearing absorbs $\frac{1}{2}$ H.P. Assuming that all loads are applied at the centre of the respective pulleys and bearings, calculate the angle of twist in the shaft at each of these points, reckoning from either end of the shaft. The modulus of rigidity is 12,500,000 lbs. per square inch.

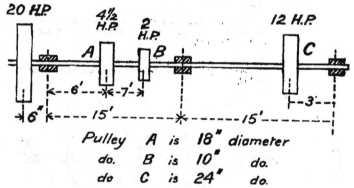

20 H.P. 4½ H.P. 2 H.P. 12 H.P.

Pulley A is 18" diameter
do. B is 10" do.
do. C is 24" do.

Answered by comparatively few candidates, and many of these made serious arithmetical blunders, especially in the mixing up of inch pounds and foot pounds of work.

Q. 51. In a certain method of making shock tests of metal, a heavy rotating disc carries a knife at a point on its circumference. The disc having been set in rapid rotation, the metal specimen to be tested, supported on two knife edges at a certain distance apart, is moved up towards the rotating disc to such a position that the knife in descending strikes the centre of the specimen and fractures it. The work absorbed in fracturing the bar is estimated from the change of velocity of rotation of the disc.

In an actual machine the diameter of the disc, which is of steel, is 12 inches, and its thickness is 4 inches. (One cubic inch of steel weighs 0·28 lbs.) The angular velocity of the disc before impact with the specimen is 36 radians per second, and after impact, 24·3 radians per second.

Calculate the number of inch-pounds of work spent in fracturing the specimen.

Criticise this method of testing the quality of a specimen of any material.

Attempted by only a few of the candidates, but well answered.

Q. 52. Show that the Lowell formula for a rectangular gauge notch is a rational formula. It is (for sharp edges at sides and sill) —

$$(Q = 3{\cdot}33\,(L - \tfrac{1}{5}\,H)\,H^{\frac{3}{2}}$$

where Q is in cubic feet per second, L and H being in feet.

Describe, with sketches, how you would measure the quantity of water flowing down a small stream.

Attempted by very few candidates, and in most cases the portion of the question dealing with the Lowell formula was badly answered.

Q. 53. Three adjacent positions, G_1, G_2, G_3 of the centre of mass G of a balance weight, at intervals of $\frac{1}{50}$ second, have been found by geometrical construction. Referred to perpendicular axes, these positions are measured in feet as follows :—

	x	y
G_1	0·167	0·078
G_2	0·352	0·146
G_3	0·487	0·242

Find approximately, by taking first and second differences, the x and y components of the velocity and acceleration of G when in the position G_2. Find also the resultant velocity and resultant acceleration for this position.

The mass of the balance weight was 351 lbs. Find the magnitude and direction of the force corresponding to the acceleration for the position G_2. Plot the points on squared paper, and on the diagram exhibit the velocity, acceleration, and force as vectors.

Attempted by very few candidates, but well answered by those who did attempt it, though in some cases the plotting was unsatisfactory.

Honours.

Results ; 1st Class, 1 ; 2nd Class, 3 ; Failed, 18 ; Total, 22.

Twenty-two candidates entered for this stage, and the work was much more satisfactory than in the preceding year. Questions 61, 62, 63, 66, and 67 were the favourite ones. Most of the answers to Question 61 were very good, the bulk of the candidates selecting division (a), but the sketching in some cases was unsatisfactory, especially with regard to the details of the feed motions. In division (b) the sketching was much better, and the details were much more carefully shown by the candidates who attempted this part of the question. In Question 62 the majority of the candidates selected division (a), but most of those omitted to explain how they would test the accuracy of the instruments employed in the experiment. The answers to Question 63 were on the whole satisfactory, the diagrams were carefully drawn, but many candidates contented themselves with dealing with only one-half of a revolution of the crank, instead of one complete revolution as was asked in the question. Very few candidates attempted Question 64, and only one secured an accurate result. Question 65 was attempted by only a few candidates, but was well answered. In Question 66 most of the incorrect answers were due to faulty arithmetic, candidates showing a sound enough knowledge of the necessary formulæ, but making serious blunders in their calculations. Question 67 was well answered. The remaining four questions, 68–71, were each attempted by only a small number of students. As a rule the work was fairly satisfactory.

Report on the Examination in Steam.

STAGE 1.

Results: 1st Class, 424; 2nd Class, 408; Failed, 496; Total, 1,328.

There were 1,328 candidates in this stage, being a slight increase compared with 1,300 last year.

SKETCHES.

The standard reached in Questions 1 and 2 is now fairly high, and the details shown often exhibit a working knowledge of the subject. Candidates are sometimes handicapped by omitting to provide themselves with compasses and straight-edges, and suffer accordingly. The sketches in Question 3 were not so good, probably because candidates were not asked for 'good sketches' as in the previous questions. On the whole there is no need to complain of the sketching, but it is very necessary that candidates should be kept up to the mark.

CALCULATIONS.

The usual difficulties were noticed as soon as candidates tried to mix the Centigrade and Fahrenheit scales, but this confusion is growing less marked as men get accustomed to the former. The use of the slide rule would save many mistakes and much labour. Several candidates drew attention to the fact that the ruling of the paper into one inch squares was not accurately done. The inch was more accurately 2·5 cm.

Q. 1. Describe, with good sketches, one, and only one, of the following, (a), (b), (c), or (d) :—

    (a) The crank shaft bearing of a horizontal or vertical engine.

    (b) The crank axle of an inside cylinder locomotive.

    (c) The piston of a gas or petrol engine, showing the packing, and the pin to which the connecting rod is attached.

    (d) The rotating part of a Parsons' or other steam turbine, showing how the vanes are fixed.

(a) The favourite section of this question, and students showed considerable familiarity with the subject.

(b) Fairly often attempted, but many had no notion where the eccentrics were put and a number showed cranks at wrong angles.

(c) Very frequently attempted, and mostly with success. There is evidently much familiarity with the petrol engine.

(d) Not often done, and attempts, when made, often sketchy and showing no familiarity with the matter.

Q. 2. Describe, with good sketches, one, and only one, of the following (a), (b), (c), (d), or (e) :—

    (a) A steam stop valve of the screw-down type.

    (b) A locomotive regulator valve of any type.

    (c) Two forms of boiler stays, stating the use of each.

    (d) The front plate of a Lancashire, Cornish, or return tube marine boiler, showing how the boiler shell is attached.

    (e) The carburettor of a petrol or oil engine.

(a) Often well done, but an astonishing number of sketches showed no provision whatever for the removal of the valve or indeed in certain cases for its ever having got there.

(b) A locomotive regulator valve is not an easy thing to sketch and many students got into difficulties and were unable to make their sketches clear.

(c) Usually done well and often attempted. A great proportion of the candidates appear to have worked in a boiler shop.

(d) Not so often tried as the preceding section and not quite so wel. done. The question offered a more promising field to the candidate who had only seen the outside of a boiler in the distance.

(e) A number of excellent answers and equally good sketches.

Q. 3. With a small experimental boiler you are finding the pressure of steam when its temperature is, say, 100° C., 110° C., 120° C., etc. Show, with sketches, exactly how you would proceed. In what way does the presence of air with the steam spoil your results ?

Often attempted by men who would have left it severely alone had it not been one of the three important questions. Every kind of answer was given. That part of the question relating to the effect of the presence of air was difficult and it was therefore marked leniently. Most of the candidates have evidently never taken part in or even witnessed experiments illustrative of this portion of the subject.

Q. 4. State the following amounts of energy in foot-pounds :—

> (a) A weight of 35 tons may fall vertically 15 feet.
>
> (b) The Kinetic Energy of a projectile of 60 lbs. moving 2,000 feet per second.
>
> (c) The Calorific Energy of 1 lb. of coal, 8,500 Centigrade pound heat units.
>
> (d) 30 lbs. of water raised from 40° F. to 103° F.
>
> (e) One horse-power-hour.
>
> (f) One kilowatt-hour.

(a) Usually correctly done.

(b) The formula was often given wrong either by omitting the figure 2 or by leaving out g.

(c) Often unattempted, but a fair proportion of correct results. The usual confusion between Centigrade and Fahrenheit units was noticed.

(d) The same remarks apply to this as to (c).

(e) The answer to this is virtually given in the table of constants and so there were many correct solutions.

(f) Many failed to work this correctly, putting the 746 in the numerator.

In answering Question 4 few of the candidates used logarithms or slide rules; they seem to prefer long methods of multiplication and division.

Q. 5. It used to be thought that by cutting off earlier and earlier in the stroke, we got better and better results. Why is this untrue ? It used to be that the slide valve was never found on economical engines; why is it now in use on many large and economical engines ?

The reason why the practice of the early cut off could easily be pushed too far was generally understood, but only in a vague manner, and hardly any thoroughly correct answers were given. Why the slide valve is now used on large and economical engines was answered in many ways and not a little ingenuity was shown; the favourite reply was to refer to the introduction of the double ported and balanced valves.

Q. 6. The mean effective pressure on the piston, both in the forward and back strokes, is 62 lbs. per square inch; cylinder, 18 inches diameter; crank, 18 inches long. What is the work done in one revolution ?

An easy question and frequently solved correctly. We are glad to think that nearly every candidate who relied upon the P.L.A.N. formula came to grief.

Q. 7. A pound of oil contains 0·85 lb. of carbon and 0·15 lb. of hydrogen. What weight of oxygen is sufficient to produce CO_2 and H_2O by combustion ? Take the atomic weights of C, 12 ; of O, 16 ; of H, 1. If 1 lb. of oxygen is contained in 4·35 lbs. of air, how many pounds of air are needed for complete combustion ?

This appeared to be a difficult question, but an astonishingly large number of perfectly correct replies were made. Hardly any who tried it got it wrong. The way in which this question was answered shows wide reading on the part of many works apprentices.

Q. 8. A slide valve is worked directly from an eccentric. The advance is 30°. When the main crank has moved 20° from the line of centres, show the position of the eccentric crank. The half travel being 3 inches, mark off this radius and drop a perpendicular on the line of centres ; what have you thus found ?

This was a very easy question, but numbers failed over it ; failed where they could probably have worked successfully a much more complicated question on the Zeuner diagram. We think the answers to this question show that the Zeuner diagram is not understood. A number lost marks by drawing a 1½ inch radius instead of a 3 inch one, they meant very possibly to be working to half scale, but it was not always possible to know whether this was so or not.

Q. 9. A formula for Regnault's total heat H will be found on the tables supplied to you ; it is the total heat which must be given to 1 lb. of water at 0° C. to raise its temperature as water to $\theta°$ C., and then to convert it all into steam at $\theta°$ C. What is the heat which must be given to 1 lb. of water at 40° C. to convert it into steam at 170° C. ?

Frequently answered correctly, and accurate knowledge upon the subject appears to be increasing. It is worth notice that a very nearly correct answer could be obtained by an entirely wrong method. A good many students subtracted the 40 from the 170 before multiplying by ·305, a serious mistake.

Q. 10. A boiler furnace-fire is about 12 inches thick. What do we know as to the way in which the combustion is going on at various places in the coal and above it and in the space just on the furnace side of the flues ? Take any state you please ; just before fresh coal is supplied or after, but you must say what the conditions are.

A number attempted this question only when they found they could do no others, and many rambling replies were therefore sent in. Some thoroughly good answers were given, but chemical knowledge was more often exhibited in Question 7 than in this.

Q. 11. F lb. is the outward radial force on each ball of a governor required to keep it in equilibrium at the distance r feet from the axis when not revolving. The following are for the extreme cases :—

r	F
0·5	100·1
0·7	144·6

The weight of each ball being 10 lbs., what is the centrifugal force of each at n revolutions per minute, the radius being r.

What are the speeds for the above values of r when the governor is revolving ?

This was obviously considered a difficult question and many of those that did attempt it arrived after ingenious struggles at incorrect solutions. The simpler form of the centrifugal force formula appears well known.

Q. 12. In a gas engine cylinder where $v = 2\cdot2$ and $p = 14\cdot72$ it was known that the temperature was 130° C. What is the temperature when $p = 1\cdot22$ and $v = 1\cdot2$?

Frequently answered, but the answer most often given was 587 deg. C., an answer obtained by treating all temperatures as though they were absolute, and even then arithmetical errors were numerous.

Q. 13. The total heat, that is, the heat H required to convert a pound of water at 0° C. into a pound of wet steam at θ° C., having a dryness fraction x, is

$$H = \theta + xL.$$

where L is the latent heat of 1 lb. of dry saturated steam. If wet steam 90 per cent. dry (that is, $x = 0\cdot9$) at 203·3 lbs. per square inch, is throttled by passing through a non-conducting reducing value to 101·9 lbs. per square inch, what is its dryness at the lower pressure? Remember that H is the same for the two kinds of steam : it keeps constant when steam is throttled.

p	θ	L
203·3	195	468·0
101·9	165	489·0

This was looked upon as a difficult question, and therefore nearly xclusively attempted by candidates who knew they could do it. A few brought in the pressure as a multiplier.

STAGE 2.

Results : 1st Class, 268 ; 2nd Class, 520 ; Failed, 323 ; Total, 1,111.

In this stage there was a considerable increase in the number of candidates, the actual figures for this and last year being 1,111 and 940 respectively.

There is very little ground for complaint as to the quality of the *sketches.* The remarks made as to *Calculations* in Stage 1 apply to Stage 2 ; the Arithmetic is not at all in a satisfactory state.

Q. 21. Describe, with good sketches, one, and only one, of the following, (a), (b), (c), or (d) :—

    (a) The crank shaft bearing of a horizontal or a vertical engine stating the diameter of the bearing.

    (b) The crank axle of an inside cylinder locomotive, inserting approximate dimensions.

    (c) The piston of a gas or a petrol engine, showing the packing, and the pin to which the connecting rod is attached. State the diameter of the piston.

    (d) The rotating part of a Parsons' or other steam turbine, showing how the vanes are fixed.

(a) This and section (c) proved to be the most popular parts of the question. The crank shaft bearing was as a rule well sketched and described, very much more information was shown than in the corresponding question in Stage 1, even when allowance is made for the difference in standard.

(b) Popular and generally well done.

(c) Very popular and rarely badly done. The facts about petrol engines are well known.

(*d*) Not often attempted, but there were a number of good answers and few "shots." .The Parsons' turbine was sketched rather more often than the impulse forms. The sketching generally in answer to this question was of a satisfactorily high quality and the proportion of marks given was therefore high, but methods of fastening the vanes do not seem to be known.

Q. 22. Describe, with good sketches, one, and only one, of the following (*a*), (*b*), (*c*), or (*d*) :—

    (*a*) A steam stop valve of the screw-down type.

    (*b*) A locomotive regulator valve of any type.

    (*c*) Three forms of boiler stays, stating the use of each.

    (*d*) The front plate of a Lancashire, Cornish, or return tube marine boiler, showing how the boiler shell and flue tubes are attached.

(*a*) This section was about equally popular with the rest, in fact there is little to choose in this respect between any of them. The stop valve was well-known in all its details, the only mistake which occurred at all frequently was, as in Stage 1, the omission of any means for inserting or removing the valve.

(*b*) This was not an easy sketch to make, and a number of views were commonly found necessary. On the whole, however, the sketches and descriptions were satisfactory.

(*c*) Mostly done well. The details of boilers are familiar to most of the students who answered this section.

(*d*) The sketches here were not of a very high standard, and a number of candidates appeared to be in doubt as to how much they should show.

Q. 23. Answer one, and only one, of the following questions, (*a*), (*b*), (*c*), or (*d*) :—

    (*a*) Describe the testing of any kind of heat engine which you have yourself seen or helped in. What measurements were made and how ?

    (*b*) How is an indicator tested ? Criticise the method which you describe.

    (*c*) How would you test the calorific power of an oil or spirit ?

    (*d*) Describe the testing of any kind of boiler for power to generate steam and for efficiency.

(*a*) This section and (*c*) and (*d*) were equally popular. Most of the candidates who selected (*a*) were evidently describing something they had seen ; in fact in numbers of cases the answers were almost complete. Measurements of I.H.P. and B.H.P. were most popular. Many answers showed electrical knowledge.

(*b*) Not often done, but from a few schools there were very good answers.

(*c*) Frequently attempted, but the information was often given as though learnt by rote. Thus a whole series of papers described a bomb calorimeter which was to be made of a material "equal to steel as regards tensile strength covered inside with gold or platinum and containing compressed oxygen to the extent of 25 atmospheres" ; further, the combustion always required exactly " two ampères at twelve volts " to start it.

(*d*) Several gave hydraulic tests, and received no marks. There were, however, many excellent answers, and a number of candidates had evidently assisted, sometimes very humbly, at actual tests.

Q. 24. The indicated work of an engine is equivalent to 206 centigrade pound heat units per pound of feed-water ; how many pounds of feed-water are required per horse-power hour ? If you had a good many examples like this to work out, how would you arrange the work so as to have no unnecessary arithmetic.

Frequently attempted, and although often correctly answered, a number of candidates showed themselves hopelessly confused with their calculations. Not a great number answered the second half of the question completely. Many numerical errors were made.

Q. 25. There is a rule concerning the velocity of a fluid before it enters a turbine wheel and the inclination of the vane and its velocity ; what is the rule ? Give the reason for it.

Scarcely ever answered. Correct ideas on the subject seemed to be only moderately well grasped by the few that essayed the question.

Q. 26. The moment of inertia of a fly wheel is 9920 in Engineers' units ; its speed changes from 10 to 10·2 radians per second ; give in foot-pounds the increase in its kinetic energy. If the acceleration was uniform and the whole change occurred in one quarter of a revolution, what excess turning moment caused it ?

Many attempted this who were evidently quite incapable of doing any part of it correctly. In spite of the many attempts hardly any candidates answered the second half correctly. A number of the better-equipped students were doubtful as to "Engineers' units," but this lack of information was not treated hardly, provided that the principles of working were correct. Candidates seem to be familiar only with linear, and not at all with angular motion.

Q. 27. A pound of oil contains 0·85 lb. of Carbon and 0·15 lb. of Hydrogen. What weight of Oxygen is just sufficient to completely burn it ? If 1 lb. of oxygen is contained in 4·35 lb. of air, how many pounds of air are needed for complete combustion ?

A fair number of correct and thoughful answers were sent up. A few thought the atomic weight of oxygen was 14.

Q. 28. The half travel of a slide valve is 3 inches, advance 30°. How far is the valve from its mid position when the crank has turned through an angle of 35° from a dead point ? Prove your method to be right.

The construction and the proof were very commonly known. Many gave a Zeuner construction which was not really necessary, but S.H.M. principles do not seem to be too well known.

Q. 29. The entropies of a pound of water and of dry saturated steam at 150° C. are 0·442 and 1·623 respectively. The volume of the dry steam would be 6·168 cubic feet.

Now there is a pound of wet steam at 150° C. whose entropy is 1·235. What is its dryness fraction ? that is, how much of it is steam, how much water ? What is its volume ? Neglect the volume of the water.

Often attempted and generally accurately done. A few attempts were made via Total Heat, and after much arithmetic a successful result was obtained. When the first part was done, the second seemed to present little difficulty. The volume of the wet steam was almost always correctly given.

Q. 30. A boiler furnace fire is about 12 inches thick. What do we know as to the way in which combustion is going on at various places in the coal and above it, and in the space just on the furnace side of the flues ? Does it depend upon the time that has elapsed since the furnace was last fed with coal ? If so, say in what state the fire is, to which your description applies.

Comparatively few complete answers were made, in spite of the number of times the question was attempted. Numbers merely discussed the matter, and seemed concerned at the thickness of the fire. Knowledge of simple chemical principles is greatly needed.

Q. 31. When the outward radial force on each ball of a motionless Watt Governor required to keep it in equilibrium at the distance r feet from the axis is equated to the centrifugal force which would exist if it were revolving, we find the following result. W lb. is a load, w lb. the weight of each ball; f friction; n revolutions per minute—

$$n = \frac{60}{2\pi} \sqrt{\frac{32\cdot2}{h}} \sqrt{\frac{W + w \pm f}{w}}$$

where h means $\sqrt{l^2 - r^2}$.

If $w = 4$, $W = 100$, $f = 0\cdot25$, $l = 1\cdot2$ feet, find the two speeds corresponding to $r = 0\cdot5$.

If you had to do this for other values of r and for other values of W, how would you arrange the work so as to have least trouble?

This being only arithmetical, a number attempted it, but many slips have to be recorded. Those that used slide rules did best. The most frequent mistake was to neglect the second square root to be taken in the h term. The arithmetic shown in this question was of a low order. Methods of saving work were seldom well known.

Q. 32. In a gas engine cylinder where $v = 2\cdot2$ and $p = 14\cdot72$ it was known that the temperature was 130° C. What is the temperature when $p = 122$ and $v = 1\cdot2$?

In doing this you have assumed the stuff to behave as a perfect gas. Why is this not correct?

Was often attempted, but nearly half forgot to add 273 to the initial temperature. Otherwise the first half of the question was commendably free from arithmetical error. Answers to the second half of the question were very interesting and showed not a little ingenuity. Unhappily, however, they also showed the most widespread errors as to the understanding of what laws a perfect gas is supposed to follow. Some thought a perfect gas was unaffected by temperature, others thought that the $p\,v/t$ formula was not obeyed if the gas received or lost heat in any way, or if there was a mixture of gases. The answers to the second part were very feeble.

Q. 33. Steam 90 per cent. dry at 203·3 lb. per square inch passes through a non-conducting reducing valve or throttle valve; and lowers in pressure to 101·9 lb. per square inch; what is its dryness at the lower pressure? Use the following information:—

p	θ	L
203·3	195	468·0
101·9	165	489·9

(Remember that $H = \theta + xL$ where θ is temperature and L is latent heat and x is the coefficient of dryness of the steam. Remember that H is the same for the steam on the two sides of the valve.)

Was often done and usually correctly. Many who failed to get the correct answer often did so owing to faulty algebra. As a rule, however, when the correct answer was not given the candidate was hopelessly confused.

Q. 34. Air is at 1600° C. in a vessel, and at the pressure p_1; it escapes through an orifice which expands outside into an atmosphere of pressure 1. Its temperature as it passes without shock into a wheel outside is not to exceed 500° C., what is p_1? Assume the adiabatic law.

Most rarely attempted, but a few answers were sent in that got full marks.

STAGE 3.

Results : 1st Class, 29 ; 2nd Class, 75 ; Failed, 135 ; Total, 239.

The number of candidates in this state was 239, compared with 176 last year, thus showing an increase of 63, or nearly 36 per cent. The work on the whole was satisfactory, and in the case of a few candidates was very good indeed. The sketches in answer to Questions 41 and 42 were generally in good proportion and exhibited a close observance of practical details. But the divorce of this kind of knowledge from that of a mathematical nature was very marked in this as in the other stages, and is specially referred to in Honours. The answers are now criticised in detail.

Q. 41. Describe, with good sketches, one, and only one, of the following, (a), (b), (c), or (d) :—

    (a) A crank shaft bearing of a large horizontal or vertical engine, giving the diameter of the bearing.

    (b) The crank axle of an inside cylinder locomotive, with the eccentric-discs, inserting approximate dimensions.

    (c) The piston and connecting rod of a gas or petrol engine. State the diameter of the piston.

    (d) The wheel of a Parsons' or other steam turbine, showing how the vanes are fixed, and how it is balanced axially against steam pressure. Also the arrangement which prevents leakage.

The choice generally fell on (a) or (c). In the answers to (a) bearings stated to be for horizontal engines were sometimes shown in which there was only provision for *vertical* wear. In (c) the answers revealed a wide acquaintance with small petrol engines. The sketches to (b) were evidently confined to students from locomotive works, and were for the most part excellent. In regard to (d) a few of the sketches were from practical experience of turbines, but many were apparently from books.

Q. 42. Describe, with good sketches, one, and only one, of the following, (a), (b), (c), or (d) :—

    (a) A large steam stop valve of good design.

    (b) A locomotive regulator valve of any type, showing the pipe by which steam is led from the steam dome to the cylinders.

    (c) Four forms of boiler stays, stating the use of each.

    (d) The front plate of a Lancashire, Cornish, or return tube marine boiler, showing how the shell, the flue tubes and the stays are attached.

Here again (a) and (c) were generally chosen. In answering (a) the candidates not infrequently spoiled an otherwise good sketch by showing a design in which it was impossible to get valve and seating either in or out of the casing. The regulator valve was not very well sketched, and its construction could seldom have been thoroughly made out from the sketch by a person who did not possess a previous knowledge of its form.

Q. 43. Answer one, and one only, of the following questions, (a) or (b) :—

    (a) How is an indicator tested? Criticise the method which you describe.

    (b) Describe the testing of any kind of boiler for strength and power to generate steam and for efficiency.

The boiler test was usually the one described, and many of the answers showed that the writers had themselves seen such tests. In other cases the candidates said, vaguely, measure this or measure that with no hint of a practical way of doing it. The efficiency of a boiler was better understood than its *power* to generate steam.

Q. 44. Why is it, that the steam turbine seems to take more advantage
of a very perfect vacuum in its condenser than a reciprocating
engine ? What are the defects of any turbine you know ? Why
do we obtain so little mechanical energy as compared with what
is shown on the Rankine Cycle ?

Some knowledge of the defects of the steam turbine was shown, but in
regard to the other parts of the question the answers were nearly always
worthless. The question was not very often attempted.

Q. 45. For any radial valve gear we have a figure which enables us
rapidly to find the half travel of the valve and the advance for
any position of the gear. Show how this is arrived at and prove
the method to be correct. Assume motions to be simple
harmonic.

Was seldom attempted, and with poor results. Candidates had some
knowledge but lacked the power to present it in a coherent and logical
form. Sometimes a proof of the Zeuner diagram was given, the travel
and advance being supposed known. In other cases Stephenson's link gear
was described.

Q. 46. Crank 1 foot, connecting rod 4·5 feet, what are the accelerations
at the ends and some other point in the stroke, if the engine
makes 200 revolutions per minute ? The piston and rod and
cross head are 420 lb. ; draw a diagram to show the force in
pounds required to produce the motion. State the scale clearly.

This was a favourite question, and it was often well answered. A rather
common error was to take the middle of the piston stroke to correspond
with the crank position half way between the dead points.

Q. 47. Prove the formula connecting latent heat, temperature, pressure
and change of specific volume when there is a change from liquid
to vapour.

This question, when attempted, which was not very often, was nearly
always completely answered, and indicated good book knowledge.

Q. 48. It has been proposed, instead of much superheating in the usual
way, to have less of this and to superheat in the receivers
between the cylinders. Assuming that the thing can be done in
a good practical way, what is your opinion of its merits ? Of
course you will give your reasons.

Was answered more frequently than the knowledge possessed by the
candidates justified. One or two condemned the method outright. A few
pointed out how the difficulties arising from a high degree of superheat
would be materially lessened, several using the $\theta \phi$ diagram very effectively
in their explanation.

Q. 49. In the following Table u is the volume in cubic feet of 1 lb. of dry
saturated steam. v is the actual volume of a pound of wet steam
(neglect the small volume of the water). What is the dryness
fraction in each case ?

In the table we give ϕ_w the entropy of 1 lb. of water and ϕ_s
the entropy of 1 lb. of dry saturated steam. Make a temperature entropy diagram. Mark the three points where the
volume is 3·2 cubic feet and draw a curve through them.

θ	u	ϕ_w	ϕ_s	v
175	3·419	0·500	1·575	3·2
150	6·168	0·441	1·623	3·2
120	14·04	0·366	1·692	3·2

A favourite question, and good marks were nearly always obtained. A mistake sometimes made was to add ϕ_s to ϕ_w in plotting the entropy line for steam.

Q. 50. The temperatures on two sides of an iron plate 0·5 inch thick differ by 10 centigrade degrees, how much heat (in centigrade pound water units) passes per square foot per second? The conductivity of iron is 0·18 in C.G.S. units (centigrade gramme water units).

A fairly favourite question, and the answers were often quite correct. Not infrequently, however, candidates went astray in the units.

Q. 51. Give the ordinary statical theory of the Watt or Hartnell form of governor, taking friction into account. If you choose the Watt it must be a modern loaded governor.

This was one of the favourite questions. It was sometimes done well but there was too much evidence of mere cram. Proofs evidently learnt by heart from a book would be given without a real knowledge of the symbols involved, and the figure would sometimes be quite inconsistent with the so-called proof.

Q. 52. Prove the formula for efficiency in the hypothetical Otto cycle (the diagram being two adiabatics and two constant volume lines), showing how efficiency is greater as clearance is less. In what way does this hypothetical diagram differ from reality? If it differs greatly, why are such calculations of any use.

Seldom attempted. The formula for efficiency in terms of the ratio of expansion was generally satisfactorily established, but little knowledge was shown in the answers to the other parts of the question.

Q. 53. When steam is throttled or passes through a non-conducting reducing valve show that the value of H remains constant; H is the total heat required to convert 1 lb. of water at 0° C. to dry or wet steam at $\theta°$ C. Find an expression for H in terms of the dryness fraction.

Steam 95 per cent. dry at 203·3 lb. per square inch passes through a non-conducting reducing valve and lowers in pressure to 101·9 lb. per square inch; what is its dryness? Use the following information. L is the latent heat of 1 lb. of dry saturated steam.

p	θ	L
203·3	195	468·0
101·9	165	489·9

This was a favourite question and the last part was generally correctly worked. Nearly every one tried the first part, but not one gave a valid reason why H remains constant. The following is typical of the line of argument: "The heat H is in the stuff at the higher pressure; none of it is lost in passing through the non-conducting valve; therefore H must be the heat after the fall of pressure."

HONOURS.

Results: 1st Class, –; 2nd Class, 5; Failed, 12; Total, 17.

As in the other stages, candidates who sketch well do not generally seem to be strong in theory, and those who do well in theory are weak in sketching. Average men seem to be divided in this way into theoretical and practical men. The best candidates are those who are interested in mechanical details of engines, but who are also interested in the scientific principles involved.

H

On the whole, both sketching and theory are of a fairly good standard. No candidate has the thorough acquaintance with theory which is expected from the highest class of student in this subject. Many candidates know what is contained in the best text-books, but they ought also to know of articles recently published in magazines and in the proceedings of Engineering Societies. There is, for example, but little knowledge of the Steam Turbine. The second law of Thermo-dynamics is easy to state, but we fear that a thorough knowledge of what the statement means is often wanting.

> Q. 68. It has been proposed, instead of much superheating in the ordinary way to have less of this, and to superheat in the receivers between the cylinders. Assuming that the thing can be done in a good practical way, what is your opinion of its merits ? Of course you will give your reasons.

No candidate suggested the use of the $t\phi$ diagram in considering Question 68.

> Q. 69. What information is necessary if we wish to convert an indicator diagram into a $p\,v$ diagram ? How is it done ? What assumptions do we make ? Although these assumptions are untrue, show that we can use the $p\,v$, or the corresponding $t\phi$ diagram in obtaining practical knowledge.

No candidate seemed to know exactly what is meant by a $p\,v$ diagram in answering Question 69.

> Q. 70. If t is temperature difference, and R is heat resistance, t/R is heat per second flowing.
> What is the heat resistance of an iron plate 0·5 inch thick, per square foot of metal, from face to face, the conductivity of iron being 0·18 in C.G.S. units (gramme water centigrade heat units) ?
> If no boiler passes more than 5,500 centigrade pound heat units per hour per square foot of metal, and the average temperature difference (flue gases and water) is 800 centigrade degrees, what is the average total heat resistance (flue gases to water) ? Compare this with what you previously calculated.

In Question 70 the arithmetic of most of the candidates was very incorrect.

> Q. 71. A Hartnell governor on a turbine shaft has a law $F = sr - a$ where F lb. is the outward radial force on each ball which would just keep the governor (if motionless) in the position in which each ball is r feet from the axis. What do s and a depend upon ?
> When the balls move let there be friction $e\,\dfrac{dr}{dt}$. Write out the equation of motion radially outwards. Let the method of regulation be such that the torque on the revolving part of the turbine is $c - br$ where b and c are constants. The speed being steady, the resisting torque having been constant, let the torque suddenly alter to another constant value ; write out the differential equation connecting speed and time. State algebraically the condition required for stability of motion (that is, no hunting).

Of all the candidates who attempted Question 71, an interesting question, carefully arranged so that the proper line of reasoning might be followed, not one gave the correct answer.

> Q. 72. Steam is flowing from a vessel through an orifice which gets larger outside. What do we know about the changes of pressure and speed of a portion of the steam as it flows ? Take the inside pressure as say 100 lb. per square inch, and the pressure outside as 2 lb. per square inch. What is the speed in the throat or narrowest place ? How is it that outside the throat the speed gets greater although the cross section is greater ?

The subject of Question 72 is of very great practical interest, yet there was no correct answer.

Q. 73. Explain how you would find the magnitude and line of action of the force corresponding to the acceleration of the connecting rod of a steam engine for any specified position of the crank. You may assume that the necessary dimensions and speed of the engine, and the kinetic elements of the rod are known.

Question 73 might easily be answered from mere text-book information, yet the answers were unsatisfactory.

In spite of these unsatisfactory details, the Examiners are fairly well satisfied with the results of the examination. Even when a candidate gets only half marks for an answer he often shows evidence of individuality, and proves that he has been thinking things out for himself. The Examiners are confident that in many cases where the reasoning is not altogether good and the real point seems to be evaded, the candidate shows signs that he will in time see things more clearly.

Report on the Examination in Practical Mathematics.

The number of candidates in this subject is increasing rapidly, as the following table for three successive years will show :—

Year.	Stage 1.	Stage 2.	Stage 3.	Total.
1904	1,000	361	137	1,498
1905	1,506	685	219	2,410
1906	2,098	1,043	346	3,487

This shows a total increase of 133 per cent. in two years, and the rate of increase is seen to be greater in the higher stages. It is satisfactory to be able to record that along with this increase in number there is no lowering of the average quality of the work. In fact, after making due allowance for the somewhat easier questions set this year, there is a distinct improvement noticed in the work of all the stages. There were many classes in the lower stages in which nearly all the candidates passed in the first class. There were some in which the work was almost wholly bad, but it is believed that these unprepared classes are fewer than formerly. Logarithms are now used with facility and with much more certainty than was the case a few years ago. There is still some looseness in writing down expressions, and especially in the use of the sign of equality " =." Thus it is not uncommon to find such a statement as

$$200 (1\cdot04)^{12} = 200 (0\cdot0170 \times 12) = 200 (0\cdot2010).$$
$$= 200 \times 1\cdot600 = 320\cdot0.$$

The candidate as a rule knows quite well what he is doing, but when dealing with more complicated expressions such slackness leads to confusion and mistakes, and should never be permitted.

A persistent feature of the examination is that although candidates can use contracted methods, as shown in their answers to Questions 1, 21 and 41, they rarely employ these methods in their arithmetical computations when working any of the other questions of the paper.

With regard to plotting, scales are, as a rule, well selected and plainly figured. There is, however, a tendency in such questions as 5, 11, 12, 13 and 27, after having marked the points, to join them by straight lines or chords, instead of by a fair continuous curve, and to measure results from this figure.

The significance of the *slope* of a curve is slowly being acquired, but, in Stage 1 especially, candidates have great difficulty in expressing themselves intelligently. The mere plotting of a curve has little value apart from the lessons the curve teaches, and students should be induced to *think* more about their work, and not be content with mere mechanical graphing on squared paper.

STAGE 1.

Results : 1st Class, 930 ; 2nd Class, 595 ; Failed, 574 ; Total, 2,099.

Q. 1. The four parts (*a*), (*b*), (*c*), and (*d*) must all be answered to get full marks :—

(*a*) Compute by contracted methods, to four significant figures only, and without using logarithms

$$3\cdot214 \times 0\cdot7423 \div 7\cdot912.$$

(*b*) Write down the logarithms of 32170, 32·17, 0·3217, 0·003217.

(*c*) Compute, using logarithms

$$\sqrt{84\cdot05 \times 0\cdot1357 \div 1\cdot163}.$$

(*d*) Express £0 17s. 9d. as the decimal of a pound.

(*a*) Contracted methods well known. Mistakes as a rule only in the fourth figure. Decimal point almost always correctly placed.

(*b*) Few mistakes ; these generally in the characteristics of the logarithms.

(*c*) The symbol of the square root instead of the index ½ gave some trouble in applying logarithms.

(*d*) Answer generally correct. The usual method was to divide the number of pence in 17s. 9d. by 240. Very few used the florin as the basis of their calculation.

Q. 2. The three parts (*a*), (*b*), and (*c*) must all be answered to get full marks :—

(*a*) If $A = P\left(1 + \dfrac{r}{100}\right)^n$ find A when $P = 200$, $r = 4$, $n = 12$.

(*b*) On board a ship there were 1,312 men, 514 women, and 132 children. State these as percentages of the total number of persons.

(*c*) When x and y are small we may take

$\dfrac{1 + x}{1 + y}$ as being very nearly equal to $1 + x - y$.

What is the error in this when $x = 0\cdot02$ and $y = 0\cdot03$?

(*a*) Common mistakes were $(1 + \cdot04)^{12} = 12\cdot48$, $1 + \frac{1}{100} = 1\cdot25$ or $1\cdot4$, $200 (1\cdot04)^{12} = 208^{12}$. One candidate multiplied the latter out in full, obtaining an answer with thirty figures.

(*b*) Fairly well done ; a few good graphical solutions.

(*c*) Not well answered as a rule.

Q. 3. The four parts (*a*), (*b*), (*c*), and (*d*) must all be answered to get full marks :—

(*a*) Write down algebraically :—The principal P multiplied by $1 + \dfrac{r}{100}$ twelve times.

(*b*) Divide 17·24 into two parts such that one quarter of the first added to one third of the second make 5·06.

(*c*) What are the factors of $x^2 - 10$?

(*d*) A wheel is 3·45 feet in diameter ; it makes 1020 revolutions rolling along a road ; what is the distance passed over ?

(*a*) A common mistake was $12\,P\left(1 + \dfrac{r}{100.}\right)$

(*b*) Pretty well done, but some, after stating the equations in x and y, could not work them out correctly.

(*c*) The factors of $x^2 - 9$ would evidently have been correctly given by almost all, but the 10 proved a stumbling block. Some said, "There are no factors." Others gave such answers as

$$x\left(x - \dfrac{10}{x}\right),\ 10\left(\dfrac{x^2}{10} - 1\ \right).$$

Common mistakes were $(x - 3\dot{3})\,(x + 3\dot{3}),\ (x - 5),\ (x - 2).$

(*d*) Fairly well done. Some think πr^2 is the circumference of a circle others use $2\pi d$, and a not uncommon answer was $3\cdot45 \times 1020$.

Q. 4. If $y = x^2 - 3\cdot4x + 2\cdot73$, calculate y when x has the values 1, 1·2, 1·4, 1·6, 1·8, 2, and 2·2. Plot these values of x and y and draw a curve. What values of x cause y to be 0 ?

Attempted by about 44 per cent. of the candidates, with very satisfactory results.

Q. 5. x and t are the distance in miles and the time in hours of a train from a railway station. Plot on squared paper. Describe why it is that the *slope* of the curve shows the speed ; where approximately is the speed greatest and where is it least ?

x	0	1·5	6·0	14·0	19·0	21·0	21·5	21·8	23·0	24·7	26·8
t	0	·1	·2	·3	·4	·5	·6	·7	·8	·9	1·0

About half the candidates selected this question. The curve was well plotted, and the places of greatest and least speed successfully indicated. Answers as to *why* the slope shows speed often amounted, when sifted, simply to the statement it is so.

Q. 6. The point B is 4 miles North and 2 miles East of the point A. What is the distance from A to B and what angle does the line AB make with the due East direction ?

The favourite optional question. Graphical solutions were common, but in these cases the scale was often too small. Of those who worked by tables, the majority were content with "63°" or "64°" for the angle, or "between 63° and 64°," or "about 63½°." Few obtained the correct angle to within 0·1° by interpolation.

Q. 7. The horse-power of the engines of a ship being proportional to the cube of the speed ; if the horse-power is 2,000 at a speed of 10 knots, what is the power when the speed is 15 knots ?

Fairly often attempted. Correct answers were frequent, but many used simple proportion obtaining 3,000 horse-power.

Q. 8. There are two maps, one to the scale of 2 inches to the mile, the other to the scale of half an inch to the mile. The area of an estate on the first map is 1·46 square inches, what is the area of this estate on the second map ?

Pretty frequently attempted but with poor results. Answers like the following occurred

$$\frac{1\cdot46 + \frac12}{2} = 0\cdot98 ; \qquad \frac{1\cdot46 + 2}{\frac12} = 6\cdot92.$$

$$\frac{1\cdot46 + 2^2}{\frac12^2} = 21\cdot84.$$

Q. 9. $$y = ax^2 + 6x^3 \; ;$$
when $x = 1$, y is 4·3, and when $x = 2$, y is 30 ; find a and b. What is y when x is 1·5 ?

Seldom attempted, but the answers were good. Quite a number discovered and pointed out the "misprint" and corrected it, and those who stuck to the equation as written were very leniently dealt with.

Q. 10. In the following table A is the area in square feet of the horizontal section of a ship at the level of the surface of the water when the vertical draught of the ship is h feet. When the draught changes from 17·5 to 18·5 feet, what is the increased displacement of the vessel in cubic feet ?

h	15	18	21
A	6020	6660	8250

Not a favourite question, nor well done, most going wrong in finding the "increased displacement," giving the difference in the areas at 17·5 and 18·5 feet, viz. 6870—6500 instead of ½ (6870 + 6500) × 1 or 6685 cubic feet.

Q. 11. The speed of a ship in knots (nautical miles per hour) has been noted at the following times :—

Speed - -	11·23	12·56	13·50	14·11	14·53
O'clock - -	4	5	6	7	8

Plot on squared paper. What is the distance passed through during the hour after 6 o'clock.

Frequently attempted. The plotting was good and there were many correct answers to the first part. But in the latter part the mistake 14·11 – 13·50 instead of ½ (14·11 + 13·50), or 13·82 as read from the curve, was common.

Q. 12. If $pu^{1·0646} = 479$, find p when u is 3·25.

Not very often attempted. Fairly well answered. Recurring mistakes :—
$pu^{1·0646} = (pu)^{1·0646}$; $pu^{1·0646} = p \times 1·0646u$.

Q. 13. The following corresponding values of x and y are given in the table :—

x	1·22	1·37	1·50
y	5·88	8·32	9·71

What is the probable value of x when y is 8 ?

A favourite question. Answers fairly good. Many took far too small a scale on one of the axes. A straight line was often taken between the points instead of a curve through them.

STAGE 2.

Results : 1st Class, 187 ; 2nd Class, 554 ; Failed, 303 ; Total, 1,044.

Q. 21. The four parts (a), (b), (c) and (d) must all be answered to get full marks :—
(a) Compute by contracted methods to four significant figures only, and without using logarithms,
$$3·214 \times 0·7423 \div 7·912.$$

(b) Using logarithms compute
$$(1\text{·}342 \times 0\text{·}01731 \div 0\text{·}0274)^{0\text{·}317}.$$

(c) Explain why we multiply a logarithm by 3 when we wish to find the cube of a number.

(d) Express £18 17s. 3d. in pounds.

(a) On the whole this was not well answered. A large number of candidates omitted the first "carrying" figure in multiplying. In many cases the last figure of the required quotient was incorrectly given, owing to this omission of the carrying figure.

(b) This was often wrong. The principal source of error was in the misplacing of the decimal point after multiplying the logarithm by the index 0·317.

(c) Some good answers were given to this, but the great bulk of the candidates are evidently accustomed to use this and similar rules without clearly understanding the theorems on which they rest.

(d) A number went wrong in this very easy question. As noticed in Q. 1, few used the florin as the base of their calculations.

Q. 22. The three parts (a), (b), and (c) must all be answered to get full marks :—

(a) If $p\,u^{1\text{·}0646} = 479$, find u when p is 120.

(b) $y = a\,x^2 + b\,x^3$. When x is 1, y is 4·3, and when x is 2, y is 30 ; find a and b. What is y when x is 1·5 ?

(c) Two men measure a rectangular box ; one finds its length, breadth and depth in inches to be 8·54, 5·17 and 3·19. The other finds them to be 8·50, 5·12 and 3·16. Calculate the volume in each case ; what is the mean of the two ? What is the percentage difference of either from the mean ?

All three parts were usually done well In (c) a good many gave themselves needless trouble by working out the volumes by uncontracted multiplication.

Q. 23. A body has moved through the distance s feet in the time t seconds and it is known that $s = b\,t^2$ when b is a constant.

Find the distance when t is 4. Find the distance when the time is $4 + \delta\,t$. What is the average speed during the interval $\delta\,t$? As $\delta\,t$ is imagined to be smaller and smaller, what does the average speed become ?

Comparatively few gave a really satisfactory answer to this question. A great many failed to grasp the notion that for average speed the distance described must be divided by the time occupied. A very considerable number seem to have a notion that in finding an average we must divide by two.

Q. 24. The three parts (a), (b) and (c) must all be answered to get full marks :—

(a) If
$$\frac{x}{y} = e^{a\theta}$$
where $e = 2\text{·}718$. If $a = 0\text{·}3$ and $\theta = 2\text{·}85$ and if $x - y = 550$, find x.

(b) When x and y are small we may take
$$\frac{1 + x}{1 + y}$$
as being very nearly equal to $1 + x - y$. What is the error in this when $x = 0\text{·}02$ and $y = 0\text{·}03$?

(c) ABC is a triangle, the angle C is a right angle. The side AC is 21·32 feet, the side BC is 12·56 feet, find the angles A and B.

(a) Well answered by a very considerable number of candidates.

(b) A good many candidates used logarithms, and a few the slide rule methods, not well adapted for finding the difference of two nearly equal quantities. In connection with this answer, a point may be noticed, viz., looseness in stating approximations. Here we have $\frac{1\cdot02}{1\cdot03} = 0\cdot99029$ . . . This was much oftener stated to be $0\cdot9902$ instead of $0\cdot9903$, the candidate stopping at the 2 in dividing out without considering the value of the succeeding figure.

(c) A point to note was the large number of candidates who were apparently unable to find an angle directly from the tangent. Many first found the hypothenuse of the given triangle, and were then able to find the angle from the *sine*.

Q. 25. A man is 100 feet above the earth which is assumed to be a sphere of 8,000 miles diameter; what is his distance in miles from the furthest point he can see on the surface? Do not give more than three figures in the answer.

Not a favourite question. Generally the formula $A = \sqrt{(C^2 - B^2)}$ was employed. A fair number expressed this in the form $A = \sqrt{(C + B)(C - B)}$ and evaluated by logs., but the majority laboriously calculated the differences of the two squares and extracted the square root of the result by the ordinary arithmetical process. The point to which attention has already been drawn in Q. 24 (b) was often conspicuous here, *e.g.*, 100 feet $= \frac{10}{528}$ miles $= 0\cdot0189$ . . . . miles. This was often stated to be approximately $0\cdot018$ miles. Of course if only two significant figures were to be retained, $0\cdot019$ should have been taken.

Q. 26. If $y = x^2 - 4\cdot2\,x + 2\cdot93$ calculate y for various values of x and plot on squared paper. What values of x cause y to be 0?

A favourite question and fairly well answered, but the diagram was often drawn on too small a scale. This generally arose in part from plotting all the values of y worked out by the candidate—the higher ones being obviously of no use for the determination of the points in question. But in nearly all cases the scale for x was too small.

Q. 27. x and t are the distance in miles and the time in hours of a train from a railway terminus. Plot on squared paper. Describe why it is that the slope of the curve shows the speed. What is the greatest speed in this case and where approximately does it occur? What is the average speed during the whole time of observation?

x	0	1·5	6·0	14·0	19·0	21·0	21·5	21·8	23·0	24·7	26·8
t	0	0·1	0·2	0·3	0·4	0·5	0·6	0·7	0·8	0·9	1·0

Often taken and, except as regards one point, usually answered well. The point which was missed was the relation between the *speed* and the *slope of the curve*. Only a few candidates showed evidence that they clearly understood how either of these *at any point on the curve* is to be estimated. There is an objectionable practice on the part of some candidates, previously mentioned, of joining plotted points of a curve by ruled straight lines. This is particularly inappropriate here.

Q. 28. A disc rotating with angular velocity a, its density ρ being 8, has an outer radius $r_0 = 50$. There is a hole in the middle whose radius r_1 is 10. Then at any place whose distance from the centre is r, there is a hoop tensile stress Q where

$$Q = \frac{5}{12}\ a^2 \rho \left(r_1^2 + r_0^2 + \frac{r_0^2\,r_1^2}{r^2} - \frac{3}{5}\,r^2 \right)$$

Taking $a = 122.5$, and arranging the formula for systematic calculation, find Q for the values of r, 10, 15, 20, 30, 40, and 50. Plot Q and r on squared paper.

Only a few candidates took this question. Good answers were somewhat scarce.

Q. 29. In the following table A is the area in square feet of the horizontal section of a ship at the level of the surface of the water when the vertical draught of the ship is h feet. When the draught changes from 17·5 to 18·5 feet, what is the increased displacement of the vessel in cubic feet ?

h	15	18	21
A	6020	6660	8250

Not often answered. The remarks under Q. 11 apply here.

Q. 30. In the following table x and y are the co-ordinates of points in a curve, which you need not draw. Tabulate the values of the average slope of the curve in each interval. Also tabulate the area between the two ordinates in each interval. You had better write in columns rather than in rows.

x	1	2	3	4	5
y	1·745	2·618	3·491	4·363	5·236

Well answered by a fair number of candidates.

Q. 31. x being distance in feet across a river measuring from one side and y the depth of water in feet, the following measurements were made :—

x	0	10	25	33	40	48	60	70
y	0	4	7	8	10	9	6	4

Find the area of the cross section. If the average speed of the water normal to the section is 3·2 feet per second, what is the quantity flowing in cubic feet per second.

A few cases occurred of the inaccurate method of estimating the mean height as the mean of equi-distant ordinates including the first and last. A certain number of candidates went wrong by taking an *even* number of *ordinates* in attempting to use Simpson's rule.

Q. 32. In a price list I find the following prices of a certain type of steam electric generator of different powers.

K kilowatts	200	600	900
P pounds	2800	7160	10420

According to what rule has this price list been made up ? What is the list price of a generator of 400 kilowatts ?

The price was usually correctly estimated, but only a moderate number made out the rule.

Results : 1st Class, 51 ; 2nd Class, 104 ; Failed, 190 ; Total, 345.

Q. 41. The four parts (a), (b), (c) and (d) must all be answered to get full marks :—

(a) Compute by contracted methods to four significant figures only, and without using logarithms,
$$3\text{·}214 \times 0\text{·}7423 \div 7\text{·}912.$$

(b) Using logarithms, compute,
$$(1\text{·}342 \times 0\text{·}01731 \div 0\text{·}00274)^{-0\text{·}317}.$$

(c) Explain why we multiply the logarithm of a by $3\text{·}5$ when we wish to find $a^{3\text{·}5}$. Start your explanation from the fact that a^3 means $a \times a \times a$.

(d) Write down the values of
$$\sin 203°, \cos 140°, \tan 278°, \sin^{-1}(0\text{·}4226)$$
$$\cos^{-1}(0\text{·}7547), \tan^{-1}(-2\text{·}7475).$$

The parts (a) and (d) were well answered. In (b) candidates often went wrong in subtracting the negative characteristic. The answers to (c) were not sufficiently complete, and were generally only valid for positive integral indices.

Q. 42. Define the scalar and vector product of two vectors. Give an illustration of each.

Some schools were totally unacquainted with the meaning to be attached to the products of vectors, and their crude guesses often served to display their ignorance of vectors in general. On the other hand, there were quite a large proportion of schools in which the answers were full and satisfactory. One candidate gave a good example of a vector product by explaining the precession of a gyroscope under the action of a couple. The favourite illustration, however, was the force action of an electric current which traverses a magnetic field.

Q. 43. The following values of y and x being given tabulate $\delta y / \delta x$ and δA in each interval, δA being the area in the interval between two ordinates. Tabulate the values of A if $A = 0$ when $x = 3$.

x	3	4	5	6	7	8	9	10	11	12	13
y	1·75	10·45	19·08	27·56	35·84	43·84	51·50	58·78	65·61	71·93	77·71

Well answered, a large proportion of candidates obtaining full or nearly full marks.

Q. 44. There is a curve, $y = a\,x^n$,
if $y = 2\text{·}34$ when $x = 2$
and $y = 20\text{·}62$ when $x = 5$
find a and n.

Let the curve rotate about the axis of x, forming a surface of revolution. Find the volume of the slice between the sections at x and $x + dx$. What is the volume between the two sections at $x = 2$ and $x = 5$?

The answers were satisfactory and the question was a favourite one. A few plotted a curve and adopted an approximate method, but the great majority proceeded by integration. There were some cases in which candidates went wrong only in the very last step, viz. the evaluation of $5^{5\text{·}75} - 2^{5\text{·}75}$, the mistake being to take $\log (5^{5\text{·}75} - 2^{5\text{·}75})$ as equivalent to $5\text{·}75 \log (5-2)$. In some cases the mistake $\int \pi y^2\, dx = \pi \dfrac{y^3}{3}$ was made.

Q. 45. K kilowatts being the average electric power actually delivered to customers from an electric station during an hour and W the weight of coal consumed per hour, the following observations were made :—

K	2560	1520	1300
W	7760	5480	5030

The maximum power which might be delivered being 13060 let $K/13060$ be called f, the load factor. Let W/K be called w, the coal per unit. [The Board of Trade unit is 1 killowatt hour.] What seems to be the law connecting w and f? Tabulate w and f when f has the values 0·25, 0·20, 0·15, 0·10, 0·05.

The answers were disappointing. An acquaintance with the subject as treated in previous examinations would have suggested a linear law between K and W. Overlooking this, candidates generally plotted f and w and were then unable to discover any satisfactory relation between these quantities.

Q. 46. Assuming the earth to be a sphere, if its circumference is 360×60 miles, what is the circumference of the parallel of latitude 56°? What is the length there of the degree of longitude? If a small map is to be drawn in this latitude with distances all to the same scale, and if a degree of latitude (which is, of course, 60 miles) is shown as 10 inches, what distance will represent a degree of longitude? NOTE.—In this question one mile means one nautical mile.

A favourite and comparatively easy question, and very well answered.

Q. 47. Fifty pounds of shot per second moving horizontally with a velocity of 2500 feet per second due north strike an armour plate and leave the plate horizontally with a velocity of 800 feet per second due east. What force is exerted upon the plate? Note that momentum and force are vectors.

Force is rate of change of momentum per second.

Momentum is mass multiplied by velocity.

The mass of 50 lb. of shot is $50 \div 32·2$.

Fairly often attempted. Many were satisfied with giving the magnitude only of the force, ignoring the direction. Some took the sum instead of the difference of the momentum vectors, and as the two were at right angles the numerical value of the answer was the same in both cases, although one was obtained on a wrong principle. On the whole the answers were poor.

Q. 48. There are errors of observation in the following values of y and x :—

x	4	5	6	7	8	9	10	11
y	6·29	5·72	5·22	4·78	4·39	4·06	3·75	3·48

It is found that the following two empirical formulæ seem to be nearly equally good :—

$$y = \frac{a}{b + x} \text{ and } y = a\varepsilon^{-\beta x}$$

Find the best values of a and b, a and β.

Not very popular. The answers were somewhat disappointing. The method of procedure was often quite wrong. Thus y and x would be plotted and an average straight line drawn through the points. Two points would then be selected on this line, by using the co-ordinates of which, the values of a, b, and a, β, would be-found. Thus the significance of the question was wholly missed.

Q. 49. If $x=a \sin (qt + e)$ expresses simple harmonic motion ; what is a ? what is q ? what is e ? Express q in terms of the periodic time. Find expressions for the speed and the acceleration.

This was a very popular question with some schools, and the answers were very full and complete. The only noticeable error was in the definition of e, the answer frequently given would have been correct if instead of a sine we had had a cosine function.

Q. 50. A sliding piece has a periodic motion. Its distance x from a point in its path is measured at twenty-four equal intervals into which the whole periodic time is divided

16·04, 16·74, 16·66, 15·86, 14·68, 13·42, 12·26, 11·16, 9·98, 8·76, 7·60, 6·68, 5·96, 5·34, 4·68, 4·14, 3·98, 4·50, 5·74, 7·46 9·36, 11·24, 13·06, 14·70.

Express x in a Fourier Series.

Not one attempted this question.

Q. 51. When air or steam is flowing through a divergent orifice from a vessel inside which at the still part the pressure is p_1 the cross sectional area A of a steam tube is such that at any place where the pressure is p

$$A^2 \left\{ x^{2/\gamma} - x^{(\gamma+1)/\gamma} \right\}$$

keeps constant, x being p/p_1 and γ [1·41 for air and 1·13 for dry or wet stream] being a known number. For what value of x (presumably in the throat) is A a minimum. Find this critical x for air and for steam.

Generally shunned. There were some complete answers, but, as a whole, the results were poor. The manipulation of the fractional indices seemed to give trouble. Thus in simplifying the equation $2 x^{\frac{2-\gamma}{\gamma}} = (\gamma + 1)^{\frac{1}{\gamma}}$ the γ in the denominator of each index would be cancelled, and the result written $2 x^{2-\gamma} = (\gamma + 1) x$. There seems to be no excuse for candidates in Stage 3 who make this kind of blunder.

Q. 52. The following values of x and y being given, find the most probable value of $\frac{dy}{dx}$ when x is three.

x	0	1	2	3	4	5	6
y	11·8	16·0	20·0	23·9	27·6	31·1	34·5

If a candidate cannot use *all* the given numbers in finding the answer let him not try this question.

There were some good answers, candidates making proper use of two diagonal lines of successive differences. But many who knew the method and the formula went astray by not attending to the minus sign of some of the differences. In some poor and almost worthless answers, the candidates plotted the points, and gave the slope of the average line, or drew the curve, guessed at the tangent and gave the slope of the latter. A plausible, but an ill-considered and a faulty method, evidently rather extensively taught, was to take first differences, then to obtain successive columns of means of adjacent numbers, the columns getting shorter until at last one number was reached which was given as the answer.

GROUP III.—PHYSICS.

BOARD OF EXAMINERS.

VIII. Sound, Light, and Heat
VIII.a. Sound
VIII.b. Light
VIII.c. Heat
IX. Magnetism and Electricity
XXIII. Physiography
(Section 1 only of Stage 1)

Professor H. L. Callendar, M.A., LL.D.,
F.R.S., *Chairman.*
Professor J. J. Thompson, M.A., F.R.S.
Professor A. W. Reinold, M.A., F.R.S.
W. Watson, D.Sc., F.R.S.

Report on the Examinations in Sound, Light, and Heat.

EVENING EXAMINATIONS.

STAGE 1.

Results : 1st Class, 185 ; 2nd Class, 149 ; Failed, 90 ; Total, 424.

The answers to this paper showed a fair general average of excellence, with comparatively few serious failures. The points of weakness were chiefly those where *exact* knowledge was required in the answers. This, however, is to be expected in the First Stage. The following remarks on the several questions may be of use to teachers.

SOUND.

Q. 1. Describe, with the aid of diagrams, the process by which sound waves are propagated through the air.

Students seem much misled by the analogy of the propagation of waves when a stone is dropped into water. They think that sound is propagated in this way. They are also much misled by the displacement curve. They thus think that sound can be propagated both longitudinally and transversely.

The question states "Describe, with the aid of *diagrams* ..."; insufficient attention was paid to this.

Q. 2. Describe some phenomena which show that sound waves can be reflected. A sharp tap is sounded in front of a long flight of stairs. What impression will the sound reflected from the stairs give to an observer in front ?

The second part of this question was seldom understood clearly.

Q. 3. Define what is meant by (*a*) simple harmonic vibration, (*b*) frequency of the vibration, (*c*) amplitude of the vibration. Illustrate your definitions by reference to the case of a simple pendulum.

When S.H.M. is described with the aid of an auxiliary point moving round a circle, it should be stated that the point moves uniformly. Amplitude is the maximum displacement from the equilibrium point.

Q. 4. An observer notes an interval of 4·5 seconds between seeing the flash and hearing the report of a gun at a distance of one mile. Find the velocity with which the sound has travelled. How would it be affected by temperature ?

It should be stated in the answer that light is propagated so quickly that the flash is seen practically instantaneously.

LIGHT.

Q. 5. A mirror hangs on one of the walls of a room ; show by means of carefully drawn diagrams that an observer will see by reflection more and more of the room behind him as he approaches the mirror.

Many of the diagrams were very crude.

Q. 6. Find the size of an image of the sun formed by a concave mirror 6 feet in radius, assuming that the distance of the earth from the sun is 100 times the diameter of the sun.

A large proportion of the candidates took the mirror as of 6 feet focal length.

Q. 7. State the laws of refraction of light, and show that it follows from your definition that the direction of a ray after passing through a plate of glass with parallel sides, is parallel to its direction before entering the glass.

Many candidates treated the angle of refraction as the angle of emergence from a parallel slab. Thus, it was stated that the angle of incidence is equal to the angle of refraction.

Q. 8. Explain what is meant by an image. What is the difference between a real and a virtual image ? In the case of a concave mirror, find the positions of the object when the image is virtual.

The *explanation* of an image was, on the whole, very badly done. A large number of candidates confined themselves to stating that it is a representation of the object. This is not an explanation, but a paraphrase.

HEAT.

Q. 9. Define what is meant by the specific heat of a substance, and explain how it can be measured.

Equal *volumes* of water at 100° C. and mercury at 0° C. are shaken up together, what will be the temperature of the mixture ? Density of mercury 13·6. Specific heat ·03.

The specific heat was frequently defined by reference to unit *volume*.

Q. 10. Describe some simple experiments which show that the vapour of water exerts an appreciable pressure on the walls of the vessel in which it is contained, and that the vapours of different liquids exert different pressures at the same temperatures.

In the "barometer tube" experiment, care should be taken to state that enough liquid is introduced to saturate the space, if the maximum vapour pressure is required.

Q. 11. Define latent heat. The latent heat of steam is 539 at 100° C How much steam at 100° C. would be required to raise 1 lb. of water at 0° to the boiling point ?

Latent heat should be defined generally, and not with particular reference to the case of water.

Q. 12. State the law of the expansion of gases at constant pressure.

Find the alteration in the weight of air in a room 8 metres long, 8 metres broad, and 4 metres high, when the temperature is raised from 0° C. to 20° C.

The height of the barometer is 76 cm.

Weight of a litre of air at 0° C. and 76 cm. = 1·3 gram.

Gases expand, per degree centigrade, by $\frac{1}{273}$ of their *volume at 0° C.* The last point is important, but was often omitted.

SOUND.

STAGE 2.

Results : 1st Class, 91 ; 2nd Class, 174 ; Failed, 37 ; Total, 302.

The answers to this paper showed in many cases a good average standard of knowledge. There were comparatively few failures. Some weakness was shown in working out numerical results, especially in regard to the relations of units. Subjoined are special details with reference to the several questions.

Q. 1. Describe an experiment showing the interference between two trains of sound waves which are travelling in nearly the same direction.

The best experiments for this are the sound analogues of Lloyd's fringes and Fresnel's Biprism (Rayleigh's Experiment.) That of stationary waves between a source of sound and the wall is not a correct answer, as the two trains are going in *opposite* directions.

Q. 2. The velocity of sound through water is 1440 metres per second ; find the percentage diminution in the volume of water produced by an additional pressure of one atmosphere.

Boyle's Law does not enter into this question. Many candidates are evidently not at home in the C.G.S. system of units. They have, therefore, attempted to convert to the F.P.S. gravitational system, and their attempt has usually ended in disaster.

Q. 3. Describe carefully the method of Kundt's tube for measuring the velocity of sound in a gas or in a solid.

The adjustment to the best position should be given—this is when the end of the rod is at a *node* (practically).

Q. 5. How would you construct a harmonicon (1) of glass strips of constant thickness, (2) of wood strips of constant length.

Scarcely attempted. Many candidates treat this as a monochord question.

Q. 6. Explain what is meant by resonance, and give examples of resonance in (a) mechanical and (b) acoustical systems.

Sounding boards in pianos, etc., do not exhibit resonance (in its strict sense), as a rule. It is there a case of forced vibrations.

Q. 7. It has been noticed that sound is sometimes transmitted over the surface of water with greater intensity during the prevalence of rain or fog than in bright sunny weather. How would you explain this result ?

The two chief causes of this effect are (i) the upward refraction caused by the warm air near the surface of the water when the sun is shining, and (ii) the acoustic clouds caused by evaporation and convection. Many candidates think a proof of an increase of the velocity sufficient.

Q. 8. An observer notes the time on his chronometer at which he hears a time gun, and the chronometer appears 25 seconds slow. If the gun is at a distance of a mile, and the temperature of the air is 15° C., find the error of the chronometer. (Velocity at 0° C., 330 metres per second.)

Candidates should use the numerical value of the velocity supplied, and not some remembered formula. The temperature reduction should be given as the square root of the absolute temperature.

Q. 9. Describe carefully how the velocity of sound in free air has been measured, and discuss the errors to which the method you describe is liable.

Any tube (*e.g.* a resonance tube) experiment is not a correct answer to this question, as the latter refers to *free* air—even Regnault's sewer experiment is not quite satisfactory. The chief errors are (i) the wind—a cross wind is not got rid of by reciprocal observations, (ii) temperature, (iii) hygrometric state, and (iv) the personal equation.

STAGE 3.

Results : 1st Class, 10 ; 2nd Class, 24 ; Failed, 16 ; Total, 50.

On the whole the answers were decidedly above the average, though owing to the comparatively small syllabus in this subject, a higher standard ought to be attained than in such subjects as Heat, Light, and Magnetism and Electricity, where the ground to be covered is so much larger.

Taking the questions in detail :—

Q. 1. Investigate the relation between the velocity of sound through a gas and the velocity of mean square of the molecules of a gas.

This question was frequently well answered, and nearly all those who attempted it were acquainted with the fundamental ideas underlying the answer.

Q. 2. Discuss the way in which determinations of the velocity of sound in a gas are used to obtain information as to the number of atoms in a molecule of gas.

Fairly well answered, though many candidates were hardly sufficiently explicit as to why the value of the ratio of the specific heats decreases as the molecule becomes more complex.

Q. 3. Write a short essay on the theory and method of production of singing flames and their use in acoustical investigations.

The answers to this question were incomplete though diffuse.

Q. 4. Prove that the velocity of propagation of a pulse along a stretched string is equal to $\sqrt{T/\rho}$, where T is the tension and ρ the mass of unit length of the string.

Well answered.

Q. 5. Describe some of the methods used to study the small movements of vibrating systems such as strings or tuning forks.

Answers very incomplete. Many candidates simply described methods of determining the frequency of the fundamental of a fork.

Q. 6. Discuss the relation between the intensity of a sound and the rate of its propagation through various media.

Seldom attempted.

Q. 7. Explain why the diatonic scale is unsuited for varied music, and describe the system of temperament in which the interval of a fifth is maintained perfect.

The answers to this question were for the most part unsatisfactory. The first part was sometimes answered fairly well. In the second part almost without exception the method of equal temperament was described.

HONOURS.

Results : 1st Class, – ; 2nd Class, 1 ; Failed, 3 ; Total, 4.

Out of four candidates, one did sufficiently well in the first paper to justify further examination. In the second paper he showed some knowledge of the mathematical theory, but little acquaintance with details of recent experimental work, although the practical paper showed that he was a very fair experimentalist.

LIGHT.

Stage 2.

Results : 1st Class, 39 ; 2nd Class, 194 ; Failed, 126 ; Total, 359.

The general character of the answers was about the same as in previous years. A little more time spent in thinking out the manner in which the answer is to be given would in most cases repay the candidate. The following notes on the answers to individual questions may be of interest to the teachers.

Q. 1. Describe carefully how you would arrange an experiment to illustrate the interference of light so that it may be visible to a large audience.

The answers to this question were not very good. A large number of candidates described apparatus for the production of interference bands, but failed to describe how the bands could be thrown upon a screen. The theory of the production of the bands was often given in a slipshod way.

Q. 2. How would you distinguish between ordinary light and plane polarised light ? Give some method of determining the plane of polarisation.

The first part was well done, but the answers to the second part were incomplete and very rarely clear. Several planes were often mentioned and mixed up, and it was sometimes difficult to follow the answers.

Q. 3. Explain the differences between the spectrum produced by a prism and one produced by a grating. Mention some of the advantages and disadvantages of each of these methods.

The fact that in a diffraction spectrum the deviation is proportional to the wave length appears to be well known. Many candidates stated that one disadvantage of a prism was the impossibility of obtaining a pure spectrum without using a focussing lens. Many curious advantages and disadvantages were invented for the purposes of answering the question. The high dispersion of a grating spectrum and the brightness of the prism spectrum were often referred to.

Q. 4. Describe a simple astronomical telescope and explain carefully, with the help of a diagram, what determines (1) the magnifying power, and (2) the field of view.

The majority of the candidates knew the essential parts of a simple astronomical telescope, but the diagrams were often very poor. Several candidates placed the object close up to the object glass. The part of the question referring to the magnifying power was fairly well done, but only one or two knew anything about the factors which determine the field of view.

Q. 5. What is meant by *total internal reflection?* Describe how this phenomenon may be employed to measure the refractive index of a liquid.

The first part of this question was well done, but the second part was not so good. A large number of candidates described unworkable methods, one of frequent occurrence involving total internal reflection at the surface of a film of liquid enclosed between two parallel glass plates.

Q. 6. Explain how caustics are formed. Give a careful drawing to scale showing the caustic due to a concave mirror when the luminous point is half-way between the principal focus and the centre of the mirror.

Fairly well answered. Some very good caustics were drawn.

Q. 7. What is meant by the terms *illuminating power, intensity of illumination?*

Describe some method by which each of these quantities may be measured.

The answers to this question showed that the difference between "illuminating power" and "intensity of illumination" was not generally known to the candidates. Correct definitions were often given, but subsequent work showed that the candidate was not clear on the subject. The descriptions of photometers were most elementary and there were very few references to any practical details. The answers to the part of the question about the measurement of intensity of illumination were very poor, amounting generally to the statement that the intensity of illumination is proportional to the strength of the source, and inversely proportional to the square of its distance.

Q. 8. Find the equivalent focal length, and the condition of achromatism for a pair of thin coaxial lenses in contact.

First part well done although many candidates got mixed with the signs they used. The second part was occasionally well done, but a good many simply stated the conditions for achromatism.

Q. 9. A patient cannot see objects clearly at a distance of less than 36 inches ; find the focal length of the glasses required to enable him to read at 10 inches.

Many candidates obtained the correct numerical answer to this question, but omitted to state whether the lens required was concave or convex. Several candidates also obtained the correct answer by a method which was entirely wrong : a method based upon the assumption that the light forms a parallel beam after passing through the lens of the eye.

STAGE 3.

Results : 1st Class, 6 ; 2nd Class, 13 ; Failed, 19 ; Total, 38.

The chief fault noticeable in the answers given by the candidates in this stage was the complete absence of any attempt to arrange the parts of an answer in any kind of sequence. Apparently the candidates wrote down the facts just as they came into their heads. Teachers ought to impress upon candidates the necessity for devoting a few minutes before starting to write out an answer to considering the order in which the facts are to be set out. Time thus spent would be more than compensated for by time saved in writing out the answer, which could be made more concise if a little forethought were employed.

Considering the questions in detail :—

Q. 1. Show that the image formed by any number of lenses can never be brighter than the object.

When attempted, this question was in general correctly answered.

Q. 2. Define principal planes and principal foci of a system of lenses, and show that when these are known the image of an object near the axis of the lens may be obtained by a simple geometrical construction. Find an expression for the ratio of the linear dimensions of the image to those of the object.

The answers to this question were sometimes very incomplete, but, on the whole, most of the candidates seemed fairly familiar with the subject.

Q. 3. Describe a zone plate ; and show that such a plate brings rays from a point on its axis to a focus. Find the distance of the focus when the object is at an infinite distance.

This question was fairly well answered, though a considerable number restricted themselves to the consideration of a plane wave incident on the zone plate.

Q. 4. State the laws of scattering of light by small obstacles, and apply them to explain the blue colour of the sky.

Fairly well answered.

Q. 5. White light, reflected from the surface of a film of oil spread over the surface of the water, is examined by a direct vision spectroscope. Describe and explain the appearance presented as the film gradually becomes thinner.

The answers to this question were often incomplete. Most candidates seemed to think that there would never be more than one band seen in the spectrum at any time.

Q. 6. Explain the functions of the diaphragms in a telescope or microscope, and investigate the best position for the diaphragm in the case of a microscope used to measure lengths with an eye-piece micrometer.

This question was not very often attempted and the answers given were without exception quite wrong. The only function of the diaphragm given was said to be to reduce the aperture of the object glass in order to reduce spherical aberration. It did not seem to occur to the candidates that if this were true the size of the objective could be cut down.

Q. 7. Write a short essay on double refraction in uniaxal crystals.

Fairly well answered.

HONOURS.

Results : 1st Class, − ; 2nd Class, 1 ; Failed, 2 ; Total, 3.

Out of three candidates one did sufficiently well in the first paper to justify further examination. In the second paper he showed some knowledge of mathematical theory, but little appreciation of the physical side of the subject. His answers were somewhat vague, and the experimental application of the theory often lacking. He did rather poorly in the practical paper.

HEAT.

STAGE 2.

Results : 1st Class, 202 ; 2nd Class, 357 ; Failed, 143 ; Total, 702.

The results of this examination were, on the whole, satisfactory, and the standard reached was better than last year, though not so good as in 1904. Some improvement might be made in neatness and clearness of working numerical results, especially in the use of abbreviated methods of multiplication, etc. Many candidates obtained absurd results by using long division and multiplication in cases where the theory was correct. The students should in this stage have some knowledge of applying with facility the small corrections so often required in practical physics. Special criticisms are added below relating to the several questions.

Q. 1. The reading of a mercury barometer is 760 mm. when the temperature is 0° C. Determine the reading at 20° C., the coefficients of expansion of mercury and of the metal of which the scale is made being respectively $1·8 \times 10^{-4}$ and $1·8 \times 10^{-5}$.

In working out a numerical example of this sort some *short* explanation should be given, *e.g.*, why the cubical expansion of mercury is required —why the envelope of the barometer is neglected, etc.

Q. 2. Explain the term *atomic heat*. How is the validity of Dulong and Petit's law affected by the variation of specific heat with temperature?

Little knowledge was shown of the variation of specific heat with temperature.

Q. 3 Describe a method of determining the mechanical equivalent of
heat. If $4\cdot2 \times 10^7$ is the numerical expression of the mechanical
equivalent of heat on the C.G.S. system and centigrade scale of
temperature, what is its value when 1 second, 1 milligram,
1 millimeter, and 1° F. are units ?

In describing a method for determining J, one that will give *accurate*
results should preferably be adopted—not, for instance, the experiment
involving the inversion of a cardboard tube containing shot, or even Hirn's
experiment.

In the second part, a common error is to take the millimetre as the $\frac{1}{1000}$
of, the C.G.S. unit of length—also to involve 32° F. in the temperature
reduction. The unit of mass does not enter into account, as it is involved
both in the unit of work and in the unit of heat.

Q. 4. Explain the terms *internal work, external work, adiabatic expansion,*
and describe an experiment for determining the ratio of the two
specific heats of a gas.

The heat used up in warming a body is *not* reckoned as internal work.
General definitions should be given—*e.g.*, not such as are applicable only to
gases under a *constant* pressure in the definition of external work, etc.
The second part requires the description of an *experiment*—the mere statement that the velocity of sound can be measured by means of Kundt's tube
is insufficient, even if the correct formula is provided.

Q. 5. Give an account of the deviations from Boyle's law. How are
these deviations accounted for ?

A common error is to suppose that directly a gas gets above the critical
temperature, Boyle's law is rigorously obeyed. The porous plug experiment
for hydrogen is erroneously stated as proving that the molecules of this gas
repel one another.

Q. 6. A vessel of 500 cc. capacity contains hydrogen saturated with
aqueous vapour at 20° C., the total pressure being 75 cm. If
the density of hydrogen is 9×10^{-5} gr./cc. and the pressure of
aqueous vapour at 20° is 1·74 cm., find the mass of the hydrogen
in the vessel.

Many knew how to correct the pressure for aqueous vapour, but had no
idea of reducing to normal temperature and pressure to find the mass.

Q. 7. What is meant by an isothermal curve.
Give the general form of the isothermals for ice, water, and
steam, drawing attention to any particular isothermal which
may be of special interest.

A continuous isothermal is required—not three separate isothermals.

Q. 8. Define the conductivity of a body.
How can the conductivity of a bad conductor such as glass be
measured ?

In defining conductivity care should be taken to state that the flow of
heat is supposed to take place perpendicularly to the two faces differing by
1 degree Cent. In the second part some stress should be laid on the points
of difference with a similar experiment for a good conductor—thus, in
any slab experiment in the case of a bad conductor, the slab is thin, while
the faces are at the observed temperatures.

Q. 9. Describe how the calibration error of a mercury thermometer is
determined, and explain how if we are given a curve showing
the calibration corrections and the corrections at the freezing
and boiling point, a curve can be drawn on which the correction
at any reading can be directly read off.

Method of calculation with detached thread should be given. Method
of plotting a correction curve little known.

133

STAGE 3.

Results : 1st Class, 14 ; 2nd Class, 34 ; Failed, 51 ; Total, 99.

The results of this examination were rather better than last year, but very few of the candidates showed much knowledge of higher practical work, or appeared to have done any reading of recent investigations outside the ordinary Stage 2 text-books. They showed fair ability in describing method and apparatus, but were unable to criticise methods satisfactorily, often raising futile objections and missing the real difficulties. Very little knowledge of accurate thermometry, or of thermodynamics was shown by any of the candidates. A large proportion of the papers were quite worthless.

Q. 1. Describe how the method of interference fringes can be applied to measure the coefficient of linear expansion of solids.

Nearly half the candidates made the measurement of expansion depend on observing the change of width of the fringes. Those who described the displacement of the fringes correctly usually contented themselves by observing that "the expansion could be found," without indicating the relation between the number of fringes, the wave-length, and the expansion.

Q. 2. Describe the methods that are used to measure with great accuracy the changes in the boiling point produced by dissolving salts in liquids.

This question was fairly answered with the exception of the precautions necessary in adjusting and testing the thermometer.

Q. 3. Describe some method by which the amount of heat radiated from a surface per second per unit area at various temperatures may be measured. Discuss the experimental evidence for Stefan's law in the case of a black body.

The majority described methods which were quite inadequate, and did not distinguish heat loss by conduction and convection. Very few were acquainted with recent work on the radiation of a black body.

Q. 4. The surface tension of water diminishes as the temperature rises. Show by the second law of thermodynamics that a soap film must cool when stretched.

There were two or three good attempts at this question, but the majority appeared to be quite ignorant of thermodynamics, and missed the point of the question entirely.

Q. 5. Define the critical temperature of a substance, and describe and criticise the methods by which it may be determined.

This was a very favourite question, and several good methods were described. Very few were able to criticise the weak points satisfactorily.

Q. 6. Point out the difficulties encountered in the attempt to liquefy hydrogen, and describe the main features of the apparatus at present employed to effect the liquefaction.

There were several good answers, and more knowledge of recent work was shown in this than in any other question. Many omitted to lay sufficient stress on the essential precautions for external protection and heat insulation of the apparatus. Some described only Pictet's method, and gave as the chief difficulty the excessively high value of the critical pressure.

Q. 7. Describe some accurate form of gas-thermometer, and enumerate the precautions and corrections required in using it.

Very few appeared to have any idea of accurate work with a gas-thermometer, or to be acquainted with Chappuis' modification of Regnault's form. The necessity of correcting for the expansion of the bulb was often omitted even by those who described the apparatus satisfactorily.

134

HONOURS.

Results : 1st Class, – ; 2nd Class, 1 ; Failed, 2 ; Total, 3.

There were three candidates for PaperI., one of whom did sufficiently well to justify further examination, and attained a similar standard in Paper II. He seemed to have a fair knowledge of theory, but little practical acquaintance with the subject, on the side of higher experimental work, though he succeeded in reaching a fair standard in the practical paper.

DAY EXAMINATIONS.

STAGE 1.

Results : 1st Class, 24 ; 2nd Class, 58 ; Failed, 68 ; Total, 160.

The number of candidates was small, but there was a large proportion of failures in some schools. The weak point was generally inaccuracy of expression. Words were used as if their meaning was quite immaterial. In some cases it looked as if the student really knew the correct answer, but from inability to express himself, or from ignorance of language, succeeded in saying exactly the opposite of what he meant.

SOUND.

Q. 1. How would you show that sound is transmitted through the air, and that it is a kind of motion and not a material emanation like an odour? What is the nature of the motion due to sound passing through the air?

Often tried, but there were few good answers.

Q. 2. An observer on the sea shore notes that the waves are breaking at the rate of 10 per minute, and that they take two minutes to reach the shore from a rock 100 yards out at sea. Find the mean wave—length, and the velocity of propagation in feet per second.

Q. 3. Describe some method which has been employed for observing the velocity of propagation of sound through air. What precautions are required to avoid errors due to wind?

These two questions were generally well answered.

Q. 4. Give illustrations showing that the loudness of a sound depends on the amplitude of vibration of the source, on the size of the vibrating surface, and on the distance of the observer from the source.

Many of the answers consisted merely in a paraphrase of the question, without any illustration.

LIGHT.

Q. 5. The sun subtends the same angle as a halfpenny at a distance of 10 feet. Give a diagram showing the size and nature of the shadow of a halfpenny cast by the sun on a surface perpendicular to the rays at a distance of 5 feet from the halfpenny.

Very seldom answered, and then badly.

Q. 6. A small object is placed six feet in front of a convex mirror of 3 feet radius. Give a diagram showing the nature and position of the image, and find its size relative to that of the object.

Often attempted, but poorly done.

Q. 7. A ray of light is incident at an angle of 30° on one face of an equilateral prism. If the path of the light through the prism is parallel to the base, find the direction of the emergent ray, and the total deviation of the ray after passing through the prism.

Very easy and fairly well answered by those who tried it.

Q. 8. An object at a distance of 10 inches from a lens, when viewed through the lens, appears to be at a distance of 30 inches from the lens. Find the focal length of the lens, and give a diagram showing the nature of the image.

The answers to this question were either good or very bad.

HEAT.

Q. 9. If the latent heat of fusion of ice is 80 calories per gramme, find how much ice would be required to cool one kilogramme of water from 20° C. to 10° C.

Generally attempted and fairly done on the whole. Many omitted to allow for the heating of the melted ice from 0° to 10° C.

Q. 10. A room contains 66 kilogrammes of air at 27° C. and 780 mm. pressure. What will be the weight of air contained (a) if the temperature falls to 2° C., (b) if the barometer falls to 715 mm. ?

Seldom tried. A few good answers, the rest worthless.

Q. 11. Distinguish between evaporation and boiling. How is the boiling point of a liquid defined, and how is it affected by pressure.

The nature of ebullition was not well understood.

Q. 12. Describe some form of maximum, and some form of minimum thermometer, and point out the defects (if any) of either instrument.

Seldom attempted, and little knowledge of details shown.

SOUND.

STAGE 2.

Results : 1st Class, 10 ; 2nd Class, 9 ; Failed, 10 ; Total, 29.

A few of the papers were very bad, but the majority appeared to be of a fair order of merit. The number sent in was too small to permit of any general conclusions of value being drawn.

LIGHT.

STAGE 2.

Results : 1st Class, 19 ; 2nd Class, 34 ; Failed, 21 ; Total, 74.

The answers to this paper were fair on the whole, with a normal proportion of good papers, and a similar proportion of failures. With regard to the several questions, the commonest mistakes made were those noted below, but many of the good papers were practically free from serious mistakes, and were clearly written and well expressed.

Q. 1. What is meant by spherical aberration ?

Make a careful drawing of the manner in which parallel rays are reflected by a hemi-spherical concave mirror.

Many of the diagrams omitted the caustic curve.

Q. 2. Determine the limits of the angle of incidence of a ray of light on one face of an equilateral prism so that the ray may be refracted at the second face, assuming the critical angle to be 45°.

The index of refraction was often taken as 3/2 instead of $\sqrt{2}$, and the angle of incidence wrongly deduced.

Q. 3. Describe the method by which Fizeau observed the velocity of light, indicating by a diagram the optical arrangements necessary.

Little knowledge was shown of the optical arrangements.

Q. 5. A rhomb of Iceland spar is laid on a page of print. How will the appearance of the print differ from that which would be observed if the Iceland spar were replaced by a slab of glass ? How does the appearance alter when the rhomb is rotated while still remaining in contact with the page ?

Many candidates thought that the brightness of the two images and their distance apart varied as the crystal was rotated.

Q. 6. A short-sighted person cannot see objects clearly at a distance greater than 6 inches. What spectacles would be required to enable him to see distant objects clearly ? If his least distance of distinct vision without glasses is 3 inches, what would it be with the above spectacles ?

There were few good attempts at the latter part of this question.

Q. 7. Describe experiments showing that radiant heat is reflected according to the same laws as light.

The experimental methods suggested were generally too rough.

Q. 8. Define dispersive power. What are the conditions that two thin prisms of different kinds of glass may give when combined, (a) no dispersion, (b) no deviation ?

In many cases dispersion was confused with dispersive power, and the answers were lacking in precision.

Q. 9. Explain what is meant by interference of light, and describe a method by which two separate beams of light from the same source may be made to interfere.

The diagrams given were generally poor, and the appearances presented were often loosely and inaccurately described.

HEAT.

STAGE 2.

Results: 1st Class, 21 ; 2nd Class, 123 ; Failed, 48 ; Total, 192.

There were comparatively few good papers, about 10 per cent. in all, and rather more than twice as many failures. The majority of the papers were poor in quality. The faults noted seemed in many cases to be due to youth and want of facility of clear expression. Subjoined are special criticisms relating to the several questions.

Q. 1. What precautions must be taken, and what corrections applied, to determine temperatures correctly to 1/100° C. by a mercurial thermometer between 0° and 100° C. ?

Freezing point and boiling point errors (or fundamental interval and one fixed point) should be given, with method of applying correction at intermediate points. Many candidates omit these, and give a number of less important points without understanding them.

Q. 2. Describe a method of measuring the specific heat of a substance of which only a small quantity can be obtained. What relation has been found between the specific heats of the metallic elements and their atomic weights ?

137

Bunsen's ice calorimeter, or Joly's steam calorimeter, are the best for this. In the former calorimeter, the tube containing the mercury should not be vertical where the surface of the mercury ends, as the changes of pressure so introduced would effect the melting point of the ice quite appreciably. Round the calorimeter should be an air space and then an ice jacket to protect from radiation.

Q. 3. Give a brief historical sketch of the discovery of the first law of thermodynamics.

A *historical* sketch is asked for. The first law should be given in definite terms—that the heat produced is proportional to the work expended, and not merely that heat appears when work is done. The answer should give a short account of the old caloric theory, and of the experiments connected with the names of Rumford, Davy, Joule and Mayer.

Q. 4. Define what is meant by the dew-point, and show how, when this is known, the amount of aqueous vapour in the air can be determined.

What is the weight of a litre of damp air at 20° C., when the dew-point is 11° C.? Vapour pressure of water at 11° C. = 1 cm.; density of air at 760 mm. and 0° C. = ·0013; density of water vapour = ⅝ths that of air.

Relative humidity is not the correct answer to the second part of the question. The saturation pressure at the dew-point is known, and hence, knowing the vapour density, the mass can be calculated. The answer is 1·205 grs.

Q. 5. Enumerate the various ways in which a liquid can lose heat, distinguishing between the cases in which heat is transformed into some other form of energy, and those in which no such transformation takes place.

In radiation, the heat energy is transformed into the energy of ether waves (until the latter strike some absorbent surface). In evaporation, part of the heat is used up in doing work against the atmospheric pressure, and part in doing internal work.

Q. 6. Show how the rise of temperature produced by the adiabatic compression of a perfect gas can be calculated.

Air at 0° C. is adiabatically compressed to half its volume; find the rise in temperature. ($2^{1\cdot4}$ = 8/3 approximately.)

First part scarcely attempted. In answering this, the equation $pv = RT$ should be assumed, and also it should be pointed out that the rise of temperature of the gas = $\dfrac{\text{Work done in compression.}}{\text{Sp. Ht. at } const. vol.}$ Note that in an adiabatic expansion the pressure does not remain constant. The answer to the second part is 91° C.

Q. 8. What is meant by saying that the internal work done when a gas expands is small? Describe experiments which have shown that the above statement is correct in the case of air.

Few understood clearly the meaning of internal work.

Q. 9. Explain carefully how the melting point of paraffin wax or sulphur may be determined by the method of cooling.

Observe rate of cooling of a *well-stirred* mass of paraffin wax. Temperature will remain nearly constant while solidification is going on. There should be no water vessel round the wax while it is cooling, as this will tend to swamp the effect, owing to the increased area of cooling, and increased thermal capacity.

Report on the Examinations in Magnetism and Electricity.

EVENING EXAMINATION.

STAGE 1.

Results : 1st Class, 709 ; 2nd Class, 708 ; Failed, 793 ; Total, 2,210.

This paper was, on the whole, rather better done than the corresponding paper last year, and this remark applies to each of the three divisions of the paper. Comments on the answers to individual questions are given below.

Magnetism.

Q. 1. A wooden ball contains a bar magnet imbedded so that the axis of the magnet lies along a diameter, but the ends do not reach the surface. Explain carefully how you would mark on the surface of the ball the points where the axis of the magnet prolonged would cut the surface.

Few of the answers were more than partially correct. It was a common mistake to float the ball in water, and then to assume the magnet to lie N. and S., and *to be horizontal.* Various tests (by compass, dip needle, bar magnet, etc.) were suggested, which would only give correct results if the earth's field could be neglected.

Q. 2. What is meant by the statement that the declination at a place is 18° west? At such a place how must a boat be steered by compass so that its course may be due east?

Well done on the whole. A curious and not infrequent blunder was to direct the helmsman to steer so that the compass pointed 18° S. of E.

Q. 3. A horse-shoe magnet is brought due south of a small compass needle, the line joining the poles of the magnet being east and west, with the north pole to the west. Describe the manner in which the compass is deflected.
Describe and explain what will happen if the keeper is placed on the magnet.

The drawings were very bad *as regards proportions.* In the first part the influence of the earth's field was generally ignored. In the second part *all* the lines of force due to the magnet were regarded as passing through the keeper.

Q. 4. How would you hold a rod of soft iron so that the influence of the earth's magnetic field upon it may be (1) as great as possible, (2) as small as possible?

Frequently well done. For the least magnetic effect almost all placed the rod horizontal, E. and W. Extremely few gave the more general answer, viz., that the rod might be placed anywhere in a plane at right angles to the line of dip.

Frictional Electricity.

Q. 5. Describe and explain the action of a gold-leaf electroscope.
Having charged the instrument positively, how would you test the sign of the charge on the inner coating of a Leyden jar without discharging or moving either the jar or the electroscope?

Answers to the first part were usually reasonable ; there were scarcely any correct answers to the second. Nearly all the candidates adopted a method by which the jar was partially discharged.

Q. 6. What is meant by the statement that a given body is at a higher potential than the earth ? Illustrate your answer by means of analogous phenomena in heat and hydrostatics.

The main part was badly answered. There were two types of answer ; the first omitted to state that it is a flow of *positive* electricity from a body to the earth that is a test of higher potential in the former ; the second, whether expressed in terms of two fluids, one fluid or Faraday tubes, merely amounted to saying that a body has higher potential than the earth if it is positively electrified.

Q. 7. A hollow metal can is placed on an insulated stand and electrified Describe the distribution of the electrification on the can and explain how you would examine the distribution experimentally.

Many knew that there is no electrification inside ; not so many stated that the density is greatest at the edges, etc. The statement that the absence of electrification can be proved by connecting the inside to an electroscope was made a good many times ; but a fair proportion knew all about the question.

Q. 8. A metal plate *A*, thickly varnished on the top, is insulated and connected to a gold-leaf electroscope, the whole being charged with positive electricity until the leaves diverge widely. When another insulated plate *B* (for instance, the cover of an electrophorus) is placed on the top of *A*, the divergence of the leaves is very little altered, but if *B* is touched the leaves fall nearly vertical. How do you explain these effects ?

There was a greater number of unsatisfactory answers to this than to any other question in the paper. The usual mistake was to assume that the touching of *B* connected the whole apparatus to earth, and allowed the electricity to escape. The common explanation in terms of " free " and " bound " electricity was sometimes given, but the number of incorrect explanations in terms of capacity and potential changes was great.

Q. 9. Describe and explain the action of a plate-glass frictional machine How would you use it to charge a Leyden jar ?

The machine was well described, but the action of the collecting combs seemed to be imperfectly understood. Some attempted to describe the Wimshurst machine, and knew very little about it.

Voltaic Electricity.

Q. 10. Describe the Daniell cell, and explain the functions of each part of the cell and the action that takes place when the poles are connected by a conducting wire.

What advantages does this form of cell possess over a simple voltaic cell consisting of plates of copper and zinc immersed in dilute acid ?

Answered by nearly all, and the best answers were very good. A large number knew nearly all about the Daniell cell. The function of the porous pot was seldom stated explicitly ; a good many stated that *bubbles* of hydrogen passed through, and then interacted with the sulphate. Some had very vague notions of polarisation. A few had apparently been taught that copper coated with hydrogen is more electropositive than zinc. Local action was frequently stated to be absent from the Daniell cell, without any mention of amalgamation of the zinc.

Q. 11. State Ohm's law, and explain the terms used.

An incandescent electric lamp takes a current of ·5 ampère when connected to a circuit of 100 volts. What is the resistance of the lamp ?

The answers to this question were too indefinite Nearly all the candidates stated that current equalled electromotive force divided by resistance, but did not explain themselves by considering any particular case of the application of the law. The arithmetical mistakes in the second part of the question were shockingly bad. An extraordinarily large number failed to divide 200 by ·5 correctly.

Q. 12. Explain how you would wind a U-shaped piece of soft iron with wire and how you would connect the wire to a battery so as to form an electro-magnet with two north poles at the tips of the U. Carefully describe the magnetic state of the iron when a current is passed through the winding.

A few good answers ; the majority were poor. Many diagrams were such that it was impossible to tell how the winding was supposed to run. The expressions "right and left handed," "clockwise and anti-clockwise," were often used ambiguously. Many failed to state the position of the consequent S. pole, or else said there would be two such poles.

Q. 13. Describe some simple form of galvanometer, and explain the method of using it.

There were a fair number of good answers, and a large number of answers of varying degrees of badness. Many candidates appeared to be acquainted with the galvanometer only as an indicator of current. Some knew that there was a suspended needle, and thought that the current was sent into it. Others described the virtues of the astatic pair, and then placed them at the centre of a large coil.

Q. 14. Assuming that the rate of production of heat by a current in a wire varies as the product of the resistance and the square of the current, compare the amount of heat developed by a current of 2 ampères in 3 minutes in a wire 3 feet long, with that produced by a current of 3 ampères in 2 minutes in 2 feet of the same wire.

Correct answers were frequently obtained, though few of the candidates made explicit reference to C^2Rt, and the arithmetic was often lamentably wrong.

STAGE 2.

Results : 1st Class, 297 ; 2nd Class, 486 ; Failed, 450 ; Total, 1,233.

There were few defects of a general kind to be noticed, and the papers, as a whole, showed improvement in some respects on last year, though there was a larger proportion of failures, but not so many as in 1904. It was evident that there were two very different types of students : (1) the student with a fair general knowledge of theory derived from books, but deficient in laboratory work and in details of practical applications ; (2) the technical electrician, familiar with details of construction and use, but weak in theoretical knowledge. It was difficult to frame questions to suit both types of student.

Magnetism.

Q. 1. A thin uniform magnet, 1 metre long, is suspended from the north end so that it can turn freely about a horizontal axis which lies magnetic east and west. The magnet is found to be deflected from the perpendicular through an angle θ (sin θ = ·1 ; cos θ = ·995). If the weight of the magnet is 10 grams, the horizontal component of the earth's field is ·2 C.G.S. units, and the vertical component ·4 C.G.S., find the moment of the magnet.

A fair percentage of candidates were successful with this question. The most common mistake was taking the vertical component of the earth's force on the S end of the magnet as downwards instead of upwards. Many had insufficient knowledge of mechanics.

Q. 2. What is a *isogonal line?*

Describe the general form of the isogonals over the surface of the earth. How are the observations made which are used in determining the isognals?

A good deal of uncertainty was shown as to the nature of isogonal lines. Only a few knew their general form over the earth's surface, and many confused them with isoclinic lines.

Q. 3. Two exactly equal magnets are attached together at their mid points so that their axes are at right angles, and the combination is pivoted so that the axes of the magnets are horizonal and they can turn freely about a vertical axis. How will the system set itself under the influence of the horizontal component of the earth's field? If the moment of each magnet is M, and the moment of inertia about the axis round which it can turn is K, what will be the period of vibration of the system?

The first part was often answered correctly. The second part scarcely ever. Very few knew how to find the magnetic moment of the compound magnet.

Q. 4. Prove that the magnetic field due to a short bar magnet at a given distance from its centre is twice as great at a point in the direction of the axis of the magnet as it is at an equi-distant point in the plane at right angles to the axis of the magnet and passing through its centre.

A large number of candidates answered this question well.

Frictional Electricity.

Q. 5. An insulated sphere having a diameter of 20 centimetres is charged. It is then connected to an electrometer by a fine wire, the deflection being 50 divisions. An insulated and uncharged sphere of 16 centimetres diameter is then joined to the first by a long wire, and the electrometer deflection falls to 32. Calculate the capacity of the electrometer.

Many candidates found no difficulty with this question. Arithmetic often bad.

Q. 6. What is meant by the term *the capacity of a condenser?*

Calculate the capacity of a parallel plate air condenser of which each plate has an area of 400 square centimetres, the distance between the plates being half a millimetre. Be careful to state the unit in which you express your answer.

Only about half the candidates gave a satisfactory definition of the capacity of a condenser. The numerical part of the question was very fairly answered by many.

Q. 7. Give a careful drawing of the lines of force due to a charged point placed near to an uncharged insulated sphere.

Usually carelessly and badly answered. The drawings were poor, and little or no explanation was given.

Q. 8. A small pith ball weighing one decigram suspended by a silk fibre and charged with positive electricity is repelled when a charged glass rod is brought near it. If the direction of the electric field of the glass rod near the ball is horizonal and its magnitude equal to 20 C.G.S. electrostatic units, when the deflection of the fibre is 45°, what is the charge on the ball?

Often answered satisfactorily.

Voltaic and Technical Electricity.

Q. 9. Describe, and explain the mode of action, of some form of sensitive galvanometer suitable for use in a place where the earth's field is much disturbed by the presence of variable electric currents.

The astatic galvanometer was given more frequently than one would have expected. As a rule, the suspended coil galvanometer was well described, but too often the mode of suspension of the coil was not given, or was stated to be glass, or quartz, or silk. Few explained why this type was to be preferred.

Q. 10. A copper disc having a diameter of 40 centimetres is rotated about a horizontal axis perpendicular to the disc and parallel to the magnetic meridian. Two brushes make contact with the disc, one at the centre and the other at the edge. If the value of the horizonal component of the earth's field is ·2 C.G.S., find the potential difference in volts between the two brushes when the disc makes 3,000 revolutions per minute.

Not often attempted, and then only by good candidates, who were usually successful with it.

Q. 11. Describe and illustrate by figures some form of self-feeding arc lamp.

Q. 12. Describe a drum armature. What are the advantages of this form of armature over the Gramme armature?

Some very good answers were sent in by the comparatively few candidates who attempted these two technical questions. The most common fault was to dilate on small details to the omission of essential features.

Q. 13. Describe carefully, stating the precautions necessary, how you would test the accuracy of an ammeter reading to about 1·5 amperes.

The voltameter method was commonly employed. Only a few used a potentiometer method.

Q. 14. Explain how the mechanical equivalent of heat may be determined by measuring the electric energy spent in heating a resistance. What instruments would you require, and how would you perform the experiment?

Many candidates gave good answers, and the majority showed good acquaintance with the principles involved. Weakness in experimental details is the chief criticism, especially with regard to the calorimetry.

Q. 15. How would you connect two equal constant cells of internal resistance 5 ohms each, if you wished to deposit copper as rapidly as possible in a voltameter of 7 ohms resistance?

A good proportion answered this question well. With the data supplied the actual relative currents should have been worked out.

Q. 16. Explain the terms *specific resistance*, and *temperature-co-efficient of resistance* of a material. What material would you employ for constructing a standard resistance, and how would you wind the wire?

A good definition of *specific resistance* was often given. Many candidates were unfamiliar with term *temperature-co-efficient of resistance*. The suitability of manganin and other alloys was put forward by most; and the non-inductive method of winding was given by almost everyone.

STAGE 3.

Results : 1st Class, 28 ; 2nd Class, 74 ; Failed, 39 ; Total, 141.

The paper was on the whole very fairly done. The results compare favourably with those of last year. Subjoined are detailed remarks on the answers to some of the questions.

Q. 1. Describe some accurate method of comparing the capacities of two condensers. Enumerate the chief precautions required?

Fairly done. General principles and methods correctly given, but details (*e.g.*, as to character of galvanometer, magnitude of resistances, errors due to absorption, etc.) often neglected.

Q. 2. Prove that if $E_1, E_2, E_3 \ldots$, are the charges on a system of conductors $A, B, C \ldots$ and $V_1, V_2, V_3 \ldots$ the potentials of these conductors, the energy of the charged system A, B, C, is $\frac{1}{2}(E_1 V_1 + E_2 V_2 + E_3 V_3 + \ldots)$.

Apply this result to find the energy in a charged Leyden jar in terms of the capacity of the jar and its charges.

Not good. The expression—"Energy$=\frac{1}{2} E V$"—was in most cases assumed. Proofs, when given, were generally unsatisfactory.

Q. 3. Define the co-efficient of self induction of a circuit. Calculate approximately the co-efficient of self induction of a long straight cylindrical solenoid of radius r and length l wound uniformly and having N turns of wire per unit length.

There were a few very good answers, but many showed cram without understanding. The expression "cutting of lines of force" is used in a vague and unsatisfactory way.

Q. 4. Describe the effects of magnetisation on the length and breadth of an iron bar magnetised longitudinally, and explain the effects of compression or extension on the permeability.

The knowledge exhibited was not above the standard of Stage 2. The effect on the length of an iron rod of applying an increasing magnetic force was rarely known. Ewing's theory was freely introduced, but none of the candidates had read Dr. Ewing's book on Magnetic Induction, or had heard of the "Villari effect."

Q. 5. Describe experiments which show that cathode rays are small particles charged with negative electricity. How has the velocity of these rays been determined ?

Q. 6. Describe some method of determining accurately the specific resistance of an electrolyte.

Well done by many.

Q. 7. Write an essay on Faraday's "magnetisation of light" including the principal results of more recent experiments.

Only attempted by a few.

HONOURS.

Results : 1st Class, - ; 2nd Class, 1 ; Failed, 12 ; Total, 13.

PAPER 1.

The quality of the work sent up was not at all satisfactory; many of the candidates made mistakes which showed they had not understood some quite elementary principles.

Q. 1. Explain how the forces in the electric field may be regarded as due to tension along the lines of force combined with pressure at right angles to them.

This question was not well done. The reasons given were either so vague as to be worthless, or else were obtained by unnecessarily lengthy and complicated mathematical analysis.

Q. 2. Explain, in detail, some method of measuring the energy lost through magnetic hysteresis, and describe some of the principal results of experiment.

Most of the candidates only knew the lengthy method of plotting and measuring up the B and H curve.

Q. 3. Describe some method of measuring the velocity of the ions in gases.

Candidates confined themselves too exclusively to the case when the the pressure of the gas is exceedingly small.

Q. 4. Find an expression for the impedance of a long straight wire traversed by a current of given frequency, and show that as the frequency is increased the current goes towards the surface of the wire.

No solution of any value was sent up.

Q. 5. Write an essay on cathode rays.

Well done by several candidates.

Q. 6. Give Lorenz's method of determining the ohm in absolute measure, and describe in detail the apparatus required for the purpose.

Q. 7. Discuss the production of electric oscillations in a circuit containing capacity and self induction, and find the effect of damping on the frequency.

These questions were also fairly well done.

PAPER II.

This paper was badly answered. Two of the candidates showed some knowledge of the mathematical theory, but little power of applying it. The remainder were very vague in their answers, and their papers were practically worthless. None of the candidates did well in the practical paper, and only one reached the pass standard.

DAY EXAMINATION.

STAGE 1.

Results : 1st Class, 47 ; 2nd Class, 61 ; Failed, 35 ; Total, 143.

On the whole, the questions were well answered. About one-third of the candidates obtained First Classes, and one-fourth failed. The Frictional Electricity portion of the paper was answered the worst.

Magnetism.

Q. 1. What is meant by the axis of a magnet ? Where is the axis of a horse-shoe magnet ? In what direction would such a magnet place itself, if placed on a wooden board floating freely in water ?

Some confusion as to the position of the axis of a magnet was shown, but the majority of the candidates were successful with the question.

Q. 2. What is meant by magnetic induction ? Give a neat sketch showing how the lines of the Earth's magnetic field in a laboratory would be distorted if the ceiling were supported on iron pillars.

Not well answered. The sketches were, as a rule, poor.

Q. 3. What are the most important points in the construction of a dip needle ? How should the axis of the needle be adjusted in taking observations of the dip ?

Most of the answers showed only a general, and often rather vague, notion of the adjustments of a dip needle.

Q. 4. A bar magnet is carried in a horizontal circle round a compass needle with its N. pole pointing always to the centre of the needle. How will the needle be affected when the magnet is north, east, south and west, respectively, of the needle, assuming that the Earth's influence on the needle is always greater than that of the magnet ?

Usually successfully attempted. The position when the magnet was north of the needle lead to some confusion.

Frictional Electricity.

Q. 5. A point-charge is placed near a conducting sphere. Describe the distribution of electricity on the sphere (a) when the sphere is insulated and unchanged ; (b) when connected to the Earth.

There was not a good answer received to this question. Very few attempted it.

Q. 6. Two insulated spheres *A* and *B* are placed near together and *A* is charged positively. How is the potential of *B* affected by the presence of *A*, and how will it be modified if *B* is touched with the finger, and *A* then removed ?

Something like half the candidates had useful notions as to potential.

Q. 7. A hollow metal vessel is insulated and charged with electricity. How is the electricity distributed, and how is the distribution modified (if at all), when a metal rod held in the hand is introduced into the vessel without touching it?

Usually badly answered. Most of the candidates avoided the question.

Q. 8. Describe the construction of a Leyden jar and the method of charging it. What do you understand by the capacity of such a jar ?

Almost every answer showed a knowledge of the Leyden jar and how to charge it. Only two or three gave satisfactory definitions of capacity. It was usually defined as the greatest quantity of electricity a jar can store.

Q. 9. How would you prove that positive and negative electricities are developed in equal quantities (a) by friction, (b) by induction?

Many candidates were obviously puzzled to prove that equal quantities of positive and negative electricity are developed by induction.

Voltaic Electricity.

Q. 10. What is meant by the Electromotive Force of a Voltaic cell? If you were given two cells, how would you test which had the greater electromotive force ?

The electromotive force of a cell was often given correctly. In the second part of the question, some ingenuity was displayed by a few candidates in developing a method. Only one gave a potentiometer method.

Q. 11. Describe how a compass needle will be affected by a current flowing in a long straight wire (a) from south to north, (b) from east to west, when the wire is placed above, below, or at the side of the compass.

A fair number of answers were correct. The east-west position of the wire confused many candidates.

Q. 12. A plate of zinc and a plate of copper are placed in dilute sulphuric acid. What action takes place, if any? How is the action modified, (1) if the zinc plate is amalgamated, (2) if it is connected to the copper plate ?

Most of the candidates found the question easy.

Q. 13. The poles of a Daniell cell are connected by one yard of fine wire, and the current observed. The length of the same wire is increased to 3 yards, and the current is thereby reduced to one-half. Compare the amounts of heat developed in the wire in the two cases.

Not often attempted, but usually successfully.

Q. 14. Insulated wire is coiled on a glass tube placed horizontal and at right angles to a compass needle, the centre of which lies on a prolongation of the axis of the tube. How will the needle be affected when the current is passed through the coil ? –Will the introduction of an iron rod or a copper rod into the tube make any difference ?

Some answers ascribed no magnetic properties to the solenoid before the metal bar is introduced. Others said that the metal bar makes no difference. But, on the whole, the question was well answered.

STAGE 2.

Results : 1st Class, 37 ; 2nd Class, 145 ; Failed, 275 ; Total, 457.

A large proportion of the candidates are unfit—either from bad teaching or from insufficient time being given to the subject—to take this stage. Not more than 8 per cent. reached a First Class standard, and a large number would not have obtained a pass in Stage 1.

Magnetism.

Q. 1. What do you understand by the terms *moment of inertia*, and *magnetic moment* of a magnet ? Explain how the magnetic moments of two magnets may be compared.

This was one of the best answered questions in the paper, though, to a large majority of the candidates, the term *moment of inertia* is a mere shibboleth.

Q. 2. A sphere of soft iron is moved in a straight line from north to south, and passes to the east of the centre of a freely suspended weak magnet. Describe how the deflection of the magnet varies with the position of the sphere.

The induced magnetism of the iron sphere was generally attributed to the suspended magnet (although the question distinctly stated that the latter was weakly magnetised), the inductive influence of the Earth's magnetism being as a rule entirely ignored. In the drawings that were given, the length of the magnet was generally represented as many times the diameter of the sphere.

Q. 3. What is meant by the critical temperature of iron ? How would you demonstrate it ? Mention any physical properties of iron (other than magnetic) which change at this temperature.

Not many answers. Recalescence was the only physical property mentioned. The temperature of recalescence was generally obtained by heating the iron in an oil bath, and was measured by a mercury thermometer.

Q. 4. A magnet of moment 1000 C.G.S. is balanced on a central knife edge. How must it be weighted if it is to remain horizontal in a place where the Earth's horizontal field is ·2 C.G.S., and the dip 45° ?

Many who tried this forgot that the Earth's magnetism would act on both poles of the magnet. Others who obtained the correct numerical result confused " force " with " moment of a force."

Frictional Electricity.

Q. 5. Explain the terms *dielectric constant* and *dielectric strength*, and illustrate the distinction between them by reference to experiment. Find an expression for the capacity of an air condenser with parallel plates.

Seldom tried, and, when tried, badly done. Scarcely a single candidate could find the capacity of a parallel plate condenser. The term "dielectric strength" was unknown.

Q. 6. Give a diagram showing how the lines of force in a uniform electric field are disturbed by inserting an insulated and unchanged conducting sphere.

Frequently well done. The chief faults were that the lines of force (1) were drawn *through* the conductor, and (2) met the conductor at all sorts of angles.

Q. 7. Find an expression for the energy of a charged condenser. If a condenser is charged, and then made to share its charge with a condenser of twice its capacity, find the loss of electric energy, and explain what has become of it.

The expression for the energy of a charged condenser was known in many cases, but the methods of obtaining it were not satisfactory. The second part of the question was, on the whole, fairly done.

Voltaic and Technical Electricity.

Q. 8. Describe the construction of a quadrant electrometer, and explain the points on which its sensitiveness chiefly depends.

Of the construction of the quadrant electrometer moderately good accounts were given, but of the points on which its sensitiveness depends, little was known.

Q. 9. The current in a circuit containing a storage cell and a resistance is 5 ampères. The difference of potential at the terminals of the cell is 1·85 volts. When the circuit is broken the difference of potential rises to 1·95 volts. Find the resistance of the cell.

This question involves an intelligent knowledge of Ohm's law, and very few candidates have that knowledge. Everyone knows the formula $C = \dfrac{E}{R}$, but few understand it. A large number obtained the correct numerical answer by assuming that a current flowed through a cell when the circuit was broken, and in many cases the drop of ·1 volt was attributed to the fall through the external resistance.

Q. 10. Describe De Sauty's (Wheatstone bridge) method of comparing the capacities of two condensers, and prove the formula employed.

Q. 11. A horse-power is 33,000 foot-pounds per minute. Find the number of watts in one horse-power, using approximate equivalents of the fundamental units if you do not remember the exact values.

Q. 12. How would you determine the efficiency of a glow lamp, and what apparatus would you require for the purpose?

Q. 13. Describe a simple form of ammeter for alternating currents.

Q. 15. Explain how the magnetic flux in a dynamo may be estimated from the magnetomotive force and magnetic resistance of the magnetic circuit.

Q. 16. Describe the construction of either a telegraph or a telephone cable, drawing attention to special points of importance for either purpose.

Of this part of the subject very little was known, and on the answers to the questions few useful comments can be made.

Q. 14. State Faraday's (or Neumann's) law of electromagnetic induction. The N. Pole of a magnet is moved rapidly downwards towards a horizontal metal plate. In which direction will the induced currents flow?

Lenz's law was generally given instead of the one asked for. The second part of the question was generally well done.

Report on the Examinations in Physiography.
Section I. of Stage 1.

EVENING EXAMINATION.

Results : Passed 126 ; Failed, 111 ; Total, 237.

A.

Q. 1. What is meant by the statement that matter is indestructible ?

Illustrate your answer by considering the burning of a candle, and explain carefully how you would perform an experiment with a candle to verify the law.

Many of the answers to the first part of this question were incomplete. The experiment of burning a candle so as to collect the products of combustion was well described, but the way in which this experiment illustrated the indestructibility of matter was not well answered.

Q. 2. Describe and explain the action of a common balance.

If the length of the right arm of a balance is 20 centimetres and that of the left is 20˙1 centimetres, what weight will have to be placed in the right-hand pan to counterpoise a weight of 100 grams placed in the left pan ?

The essential points of a common laboratory balance were generally omitted. Most candidates gave an elementary description of an ordinary pair of scales. The underlying principle of the lever was known and the second part of the question was well answered.

Q. 3. The wheel of a bicycle is 30 inches in diameter and is observed to make 100 revolutions in a minute. What is the speed with which the bicycle is moving ? What are the speeds of the points on the tyre of the wheel which are at a given instant at the highest and lowest points respectively.

The first part of this question was well answered. The second part was only occasionally attempted and only once was the correct answer given.

Q. 4. What is the function of the pendulum of a clock ?

What would be the effect on the rate of the clock (1) of increasing the size of the bob, the length of the pendulum remaining constant, (2) of increasing the length and keeping the size of the bob constant ?

The first part was badly answered. The function of the pendulum is to "tick seconds" and the function of the pendulum is "to regulate the clock" were the common answers. The second part was well done.

B.

Q. 5. What is meant by the term specific heat ?

Describe carefully an experiment to show that iron and lead have different specific heats.

A few correct definitions of specific heat were given, but the majority missed out one or more essential points in the definition. The unsatisfactory method of showing the difference in the specific heats of iron and lead by dropping balls of these substances at a high temperature on to a sheet of beeswax was often given.

Q. 6. Water is said to boil at 100° C. ; criticise this statement and point out where it is defective.

Describe an experiment to illustrate your answer.

Well done. The effect of change of pressure was generally known and good illustrations were given.

Q. 7. What are the laws of refraction of light ?

Explain, illustrating your answer by a carefully drawn diagram, why the water in a swimming bath appears shallower than is actually the case.

Snell's law was only given two or three times. The majority of the candidates stated that when a ray of light passed into a denser medium it was refracted towards the normal and vice versa. The second part of the question was not well answered, many of the candidates, in order to explain the phenomenon, finding it necessary to assume that light in passing into a rarer medium was bent towards the normal. The apparent position of a point upon the bottom of the bath was seldom given, the majority of the candidates simply indicating the direction in which it lay.

Q. 8. Describe how a spectrum may be projected on a screen, and explain carefully the functions of each of the parts of the apparatus you would employ.

What will be the appearance of the spectrum if the slit is opened very wide ?

The lens was generally omitted. When it was introduced its function was not explained. Nearly all the diagrams given were very badly drawn and out of proportion. The appearance of the spectrum with a wide slit was given as " blurred" or "indistinct," but the reasons were not forthcoming.

C.

Q. 9. Describe, giving a sketch of the apparatus employed, how you would remove oxygen and water vapour from atmospheric air.

Several candidates explained how to remove oxygen from the air, but only a few knew how to get rid of water vapour.

Q. 10. What is the composition of iron rust.

Describe an experiment to prove the composition of iron rust.

Fairly well answered.

Q. 11. Describe how you would prepare carbon dioxide, giving a sketch of the apparatus.

Describe three experiments illustrating the properties of carbon dioxide.

Very well done.

Q. 12. Describe the composition and general properties of limestone, lime, common salt, washing soda, and caustic soda.

The composition and properties of limestone, lime, and common salt were satisfactorily given. Washing soda and caustic soda gave trouble to many.

Day Examination.

Results : Passed, 108 ; Failed, 76 ; Total, 184.

A.

Q. 1. What are the principal features of difference between the metric and the British systems of weights and measures ? If 1 pint = ·567 litre, and 1 gram = ·002204 lb., find the weight of a pint of water.

Fairly well done. The commonest mistakes were (1) the metre represents a certain natural length exactly and could be easily replaced if lost ; (2) no relation whatever between British units of weight and volume.

150

Q. 2. A piece of sulphur at one end of a balance beam is in equilibrium with a piece of brass at the other end. How will the horizontality of the beam be affected when (1) the brass alone, (2) the whole system—beam, brass and sulphur—is immersed in water?

Usually done correctly.

Q. 3. A railway train is moving round a circle with uniform velocity. What are the forces which act upon it? Why must the outer rail be raised above the inner?

Not more than five candidates realised that the centripetal force is exerted upon the train by the rails. This force was described as "pulling the train from the centre of the curve." The statement that inertia was one of the forces was frequent. No one knew exactly the effect of elevation of the outer rail. Most stated only that it was there to prevent the train running off the line.

Q. 4. What is meant by the energy of a swinging pendulum? Is the energy the same when the bob is at the top as when it is at the bottom of its swing? If not, how do they differ?

Many knew that the energy was sometimes kinetic and sometimes potential; but the names were confused, and very few knew that the sum of the two is nearly constant throughout the swing.

B.

Q. 5. Explain how the fixed points are marked on the stem of a thermometer. What is the effect on the indication of a thermometer immersed in boiling water of adding some common salt to the water?

A good many omitted to say that the ice should be melting. One or two candidates referred to the facts that the ice should be pure, and that the barometer should be read in the case of the boiling point.

Q. 6. It is possible to extinguish the flame of a candle by passing over it (without touching the wick) a short coil of thick copper wire. Explain why the candle is extinguished?

Most of the candidates knew the general lines of the explanation; but many answers were incomplete in the respect that the necessity for the temperature to be above a certain value for combustion to continue was not stated.

Q. 7. If you look at a telegraph post through a slab of glass held some distance from the eye you notice that the part of the post seen through the glass varies in position as the glass is rotated. Draw a picture to illustrate this effect, and explain it.

Very seldom attempted.

Q. 8. A dark blind covers the window of a room so that light only enters by a narrow horizontal chink at the bottom. How would you hold a glass prism so as to see the chink through the prism, and what would the appearance be like? Draw a picture to illustrate your answer.

There were a few incomplete answers.

C.

Q. 9. Describe any methods you are acquainted with for preparing hydrogen. What are its physical and chemical properties?

Better done than any of the other questions. The commonest mistake was confusion of the physical and chemical properties.

151

Q. 10. What is "common salt"? What are its properties? What experiments would you make to ascertain its nature?

Only a few knew how to show that salt contains sodium and chlorine.

Q. 11. What would be the effect of putting into an oven and raising to a high temperature, (1) wood, (2) iron, (3) marble, (4) washing soda? Would the results be the same if the substances were heated in a Bunsen flame?

Many gave only physical effects, *e.g.* change of temperature, colour and state in the case of iron, and most of the answers were incomplete.

Q. 12. How does spring water generally differ from rain water? Why is pure rain water not pleasant to drink? How can it be made more palatable?

It was sometimes stated that the soil acted as a filter in the case of spring water. Softness and hardness were frequently mentioned without being understood, *e.g.*, rain water was stated to have a soft taste.

GROUP IV.—CHEMISTRY AND METALLURGY.

BOARD OF EXAMINERS.

X. Inorganic Chemistry
X.*p.*   „
    (Practical)
XI. Organic Chemistry
XI.*p.* „   „
    (Practical)
XIX. Metallurgy
XIX.*p.*   „   (Practical)
XXVI. Elementary Science
of Common Life (Chemistry)
	Professor W. A. Tilden, D.Sc., F.R.S.,
	Chairman.
	Professor W. H. Perkin, Junr., Ph.D.,
	F.R.S.
	Professor W. Gowland, Assoc. R.S.M.
	Professor W. P. Wynne, D.Sc., F.R.S.

Report on the Examinations in Chemistry.

Evening Examinations.

Inorganic Chemistry, Theoretical.

Stage 1.

Results : 1st Class, 759 ; 2nd Class, 671 ; Failed, 616 ; Total, 2,046.

There is a consensus among those who have read the papers that, on the whole, they represent a marked improvement on those of former years. There is much less of the hopeless rubbish which was at one time so characteristic of the answers in this stage. But while on the whole satisfactory, the papers seem to indicate a certain amount of neglect of some fundamental subjects to which the attention of the teachers ought to be directed. Of these, the most important is represented by Q. 4, which asks for an explanation why it is wrong to represent the composition of atmospheric air by a formula, such as N_4O. For years past the Examiners have been endeavouring to suppress this practice, which was at one time very common, and was evidently the result of widespread erroneous teaching. Even now the answers to this question show, in a large proportion of cases, that the students do not apprehend correctly the nature of the error involved in the use of a formula. It seems to be thought that the formula is to be objected to on the ground that it ignores the small amounts of water vapour, carbon dioxide, and other gases present, along with the oxygen and nitrogen, and therefore does not represent truly the composition of atmospheric air. It ought to be made more clear to them that the fundamental mistake lies in using a formula which implies definite chemical composition, and the existence of a definite compound with definite properties, rather than a mere mixture of two things which are not present in fixed and invariable proportions, and, being merely mechanically mixed together, are capable of being separated by merely mechanical processes. More care should be taken by the teachers to explain the meaning and application of chemical formulæ.

Q. 12 consists of an easy problem in the calculation of weights and volume . Rather unexpectedly, this was attempted by a smaller proportion of the candidates than usual, and by them often unsuccessfully.

Attention should be drawn to the fact that there is a tendency to write symbols carelessly. Such instances as *PB* for *Pb*, *MN* for *Mn*, *Co* for *CO*, were quite common.

153

STAGE 2.

Results : 1st Class, 229 ; 2nd Class, 989 ; Failed, 646 ; Total, 1,864.

The number of papers in this stage which may be designated absolute failures appears to be smaller than it used to be, but, on the other hand, the papers that are distinctly good are very few. A striking feature is the large amount of inaccurate statement which may result from the mistaken effort on the part of many candidates to attack questions concerning the subject matter of which they have no real knowledge. The result is that many papers are received containing some good answers, together with some which seem to show a want of apprehension of principles, and a strange ignorance of facts. To tabulate the chief properties of chlorine, bromine, and iodine so as to show their relation to one another, and to indicate that they belong to the same family of elements, would appear to be a requirement which would be easily met by students even at this early stage, but though many tabular statements were put in there were few attempts to institute the comparison desired. Then, in regard to facts, great ignorance was displayed : for example, (Q. 21) one volume of CO was said to combine with one volume of oxygen ; (Q. 22) calcium carbonate was said to be decomposed by boiling in the water, and CaO precipitated ; (Q. 26) a common mistake was to represent $CrSO_4$ or $FeSO_4$ as replacing the alkali sulphate in chrome and iron alums ; (Q. 24) the manufacture of bleaching powder was described, but the action of acids was almost always incorrectly represented. As nearly all candidates who attempted this question state that chlorine is liberated by the action of carbonic acid on bleaching powder, it may be as well to explain here that whatever constitution is attributed to bleaching powder, hypochlorous acid, and not chlorine, is the volatile product. This can be expressed by either of the following equations, which show that the chloride part of the molecule is unaffected by carbonic acid or carbon dioxide in the presence of water.

I. $CaCl_2Ca(ClO)_2 + CO_2 + H_2O = CaCl_2 + CaCO_3 + 2HClO$

II. $2CaCl(ClO) + CO_2 + H_2O = CaCl_2 + CaCO_3 + 2HClO$

The peculiar chlorinous smell of bleaching powder is due to hypochlorous acid liberated in this way. Chlorine is evolved only when a strong acid is used.

STAGE 3.

Results : 1st Class, 21 ; 2nd Class, 158 ; Failed, 218 ; Total, 397.

The papers were for the most part of poor quality. Two questions in particular were answered in an unsatisfactory manner.

Q. 46. Explain carefully how the equivalent, atomic weight and molecular weight of mercury *or* of zinc have been determined.

Q. 48. Define the term "acid." In the light of your definition give reasons for assigning or refusing the name "acid" to aqueous solutions of the following :—Hydrogen sulphide, ordinary sodium phosphate, sodium bi-sulphate, copper sulphate, ethyl alcohol.

The doctrine of ions completely overshadows facts in the view of these students, and seems to have been used by their teachers without sufficient preparatory experimental or explanatory foundation.

Wild answers to other questions are quite common, such as "anhydrous hydrogen peroxide has been prepared by the direct combination of measured quantities of ozone and hydrogen," or "ammonium amalgam is prepared by grinding ammonia and mercury together in a mortar." Very few knew anything about anhydrous hydrogen peroxide, the formulæ of the carbonyls were seldom given correctly, and the answers about barium carbonate and barium hydroxide were very bad.

Added to the lack of chemical knowledge, the misapplication of words and the grotesque spelling were in too many cases deplorable. The word "approximate" is commonly understood by these candidates to mean "inaccurate," as in the paper of 71530, who writes concerning the law of

Dulong and Petit, that "though two (*sic*) approximate to afford a direct method for finding atomic weights," &c. Another frequently occurring expression is "solution of brine," meaning a solution of common salt.

Attention has been repeatedly drawn to the unsatisfactory answers in Section II. and the Examiners cannot but express their belief once more that the majority of the candidates who attempt these questions have none of that knowledge of manufacturing processes obtained at first hand or from the pages of the larger treatises which is prescribed by the syllabus.

HONOURS.

Results : 1st Class, 1 ; 2nd Class, 7 ; Failed, 12 ; Total, 20.

The most prominent defects in these papers on Theoretical Chemistry arise from imperfect knowledge of the current literature of the subject. Many answers were given to the question (62) about nitrogen trioxide, but none were satisfactory, and no candidate could show much knowledge of the application of electrolytic methods in Organic Chemistry (Q. 63). The chemistry of iodine compounds was also very imperfect in most cases, such compounds as the polyiodides, iodonium and iodoxy compounds being generally ignored, and even the iodates and periodates were imperfectly described. Out of 20 candidates, 1 was awarded First Class and 7 Second Class Honours.

INORGANIC CHEMISTRY, PRACTICAL.

STAGE 1.

Results : 1st Class, 439 ; 2nd Class, 722 ; Failed, 306 ; Total, 1,467.

The results are, on the whole, fair. The most unsatisfactory features of the work arise from lack of thought. In the first exercise the students were asked to apply heat to a powder in a dry test tube and record the effects observed. The powder consisted of a mixture either of mercuric iodide and zinc oxide or of mercuric iodide and cuprous iodide. Instead of following instructions many of the candidates proceeded to apply litmus, lime water, etc., and then to write out a formal table on the "experiment, observation inference " plan, wholly ignoring the facts to be observed. The training of the intelligence, which should be the highest aim of teaching, is not yet the definite and paramount aim of many science teachers. The same defect is also apparent in the answers to the other two exercises. A large number of candidates fail to distinguish between "loss of weight" and "residue," thus giving wrong results of experiments otherwise correctly done. If this mistake arises, as is possible, from misunderstanding of the word "residue," it ought to be put right by the teachers. This is by no means the first time that this kind of error has been noticed.

STAGE 2.

Results : 1st Class, 556 ; 2nd Class, 636 ; Failed, 444 ; Total, 1,636.

The general impression derived from a perusal of these papers is, as in previous years, the superiority of the quantitative over the qualitative work. A feature to be regretted is the number of cases in which things not present are found in the substances supplied for qualitative analysis. This generally arises from imperfect separations, *e.g.*, when lead is present the candidates also find aluminium. There is also, in certain schools, a tendency to make "shots" at supposed constituents of the mixtures by means of individual tests without attempting separations, and the condition of valency in which iron, for example, occurs is very rarely ascertained. There is no excuse for slipshod work of this kind if the students have had only a reasonable amount of practice, as the use of books is allowed during the examination. It would almost appear from the results sent in by some candidates that they have used the book for the first time in the examination room. In the theoretical paper the customary ignorance of the explanation of analytical processes and reactions was displayed. It would appear that very little teaching is given in this direction.

STAGE 3.

Results: 1st Class, 11 ; 2nd Class, 155 ; Failed, 413 ; Total, 579.

The qualitative analysis was fair on the whole, but not so good as might be expected in this stage, the majority of the candidates receiving only from 30 to 40 marks out of the 75 allotted to this part of the work. The chief mistakes may be grouped under the following heads :—

(a) Arsenic acid often recorded as phosphoric acid, being missed in group ii., and noticed on the application of the molybdate test.

(b) In not a few cases phosphates were not looked for in group iii., and calcium and zinc consequently escaped recognition.

(c) The phosphate separation was in many cases not carried out properly, with the result that calcium phosphate was recorded as alumina.

(d) With five exceptions the valency of the iron and arsenic was not investigated.

The quantitative work was for the most part quite inaccurate, the percentage of carbon dioxide being usually returned 20 or 30 per cent. too high. The estimation of copper gravimetrically was almost invariably 5 or more per cent. too high. This was due to the use of caustic soda or potash as a precipitant, thus contaminating the cupric oxide with iron and with carbonate of calcium, both of which were present in the mineral. Those candidates who precipitated and weighed the copper as sulphide got fairly good results.

HONOURS.

Results : 1st Class, - ; 2nd Class, 6 ; Failed, 8 ; Total, 14.

The work given was the following :—

JULY 4TH, 1906.

10 A.M. to 5 P.M.

The solution given contains one salt. Identify it and estimate by two methods the amount present per litre of solution.

The solutions given to alternate candidates contained 50 grams per litre of phosphite or hyposulphite of sodium.

One only succeeded in identifying the salt, and his estimations were not only wide of the mark, but did not agree together.

JULY 5TH, 1906.

10 A.M. to 5 P.M.

The solution given contains the chloride of tin together with a small quantity of iron.

Estimate the amount of stannous chloride present and the total amount of tin per litre.

Most of the candidates estimated the total tin with fair accuracy, but the amount of stannous chloride was usually 10 to 20 per cent. wrong.

JULY 6TH, 1906.

10 A.M. to 5 P.M.

From the salt supplied prepare the corresponding organic base. If solid, recrystallise it and determine the melting point ; if liquid, distil and determine the boiling point.

Prepare a crystallised specimen of one derivative, not a salt.

Determine whether this is a primary, secondary, or tertiary base, and make some experiments with the object of discovering its constitution.

Diphenylamine and benzidine sulphates were given to alternate candidates. The work was generally very unsatisfactory. The best of the candidates got a clean crystallised specimen of the base and determined its melting point ; one or two ascertained the character of the base as primary or secondary, but the specimens of derivatives handed in were not what they professed to be. One candidate was unable to commence work, not knowing how to proceed, another obtained salicylic acid from the material supplied, and a third discovered that it was tannin and proceeded to make gallic acid from it ! In these and several other cases the candidates should not have been admitted to the examination, as they had confessedly received no proper preparation in practical organic chemistry.

Eight out of fourteen candidates failed, the remaining six being placed in the second class.

ORGANIC CHEMISTRY, THEORETICAL.

STAGE 1.

Results : 1st Class, 39 ; 2nd Class, 136 ; Failed, 86 ; Total, 261.

The papers represented approximately the standard of former years. Q. 10 relating to fermentation was answered in the least satisfactory manner, after making due allowance for the fact that the subject is difficult, and any approach to a complete answer was not to be expected at this stage.

STAGE 2.

Results : 1st Class, 46 ; 2nd Class, 107 ; Failed, 98 ; Total, 251.

On the whole the papers were good. The only question which calls for remark is No. 32, relating to alizarin, which was attempted by few, and only in one or two cases with much success.

STAGE 3.

Results : 1st Class, 1 ; 2nd Class, 23 ; Failed, 11 ; Total, 35.

The answers in this stage were more satisfactory than last year, and call for little detailed comment. Q. 45 relating to the "Grignard reaction" and Q. 46 concerning the constitution of papaverine or atropine were generally avoided. Neglect of the former is remarkable in view of the fact that the chemical journals for the last two years have teemed with applications of the method, and it was expected that the teachers would be alive to its importance.

HONOURS.

See Report on Inorganic Chemistry, Theoretical, Honours.

ORGANIC CHEMISTRY, PRACTICAL.

STAGE 1.

Results : 1st Class, 76 ; 2nd Class, 50 ; Failed, 39 ; Total 165.

This work was well done on the whole.

STAGE 2.

Results : 1st Class, 76 ; 2nd Class, 65 ; Failed, 74 ; Total, 215.

The descriptive written part of the examination was not very satisfactory. In writing out instructions for the production of some compound, which the candidate had himself prepared, sufficient detail was not given, and generally no attention whatever was paid to the quantities of materials used or the yield obtained.

In the practical work the second exercise was not well done. As a rule the candidates, in spite of the precise instructions to the contrary given in the question, devoted all their efforts to identifying the substance by means of colour reactions, and paid little or no attention to ascertaining its chief characters.

STAGE 3.

Results : 1st Class, 30 ; 2nd Class, 20 ; Failed, 21 ; Total, 71.

The practical work was very poor. The preparation of the silver salt was carried out successfully, so far as could be judged from the written accounts (often very brief), but the preparation for analysis did not seem to be understood. The salt was drained on a tile, or on filter paper, or in a desiccator or on a water bath, and analysed in a wet state, as some of the candidates even pointed out ! Four candidates out of thirty-five alone had the good sense to dry the salt in a steam oven until the weight was constant before proceeding to decompose it by heat.

It is difficult to imagine how students could have reached this stage without being instructed in such elementary matters.

HONOURS.

See Report on Inorganic Chemistry, Practical, Honours.

DAY EXAMINATIONS.

INORGANIC CHEMISTRY, THEORETICAL.

STAGE 1.

Results : 1st Class, 235 ; 2nd Class, 127 ; Failed, 65 ; Total, 427.

Though many of the answers were childish in style, indicating the youth of the candidates, the papers were on the whole creditable, and the diagrams were much better than those of the Evening Students. The work represents an improvement on the results of last year.

STAGE 2.

Results : 1st Class, 93 ; 2nd Class, 334 ; Failed, 253 ; Total, 680.

There were a few excellent papers, but the majority were very weak, and many wholly unfit to present themselves in Stage 2.

It is remarkable what a large number of students persist in the belief that steam is decomposed by red hot copper, and how many introduced this idea into their answers to Q. 1 about the method of determining the composition of water by weight. There is also rather more evidence than usual of pure cram. The preparation of marsh gas for example is represented by many as resulting from "the action of caustic soda on sodium acetate," or even "by adding excess of caustic soda to acetic acid," the statement being accompanied by a picture of a glass flask with thistle funnel and delivery tube, and with a correct equation, showing that the method has never been seen in operation, but has been learned simply from a book.

INORGANIC CHEMISTRY, PRACTICAL.

STAGE 1.

Results : 1st Class, 100 ; 2nd Class, 55 ; Failed, 42 ; Total, 197.

The results are similar to those of last year. The answers to Exercise B show that many of these students have learned to weigh with tolerable accuracy, but in Exercise A they do not show that their powers of observation have been much cultivated, for the majority of the candidates who were supplied with pure sulphur found impurity which was not present.

In connection with Exercise C the results were very poor. Nearly all the candidates used a form of apparatus in which a volume of water supposed to be equal to the volume of gas produced was syphoned off and measured. The varied and usually erroneous results obtainable with this form of apparatus in the hands of careless experimenters are well illustrated by the answers of one set of 28 candidates who all used it. Of these, two obtained approximately the correct amount of gas, three rather too little, and the remainder from *two* to *five times* the correct amount.

STAGE 2.

Results: 1st Class, 90 ; 2nd Class, 226 ; Failed, 88 ; Total, 404.

Notwithstanding that a large proportion of the candidates secure marks sufficient for a pass, the work is not well done.

In spite of the precise instructions given by the Examiners, only about half the candidates made a separate examination of the soluble and insoluble constituents of the mixture. Zinc in Mixture II. was missed by about 90 per cent. of the candidates, while a very large number found chlorine in Mixtures I. and II. This was often traced to the common mistake of the thoughtless worker, which consists in dissolving the substance in hydrochloric acid and then testing for a chloride.

In the quantitative exercise the most common mistake was in the identification of the gas, which was nitrogen. Nearly half the candidates reported it to be ammonia, notwithstanding that they used an apparatus for collecting it filled with water.

The equations to be found in the written paper were often ludicrous, and there is too much uncertainty about the formulæ of common things, especially salts of silver.

Report on the Examinations in Metallurgy.

THEORETICAL.

STAGE 1.

Results : 1st Class, 48 ; 2nd Class, 55 ; Failed, 42 ; Total, 145.

The standard of attainment in this stage is similar to that of last year. It is, however, encouraging to observe that the gradual improvement exhibited during recent years continues to be maintained, there being but few really worthless papers among the failures.

In making sketches, the candidates generally showed great weakness ; not only was the execution poor, but often the parts of furnaces were confused and drawn entirely in wrong proportions.

Another point to which the attention of the teachers in a few schools is called, is the failure of their students to grasp the fact that metallurgical processes are not identical with assay methods, but are concerned with materials in large quantities, and under conditions in which cost is the controlling factor. Hence, for example, sodium carbonate, however useful it is in assaying operations, would be precluded from use in a blast furnace on account of its cost alone.

The attention of teachers is again called to the reprehensible practice followed by a large number of candidates of selecting the questions they attempt to answer from Sections I. and II. only. Specialising at this early stage can only result in an imperfect and unsatisfactory knowledge of elementary metallurgy, and cannot be too strongly condemned. Even to those who propose entering into, or are already engaged in, iron and steel works, it is essential that they should have an acquaintance with the metallurgy of the other metals.

The remarks which follow on the answers to individual questions are confined to those only which call for special comment.

SECTION I.

Q. 2. Explain the terms "welding" and "annealing" as applied to metals, and "dressing" as applied to ores. Give an example of each of these operations.

Many good answers, but in too many cases the term "dressing," even when correctly explained, did not appear to be understood, the examples given of the process being quite wrong. The simple *crushing* of gold ores in a stamp battery was often cited as an example, as was the case last year, no reference being made to the subsequent operations which constitute the real dressing of the ore.

Q. 3. What flux or fluxes would you use respectively when smelting :—
(a) an ore with a siliceous gangue, (b) one with a calcareous gangue in a blast furnace, in order to obtain a fusible slag? State your reasons for using these fluxes.

Fairly well answered as a rule. The advantages of the use of two fluxes in increasing the fusibility of slags in each case were known to only one or two candidates.

Q. 4. State the principles on which the manufacture of coke from coal depends. Describe the working of a charge of coal in any oven known to you.

There were too many weak answers to this simple question. The principles were generally very imperfectly stated, and the descriptions of the working of a charge were poor, and if carried out in practice would result in the combustion and not the coking of the coal.

SECTION II.

Q. 6. Give an account of the composition and general characters of the chief iron ores. Why cannot Cleveland iron ore be used for the production of Bessemer pig iron?

Not generally attempted. Great ignorance was displayed of the compositions and characters of the ores found in this country. Clayband ore seemed to be almost unknown, and only one candidate correctly explained why Cleveland ore was unsuitable for the production of Bessemer pig iron.

Q. 7. Describe and make a sketch of a basic open hearth furnace. Give a description of the lining.

Only a few good answers, the sketches being as a rule very poor, and representing text-book forms of old furnaces.

SECTION III.

Q. 9. Name the chief re-agents in use at works for the precipitation of gold from its solutions. Give the reactions which take place in each case.

Very few answers and all poor.

Q. 10. Describe and make a sketch of a *modern* hand-worked reverberatory furnace for the chloridising roasting of silver ores.

Only eighteen answers, and eleven failed to obtain any marks. Only one candidate had a satisfactory knowledge of the form and construction of this simple furnace. By some candidates the furnace was drawn with a concave bed and a tap-hole, showing that they were quite ignorant of the

160

operation of chloridising roasting. All students in this stage ought to be able to make a sketch of the hand-worked four or five hearth reverberatory furnace required in this question.

Q. 11. How would you treat an ore of the following composition for the extraction of the lead it contains?

Galena - - - 50 per cent.
Calc spar - - - 50 per cent.

Give the chemical reactions which take place.

Only two correct answers. In the majority of the answers it was proposed to flux the calc spar, whereas it should be separated by dressing, and the dressed product then treated in a furnace of the Flintshire type.

Q. 12. State the principles and chemical reactions on which the processes for the extraction of mercury from its ores depend.

Great weakness shown in the answers. Instead of a statement of the principles, the process and plant were usually described; the plant given being in every case an obsolete form of furnace and condenser, now only of historic interest. Answers of this character are never awarded marks.

Section IV.

Q. 14. Describe and make a sketch of a water-jacketed blast furnace for smelting copper ores. Why are water jackets used?

There were only four good answers to this question, but it was not attempted by many candidates. The modern water jacket furnace is of such great importance and in such extensive use that every student, even in Stage 1, should be acquainted with its form and the principles on which it is constructed, and there can be no valid excuse for the ignorance shown by the candidates from some of the schools in their answers to this question.

Q. 15. Describe the process of refining tin. State the changes which take place in the operations.

Several candidates omitted the operation of liquation which is essential before the metal is "boiled" or "tossed."

Q. 16. Name the common alloys in which zinc is an important, but not the chief constituent. Give their compositions and industrial uses.

Some fairly good answers. In the others the compositions given were too often mere guesses, as were also the industrial uses of the alloys.

Stage 2.

Results : 1st Class, 27 ; 2nd Class, 73 ; Failed, 39 ; Total, 139.

The number of candidates taking the examination in this stage was considerably greater than last year, 139 papers having been received, as compared with 115 in 1905.

The general standard reached was on the whole better than last year, in fact, many of the answers to questions in this stage were more complete and showed a wider knowledge of the subject than some in Stage 3. That the identification of samples of ores and metallurgical products still leaves much to be desired will be evident from the fact that typical samples of ganister were frequently described as limestone, galena and cerussite as grey iron, brass as copper, and white iron as copper matte.

Some of the sketches were good, but as a rule they were poor and inaccurate. In not a few instances, the same mistakes occurred in a number of papers from the same school, which indicates either that inaccurate diagrams or faulty text books are employed for teaching.

In the identification of specimens, also, similar mistakes often occur throughout an entire school. Such mistakes cannot be coincidences, and appear to indicate that a limited number of specimens only are shown the students. It cannot be too strongly impressed upon teachers, that not only should an ample supply of specimens be provided for the students, but they should be afforded facilities for actually handling them.

A striking point revealed by the examination is the ignorance of many of the candidates of the composition of the more common alloys. German silver, in several instances, was described as an alloy of silver and copper; soft solder as a mixture of lead and zinc or tin and zinc, and ferro-nickel as a steel containing 5 per cent of nickel.

SECTION I.

Q. 21. Distinguish between the following metallurgical terms :—(a) "Malleability" and "Ductility" ; (b) "Forgeability" and "Weldability" ; (c) Give characteristic examples of each.

In most cases this question was answered correctly ; a few candidates, however, confused the terms "Forgeability" and "Weldability" and in two instances the candidates thought that an essential feature of welding was that the metals should be cold.

Q. 22. How much brown iron ore ($2 Fe_2O_3$, $3 H_2O$) will be required to convert one ton of a gangue of the following composition into a mono-silicate slag ?

Calc Spar ($CaCO_3$) - - - - - 50 per cent.
Quartz - - - - - - - 50 „
  Atomic weights : Fe = 56, Ca = 40, Si = 28, C = 12.

Only three of the 31 candidates who attempted this question obtained a correct result, several lost a few marks for arithmetical errors, but the majority failed to obtain good marks either from their not knowing the general formula for a mono-silicate or from their attempting to produce one with Fe_2O_3 in its composition.

Q. 23. Describe, with the aid of sketches, a modern water-bottom gas producer and give the approximate composition of the gas you would expect to obtain from it.

Forty-two candidates attempted this question, and in a few instances good sketches and descriptions were given, but the majority of the answers were poor. Some candidates thought the producer they described would give a gas mainly composed of either hydrogen or carbon dioxide, while several considered that nitrogen would not enter into its composition at all.

Q. 24. Name and briefly describe the six specimens submitted to you.

Although the specimens were perfectly typical ones, no less than 70 candidates failed to obtain half marks. The specimens, which were of a simple character, were :—Iron Pyrites, Ganister, Blue Metal, Galena and Cerussite, White Iron, and Brass. As was pointed out in last year's Reports, it is still evident that facilities are not afforded the students in many institutions for recognising ores, metallurgical products, and materials. In addition to adequate facilities for handling specimens at schools, the students should be encouraged to make collections of their own. They should also be taught to make rough tests for the hardness of the materials with a pocket knife, then such mistakes as describing ganister as limestone, blue metal as blast furnace slag, and brass as chromium are hardly likely to occur. A small pocket lens would aid the students greatly in identifying specimens.

From the answers given to this question, it is evident that very little attention is given to this important branch of the subject in the majority of schools.

SECTION II.

Q. 25. Describe fully, with the aid of sketches, an ordinary Whitwell hot blast stove.

A few good answers were given to this question, but the majority were weak. Some students gave the original form of Whitwell stove, while others described the old pipe stove. Some of the sketches were good.

L

Q. 26. Give an account of a *modern* automatic method for charging a blast furnace smelting iron ores. Make a sketch of the appliances.

The same remarks apply to this question as to a similar one set last year. In many cases the ordinary "cup and cone" was described as an automatic method for charging a blast furnace. Several candidates from one school described with sketches an ordinary bucket elevator for this purpose. It is hardly possible that a number of mistakes of this nature can be due entirely to the imagination of the students.

Q. 27. In what respects does the Thomas-Gilchrist or "basic" process differ from the Bessemer or "acid" process? Describe a converter used for the basic process.

Some really good answers were given by candidates who were evidently well acquainted with modern steel works practice. On the whole this question was well done.

Q. 28. Classify the processes employed in the manufacture of steel. State the principles and chemical reactions on which each is based.

This question, like the last, was often well answered and good marks were obtained by many of the candidates who attempted it. The chemical principles and reactions were, however, too frequently omitted.

SECTION III.

Q. 29. Describe and make a sketch plan and elevation of a simple cyanide plant for the treatment of sands.

Generally speaking, this question was answered in an unsatisfactory manner; the majority of the sketches were poor and the descriptions inaccurate. In several instances the strengths given for the cyanide solutions were quite wrong. A few candidates gave a very good description of the chemistry of the process.

Q. 30. State the principles and chemical reactions on which the "parting" of gold and silver bullion by sulphuric acid depends. Give an outline of the operations.

Some of the candidates evidently understood the principles of the process, and gave the chemical reactions accurately, but others gave details of methods employed for parting bullion in a laboratory for assaying purposes, substituting sulphuric acid for the ordinary nitric acid parting mixtures. The use of white iron vessels for parting was generally omitted.

Q. 31. How would you treat an ore of the following composition, in order to obtain marketable lead and silver :—

Galena	20
Cerussite	45
Calc Spar	15
Quartz	20
	100

Silver, 20 ounces per ton.

Not well done by the majority of those who attempted this question. Several candidates suggested the concentration of the lead by means of Wilfley, and other concentrators, in spite of the high percentage of cerussite present.

In several cases, where treatment of the ore in a blast furnace was suggested, the addition of iron ore as a flux was omitted.

Q. 32. How may the silver in a pyritic silver ore be made soluble in water and in brine respectively?

How may the silver solutions be treated for the production of the metal in ingots?

163

The students who attempted this question generally gave their answers accurately. In a few instances the Ziervogel process was not given for converting the silver in a pyritic ore into sulphate, and some did not mention the possibility of having to add more pyritic material in order that the roasting should be effective.

Section IV.

Q. 33. How would you smelt copper refinery slag in order to obtain the copper it contains? Explain the chemical changes which take place by equations.

Only attempted by 16 candidates, of whom only seven gave passably good answers. Most of the students preferred to treat the slag in the fourth operation of the Welsh copper process, for the production of "white metal." In only two cases was the possibility of smelting in a blast furnace mentioned.

Q. 34. Describe and make a sketch of a *modern* barrel converter for Bessemerising copper regulus. Give a brief account of the working of a charge.

Some good answers. Several candidates described an ordinary vertical converter with bottom tuyères, and lost marks accordingly.

Q. 35. State fully the conditions which are essential in distilling zinc ores in order to obtain the zinc as metal. Why cannot a blast furnace be used instead of retorts?

Many candidates enumerated the essential conditions for the distillation of zinc ores satisfactorily, but they failed to show why it is practically impossible to use a blast furnace instead of retorts. A few only mentioned the facts that both carbon dioxide and air will oxidise volatilised zinc and that the large quantity of escaping gases from a blast furnace would render the condensation of the zinc as metal impossible.

Q. 36. Give an account of the physical properties, composition, and chief uses of the following alloys:—Muntz metal, German silver, soft solder, and ferro-nickel.

Only ten satisfactory answers were given to this question. It is surprising to note that several candidates in this stage had no idea of the compositions of the four simple alloys given in the question: several thought Muntz's metal was composed of copper and tin, while others thought soft solder was composed of lead and zinc.

Stage 3.

Results : 1st Class, 12 ; 2nd Class, 21 ; Failed, 25 ; Total, 58.

There is an increase of 8 in the number of papers sent in as compared with last year, and it is satisfactory to note that there is a marked improvement in the quality of the answers of the candidates generally. The weakest point in all the papers, with two or three exceptions, was the recognition of metallurgical materials (Q. 42). This was deplorably bad, although the specimens were all extremely characteristic, and comprised only materials in every-day occurrence in works. It was even worse than in Stage 2.

In the answers to the other questions, obsolete processes and plant occurred much less frequently than hitherto.

Section I.

Q. 40. State fully the physical characters and composition which coke should possess for use in a blast furnace smelting iron ores for Bessemer pig.

The answers as a rule were only moderately good. No mention was made in many papers of ash and phosphorus, and the percentages of carbon given in some can only have been mere guesswork.

Q. 41. How would you proceed to obtain a continuous record of the variations in temperature of a reverberatory furnace ? Describe the pyrometer you would employ and state how you would calibrate it.

Several good answers, but the majority of candidates can never have seen, and certainly not used, a recording pyrometer.

Q. 42. Name and briefly describe the six specimens submitted to you.

Attention has been called above to the extremely bad answers to this question.

The following examples will suffice to show the ignorance of some of the candidates :—

Copper refinery slag containing shots of copper was variously named copper regulus, tap cinder, brown hæmatite, tinstone, white cast iron, iron pyrites and mispickel ; while *coarse metal* was said to be cinnabar, ferro-manganese, grey slag from lead smelting, zinc blende, steel furnace slag, tap cinder, magnetite, wolfram, tinstone, &c.

If candidates would only try the hardness of the specimens, as has been already pointed out under Stage 2, most of these glaring mistakes would not be made.

19 candidates recognised only one of the six specimens and 10 failed to recognise any.

Section II.

Q. 43. Describe and make sketches of the lower half of a *modern* blast furnace for smelting iron ores, showing two methods of cooling the boshes.

This easy question was attempted by only about one-third of the candidates. There were a few excellent answers, but the others showed a very imperfect acquaintance with the construction of a modern water-cooled bosh.

Q. 44. Describe the manufacture of steel as carried on in a tilting furnace by a continuous process. State the chemical changes which take place from charging to tapping.

Generally well answered.

Q. 45. How are malleable iron castings produced ? Explain exactly why the final treatment, to which the castings are subjected, renders them malleable.

The method of preparing malleable iron castings was generally given correctly, but the cause of the malleability was in too many answers attributed solely to the removal of carbon and not to the change of the carbon from the combined to the finely graphitic state.

Section III.

Q. 47. Give a brief account of the cyanide plant you would erect, and the treatment you would adopt for the extraction of gold from an ore, the whole of which has been ground to slimes.

Answers very poor ; only 7 candidates out of 30 who attempted the question obtained more than half marks. The treatment of gold ores by the cyanide method and the arrangement of the plant is evidently very imperfectly taught in most schools. The majority of the candidates had no knowledge of either the decantation or the filter press method, and confused the treatment of slimes with that of sands. Impracticable arrangements of the plant were sketched. Some gave ferrous sulphate as the precipitant for the gold.

Q. 48. Describe and make a sectional sketch of the lower half of a *modern* rectangular water-jacketed furnace for smelting lead ores. How does the hearth differ from that of a copper smelting blast furnace ?

Rarely attempted. Answers with two exceptions very bad. In some cases a poor drawing of a copper furnace was given At this stage all students ought to be well acquainted with the form and construction of typical modern water-jacketed furnaces used in copper smelting and lead smelting respectively.

SECTION IV.

Q. 49. State as fully as possible the conditions which are essential to success in the "pyritic" or "raw sulphide" smelting of copper ores.

Somewhat less than half of the candidates attempted this question, and the answers, with a few exceptions, were extremely disappointing.

This important smelting process appears not to have been taught in many schools, or if taught, the teaching is far from efficient. As the process is now coming extensively into use wherever the ores are pyritic, and is rapidly replacing the old methods on account of its greater economy, all students at this stage ought to be well acquainted with it, and especially with the conditions under which it can be successfully employed.

Q. 50. State fully how you would treat, on a large scale, "white metal" containing 10 ozs. of gold per ton, in order to obtain the gold and the copper in marketable forms. If the white metal contained 100 ozs. of silver per ton, in addition to the gold, how would you proceed?

This question on practical work was attempted by rather less than one-third of the candidates and was fairly well answered.

Q. 51. Describe the Mond (nickel carbonyl) process for the extraction of nickel from a copper nickel matte.

The chief errors in the answers were :—treating the matte with water gas *without* previous calcination, and changing the copper nickel oxide into the volatilizer without previous reduction.

HONOURS.

Results : 1st Class, 2 ; 2nd Class, 1 ; Failed, 7 ; Total, 10.

PAPER 1.

There were only 10 candidates, the number last year being 16. Eight were examined in Section II. Iron and Steel, and two in Section III. : Gold, Silver, Lead, &c.

Four only in Section II. obtained sufficient marks to qualify them for admission to the practical examination and the examination in Paper II.

The average standard of attainment of the whole of the candidates was practically the same as last year, but the average of the qualifying marks obtained by those who passed the examination in this paper was much lower, and closely approached the minimum required.

The greatest weakness was shown in the answers to the questions on working drawings and on the microstructure of steel.

None of the candidates had a clear understanding of what is meant by working drawings. They are the drawings which are required by the furnace builder to enable him to erect a furnace, and for a reverberatory furnace usually comprise the following :—

1. Vertical section on the median line.
2. Horizontal section at the datum line and plan of the foundations.
3. Vertical transverse section at the widest part of the bed.
4. Vertical transverse section through the firebox.
5. Front elevation.
6. Side elevation.
7. Plan.

PRACTICAL.

STAGE 1.

Results : 1st Class, 36 ; 2nd Class, 41 ; Failed, 20 ; Total, 97.

The number of papers sent in for this stage was practically the same as last year, there being 97 papers as compared with 99 in 1906. The standard attained by the majority of the candidates was good, while those who failed to pass showed a better knowledge of the subject than those who failed last year. Thirty-six qualified for the First, and forty-one for the Second Class.

In the preparation of the alloys, a number of the candidates were evidently unsuccessful owing to the furnaces at their disposal not giving a sufficiently high temperature for alloying the copper and iron in the copper-zinc-iron alloy, and the copper and nickel in the copper-nickel-zinc alloy, which they had to prepare.

It is possible that in some instances the low temperature may have been due to the furnaces not being prepared for the candidates before the hour of the examination. In all laboratories, especially those in which the draught of the chimneys is not particularly good, the fires should be lighted some time before the commencement of the examination.

In a number of instances in the preparation of the copper-zinc-iron and the copper-zinc-nickel alloys, the results were masses of metal with pieces of iron or nickel distributed through them. Some candidates did not cover their metal with carbon, during the fusion, while a few used coke as a covering, but this cannot be considered satisfactory.

As was also the case last year, many of the samples of metal were not properly cast, and in others the fractured surfaces indicated that the ingredients had not been weighed in the proper proportions before melting.

The preparation of coke from the samples of coal supplied was well done by most of the candidates, but in some cases the temperature at which the coking had been performed was too low. The results of the examination show, however, a general improvement on those of last year.

STAGE 2.

Results : 1st Class, 30 ; 2nd Class, 48 ; Failed, 38 ; Total, 116.

The number of papers sent in showed an increase of 27 on those of last year.

The exercises given were as follows :—

(C) Extract the silver, by a dry method, from the German silver supplied.

(D) Extract the lead from the ore-galena and zinc-blende supplied.

(CC) Extract the silver from the "hard" lead supplied.

(DD) Extract the lead from the "grey" slag supplied.

Exercises C and CC were, as a rule, correctly carried out, although, in the case of the latter, the impurities were not always removed by scorification. Some candidates did not give sufficient attention to the temperature necessary for the cupellation of the lead for silver, and many did not properly clean the beads obtained, thus getting inaccurate results.

Exercises D and DD were performed in a satisfactory manner by about 50 per cent. of the candidates. In some cases insufficient reducing agent was added, resulting in a very low extraction.

Little attention seems to have been paid to the remarks made in the report of last year regarding the necessity for removing all adherent slag or other material from the buttons of lead and silver before weighing. The weight of a button coated with slag cannot possibly give the correct weight of the metal. In future, the marks awarded to candidates who do not return properly cleaned buttons will be few or none.

STAGE 3.

Results: 1st Class, 19 ; 2nd Class, 36 ; Failed, 26 ; Total, 81.

The number of candidates last year was 77 ; on that there is an increase of four in the present.

The work compares most favourably with that of previous years except in the determination of phosphorus in pig-iron. This exercise was attempted by 47 candidates, of whom 22 failed to obtain a single mark. In most of the latter cases the failures would seem to have been chiefly due to defective manipulation. The results ranged from 0·56 to 4·40 per cent.

The determination of lime in dolomite was, as a rule, fairly well done, but several candidates omitted to separate the silica or the iron and alumina, before precipitating the lime, and others had imperfectly ignited the calcium oxalate precipitate.

The determination of gold and silver in copper was also fairly satisfactory, but the best method was not generally selected. The ordinary mixed "wet and dry" method (with the addition of lead acetate to the original solution) should have been used. Scorification could only be successful in experienced hands.

HONOURS.

Results : 1st Class, 2 ; 2nd Class, 1 ; Failed, - ; Total, 3.

The three candidates who were finally qualified for admission to the practical examination in the Metallurgical Laboratory at South Kensington and the examination in Paper II., presented themselves, and all passed.

The practical work in the laboratory was well done and the questions in Paper II. were generally well answered.

Report on the Examinations in Elementary Science of Common Life (Chemistry).

EVENING EXAMINATION.

Results : 1st Class, 151 ; 2nd Class, 130 ; Failed, 81 ; Total, 362.

The students of this subject have acquired a knowledge of a great many facts, but whether from youth and inexperience, or defective teaching, they have not learnt to use these facts intelligently. Hence, many of the statements in their papers are not answers to the questions given, but apparently represent all they know about the subject. Several misconceptions are also very prevalent, e.g., that air from the lungs is carbon dioxide and nothing else, that coal contains coal gas, etc. Another point which requires attention is the unusual amount of irrelevant matter, quite unconnected with the subjects of the several questions, contained in many of the papers.

These are defects which can be eliminated by the use of a little care on the part of the teachers, and some practice in writing answers to questions.

DAY EXAMINATION.

Results : 1st Class, 187 ; 2nd Class, 131 ; Failed, 38 ; Total, 356.

The papers were, on the whole, good, but the chief defect generally noticeable seems to arise from the tendency to keep the facts acquired in compartments, and the inability to apply them in new and unfamiliar cases.

Questions in Section IX. of the Syllabus were answered less frequently than those in the other Sections.

168

GROUP V.—GEOLOGY, MINING, AND PHYSIOGRAPHY.

BOARD OF EXAMINERS.

XII. Geology	J. W. Judd, C.B., LL.D., F.R.S., *Chairman.*
XIII. Mineralogy	Sir J. N. Lockyer, K.C.B., LL.D., F.R.S.
XVIII. Principles of Mining	B. H. Brough, A.R.S.M., F.G.S.
XXIII. Physiography	

Report on the Examination in Geology.

The very marked increase in the number of papers in this subject which was noticed last year has been more than maintained in the present year ; and, what is of still greater importance, the striking improvement in the answers is as conspicuous as it was in 1905. There is clear evidence from a perusal of the papers sent in that both teachers and students are keenly alive to the interest of the subject, and to the value of Geology as a means of education, both in encouraging out-of-door studies and in inculcating habits of observation.

STAGE 1.

Results : 1st Class, 64 ; 2nd Class, 87 ; Failed, 62 ; Total, 213.

It is in this part of the examination that the results are least satisfactory. There is a slight falling off in numbers, and the answers are not quite so good as last year. But the answers are evidently written by pupils with very little literary training and small powers of expression. Teachers have a difficult task in explaining the characters of rocks and minerals to pupils who have no knowledge whatever of the elements of chemistry and physics. But it is evident that effort on the part of the teachers and interest on the part of the students have not been lacking. The percentage of Failures is slightly greater than last year, but the proportion of First to Second Class is about the same.

Q. 1. Explain the terms Volcanic and Plutonic, as applied to Igneous rocks, and give an example of (*a*) a Vitreous Volcanic rock, (*b*) a Clastic Volcanic rock, (*c*) a Basic Plutonic rock, (*d*) an Acid Volcanic rock.

This question is fairly well answered, the distinction between Plutonic and Volcanic rocks being clearly understood. The choice of examples is not, however, equally satisfactory, and many are puzzled to name a Clastic Volcanic rock.

Q. 2. State the chemical composition of (*a*) the Felspars, (*b*) the Hornblendes and Augites. Name rocks in which the following minerals occur as essential constituents :—(*c*) Orthoclase Felspar, (*d*) Labradorite, (*e*) Common Augite, (*f*) Common Hornblende.

While most of the candidates show a knowledge of the composition of the Felspars, far less acquaintance with the composition of the Ferromagnesian Silicates is displayed. The selection of examples of rocks was, on the whole, satisfactory.

Q. 3. Describe the structures found in the following varieties of Limestone :—(*a*) Oolite, (*b*) Chalk, (*c*) Travertine, (*d*) Stalactite, (*e*) Crystalline Limestone.

The chief difficulties which the candidates experience are in describing the structure of Travertine and Crystalline Limestone. The descriptions of Chalk and Oolite are often very good indeed.

Q. 4. Strata of Lias and Oolite, with a dip of about 30°, are found covered unconformably by horizontal Cretaceous Strata. Draw a section to illustrate these relations.

The attempts at section-drawing are often very crude and incomplete. There is in many cases no attempt to indicate the different mineral characters of the beds by the use of conventional shading. It would evidently be of great advantage to the pupils if the teachers made a point of seeing that their own blackboard drawings are not of too sketchy a character, and that the pupils are given some practice in section-drawing. Some candidates show Oolite and Lias beds alternating with one another repeatedly.

Q. 5. Represent, in a diagrammatic section, the escarpment formed in a bed of limestone resting on clay, with an outlier of the limestone outside the escarpment.

The chief error in the drawing of this section is a failure to indicate that the outlier is really part of the same limestone bed that forms the escarpment. In a few cases, where the outlier is represented at a much lower level than the escarpment, a fault is given to account for the position of the beds, but in many cases the necessity for showing the cause of such relations is not appreciated.

Q. 6. Give an account of the formations known as Wealden and Lower Greensand and the nature of the fossils found in each of these formations.

The few answers given to this question exhibit little knowledge of the subject. The contrast between a fresh water and a marine fauna and flora is very rarely brought out in the descriptions.

Q. 7. Describe the internal structure of (a) a Scoria or "Cinder" Cone, (b) a Lava Cone, (c) a Composite Volcanic Cone. Your descriptions should be accompanied by sketches.

While the characters of a Cinder and a Lava Cone are fairly well described and illustrated, many of the candidates fail to realise the distinctive features of a "Composite" Cone.

Q. 8. What are the distinctive characters of the structures known as (a) Stratification, (b) Cleavage, (c) Foliation? In what classes of rocks are these several structures found, and how have they respectively originated?

Stratification and Cleavage are well understood, though some of the candidates make the mistake of saying that the direction of Cleavage is always at right angles to that of Stratification. About Foliation the ideas of the candidates are much more vague, and some even confound Foliation with Folding.

STAGE 2.

Results : 1st Class, 45 ; 2nd Class, 73 ; Failed, 50 ; Total, 168.

There is a marked increase in the number of students in this stage as compared with last year, which is not accompanied by any serious decline in the quality of the answers given to the questions. Some portions of the subject, however, do not appear to have received adequate attention from teachers.

Q. 21. Name the six chemical elements which occur in the greatest abundance in the Earth's Crust, and six which occur most commonly in Meteorites. Point out the differences in the proportions of the several elements in the Crust of the Earth and in Meteorites.

The subject of this question does not appear to have been well taught. Less than half the candidates select the question, and of these the majority are only acquainted with the six most common elements in the Earth's Crust. Many give oxygen and silicon as the predominating elements in Meteorites, failing to refer to iron and nickel ; while very few bring out clearly the unoxidized nature of the materials as the characteristic feature of Meteorites.

Q. 22. Describe the principal species of Mica which occur as rock constituents, indicating the particular class of rocks in which each of these species occurs.

Most of the candidates are acquainted with the chief characters of Muscovite and Biotite, but do not recognize the existence of any other kinds of Mica. Instead of stating the class of rocks in which the several species of Mica occur, they give a list of names of micaceous rocks.

Q. 23. State the mineralogical constitution and the structure of common basalt, and indicate the relations to basalt of the following rocks :—(a) Tachylyte ; (b) Gabbro ; (c) Variolite ; (d) Amygdaloidal Melaphyre.

This question, which is selected by a considerable majority of the candidates, is, on the whole, very well answered. Among the mineral constituents of Basalt, olivine, magnetite and glass are frequently omitted. Very few appear to be acquainted with Variolite, and the nature and mode of origin of Amygdaloids is not well understood.

Q. 24. Give an account of the nature and origin of (a) Slickensides, (b) Crushed and impressed pebbles, (c) Friction Breccias, (d) Mylonites.

Also answered by a majority of the candidates. A considerable amount of knowledge is shown concerning Slickensides and Friction Breccias ; but the statements about Crushed and Impressed Pebbles are evidently guesses, based on the name and its association, while little knowledge is shown concerning Mylonites.

Q. 25. Describe the composition and modes of occurrence of Septaria, and explain their origin.

This question, which is selected by only a few of the candidates, is by no means so well answered as might have been anticipated.

Q. 26. Draw a section showing beds of limestone and slate traversed by reversed step-faults and overlain by false-bedded sands.

Selected by nearly all the candidates, and fairly good drawings are given. In some cases, however, the diagram is incomplete, the most prevalent error being a failure to make clear the unconformable relations of the false-bedded sands to the faulted strata below.

Q. 27. Give an account of the nature and origin of different varieties of Volcanic Bombs. What are Pseudo-volcanic Bombs, and how are they formed ?

That this subject is still imperfectly taught is shown by the circumstance that very few of the candidates attempted an answer to the question. Of this small number scarcely any show any real knowledge concerning the nature and origin of Volcanic Bombs and the objects which simulate them.

Q. 28. Describe the composition, structure and relations of the rock called Troctolite (" Forellenstein ").

The half a dozen candidates who alone selected this question give good answers to it—some of them excellent ones. But it is evident that practical petrological teaching at this advanced stage is not as good as could be desired.

Q. 29. Describe the relations of the Coal Measures in the Midland Coalfields of England to the strata which lie above and below them respectively.

This question when selected is not very satisfactorily answered. Many of the candidates appear to think that a general statement of the carboniferous succession is all that is required. At present there does not seem to be much geological teaching with an economic bearing.

Q. 30. Give an account of the nature and mode of formation of the chief deposits of iron-ore which are of economic importance.

It is evident that the teaching had not covered the subject of this question. The answers are few and very imperfect in almost all cases.

Q. 31. Describe, with the aid of sketches, the jointing of limestone rocks and explain how the operation of quarrying is facilitated by the presence of joints.

The subject of joints had clearly been well taught and as a rule their economic value and importance are recognised. The one point upon which there is some ambiguity is the necessity of bedding planes as well as of two sets of joint planes for the quarrying of cuboidal blocks.

STAGE 3.

Results : 1st Class, 18 ; 2nd Class, 13 ; Failed, 9 ; Total, 40.

In this stage there is not only a marked increase in the number of candidates, but a very considerable improvement is manifested in the character of the answers. Many of the descriptions given of the Radiolarian Ooze are very full and complete, the most serious error (which is only seen in a few cases) is the failure to recognize the siliceous character of the skeletons of Radiolaria. It is a strange circumstance that some among the candidates, who give fair descriptions of the Radiolarian Cherts, argue that the occurrence of these among upraised stratified rocks must be regarded as an evidence *in favour of* the permanence of Ocean-basins. In connection with Question 42, it is a very gratifying circumstance to find that some of the candidates have evidently visited the dry valleys of Yorkshire and Derbyshire, while one of them has evidently made a personal examination of the Mole Valley. The accounts given of the appearances witnessed in these valleys, and of the methods of experimenting with a view to determine the actual courses of the underground streams, are in every way admirable. It is not apparent from the papers whether these geological excursions had been made under the guidance and direction of the teacher, or had been undertaken by the students upon their own initiative. In the Question on Coral Reefs (43) a good deal of ignorance was shown concerning the important part played by Calcareous Algæ ("Nullipores"), Foraminifera, and other organisms in forming reefs. This, however, is probably due to the imperfect accounts given in most of the text-books. Neither in the answers to Question 44 (Spherulites and Lithophyses), nor in that to Question 46 (Peridotites), is a very satisfactory knowledge of Petrology shown. Probably few of the schools are provided with the microscopes and specimens necessary for teaching the subject practically. Side by side with several very weak answers to Question 45 (on a comparison of the Faunas of the Crag and Glacial periods), there were two or three very full and complete ones, showing much knowledge and intelligence on the part of the candidates. On the whole, we consider the results in this stage to compare very favourably with those of last year. They afford evidence of excellent and, we think we may add, enthusiastic teaching, and the way in which out-of-door work has been undertaken is most praiseworthy.

HONOURS.

Results : 1st Class, 5 ; 2nd Class, 6 ; Failed, 1 ; Total, 12.

There is the same number of Honours papers in Geology this year as there was in 1905 ; but the Failures are fewer and the First Classes more numerous. There is a very considerable improvement in the quality of the answers, especially to the Palæontological questions. It was an unfortunate circumstance that one of the candidates, who had to be placed in the Second Class, after giving excellent answers to three questions, stated that he was unable to attempt a fourth for want of time. His failure to complete the paper was undoubtedly owing to the undue amount of time which he had devoted to the three questions answered. There is evidence in nearly all the papers sent in of much careful reading and study, and the papers certainly reach the highest University standard. The greatest weakness is shown in the subjects of Petrology and Stratigraphical Geology. The want of success in Petrology is probably due to insufficient equipment of the schools. The weakness in Stratigraphical

Geology is less easily accounted for, seeing that provision was made for
students residing in different areas by giving a choice for description of
a Palæozoic, a Mesozoic and a Cainozoic formation. It is surprising
to find that few candidates appear to be aware of the fact that Garnets,
of several species, form important constituents of some igneous, as well
as of many metamorphic rocks.

Report on the Examination in Mineralogy.

There is an increase in the number of papers as compared with 1905.
The teaching still seems to be excellent in this subject, the percentage of
failures being still very low, though there is a decline in the number
obtaining a First Class. The only ground of regret is that the subject is not
more generally taught, especially in the mining districts.

STAGE 1.

Results : 1st Class, 19 ; 2nd Class, 24 ; Failed, 5 ; Total, 48.

In the increased number of papers in this stage there are very few
failures, but the number of First Classes is not quite as high as was the
case last year. The great increase is in the number who obtained a
Second-Class.

Q. 1. Draw (a) an Octahedron, (b) a Rhomb-dodecahedron, (c) a combination of these two forms. Name a common mineral which
is found crystallised in each of these forms.

Of the rather more than half the candidates who attempted this
question, the great majority find no difficulty in drawing the Octahedron
and the Rhomb-dodecahedron. But a considerable number experience
difficulty in representing a combination. Without an opportunity of handling
models of crystals, it is to be feared that such difficulty will always be felt.

Q. 2. Name (a) a mineral which exhibits Adamantine lustre, (b) one
showing Vitreous lustre, (c) one with Metallic lustre, (d) one
with Submetallic lustre, (e) one with Earthy lustre. State
what is meant by (f) Dichroism, and (g) Trichroism.

Good answers are the rule as far as the first part of the question is
concerned, and good selections are made of minerals exhibiting different
varieties of lustre. Dichroism and Trichroism are, however, seldom
well understood, confusion with particolour, play of colours, and even
dimorphism being frequent.

Q. 3. Give the names of the minerals which exhibit magnetic properties,
and state how you would test the magnetism of a mineral.

This question is only moderately well answered, and very few of the
candidates recognise the existence of "polarity" in magnetic minerals.

Q. 4. Calcite and Aragonite are said to be "dimorphous forms of the
same chemical compound." Explain what is meant by this
statement.

Most of the candidates appear to understand the term "dimorphism."
The difference of crystal form is generally recognised, though often badly
expressed, but the difference in other physical properties of Calcite and
Aragonite are seldom referred to.

Q. 5. Describe the minerals which are sulphides of iron, lead and zinc,
respectively.

Well answered except in certain cases, where neither Marcasite nor
Pyrrhotite are enumerated among the iron-sulphides.

Q. 6. What is a Pseudomorph? Describe three commonly occurring pseudomorphs, stating how each has been formed.

This question was not so frequently attempted as the last, but those who selected it appear to have understood what pseudomorphism really is, difficulties in definition appearing to be due rather to want of powers of expression, than to want of knowledge of the subject.

Q. 7. What is the crystalline form of Native Sulphur? How and where has this mineral been formed.

Selected by very few candidates. Some of these give excellent answers, but others rather indifferent ones.

Q. 8. From what sources is the metal Tin obtained? State the modes of occurrence of tin-ores.

More than half the candidates attempted this question, and the answers are uniformly good.

Q. 9. What are the chief minerals which occur as "veinstones" in association with ores? Give the chemical composition of each of these veinstones.

Among the few candidates who selected this question there is a strange want of clear perception of the difference between "veinstones" and "ores."

Q. 10. Name the three specimens placed before you; give the chemical composition of each, and the system in which it crystallises. Also make a qualitative blowpipe-analysis of each of the two powdered minerals supplied to you. State your results clearly; if any chemical symbols or abbreviations are used, write them *distinctly.*

Of the minerals given, Actinolite (Hornblende) is seldom recognised. Selenite is generally rightly named and described, and the candidates are equally successful with the Stibnite. The blowpipe work is fairly well done. In the powdered Barium Carbonate, Calcium and Strontium are often found, and the Barium is sometimes missed. Nearly all determine the Cuprite.

STAGE 2.

Results : 1st Class, 6 ; 2nd Class, 16 ; Failed, 2 ; Total, 24.

In this stage the number of candidates is rather less than last year, but the number of failures is equally small. The proportion of First to Second Class is this year rather lower than in 1905. On the whole, the results may be regarded as very satisfactory, there being good evidence of careful teaching.

Q. 21. Draw a commonly occurring crystal of Augite, indicating the forms present in it. How do crystals of Augite and Hornblende generally differ from one another?

Selected by one-third of the candidates, all of whom, with two or three exceptions, give good and correct answers.

Q. 22. What are the chief precautions necessary in taking the specific gravity of a crystal or cut gem by means of a chemical balance?

Also attempted by one-third of the candidates, who give intelligent and fairly good answers.

Q. 23. Describe exactly what is seen when a section cut from a crystal of Hornblende is rotated in a polariscope or polarising microscope, (a) over a single Nicol prism, (b) between crossed Nicols.

The same proportion of the candidates selected this as attempted the two previous questions. The great defect in the answers is a failure to recognise the distinctive appearances when the crystal sections are cut in different directions. It is to be feared that few of the candidates have an opportunity of seeing these appearances for themselves.

Q. 24. In what respects do crystals of Orthoclase, Microcline, and Oligoclase resemble one another, and in what respects do they differ ?

This question was attempted by a much smaller number of candidates. The answers are correct, but unnecessarily verbose. Instead of confining themselves to definite points of resemblance and difference, the candidates write long descriptions of the three minerals.

Q. 25. Describe the three models placed before you, giving a sketch of each to show which axis you place in an upright position. In each case name a mineral that crystallises in the form shown.

Although the answers to this question are *generally* correct, there is one very prevalent error, namely, in the position of the axes in the Tristetrahedron. This mistake is probably due to trusting to drawings instead of handling models of the crystals.

Q. 26. Name the three specimens placed before you ; give the chemical composition of each, and the system in which it crystallises. Also make a qualitative blowpipe-analysis of each of the two powdered minerals supplied to you. Tabulate the results, stating how each was obtained ; if any chemical symbols or abbreviations are used, write them *distinctly.*

This question was only moderately well answered. Of the minerals for determination Zincite is almost always correctly identified, Molybdenite is frequently mistaken for Graphite, while no candidate correctly identified Brucite. The blowpipe-work is much better done, the elements present both in Cobaltite and Pyrohisite being found, though the inferences drawn are sometimes less satisfactory.

Q. 27. Describe the mineral Nepheline—its crystalline form, chemical composition, and physical properties—stating the chief rocks in which it occurs as an Essential Constituent.

About one-fourth of the candidates who attempted this question answer it very well.

Q. 28. Give an account of the Sodium, Potassium, and Ammonium Chlorides occurring as minerals, describing the mode of occurrence and origin of each.

One half of the candidates selected this question, and give good answers, except with respect to the origin and mode of occurrence of Ammonium Chloride—a subject which does not appear to have been properly taught.

Q. 29. Describe the Oxides of Iron (both anhydrous and hydrous) which are used for the extraction of iron.

Well answered in nearly all cases, full and complete accounts of the several minerals being given.

Q. 30. Give an account of the mineral Talc, its composition and properties, the forms which it assumes, and the uses to which it is put. Point out the difference between the commercial and scientific uses of the term " talc."

Very few candidates attempted this question ; only one of them is aware of the difference between the commercial and the scientific use of the term "talc " ; and, generally, the uses of the mineral are entirely ignored.

Q. 31. Describe the chief minerals which constitute ores of Silver.

This was the question in the Technical Series which was most often selected, and it is extremely well answered.

Q. 32. What is known concerning the nature and origin of Jet, Amber, and Emery ? Why are these substances no longer regarded as minerals ?

One fourth of the candidates attempted this question, but many of them appear to be vague in their ideas concerning the modern definition of "minerals." Usually the organic origin of Jet and Amber is recognised as putting them outside the category, but the mixed composition of Emery is not appreciated as leading to its being classed as a rock rather than a mineral. Some are quite unacquainted with the composition of Emery.

STAGE 3.

Results : 1st Class, – ; 2nd Class, 7 ; Failed, 4 ; Total, 11.

The few candidates in this stage show a very fair knowledge of the subject. In 1905, the students taking this stage were of exceptional ability, no less than five being awarded a First Class. This year, while the failures are one more than in 1905, the remaining candidates attain only to a Second Class standard.

The question on "Hardness-Figures" was only well answered by one or two candidates, most of them regarding the Sclerometer as only an instrument for determining comparative hardness. In one case "Exner" was taken as the name of a mineral! In the question on the use of the polariscope, the difference between the effect seen when the rays are parallel and when they are convergent is seldom appreciated. "Schiller" is treated by some as merely a variety of lustre, the fact that reflection takes place only in certain positions being missed. The accounts given of Uralite, Apatite, and the Stassfurt Salts are, on the whole, disappointing, and the economic questions involved in the use of certain materials for incandescent gas-mantles have apparently not been taught. On the other hand, the identification of minerals and their study with the blowpipe have evidently received much attention, and the results are satisfactory.

HONOURS.

Results : 1st Class, 2 ; 2nd Class, – ; Failed, 2 ; Total, 4.

Four candidates presented themselves, two of whom sent in very admirable papers that would be regarded as very creditable indeed in any University Examination, and these are placed in the First Class ; two failed.

Report on the Examination in Principles of Mining.

The following Table gives the number of candidates this year and last:—

Year.	Stage 1.	Stage 2.	Stage 3.	Honours.	Total.
1905	964	849	321	74	2,208
1906	951	738	484	128	2,301

The comparison shews an increase of 93 candidates, there being a larger number of entries in Stage 3 and Honours, but a falling off in Stages 1 and 2.

STAGE 1.

Results : 1st Class, 236 ; 2nd Class, 417 ; Failed, 298 ; Total, 951.

Compared with the previous year the papers in this Stage shew little change. They are up to the average of last year in matter, and shew a distinct improvement in neatness and style. The papers in one parcel are exceptionally bad, and have lowered the general average.

With regard to the questions severally, the following points may be noted :—

BRANCH A.

Q. 1. What is anthracite, and what are its special properties and uses? Where is it mined?

This question is answered very well on the whole. The only faulty portion is in regard to the uses. Even Welsh candidates, familiar with the mining of anthracite, appear to have hazy notions as to the uses of that material, and many refer to it as being largely employed in the Navy. No reference is made to its use in stoves. By a curious mental confusion several candidates describe anthracite as a dangerous explosive.

Q. 2. Describe the operation of shot-firing with an explosive on the "permitted list." (Sketches required.)

In very many cases this question has been carelessly read, and much time wasted in descriptions of the actual drilling and the preparation of the shot hole. Comparatively few candidates lay stress on the essential acts that have to be performed in the interest of safety, such as the careful examination for gas, the watering of any coal dust that may be present, and the use of clay for tamping. In some cases vague ideas as to "permitted explosives" obtain, even ordinary gunpowder being sometimes regarded as an explosive on the permitted list.

Q. 3. What precautions should be taken in withdrawing timber when the roof is bad? (Sketch required.)

This question is answered very well. Candidates appear to be fully aware of the common-sense precautions that have to be taken in withdrawing timber, and generally describe the old dog and chain or one of the modern timber-withdrawing appliances. The Sylvester pulling-jack is as a rule accurately described, but generally inaccurately sketched, the candidates connecting both the withdrawing chain and the chain anchoring the machine to the firm prop to opposite ends of the notched bar. Many of the candidates can have had no practical knowledge of withdrawing timber, as they recommend, after examining, to place the setting of chocks before beginning to draw timber, so that they would use more timber than they save.

Q. 4. Describe the pit-bottom arrangements at some colliery with which you are acquainted. (Sketch required.)

This is a favourite question, and is answered satisfactorily on the whole. There appears to be a good knowledge of the arrangements for convenient and rapid handling of wagons at the pit bottom, and the different practice in various districts is well indicated. Good sketches, however, are few.

Q. 5. Describe the best form of wheels for mine wagons, and the most economical method of greasing their bearings. (Sketches required.)

This also is a favourite question; but much time has been wasted by a discussion of the relative merits of fast and loose wheels. The methods of greasing are well and clearly described. Reference is frequently made to automatic greasers of the corrugated wheel type. In South Wales the candidates generally describe the Rowbottom wheel, loose on the axle with the oil chamber in the body.

Q. 6. In what manner should a cage be attached to the winding rope? (Sketch required.)

The sketches given in answer to this question are poor, but the descriptions are generally accurate. Most of the candidates appear to realise the importance of a good capping to the rope, although in describing the capping many think that the rope is brought through the large link connecting the bridle chains together and then bent back and held in place by two flat cheeks of iron. This idea is to some extent excusable, as in a dusty mine with a well oiled rope the student might easily draw such a conclusion from a casual examination of the end of the rope.

Q. 7. Explain the action of the plunger pump used in mines, and state its advantages over a bucket lift. (Sketch required.)

This question is that least frequently attempted, and is poorly answered. Even from the satisfactory replies, it is obvious that the knowledge was purely theoretical. There appears to be general ignorance as to the difference between the plunger and the bucket lift. It is possible that the lack of good answers is due to the fact that the old type of engine at the surface with the rods going down the shaft has been largely displaced during recent years by the direct-acting steam pump placed underground.

Q. 8. Supposing 40,000 cubic feet of air per minute to be passing through an airway 8 feet 9 inches wide and 7 feet 3 inches high, what is the velocity of the air per second.

This question has elicited a large number of correct answers with the working clearly stated. A few give the quantity of air per second and the velocity per minute, but as a rule the ideas are correct and the mistakes made are in the arithmetic.

Q. 9. Explain the action of any centrifugal fan with which you are acquainted. (Sketch required.)

Most of the answers shew a very good knowledge of the action of a centrifugal fan, but the sketches leave much to be desired.

Q. 10. Describe the safety lamp with which you are most familiar, and state the method of locking adopted. (Sketch required.)

This is a favourite question, and is answered very satisfactorily with good sketches. Of those who attempt the question, about 64 per cent. describe locking by lead rivets, 28 per cent. magnetic locks, and 8 per cent. the old-fashioned screw.

Branch B.

Comparatively few candidates entered in Branch B., many, as in previous years, being coal miners who had obviously wandered unintentionally into this Branch. Their answers are too poor to enable useful deductions to be drawn from them. There are good papers from a few classes in Cornwall and in iron-ore districts.

Q. 11. Give particulars of the nature and extent of any workable mineral deposit (other than coal) with which you are acquainted.

This question when attempted elicited good descriptions of tin-ore and iron-ore deposits.

Q. 12. Describe the operation of shot-firing with an explosive of the nitro-glycerine class. (Sketches required.)

This question is, on the whole, satisfactorily answered.

Q. 13. What precautions should be taken in withdrawing timber when the roof is bad ? (Sketch required.)

The answers are not so good as those to the similar question in Branch A., attention being devoted to bad timber rather than to bad roof.

Q. 14. Describe the operation of filling mineral into a skip in an inclined shaft. (Sketch required.)

This question is answered well, and there are some excellent sketches.

Q. 15. Describe the best form of wheels for mine wagons, and the most economical method of greasing their bearings. (Sketches required.)

178

The answers are poor ; one candidate, for example, states that "the most
economical way of greasing the wheels of a train is to drop candle grease
into the bearings ". The poorness of the answers is probably due to the
fact that lubrication is not carried out so systematically at ore mines as it
is at collieries.

Q. 17. Explain the action of the plunger pump used in mines and state
its advantages over a bucket lift. (Sketch required.)

A metal miner ought to have been able to answer this question without
difficulty, seeing that pumping engines are provided at nearly every metal
mine. It was, however, rarely attempted.

Q. 19. Why are the working places of quarries usually arranged in steps
or terraces ? (Sketch required.)

The answers are very poor. Much ignorance is shewn regarding the
nature of open-workings, and in the sketches the beds are invariably
represented as horizontal.

Q. 20. Give a detailed description of the various kinds of candles used
by miners, stating their relative advantages and disadvantages.

The answers are poor. Candidates do not appear to be acquainted with
the size and weight of candles, and rarely point out the advantages of one
kind over another.

STAGE 2.

Results : 1st Class, 111 ; 2nd Class, 447 ; Failed, 180 ; Total, 738

In this Stage, the papers, as a rule, shew that there have been most
careful training on the part of the teachers and accurate and painstaking
work on the part of the candidates. They are fully up to last year's
standard.

BRANCH A.

Q. 21. Describe fully any deposit of fireclay, oil shale, or stratified ironstone with which you are acquainted.

This question is answered very badly. Those who attempted it described
fireclay, oil shale, *and* ironstone in the most elementary manner. Oil shale
is generally stated to be "clay or mud consolidated by time or pressure."
Every student who has attempted this question uses these actual words
with only the slightest variation, and all appear to be ignorant that the
term "oil shale" should be confined to shale containing sufficient petroleum
to permit its extraction by a process of distillation.

Q. 22. Give particulars of the results obtained in the search for coal
under the secondary rocks of this country.

This question is less frequently attempted than any other, and there is
not a single answer shewing an intelligent appreciation of what the
question means. Many of the candidates shew a lamentable lack of
knowledge of Elementary Geology, and many give theories as to the formation of coal, and the most elementary geological descriptions of
Mesozoic rocks. Only three or four candidates appear to have heard of
the search for coal in the south-eastern counties of England.

Q. 23. Describe one of the coal-cutting machines of the disc type.
(Sketch required.)

The answers to this question are generally good, but with few exceptions
the sketches are poor. The question is a popular one, and the construction
and mode of operation of coal-cutting machines are well understood.
Indeed the answers are better than those to similar questions in previous
years. Either this portion of the syllabus is receiving more attention from
teachers or the machines themselves are coming into more general use.

Q. 24. Describe the method of "spilling" or "forepoling" for driving through loose, watery, or running ground. (Sketch required.)

Except that many candidates describe the method of sinking by spilling instead of driving by spilling, the answers are quite satisfactory. The confusion of spilling in sinking with driving through loose ground extends even to candidates from the north of England where the process has been largely employed, and where the term "spilling" is usual. "Piling" is perhaps a more usual term in other localities. Some excellent descriptions are given by candidates who obviously have had practical experience of the process.

Q. 25. What is meant by the term "self-acting incline"? State the conditions under which such "inclines" may be used, and the precautions to be adopted for the safety of persons employed in connection with them. (Sketch required.)

The answers shew that the working and arrangement of a self-acting incline and the precautions demanded by the Coal Mines Regulation Act are well known. In some cases, however, there are hazy ideas as to the conditions under which such inclines may be used, and very crude ideas as to the gradients.

Q. 26. Describe an aerial ropeway. In what circumstances is this method of haulage most suitable? (Sketch required.)

Very few candidates have heard of an aerial ropeway. Most regard it as meaning an endless rope over the tubs. Some have vague ideas of the system and of the circumstances in which it is most suitable, but there are very few really satisfactory answers.

Q. 27. What are the chief causes of the deterioration of winding ropes, and what remedies are used?

The answers are full and accurate. Corrosion is usually given as the chief cause. It is extraordinary to find in many cases the friction caused by the rope passing over the pulley and the strains and jerks due to starting the load put down as the chief causes of the deterioration of winding ropes. These strains are not nearly so common as often believed. A good winding-engine man starts his cage without the least jerk, and a good engine-wright sees that both ropes are adjusted to the proper length so that no slack rope exists at the moment of lifting. In reference to corrosion, the common idea appears to be that it is entirely due to acid water. Ordinary oxidation is not mentioned and it is assumed that oxidation takes place only in wet shafts, it being forgotten that the rope is continually subjected to the action of rain and of moisture in the atmosphere.

Q. 28. What horse-power is required to lift 18,000 gallons of water per hour from a dip working 1,500 yards distant from the shaft, the average gradient of the road being 1 in 5? The friction in the pipes is to be neglected.

This is a favourite question and the correct answer (81·81 horse power) is frequently given, and the working neatly and systematically shewn. The popular mistake is to neglect to reduce the gallons of water per hour to gallons per minute. It is curious to find candidates taking the trouble to determine the hypotenuse by Euclid's 47th proposition, or by finding the cosine of the angle. One candidate, after doing the latter correctly found the horse power to be 289,332.

Q. 29. What effect has "splitting" the air on the ventilation of mines, and what benefits are to be gained by increasing the size of airways?

This favourite question is answered very intelligently. The chief advantages of splitting the air are realised, and there is a general knowledge of the benefits to be gained by increasing the size of the airways.

Q. 30. Describe the construction of a travelling belt for coal picking and conveying. Explain how the belt is driven, and what arrangements are made for taking up any slack on the belt. (Sketch required.)

All sections of this question are well answered, but in a few cases there is a little confusion as to the terms "conveying" and "slack" used in the question. Some few descriptions are given of the conveyor recently introduced for use underground at the long wall face, and in some instances taking up "slack" is misunderstood to mean small coal.

BRANCH B.

Comparatively few candidates entered in this Branch, and as usual several of these evidently should have entered in Branch A.

Q. 31. Describe any one important deposit of ore, *or* of slate, *or* of rock salt with which you are acquainted.

This question is rarely attempted and there are only a few good descriptions given.

Q. 32. What are "gossans"? How are they formed, and what indications are afforded by them?

There are some good answers to this question from Cornish candidates.

Q. 33. Describe an arrangement for automatically rotating the drill in a compressed-air percussive rock-drill. (Sketch required.)

When attempted, this question is well answered with good descriptions and sketches of the rifled bar and rack mechanism.

Q. 34. Describe the method of "spilling" or "forepoling" for driving through loose, watery, or running ground. (Sketch required.)

This question is well answered, notably by candidates from an iron-mining district.

Q. 35. What is meant by the term "self-acting incline"? State the conditions under which such "inclines" may be used, and the precautions to be adopted for the safety of persons employed in connection with them. (Sketch required.)

This question is well answered by the metal-mining candidates.

Q. 36. Describe an aerial rope-way. In what circumstances is this method of haulage most suitable? (Sketch required.)

One would have expected all the candidates in Branch B to have attempted this question, as this method of transport is in very many cases specially adapted for metal-mining districts. There are, however, but few good answers.

Q. 39. What effect has "splitting" the air on the ventilation of mines, and what benefits are to be gained by increasing the size of air-ways?

This question is not so well answered as it was by candidates in Branch A. Metal-mining candidates appear to be imperfectly acquainted with the practice, and simply refer to air-sollars and brattices used to divert and direct air currents. The virtues of larger air-ways are, however, fully realised.

Q. 40. Describe the construction of any form of gyratory rock- and ore-breaker. (Sketch required.)

This question is rarely attempted. The answers are very poor. The gyratory rock-breaker appears to be but little known, candidates usually describing jaw-crushers only.

STAGE 3.

Results : 1st Class, 88 ; 2nd Class, 178 ; Failed, 218 ; Total, 484.

Compared with 1905 there is a remarkable increase in the number of the candidates, and, although the proportion of first class papers is slightly below that of last year, a general improvement is noticeable. A number of candidates, however, entered who should properly have contented themselves with Stage 2. Such candidates do not realise that in this Stage a high standard of knowledge is expected.

The great majority of the candidates select the coal mining Branch A. The instruments for ascertaining the inclination and direction of bore holes (Q. 41) are well described. Q. 42, on blasting in a dusty mine where gas is sometimes found, is well answered in very many cases, but in others there is a surprising ignorance of the requirements of the Coal Mines Regulation Act. There is remarkable variety in the explosives recommended, the most popular being ammonite, carbonite, saxonite, roburite, westphalite, electronite, and bellite. Failure to read Q. 44 carefully has led to the introduction of superfluous details regarding the Kind-Chaudron method of sinking. Q. 45 is a favourite one, and there are some excellent detailed answers. The answers to Q. 46 shew that recent Continental progress has been carefully followed. In answering Q. 47, on winding with an endless rope, some candidates describe methods of haulage, but there are good descriptions of the Koepe and Craven systems of winding. Q. 48, on electric pumps, is not a very popular one, but when attempted is well answered. The problem (Q. 49) on ventilation is usually accurately solved, the correct answer being 62·36 per cent. Q. 50, on precautions in using electricity, is not answered as fully as might reasonably have been expected. The special rules established under the Coal Mines Regulation Act regarding the use of electricity in mines do not appear to have been adequately studied.

In the metal-mining Branch B. the papers are few but of excellent quality. Q. 52 has elicited some good descriptions of the operation of shot-firing and of the precautions for obviating the evil effects of dust and smoke. There are, however, some very vague ideas as to the composition of blasting gelatine. Q. 55, on working thick beds of ore, is well answered, and some excellent sketches are given. Q. 56, on magnetic separators, is well answered by Cornish candidates, who appear to have studied such machines in operation. In answer to Q. 57 there are some good descriptions of the Whiting hoist.

HONOURS.

Results ; 1st Class, 23 ; 2nd Class, 47 ; Failed, 58 ; Total, 128.

From the fact that there are 54 more candidates in Honours than in the previous year, it is evident that the attention devoted to higher technical education in the mining centres continues to increase. There is a notable absence of candidates from metalliferous mining districts. The majority of candidates appear to have had the practical experience required by the Act of 1903 of students presenting themselves at examinations for colliery managers' certificates. Certainly the candidates generally give clear proof of extensive practical experience ; whilst a gratifying feature in the examination is the fulness and intelligence with which the questions based on recent investigations are answered. Important papers read before the various mining institutes and the reports of H.M. Inspectors of Mines have obviously been diligently studied. Compared with the previous year the general improvement is marked. There are fewer candidates of exceptional brilliancy, but more of average merit ; and even among the unsuccessful there is a complete absence of the utterly unfit.

182

Report on the Examinations in Physiography.

EVENING EXAMINATION.

WHOLE OF STAGE 1.

Results : 1st Class, 163 ; 2nd Class, 139 ; Failed, 49 ; Total, 351.

Although there is a great decrease in the number of candidates sent in for the examination the numbers shew no falling off from the high standard of last year. We find that the percentage of Failures is about the same as in 1905, and the proportion of First to Second Classes similar to that of last year.

It is evident that, under existing conditions, very weak candidates are not now sent in for the examination, as was the case in former years, and that those who sit have been really well taught. Quite a large proportion have obtained very high marks, and a few have even reached the maximum. The answers to the questions in the First Series shew that the experiments and illustrations suggested in the Syllabus have been employed by the teachers and understood by the students. In the replies given to all the questions there is an absence of the kind of language, so prevalent formerly, which indicated that the students had been "crammed" from text books. On the contrary, we now find clear evidence of much intelligent and patient teaching, and the results are given in terms which show that the candidates are not repeating statements learned by rote, but have learned to think for themselves.

The following remarks apply to the way in which the several questions are answered :—

Q. 21. Water, in a Florence flask, is warmed over a spirit lamp, coloured particles being thrown into it from time to time. State what is seen and the explanation of the phenomena.

The answers to this question are, on the whole, very satisfactory. Many candidates give intelligible diagrams, and the descriptions are usually correct, the most prevalent error being a reversal of the direction of the currents at the sides and the middle of the flask. A few candidates misunderstood the object of the question, and describe the downward movement seen on the application of heat to a flask with a narrow tube attached (due to the expansion of the glass before the liquid). Of course, such an effect would be scarcely perceptible in a vessel with so wide a neck as an ordinary Florence flask. On the other hand, some students shew great intelligence in describing everything that is seen, such as the collection and rising, first of air-bubbles and then of steam-bubbles in the liquid as it is warmed.

Q. 22. Explain what happens when a piece of potassium is thrown into a vessel of water.

This question was selected by a much smaller proportion of the candidates than the preceding one, and the answers are, on the whole, less satisfactory. In very few cases is the whole sequence of the phenomena— the rapid movements of the fragment, the assumption of the globular form, the bursting into flame of marked colour, the gradual diminution in size and final disappearance of the fragment, and the alkaline character given to the water—correctly and fully described. The causes of the movement and the production of flame are very seldom well understood.

Q. 23. Describe and illustrate by diagram two different forms of lever.

More than half the candidates selected this question, and the great majority of these give clear and correct answers. The examples are well selected, and intelligently described, and the diagrams are, as a rule, satisfactory.

Q. 24. What chemical element is common to air and water ? State the chief properties of this element.

A very large majority of the candidates selected this question, and, as a rule, the answers are very good. All the principal properties of the gas (oxygen) are fairly described, the chief ones not noticed being the specific gravity, absence of acid characters, and solubility.

Q. 25. On a cloudless evening after a hot summer's day, a mist is found covering the surface of the grass at nightfall. Explain the reason of this.

The answers to this question are not quite so full and satisfactory as could be wished. A great many candidates altogether miss the import- ance of the "hot day" in promoting evaporation, and of the "cloudless evening" in permitting radiation from the grass. In the explanation of what takes place there is the same confusion of ideas and language, though to a less extent, that we have remarked upon in former years with questions on similar subjects. The air is said to be condensed into dew, which is said to be formed by cold air rising and mixing with warm air, and generally the fact of the absorption and separation of water in the air is missed by the candidates.

Q. 26. Explain, by the aid of a diagram, the formation of a spring. Why is spring-water generally "harder" than river-water ?

The answers from some schools include intelligent diagrams showing the mode of formation of springs at the junction of pervious and impervious strata, but in other cases the drawings are very imperfect or quite im- possible. While the cause of the "hardness" of water is very generally understood, there is a great want of appreciation of the fact that river-water is a mixture of the hard spring-water with the "softer" water which, falling as rain, has merely flowed over the surface and has not therefore dissolved much mineral matter. The subject is evidently one in which there is need for more careful and exact teaching.

Q. 27. State what is likely to happen if an empty bottle is tightly corked and let down to a great depth in the sea, and give the reason.

Many of the candidates have taken "tightly corked" as meaning not simply securely corked, but having the cork arranged so that it could not possibly move. Under these conditions they have correctly stated that the bottle would be crushed. As a rule the effects of pressure at great depths in the ocean are very well understood. Some candidates have taken "let down to a great depth " not as being carried down by sounding apparatus, but as being merely thrown overboard, in which case they state correctly that it would float. It is gratifying to find that even where the object of the question has been misunderstood, a considerable amount of intelligence is shown in grappling with it.

Q. 28. Why have volcanic mountains a conical form ? What are volcanic craters and how are they formed ?

As is so often the case with questions connected with volcanic phenomena, the loose and unscientific language so frequently employed, even in text- books, leads to vague and inexact answers. The first part of the question is usually answered much better than the second part, but even in the first part there is a want of clear understanding how materials thrown up from a central point must, in falling and rolling over one another, give rise to the characteristic volcanic cone. The relation of the crater to the explosive action is by no means well grasped.

Q. 29. What is the age of the moon when seen (*a*) in the south-western direction at sunset, (*b*) in the eastern direction at sunset?

This question was selected only by a minority of the candidates. The answer to the first part is more often correct than that to the second part, but there is some confusion of ideas between the actual (invisible) new moon, and the young crescent moon. In some cases diagrams (more or less erroneous) are reproduced to illustrate the phases of the moon, and it is clear that the positions of the moon at different ages had not been learnt by actual observation. The fact that so few selected this very simple question, and that in many cases reliance was placed upon statements made in books, rather than upon observation, is disappointing.

Q. 30. How is the position of a place on the earth's surface defined ? State the datum lines from which the measures are reckoned.

This question was selected by about two-thirds of the candidates, and the answers are almost uniformily correct and clearly expressed.

Q. 31. Describe the principle on which the distance of the moon is determined. Name two observatories chosen to make the measurement, and state why they were chosen.

Very few (less than one-eighth) of the candidates selected this question, but some of these give very excellent answers. In certain cases there is a want of understanding of the principles involved, this being shown by ignorance of the importance of selecting observing stations as far apart as possible. It is clear that this part of the subject has not been so well taught as that dealt with in the preceding question.

Q. 32. Describe, or illustrate by diagram, the arrangement taken up by iron filings if sprinkled on a glass plate under which a bar magnet is placed horizontally in contact.

This was a very favourite question, and is answered by nearly all the candidates. As a rule, the answers are correct, but when a diagram is given, this in many cases is drawn in a very slovenly manner and gives only a very imperfect idea of the real distribution of the lines of force. It would appear that, in many cases, the drawings and descriptions are the result of more or less imperfect recollections of drawings seen in books, rather than of a careful study of what is witnessed when the experiment is actually tried.

STAGE 2.

Results : 1st Class, 169 ; 2nd Class, 144 ; Failed, 118 ; Total, 431.

The number of papers sent in for this Stage also shows a great decline (from 751 for 1905 to 431 for 1906). But it is gratifying to be able to state that the quality of the answers shows a very marked improvement. There is, indeed, an actual increase in the number of First Class awards, in spite of the great diminution in the total number of papers, while the decrease in numbers falls upon the Second Classes and Failures. Not only would there appear to be a withdrawal of imperfectly instructed candidates, but we find evidence of, what has been lacking in former years, thorough teaching, in conformity with the Syllabus for this stage, and in advance of that required for Stage 1. Many of the candidates now give good answers, both to the Astronomical and to the Meteorological and other questions. On the whole, however, the candidates show a greater acquaintance with the Astronomical than with the other questions, and there is still a tendency apparently among teachers to confine their instruction to Astronomical subjects, under the belief that other questions are sufficiently provided for by the teaching in Stage 1.

Q. 41. Explain the conditions which are favourable to the formation of Hoar-frost. What is meant by "Dew-point"?

The answers to this question are, as a rule, very good, and show a great advance in knowledge as compared with the answers given to similar questions in former years. The chief mistakes made are as follows :—

Some candidates describe the formation of dew, and add that when the dew drops are frozen they become hoar-frost. There is a failure to recognize that the minute water particles are frozen while they are being deposited. The *local* cooling of the air near the ground by the contact with good radiators is often missed. Confusion sometimes follows from the idea that radiators in giving off their heat must so warm the air that a layer of *heated* air covers the ground, the importance of the contact of vapour-laden air with the cooled ground being overlooked. Dew-point is generally well explained, but in some cases it is spoken of as a condition of the atmosphere instead of as a definite temperature in relation to the humidity of the atmosphere.

Q. 42. Enumerate the chief instruments employed at a meteorological station, and state the exact nature of the record yielded by each of these instruments.

This question is, on the whole, well answered, and the candidates show an acquaintance with all the chief meteorological instruments. In some cases seismographs and even telescopes are included among the meteorological outfit! and, as a rule, the value and importance of self-registering instruments are not recognized. With these two exceptions, which apply only to a minority of the papers, the answers to this question are full and satisfactory.

Q. 43. How do the observations of Sun-spots help us to determine the period of the Sun's rotation and the direction of its axis in space?

A question very generally selected and usually well answered. The following are the points on which confusion of ideas is sometimes shown. The varying rates of movement in different solar latitudes; and the apparent variation in the path followed by the spots at different periods of the year—this being ascribed to changes in the position of the Sun's axis rather than to the varying position of the Earth. The general nature of the observations, and their results, are on the whole well understood, and the reasoning required in the second portion of the question is given in clear terms.

Q. 44. Explain the use of the Dip Circle. What deductions have been made by comparing annual values for different years?

The answers to this question are by no means so good as those to the preceding ones. The very frequent confusion between "dip" and "declination" is often exhibited, and the necessity of swinging the needle in the plane of the magnetic meridian in order to obtain accurate results is frequently overlooked. While the fact that the dip is not constant appears to be generally recognized, little exact knowledge is shown concerning the nature of the secular variations, or its relation to other phenomena. There are a few full and very good answers, but, as a rule, the information exhibited is below what might fairly be expected from candidates in this Stage.

Q. 45. Give an account of the causes and directions of the Trade Winds.

On the whole, this question is well and correctly answered. In a few cases the direction of the winds is mis-stated, being named (like sea currents) from the point *towards* which they blow instead of from the points *from* which they blow. The causes of the Trade Winds are correctly stated, but while the easterly deflection, due to the earth's rotation, is referred to, few give a clear and full statement that the actual direction is due to the composition of two forces acting in different directions. Good diagrams are very commonly given.

Q. 46. Describe the nature and composition of Globigerina Ooze. Where and under what conditions does this material occur, and how are specimens of it obtained?

The answers to this question, although correct so far as they go, do not exhibit the amount of knowledge that might be fairly expected. There is some confusion about the chemical composition of the Ooze, a number of the candidates describing it as siliceous, while others confuse calcium and calcium carbonate. The microscopic features of the Ooze are by no means fully described, and a want of knowledge concerning the nature of the organisms composing it is prevalent. The statements as to localities and depth in which the Ooze is found are very vague and wanting in precision in most cases. Nearly all candidates appear to be under the impression that our knowledge of the Globigerina Ooze is derived from the study of the minute samples brought up in sounding apparatus, and are not aware that large quantities are obtained by means of the dredge.

Q. 47. What are Isotherms? What are the chief classes of Isotherms employed by meteorologists, and upon what data are they drawn?

The meaning of "Isotherms" is generally understood, but they are treated as being the result of simultaneous temperature observations taken all over the globe. As the special importance of average or maximum and minimum temperatures for different months or different seasons of the year is not usually recognised, the actual data on which Isotherms are drawn by mineralogists is not understood. The candidates evidently depend on the etymology of the word to explain the subject, and have not received specific instruction, which would have enabled them to fully answer the question. Many candidates refer to "Geo-isotherms," and give good definitions of them, but these could scarcely be included among the Isotherms employed by meteorologists.

Q. 48. Give examples of glassy and stony lavas, and describe the products which are formed by the escape of gases from each of these kinds of lava.

Very few attempt to deal with this question, and the answers given are, on the whole, very unsatisfactory. With the exception of the recognition of Obsidian as a volcanic glass, the students appear to have had scarcely any knowledge at all upon the subject. Even Pumice appears to be little understood, and its true nature as the result of the "frothing" of a *glassy* lava is seldom clearly stated. Good teaching on this part of the subject is still greatly needed.

Q. 49. Name the elements of a comet's orbit. What is meant by a periodic comet? What explanation has been given of their periodic nature?

This question proved to be beyond the scope of teaching of most of the candidates. The majority of the small number of candidates who selected the question have scarcely any idea of what is meant by the elements of a comet's orbit. The question of comets has not been wholly neglected in the teaching, for most of the candidates are only able to give clear explanations of the difference between periodic and non-periodic comets, and a considerable amount of matter is introduced which is irrelevant to the question. The theories proposed to account for the total disappearance of comets appear to be quite unknown.

Q. 50. What is meant by "the proper motion" and "motion in the line of sight" of a star? Describe generally how the former has been determined.

This question also proved to be beyond the general astronomical teaching given to the students. "Proper motion" is spoken of as the equivalent of absolute motion, instead of the component at right angles to the line of sight. The relation of the proper motion and the motion in the line of sight to the *actual* motion of the star is very seldom clearly explained. Some candidates confused proper motion with parallax. Photographic methods were seldom referred to, and altogether the portion of the question dealing with the determination of the proper motion of stars was very inadequately treated.

Q. 51. Explain the cause of "nutation"? What effect has nutation on the path of the celestial pole?

Taking into account the rather advanced character of this question, the answers to it must be regarded as fairly satisfactory. The effect of nutation in introducing irregularities in the precessional movement is well stated, and some candidates give an account even of the minor nutations depending upon the revolution of the moon's orbit. The explanations attempted of the causes of nutation are not equally good. There are a few instances of serious error, such as nutation being confounded with precession, and nutation being described as resulting in a wavy movement of the earth in its orbit.

Q. 52. Describe the physical surface features of Jupiter. What deductions have been made from such observations ?

The knowledge of the candidates is generally limited to the belts and the great red spot, other surface details being omitted. The deductions concerning the rapid rotation of the planet are frequently omitted. There are a number of cases in which the markings on Mars and even on Saturn are described as belonging to Jupiter.

STAGE 3.

Results : 1st Class, 2 ; 2nd Class, 6 ; Failed, 13 ; Total, 21.

There is this year a decrease in the number of papers in this Stage. As is usually the case in Stage 3, only a small proportion of the candidates exhibit any extended knowledge of the subject, and the answers to the questions are rarely better than those of Stage 2. The answers to the questions in Terrestrial Physiography (63 and 64) show very small grasp of the subjects treated, and abound with errors that indicate a total want of advanced teaching. The answers to the astronomical questions (65 and 66), except in about half a dozen papers, are very defective and disappointing. In most cases they are based on mere guesses and not upon knowledge.

In addition to the ordinary papers, there are 25 papers sent in from Training Colleges, and these exhibit the faults already referred to in an exaggerated form. In reading these papers from Training Colleges, we are impressed by the conviction that the teaching must be given to these students by persons who have only a superficial and "popular" knowledge of scientific subjects. Minerals are spoken of as chemical elements ; the vessels enclosing the instruments attached to sounding lines are said to be filled with the vapour of mercury ; divers are spoken of as exploring the bed of the deep ocean ; and slow-action thermometers are referred to as appropriate instruments for determining ocean temperatures. These are only a few of the indications of feeble and unsatisfactory teaching which we have noticed in these papers.

DAY EXAMINATION.

There is again a great falling off in the number of papers taken at the Day Examinations, though the quality of the answers is well maintained, and, in some respects, shows marked improvement.

WHOLE OF STAGE 1.

Results : 1st Class, 83 ; 2nd Class, 72 ; Failed, 11 ; Total, 166.

As compared with the results of 1905, we find a considerable improvement in the elementary papers (Whole of Stage 1). The percentage of failures is remarkably low, while one half of the candidates earn sufficient marks to place them in the first class.

Q. 21. With a strong light in a darkened room, I throw the shadow of a red-hot poker on a screen, describe and explain what is seen.

It would appear from the fewness and the poverty of the answers to this question that this experiment had been seldom shown, and scarcely ever adequately explained. Beyond a reference to wavy motion, the descriptions seldom advanced ; the reference to upward currents and to the varying refracting effects on the light passing through air of different densities was never given.

Q. 22. State what happens when sulphuric acid is poured upon iron filings. How would you collect the gas that is formed and examine its properties ?

In the case of this question, it was evident that the candidates had seen or actually performed this, or a similar experiment, and understood it thoroughly. The pneumatic trough was well described or figured, and the chief deficiencies in the answers were the want of reference to the evolution of heat, and in certain cases to some important properties of hydrogen. Occasionally the gas evolved was described as sulphur dioxide.

Q. 23. Define mass. Name units of mass in British and French systems of weights.

This question was very generally selected, and the answers were nearly always correct, so far as the verbal definition went. But some candidates who proceeded to "explain" the meaning of the definition, gave evidence that they did not realise the real distinction between mass and volume. The difference of British and French standards was generally correctly given.

Q. 24. Name the chief properties of hydrogen and describe one method of preparing it.

Although the subject matter of this question had much in common with that of Q. 22, the candidates showed great intelligence and discrimination in their answers. The manner in which the practical details in preparing the gas, such as looking for traces of air by testing small quantities of the gas, showed that the experiment had been witnessed, if not actually performed, by the candidates. The answers were, on the whole, excellent.

Q. 25. After a bright starlight night in winter, that has succeeded a wet day, there is a heavy deposit of hoar frost. Explain the reason of this.

This question was well answered in the case of some schools, but badly answered in others. The chief errors in the defective answers were the want of recognition of the effects of radiation with a clear sky, and the notion that dew is deposited at the outset, and that on a winter's night the freezing of this dew gives rise to the hoar frost.

Q. 26. How do the waters of different rivers differ in respect to hardness? Explain the reasons of these differences.

There were a few excellent answers to this question, but in the majority of cases the candidates showed a want of appreciation of the important part played by calcium carbonate, and of the action of carbon dioxide when dissolved in natural waters.

Q. 27. Explain how animals are able to live at great depths in the ocean, under the pressure of the water, and state what happens when these animals are brought suddenly to the surface.

Very few candidates selected this question, and among these only a small minority showed a knowledge of the pressure conditions in the deep ocean, and of the manner in which external is counterbalanced by internal pressure in the organisms. Many stated that the only difficulty arising in the case of these animals was the want of dissolved oxygen in the water.

Q. 28. Describe the forms of lava-streams, and state what is known of their composition.

The answers to this question were generally very incomplete. Very few candidates showed a knowledge of the fact that lavas are composed of a mixture of silicates, though they write about "acid" and "basic" varieties. Much is written about the varying degrees of fluidity in lavas, but the resulting characters displayed in the form and appearance of the lava streams are not referred to.

Q. 29. State three methods of proving that the earth rotates on its axis. Describe in full one of these methods.

The results in the case of this question were very unequal. In many cases indirect evidence was taken as sufficient, and the diurnal movements of the heavenly bodies were described. In some schools, however,

Foucault's pendulum was well and clearly described, the most prevalent error being a supposition that the pendulum would make a complete revolution in 24 hours in any latitude. The *principle* of the observations was, however, well understood.

Q. 30. Explain why only one side of the moon can be seen from the earth.

Two classes of errors were displayed in the answers to this question, which were by no means good. Some candidates were quite unaware of the fact that only one side of the moon is ever exhibited to the inhabitants of the earth. These contented themselves with the statement that, the moon being a sphere, we can never expect to see more than one half of it *at once*. Those who were aware of the real facts of the case very often stated that the phenomena result from the moon not rotating on its axis at all.

Q. 31. How do observations of Jupiter's satellites help us to determine the distance of the earth from the sun ?

It is evident from the answers given to this question that teachers have directed their attention to the results of actual observation—numerical details being often given—rather than to making the pupils thoroughly understand the principles on which this kind of determination depends. Explanation is evidently required of the cause of the differences between the observed and calculated times of the eclipse, when the earth is in different positions in its orbit.

Q. 32. By what simple means can the law of attraction and repulsion of magnets be demonstrated ?

In the case of this question, complete knowledge of the subject was very generally, almost universally, shown, and the answers were both full and correct. The question was selected by nearly all the candidates.

STAGE 2.

Results : 1st Class, 27 ; 2nd Class, 31 ; Failed, 23 ; Total, 81.

In this stage, although the exceptionally high results attained last year are not maintained, yet they still come up to a very good average, as compared with previous years.

Q. 41. Describe the principal forms of clouds, and explain the differences in their appearance.

The answers to this question were, on the whole, very good. The different varieties of cloud were known (the "nimbus" being most frequently omitted), and a considerable amount of intelligence was shown in explaining the causes of the diversity in appearance.

Q. 42. Describe the chief forms of self-registering meteorological apparatus.

The answers to this question were far less satisfactory. Many candidates quite disregarded the word *self-registering* instruments, and described ordinary barometers and thermometers, while many thought that the sun-dial maximum and minimum thermometers and even seismographs come within the category of self-registering meteorological instruments.

Q. 43. Explain what is seen when sunlight is observed through a spectroscope. How is the spectrum affected when much water vapour is present in the atmosphere ?

While a fair acquaintance with the ordinary solar spectrum is shown in the answers, it is only too evident that few of the candidates have learnt anything about the rain-bands, and that still fewer have ever seen them.

Q. 44. Describe how in London a true north and south line can be determined by means of a horizontal magnetic needle.

Though not often selected, this question when attempted was invariably answered correctly and fully.

Q. 45. Explain the origin and describe the courses of the great surface currents of the Atlantic Ocean.

The "courses" of the various currents were usually correctly described, but their "origin" was not well understood. Convection was often referred to, but usually there was no mention of the action of prevailing winds.

Q. 46. What are the chief materials brought up from the *deepest* portions of the ocean by dredging operations?

Although the word *deepest* is emphasised in the question by means of italics, a large proportion of the candidates ignored it, and described all deep-water deposits, including globigerina ooze. The manganese nodules &c., were referred to by a considerable number, but almost complete ignorance was shown of the existence of scattered boulders, volcanic materials, zeolite crystals, and meteorite débris.

Q. 47. What are Isobars? What observations are required in order to draw them? What deductions can be drawn from their study?

This question was generally well answered. Some candidates neglected any reference to the need of correction in the barometric readings for altitude and temperature. The weakest portions of the answers, however, were the attempts to explain how a study of the Isobars enables meteorologists to deduce conclusions concerning wind force and direction, and, in some cases, of the character of the weather in the immediate future.

Q. 48. State what you know concerning the nature of, and the forms assumed by, the deposits which accumulate round geysers.

In some schools there seems to have been no teaching on this subject, and even the siliceous nature of geyser deposits was unknown. In other schools a fair general knowledge of the *nature* of the deposit was exhibited, but very little was known of the cones, basins, or terraces formed around geyser vents. Comparatively few candidates selected this question.

Q. 49. Describe the motion of Venus round the sun as observed from the earth. What is known about the period of rotation of this planet?

The answers to this question were almost always very incomplete. The portion about which most knowledge was shown was the apparent movement of Venus in the heavens. With regard to the "rotation" period, those candidates who did not confound rotation with revolution evidently gave mere guesses on the subject.

Q. 50. What is the physical cause of the precession of the equinoxes? Describe an experiment to illustrate precession.

Very diverse results were seen in the case of different schools. In some the phenomena and causes of precession had evidently been well explained and illustrated by means of spinning tops or gyroscopes. But in other cases the poverty of the answers indicated that there had been very little exact teaching given.

Q. 51. Describe fully the system adopted for classifying stars according to their brightness.

In only one or two cases were good and full answers given to this question, and we must conclude that in most schools there has been no teaching, worth the name, on the subject. As a rule, there was no reference whatever to exact numerical estimates adopted by astronomers, or to the photometric methods which render such systems of classification possible.

Q. 52. Describe the chief different forms assumed by nebulæ. What is known about their general distribution in the heavens?

While a general fair knowledge of the character of nebulæ, especially the spiral, annular, and irregular forms, was shown, and the fact of their abundance in the region of the Milky Way was usually stated, there was much less exact knowledge of the subject shown than could be wished. The statement of the varieties of type was far from exhaustive—all reference to planetary nebulæ being usually omitted—and of the distinction in the character and distribution of the gaseous and non-gaseous nebulæ nothing seems to be known. Very few candidates, however, selected this question.

GROUP VI.--BIOLOGY, PHYSIOLOGY, AND HYGIENE.

BOARD OF EXAMINERS.

XIV. Human Physiology	Professor L. C. Miall, F.R.S., *Chairman.*
XV. General Biology	Professor J. B. Farmer, D.Sc., M.A., F.R.S.,
XVI. Zoology	F.L.S.
XVII. Botany	Professor F. Gotch, M.A., F.R.S.
XXV. Hygiene	Col. J. L. Notter, M.A., M.D.

Report on the Examinations in Human Physiology.

EVENING EXAMINATION.

The work in the first and second stages of the Evening Examination for 1906 shows a distinct improvement over that of previous years. This is evidenced by the intelligent character of the answers of a considerable number of the candidates, by the increased extent to which candidates realise the bearing of the examination questions, and above all by the small number of those totally inadequate answers which have in previous years been but too common. This improvement may, it is hoped, be considered as showing a corresponding improvement in the efficiency of the teaching and is an indication that teachers have realised the value of supplementing their work by such simple demonstrations as are set forth in the printed syllabus. A further satisfactory feature of the written work of candidates in these stages is the general improvement in writing and in spelling, the defects to which attention was drawn in the report for 1905 being much less conspicuous. As the total number of candidates in the first and second stages was slightly larger than in 1905, it seems improbable that the favourable result is due to the dropping out of the lowest class candidates, and it thus affords grounds for believing that the teaching has become more efficient. If this belief is substantiated it is a very satisfactory feature of the whole work.

STAGE 1.

Results : 1st Class, 337 ; 2nd Class, 482 ; Failed, 225 ; Total, 1044.

The number of candidates who attained the standard necessary for first-class amounted to 32 per cent. as compared with 29 per cent. in 1905, but only 22 per cent. of the candidates failed, whereas 27 per cent. failed in 1905. There are still many instances of incapacity to answer questions which involve the description of some simple structure or physiological process, and examples of this in reference to Questions 1, 3, 4, 6, and 7 will be found in the appended remarks.

Q. 1. What gives the blood its red colour ? Explain the importance of the colouring material. Does the colour ever change, and, if so, under what circumstances ?

This question was answered by nearly all candidates. The colour of a dilute solution of defibrinated blood should be demonstrated, as also its change by taking away the oxygen through any so-called reducing agent, ammonium sulphide, etc. The change of colour is not brought about by CO_2 but by loss of some oxygen.

Q. 2. Draw a diagram representing the general distribution of the vessels through which the blood circulates. Describe the general structure of the finest branches of this circulatory system.

The drawings which illustrated many answers to this question were not satisfactory. A familiar mistake in many instances was the character of the wall of the capillary vessels, which are formed by a single layer of flat cells in no way resembling mucous membrane cells.

Q. 3. What chemical elements are present in albumin, gelatine, starch, fat and sugar? Give an example of the occurrence of each of these in familiar articles of food. What happens if you heat albumin and sugar respectively so as to char them?

The question was well answered except as regards the final part. It was evident that some groups of candidates had observed what happens if albumin and sugar are heated so as to burn them, whilst others had never been shown this simple way of distinguishing between a nitrogenous compound and a carbohydrate.

Q. 4. What is the average rate of breathing per minute. Give the general composition of the atmosphere and of the expired air respectively. How would you show the peculiar characters of the latter?

This question was taken by nearly all candidates and was generally well answered. The composition of the atmosphere and expired air was often given to two places of decimals, which is absurd, and as regards expired air of no value. Such gross mistakes as the inclusion of hydrogen among the atmospheric gases were occasionally made, but were rarer than in previous years.

Q. 5. Describe the general structure, position, and chief functions of (a) the parotid glands, (b) the pancreas, (c) the liver.

The answers do not call for any special comment, being generally satisfactory.

Q. 6. What groups of bones are present in the palm of the hand and the digits? Explain how it is possible for the hand to turn round, and for the thumb to meet each of the finger tips.

The groups of bones were generally given correctly, but the explanation of the movements allowed by the articulations was inadequate in almost all cases. It was not realised that the first carpo-metacarpal articulation is a saddle joint allowing movements round two axes.

Q. 7. What is the temperature of the body as determined (a) by the Fahrenheit thermometer, (b) by the Centigrade thermometer. How does it come about that this temperature remains steady whether we are living in summer heat or in winter cold?

There is still an uncertainty as to the two thermometric scales. Since in the case of the body temperature the first scale is used (clinical thermometers) whilst in physiology the second (Centigrade) scale is always referred to, the comparison between the two must be actually demonstrated by teachers.

Q. 8. Describe the position, general structure and functions of the diaphragm, illustrating your answer by appropriate drawings.

The weak point in most of these answers was the nature of the diagrammatic drawings. Weak candidates still describe the diaphragm as a muscular structure which by contracting moves the ribs and thus causes inspiration. However, the majority of answers were much more intelligent than in previous years.

Q. 9. What nervous structures are concerned in reflex actions? Give two examples of such actions.

This question was satisfactorily answered by very few of the candidate; Simple reflexes which occur in the body should be actually demonstrated; there are a number of respiratory ones, coughing, sneezing, etc., also several in the eye, pupillary contraction to light, blinking, etc.

Q. 10. Make a drawing to show the general position of the various structures contained in the eyeball. What is the blind spot, and why is it blind?

The drawing was in most cases correctly given as regards the chief details. In connection with the reason why the blind spot is blind there seemed to be evidence of want of intelligent thought.

STAGE 2.

Results : 1st Class, 169 ; 2nd Class, 559 ; Failed, 151 ; Total, 879.

The work was a considerable improvement on that of previous years, the percentage of those obtaining the standard of first class was higher, being 19 per cent. as compared with 13 per cent. in 1905, whilst only 17 per cent. of the candidates failed to reach the pass standard ; in 1905 there were 32 per cent. of failures. The inaccuracies to which attention was drawn in the report for 1905 were much less conspicuous, and although there was still evidence of inequality in different batches of papers, the poor batches were not so inadequate as in previous years. The answers were distinctly more intelligent as a whole, and this appears to indicate that the teaching has improved as regards efficiency.

Q. 21. Classify from the point of view of their action the various substances in the digestive secretions which alter the constituents of the food, and indicate the organs which are concerned in their production?

The point of view indicated by the term "classify" was not taken by the great majority of those who attempted this question. No classification into sugar-forming, fat-splitting and proteolytic enzymes was made, although many facts were correctly given.

Q. 22. What is understood by the expression "arterial blood pressure"? In what respects does the blood pressure differ in the various parts of the vascular system? Explain what happens to the arterial blood pressure when the spinal cord is divided.

There is still considerable confusion between the pressure distribution in a system and the varieties of flow of liquid in such a system. By means of a water supply and some elastic tubing the main features of pressure and flow can be demonstrated.

Q. 23. Describe the minute structure of an intestinal villus. What are the nature and course of the channels by which the absorbed constituents of the digested food reach the general systemic circulation?

This question was answered very well by some candidates, and fairly by most of those who attempted it. The weakest feature was the description of the villus.

Q. 24. Describe the situation and structure of the lungs. What is artificial respiration, and how would you employ it the case of an apparently drowned person?

Fairly well answered by most candidates, and, as regards the second part, quite intelligently by the great majority.

Q. 25. By what organs are substances excreted from the body? Briefly explain any alteration in the different excretions resulting from (a) muscular exertion, (b) absence of food, (c) warm surroundings.

The alterations in the different excretions under the various conditions indicated in the latter part of this question were not satisfactorily explained. The question demanded intelligent appreciation of the general principles of metabolism.

Q. 26. Of what substances is a bone composed ? Describe with the aid of appropriate drawings the general and microscopic structure of a long bone, such as the femur.

The answers were on the whole satisfactory, and the drawings were in most cases appropriate and good. The least satisfactory feature of the majority of answers was that concerned with the composition of bone.

Q. 27. Enumerate the cranial nerves, stating in general terms the functions of each. State briefly the part of the central nervous system to which each is attached.

Those who attempted this question answered it fairly well, and in some instances excellently.

Q. 28. Give a short description of the situation, general structure and functions of (a) the crystalline lens, (b) the olfactory mucous membrane, (c) the circumvallate papillæ.

As a whole this question was poorly done, although there were a few very good answers. The functions of the crystalline lens were in many cases wrongly described, and there is still the tendency among weaker candidates to use the two expressions, "refraction" and "reflection" indiscriminately.

STAGE 3.

Results : 1st Class, 10 ; 2nd Class, 21 ; Failed, 27 ; Total, 58.

There were 58 candidates in this Stage, as compared with 42 in 1905. The work of the best candidates showed distinct improvement, and the percentage of failures was slightly smaller than in the previous year. The Stage demands from candidates practical acquaintance with microscopic work (see Question 41), and some knowledge of the simpler operations used in physiological chemistry (see Question 42). The new syllabus for next year will increase these requirements, and, by limiting the candidates to those who have already taken Stage 2, will prevent this Stage being attempted by those who are quite unqualified to enter upon it.

Q. 41. Identify and describe with appropriate drawings the structural features of each of the two specimens A and B provided for microscopic examination.

The specimens were first a section through the cardiac end of the stomach, which, being doubly stained, showed more distinctly the two types of gland cells, and secondly, a section through the spinal cord, so stained as to show very beautifully the nerve cells with their contained granules. The stomach section was poorly described, and in the great majority of cases was not identified. The cord section, although identified, was adequately described by only a few of the candidates.

Q. 42. By what method can dextrose be detected in a solution ? In what respects does dextrose differ from lactose and maltose ? Where is dextrose found in the body, and what is its physiological importance ?

This question was not well answered by any candidate. It would thus appear that the simple methods used in physiological chemistry for the examination of carbohydrates had not been practised by candidates. Attention is drawn to the terms of the new syllabus for 1906, as regards this.

Q. 43. Describe the peculiarities of the circulation in the mammalian fœtus, illustrating your answer by diagrams.

Only attempted by a few candidates, whose answers were either quite good or very poor. The subject is one of very considerable importance, but is apt to be omitted by teachers, and, although given in most text books of even an elementary kind, is apt to be passed over by students as unnecessary.

Q. 44. Enumerate the nitrogenous substances which are found in the urinary excretion. What is known as to their formation in the body?

Fairly well answered by most candidates, and quite well by a few. One of the most definite substances as regards its formation, hippuric acid, was omitted almost universally, although its formation in the kidney from glycocoll and benzoic acid is one of the best known instances of a synthesis occurring within a body tissue.

Q. 45. By what tracts of nerve fibres do nervous impulses pass along the spinal cord from the cerebral hemispheres to the muscles, and from the posterior spinal roots to the cerebral hemispheres?

Those who attempted this question generally gave a fairly correct account of the principal tracts of nerve fibres in the spinal cord. In the new syllabus for this stage it is stated that one question will always deal with the structure and functions of the central nervous system.

Q. 46. Describe the situation, structure, and innervation of the aqueductus cochleæ. What is believed to be the function of its different parts?

Fairly well answered by those who attempted it, and excellently by several candidates. The answers call for no special comment.

HONOURS.

Results : 1st Class, — ; 2nd Class, 1 ; Failed, 1 ; Total, 2.

There were two candidates for Honours, both of whom did sufficiently well to justify a further practical examination. The practical examination was, as in the previous year, divided into three groups, dealing with histology, physiological chemistry, and experimental work respectively ; periods of from three to four hours were assigned to each group. It is desirable to make it clearly known that in order to attempt with any success this part of the examination, candidates must have worked at all these branches of the subject in a physiological laboratory which is equipped for the purpose.

DAY EXAMINATION.

The work of these candidates was very different in the two stages. In Stage 1 it was quite good and showed great improvement on previous years ; the answers were for the most part intelligent and to the point, indicating that for this stage the teaching has become distinctly more efficient. Gross faults of spelling, bad writing, and grammatical errors were comparatively rare. As regards the second stage, the results were disappointing, for, although the number of inadequate answers was decreased as compared with previous years, the number of good papers was less than in 1905. It is probable that candidates for this second stage still trust very largely to getting up by heart certain text-book descriptions, and this was notably the case in the answer to Q. 25. There were, however, some very good consecutive papers among many ones of mediocre value. Thus four consecutive papers all obtained the first class standard. On the other hand, in six consecutive papers and in eight other papers there were respectively two and four failures and only two first class.

STAGE 1.

Results : 1st Class, 77 ; 2nd Class, 53 ; Failed, 31 ; Total, 161.

The work, like that of the similar stage in the Evening Examination, showed a great improvement on previous years. Whereas in 1905, 29 per cent. of the candidates failed to reach the pass standard, only 19 per cent. failed in the 1906 examination. Certain batches of papers were particularly good. Thus, one batch comprised 20 first class, 4 second class, and only 1 failure; whilst another batch comprised 21 first class, 7 second class, and only 2 failures.

Q. 1. Compare the appearances presented when a drop of blood and a drop of milk are spread out on each of two slides and examined under the microscope.

The weak point in the answers to this question was the description of the microscopic characters of milk, which many candidates have evidently not seen for themselves.

Q. 2. Describe the right side of the human heart, stating precisely what blood vessels are connected with it. In what respects does the blood on the left side of the heart differ from that on the right side?

Fairly well answered by most candidates. No reference was made to the circumstance that as heat is given up by the blood to the air in the lungs, the blood on the left side is cooler than that on the right side of the heart.

Q. 3. What substances make milk, bread, butter, potatoes, meat, and eggs valuable articles of food?

This question calls for no special comment. It was generally well answered by the great majority of the candidates.

Q. 4. Describe the situation of the small intestine, naming its various parts. What changes do the food principles undergo in this structure, and by what agents are they produced?

Fairly well answered by most candidates, and excellently by a considerable number.

Q. 5. Explain by appropriate diagrams the mechanism by which we are enabled to take a deep breath. Supposing that a hole existed between the ribs on the left side, how would this affect the mechanism? Explain any effect which you describe.

On the whole, this question was inadequately answered. The real significance of the diaphragm is not generally appreciated; it does not alter the position of the ribs, as many candidates assert. The latter part of the question was answered correctly by only a few candidates.

Q. 6. Describe the general disposition of the various groups of vertebrae, and the mode in which the vertebral column is related (a) to the skull, and (b) to the pelvis.

Satisfactorily answered by the great majority of candidates, who evidently know the main features of this portion of the skeleton. Many of the drawings were quite good.

Q. 7. Make a drawing to show the shape and relative positions of the kidneys, ureters, and bladder. What forms of tissue are present in these structures?

The weak point in the answers to this question is that of the forms of tissue present. Cellular secreting tissue and blood vessels in the kidney, involuntary muscle in the bladder wall, were given by only a few candidates.

Q. 8. Describe the position, general structure, and chief functions of (a) the portal vein, (b) the radius, (c) the parotid glands.

The radius still seems to present a difficulty to candidates, who do not realise its great mechanical importance in connexion with the movements of the hand.

Q. 9. What are the general structure and functions of the skin, and how do these differ from those found in the lining of the mouth?

Satisfactorily answered by the majority of candidates. There is still a tendency to regard the skin as an organ for excreting in large quantity the waste products of the body.

Q. 10. Can any movements be produced in the brainless frog, and if so, by what means? How would such movements differ from those which occur in the normal animal?

As in previous years, this question presents difficulties which few candidates are able to face. The movements are in themselves the same whether the frog is brainless or entire; they differ in the circumstance that in the brainless frog they only occur in response to definite stimulation of the sense organs in the skin, etc.

STAGE 2.

Results : 1st Class, 22 ; 2nd Class, 87 ; Failed, 25 ; Total, 134.

The work of the candidates in this stage was not quite as good as that in previous years. The number of those who failed to attain the pass standard was, however, less than in 1905, amounting to 19 per cent., as compared with 20 per cent. The falling off was due to the smaller number of really good answers, only 16 per cent. attaining a first class standard, as compared with 32 per cent. in 1905. The reason for this is indicated in the detailed remarks.

Q. 21. Enumerate the substances present in blood plasma. What are the differences between blood plasma, serum, and defibrinated blood?

In answering this question very few candidates showed an intelligent appreciation of the fluid part of the circulating blood, that is, blood plasma. Its proteids, salts, and extractives (such as urea, dextrose, and fat) should have been given in the enumeration. The greater part of the allotted marks were given for this part of the question.

Q. 22. Describe the structural and functional peculiarities of a capillary system. What instances are there of one set of blood capillaries being succeeded by a second set, and what must be the effect of such an arrangement?

Fairly well answered by the great majority of candidates, but the bearing of the last part of the question was not appreciated even by good candidates.

The effect of such an arrangement is to cause necessary changes in both the pressure and the rate of flow.

Q. 23. Describe the microscopic character of starch as found in the potato. What is its chemical constitution? By what chemical tests can it be recognised, and to what extent can it be changed into other compounds?

Very well answered by a few candidates, and fairly well by most.

The change of starch into sugar by (a) saliva and (b) boiling with an acid is so easily demonstrated that it should be carried out before students. Trommer's test for sugar should also be demonstrated.

Q. 24. What do you know as to the situation, structure, and functions of the lacteals and the thoracic duct? Describe the character of the fluid which they contain.

On the whole, this question was the most satisfactorily answered of any in the paper. There was some uncertainty as to the precise situation of the thoracic duct, but this was not expected to be given in detail.

Q. 25. What varieties of cartilage are found in the body? Describe the microscopic structure of cartilage and tendon respectively.

The great majority of answers to this question were distinctly inferior, for although the structure of cartilage was known in a general way, that of tendon was wrongly described by most candidates. Many regarded it as muscular, others as composed of elastic tissue, and scarcely any one referred to the well-known "tendon cells."

Q. 26. Describe the structure and course of the uriniferous tubules, illustrating your answer by appropriate diagrams. What is the chief physiological purpose of the various parts of such tubules?

The first part of this question was satisfactorily answered by most candidates. The second part presents some difficulties, and was only seriously attempted by comparatively few. What was desired was the distinction in function between the glomerular and the convoluted portions.

Q. 27. Describe the nervous and muscular structures which are concerned in producing the respiratory enlargement of the thorax. Where is the respiratory centre situated, and what circumstances arouse its activity?

Fairly well answered by most candidates as regards the first part, but the second part was only answered satisfactorily by few. The respiratory centre in the medulla is aroused by two agencies: (1) the increased venosity of the blood which circulates through it, (2) the arrival of nervous impulses up afferent nerves.

Q. 28. Describe the structure of the retina. What parts of this tissue are those which primarily respond to the action of light? Give reasons for any statement which you make on this subject.

Well answered by a considerable number of candidates, and thus calls for no special remarks.

Report on the Examination in General Biology.

SECTION 1 OF STAGE 1.

Results : Passed, 82 ; Failed, 109 ; Total, 191.

The candidates continue to reproduce, often in copious detail, the information supplied in class, but the majority are practically untrained in observation or experiment. Drawing from the object needs to be practised.

Q. 1. How would you illustrate the effect of dissolved food upon the growth of young seedlings? Methods which have actually been tried should be mentioned.

Q. 2. What experiments prove that a green plant draws nourishment from the air?

The methods were described with insufficient detail; in bad cases all the information was supplied by the syllabus. Indications that the candidates were describing experiments which they had actually seen were the exception.

Q. 3. Make an enlarged drawing of some winter bud cut lengthwise; introduce a piece of the stem and an old leaf-base.

The drawings were usually poor. Axillary buds were rarely mentioned or drawn.

Q. 4. Describe the life-history of some moth or butterfly; mention the food plant, and give the dates at which pupation and the emergence of the winged insect may be expected.

Well done on the whole.

Q. 5. Draw in side-view a tadpole in which the limbs are just appearing. The drawing should be about three inches long.

The drawings were very poor. The dorsal and ventral tail-fins were generally omitted.

Q. 6. Describe a bird's wing, and point out some of the arrangements which render it effective in propelling the body through the air.

The muscles of flight were not noticed. The rotation of the quills was often omitted.

Q. 7. Give a short acccount of the foot of a fowl or any other common bird.

No one mentioned the extensor tendons, and few knew of the flexor tendons. The spur was often called a digit. The tissues were often inaccurately described ; thus the foot was said to be "covered with cartilage," or "with bony scales," or "with hard flesh tissue," or to be provided with "muscular pads."

Q. 8. Name some common animal which lives in societies, and show how the members of the same society co-operate for one another's advantage.

The rabbit was often said to raise its tail as a danger-signal.

Q. 9. Point out some of the differences between the eye of a sheep and the eye of a cat.

The form of the pupil of the sheep's eye was unknown to many candidates.

Q. 12. Illustrate by drawings and explanations the structures, peculiarities and uses of the feather supplied.

The candidates showed little power of observation ; for example, the aftershaft was generally left out. On the other hand, the barbules, which could not be seen without a microscope, were carefully described and drawn. Only a few of the drawings were successful.

WHOLE OF STAGE 1.

Results : 1st Class, — ; 2nd Class, 17 ; Failed, 51 ; Total, 68.

Q. 21. Try to account for the fact that the frog has practically no neck and no tail ; show that the statement is not exactly true.

No one attempted to explain why the tail is lost during transformation.

Q. 22. Mention some peculiarities of the stomach and lung of the frog.

The structure of the frog's lung was not described moderately well by any candidate.

Q. 23. Show that a frog's skin is adapted to aid in respiration.

The skin was believed by many candidates to admit air by pores.

Q. 25. Why should the frog's blood be kept moving ? To what extent is the circulation in a frog a double one ? What is the advantage of the double circulation ?

The term "double circulation" was not generally understood.

Q. 27. What proofs can be given that sepals and petals are peculiar kinds of leaves ? Is there any part of a flower which is a peculiar kind of stem ?

Many candidates said that the style or the pistil was a prolongation of the stem.

Q. 32. Illustrate by drawings and explanations the structure and uses of the feather supplied.

The same faults were remarked as in Section 1., Q. 12,

Results : 1st Class, 22 ; 2nd Class, 38 ; Failed, 35 ; Total, 95.

Many of the candidates wrote too much, filling page after page with irrelevant matter.

Q. 41. Show that the circulatory system of the frog agrees in its general plan with the circulatory system of the dogfish, and indicate the chief points in which it differs.

Candidates do not realise that they must themselves point out the resemblances and differences. Many described the circulatory system of each animal in turn, without attempting any comparison.

Q. 42. Describe the iris and pupil of a sheep's eye, and make a diagram to show the relative position of the cornea, lens, and iris.

Most of the candidates cannot have seen a sheep's eye for themselves ; its pupil was usually described as circular.

Q. 45. Describe the air-spaces of a leaf. How can it be made evident that they communicate with the stomates and with one another ?

The second half of this question was answered poorly.

Report on the Examination in Zoology.

STAGE 1.

Results : 1st Class, 8 ; 2nd Class, 40 ; Failed, 10 ; Total, 58.

Q. 1. Give an account of the habitation and mode of life (feeding, loco-motion, self-protection) of a crayfish. How is a crayfish enabled to enlarge notwithstanding its hard skin ?

The candidates showed a fair knowledge of the structure and habits of the crayfish. The most frequent mistakes were :—(1) no mention was made of the vegetable food of the crayfish, (2) the swimmerets were described as of practical importance in swimming, and (3) the carapace was said to split lengthwise during the moult.

Q. 4. What is the use of the cloudy masses attached to opposite sides of the yolk of a fowl's egg ?

The answers were very poor in all cases.

Q. 6. Mention points in which a Hydra resembles a plant, and other points in which it resembles an animal.

The tentacles on the inhalent aperture were repeatedly described as cilia, and the position of the two apertures was often reversed.

Q. 7. Show how a full-grown frog is enabled to live either in air or in water.

The ingestion of solid food as a characteristic of animals was often left out.

Q. 8. Give short definitions of birds, amphibians and fishes.

The answers dwelt too exclusively upon the respiratory adaptations of the frog.

Q. 9. Mention a number of common Arthropods which live in water. Show that they do not all belong to one class.

Little was known about aquatic insects and arachnids.

Q. 10. To what classes do the following animals belong :—snake, eel, slug, bat, pigeon ? Give reasons in each case.

Q. 11. Name the chief divisions of the mollusca, and give examples of each.

Q. 12. What peculiarities distinguish feathers which aid in flight from feathers which merely prevent loss of heat?

These were often answered well.

Results : 1st Class, 4 ; 2nd Class, 16 ; Failed, 19 ; Total, 39.

Q. 21. Show that the lower jaw is differently connected to the skull in a mammal and a bird.

The mobility of the bird's quadrate was not mentioned.

Q. 25. To what divisions of the animal kingdom would you refer the following animals :—

    (a) A segmented animal with lateral appendages and tentacles on the head ; a true coelom surrounds the alimentary canal.

    (b) The body naked and provided with one pair of gills not in communication with the alimentary canal ; the mouth armed with pointed jaws and a rasping tongue.

    (c) Compound animals breathing by perforated pharynx ; the nervous system greatly reduced.

No candidate got all three right ; (a) was often thought to be an arthropod, and (c) a sponge.

Q. 26. Show by a zoological comparision of the equatorial forests of Africa and America that similarity of climate does not necessarily bring with it similarity in the animal life.

There was much theorising, and too few facts were mentioned.

Q. 27. Trace the chief stages in the life history of a stalked barnacle.

Q. 30. Describe the structure, origin and contents of the ephippium of Daphnia.

Such knowledge of the special types as would be gained by actual dissection was rarely to be found.

Results : 1st Class, 3 ; 2nd Class, 4 ; Failed, 3 ; Total, 10.

Q. 32. What structures in the larva of Chironomus indicate that its progenitors breathed air in the larval stage?

No candidate got any marks on this question.

Q. 35. Describe the large intestine of the rabbit, and give illustrative sketches. Discuss the uses of some of the peculiar structures to be remarked in it.

There was little or no indication of such knowledge as would be gained by actual dissection.

Q. 37. Identify the five animals contained in the tube and refer them as nearly as you can to their place in the system. Some are of microscopic size.

The animals were :—Ephyra of Aurelia, recognised by 8 out of 9 candidates ; Ascidian tadpole, by 1 ; Daphnia, by 5 ; Zoaea of crab, by 7 ; Bugula, by 4. It is evident that several candidates did not know by sight all the animals named in the syllabus.

Q. 38. A piece of skin armed with calcareous teeth is supplied. Remove and mount several teeth, and draw them with aid of the microscope.

The calcareous teeth were not removed in the best way, but usually scraped off. Most of the drawings were poor.

HONOURS.

No candidate attempted the Honours paper.

Report on the Examinations in Botany.

EVENING EXAMINATION.

The work on the whole shows an improvement on that of last year, but there is still a noticeable deficiency in definiteness in the answers. Many candidates appear to think that lack of knowledge can be compensated for by diffuse writing ; but it should be remembered that a short clear answer that really grapples with the points raised in the question set will always secure the highest marks. Too little attention is also paid to the desirability of illustrative sketches.

STAGE 1.

Results : 1st Class, 159 ; 2nd Class, 344 ; Failed, 150 ; Total, 653.

Q. 1. Refer the specimen placed before you to its natural order, giving your reasons ; describe it, taking its organs (*when present*) in the following order :—

Stem,	Flower,	Gynaecium,
Leaves,	Calyx,	Fruit,
Inflorescence,	Corolla,	Seed.
Bracts,	Androecium,	

The specimen set was *Scilla nutans*. As might have been expected, it was commonly correctly assigned to Liliaceæ, but the features for the correct description of which care was needed were too often overlooked.

Q. 2. Describe carefully the arrangements of the flowers and fruits of *either* the wallflower *or* the wild mustard. Explain as fully as you can the use to the plant of the arrangement in the example you select.

This question was very often taken, and usually rather badly done. Much time was devoted to description of the *structure* of the flowers and fruit and no attention paid to their *arrangement*. Few appreciated the significance of the terminal grouping of the flowers, or the method by which they are kept well above the fruits.

Q. 3. What is meant by transpiration? What is the use of the process to the plant? How would you ascertain the rate of transpiration in any given instance?

This was sometimes very well done. The experiments had clearly been made by the better candidates. Others, on the contrary, have confused ideas as to what transpiration really is, and they often included a discussion of root pressure in their answers! Experiments were often described which either could not be carried out at all or from which no *quantitative* inferences could be drawn.

Q. 4. Mention plants that possess stipules. Explain in each case the exact use of the stipules to the plant that bears them.

Comparatively few attempted this question with much success. The examples were often rather ill chosen, and the correlation between form and function was generally badly elucidated.

Q. 5. Give an example of (1) a plant that climbs by means of leaf structure, (2) a plant that climbs by means of stem structure. Carefully describe the process of climbing in the case of one of them.

The pea was the commonly selected example, and most candidates contented themselves with the statement that the tendril is a modified *leaf*. This is, of course, incorrect, as these organs are derived from *leaflets*. The actual *process* of climbing was seldom touched on in any detail. Some candidates selected the hop, but they scarcely ever mentioned the *hairs* on the stems of this plant.

Q. 6. What do you understand by phyllotaxis? Illustrate your answer by four examples which you have specially studied.

This question was not well done. Book illustrations were given instead of names and diagrams of plants that had really been studied.

Q. 7. To what structures is the green colour of a plant due? Explain what happens to it when you allow a green leaf to soak for some time in alcohol.

Often well done, but others had evidently never observed the action of alcohol on leaves.

Q. 8. Describe three fruits that are adapted for dispersal by animals, and explain the nature of the adaptation in each case.

This question was commonly done well. But the examples were frequently not well chosen so as to illustrate *different modes* of dispersal.

Q. 9. What is meant by the vernation and the venation of a leaf? Illustrate your answer by a description of two examples.

This was often badly answered. The illustrations were very imperfectly described.

Q. 10. In what way do monocotyledons differ from dicotyledons? Give three examples of each group.

This was commonly done well, but too many still adhere to the error that dicotyledons always possess exalbuminous seeds.

Q. 11. Explain the effect of pruning a shrub or tree, taking any definite example you may select as an illustration.

This was seldom attempted, and whilst a few good answers were sent in, the majority were almost worthless. The *effect* was imperfectly known, and the *reason* for the effect was usually merely guessed at.

STAGE 2.

Results : 1st Class, 65 ; 2nd Class, 200 ; Failed, 145 ; Total, 410.

Q. 21. Refer the specimen placed before you to its natural order, giving your reasons, and describe it fully, taking its organs (*when present*) in the following order :—

Stem,	Flower,	Gynæcium,
Leaves,	Calyx,	Fruit,
Inflorescence,	Corolla,	Seed.
Bracts,	Andrœcium,	

The specimen set was Iris xiphioides. It was generally fairly well done, although some candidates mistook the petaloid styles for petals.

Q. 22. Give an account of the gametophyte of the pine and compare it with that of the fern.

This was often attempted, and was very unevenly done. Some of the answers were extremely good, others hopelessly bad. Some confusion exists as to the limits of the generations. The latter part of the question was almost always badly done.

Q. 23. Explain the nature and mode of the origin of " knots " and of "silver grain " in timber.

Comparatively few candidates attempted this question, but it was sometimes very well done.

Q. 24. How would you make a pure culture of Mucor or Eurotium ? State *fully* the precautions you would take.

Many worthless answers were sent in. The real nature and use of the precautions were often quite ignored. Hardly anyone seemed to know what a pure culture really is.

Q. 25. Describe the flowers of the willow, and explain how pollination is effected in these plants.

Most of those who attempted this question confined themselves chiefly to the inflorescence. Too many stated that pollination is effected by the wind, completely ignoring the nectaries and the other entomophilous characters of the flowers. Very few seemed to have observed the plant when actually in flower.

Q. 26. What conditions are essential in order that a green leaf may form starch ? Give an account of the experimental evidence on which your answer is based.

This question was often fairly well done, but many of the answers were incomplete—thus some omitted to mention the need of carbon dioxide.

Q. 27. Mention three carnivorous plants that occur in Britain, and describe the structures that are adapted for catching or trapping the animals in each case.

Nepenthes was often given as an example, although it is not a British plant. Arum and Lathræa are not carnivorous plants.

Q. 28. Describe in the case of any seedling you may select how the structure characteristic of the root changes into that met with in the young stem. What do you think is the use of the change to the plant ?

Seldom attempted and almost always badly done.

Q. 29. Describe and compare the fruits of the rose, fig, strawberry, and mulberry.

This was often very carelessly done, and the *comparison* was, as usual, a weak point in the majority of answers.

Q. 30. What is meant by sclerenchyma ? Give some account of its mode of occurrence in stems, and show how it is of use to the plant.

Very rudimentary knowledge was shown as to the nature of sclerenchyma. It was often confounded with water-conducting tissue. The mechanism of strengthening tissue as a whole seems not to be appreciated.

Q. 31. Give an account of the modes of *vegetative* reproduction met with in a fern, a snowdrop, and a bramble.

Sometimes this was well answered, but most of those who attempted the question showed very little real knowledge of the main facts.

STAGE 3.

Results : 1st Class, 11 ; 2nd Class, 21 ; Failed, 12 ; Total, 44.

The work was on the whole fair, but the conclusions to be drawn from experiments, *e.g.*, on geotropic phenomena, were in most cases not well reasoned, and they often rested on too narrow a base. Many answers failed to get high marks on account of inaccuracies due to mere guessing.

Q. 41. Identify the specimen provided, and comment on its morphology.

The specimen was Viburnum Lantana, and it was often correctly known ; a common error lay in referring it to Umbelliferæ, a mistake betraying gross ignorance of natural orders. Very few really good accounts were given of the morphology.

Q. 42. Give an account of the principal modifications in floral structures encountered in the Scitamineæ *or* in the Myrtaceæ.

This question was frequently attempted. Nearly all candidates showed some knowledge of the Scitamineæ as exemplified by Canna, but few were really able to deal with the order as a whole.

Q. 43. Discuss the ecological conditions that may determine the formation of the " Heather-moor," and give some account of the composition of the flora of such moor.

Many candidates attempted this question, but the answers were in many cases almost worthless. Much guessing was obvious, and few had any real acquaintance with the real conditions that determine plant formations.

Q. 44. What are the chief reserve-substances of food stored in the seeds of plants ? State how they may be severally identified.

This was often rather well done, and candidates showed that they had really obtained first-hand knowledge of the reactions involved.

Q. 45. Write a life history of *either* Erysiphe *or* of Tilletia, and include in your answer a discussion of the parasitic habit of the form you select.

This was very seldom well done. The latter part of the question was hardly ever properly attempted.

Q. 46. Write a short account of the Conjugatæ, as illustrated by British genera.

Often attempted with fair success.

Q. 47. What is meant by geotropism ? Write a careful account of any three experiments you may have performed in order to investigate the geotropic phenomena in roots.

The descriptions of experiments were often fairly done, but the experiments themselves were seldom well chosen. It would appear that the subject of irritability is not well dealt with ; it is one that students commonly find difficult. Thus the *stimulus* given by gravity was frequently confounded with the geotropic *response*. Again the special case of taproots was almost exclusively referred to, and hence the evidence derived from a study of shoots and lateral roots was ignored. A more careful study of these phenomena is most important, since they offer so excellent an opportunity for enabling the student to obtain a real insight into the nature of irritability in general.

Q. 48. Give an account of the structure of the fossil known as Lyginodendron, and include in your answer a discussion of its affinities with existing groups of plants.

This question was seldom attempted with any great measure of success.

HONOURS.

Results : 1st Class, — ; 2nd Class, 3 ; Failed, 9 ; Total, 12.

Some of the work sent in was of considerable merit, but the answers to certain questions betrayed great ignorance on matters of general biological importance. Thus no candidates were able to discuss adequately the question of "acquired characters"; very few realised the real difficulties encountered in explaining root-pressure, and no one attempted to deal with the symbiotic associations as illustrated by Bacteria. There seems evidence to show that students have attended certain courses of advanced lectures, but have done little work independently of these.

DAY EXAMINATION.

The general average of the work in Stages 1 and 2 was fairly good, but the number of really first-class papers, especially in Stage 2, was smaller than might have been expected. In this respect there was no difference between Training College and other students.

Many candidates seem to think that they will be judged by the quantity, rather than by the quality, of what they write, and the instruction that the answers are to be strictly confined to the questions proposed is, in very many cases, completely ignored.

STAGE 1.

Results : 1st Class, 72 ; 2nd Class, 47 ; Failed, 24 ; Total, 143.

Q. 1. Refer the specimen placed before you to its natural order, giving your reasons ; describe it, taking its organs (*when present*) in the following order :—

Stem	Flower	Gynæcium
Leaf	Calyx	Fruit
Inflorescence	Corolla	Seed
Bracts	Andrœcium	

The specimen set was *Campanula glomerata*.

The description was in some cases very good, in others extremely careless. Some candidates evidently had decided from memory what they thought they ought to see, and thus committed the most absurd errors.

Q. 2. Mention two plants that possess bulbs. Describe and explain carefully the structure of the bulb of one of them.

This question was nearly always attempted, but beyond text-book generalities, real knowledge was shown only by a few candidates. The examples commonly selected were the onion and hyacinth, but the real nature of the scales (*i.e.*, persistent bases of foliage leaves) seemed to be known only to very few. This implies that the objects themselves had at best been very imperfectly studied.

Q. 3. Give some account of the modes of climbing to be met with in British climbing plants.

Foreign examples were often selected, and they were not often well chosen to illustrate the *various* methods of climbing.

Q. 4. What are "sleep movements"? Describe fully these movements in any example you may have studied.

This question was very seldom attempted. It is difficult to understand why so widespread a phenomenon should have been so little studied.

Q. 5. Describe, and, as far as you can, explain the appearance of a seedling that has been grown in continuous darkness.

This was often intelligently answered, and candidates who had obviously made observations on actual plants secured high marks.

Q. 6. Write a short account of seed distribution in either the Compositæ or Rosaceæ.

The answers were rather meagre, very few examples being known. Fruits illustrate so well the diversity ultimately reached by structures originally similar, that they should receive more attention. Such collections are easy to make and are very instructive.

Q. 7. What is meant by the terms symbiosis, saprophyte, parasite? Mention and *briefly* describe *one* example of each.

Seldom attempted, but a few very good answers.

Q. 8. Explain what is meant by the torus. Compare the torus in the Ranunculaceæ and the Umbelliferæ.

This question was seldom attempted, and was never well done. The structure of an epigynous flower seems not yet to be understood.

Q. 9. Describe, and state the functions of the cotyledons in any *three* of the following plants :—pea, buckwheat, castor oil plant, mustard.

This question was badly done by those who attempted it.

Q. 10. Describe a twig of *either* hawthorn *or* furze (*ulex*), and explain the morphological nature of the thorns in the example you select.

The answers were very uneven, some good, others very poor.

Q. 11. How is the plant enabled to take in the gases present in the atmosphere? Which of these gases are useful to the plant, and what is the nature of the use in each case?

Some very wild answers were returned. Phosphorus and carbon were even stated to be gases by some candidates. A few, however, showed real knowledge.

STAGE 2.

Results : 1st Class, 16 ; 2nd Class, 61 ; Failed, 9 ; Total, 86.

Q. 21. Refer the specimen placed before you to its natural order, giving your reasons ; describe it, taking its organs (*when present*) in the following order :—

Stem	Flower	Gynæcium
Leaf	Calyx	Fruit
Inflorescence	Corolla	Seed
Bracts	Andrœcium	

The specimen set was *Lupinus polyphyllus.*

It was often very well described.

Q. 22. When a leafy shoot is gathered it soon begins to wither. Explain as fully as you can the nature of the events that lead to "withering."

This question was very unevenly answered. The principal source of mistakes lay in confusing turgidity of the cells with nutrition, and with photosynthesis.

Q. 23. Describe fully the flowers of the campanula, and show how the seeds of this plant are dispersed.

Few appreciated the mechanism for ensuring cross pollination, and no one explained correctly how the seeds are dispersed.

Q. 24. What is bark? Briefly describe the mode of its formation in a stem.

Some good answers were sent in, but the greater number of those who attempted the question seemed to possess little knowledge beyond that conveyed in a black-board demonstration.

Q. 25. Describe the structure of a root as seen in longitudinal sections and indicate the nature of the functions of the different parts.

With some few exceptions, this question was badly answered. Many even omitted all reference to the root-cap.

Q. 26. Describe the reproductive organs of Pellia, and compare them with those of a moss.

This question was often rather well done.

Q. 27. Describe the flowers of either the oak *or* of the beech, and explain the structure of the "fruit" in the example you select.

Seldom attempted, but well done by a few.

Q. 28. Explain fully why it is that plants commonly thrive better in a soil that has been deeply dug or trenched than in a soil that has remained undisturbed for several years.

This question was well answered by most of those who attempted it. The significance of aeration and drainage was well appreciated.

Q. 29. What are the points of essential similarity and difference between the mode of nutrition of a green plant and of a fungus?

Many candidates returned good answers, but others were extraordinarily bad. Some seemed to think that starch is the most important food of fungi, others went so far as to assert that the fungus has to make starch out of the materials it obtains from its host!

Q. 30. What is meant by sclerenchyma? Give some account of its occurrence in stems and show how it is useful to the plant.

This question was very badly answered by nearly all who attempted it. It is clear that the candidates had never really observed the structures that can easily be seen, even by the aid of a low power of the microscope, in the stem of an ordinary herbaceous plant.

Q. 31. Describe fully the gametophyte of Pinus, and show in what points it (a) resembles, (b) differs from, that of a fern.

Very seldom well done. The comparison was nearly always very badly drawn.

Report on the Examinations in Hygiene.

EVENING EXAMINATION.

STAGE 1.

Results : 1st Class, 475 ; 2nd Class, 722 ; Failed, 98 ; Total, 1,295.

For the first part of the examination 1295 papers were sent in ; this is a decrease on the number who presented themselves for examination last year. Of these students the numbers who were placed in the First Class were 36 per cent. ; of those entitled to a Second Class, 55 per cent. ; and those who failed to secure a minimum of marks were 7 per cent.

The general results of this examination may be said to be very good. Some of the papers were excellent, and the whole standard of the examination is distinctly improved. There appears to be a better organized system of instruction, and the answers to the several questions show intelligence on the part of the students, who appear to take an interest in the subject. The answers, too, are not given so constantly in a set form, but appear more frequently in the words of the students themselves; there is a marked improvement in this respect. There is also an absence of teaching by rôte, which was very prevalent in the earlier examinations in this subject. The failures were largely due to non-compliance with the rules, which, perhaps foreign students had some difficulty with. The worked papers in Stage 1 showed a distinct advance this year.

ELEMENTARY HUMAN PHYSIOLOGY.

Q. (a) Write a short account of the structure and functions of the skin.

This question was a very popular one, and, as a rule, was well answered, some of the replies being excellently illustrated.

Q. (b) Where are the salivary glands situated? What action has the juice secreted by these glands upon food taken into the mouth?

A considerable number tried this question and usually answered it well

Q. (c) Explain the following terms:—Serum, cartilage, peptone, chyme.

This was not a very favourite question, but those who attempted it had a competent grasp of the requisite knowledge.

Q. (d) What are the changes which take place during respiration (1) in the air breathed, (2) in the blood?

The replies to this question were fairly good, some excellent answers being received.

HYGIENE.

Q. 1. Name three common sources of drinking water, and, in respect of each, point out the probable risks of pollution, and how they can be best prevented.

This question seemed to appeal to many, and the majority of the answers given were distinctly good.

Q. 2. What rules and precautions should be observed in the storage of water in a house? Explain the chief risks attaching to this practice.

Few questions were better answered than this; it was attempted by the greater number of candidates, many of whom submitted sensible answers.

Q. 3. What is carbon dioxide? What are its sources, and what part does it play as a sign of good or bad ventilation?

This again was a favourite question, and usually well done.

Q. 4. What is the use of food? Explain the chief changes which a piece of bread undergoes during the act of digestion.

On the whole this was not so well done. Many students gave a good explanation of the uses of food, but it was curious to note how many failed to give an intelligible account of the digestion of such a common article of diet as bread.

Q. 5. What diseases are occasionally caused by milk, and how should milk be collected, stored, and distributed?

But a small number attempted this question, but those who did gave satisfactory replies. The importance of the sanitary problems connected with the milk trade is so great that the attention of teachers should be directed to the emphasizing of the essential facts and principles to all students.

O

Q. 6. What are the advantages of woollen clothing? Explain its action in preventing chill; explain also the more important points to be borne in mind in making clothing of any kind.

A very popular question. Nearly every candidate tried it, and, as a rule, answered it well.

Q. 7. How should an ash-pit be constructed, and why is it likely to become a nuisance?

This was another favourite question, and was wonderfully well done.

Q. 8. What is the use of traps, as met with in a drain-system? Where are these contrivances usually placed, and what are the common causes of their being rendered useless?

Taken as a whole, this was not a popular subject. Some of the replies were very good indeed, but it was curious to note how few had intelligent ideas as to how drain traps are rendered useless.

Q. 9. A child falls out of a swing, cutting the forehead badly, with much bleeding, and becomes unconscious; what would you do?

Considering the simplicity and practical nature of this question, the generality of replies to it were disappointing; a considerable number of students failed to grasp the value of direct pressure so applied as to check bleeding.

STAGE 2.

Results : 1st Class, 262 ; 2nd Class, 791 ; Failed, 125 ; Total, 1,178.

For this part of the examination 1,178 papers were sent in ; this also is a decrease on the number for last year. Though in the main satisfactory, they were not quite so good as those sent in for the more elementary paper. Indeed, some of the answers suggested that the candidates should have attempted Stage 1 rather than Stage 2.

Of the 1,178 papers examined, 22 per cent. were placed in the First Class, 67 per cent. in the Second Class ; and 10 per cent. failed. Generally, the papers in this stage showed a decided advance over previous years in the way the questions were answered, and point to a more organized system of teaching adopted by the teachers.

ELEMENTARY HUMAN PHYSIOLOGY.

Q. (a) What is meant by inspiration and expiration? How are they brought about, and what changes takes place in the air and blood as the result of them?

Very few candidates failed to answer this question, and many of them gave excellent accounts of the physiology of respiration.

Q. (b) Give a short account of the teeth, noting their number, names, situation and general structure.

This was a very favourite question, many of the replies being excellently illustrated.

Q. (c) Mention the changes which a piece of bread and a piece of cheese would respectively undergo in the mouth and stomach.

The replies to this question were somewhat unequal ; a considerable number of candidates failed to appreciate that bread is mainly starch, and cheese mainly proteid, and that the former would undergo essentially different changes in the mouth to what the latter would.

Q. (d) Give a brief description of the pancreas, and explain its function.

This question was not a very popular one, but when attempted it elicited good replies,

HYGIENE.

Q. 21. What quantity of water per head of population is required in a non-manufacturing town, and how is it divided among the various uses?

It was very noticeable how few tried to answer this question; when attempted the replies were good and accurate.

Q. 22. What methods would you adopt for the purification of a domestic water supply? Discuss the value of any three filtering media in general use.

This was quite the most popular question in the paper and productive of some really good answers.

Q. 23. Mention the chief factors concerned in the natural ventilation of a dwelling-room. Explain their effect.

Although attempted by the greater number of candidates, it cannot be said that the answers were good. Many seemed not to have read the question carefully, and in place of mentioning and discussing the effects of the chief factors concerned in natural ventilation, such as action of winds, variations and weights of masses of air, the effects of temperature, etc., they gave long descriptions of appliances for ventilation.

Q. 24. What is meant by " relative humidity of the atmosphere "? State the figures for an average condition. Describe two ways of ascertaining the degree of relative humidity.

This question was wonderfully well answered, and considering the general difficulty of the subject many of the replies were distinctly good.

Q. 25. What are the constituents and the variations in their proportions in cow's milk and in fresh butter? In what respect does the latter differ from margarine?

A comparatively small number tried this question, but those who did gave very satisfactory answers.

Q. 26. What are the important points as regards the material, position, size and course of a soil-pipe? Give your reasons for considering these details important.

Considering its practical nature, the question was badly answered, as a rule. The greater number appeared to be ignorant of what is meant by a soil-pipe, and described a drain ; it is apparent that elementary instruction on a very simple and common sanitary appliance in every house has been neglected in many schools.

Q. 27. Describe in detail the methods of applying (a) the smoke test ; (b) the water test ; (c) any "scent" tests you may be acquainted with, to a system of house drainage.

In contrast to the last question, this was remarkably well answered, many candidates having evidently a practical acquaintance with the methods they were asked to describe.

Q 28. Explain the physical modes in which heat is propagated. How are these modes of propagation utilised in warming buildings, and what are their several advantages?

This was a very popular question and was answered remarkably well.

Q. 29. Name the periods during which children from infected houses should be excluded from schools in case of the following diseases : (a) small pox ; (b) measles ; (c) diphtheria. What is meant by the incubation period?

The second part of this question was nearly always well answered, but in attempting to answer the first part the greater number failed to distinguish between the period of infectivity of an actual case of one of the named diseases and the period of incubation. Occasionally some of the answers were extremely good, being lucid and showing a remarkable grasp of the facts.

STAGE 3.

Results : 1st Class, 20 ; 2nd Class, 66 ; Failed, 118 ; Total, 204.

For this part of the examination 204 papers were sent in. Of these 9 per cent. were placed in the First Class, 32 per cent. in the Second Class, and 57 per cent. failed. There was not the same improvement in the papers this year as has been remarked in those sent in for the more elementary part of this examination. It is very evident that many students presented themselves for this part of the examination who could not have taken a First Class in Stage 2, and it is doubtful even if they would have passed in that stage. A higher standard of knowledge is required to pass in this stage, and no student should attempt this examination before he has obtained a First Class in Stage 2, and increased his knowledge by a study of the more advanced subjects noted in the syllabus.

ELEMENTARY HUMAN PHYSIOLOGY.

Q. (a). What is meant by inspiration and expiration? How are they brought about, and what changes take place in the air and blood as the result of them?

On the whole this question was not well answered. The changes which take place in the blood were in many cases not referred to.

Q. (b). Give a short account of the teeth, noting their number, names, situation and general structure.

This was a favourite question and generally fairly well answered. Contrary to what is usually the case, there were comparatively few good sketches.

Q. (c). Mention the changes which a piece of bread and a piece of cheese would respectively undergo in the mouth and stomach.

This was not a favourite question. It was indifferently answered by those who attempted it.

Q. (d). Give a brief description of the pancreas, and explain its function.

Comparatively few students attempted this question. Some really good answers were given, but there were many who failed to give a description or explain the function of the pancreas. On the whole the question was not well answered.

HYGIENE.

Q. 41. The water supplies from three districts are derived respectively (a) from moorland ; (b) from a shaft sunk in mountain limestone ; (c) from a stream supplied by springs from the chalk. State the probable characteristics of these several waters, and shortly epitomise in respect of each the special hygienic precautions to be borne in mind.

Nearly every student attempted this question. Some of the answers were excellent. A large number, however, did not distinguish between the "temporary" and "permanent" hardness of water, and attributed the hardness in water in the mountain limestone to salts of lime which could be removed by boiling, etc. On the whole, the question was not well answered.

Q. 42. Upon what conditions does the danger of contamination of drinking water by lead depend, and how can it be minimised? State how you would make an estimation of lead in a water sample.

This was a favourite question, but the replies were very unequal. All the students were alive to the danger of contamination of drinking water by lead, but comparatively few gave complete answers as to how to minimise the danger. The use of lead pipes is the real source of danger in the large majority of cases. The last part of the question was very indifferently answered.

Q. 43. Whence is the energy for the work of the human body obtained?
Explain this in reference to the theory of the nutritive value of
food stuffs. Is all the energy expended in visible work; if not,
what becomes of it?

This question was attempted by the majority of the students; the first
and last parts were fairly well answered, but there were few who attempted
to connect the energy available for work with the nutritive value of food
stuffs.

Q. 44. What is the alcoholic strength of whisky and that of beer? How
are these fermented drinks prepared, and what are the usual
adulterations (if any)?

Comparatively few attempted this question, and of these very few had
any knowledge of the alcoholic strength of whisky or malt liquors. As a
a rule, the majority were familiar with the ordinary preparation of fermented
drinks; they were, however, prepared to accept a large list of articles used
as adulterants.

Q. 45. Describe two unhealthy subsoils. Explain why they are undesir-
able as sites for dwellings, and how they may be improved.

This question was attempted by almost every student and was very
indifferently answered. Comparatively few named any subsoil, and the
large majority limited their answers to the construction of buildings.
Nearly all made reference to "made" soil as a subsoil—which it is not.
The question, although a very simple one, was not well answered.

Q. 46. Describe the arrangement of a system for the bacterial treatment
of sewage, and state the conditions under which the micro-
organisms discharge their functions.

The answers to this question were very uneven and in a large number of
cases distinctly bad. A large number confused the biological methods, as
usually understood, with broad irrigation and intermittent downward
filtration; others added chemicals to the sewage. On the whole, the
question was indifferently answered.

Honours.

Results: 1st Class, –; 2nd Class, 5; Failed, 17; Total, 22.

For the first part of the examination twenty-two papers were sent in.
Of these five obtained the minimum number of marks, but had still to
qualify in the practical part of the examination. Only three candidates
obtained marks above the minimum. On the whole, the answers were not
of so high an order as those sent in in former years. Some of those students
who competed would hardly have passed Stage 2, and in one or two cases
there is evidence of a want of the general education and knowledge
necessary as a foundation for any high honours in a very special and
technical subject.

The following remarks apply only to the papers.

Q. 61. Discuss the hygienic importance of the presence in water of each
of the following constituents: protozoa, nitrites, excess of
nitrates, excess of lime and magnesia salts, excess of chlorides,
insoluble mineral matter in suspension.

All the candidates attempted this question, except two. Only two
obtained really good marks or gave anything like complete answers.

Q. 62. Describe the origin and different composition of soils and subsoils.
Discuss the conditions which influence the healthiness or un-
healthiness of various soils.

The same remarks apply to this question as to the preceding one. The
answers, in the large majority of cases, were very short and sketchy.

Q. 63. What points would you take into consideration when deciding whether or not a sewage effluent was fit to be discharged into a stream? Describe how you would estimate volumetrically the nitrogen in an effluent.

This question was indifferently answered by nearly all the students. Few gave correct replies to the last part of the question, and a large number simply stated a method for ascertaining the nitric acid in a sample of water. They took into no account the nitrogen in the free ammonia or nitrous acid.

Q. 64. Explain the principle and use of the mercurial barometer, and point out the corrections which are necessary when the most exact readings of the barometer are required.

This question was a favourite one, but was answered badly. The corrections for temperature and height above sea-level were omitted or wronglv expressed.

Q. 65. What do you understand by the term "standard death-rate"? Describe precisely the method of obtaining the comparative mortality figure for any county or large urban district.

This was not a favourite question, and very few who attempted it showed any knowledge of the meaning of the term or how it is obtained.

Q. 66. What is the definition of "Alkali works"? Mention the chief provisions of the Alkali, &c., Works Regulation Act, 1881.

This question was attempted by only five students, and of these only one had any knowledge of the Act or its chief provisions.

HONOURS PRACTICAL EXAMINATION.

The practical examination this year was on much the same lines as that given in the years 1904 and 1905. Five students presented themselves for this part of the examination. The results are very satisfactory and, when compared with last year, the work done is far better in every way. All the students were more or less familiar with the technique of practical work, while some had an excellent knowledge of the subject.

The candidates appear to have had a good training in the technical colleges, and this has widened the practical side of the subject and imparted a larger interest to it. The difference in the work and knowledge shown by the students this year compared with what was found two years ago when the examination was first established is really remarkable and is most satisfactory in every way.

Q. 1. Submit the sample of water marked A to qualitative (including physical characters) and quantitative examination, so as to pass an opinion as to the fitness of the water for drinking and cooking purposes.

The reasons for your opinion and the methods by which you arrive at those reasons must be briefly stated in your report.

N.B. – The total solids of the water and the oxygen required to oxidize organic matter need not be estimated.

All the candidates attempted this question. Two of the students made a good analysis of the sample of water. As a rule the qualitative examination was not well done. The majority of the candidates relied too much on their notes.

In the quantitative analysis the free and albuminoid ammonia, the chlorine and hardness were attempted with varying success.

In their report the candidates did not bring their knowledge to bear on the results obtained, and in some cases failed to express any opinion. The interpretation of their results is in all cases a very important feature in an examination of this kind and should receive more attention than appears to have been given to it.

Q. 2. Determine the amount of gluten in the sample of flour marked
B ; express the result as a percentage.

The water is 16 per cent. and the ash is 0·4 per cent. Report
on the quality of the flour.

Of those who attempted this question only one gave an approximate
result. The report also was indifferent. The students were not well
prepared in the technique necessary to make this analysis.

Q. 3. Name the parasites shown under the microscopes 1, 2 and 3 ; give
a brief account of their life-histories ; and describe the symptoms
which they produce in the human body.

Three candidates attempted this question. Two gave fairly satisfactory
replies as to the names of the parasites, but failed to describe the life-history
or the symptoms which the parasites produce in the human body. On the
whole the question was not well answered.

DAY EXAMINATION.

STAGE 1.

Results : 1st Class, 89 ; 2nd Class, 136 ; Failed, 6 ; Total, 231.

This year, for this part of the examination, 231 papers were sent in. Of
these, 38 per cent. obtained a First Class, 58 per cent. a Second Class,
and 2 per cent. failed. This result is extremely satisfactory, and compares
favourably with last year. The whole of the papers are distinctly above the
average. There certainly is such a marked improvement in the papers that
it is evident there has been much more systematic teaching, and the instruction given has been such that the students understood it and took an
interest in the subject.

The following remarks have reference to this part of the examination.

ELEMENTARY HUMAN PHYSIOLOGY.

Q. (a) Give a general account of the structure of the lungs, and of the
parts by which these communicate with the air.

The majority of candidates attempted this question, giving good and
accurate replies illustrated by some excellent diagrams.

Q. (b) Where and how is the gastric juice formed ? What are its composition and uses ?

This was not a favourite question. When attempted, the answers were
good as a whole.

Q. (c) What bones form the shoulder-joint ? Compare its structure with
that of the hip-joint.

The first part of this question was well done, but many candidates broke
down when they came to compare the general structure and arrangement of
the shoulder with the hip-joint.

Q. (d) Give a short description of the heart and its mechanism.

A very favourite question, usually well answered and satisfactorily
illustrated.

HYGIENE.

Q. 1. State how water may be contaminated after it enters a dwelling
from the street main, and how such pollution can be prevented.

The general run of answers to this question was good, and in not a few
cases the replies showed a comprehensive grasp of the practical points
raised by the question.

Q. 2. What do you understand by temporary and permanent hardness of water ? How may temporary hardness of water be removed ?

Nearly every candidate replied to this. Some of the answers were very good, the writers evidently having a competent grasp of the chemistry of the subject.

Q. 3. What is meant by "natural ventilation," and upon what physical laws does it depend ?

This subject had evidently been well taught, nearly all the answers to this question being clear and accurate.

Q. 4. What are the essential objects of cooking processes ? Explain the changes which meat and bread undergo respectively when baked.

In this question candidates found an old friend and a congenial subject on which to write. Judging by the answers generally, this topic had been well taught.

Q. 5. What is the average composition of milk ? Why is milk the best food for young children ?

One of the most noteworthy features of this examination was the manner in which this question was handled. One was surprised to see the accuracy of the figures quoted.

Q. 6. Describe the conditions which cause dampness in house-walls. What preventive measures would you advise ?

This was a favourite question ; some of the illustrations being very good.

Q. 7. What are the important points to bear in mind in dealing with the storage and disposal of house refuse ?

Here again candidates found an easy and congenial subject on which to write. The greater number of replies were distinctly good.

Q. 8. What is the value of exercise in development, and to what particular objects should such exercise be directed in school life ? What forms of exercise are best adapted to meet these particular objects ?

One expected to find this question indifferently handled. On the contrary, when attempted, and that was fairly often, it was wonderfully well done. In fact, it was one of the most satisfactory features in the whole examination, as it could not be readily answered from the ordinary text books, but needed some reflection and initiative on the part of candidates.

Q. 9. How would you distinguish between an epileptic fit and a fainting fit ? Indicate the nature of the first aid you would give in each case.

This question was not such a favourite as one expected to find it ; but when attempted was invariably well done.

Judging this Stage 1 (Day) Examination as a whole, the papers submitted were distinctly good, and far better than those of some previous years.

STAGE 2.

Results : 1st Class, 48 ; 2nd Class, 188 ; Failed, 37 ; Total, 273.

For this part of the examination 273 papers were sent in. Of these, 17 per cent. obtained a First Class, 68 per cent. a Second Class, and 13 per cent. failed.

On the whole, the examination in Hygiene may be said to be satisfactory ; perhaps the papers in the Elementary Human Physiology were not quite so good, though many excellent answers were given. It should be impressed on students before commencing their papers, to carefully read through the questions they propose to answer. That they had not done so in all cases is shown by the numbers who attempted Questions 21 and 30. In the former, domestic filtration and cisterns for the storage of water were discussed, while in the latter the isolation of the patient and nursing were entered into. These answers were good, but they had no reference to the questions in the paper.

The following remarks have reference to this part of the examination.

ELEMENTARY HUMAN PHYSIOLOGY.

Q. (a) Describe the difference between an artery and a vein, and explain how these differences affect the circulation of the blood.

Nearly every candidate attempted this question, and many excellent answers were given; but a few were quite ignorant of the difference between an artery and a vein.

Q. (b) Describe the position, form, general structure, and function of the stomach.

This question was a very favourite one, and the replies to it were, as a rule, good. The students have been carefully and well instructed on the processes of the digestion of food, etc.

Q. (c) What bones go to make up the foot and ankle? Describe briefly the human foot, and show its special adaptation to the act of walking.

Comparatively few attempted this question, but those who did gave excellent answers.

Q. (d) Where is the spleen placed in the body? What is its shape, general structure, and appearance?

Many candidates attempted this question, and some excellent answers were given. In point of fact, some of the answers were surprisingly good, and show a well-grounded knowledge of the subject.

HYGIENE.

Q. 21. State in detail the method usually adopted for the purification of water from rivers, springs, etc. Explain the action that takes place in such method, and how the water should be stored after purification and before delivery.

Every student attempted this question, and in the large majority of cases the answers were good. Many, however, were unfamiliar with the action that takes place in sand filtration; others entered into the question of domestic filtration by means of the Chamberland filter, although the question referred to water "before delivery" to the consumer. Comparatively few gave a good description of a service reservoir or stated how water should be stored after filtration. A few suggested that it was stored in the water mains.

Q. 22. How is the amount of pollution of air in a crowded space estimated, and why is the amount of carbon dioxide always taken into account?

This question brought very few good answers. A very large number attributed poisonous qualities to the small amount of carbon dioxide present in the air, and only a few grasped the idea that it is taken as *an index* of organic impurity. On the whole, the question was indifferently answered.

Q. 23. What is meant by the expressions: (a) relative humidity, (b) dew point? Describe a method of ascertaining the dew-point.

This was a favourite question. Comparatively few gave a correct definition of relative humidity, although nearly all were familiar with the dew-point. In many cases the last part of the question was indifferently answered.

Q. 24. What do you understand by the term "proximate alimentary principles"? State the amount of these principles necessary in a diet for (a) ordinary work, (b) hard work.

The majority of the students attempted this question. The first part was indifferently answered, very few gave a correct definition of the term "proximate alimentary principles." The last part of the question was, as a rule, well answered. Only about three candidates gave the more recent numbers for diets in ordinary and hard work.

Q. 25. Name the parasites which may be transmitted to man by eating meat, and describe their appearance in the flesh of animals.

Very few candidates attempted this question, and only comparatively few of these gave any description or were able to name the parasites connected with meat supplies.

Q. 26. What is the difference between the high and the low pressure system of hot water heating? Describe shortly the arrangements of each, and state their relative merits and demerits.

Nearly every student attempted this question, and the answers were by far the best on this paper. Few mistakes were made, all being quite familiar with these systems of heating.

Q. 27. Describe the best form of w.c. for houses, for factories, for schools. Illustrate your answer by sketches.

The first part of this question was very well answered and, as a rule, the sketches given were good. The answers given to the last part were quite the reverse; there were few sketches and those who attempted them had never seen a trough closet, which was the one generally suggested. Very many gave an ordinary w.c., the base of which entered a common drain pipe. Under such a condition the basin would never be cleansed and the pipe would be foul. This question was not well answered.

Q. 28. Mention the strengths and the way in which each of the following disinfectants should be used:—Carbolic acid, perchloride of mercury, chloride of lime, sulphurous acid, formalin.

Those who attempted to answer this question had no idea of the strengths of the various disinfectants named, when used in a sick room or house. They were familiar with the names and knew how to apply them; but in the large majority of cases their knowledge ceased there.

Q. 29. Describe the suitability of the following sites for houses:—Rock, sand or gravel, chalk, clay, and alluvial drift. State how these soils influence health.

A very favourite question, but answered very unequally. Some good replies were given; but on the whole the answers were disappointing.

Q. 30. An outbreak of diphtheria having occurred in a school, what precautions would you take with regard to the school-buildings and appliances?

This question was a favourite one. Very many students dealt with the isolation, disinfection, and nursing of the patient, which was not asked for. Others entered into details as regards disinfection by sulphur. Only a few referred to the drainage and sanitary arrangements of the lavatories, etc., or to any possible source of danger in or around the buildings. Very few gave any method other than that of burning sulphur for disinfecting a room, and evidently the practice of spraying the walls, which is more effective, has not been referred to. On the whole, the answers were somewhat disappointing.

Report on the Examinations in Agricultural Science and Rural Economy.

Results : 1st Class, 11 ; 2nd Class, 15 ; Failed, 12 ; Total, 38.

The improvement noted in the last report may be again seen ; there is a little more evidence from the answers that experiments have been actually carried out before the class. But a great deal of teaching by rote still goes on, and energy is wasted over an elaborately technical nomenclature of the parts of a plant, to the neglect of the study of their functions in a simple and common-sense fashion. At this stage of the subject, technical terms like cotyledon, pericarp, phloem, &c., are not only an added burden to the student, but they are positive hindrances to his understanding of the facts. The sketches are still very bad.

Q. 1. Draw a sketch of a young seedling of wheat or barley, naming the various parts visible to the naked eye. Make another drawing showing the same seedling as growing in the open ground about a month later.

The first stage of the seedling was often correctly drawn, but not the later one. Nobody appeared to have seen a young plant from the open ground, with its adventitious roots and tillering.

Q. 2. Describe experiments to show that growing plants require air. What changes do they bring about in the air.

Most of the answers began "enclose a plant in an air-tight box and pump out all the air." Teachers should set their faces against such description of hypothetical experiments, and insist on being told how a thing is to be done in real life.

Q. 3. If you have made the experiment of weighing dried seeds and seedlings in successive stages of growth, say in which stage a loss of weight, and in which a gain in weight was observed. Give the reasons of these changes in weight.

Answers confused, because they showed no appreciation of the relative magnitude of loss by respiration and gain when assimilation begins.

Q. 4. Describe experiments to show that all parts of the young root and the young shoot of a plant do not grow at the same rate.

Generally correct.

Q. 5. How would you show the difference in the production of starch by the white and green parts of a variegated maple or geranium leaf ? What is the cause of this difference in the parts ?

Q. 6. How is charcoal made ? Name a few substances from which it may be prepared. What effect has the gas produced by burning charcoal on lime-water ? What names do chemists give to charcoal, and to the gas which it produces on burning ?

These two questions were well answered.

Q. 7. Draw a sketch showing what is seen on cutting an apple down the middle. Explain the nature of each part.

The sketches were quite unrecognisable, yet some of the answers were stiff with botanical equivalents for skin, flesh, core and pips.

Q. 8. What is the value to the plant of (1) the spines upon gorse ; (2) the prickles upon a rose bush ?

Most candidates knew that prickles kept off animals, but not that rose thorns were also useful for climbing.

Q. 9. As the trunk of a tree increases in thickness, where does the new growth take place ? If a ring of bark be taken off can the tree repair the damage ?

The teacher wants to try and forget all about phloem and xylem, and to make his class look at a tree as does an intelligent countryman, who knows that a certain layer is alive and will grow when the tree is wounded, and that it will unite to other similar layers, as in budding or grafting.

Q. 10. A wheat crop may weigh several tons per acre though only two bushels of seed were put in ; from whence does this large amount of matter come ?

Answers rather confused because they did not recognise the relative quantities of combustible matter and ash in a crop.

Q. 11. Describe carefully some section of soil and subsoil which you have seen in a quarry or railway cutting, illustrating your remarks by a sketch. What does this section teach as to the manner in which a soil may be produced ?

Well answered.

Q. 12. If you work on a clay soil when it is in a wet state, how will its behaviour be affected (1) as regards rain falling on the land, (2) as regards its cultivation when dry ?

Rather confused.

STAGE 2.

Results : 1st Class, 36 ; 2nd Class, 103 ; Failed, 43 ; Total, 182.

SECTION A.—TILLAGE AND CROPS.

The answers this year showed a marked improvement and indicated better and more systematic teaching.

Q. 1. What points have to be specially attended to if a good tilth is to be obtained in spring on a heavy clay soil ? What previous treatment of the land will aid in obtaining this result ?

Generally well answered, though too many candidates were content to say merely " plough again in the spring" without indicating the necessity of catching the soil in the right state of dryness.

Q. 2. How much straw would you expect to obtain on an average from 100 acres of arable land farmed on the Norfolk four-course rotation ? How much farmyard manure would this straw produce ?

Fairly answered.

Q. 3. What variety of barley is chiefly grown in your part of the country ? What are its chief characteristics as compared with other barleys ? What yield per acre would you expect to obtain both of grain and straw ?

Fairly answered, but candidates should give their answers in statute bushels and acres ; often the Examiner can only infer that the bushel of which the candidate is talking represents some unknown local measure.

Q. 4. Give the average weights of a bushel of wheat, barley, and oats. How are these affected by a wet or a dry season ? What are the characteristic appearances in each of these grains by which their quality is judged ?

Candidates seem to have little idea of what a good sample of corn ought to look like.

Q. 5. Mention the chief leguminous crops grown by the English farmer, the circumstances under which each would become especially suitable for cultivation, and the uses to which each is put.

Q. 6. Under what conditions of soil and climate would it be advisable to grow oats instead of barley or wheat? How much seed per acre would you employ for an oat crop, what produce would you expect if ordinary or Tartar oats were grown, and what would be the weight per bushel in each case?

These two questions were fairly answered.

Q. 7. Set out two rotations designed to include a potato crop as one of the most important items, and explain the reasons for the arrangement suggested.

Indifferently answered. Candidates seemed to have little idea of the practice prevailing in the potato growing districts.

Q. 8. Describe how you would proceed to lay a piece of land down to permanent grass. What seeds would you sow, and in what quantities? State the character of the land you have in view.

Well answered.

Q. 9. Discuss the differences which should be observed in the management of a good pasture, and of meadow land mown every year for hay, if both are to be kept in a profitable condition.

Candidates forgot that farming does not simply consist in applying manure; very little was said about rolling, dragging, paring anthills, moving dung, etc., all necessary items in the management of grass land.

Q. 10. Describe the construction and arrangement of the knives of a reaping machine. How are they sharpened?

Well answered.

SECTION B.—HORTICULTURE.

The answers were neither so numerous nor so good as in former years, and need not be dealt with in detail, since they call for no special comment or elucidation.

SECTION C.—ANIMAL HUSBANDRY.

Both the numbers and the quality of the answers in this section were much better than usual, the only defect about the answers, speaking generally, was that they were too exclusively local and showed little or no acquaintance with general farming customs in other parts of the country.

Q. 1. Describe the management of either a (a) Sussex, (b) Devon, or (c) Aberdeen-Angus steer from its birth until it is killed as fat.

Q. 2. Describe the dentition of the horse, and explain how its age is judged thereby.

These two questions were well answered.

Q. 3. What advantages are the cross-breds supposed to have over pure-bred stock for the purposes of the ordinary farmer? Mention some crosses that are commonly made among both cattle and sheep.

Here certain local crosses were mentioned, but seldom such standard crosses as the "Blue grey," or the use of a Down ram on the commoner breeds of sheep.

Q. 4. Write a brief account of the management of some one breed of pigs. Explain how you would feed the young pigs until they were ready for market. At what weight would you sell them?

Q. 5. Describe the operations incident to the shearing of any breed of sheep with which you are familiar. What weight of wool would you expect, and what price ruled for it last season?

Q. 6. By what characters would you decide whether a bullock were ready for market or not? About how much average increase per diem will a good bullock make from its birth until it is killed? What proportion should the dressed carcase bear to the live weight?

These three questions were very fairly answered in a practical way.

Q. 7. For what reasons does the farmer prefer linseed or cotton cake for feeding dairy cows or fattening beasts? Is there any justification for the difference in the price of these two feeding stuffs?

Very few candidates discussed the relative merits of linseed and cotton cake.

Q. 10. Describe the process of butter making from the milk onwards.

While some of the answers were excellent, others showed a curious ignorance of such important points as the souring of the cream.

Section D.—Chemistry of Plant and Soil.

The general average was seriously lowered by one or two classes which had not been taught on lines that would enable them to deal at all with the questions. The few who had been taught sent in very fair papers calling for no special comment.

Section E.—Chemistry of Manures and Crops.

The answers were not very numerous, but were generally sound.

Q. 1. Would an application of sulphate of lime (gypsum) or phosphate of lime to land produce a similar effect as an application of lime? Give the reasons of your answer fully.

The distinction between lime as a free base, and sulphate or phosphate of lime as neutral salts was only appreciated by a few candidates, yet it should be pressed home upon students.

Q. 4. What difference in composition would you expect between cake-fed and ordinary dung in both the soluble and insoluble portions of the manure?

The differences in composition are important, and should be carefully taught to students. The value of cake-fed dung lies in its higher proportion of amides and ammonia salts, representing the digested albuminoids of the richer food.

Section F.—Chemistry of Animals and Foods.

Larger numbers presented themselves this year and the quality of the answers also rose.

Q. 2. What is meant by the digestibility of a food, and how is it ascertained experimentally.

The answers often showed confusion between the nitrogen retained by the animal and that excreted in the urine. Very often the former alone was regarded as representing the digested nitrogen.

Q. 3. What difference is there between the digestive organs of ruminants and non-ruminants? What influence has this difference in the digestive apparatus on the kinds of food suitable for each class of animal?

Q. 4. What is approximately the composition of the increase in live weight put on by a bullock during the latter stages of fattening? How does it differ in composition from the increase during earlier stages of growth?

Q. 6. What percentage of the cellulose in the food will be digested by an ox? Has the digestible cellulose the same nutritive value to the animal as other digestive carbohydrates? Give the reasons for your answer fully.

Q. 7. From which constituents of food can ·fat be produced? In selecting a fattening food what composition would you especially desire? What must be the character of the animal, and under what conditions should it be placed if rapid fattening is desired?

Q. 8. How has it been shown experimentally that the production of work by an animal does not depend upon the amount of albuminoids in its food?

These five questions were generally well answered.

Q. 9. What is meant by the manure value of a food? Compare the manure values of linseed and cotton cakes, of maize and beans?

Here the information lacked definiteness; candidates had no idea of the quantities involved.

Q. 10. By what different agents may milk be curdled? Does milk curdle more quickly when warm or when cold? Which constituents of the milk are found in the curd, and which in the whey?

Indifferently answered. Generally, milk was said to be curdled by "bacteria," in contradistinction to curdling by acid or by rennet. Yet the bacteria only act by secreting acids or enzymes.

HONOURS.

Results : 1st Class, – ; 2nd Class, 2 ; Failed, 3 ; Total, 5.

The answers sent in to the Honours questions did not attain a high standard ; it was evident that the candidates had some acquaintance with the subject matter of each question, but had not passed beyond a mere general idea to the exact knowledge demanded. For example, in Q. 3 (Part I., Agriculture) the answers indicated that the nitrogen, phosphoric acid and potash of a purchased food were in the main left on the farm in the dung, and so could be valued to the incoming tenant, but the basis on which this is now done as an ordinary part of farm valuations was not given, nor was any reference made to the crucial distinction between the old scale of compensation based on the cost of the food and the new one which depends on its composition. Q's. 2 (on rates and taxes), 5 (on the cost and production of a milch cow), 7 (on finger and toe) were better answered, but in Q. 4 (on the continuous growing of cereal crops) no one knew of Mr. Prout's long and successful management of a farm exclusively devoted to cereal growing, although a further account of it appeared in the last volume of the Journal of the Royal Agricultural Society.

The papers submitted for Honours in Horticulture were sound as far as they went, but all showed that the candidates lacked experience of market gardening.

DAY EXAMINATION.

STAGE 1.

Results : 1st Class, 1 ; 2nd Class, 1 ; Failed, 2 ; Total, 4.

The answers were too few in number to call for detailed comment.

STAGE 2.

1st Class, 22 ; 2nd Class, 49 ; Failed, 24 ; Total, 95.

SECTION A.—TILLAGE AND CROPS.

With the exception of the papers from one class, the answers generally showed an improvement. There was evidence of better teaching, but candidates still show a tendency to regard farming operations from too exclusively a chemical point of view, to the neglect of the general economy of the farm and the important factor of the tilth of the soil.

Q. 1. What differences in the character of the plough slice are brought
about by a short or a long mould board in a plough ? For what
class of land is each best suited ? How is the shape of the plough
slice adjusted by the ploughman ?

The character of the work done by a long or short mould board was
generally known, but opinions were about equally divided as to which was
more suitable to heavy land.

Q. 2. What difference in fertility would you expect to find between soil
and subsoil ? Is anything to be gained by working the land
more deeply than customary ; distinguish between the effects of
deep ploughing and subsoiling.

The majority of candidates still regard the subsoil as composed of coarser
materials than the soil, and do not in consequence recognise how unworkable a clay subsoil may be if brought to the surface. Nor was the
importance of organic matter of the soil and its accompanying bacteria
sufficiently recognised.

Q. 3. What are the chief improvements effected (1) in a heavy clay soil,
(2) in a light sand, by laying it down to temporary grass for two
or three years ?

This was generally soundly answered.

Q. 4. What is meant by bare and bastard fallows respectively ? For
what reason do some farmers give their land an occasional bare
fallow, and on what class of land is the practice likely to be
useful ? Calculate the cost per acre of a bare fallowing.

It should be borne in mind that almost the only justification of a bare
fallow is the need of restoring the tilth of a heavy clay soil.

Q. 5. What are the most troublesome weeds of arable land in your part
of the country ? Describe the class of soil you are dealing with
and what are the most effective means of eradicating or keeping
under the weeds in question ?

More observation should be given to the weeds characteristic of different
classes of land.

Q. 6. A farmer has some good grazing land ; what rules should he follow,
and what details should he look to, to secure that it remains in
fine condition ? Indicate some of the best methods of improving
poor pasture.

Here the answers turned almost wholly on manuring, to the neglect of
such practical questions as careful stocking to keep the grass properly
eaten off, harrowing, rolling, cutting anthills, and other details attended to
by the skilful grazier.

Q. 7. Under what conditions will farmyard manure of high quality be
produced, and how should it be managed and stored so as to
retain its manurial value to the full ?

Fairly answered, though not enough was said of the value of keeping
the manure undisturbed and well trampled down in the yard until it is
ready for the land.

Q. 8. Describe the leading varieties of mangels ; state which is the hard-
iest, which the heaviest cropper, and which the richest. Describe
the routine of cultivation for the mangel crop.

Little was known of the varieties of mangold and of their relative
values.

Q. 9. To what attacks of disease or insect pests is the oat crop subject,
and what remedies can be applied ?

Well answered by a few candidates.

Q. 10. Work out the cost of a day's labour of a horse, taking into account food, attendance, and depreciation.

Candidates generally showed an improvement in their knowledge of costs.

SECTION B.—HORTICULTURE.

A small but good set of candidates, possessing a sound general knowledge of Horticulture, and able to express themselves clearly. The questions call for no detailed comment.

SECTION C.— ANIMAL HUSBANDRY.

Numbers small, but the work in this section shows improvement ; there was more definiteness in the answers, quantities were given and costs realised.

SECTION D.—CHEMISTRY OF PLANT AND SOIL.

A fair set of answers, marred, as in Section E, by the fact that the candidates had often begun to learn Agricultural Chemistry without any training in the pure science. Often an answer would read very correctly until some passage would reveal that the writer had got up the question without any real understanding of the subject, from sheer inability to grasp the meaning of a chemical change.

Q. 1. Lime is often said to sink in the soil. What is meant by "lime" in this connection, and how far is the statement justified ? What solvent actions are at work removing "lime" from the soil?

Few candidates knew that a layer of chalk or lime applied to the surface of grass land will be found, after a time, a little distance below the ground level, owing to the action of earthworms. This process is not seen in arable land, and is quite distinct from the removal of calcium carbonate by solution. Teachers might impress upon their students that rain water cannot become charged with carbon dioxide by passing through the air (law of partial pressures) ; it is only when in contact with the soil gases that the soil water acquires any considerable proportion of carbon dioxide.

Q. 4. Have the roots of a plant any solvent action upon the inorganic materials of the soil ? Describe experiments to illustrate your answer and discuss the evidence that they afford.

Nearly all the candidates ascribed considerable solvent power to the acid root sap, a theory which is generally discredited nowadays. Few candidates mentioned that the roots do excrete carbon dioxide, and that this is quite capable of etching the marble slab in Sach's well-known experiment. One or two candidates said the acid excreted was acid potassium phosphate, but did not explain why a plant should excrete two of the constituents it is always trying to obtain from the soil. Czapek's observation of the excretion of acid potassium phosphate only referred to germinating seedlings.

Q. 6. How is humus formed in the soil, and what does it contain ? Under what circumstances will the so-called "sweet" or "sour" humus be produced ?

Many candidates regarded nitrification as part of the action of making "sweet" humus, denitrification as the corresponding action bringing about "sour" humus.

Q. 3. What are the factors regulating the temperature of the soil ? Discuss their relative importance and illustrate your reasons by practical examples.

It was not sufficiently recognised that the greater or less evaporation of water is the chief factor in regulating the temperature of the soil.

Section E.--Chemistry of Manures and Crops.

The failures were mostly from one class which had not been taught to the necessary standard.

Q. 2. What essential difference in composition is there between the liquid and the solid portions of an animal's excrement, and which is the more valuable as manure? Which of the two is more subject to loss and how?

Few candidates appreciated the fact that since the solid excrement represents those portions of the animals' food which have resisted digestion, it will continue to resist the putrefactive bacteria in the soil and decay but slowly.

Q. 3. What plant food does the soil obtain from air and rain? Under what conditions would this supply be increased or diminished? Give the amounts received in pounds per acre where this is possible.

Quantities, which are all important in this connection, were rarely given. It is not correct to say that after a thunderstorm there is an increase in the nitrates in the rain water.

Q. 7. Name crops specially benefited by nitrate of soda, and others on which it has generally but little effect. How would its value be affected by very early or very late applications? Is it generally wise to use nitrate of soda alone? If not, what else should be applied to the crop?

Candidates generally were correct in connecting the value of nitrate of soda for wheat with the growth of the latter during the winter, and the small value of the same manure for turnips with their growth under conditions rendering nitrification active; but as regards late applications of nitrate they did not lay enough stress on the fact that a cereal crop almost ceases to take nitrates from the soil after the time of its flowering.

Section F.—Chemistry of Animals and Foods.

The few answers call for no comment.

SCIENCE EXAMINATIONS, 1906.

SUMMARIES OF THE RESULTS.

Details of Successes and Failures in each Stage of each Subject at the Evening Science Examinations, 1906.

SUBJECT.	HONOURS				STAGE 3.				STAGE 2.				STAGE 1.			
	1st Class.	2nd Class.	Failures.	Total.	1st Class.	2nd Class.	Failures.	Total.	1st Class.	2nd Class.	Failures.	Total.	1st Class.	2nd Class.	Failures.	Total.
I. Practical Plane and Solid Geometry	7	14	21	42	26	81	104	211	253	436	218	907	649	518	658	1,825
II. Machine Construction and Drawing	3	12	67	82	102	236	365	703	671	1,669	1,474	3,814	1,718	1,724	1,706	5,148
III. Building Construction and Drawing	6	24	180	210	177	407	337	921	605	1,437	655	2,697	918	1,282	1,208	3,408
IV. Naval Architecture	4	9	66	79	27	63	98	190	79	175	76	330	134	119	78	331
V. Mathematics	—	—	—	—	—	—	—	—	See	below.			930	395	574	2,099
Vp. Practical Mathematics	1	—	1	2	51	104	190	345	187	554	303	1,044	142	226	150	518
VIa. Theoretical Mechanics (Solids)	1	3	18	22	19	45	25	89	108	361	205	674	71	89	52	212
VIb. " " (Fluids)	—	—	—	—	27	28	11	66	78	169	68	303	639	507	541	1,705
VII. Applied Mechanics	—	—	—	—	8	110	133	251	176	744	349	1,269	185	149	90	424
VIII. Sound, Light, and Heat	—	1	3	4	—	—	—	—	—	—	—	—	—	—	—	—
VIIIa. Sound	—	1	2	3	10	24	16	50	91	174	37	302	—	—	—	—
VIIIb. Light	—	1	2	3	6	13	19	38	39	194	126	359	709	708	793	2,210
VIIIc. Heat	1	—	—	—	14	34	51	99	202	337	143	702	759	671	616	2,046
IX. Magnetism and Electricity	1	7	12	20	28	74	39	141	297	486	450	1,233	439	722	306	1,467
X. Inorganic Chemistry	†	See	X.	14	41	138	218	397	229	989	646	1,864	39	136	86	261
Xp. " " (Practical)	†	See	Xp.	—	11	165	403	579	556	638	444	1,636	76	50	39	165
XI. Organic Chemistry	—	6	1	—	1	23	11	35	46	107	98	251	64	87	62	213
XIp. " (Practical)	5	—	2	12	30	20	21	71	76	65	74	215	19	24	3	48
XII. Geology	2	1	1	4	18	13	9	40	45	73	50	168	337	482	225	1,044
XIII. Mineralogy	—	—	—	3	—	7	4	11	6	16	2	24	—	17	51	68
XIV. Human Physiology	—	1	—	—	10	21	27	58	169	559	161	879	82	40	109	191
XV. General Biology	—	—	—	—	—	—	—	—	22	38	35	95	—	—	10	38
XVI. Zoology	—	—	—	—	—	—	—	—	—	—	—	—	139	344	150	653
" Stage I., Section I.	—	—	—	—	—	—	—	—	—	—	—	—	236	417	298	951
XVII. Botany	—	3	9	12	3	4	3	10	4	16	19	39	48	65	42	145
XVIII. Principles of Mining	23	47	58	128	11	21	12	44	65	200	145	410	36	41	20	97
XIX. Metallurgy	2	1	7	10	88	178	218	484	111	447	180	738	2	7	8	17
XIXp. " (Practical)	—	—	—	—	12	21	25	58	27	73	39	139				
XX. Navigation	—	—	—	—	19	36	26	81	30	48	38	116				
	—	—	—	—					11	24	11	46				

SUBJECT.															
XXIII. Physiography, except Stage I., Section I.	—	—	—	—	2	6	13	21	169	144	118	431	163	139	49	351
XXIII. Physiography. Stage I., Section I.	—	—	—	—	—	—	—	—	—	—	—	—	*126	—	111	237
XXIV. Agricultural Science and Rural Economy	—	2	3	5	20	—	—	—	30	103	43	182	11	15	12	38
XXV. Hygiene	—	5	17	22	—	66	118	204	262	791	125	1,178	475	722	98	1,295
XXVI. Elementary Science of Common Life	—	—	—	—	—	—	—	—	—	—	—	—	151	130	81	362
TOTALS	55	161	503	709	770	2,027	2,644	5,441	4,917	11,906	6,648	23,171	9,777	10,429	8,724	28,930

* Passes. † Honours in Subjects X. and XI. and in Subjects Xp. and XIp. are combined.

SUBJECT.	Stages.	1st Class.	2nd Class.	Failures.	Total.
	1	632	1138	1,423	3,193
	2	241	899	843	1,983
	3	154	461	253	868
V. Mathematics	4	5	4	5	14
	Hons. Div. I. { 5	5	48	52	105
	6	79	198	112	389
	7 }	25	24	12	61
	Hons. Div. II.	—	1	2	3
TOTALS		1,141	2,773	2,703	6,617

Total Number of Successes in all Subjects · { 1st Class · · · 16,660 } 43,646.
                                             { 2nd Class · · · 26,986 }

Details of Successes and Failures in each Stage of each Subject at the **Day** Science Examinations, 1906.

SUBJECT.	STAGE 2.				STAGE 1.			
	1st Class.	2nd Class.	Fail- ures.	Total.	1st Class.	2nd Class.	Fail- ures.	Total.
I. Practical Plane and Solid Geometry - - -	19	42	28	89	68	28	32	128
V. Mathematics - - -	—	See	below.	—	—	—	—	—
VIa. Theoretical Mechanics (Solids) - - - -	22	62	89	173	20	56	53	129
VIb. Theoretical Mechanics (Fluids) - - -	5	13	20	38	11	43	14	68
VIII. Sound, Light and Heat -	—	—	—	—	24	58	68	160
VIIIa. Sound - - - -	10	9	10	29	—	—	—	—
VIIIb. Light - - - - -	19	34	21	74	—	—	—	—
VIIIc. Heat - - - -	21	123	48	192	—	—	—	—
IX. Magnetism and Electricity	37	145	275	457	47	61	35	143
X. Inorganic Chemistry - -	93	334	253	680	235	127	65	427
Xp. „ „ (Practical)	90	226	88	404	100	55	42	197
XIV. Human Physiology - -	22	87	25	134	77	53	31	161
XVII. Botany - - - -	16	61	9	86	72	47	24	143
XXIII. Physiography, except Stage I., Section 1. - - -	27	31	23	81	83	72	11	166
XXIII. Physiography, Stage 1, Section I. - - -	—	—	—	—	*108	—	76	184
XXIV. Agricultural Science and Rural Economy - -	22	49	24	95	1	1	2	4
XXV. Hygiene - - - -	48	188	37	273	89	136	6	231
XXVI. Elementary Science of Common Life - - -	—	—	—	—	187	131	38	356
Totals - - -	451	1,404	950	2,805	1,122	868	497	2,487

* Passes.

SUBJECT.	Stage.	1st Class.	2nd Class.	Failures.	Total.
V. Mathematics - - -	1	398	542	208	1,148
	2	306	1,167	487	1,960
	3	88	193	115	396
	4	—	1	1	2
	5	36	14	7	57
	6	3	4	3	10
	7	—	—	—	—
Totals - -	—	831	1,921	821	3,573

Total Number of Successes in all Subjects { 1st Class - - 2,404 } 6,597.
{ 2nd Class - - 4,193 }

231

COMPETITIONS FOR ROYAL EXHIBITIONS, NATIONAL
SCHOLARSHIPS, AND FREE STUDENTSHIPS, 1906.

Competitions for Royal Exhibitions, National Scholarships, and Free Studentships, 1906.

NAMES OF SUCCESSFUL CANDIDATES.

Name.	Age.	Occupation.	Place.	Award.
Stock, Walter H. -	21	Engineer's Apprentice.	Swindon - -	
Robertson, John M. -	20	Engine Fitter's Apprentice.	Pembroke Dock -	
Nixon, John C. -	18	Student - -	Southsea - -	
Page, Thomas W. -	19	Student - -	Ipplepen, Newton Abbot	Royal Exhibitions.
Brearley, Charles A. -	19	Machine Tool Maker's Apprentice.	Halifax - - -	
Cobbett, William F. -	19	Engine Fitter's Apprentice.	Gosport - - -	
Schofield, Herbert -	23	Student - -	Halifax - - -	
Rowell, Henry S. -	20	Engineer's Apprentice.	West Benwell, Newcastle-on-Tyne	
Brooks, Joseph J. -	20	Shipwright's Apprentice.	Devonport - -	
Connor, Albert C. H.	21	Engine Fitter's Apprentice.	Gillingham, Kent -	National Scholarships for Mechanics (Group A.)
Hickey, Frederick -	19	Shipwright's Apprentice.	Southsea - -	
Mead, William H. -	17	Engine Fitter's Apprentice.	Southsea - -	
Lowe, Arthur C. -	21	Engineer's Apprentice.	Harrogate - -	
Bloor, Frank R. -	20	Engine Fitter's Apprentice.	Gillingham, Kent -	Free Studentships for Mechanics (Group A.)
*Airey, John - -	21,	Engineer - -	Bradford, Yorks -	
Plumbridge, Douglas V.	18	Laboratory Assistant.	Isleworth - -	
McCance, Andrew -	17	Student - -	Glasgow - -	National Scholarships for Physics (Group B.)
Royds, Thomas -	22	Student - -	Oldham - -	
Lomax, Henry J. -	18	Student - -	Darwen - -	
Brown, John N. -	16	Student - -	London - -	
Pattenden, Edward F.	18	Student - -	Whitstable - -	Free Studentship for Physics (Group B.)
Bramley, Arthur -	27	Teacher - -	Elland, Yorks -	
Atkinson, Harold W.	23	Teacher - -	New Mills, Stockport	
Bridge, Fred -	19	Weaver - -	Burnley - -	National Scholarships for Chemistry (Group C.)
Naish, William A. -	20	Assayer's Assistant.	Handsworth, Birmingham	
Comber, Norman M.	18	Student - -	Brighton - -	
Ward, Percy G. -	19	Student - -	Brighton - -	
Briscoe, Henry V. A.	17	Student - -	London - -	Free Studentship for Chemistry (Group C.)
Richards, Rowland M.	20	Student - -	Manningham, Bradford	National Scholarships for Biology (Group D.)
Orton, James H. -	22	Dental Mechanic	Bradford, Yorks -	
Barratt, Katie -	22	Student - -	Swanley, Kent -	
Thompson, James L.	19	Student - -	London - -	Free Studentship for Biology (Group D.)
Haworth, Abraham -	19	Compositor -	Burnley - -	National Scholarships for Geology (Group E.)
Cundy, Arthur T. -	20	Assistant in Mining School.	Redruth - -	
Lee, Ernest - -	20	Weaver - -	Burnley - -	

* Extra Free Studentship transferred from Group E.

COMPETITION FOR WHITWORTH SCHOLARSHIPS AND EXHIBITIONS, 1906.

Competition for Whitworth Scholarships and Exhibitions. 1906.

Name.	Age	Occupation.	Place.	Value of Scholarships and Exhibitions awarded.
I. SCHOLARSHIPS (tenable for 3 years).				
Turner, Frederick G. -	22	Student (late Engine Fitter's Apprentice)	London - - -	£125 a year each.
Hogg, William E. -	25	Student (late Engineer) -	London - -	
Winn, Sidney G. -	20	Engineer's Apprentice -	London - -	
Lees, Samuel - -	20	Student (late Engineer's Apprentice)	Manchester - -	
II. EXHIBITIONS (tenable for 1 year).				£
Cobbett, William F. -	19	Engine Fitter's Apprentice	Gosport - - -	50
Mead, William H. -	17	Engine Fitter's Apprentice	Southsea - - -	50
Williams, Arthur -	21	Student (late Engineer's Apprentice)	Brymbo, Wrexham -	50
Bradley, James -	20	Student (late Engineer) -	Hollinwood, Lancs. -	50
Morgan, George E. -	19	Engine Fitter's Apprentice	Portsmouth - -	50
Connor, Albert C. H. -	21	Engine Fitter's Apprentice	Gillingham, Kent -	50
Mitchell, Edgar J. -	18	Engine Fitter's Apprentice	Devonport - -	50
Dawe, George O. -	18	Engine Fitter's Apprentice	Devonport - -	50
Bate, Ernest - -	22	Student (late Engineer's Apprentice)	London - - -	50
Turner, Henry W. -	19	Engine Fitter's Apprentice	Portsmouth - -	50
Coombe, William H. C.	18	Engine Fitter's Apprentice	Devonport - -	50
Vigers, Edwin M. -	23	Engine Smith - - -	London - - -	50
Widdecombe, Ronald E.	18	Engine Fitter's Apprentice	Saltash - - -	50
Rogers, Frederick R. .	19	Engine Fitter's Apprentice	Devonport - -	50
Cothay, Frank H. -	21	Engineer - - -	Sunderland - -	50
Vernon, Sidney - -	20	Engineer's Draughtsman -	Abbey Wood, Kent -	50
Bloor, Frank R. - -	20	Engine Fitter's Apprentice	Gillingham, Kent -	50
Burley, George W. -	21	Engineer - - -	Meersbrook, Sheffield	50
James, Robert - -	19	Engine Fitter's Apprentice	Pembroke Dock -	50
Gladwyn, Sidney C. -	20	Engineer - - -	London - - -	50
Worton, Frederick C. -	22	Turner - - - -	London - - -	50
Airey, John - -	21	Engineer - - - -	Bradford (Yorks) -	50
Wright, Charles A. -	21	Student (late Engineer's Apprentice)	Preston - - -	50
Weaver, William G. -	21	Student (late Engine Fitter's Apprentice)	Brighton - -	50
Stokes, William E. -	20	Engineer's Apprentice -	London - - -	50
Bardo, Thomas B. -	20	Engine Fitter's Apprentice	Sheerness - -	50
Baily, Alfred - -	22	Student (late Turner) -	Oldham - - -	50
Buchanan, John S. -	22	Engineer's Draughtsman -	Cambuslang, Glasgow	50
Palmer, Albert E. -	22	Engineer - - - -	Sunderland - -	50
Maskell, Henry W. -	19	Engineer's Draughtsman -	London - - -	50

BOARD OF EDUCATION, SOUTH KENSINGTON, LONDON, S.W.

SCIENCE EXAMINATIONS, 1907.

REPORTS, &c.

REPORTS ON THE SCIENCE EXAM-
INATIONS, AND SUMMARIES OF THE
RESULTS. NAMES OF SUCCESSFUL
CANDIDATES IN THE COMPETITIONS
FOR ROYAL EXHIBITIONS, NATIONAL
SCHOLARSHIPS, FREE STUDENTSHIPS,
AND WHITWORTH SCHOLARSHIPS AND
EXHIBITIONS.

LONDON:
PRINTED FOR HIS MAJESTY'S STATIONERY OFFICE,
By WYMAN AND SONS, LIMITED, 109, FETTER LANE, E.C.

And to be purchased, either directly or through any Bookseller, from
WYMAN AND SONS, LIMITED, 109, FETTER LANE, FLEET STREET, E.C.; or
OLIVER AND BOYD, TWEEDDALE COURT, EDINBURGH; or
E. PONSONBY, 116, GRAFTON STREET, DUBLIN.

1907.

Price Sixpence.

CONTENTS.

NOTE.—The Board of Education publish herein sections of the Reports of the Examiners, which will be of service to those engaged in teaching classes under the Board.

GROUP I.—PURE AND APPLIED MATHEMATICS.

BOARD OF EXAMINERS.

V.—Pure Mathematics	Rev. J. F. Twisden, M.A., *Chairman.*
VI.—Theoretical Mechanics	A. R. Willis, M.A., D.Sc.
XX.—Navigation	P. T. Wrigley, M.A.
XXI.—Spherical and Nautical	Major P. A. Macmahon, R.A., D.Sc., F.R.S.
Astronomy	H. B. Goodwin, M.A., late R.N.

Report on the Examinations in Pure Mathematics.

EVENING EXAMINATIONS.

STAGE 1.

Results : 1st Class, 515 ; 2nd Class, 1,245 ; Failed, 1,113 ; Total, 2,873.

A.

On the whole the work in ARITHMETIC was well done. The following points may be noticed :—

Q. 2. Assume that a metre equals 3·281 ft. ; find, as a decimal true to the nearest second place, how many square metres there are in 10 square yards. The distance between two railway stations is 125 kilometres ; find the distance in miles and a decimal true to the nearest third place.

Work in approximate decimals should, as a rule, be carried a place or two further than what the answer demands.

Q. 3. How many square yards are there in an acre ?

A rectangular piece of ground has an area of one acre, and its length is twice its breadth ; find the length and breadth to the nearest tenth of a yard. Verify your result by multiplying the length by the breadth, and explain any discrepancy that you find. If a border 5 yards wide were trenched round the acre, find the fractional part of the acre which remains untrenched.

Was not taken so often as some of the other questions, but it came in for several good answers.

Q. 5. (a) A man buys 2½ per cent. Consols at 86⅝ ; find the rate per cent. of the interest which accrues.

(b) A man invests £1,280 in a 3 per cent. stock, and gets from it a yearly income of £36 16s. 0d. ; find the price of a hundred pounds of the stock.

The price of the stock, in (b), was commonly given in a fractional or decimal form, *e.g.,* £104⅔₃, instead of £104 7s.

Q. 6. Find at what time between 12 and 1 o'clock the hands of a clock are exactly opposite each other.

At what times between 1 and 2 o'clock will the hands be at right angles to each other ?

A few students answered this question correctly.

9897. 2625—Wt. 23129. 12/07. Wy. & S. 6175r.　　　　　　　　A

B.

The work in GEOMETRY was fairly well done. The questions most often attempted were Q. 7 and Q. 10.

Q. 8. *ABC* and *DEF* are two triangles, and it is given that the sides *AB*, *AC* are equal to the sides *DE*, *DF* respectively ; also it is given that the angle *ABC* equals the angle *DEF*. Under what circumstances cannot we draw the conclusion that the triangles are equal in all respects ?

Draw a triangle which has two sides 2 in. and 1¼ in. long, and the angle opposite to the shorter side equal to a third of a right angle. From the same data draw a second triangle not equal in all respects to the former, and show from your diagrams that the third side of one triangle is more than twice as long as the third side of the other triangle.

The answers to this question suggest the following remark : There are two triangles *ABC* and *abc* ; the sides *AC*, *CB* of the one equal the sides *ac*, *cb*, of the other, each to each ; also the angle *A* equals the angle at *a*. With these data, most of the students think that they are justified in drawing the conclusion that the triangles are equal in all respects. This calls for the attention of the teachers. The same weakness was shown in the answers to Q. 22.

Q. 9. Show that, of all straight lines that can be drawn to a given straight line from a given point outside it, the perpendicular is the shortest.

Show that the locus of a point which is equidistant from two fixed points is the perpendicular bisector of the straight line joining the two fixed points.

The locus in the second part was seldom completely made out.

Q. 10. Define parallel straight lines, parallelogram, rhombus, square.

Show that parallelograms on the same base and between the same parallels have equal areas.

Two four-sided figures are on the same base, and between the same parallels ; also the sides opposite to the base are equal ; show that the areas are equal.

The definitions were often unsatisfactory, *e.g.*, it was seldom stated that two parallel lines must be in one plane.

In the deduction it was almost invariably assumed that the sides opposite to the base are not merely equal, but are equal to the base.

Q. 11. *AB*, *CD*, *EF* are three given parallel straight lines such that a straight line, cutting them in *P*, *Q*, *R* respectively, makes *PQ* equal to *QR*. If any other straight line cuts them in *X*, *Y*, *Z* respectively, show that *XY* is equal to *YZ*.

ABC is a triangle, and through *D* the middle point of *AB* a parallel is drawn to *BC*, cutting *AC* at *E* ; show that *DE* is half as long as *BC*.

Was often attempted, but the answers were seldom well given.

Q. 12. Show how to construct a rhombus which has one diagonal of given length, and whose area equals that of a given square.

As might have been expected, this question was seldom attempted, and most of the attempts failed. There were, however, a few good answers by the best students.

C.

In ALGEBRA, the questions in elementary rules and in simplifications were often well answered. The answers to the other questions often failed.

Q. 13. (*a*) Find the sum of
$(x^2 - 2x + 3)(x^2 + 3x - 5)$ and $(x^3 - 3x - 1)(x + 3)$

(*b*) Find the value of the sum, when x equals $-\frac{2}{3}$.

The result of the substitution, in (*b*), was often wrong.

Q. 15. (a) Find the following expressions in factors :

(i) $16x^4 + 4x^2y^2 + y^4$.

(ii) $6 (3a + b)^2 - 5 (3a + b) (a + 2b) + (a + 2b)^2$.

(b) Write down $x^2 - 11x - 42$ in factors, and find between what limits x must lie, if the expression is to have a negative value.

Was not very often taken. Few of the students showed, by their answers to (b), that they understand that, if the product of two factors is negative, one of the factors must be positive and the other negative. Consequently the reasoning was nearly always inconclusive.

Q. 18. There are three heaps of apples A, B, and C ; a number of apples equal to a ninth part of the whole number of apples is taken out of A and added to B; next a number of apples equal to a twelfth part of the whole number is taken out of C and added to A ; the three heaps now contain equal numbers of apples. If there were originally 80 apples in B, find how many there were originally in A and in C.

Was attempted fairly often. Occasionally a brief calculation led to a correct result. In most cases no result, or an incorrect result, followed a page, or even two pages of work.

STAGE 2.

Results : 1st Class, 472 ; 2nd Class, 898 ; Failed, 530 ; Total, 1,900.

The work in this Stage was, on the whole, distinctly better than the work in Stage 1. and, perhaps, showed an improvement on the work of last year.

A.

In GEOMETRY the questions most frequently answered were Q.'s 21, 22, 23.

Q. 22. Show that chords of a circle, which are equidistant from the centre, are equal, and subtend equal angles at the centre.

In a circle whose centre is O, there are drawn two chords, AB, CD, which meet when produced at E, and OE bisects the angle BED ; show that AB is equal to CD.

The assumption mentioned in the remark on Q. 3 was of frequent occurrence in the answers to this question. It is unnecessary to repeat what has been said above.

Q. 23. A tangent is drawn to a circle, and from the point of contact a straight line is drawn to cut the circle. Show that the angles between this straight line and the tangent are equal to the angles in the alternate segments of the circle.

What is the meaning of the word alternate in the foregoing sentence ?

Show how to divide a circle into two segments, so that the angle in the one segment may be five times the angle in the other.

In an examination in Geometry it may be fairly expected that geometrical methods should be employed. Such a direction as "Make BAE an angle of 30°" contravenes this rule.

Q. 24. If two chords of a circle intersect, show that the rectangle contained by the parts of the one is equal to the rectangle contained by the parts of the other.

Find a point P on the diameter AB of a given circle, such that twice the rectangle $AP . PB$ is equal to the square on the radius.

Scarcely anyone treated the rider correctly, though it is not very hard.

Q. 25. In a circle of radius 2 inches construct a regular octagon.

If A, B, C, D be consecutive angular points of the octagon, show that the triangle ABD has one of its angles twice another, and the remaining one five times that other.

The construction was often well made, and the other points of the question were made out, though seldom in good form.

Q. 26. AB is a diameter of a given circle ; show how to place in the circle a chord of given length which shall be divided into given parts by AB.

Make the construction in the case when the radius of the given circle is 2 in., the length of the chord 3 in., and the lengths of the parts $2\frac{1}{2}$ in. and $\frac{1}{2}$ in.

Was not often attempted ; but a few of the attempts were well made by the best candidates.

B.

In ALGEBRA, the work was, on the whole, well done.

Q. 27 (a) If
$$a + \sqrt{b} = x + \sqrt{y},$$
where a and x are rational and $\sqrt{b}$ and $\sqrt{y}$ are irrational, show that a must equal x, and b must equal y.

In this sentence, what is the meaning of the word "irrational"?

Many of the students answered in such a way as to show that their notion of what constitutes a proof is rather vague.

Q. 28. (a) Reduce the following expression to its simplest surd form :—
$$\frac{3 - \sqrt{5}}{(\sqrt{3} + \sqrt{5})^2} + \frac{3 + \sqrt{5}}{(\sqrt{3} - \sqrt{5})^2}$$

(b) Find a fourth root of
$$17 + 12\sqrt{2}$$
in the form
$$a + \sqrt{b}.$$

Q. 29. (a) Show that the expression
$$12x^3 + 25x^2 - 31x + 6$$
vanishes when $x = \frac{1}{4}$, and when $x = -3$; hence find its factors.

(b) Solve the equation
$$x^4 - 4x^2 + 1 = 0,$$
expressing the four values of x, (i) in their simplest surd form, (ii) as decimals correct to four places, having given
$$\sqrt{2} = 1\cdot11421, \quad \sqrt{6} = 2\cdot44949.$$

Q. 30. (a) Solve the equations :—

(i) $\sqrt{(x + 2)} - \sqrt{(x + 1)} = \sqrt{5}$.

(ii) $3x - 4y - 9z = 13, \quad 5x - 6y + z = \frac{2}{3}$,
$x + 2y - 21z = 30$.

(iii) $\dfrac{x}{x - a} = \dfrac{4a - 2b}{x - b}$.

(b) On solving (i) you will probably find that x is equal to $-\frac{1}{4}$. Explain the result obtained by substituting this value of x in the equation.

Were often well answered, except that scarcely any one gave a good explanation of Q. 30 (b).

Q. 31. (a) Find the condition that the roots of the equation
$$x^2 + px + q = 0$$
are imaginary, and show that the roots of
$$x^2 + 2(a + b)x + 2(a^2 + b^2) = 0$$
are imaginary.

(b) Show that the roots of
$$\frac{1}{x-1} + \frac{2}{x-2} + \frac{3}{x-3} = 0$$
are real and unequal.

(c) Show that the greatest value which the expression
$$1 + 7x - 3x^2$$
can have for real values of x is $5\frac{1}{12}$.

Parts (a) and (b) were fairly well answered, but scarcely any one knew how to treat Part (c).

Q. 32. There are two areas A and B, and A contains just as many square yards as B contains square metres. Find the ratio of A to B as a decimal, assuming that a metre equals 3·281 ft.

A certain area contains 756·25 square yards. If the area is represented by 100, find the number of feet in the unit of length.

Was answered as often and as well as could be fairly expected.

C.

In TRIGONOMETRY most attention was paid to Q.'s 33, 34, 35, and they were often well answered.

Q. 36. (a) Show that in any triangle ABC
$$\frac{a}{\sin A} = \frac{b}{\sin B} = \frac{c}{\sin C}.$$
(b) Find expressions for the area of a triangle
(i) in terms of two sides and the included angle ;
(ii) in terms of the angles and a side.

In the answers to (a) the case in which one of the angles of the triangle is obtuse was often omitted or not fully treated. Part (b) was seldom answered.

Q. 37. Write down the formula for the tangent of the half of any one of the angles of a triangle, in terms of the sides.

The sides of a triangle are 13, 14, and 15 ft. long ; employ the formula to calculate its smallest angle.

In a good many cases the work stopped at $\tan \frac{1}{2} A = \frac{1}{2}$.

Q. 38. From the vertex A of a triangle ABC a perpendicular is drawn to cut the base (or base produced) in D. Given the angles of the triangle and the length of BD, explain how to calculate the length of CD, without first calculating a side of the triangle.

Apply the method to the following case :—The angles B and C are 33° 28′ and 111° 45′ ; the length of BD is 2,000 ft. ; find the length of CD, and hence that of the side BC.

Is an easy question, but it was not answered as often as might have been fairly expected.

Results : 1st Class, 225 ; 2nd Class, 511 ; Failed, 215 ; Total, 951.

The work in this Stage was, on the whole, well done, and the results compare favourably with those of last year.

A.

Q. 41. Perpendiculars AD, BE are drawn to the sides BC and CA of a triangle ABC ; BF is drawn at right angles to AB to meet ED produced in F. Show that the angles FBD and DEB are equal.

Was fairly often attempted, and was well answered in a variety of ways.

Q. 42. If two triangles are equiangular, show that their corresponding sides are proportional.

$ABCD$ is a quadrilateral inscribed in a circle, and E is the point of intersection of its diagonals ; show that

$$AE \cdot CD \cdot CB = CE \cdot AD \cdot AB.$$

Q. 43. Show that the straight line which bisects an angle of a triangle divides the opposite side into segments having the same ratio as the other two sides of the triangle.

Points D, E, F are taken on the base BC of a triangle ABC such that the angle at A is trisected by DA and EA, and is bisected by FA ; show that

$$BD \cdot FE : DF \cdot EC : : AB : CA.$$

These were the questions most generally chosen from Section A. The riders as well as the propositions were frequently made out.

Q. 44. State what are the relations that must exist between the sides and between the angles of two polygons, which are similar to each other.

Define a regular polygon.

Two similar polygons (which are not regular) are inscribed in circles, whose centres are O and P respectively. Let AB be a side of the former polygon homologous to a side HK of the latter polygon ; show that the triangles AOB and HPK are similar.

Explain how it follows that the polygons are to each other in the same ratio as the triangles.

In many cases the relations asked for were not clearly stated ; and in the rider, the angles AOB and HBK were often unwarrantably assumed to be equal.

Q. 45. Show that the common tangents of two circles cut the line joining their centres in two points P, Q, which divide that line internally and externally in the ratio of the radii. Show also that the middle point of PQ divides the line joining the centres of the circles into segments which are proportional to the squares on the radii.

Very few solved the second part.

Q. 46. Lines OP, OQ, OR radiate from O, the centre of a given circle, and no one of the angles POQ, QOR, ROP exceeds an obtuse angle ; construct points A, B, C in the rays respectively, such that the triangle ABC may be circumscribed about the circle.

Was not often attempted.

B.

Q. 47. (a) Show that the sum of any positive number and its reciprocal is in no case less than 2.

If a, b, c be different positive numbers, show that

$$bc (b + c) + ca (c + a) + ab (a + b) > 6abc.$$

(b) Show that four times the sum of the cubes of any two different numbers is greater than the cube of the sum of the two numbers.

(c) Show that the difference of the squares of any two odd integers is exactly divisible by 8.

Of the three parts of this question, (b) was answered best. In (c) the mistake was frequently made of taking *consecutive* odd numbers instead of *any* odd numbers.

Q. 48. (a) Find the least value of $x + \dfrac{n^2}{x}$, when n is a positive whole number.

(b) Of all positive values of x, find that for which $\dfrac{48x}{(x + 4)^2}$ takes its greatest value, and explain how the value of the fraction changes as x increases from zero to a very large value (*s.g.*, 10,000).

Was fairly well done in many cases.

Q. 49. Solve the following equations :—

(a) $37x^{\frac{1}{2}} + 8x^2 = 216x^{-1}$.

(b) $x^2 + y = x + y^2 = a (x + y)$.

(c) $xy = z^2$, $x + y + z = 7$, $x^2 + y^2 + z^2 = 21$.

There was more success with (c) than with (a) or (b) ; but many of the answers to (c) were somewhat marred by the candidates substituting their numerical values of x and y in the third equation instead of in the second, and thus arriving at a double value of z.

Q. 50. Define a series of numbers in geometrical progression.

(a) Find the continued product of the first n terms of a geometrical series, and how it is related to the nth term of that series.

(b) If the common ratio of a geometrical series is but a little greater than unity, show that the sum of the first n terms differs but little from n times the arithmetic mean of the first and last term.

Not more than five or six candidates sent up really good answers to (b).

Q. 51. (a) In the case when n is a positive integer, write down the first four terms and the middle term of the expansion of $(1 - x)^{2n}$ by the Binomial Theorem, and reduce the middle term to its simplest form.

(b) Show that the total number of combinations of n things taking some or all of them at a time is $2^n - 1$.

(c) Find by the Binomial Theorem the value of $(1 + \tfrac{1}{500})^6$ correct to five places of decimals.

Q. 52. In uniformly accelerated motion, other things being equal, the distance described from rest varies as the square of the final velocity. Under these circumstances two bodies describe distances such that their final velocities are as 4 to 5. Also the final velocity of a body describing a distance equal to the sum of those distances is two-thirds of the final velocity due to 1230 ft. Find the two distances.

Were very well answered by a great majority of the candidates.

C.

Q. 53. (*a*) From the formula

$$\sin (A + B) = \sin A \cos B + \cos A \sin B,$$

by changing *A* into 90° + *A*, deduce the corresponding formula for

$$\cos (A + B).$$

(*b*) Show that

$$\cos (30° + A) + \cos (60° + A) = \tfrac{1}{2} (\sqrt{2} + \sqrt{6}) \sin (45° - A).$$

(*c*) Show that

$$a_1 \sin (px - \beta_1) + a_2 \sin (px - \beta_2)$$

can be expressed in the form

$$A \sin (px - B).$$

(*a*) and (*b*) were usually made out correctly, but there were not many completely satisfactory answers to (*c*).

Q. 54. (*a*) If

$$A + B + C = 180°,$$

show that

$$\sin (120° - A) + \sin (120° - B) + \sin (120° - C)$$

can be reduced to four times the product of the sines of three angles.

(*b*) Find the relation between *A* and *B* when

$$\cos A - \sin A = \cos B + \sin B.$$

In (*b*) a factor, $\sin \tfrac{1}{2} (A + B)$, on both sides of the equation, was frequently neglected.

Q. 55. Establish the formula

$$\sin \frac{A}{2} = \pm \tfrac{1}{2}\sqrt{1 + \sin A} \pm \tfrac{1}{2}\sqrt{1 - \sin A,}$$

and explain with the aid of a diagram why $\sin \dfrac{A}{2}$ may have any one of four values when only $\sin A$ is given.

Find which signs must be taken when $A = 400°$.

A good explanation of the second part, with the aid of a diagram, was sometimes made, but often this part was left undone.

Q. 56. (*a*) Extract the square root of

$$\cos \theta + \sqrt{\cos 2\theta}.$$

(*b*) Extract the square root of

$$\sqrt{2} + \sqrt{3},$$

and show that the result is a verification of the result obtained in (*a*).

(*a*) Was frequently done rightly, and also the first part of (*b*); the verification was established only now and then.

Q. 57. Let *O* be a point within the triangle *ABC* such that each of the angles *AOB*, *BOC*, and *COA* may equal 120°, and let *OA*, *OB*, *OC* be denoted by *x, y, z*; show that

$$a^2 (y - z) + b^2 (z - x) + c^2 (x - y) = 0.$$

This was not very often attempted, but when taken in hand the relation was usually correctly made out.

Q. 58. Find the area of a regular polygon of n sides inscribed in a circle of radius r, and deduce the area of the circle.

Find the ratio of the area of a circle to that of a regular polygon of 16 sides inscribed in it ; (i) in a surd form, (ii) as a decimal correct to three places, having given $\sqrt{2} = 1\cdot4142$.

The weak point in the answers was the deducing of the area of the circle ; comparatively few worked out the result as the limiting case of the polygon, when n becomes indefinitely great.

STAGE 4.

Results : 1st Class, 4 ; 2nd Class, 3 ; Failed, 6 ; Total, 13.

The work sent up was good as far as it went, but in some cases only two of the four subjects of the paper seem to have been studied.

The questions in Descriptive Geometry and Solid Geometry were those most often taken ; two or three candidates sent up excellent answers in Spherical Trigonometry, whilst most of the others neglected this subject ; in Geometrical Conics Q.'s 70 and 71 were answered a few times, but Q. 72 was not attempted.

HONOURS IN DIVISION I.

Results : 1st Class, 5 ; 2nd Class, 52 ; Failed, 53 ; Total, 110.

This paper was attempted by as many as 109 students.

The results very closely resemble those obtained last year. Many of the questions were completely answered several times, and all of them were completely answered at least once, except that in no case was more than the first part of Q. 89 answered.

As usually happens, the questions in Geometry (87–91) were less often taken than the others. Much of the highly marked work was well done, but there was a general tendency to undue length in the algebraical work.

About a third of the whole number of students, who took the paper, obtained fewer than 100 marks. It is hard to resist the impression that most of them would have done well to have qualified for the Third Stage paper. However, that is a matter which they, in conjunction with their teachers, must settle for themselves.

STAGE 5.

Results : 1st Class, 81 ; 2nd Class, 211 ; Failed, 132 ; Total, 424.

The results in this Stage did not reach so high a standard as those of last year. The questions on the whole proved a little more difficult than usual, although all of them, except Q. 2, were well answered several times.

In Descriptive Geometry :—

Q. 1. A right circular cone with a base of 2 inches radius, and an altitude of 6 inches, stands upon the horizontal plane, and is cut by a plane which bisects the axis and is inclined 30° to the horizontal. Construct the plan of the section, and the development of the portion of the surface of the cone between the vertex and the cutting plane.

Was frequently attempted, and most of the attempts succeeded in regard to the plan of the section ; a fair number also constructed the development.

Q. 2. A hyperboloid of revolution has a vertical axis, and its generating lines are inclined 25° to the axis, the shortest distance between them and the axis being $1\frac{1}{2}$ inches.

Draw the elevation of the surface, and construct the traces of the tangent plane at any given point on the surface.

Was on a part of the Syllabus that the candidates do not appear to have studied.

Q. 3. A straight line is drawn through the point (5, 9) inclined at 45° to the axis Ox of rectangular co-ordinates. This straight line is cut in points P, Q by the lines

$$x + 3y = 20, \ 7x + y = 120$$

which pair of lines themselves intersect at T.

Show that the triangle PQT is isosceles, and give the length of the equal sides, and the tangent of the angle at the vertex.

Was generally well done; a common mistake, however, was to make the tangent of the angle at the vertex $+ \frac{4}{3}$ instead of $- \frac{4}{3}$.

Q. 4. Show that

$$r^2 - 2ar \cos \theta - 3a^2 = 0$$

is the polar equation of a circle whose centre lies on the initial line.

If OP be any radius vector of this circle, and a point Q be taken on OP, produced if necessary, so that $OP.\ OQ = 6a^2$ find the equation of the locus of Q, and show that it is a circle whose radius is double the radius of the given circle.

The candidates seemed ill at ease with polar co-ordinates; thus the first part was often proved by transposing to rectangular axes.

Q. 5. Show that the points of bisection of all parallel chords of a parabola lie on a straight line.

In the parabola $y^2 = 6x$ chords are drawn through the fixed point (9, 5). Show that the locus of middle points of these chords is the parabola

$$y^2 - 5y - 3x + 27 = 0.$$

Q. 6. If $y = mx$, and $y = m'x$ be the equations of a pair of conjugate diameters of the ellipse

$$\frac{x^2}{a^2} + \frac{y^2}{b^2} = 1,$$

show that

$$mm' = - \frac{b^2}{a^2}.$$

Show that the lines

$$10y^2 - 7\ xy - 6x^2 = 0$$

coincide in direction with a pair of conjugate diameters of the ellipse

$$3x^2 + 5y^2 - 15 = 0$$

An ellipse is drawn so as to pass through the angular points of a rectangle whose sides are of the length $8a$, $6a$ respectively, and to have its diagonals as conjugate diameters. Show that its eccentricity is $\frac{\sqrt{7}}{4}$, and mark the foci.

Q. 7. Indicate the form of the curve whose equation referred to rectangular axes is $x^2 - y^2 = a^2$, and draw the asymptotes.

If the curve be referred to the asymptotes as co-ordinate axes, find its equation.

A and B are fixed points, and AC is a fixed straight line. If a line drawn through B meet AC in Q, and a point P be taken on this line, produced if necessary, so that $PA = PQ$; show that the locus of P is a hyperbola whose centre is the middle point of AB.

Q.'s 5 and 6, and the first part of Q. 7 received many good answers.

Q. 8. Mark on a diagram the position of the focus and directrix of the parabola whose equation is

$$x^2 - 2xy + y^2 + x - 3y + 3 = 0$$

and give the magnitude and position of the axes of the conic

$$16x^2 - 44xy + 49y^2 = 60.$$

In the first case the equations of the tangent at the vertex and of the axis of the parabola were usually found, but only a few of the candidates were able to mark on a diagram the focus and directrix.

Q. 9. Define the differential coefficient of $f(x)$ with respect to x, and find from first principles the differential coefficients of x^5 and $\cos x$.

Write down the differential coefficients of

$$(a^2 + x^2)^{\frac{3}{2}}, \quad (b^2 - x^2)^{\frac{2x}{a}}, \quad \tan^{-1}\left(\frac{3x}{a}\right).$$

Water is poured at a constant rate into a conical glass, which is filled in 2 minutes, the height of the cone being 12 inches. At what rate, in inches per minute, is the surface of water rising, (1) when the glass is filled to half its height, (2) when half the liquid has been poured in.

The first half of this question was often answered; the problem was worked out correctly a few times.

Q. 10. The graph of $f'(x)$ is the parabola

$$y + 2 = 3(x - 1)^2.$$

What information does this give you respecting $f(x)$?

Find a minimum value of

$$\left(\frac{x^2}{3} + 2 + \frac{5}{x^2}\right)$$

and show that there is no maximum value.

Find the circular cylinder of largest volume which can be cut from a sphere of radius 6 inches, the plane ends being perpendicular to the axis.

The minimum value and the maximum volume were often found rightly.

Q. 11. Find the following indefinite integrals :—

$$\int \frac{x^3 + a^3}{2x}\,dx, \quad \int (3 - 2x)^{\frac{2}{3}}\,dx, \quad \int \cot x\,dx,$$

$$\int \frac{dx}{1 - e^x}; \text{ also evaluate the integrals}$$

$$\int_1^2 \frac{dx}{5 - x^2}, \quad \int_0^{\pi} \sin^2 x\,dx, \quad \int_0^{\pi} \tan^2 x\,dx.$$

The integrals were made out with a fair measure of success; a common mistake in the last one was to put $\tan^2 x = \sec^2 x + 1$.

Q. 12. Indicate in a diagram the curves $yx^{1 \cdot 2} = 2$ and $yx^{1 \cdot 5} = 2$.

At what angle do these curves intersect each other? Find the area of the closed figure bounded by these curves and the ordinate corresponding to $x = 2$.

What is the distance of the centre of gravity of this area from the axis of x?

The diagram was often omitted, and this failure to represent the curves graphically often led to the limits of integration being taken incorrectly.

12 GROUP I.—MATHEMATICS.

Results: 1st Class, 25; 2nd Class, 52; Failed, 26; Total, 103.

In Solid Geometry, Q.'s 21 and 22 were nearly always taken, Q. 23 only three or four times.

Q 22. Find the angle between two intersecting straight lines whose direction-cosines are l, m, n, and l', m', n', respectively.

The straight line which passes through the points (11, 11, 18,) (2, —1, 3,) is intersected by a straight line drawn through (17, 19, 8) at right angles to the axis Oz.

Show that the two lines intersect at an angle of 45°.

It was a common mistake to assume that a line at right angles to Oz must necessarily intersect Oz.

In Differential Calculus :—

Q. 25. Explain the meaning of partial differentiation of a function of two independent variables.

If $x = r \cos \theta$, and $y = r \sin \theta$,

Show that $\left(\dfrac{\partial r}{\partial x}\right)_{y \text{ constant}} \times \left(\dfrac{\partial x}{\partial r}\right)_{\theta \text{ constant}} = \cos^2\theta$,

and illustrate this geometrically.

If $\tan u = \dfrac{\cos x}{\sinh. y}$ and $\tanh. v = \dfrac{\sin x}{\cosh. y}$,

show that $\dfrac{\partial u}{\partial x} = \dfrac{\partial v}{\partial y}$ and $\dfrac{\partial u}{\partial y} = -\dfrac{\partial v}{\partial x}$.

The geometrical illustration was not often given.

Q. 26. If $u = \dfrac{1}{r}$, where (r, θ) are the polar co-ordinates of a point, and p the length of the perpendicular from the origin on the tangent to a curve at the point (r, θ), show that

$$\frac{1}{p^2} = u^2 + \left(\frac{du}{d\theta}\right)^2$$

In the case of the curve $r^3 = a^3 \cos 3\theta$ find the angle which the radius-vector at any point makes with the tangent to the curve, and show that the locus of the foot of the perpendicular from the origin on the tangent is given by the equation,

$$r^3 = a^3 \cos^4\frac{3\theta}{4}.$$

In dealing with the locus, candidates frequently confused the vectorial angle of the foot of the perpendicular with that of the corresponding point on the given curve.

Q. 28. Show how to obtain the expansion of $f(x + h)$ in ascending powers of h, stating clearly the assumptions made.

Give the first three terms in the expansion of $\log_e \cos (x + h)$ in ascending powers of h.

Given $\log_{10} (\cos a°) = A$, calculate the approximate value of $\log_{10} (\cos a°. 0'. 10'')$, and give the numerical value if $\cos a° = \dfrac{4}{5}$.

Explain the application of this expansion in interpolation in a table of logarithmic cosines tabulated for every minute of angle.

Was seldom taken, and hardly anyone got over the difficulty of differentiating $\log_{10} \cos x°$.

In Integral Calculus :—

Q. 27. Find the following indefinite integrals ;

$$\int \frac{dx}{(x+4)\sqrt{x^2+3x-4}}; \qquad \int x^2 \log(a+x)\,dx;$$

$$\int \cos 2x.\sin^2x\,dx;$$

and show that
$$\int_0^\infty \frac{x^4\,dx}{(1+x^2)^5} = \frac{3\pi}{256}$$

and
$$\int_0^\infty \frac{x^5\,dx}{(1+x^2)^6} = \frac{1}{60}.$$

Q. 29. A uniform thin elliptic lamina has its major and minor axes of lengths $2a$, $2b$, respectively.

Find (1) the centre of gravity of one of the quadrants into which it is divided by the major and minor axes :

(2) The moment of inertia of this quadrant about the minor axis, also the moment of inertia about the parallel axis through its centre of gravity.

Q. 30. Apply the integral calculus to obtain the volume of the solid generated by the revolution about its minor axis of the portion of a given elliptic area included between the minor axis and a latus-rectum.

Find also the whole area of the bounding surface of this solid of revolution.

Q.'s 27, 29, were usually made out, but in Q. 30, candidates showed much weakness in dealing with the solid of revolution, though some of them, starting from the formulæ

$$2\int_0^{ae} 2\pi x\,ydx, \quad \text{and} \quad 2\int_{b^2}^b 2\pi x\frac{ds}{dy}\,dy + 4\pi ae\frac{b^2}{a},$$

easily obtained the required results.

Q.'s 31, 32, on differential equations were generally taken, and in many cases were well answered.

The work sent up in this Stage included some excellent papers, and, on the whole, was distinctly satisfactory.

STAGE 7.

Results : 1st Class, — ; 2nd Class, 6 ; Failed, 2 ; Total, 8.

Of the 8 candidates, one was very weak ; each of the other seven made out three or four questions fairly completely, and did portions of some others, but no one attained the standard of a First Class in this Stage.

HONOURS IN DIVISION II.

Result : 1st Class, — ; 2nd Class, — ; Failed, 1 ; Total, 1.

There was only one candidate ; his work did not reach the standard of a pass in Honours.

DAY EXAMINATIONS.

STAGE 1.

Results : 1st Class, 195 ; 2nd Class, 287 ; Failed, 101 ; Total, 583.

The work is of about the same standard as that of the Day Examination of last year.

A.

Q. 1. What is a prime number ?

Write down the prime numbers that are greater than 10 and less than 20.

Find the value of

$$\frac{1}{3} + \frac{1}{5} + \frac{1}{7},$$

as a decimal true to four places.

What is the value of 5·91374 true to the nearest third place of decimals.

A common mistake was to give 0·6761 instead of 0·6762 for 0·67619 . . . . true to four places.

Q. 2. Assuming that a metre equals 3·281 feet, find which is longer, 10 miles or 16 kilometres. How much per cent. of the shorter length must be added to it so that it may equal the longer length ?

The area of a hectare being 10,000 square metres, express a hectare as a decimal of a square mile.

Comparatively few found the correct results to all the parts of this question, though the methods were usually right.

Q. 3. Two trains, *A* and *B*, are moving uniformly in opposite directions along parallel rails. *A*'s pace is 9-10ths of *B*'s pace ; find the rates per hour at which they are moving, if 10 minutes after passing each other they are 14¼ miles apart.

Was not often attempted, but nearly all who tried it sent up a correct solution.

Q. 5. A man buys eggs at 1*s.* 3*d.* a dozen, and sells them at 11*s.* 8*d.* per hundred ; find his gain per cent.

How many eggs must he sell in order to make a profit of £1.

It was a frequent error to say the gain was 15 per cent. when the profit on 100 eggs had been found to be 15 pence.

B.

Q. 7. Draw a straight line *AB*, and by use of your ruler and compasses find the middle point of *AB*.

Prove that your method is correct.

How would you proceed to obtain the middle point when *AB* is longer than the diameter of the greatest circle that can be drawn by your compasses ?

Q. 8. In a triangle *ABC* the angle *ABC* is greater than the angle *ACB* ; show that the side *AC* is greater than the side *AB*.

AC is a diagonal of a parallelogram *ABCD*, and *AC* is less than the side *AB* ; show that the angle *ABC* is less than the angle *CAD*.

These two questions were often well answered.

Q. 9. State the axiom on which your proof of the following theorem
depends :—If a straight line fall on two parallel straight lines it
makes the alternate angles equal to one another.

Give the proof of the theorem.

In the quadrilateral $ABCD$ the sides AB and CD are parallel
and AB is half as long as CD; each of the diagonals AC and
BD is as long as CD. Choosing a length of about 2 inches for
AB, construct the figure accurately to scale.

Very many had an erroneous idea of the axiom required, and gave
instead the definition of parallel straight lines.

Q. 11. Two given unequal parallelograms are equiangular to each other ;
show how to draw a straight line which shall divide the larger
into two parallelograms, one of which shall be equal to the
smaller given parallelogram.

There were a few correct solutions ; not many selected this question.

Q. 12. Show that in a right-angled triangle the sum of the squares on the
sides containing the right angle is equal to the square on the
side opposite the right angle.

Construct a square so that its area may be five times the area
of a given square.

Though often attempted, the second part was seldom correctly constructed.

C.

Q. 13. Multiply together

$(a + b + c) (- a + b + c) (a - b + c) (a + b - c).$

In the result you obtain, substitute $a^2 + b^2$ for c^2, and show
that the product then reduces to $4a^2b^2$.

The multiplication was often wrong. Very few made out the final result.

Q. 14. (a) Divide $x^3 - y^3 - z^2 + 2yz$ by $x + y - z$.
(b) Divide $(3a + 2b + c)^2 - (a + 2b + 3c)^2$ by $a + b + c$.

Q. 15. (a) Find the following expressions in factors :
(i) $1 - a^2 + 4ab - 4b^2$.
(ii) $6x^2 + xy - 12y^2$.
(iii) $a^4 + b^4 - c^4 - 2a^2b^2$.
(b) Write down the expression $x^2 - 9x + 14$ in factors, and find
for what values of x the expression will have a positive value.

Questions 14 and 15 (a) were well done. In Question 15 (b) not many
got further than writing down the given expression in factors.

Q. 16. (a) Simplify the following expressions :
(i) $\dfrac{n}{x - n} + \dfrac{n + 1}{x + n + 1} - \dfrac{2nx}{x^2 + x - n(n + 1)}$

(ii) $\left(\dfrac{x}{1 + \frac{x}{y}} + \dfrac{y}{1 + \frac{y}{x}} \right) \div \left(\dfrac{x}{1 - \frac{x}{y}} - \dfrac{y}{1 - \frac{y}{x}} \right)$

(b) Find the numerical value of

$\dfrac{y - 2x}{2y + x},$

when $x = \dfrac{1}{4}$ and $y = -\dfrac{1}{6}$.

As a rule, this was done only moderately well.

Q. 17. Solve the following equations :—

(a) $\dfrac{3}{x-2} + \dfrac{4}{x-3} = \dfrac{7}{x-4}$.

(b) $\dfrac{x-1}{2} + \dfrac{y-2}{3} = 1$, $2x + 3y = 2$.

(c) $\dfrac{x+m}{x-n} + \dfrac{x+n}{x-m} = 2$.

Q. 18. Divide £150 between A, B, and C, so that B and C together may receive £20 more than A, and that B's share may exceed C's by $2\frac{1}{2}$ times as much as A's exceeds B's.

There were many very good answers to these two questions.

STAGE 2.

Results : 1st Class, 70 ; 2nd Class, 401 ; Failed, 133 ; Total, 604.

The results are not quite as good as those of the Day Examination of last year.

A.

Q. 21. State what is meant by the projection of a finite line upon another line.

Show that in an obtuse-angled triangle the square on the side opposite to the obtuse angle is equal to the sum of the squares on the other two sides, together with twice the rectangle contained by either of them and the projection of the other upon it.

The base BC of an acute-angled triangle ABC is produced through B to D, and through C to E, so that $DB = BC = CE$, and AD, AE are joined ; show that

$$AD^2 + AE^2 = AB^2 + AC^2 + DC^2.$$

Q. 22. From one end of a diameter of a circle a straight line is drawn at right angles to the diameter. Show that the line so drawn does not cut the circle.

Define a tangent to a circle.

P is a given point outside a circle, whose centre is A. Show how to produce AP to Q, so that the tangent of the circle drawn from Q may be twice as long as the tangent drawn from P.

Q. 23. If two opposite angles of a quadrilateral are together equal to two right angles, show that a circle can be described through the four corners of the quadrilateral.

$ABCD$ is a quadrilateral inscribed in a circle ; the sides AB, DC are produced to meet at E, and the sides BC, AD are produced to meet at F ; show that the bisectors of the angles at E and F are at right angles to one another.

Q. 24. Show how to inscribe a circle in a given triangle.

A circle inscribed in a triangle ABC touches the sides at points D, E, F ; find the angles of the triangle DEF in terms of the angles of ABC.

The bookwork propositions in these questions were on the whole well written out, the chief defect being in Q. 24, where the candidates frequently omitted the proof that the circle *touches* the sides of the triangle. The deductions in the latter part of these questions were done correctly fairly often.

Q. 25. Let AB be the straight line joining A and B, the centres of two intersecting circles ; let the common chord of the circles cut AB in M. From any point N in AB draw a line NP at right angle to AB, and from any point in NP let tangents be drawn to the circles ; show that the difference between the squares on the tangents equals twice the rectangle $AB . MN$.

Q. 26. Find the locus of a point which moves so that the sum of the squares of its distances from two fixed points is constant.

Construct the locus to scale when the fixed points are two inches apart and the sum of the squares is 10 square inches.

These two questions were not often selected, but were rightly made out a few times.

B.

Q. 27. (*a*) If

$$x = \frac{1}{1-y}, \text{ and } y = \frac{1}{1-z},$$

show that

$$z = \frac{1}{1-x}.$$

(*b*) Show that the square of

$$\sqrt{\left\{\frac{a + \sqrt{(a^2 - b)}}{2}\right\}} + \sqrt{\left\{\frac{a - \sqrt{(a^2 - b)}}{2}\right\}}$$

reduces to $a + \sqrt{b}$.

(*c*) Find the square root of $(x - 9)(x - 1)^3 + 64x$.

(*a*) was not often made out ; (*c*) was well done a good many times.

Q. 28. (*a*) If $a^2 - 5ab + 6b^2 = 0$, show that b must be either the half or the third of a.

(*b*) Show that the square of any odd number increased by 3 is divisible by 4.

(*c*) Explain whether there be such an odd number that its square, diminished by 3, is divisible by 4.

Often answered ; the reasoning was usually well given.

Q. 29. Solve the equations

(*a*) $\dfrac{2x}{x-1} + \dfrac{3x-1}{x+2} = \dfrac{5x-11}{x-2}$.

(*b*) $\dfrac{x}{3} - \dfrac{y}{4} + \dfrac{z}{6} = 16$, $\quad \dfrac{x}{9} + \dfrac{y}{12} - \dfrac{z}{4} = 1$, $\quad \dfrac{x}{5} - \dfrac{y}{16} - \dfrac{z}{8} = 5$.

(*c*) $(2a - b - x)^2 + 9(a - b)^2 = (a + b - 2x)^2$.

(*a*) was frequently solved ; (*b*) less often ; (*c*) a few times.

Q. 30. (*a*) If a, β are the roots of the equation

$$x^2 - ax + b = 0,$$

show that

$$a + \beta = a \text{ and } a\beta = b,$$

without solving the equation. Also find the value of $a^2 + \beta$ in terms of a and b.

(*b*) Without solving the equations, find two relations between the roots of $x^2 - ax + b = 0$ and the roots of $bx^2 - 2ax + 4 = 0$.

The answers, especially those to (*b*), were very feeble.

Q. 31. Find the ratio of two numbers, which are such that their product is a mean proportional to the sum of their squares and the difference of their squares.

Also express the ratio as a decimal true to three places.

N.B. $\sqrt{5} = 2\cdot236068$.

Q. 32. There are four vessels of equal capacity ; and wine is poured into them, so that ⅝th of the first, ¼th of the second, ⅔th of the third, and ⅓rd of the fourth are filled with wine.   The first is then filled up with water, and from this mixture the second is filled up, again from this second mixture the third is filled up, and in like manner the fourth is filled up from the third.   What is the ratio of wine to water in the fourth vessel ?

These two questions were less often tried than the others in this section, but occasionally they received good answers.

C.

Q. 33. (a) Define the terms logarithm, mantissa, characteristic.

Referring to the logarithms given below, write down the logarithm of 535·51, and also the logarithm of 0·053551.

(b) From logarithms given below find the logarithm of 27 and that of 125 ; also calculate the numerical value of

$$(27)^{0·25} \div (125)^{0·3}.$$

(c) If

$$\log (x^2) = -\frac{3}{5},$$

find the value of x.

Was on the whole satisfactorily answered, but many failed to make out (c).

Q. 34. (a) Define a degree, a minute, and a second of angle.

Explain what is meant by the number commonly denoted by the Greek letter π, and write down its approximate value, true to four decimal places.

(b) If an angle of 90° is represented by $\frac{\pi}{2}$, find the number of degrees, with the odd minutes and seconds, in the unit of angle. By what name is that unit commonly called ?

(c) Calculate the numerical value of $\frac{\pi}{\log 3}$.

The definition of a degree was often faulty ; e.g., "the 360th part of a circle" ; on the other hand there were several careful and correct definitions.

Q. 35. (a) Draw an appropriate diagram, and, with reference to it, define the sine, the tangent, the cosine, and the cotangent of an angle less than 90°.

(b) Express the sine, the cosine, and the cotangent of an angle in terms of its tangent.

(c) Show that $\sin \theta \tan \theta$ is greater than $2(1 - \cos \theta)$, when θ is a positive angle less than 90°.

The last part, (c), was seldom well done ; what was usually given was merely a verification for a particular value of θ.

Q. 36. (a) Construct the positive angle less than 180° whose tangent is $-\frac{3}{2}$, and find the sine and the cosine of the angle correct to two places of decimals.

(b) Establish the following relations, in which A denotes an acute angle :—
(i) $\cos (180° - A) \tan (180° - A) = \sin A.$
(ii) $\sin (90° + A) \cos (90° + A) + \sin (90° - A) \cos (90° - A) = 0.$

(c) Taking the tangent of 31° as 0·6, how many degrees are there in each of the positive angles (less than 360°) whose tangent is $- 0·6$?

There was much vagueness and confusion in many of the answers. As usual, angles greater than a right angle proved to be outside the range of knowledge of the candidates.

Q. 37. Write down the formula for the sine of the half of any one of the angles of a triangle, in terms of the sides, and explain the notation.

The sides of a triangle are 491, 682, and 827 feet long ; employ the formula to calculate its largest angle.

Q. 38. Show how to find the remaining parts of a triangle when two angles and the side adjacent to both are given.

The distance between two stations P and Q on the sea shore is 1,000 yards ; the line joining P with a buoy B subtends an angle of 38° at Q, and the line BQ subtends an angle of 65° at P. Find the distance of the buoy from P.

The problems were often worked correctly, but the explanation required in the first part of Q. 38 was not well given.

STAGE 3.

Results : 1st Class, 26 ; 2nd Class, 47 ; Failed, 21 ; Total, 94.

The work in this Stage quite reaches the standard of last year.

A.

Q. 41. If two triangles have one angle of the one equal to one angle of the other, and the sides about the equal angles proportionals, show that the triangles are equiangular to one another, and that those angles are equal which are opposite to the homologous sides.

What is meant by " homologous sides " ?

Perpendiculars AD, BE are drawn to the sides BC and CA of a triangle ABC. Let ED and AB be produced to meet in O ; show that OD is to OE as triangle ADB is to triangle AEB.

Q. 42. If a straight line be divided into any two parts, show that a rectilinear figure described on the whole line exceeds the sum of the two similar figures similarly described on the two parts by twice the similar figure similarly described on the mean proportional between the parts.

Show that either of the complements is a mean proportional between the parallelograms about a diagonal of a parallelogram.

Q. 43. Given two squares P and Q, and a straight line AB, show how, by a geometrical construction, to find a point E in AB such that the ratio of AE to EB may equal the ratio of P to Q.

Q. 44. Having given the sum of the squares on two straight lines, and also the rectangle contained by the lines, show how to construct them.

Draw a circle of radius two inches, and inscribe in it a rectangle having an area of 5 square inches.

Q. 45. A point O is taken within a triangle ABC, and from A, B, and C lines are drawn through O to cut the opposite sides in D, E, F ; show that

$$BD \cdot CE \cdot AF = DC \cdot EA \cdot FB.$$

If the line drawn through O bisects the angle CAB, and if FE is parallel to BC, show that AB equals AC.

Q. 46. $ABCD$ is a given quadrilateral ; show how to construct another quadrilateral with its angular points P, Q, R, S on the four lines AB, BC, CD, DA respectively, and with its sides drawn parallel to four given directions.

In GEOMETRY, Qs. 41, 43 and 45 were those most often chosen ; Qs. 41 and 45 were on the whole well answered ; in Q. 43 several candidates assumed that the ratio $a^2 : b^2$ was equal to $a : b$, which showed to what little advantage they had studied the subject of ratio.

Of the remaining questions in this section, the first part of Q. 42 was made out by a fair number, and the second part by a few ; there were five or six complete answers to Q. 44, and two or three to Q. 46.

B.

In ALGEBRA the work was very satisfactory, many good answers being made in the case of each of the questions.

C.

In TRIGONOMETRY all the questions were fully answered except Q. 56, which no one attempted.

Q. 56. If a, b are the adjacent sides of a parallelogram, and θ, ϕ the acute angles between the sides and between the diagonals respectively, show that

$$\frac{a}{b} \sin \phi = \sin \theta \cos \phi \pm \sqrt{(1 - \cos^2\theta \cos^2\phi)}.$$

If $\theta = \phi$, show that

$$\cos \theta = \frac{a^2 - b^2}{2ab},$$

where a denotes the longer side.

STAGE 4.

Results : 1st Class, 2 ; 2nd Class, — ; Failed, — ; Total, 2.

Both the candidates in this Stage sent up good papers.

STAGE 5.

Results : 1st Class, 6 ; 2nd Class, 12 ; Failed, 10 ; Total, 28.

Of the 28 candidates, about half answered fairly well, but the work as a whole is less satisfactory than that of last year.

STAGE 6.

Results : 1st Class, 1 ; 2nd Class, 1 ; Failed, 2 ; Total, 4.

Four papers were sent up ; one was good, one fairly good, the two others weak.

STAGE 7.

Results : 1st Class, — ; 2nd Class, 1 ; Failed, — ; Total, 1.

The paper sent up was creditable, but did not reach the standard for a First Class.

Report on the Examinations in Theoretical Mechanics.

EVENING EXAMINATIONS.

DIVISION I. (SOLIDS).

STAGE 1.

Results : 1st Class, 141 ; 2nd Class, 193 ; Failed, 117 ; Total, 451.

The work in this Stage was much as usual, and does not call for any general remarks. The following may be worth the attention of the teachers.

Q. 2. State how to find the centre of gravity (or centre of mass) of two particles of given masses.

ABC is a triangle formed by three uniform rods, whose thickness is not to be considered. AB is 5 ft. long and weighs 4 lbs., BC is 4 feet long and weighs 1 lb., CA is 3 ft. long and weighs 2 lbs. Find the centre of gravity of the rods, and show, in a carefully drawn diagram, the position taken by the triangle when hung up by the point A.

The centre of gravity was found correctly in a good many cases ; but it seldom or never occurred that the triangle was rightly constructed with AG vertical.

Q. 4. If three forces of given magnitude are in equilibrium at a point, state the construction by which the angles between their directions can be found.

If the forces contain 5, 7, and 9 units, make the construction in a carefully drawn diagram.

It is proved in Geometry that any two sides of a triangle are together greater than the third side ; what is the corresponding property of three forces in equilibrium at a point ?

The actual arrangement of the forces was often not shown, even when the triangle had been correctly drawn. In only a few cases was the approximate number of degrees in the angles given.

Q. 6. A straight uniform bar 2 feet long is supported horizontally by pegs placed symmetrically 3 inches from either end. If the weight of the bar be 5 lbs., what weight must be placed on one end so that the pressure on one of the pegs may be wholly relieved ?

The number of pounds in the weight (15) was often found, but there was seldom a good reason assigned for this weight wholly relieving the pressure on one of the pegs.

Q. 7. One of the supports of a rod is a smooth fixed point ; in what direction is the reaction of that point exerted ?

A uniform rod AB can turn freely round a hinge at A, and rests against a fixed point C, which is so placed that C is on a lower level than A, and that AB is inclined at an angle of 45° to the vertical ; also AC is ⅔ths of AB. Draw a diagram to scale showing the forces which act on the rod ; also draw a triangle for the forces.

This is an instructive question. Of course there were many failures ; but there were several good answers, as many perhaps as could be fairly expected.

Q. 8. When is a force said to do work ?

Two weights of 10 lbs. and 15 lbs. respectively are joined by a fine thread which passes over a smooth fixed pulley. The heavier weight is allowed to fall and to draw up the lighter weight. When it has fallen 6 ft. how much work has been done by the first weight, and against the second weight ? What is there to show for the difference between these two quantities ?

Many found the 90 and 60 foot-pounds and the excess of 30 foot-pounds, but very few seemed to understand that this excess is represented by the Kinetic energy of the weights and pulley.

Q. 10. Describe Atwood's machine and show how it may be employed to determine the numerical value of the acceleration due to gravity.

Weights of 4 and 5 lbs., connected by a string which passes over a smooth fixed pulley, are held at rest and then gently released so that motion ensues ; how soon will the system be moving with unit velocity ?

The determination, by Atwood's Machine, of the numerical value of the acceleration due to gravity was often omitted, and in other cases seldom well explained.

Q. 11. Describe a simple pendulum and state the property of its small oscillations.

What is the effect upon the number of oscillations performed in a given time

(i) of increasing its length,

(ii) of transferring it to a place where the force of the earth's attraction is less ?

Of course, an oscillation is small when the arc through which the oscillating body moves is small. Now, very few seemed to understand that small arcs may have different lengths, e.g., one small arc may be two or three times as long as another small arc, and consequently only a few distinctly realised the property of the simple pendulum, viz., that its small oscillations are (sensibly) made in a given time, whatever be the length of the arc, provided it be small.

Stage 2.

Results : 1st Class, 157 ; 2nd Class, 338 ; Failed, 192 ; Total, 687.

Much of the work showed an adequate grasp of principles, and the examination may be considered to be satisfactory.

The most noticeable failure was in regard to the polygon of forces ; nearly all the candidates failed to distinguish between "a force acting along a line" and "a force represented in direction by a line." The attention of teachers may be called to this matter.

Q. 21. Find the unit of acceleration when the units of length and time are 1 yard and 1 minute respectively.

Candidates often failed to understand that they should have compared the magnitude of the unit of acceleration with that which obtains when the units of length and time are 1 foot and 1 second respectively. Many gave as the answer 1,200 yards per minute.

Q. 22. Ox, Oy are two lines inclined at a given angle ; one particle, whose mass is m, moves along Ox with a velocity u ; another, whose mass is n, moves along Oy with a velocity v ; they start together from O. Show in a diagram the line along which the centre of gravity moves, and find its velocity along that line.

Few were able to find the velocity of the centre of gravity.

Q. 25. A labourer having to move roots, or earth, or stones a considerable distance (such as a hundred yards), puts them into a wheelbarrow, and thereby can transfer at one journey about 1½ cwt. of material. Explain the mechanical principles on which he derives advantage from the use of the machine.

A wheelbarrow is sometimes cited as an instance of a lever ; explain this. Explain also the use of the wheel.

The answers were generally very fair ; few were entirely satisfactory.

Q. 26. Explain why a ladder cannot be placed in an inclined position on smooth pavement against a rough wall. A ladder is placed on a rough pavement against a rough wall (the co-efficient of friction being in each case ·5) and is in limiting equilibrium when inclined at an angle 30° to the horizontal ; find the position of its centre of gravity.

Usually well done. There were some mistakes in signs in writing down the equation of moment.

Q. 27. A heavy rod, 10 feet long, has a cord 20 feet long attached to its ends and passing over a smooth peg ; find the position in which it will rest if the centre of gravity divides its length in the ratio of 2 to 3.

Fair, but a sufficient explanation was not often given.

Q. 28. Let a square $ABCD$ represent a cube, with its face AB on a rough horizontal plane, and let the angle of friction be ϕ. There is a pulley at a point E over which passes a thread DE, fastened to D and carrying a weight P at the hanging end. Also DE is inclined at an angle a to the vertical. When P is just on the point of turning the cube round A, and of making it slide simultaneously, show that

$$\cot a + \cot \phi = 2.$$

Also find the ratio of P to W in this case.

When seriously attempted, this question was well done.

Q. 29. Define "work" and "kinetic energy." Draw an indicator diagram and show how to interpret it.

There was frequent failure to explain why the area represents the work done.

Q. 30. A chain is held vertically with one end on the ground ; if it be let down till all is on the ground, how many units of work have been done by gravity?

A right-angled triangle ABC represents a smooth inclined plane ; a chain just covers the incline AB and the height AC. If a small preponderance is given to the end B, find the work done by gravity up to the instant at which the chain leaves the incline, the hanging parts of the chain continuing vertical throughout the motion.

Few made use of the principle that the work done by gravity is given by the difference of potential at the initial and final positions.

Q. 32. Show graphically that the path of a projectile *in vacuo* is a parabola.

A tower, of height h, stands upon a horizontal plane ; from a point O in the plane the direction of projection passes through the summit of the tower. Show that for the projectile to strike the base of the tower the velocity of projection must be proportional to the distance from O to the summit.

Well done, but a simple geometrical proof was rare.

STAGE 3.

Results : 1st Class, 18 ; 2nd Class, 75 ; Failed, 39 ; Total, 132.

The examination shows that the majority of the candidates have carefully studied the subjects included in this Stage.

Q. 41. Let P be a point on the circumference of a wheel which rolls, in a vertical plane, along a straight line. At a given instant P is in a certain position in the plane ; find its position when the wheel has made half a revolution from that instant ; find also the length of the intervening path of P.

If at any instant P is in contact with the line, explain in what direction it begins to move after contact.

The few that attempted this did well generally. The best answer to the last part regarded the circumference of the wheel as the limit of a polygon.

Q. 42. Define simple harmonic motion, and show how it may be practically realised.

Prove that the acceleration is proportional to the distance from the centre, and that the period is independent of the amplitude.

Very well answered.

Q. 43. What are the laws of the variation of the force of the earth's attraction—

(i) for points inside the surface,
(ii) for points outside the surface?

If L, l be the lengths of the seconds pendulums at the surface of the earth and at a height h, show that the earth's radius is—

$$\frac{\sqrt{l}}{\sqrt{L}-\sqrt{l}} h$$

The law for points inside the surface was very often not known.

Q. 44. $ABCD$ is a quadrilateral formed by four equal rods without weight, connected by smooth hinges ; also it is stiffened by a fifth rod AC ; it is hung up by A, and carries equal weights (W) at B and D. Find the stress set up in AC, by virtual work (or virtual velocities). Also verify your result by resolving the forces.

There were frequent failures to verify the result by resolution of forces.

Q. 45. A heavy chain rests in a vertical plane on the rough convex perimeter of a vertical polygon, passing over small smooth pulleys at the angular points. Show that, in limiting equilibrium, the line joining the ends of the chain is inclined to the horizontal at an angle equal to the angle of friction.

A few candidates gave perfect answers.

Q. 46. State what is meant by relative motion, and give an example.

ABC is an inclined plane capable of moving freely with its base horizontal. A body, whose mass is m, is placed on the plane ; show how the plane must move so as to keep the body at rest relatively to the plane. Also find the pressure on the plane.

Very seldom well done. Candidates failed to see that the resultant acceleration of the particle must be perpendicular to the plane.

Q. 47. A particle is placed on the highest point of a smooth circle, and is allowed to slide down ; find the position of the directrix and of the focus of the parabola which it describes after leaving the circle.

The first part was commonly well done ; the second part occasionally.

Q. 48. A plane is at right angles to the axis of a cylinder at the middle point ; let a line be drawn in the plane to touch the cylinder. Find the moment of inertia of the cylinder about the line.

Let the cylinder oscillate about the line as an axis. Consider two cases : (a) when the length (l) is very great, (b) when it is very small, in comparison with the radius (r). Show that the time of a small oscillation in the former case is to the time in the latter case as l is to $r\sqrt{15}$, very nearly.

Q. 49. Find the moment of inertia of a triangle about an axis through an angular point perpendicular to its plane.

An isosceles triangular lamina swings about its vertex in a vertical plane at right angles to its own plane ; find the time of a small oscillation.

These two questions were often well done.

Q. 50. Investigate the motion of a conical pendulum.

At what angle is the arm inclined when it revolves in the time of its complete oscillation as a simple pendulum ?

The answer to the second part is that the arm must be vertical. This question was unduly puzzling to candidates, and allowance for this was made in assigning the marks.

Q. 51. A perfectly flexible chain is wrapped round a cylinder, and one end is fastened to the cylinder. The axis of the cylinder is horizontal, and round it the cylinder turns freely. If a very small preponderance is given to the other end of the chain, so that it begins to run down, find the velocity of the hanging end when one turn of the cylinder is completed. Also find the acceleration.

Q. 52. A light elastic string stretches ¼ inch for every lb. of tension. If when the string is vertical and unstretched, the upper end being fixed, a weight of 3 lbs. is attached at the lower end and gently released, find how far it will fall before coming to rest and the time of a complete oscillation.

These two questions were well done by the best candidates.

DIVISION II. (FLUIDS).

STAGE 1.

Results : 1st Class, 73 ; 2nd Class, 84 ; Failed, 28 ; Total, 185.

The work creates a favourable impression and the small number of failures is noticeable. Great care and neatness were the rule and not the exception. The illustrations given were numerous and varied.

Q. 2. State the principal elementary property of the centre of gravity of a body. Also state where the centre of gravity is situated in each of the following cases, viz. : (1) two particles whose given masses are unequal, and which are a given distance apart, (2) a square, (3) a cylinder.

What supposition is generally implied when we speak, without qualification, of the centre of gravity of a sphere, of a cylinder, &c. ?

A square is made up of two triangles, each of uniform density, but one of them twice as heavy as the other ; find where the centre of gravity of the square is situated.

The book-work was very well done.

Q. 3. Distinguish between energy and momentum.

A body is projected vertically upwards in a vacuum with a velocity of 100 feet per second. Draw a diagram to show the changes in its kinetic and potential energies.

Candidates, even when they had clear ideas about energy, were seldom able to draw a diagram.

Q. 5. A cubical box is filled with water (the weight of the water is not to be considered) and has a cylinder projecting from one face in which there works a water-tight piston (say a square inch in area) ; show, with the aid of a carefully drawn diagram, how the pressure is transmitted to the faces of the cube.

Continue your statement by explaining the need of a safety valve, when the pressure per square inch becomes large, and how the valve acts.

Q. 6. What circumstances determine the pressure of a liquid at an internal point of the vessel containing it ?

A vessel of circular cross section has a height 10″ and lower and upper diameters 4″ and 3″ respectively. Find, when it is filled with water,

(a) the pressure at a point in the base,

(b) the resultant pressure on the base.

These two questions were usually answered with intelligence.

Q. 7. What do you understand by the resultant pressure of a liquid upon an immersed body ?

A cube, edge 1 foot, is immersed with its centre 12 feet below the surface of water : find the resultant pressure of the water upon it.

Not well done on the whole. The line of action of the resultant pressure was often ignored and the cube taken with a face horizontal.

Q. 8. When a body floats, what is the magnitude and what is the direction of the resultant of the fluid pressures ?

State the conditions that must be fulfilled when a body floats.

Q. 9. What is meant by " atmospheric pressure " ?

Express its normal amount in lbs. per square inch.

At what depth must a horizontal surface be placed in water that the pressure on it may be 60 lbs. per square inch.

Q. 10. State what are the fixed points of a Mercurial thermometer, and explain in what sense they are fixed.

When the fixed points are given what is meant by a degree of temperature (a) on the centigrade scale, (b) on Fahrenheit's scale ?

When the reading on the centigrade scale is — 3°, what is the corresponding reading on Fahrenheit's scale ?

These three questions were well answered.

Q. 11. How does the volume of a given mass of gas change when both its temperature and pressure are altered ? An iron cylinder at 13° C. contains gas at a pressure of 5 atmospheres ; if the cylinder is made to withstand the pressure of 10 atmospheres with a factor of safety equal to 2, find the temperature to which the gas may be heated before the cylinder will burst.

The meaning of the term "factor of safety" was not always known ; it was common to add on two atmospheres to the ten atmospheres instead of multiplying the ten by two.

Q. 12. Describe the condensing air-pump.

Show that after n strokes the density of the air in the condenser is multiplied by

$$1 + n \frac{V'}{V},$$

where V, V' are the volumes of the condenser and cylinder respectively.

The explanation given often did not suffice.

Stage 2.

Results : 1st Class, 108 ; 2nd Class, 173 ; Failed, 52 ; Total, 333.

Q. 21. Find the moment of inertia in the two following cases, viz. :—(a) of a circular lamina about a diameter, (b) of a cylinder about a diameter of one end.

Mention a question in hydrostatics which depends on the moment of inertia of a lamina.

The moment of inertia of a cylinder was often carelessly done. The other parts of the question were fairly well answered.

Q. 23. State what is meant by the resultant pressure of a liquid on a given curved surface.

A cylinder is held in a given inclined position under water, find the magnitude and direction of the resultant pressure of the water on its curved surface, and compare it with the whole pressure on the curved surface. $N.B.$—You are not asked to find the line of action of the resultant.

Was not often attempted, and most of the attempts failed.

Q. 24. Find the centre of pressure of a triangle immersed in homogenous liquid with one side in the surface.

Was often well done, except that when the depth of the centre of pressure had been found, its position (on the median) was not given.

Q. 25. Find the conditions that must be fulfilled when a body floats.

A hollow cone (whose weight is put out of the question) floats in water when it contains a liquid whose specific gravity is n ; find the depth of the vertex below the surface of the water when the depth of the liquid in the cone is h.

How would it affect the answer if the weight of the cone were considered ?

Under what circumstances would the liquid sink the cone ?

This question was often taken, and was well answered by the better students.

Q. 26. A body, of specific gravity ·75, weighing 5 lb., dips into water and is supported partly by the buoyancy of the water and partly by an attached string which passes over a smooth pulley and carries at its other end a weight of 1 lb. hanging freely in the air. How much of the body is immersed ?

Q. 27. A thin cylinder is subjected to internal fluid pressure ; find the tension of the material of the cylinder.

A long strip, a quarter of an inch wide, is cut off from a thin plate of metal, and found to be just able to carry safely a weight of 500 lbs. The plate is formed into a cylinder which can just bear with safety an internal fluid pressure of 4,000 lbs. per square inch ; find the radius.

These two questions were very often taken, and, in most cases, were well done.

Q. 28. Explain the construction and principle of a mercury barometer. The tube of a barometer has a cross section of 1 square cm. and the lengths of a mercurial column and of the Torricellian vacuum are 77 cms. and 8 cms. respectively. If 1 cubic cm. of air is passed up into the vacuum show that the mercury column will be depressed 5·65 cms.

The answers to the first part were often long, and yet the explanation of the principles involved was often defective. The numerical example was often right.

Q. 29. A receiver provided with a stop-cock contains air at pressure p' which is greater than the atmospheric pressure P; the temperature is t, the same as that of the atmosphere. The stop-cock is opened and is shut again as soon as the air is at atmospheric pressure.

Is the temperature now greater or less than t.

If the air again becomes of temperature t, will its pressure p_1 then be greater or less than P?

Compare the mass of air now in the receiver with what it was originally.

The fall of temperature was often rightly explained. The answers to the other parts of the question were, in most cases, not good.

Q. 30. State the relation between the volume, the pressure, and the temperature of a given quantity of perfect gas.

A certain quantity of air has a volume of 10 cubic decimetres when under the pressure due to 0·7 metre of mercury and at a temperature of 7° C.; another quantity of air has a volume of 5 cubic decimetres when under the pressure due to 2·1 metres of mercury and at a temperature of 27° C. If the two quantities are made to occupy a volume 8 cubic decimetres at a temperature of 23° C., find the pressure.

Was generally well done. Both this question and Question 29 showed that many of the students do not clearly understand that the formula $VP = KT$ refers to a definite quantity (or mass) of gas.

Q. 31. If the atmosphere be at rest and the temperature constant, show that at points, whose heights are in arithmetical progression, (the common difference being small) the pressures are in geometrical progression.

Show that difference in height in feet between the stations where the barometer readings are H_1 and H_2 is

$$\frac{k}{g} \log_e 10 \, (\log 10 \, H_1 - \log_{10} H_2)$$

and discuss the value of k.

Was not often taken, but several of the answers were good, except that the discussion of the value of k was often defective.

Q. 32. State and prove the theorem (called Torricelli's Theorem) for the velocity of water issuing from a hole in a side of the containing vessel.

Explain what is the vena contracta.

The level of water in a pond is constant. There is a sluice, the gate of which is shut. A circular hole 1¾ of an inch in diameter is bored in the gate with its centre 3 inches below the surface. Assuming that the actual outflow is ⅝ths of the theoretical outflow, find how many gallons flow out in 24 hours. ($N.B.$ 7 $\pi = 22$.)

Was taken rather often, and in most cases was fairly well done. The loss of potential energy of the water in the vessel, due to the efflux, was seldom well explained, and the numerical result was often wrong.

STAGE 3.

Results : 1st Class, 12 ; 2nd Class, 40 ; Failed, 20 ; Total, 72.

It may be said that generally when the questions are such as can be answered by what the students have seen in their text books or learned from their teachers, the answers are often well and intelligently given. But when a question requires a not very obvious application of what has been learned, weakness is commonly shown. Of course, it is to be expected that such questions will come in for fewer good answers than the others ; but, allowing for this, the good answers were but few.

Q. 41. When the angular velocity of a body moving in one plane is represented by

$$\frac{d\theta}{dt},$$

what points have to be attended to in regard to θ ?

Ox and Oy are two lines at right angles to each other ; A, B, are two points fixed in a rod which is constrained to move in such a way that A is always in Ox, and B in Oy. If at any instant A is moving with a given velocity (V) along Ox, find the velocity of B along Oy, and the angular velocity of AB.

The point, that θ must be measured from some fixed direction, was often missed.

Q. 42. Investigate a formula for the resultant pressure of a liquid on a curved surface.

Find it in the case of the portion of a hemispherical bowl cut off by a vertical plane through the centre ; the bowl being 1 foot in diameter and filled with water.

The diagrams, illustrative of the second part, often showed a curious perverseness. A hemispherical bowl can hardly be full of water unless its circular rim is horizontal, yet the bowl was often drawn with the rim vertical. Moreover the position of the centre of gravity of a semicircle was often not known.

Q. 43. State briefly the meaning of the equation

$$dp = \rho \left(X\, dx + Y\, dy + Z\, dz \right).$$

Explain the notation, and prove the equation.

A closed hollow sphere is full of water ; it turns with a given constant angular velocity round a vertical axis coinciding with a diameter ; find the pressure of the water at any point of the great circle, which is at right angles to the axis.

Find the result in pounds per square foot, when the radius is 3 ft. and the sphere makes one turn per second.

(N.B. $\pi^2 = 10$).

The proof when attempted often failed, and the numerical result was seldom found.

Q. 44. An elliptical lamina is immersed, at a given depth in liquid, with its major axis vertical ; investigate the position of the centre of pressure.

How is the result connected with pendulum motion ?

The radius of gyration, needed for answering this question, was seldom found correctly. Of course, it can be found from known properties of the Moment of Inertia with little or no integration. Instead of using these properties many of the students tried to find it directly, and failed for want of sufficient skill in integration.

Q. 45. A uniform rod AB is attached to a fixed point P, round which it can turn freely, and AP is longer than BP. The fixed point P is within a vessel so large as not to interfere with the freedom of AB's motion. Suppose that the vessel is slowly filled with water. The specific gravity of the rod being less than that of water, state what are the various positions that AB will take up until it is covered by the water, and prove the statement.

If we suppose that $AP = 2 BP$, and that the specific gravity of the rod is 5-4ths of that of water, find how the motion of the rod in this case will differ from that of the rod in the former case.

Was attempted fairly often. In many cases the attempt failed ; in others the success was no more than partial, e.g., no one found out that when the water has risen to a certain height and the rod begins to turn, it moves in such a manner that while passing from the vertical to the horizontal position the length of the rod out of water continues constant, and that the like will be true when the water rises above P. In the first case, however, the rod continues to rise and finally comes to rest with A above B ; in the second case the rod gradually falls back and finally comes to rest with A in its old position.

Q. 46. There is a cone of uniform density, and a particle, whose weight is 1-nth of that of the cone, is placed at its vertex. The cone is put into water with its vertex downward ; find the condition of its not sinking.

Find also what further condition must be fulfilled, if it is to float permanently with its vertex downwards.

The condition of permanent or stable flotation was seldom understood ; and when it seemed to be understood, the particular case was rarely worked out correctly.

Q. 47. Given the formula for a perfect gas, viz., $vp = Rt$, explain the notation, and state the physical laws which it expresses.

Show that R denotes a certain number of units of work. If v denotes the volume of the unit of mass of air, find R in kilogramme-metres, having given that at a temperature of 0°C. and under a pressure of 760 m.m. of mercury, whose density is 13·6, a cubic metre of air weighs 1·2932 kilogrammes.

The correct numerical value of R was seldom found.

Q. 49. Assuming Boyle's law to be true, show that at a given temperature the mean velocity of the molecules of a gas is constant.

The mean velocity of the molecules of hydrogen at the temperature of melting ice is 185,900 cm. per sec. ; find the density of the gas at atmospheric pressure.

N.B. $g = 9·8$, see also the data in Q. 47.

The proof, that $p = \frac{1}{3}\rho V^2$, was attempted fairly often, but seemed to be imperfectly understood. The numerical work often contained serious errors.

Q. 50. Why is the pressure inside a soap bubble greater than the pressure outside ?

Investigate an expression for the excess of pressure in terms of the surface tension and the diameter.

Q. 51. A clean glass tube of fine bore is dipped vertically into water. Draw a diagram to show how the surface tension acts in keeping the water raised in the tube, and show that under certain conditions the height of the raised water is inversely proportional to the diameter of the tube.

These two questions were often taken and were in most cases answered well or fairly well.

Q. 52. ABC is a triangle having a right angle at C, and we will suppose that it represents a rectangular prism whose height is the unit of length. The prism is in equilibrium under stresses on its three faces, viz., a normal pressure X per square unit on BC and of Y per square unit on CA ; find the stress on AB.

Show that your results include, as a particular case, that in which the stresses are due to fluid pressure.

Many of the answers to this question were wrong. Of those which could be hardly described as wrong, few brought out plainly that the stress on AB is made up of a normal stress $X \sin^2 A + Y \cos^2 A$ and a tangential stress $(X-Y) \sin A \cos B$.

HONOURS.

Results: 1st Class, — ; 2nd Class, 2 ; Failed, 1 ; Total, 3.

Three students attempted the Honours questions. The work sent up by two of them comprised a few answers which were good in substance, though somewhat deficient in style.

DAY EXAMINATIONS.

DIVISION I. (SOLIDS.)

STAGE 1.

Results: 1st Class, 18 ; 2nd Class, 53 ; Failed, 46 ; Total, 117.

The number of students in this Stage shows only a slight falling off, in comparison with the number of last year. The work, on the whole, was fairly good, quite as good as it was last year. A few of the best papers were very good. Some points in the answers may be worth notice.

Q. 3. Draw an isosceles triangle and indicate accurately the position of its centre of gravity.

If it be divided by a straight line passing through this point parallel to the base, will the portions of the area on either side of the dividing line be of equal area ? Give an explanation of your answer.

Very few understood that the line through the centre of gravity divides the triangle into parts of which one is four-fifths of the other.

Q. 5. Draw a diagram of a single movable pulley.

If the two parts of the rope are parallel, why must the tension be half the weight ?

If the free end of the rope were pulled horizontally, why would it be impossible for the pulley to stay at rest ?

Was not very well answered. Few understood that, under the conditions usually presupposed, the tension of the rope is the same throughout.

Q. 6. Explain the properties of an equal arm balance according as the centre of motion is above, coincident with, or below the centre of gravity of the beam.

Thence show that great sensibility is not compatible with great stability, giving accurate definitions of these terms.

This is a rather difficult question, but a few of the students sent up fairly good answers.

Q. 8. A mass of 1,000 lbs. is placed on a rough horizontal plane; what is the coefficient of friction if a force of 700 lbs. weight acting at an angle of 30° to the horizontal is on the point of moving it?

The mistake that so often occurs in questions of this kind occurred often on the present occasion. The pressure on the plane was supposed to be 1,000 lbs., instead of 1,000 lbs. diminished by the vertical component of the force of 700 lbs.; so that the friction was taken as 1,000 μ, instead of 650 μ.

Q. 9. Find the effective horse-power of an engine which draws a train of 100 tons, at 20 miles an hour, up an incline of 1 in 500; taking the resistance due to air, friction, &c., as 10 lbs. per ton.

Not more than a few understood that the power of the engine is used up, (a) in dragging the train against friction along the base of the plane; (b) in lifting the train through the height, i.e., through base ÷ 500.

Q. 10. What is meant by the composition of two velocities? Give an example.

A body P is moving at the rate of 12 miles an hour, in a direction 30° to the north of east; find—by a construction, or otherwise—its velocity eastward and its velocity northward.

A second body Q is moving due east at the rate of 15 miles an hour, along a line AB; at a certain instant Q is due north of P at a distance of 10 miles; find the distance between P and Q at the instant P crosses AB.

Q. 11. Give the formulæ for motion in a straight line under constant acceleration.

With what constant acceleration must a balloon ascend vertically in order to reach a height of 1,000 feet in 1 minute?

These two questions were fairly well done.

Q. 12. A body moves uniformly in a circle. Without going into any calculation, explain why it must be acted on by a constant force, directed to the centre.

A body moves with a constant velocity in a circle, which it describes 480 times a minute; the radius of the circle is 3 feet; and the force which keeps the body in the circle, equals a weight of 10 lbs. Find the mass of the body. ($N.B.$ $\pi^2 = 10$).

The required explanation was seldom good. In the example, g was often omitted, so that the answer came out $\frac{1}{16}$th of an ounce, instead of $\frac{1}{4}$th of a pound.

STAGE 2.

Results: 1st Class, 15; 2nd Class, 29; Failed, 19; Total, 63.

There was a large falling off in the number of papers, as compared with the number of last year; but, perhaps the work sent up was on the whole better than usual.

Q. 22. State what is the position of the centre of gravity of (1) a triangle, (2) a cone, (3) the arc of a semicircle.

Find the centre of gravity of the part of a square which is left, when a corner has been cut off by a line which is parallel to one diagonal, and which cuts off the $1/n^{\text{th}}$ part of the other diagonal.

The second part of this question is rather hard, that is, requires care, and the mistakes were many.

Q. 25. Describe some form of weighing machine in which the indication does not depend upon the position of the body weighed upon the platform. Explain the action.

Few took this question, and not many of them understood it.

Q. 26. AB is a rod projecting horizontally from A, a point in a wall ; C is a point in the wall below A, and D is a point in AB ; CD is a strut with smooth attachments at C and D. Let a weight W be hung from B ; show in a diagram, the forces which keep AB at rest, and draw a triangle for them.

In the particular case when
$$AC = AD = AB \div 2,$$
show that the thrust of the strut is
$$2W \sqrt{2}.$$
Also find the force tending to pull AB away from the wall, and the line along which it acts.

A few—about ten—of the students treated this question well, showing correctly in diagrams the forces and the relations between them. Most of the others failed to treat rightly the action at A.

Q. 28 A body moves through a distance of 6 ft. and is acted on by a force P, which varies continuously, and has at first a value of 5 lbs. ; at the ends of the successive feet its values are 8, 10, 11, 9, 4, 1 lbs. Find the number of foot pounds of work done, and the mean value of P. Illustrate your results by a diagram drawn to scale.

Very few knew Simpson's Rule, and consequently did not get the area of the graph as accurately as the data permitted.

Q. 29. A body slides down a smooth inclined plane, find the acceleration and the pressure on the plane.

If the plane were rough, how would the roughness affect the acceleration ? Would the pressure be affected ?

Find the acceleration and the pressure on the plane in the case in which the length of the plane is three times its height, and the coefficient of friction is $\frac{1}{5}$.

Was fairly well done.

Q. 30. Draw a diagram to show *all* the forces acting upon a marble which moves freely in a horizontal circular tube with uniform acceleration f; taking the marble to weigh 1 oz., and the diameter of the circle to be 1 foot.

If the tube is in a vertical plane and the marble starts from rest at the highest point, find the pressure on the tube when the marble is at its lowest position.

Was seldom well answered.

Q. 31. An inclined plane AB and a point P above it are given. Of all straight lines drawn from P to AB, find that along which the descent is made in the least time.

Let t denote the time in which a body would fall vertically from P to AB, and t_1 the time down the line of quickest descent; show that
$$\frac{t}{t_1} = \sqrt{\frac{1 + \sec a}{2}},$$
where a denotes the inclination of the plane.

Was fairly well done. However, the first part of the question is to be found in many text books, and the second part does not require much geometry.

Q. 32. Write down and explain the equation of work and kinetic energy.

A weight of 2 lbs. falls from a height of 1 foot upon the head of a vertical nail, weighing $\frac{1}{4}$ oz., in a horizontal wooden board, and drives it in $\frac{1}{8}$ inch ; find the average resistance of the wood.

Was several times answered approximately, *i.e.*, the mass of the nail was neglected.

Division II. (Fluids.)

Stage 1.

Results : 1st Class, 39 ; 2nd Class, 32 ; Failed, 22 ; Total, 93.

There were few candidates.   Over 50 per cent. were well prepared for the examination.

Q. 10. State Boyle's law and explain the nature of the limitations to which it is subject.

> A piston is situated in the middle of a closed cylinder a foot long and there are equal quantities of air on each side of it. The piston is pushed gradually until it is at a distance of 1 inch from one end. Compare the pressures on each side of the piston.

From this question it was evident, as frequently pointed out in these reports, that many candidates did not realize that Boyle's law refers to a given mass, or quantity, of air.

Q. 9. Describe a Nicholson's Hydrometer, and explain how it is used for finding the specific gravity of a solid body.

> A Nicholson's Hydrometer is found to sink to the standard point (a) when 720 grains and a certain body P are in the upper pan ; (b) when 765 grains are in the upper pan and P in the lower pan. What conclusion can you draw from these data ? What more must you know before you can infer the weight of P and its specific gravity?

Q. 11. Explain how the column of mercury in a barometer is supported, and why the column is sometimes higher and sometimes lower.

> It is given that the elastic force of the vapour of water at 60° F. equals the pressure of 0·52 inches of mercury. A barometer stands at 30·15 in. and the temperature is 60° F. Suppose that a little water—enough to occupy about a tenth of an inch of the tube—got into the barometer and came into the vacuum space at the top of the mercury ; how would it affect the reading of the barometer, and why ? How would the reading be affected if the temperature rose, and how, if it fell ?

Q. 12. A tube 61 inches long, closed at one end and open at the other, is held upright in a vessel of mercury.   At first the closed end is 30 inches above the surface of the mercury, which is on the same level within and without the tube. The tube is raised slowly. Explain why the surface of the mercury in the tube rises.

> If the barometer stands at 30 inches and the closed end of the tube described above is raised to 60 inches above the surface of the mercury, what is the height of the mercury within the tube, above the surface of the mercury outside the tube ?

> [N.B. $\sqrt{5} = 2\cdot236$.]

The answering to these three questions gives rise to the remark that candidates should be taught not to give irrelevant detail in answering. The question should be carefully read in order to see the precise point, and the answer then directed to it. A short time spent in instructing students in a proper method of answering would be well employed.

Stage 2.

Results : 1st Class, 8 ; 2nd Class, 4 ; Failed, — ; Total, 12.

There were only 12 candidates and the quality of the work was good.

Some want of accuracy in calculation was shown in the answering of Question 29.

Q. 29. Describe a diving bell.

> A cylindrical bell, 7 feet in height, is lowered until the top of the bell if 26 feet below the surface. If the water rises 2·9 feet within the bell, find the height of the mercury barometer, assuming the specific gravity of mercury to be 13·6.

Report on the Examinations in Navigation and in Spherical and Nautical Astronomy.

NAVIGATION.

STAGE 1.

Results : 1st Class, 3 ; 2nd Class, 15 ; Failed, 4 ; Total, 22.

The number of papers sent in, viz., twenty-two, was slightly larger than usual.

The practical questions were fairly well answered, and the definitions asked for were generally given correctly, but otherwise the knowledge of theory was but small.

Q. 2. Describe the Mariner's Compass, explaining particularly the terms : Bowl, Binnacle, Lubber Point, Gimbals.

> Two ships A and B are at anchor, the true bearing of A from B being known to be N. 70° E., and the variation of compass 15° 20′ W.
>
> If the compass bearing of B from A is found to be S. 87° W., find the deviation.

In several cases the first part of the question was very well done, but the answers to the easy numerical example which formed the second part were often inaccurate.

Q. 3. Explain what is meant by parallel sailing, and investigate the formula employed.

> Two ships in latitude 40° S., which are 300 miles apart, each steam due North at 10 knots. After what interval will they be 350 miles apart ?

The answers generally were unsatisfactory, and none of the candidates appeared to be acquainted with the easy trigonometrical proof of the formula employed.

Q. 5. Describe the Traverse Table, and explain its use.

> By means of this Table solve the equations
>
> (1) $x = 191 \sec 49°$
>
> (2) $118 = 146 \cot y,$
>
> explaining the processes employed.

The descriptions given of the Traverse Table were somewhat vague, and the useful applications of the Table to the solution of plane right-angled triangles in general seem to be very generally neglected.

Q. 8. A ship sails from Vigo (lat. 42° 15′ N., long. 8° 40′ W.) S.W. ½ W. until she finds herself in lat. 37° 27′ N. What is then her longitude ?

In this, and other of the practical questions, much confusion was evident as to the distinction between departure and difference of longitude, which cannot be too strongly impressed upon the beginner.

STAGE 2.

Results : 1st Class, 8 ; 2nd Class, 22 ; Failed, 9 ; Total, 39.

The results in this Stage were of an average character, and a few excellent papers were sent in. The practical questions were upon the whole very correctly worked, and the theoretical knowledge shewn was perhaps a little more satisfactory than usual.

SPHERICAL AND NAUTICAL ASTRONOMY.

STAGE 1.

Results : 1st Class, 1 ; 2nd Class, 2 ; Failed, — ; Total, 3.

Only three papers were received in this Stage, all of which showed a fairly satisfactory knowledge, and one obtained 74 per cent. of the total marks. No candidate availed himself of the option to substitute questions in Spherical Astronomy from Section III. for the practical questions in Nautical Astronomy from Section II.

STAGE 2.

Results : 1st Class, 4 ; 2nd Class, 12 ; Failed, 1 ; Total, 17.

Of the 17 candidates, four took the questions in Spherical Astronomy, and the papers of two of these were very good.

In the remaining 13 papers the practical work from Section II. was generally well done, but the theoretical portion was less satisfactory. The practical question (No. 32) on fixing a ship's place by the method of position-lines was very correctly worked by nearly all those who attempted it, but the equally useful method of fixing position by a combination of a single position-line with the bearing of a known point of land (No. 25) seems not so well understood.

It would perhaps be well if it were impressed on students that it is unnecessary to correct elements from the Nautical Almanac to the tenth of a second, as such minute accuracy has no meaning in nautical calculations, and much time is lost thereby.

NAVIGATION AND SPHERICAL AND NAUTICAL ASTRONOMY.

STAGE 3.

No papers were received in this Stage.

HONOURS.

Result : 1st Class, — ; 2nd Class, 1 ; Failed, — ; Total, 1.

One paper only was sent in, the questions answered being taken wholly from Section A., Navigation and Nautical Astronomy. Slightly more than half marks were awarded to the paper.

GROUP II.—ENGINEERING.

BOARD OF EXAMINERS.

I. Practical Plane and Solid Geometry	Professor John Perry, M.E., D.Sc., LL.D., F.R.S., *Chairman*.
II. Machine Construction and Drawing	J. Harrison, M.I.M.E., Assoc. M. Inst. C.E.
III. Building Construction and Drawing	Professor W. E. Dalby, M.A., M. Inst. C.E.
IV. Naval Architecture	J. Slater, F.R.I.B.A.
VII. Applied Mechanics	Professor Henry Adams, M. Inst. C.E.
XXII. Steam	C. E. Goodyear.
V*p*. Practical Mathematics	Professor T. Hudson Beare, B.Sc., F.R.S.E., M. Inst. C.E.

Report on the Examinations in Practical Plane and Solid Geometry.

EVENING EXAMINATION.

The number of candidates in this subject continues to increase, the rates of increase in comparison with the numbers last year being 5½ per cent. in Stage 1, 9½ per cent. in Stage 2, 27 per cent. in Stage 3, and 12 per cent. in Honours.

As regards quality, the work in Stage 1 was very satisfactory, except for a prevalent weakness in two portions of the subject, viz., in problems on the construction and tangency of circles, represented by Questions 2 and 5, and in problems on the line and plane, for illustration of which refer to Question 10. The same faults were noticed in last year's report, and have not yet been rectified in the classes. The defective answers to these three questions are mainly responsible for the smaller proportion of successes this year. In other parts of both Plane and Solid Geometry, and in vector work, a large amount of good work was done.

In Stage 2, the answering was not so good as in 1906, which was an exceptionally good year. This was partly owing to the character of the examination paper, and partly to a want of thorough knowledge in the more abstract and fundamental parts of Solid Geometry, as tested by Questions 28 and 32 on the line and plane. This portion of the subject merits more attention than appears to be given to it, and probably requires improved methods of teaching. Questions 26 and 27, on vectors, would no doubt present new features to many candidates, so that the comparatively low average marks obtained for them was to be expected. On the whole the work gave evidence of a large amount of earnest and efficient teaching in the subject.

In Stage 3 and in Honours the answering was even better than in 1906; in Stage 3 especially, the questions proved to be better within the capabilities of the well-taught student.

Detailed criticisms of the answers follow.

STAGE 1.

Results: 1st Class, 574; 2nd Class, 602; Failed, 752; Total, 1,928.

Q. 1. Take from the tables the chord and tangent of 22°. Construct an angle of 22° by using the value of the chord, and a second angle of 22° by using the tangent. Verify the results by measuring the two angles with your protractor, writing down, to the first decimal, what each angle measures.

The values of the chord and tangent were usually taken correctly from the tables, and in most cases a proper construction was used for the angle, but the radius was often taken too small to ensure any great accuracy.

Q. 2. The given figure is symmetrical about the axes AA, BB. The circular arcs PAP, PBP join tangentially at P. Draw the figure to the given dimensions, which are in millimetres, determining by construction the centres of the two arcs PBP, and the four points P.

N.B.—No credit will be given for a mere copy of the diagram.

This question was badly answered. The constructions for determining the centres of the two arcs were nearly always wrong in principle, and comparatively few could even find the points of junction of the circular arcs. More attention should be given to the properties of circles.

Q. 3. The building plot S is drawn to a scale of ½ inch to 10 yards. Find the area of the plot in square yards.

A rectangular plot of land of the same area has the frontage (or side) AA. Find the depth (that is the other side) of the plot in feet, and draw the rectangle to scale.

This was a favourite question and the answering was fairly good. But a number of the candidates divided the figure very clumsily into a large number of triangles instead of into two with a common base, thus making several multiplications necessary instead of only one. Errors in scaling were not so numerous as in past years, but some candidates require more training in reading directly to scale, and there is still too much clumsy arithmetic in evidence.

Q. 4. The circular plate P turns about the axis C, set eccentrically, thus forming a cam. The slider S has its lower end A resting on the cam, and thus receives an up and down motion. Mark successive positions of A corresponding to angular positions of the cam of 30°, 60°, 90°, 120°, 150° and 180° from the given position.

Was not very frequently chosen, but the attempts were usually very successful.

Q. 5. Draw the figure to the given dimensions, linear scale ⅛th. It represents two pulleys, connected by a crossed belt $CAACBBC$. Mark the arcs of contact of the belt. Measure the total length of the belt. The circular portions may be measured by using tracing paper and a pricker, or otherwise.

This question was commonly attempted, but the work was not of any great merit. The arcs of contact of the belt were seldom correctly marked; errors of scale were frequent, and sometimes answers were given without any indication of the method by which they were obtained. Measurement of the arcs by means of tracing paper was frequent, but not very accurately carried out.

Q. 6. Construct a parallelogram $AABB$ on the given side AA such that the angle AOA between the diagonals shall measure 115° and the side AB shall be ⅔ AA.

Was frequently attempted, but the answers were generally poor. The ratio of the sides was usually found correctly, and occasionally a segment containing an angle of 115° was constructed, but very few could proceed further, and for the final figure the great majority relied on pure guessing.

Q. 7. In a survey the following measurements were made, lengths being in chains and angles being reckoned anti-clockwise from the east.

$$AB = 32 \underset{16°}{}, \quad BC = 51\cdot3 \underset{142°}{}, \quad CD = 67 \underset{41\cdot4°}{}.$$

Plot the points A, B, C, D to the scale of ½ inch to 10 chains. Measure from your drawing the length and direction of AD. Also give the easterly and northerly components of AD.

This question was only moderately well answered. In too many cases the angles were set off wrongly, usually from the preceding vector instead of from a fixed zero direction, and other mistakes in measuring the angles occurred.

Q. 8. A load W of 400 pounds is carried from overhead beams in the manner shown, where A and B are two bars pinned to the beams and to each other.

Find the pull in each bar. Find also the horizontal force pulling the beams towards each other.

Fairly often attempted. The pulls in the bars were usually correctly given, but many went wrong with the horizontal pull, giving the sum of the pulls on the two beams, or else the result obtained by measuring the other diagonal of their original parallelogram, that is, the magnitude of the vector difference of the two pulls.

Q. 9. You are given the plan of a lawn sprinkler which revolves about O. Water leaves at A with a speed through the nozzle of 50 feet per second, as indicated. The rotation of the arms causes the nozzle A to move with a speed of 10 feet per second in a direction perpendicular to the radius OA, as shown.

Find the actual velocity of the jet, measuring its speed and showing its direction.

Not very frequently attempted, but usually well answered.

Q. 10. A geometrical model is made by soldering together at O three pieces of wire OA, OB, OC. You are given the plan with OA, OB resting on the horizontal plane, and OC inclined upwards, the height of C being indexed in millimetres.

(a) Draw an elevation of the model on xy.

(b) Draw a new elevation on a second xy so chosen as to exhibit an edge or a profile view of the plane containing AOC. Show the traces of this plane in reference to your new xy, and measure the inclination of the plane to the horizontal.

The first part (a) was nearly always well done, but in (b) few could choose the new xy properly, and some of those who successfully accomplished this failed to indicate the traces of the plane. More attention should be given to, and improved methods adopted in, the teaching of the fundamental parts of descriptive geometry.

Q. 11. A and B are two branches of a sheet metal pipe of square section. Draw an elevation of the pipe on $x'y'$. Also by developing A, draw the shape to which the flat piece of metal forming this part must be cut.

This question was very often successfully attempted.

Q. 12. A cast iron cover or lid is shown in plan and in pictorial projection. From the plan project an elevation on xy, the lower part of the cover resting on the horizontal plane, and vertical dimensions being taken from the pictorial view, in which vertical lines appear full size.

SS is a vertical section plane. Draw a sectional elevation on $x'y'$ (parallel to SS), the front portion SAS of the cover being supposed removed.

Frequently attempted and well done. The first elevation presented no difficulties, and the sectional elevation was satisfactorily drawn. In spite of the small scale adopted for the figure, the answers were fairly accurate and complete. It is evident that candidates have a liking for the projection of simple figures.

Q. 13. The figure is the dimensioned roof plan of a house. The roof planes A and B are both inclined to the horizontal at 33°. Find the length and inclination of the valley rafter CD, that is of the line whose plan is cd.

N.B.—Employ a scale of ¼ inch to 1 foot. The diagram need not be copied.

Was frequently attempted and often with complete success. The adverse criticism offered in reference to Q. 10 must therefore be qualified to some extent. Candidates can deal with lines better than with planes.

Q. 14. Two views of a tusk tenon joint are shown. Represent the portion *A* (removed from *B*) in pictorial projection, in a manner similar to that used for the cube, where lines parallel to *oy* and *oz* are drawn horizontally and vertically, to a scale of full size, and lines parallel to *ox* are drawn by using the 45° set-square, and to a scale of half size.

N.B.—The figure need not be copied, dimensions being taken directly from the diagram.

Very commonly attempted, and, as in similar questions of previous years, very well answered. This kind of projection is attractive to the majority of students.

STAGE 2.

Results: 1st Class, 264 ; 2nd Class, 431 ; Failed, 298 ; Total, 993.

Q. 21. Take from the tables the chord and tangent of 22°. Construct an angle of 22° by using the value of the chord, and a second angle of 22° by using the tangent. From each of these angles determine the sine of 22°, and compare the mean of the two values with the true value of sine 22°.

This question was very well answered as a rule, but many employed too small a scale. A few were evidently not clear as to the meaning of the tables. Some candidates marked off the angle by means of a protractor.

Q. 22. The building plot *S* is drawn to a scale of ½ inch to 10 yards. Find the area of the plot in square yards. The portion *LL* of the boundary may be replaced by a well-judged "equalising line."

A rectangular plot of the same area has the frontage (or side) *AA*. Find the depth (*i.e.*, the other side) of the plot and draw the rectangle to scale.

A favourite question. The answers were usually fairly correct, but the methods of working were often somewhat faulty. Some candidates found the area first in square inches and then converted it into square yards, instead of scaling the original measurements in yards. Some divided the whole area into rather wide strips, and applied Simpson's or the "mid-ordinate" rule, not realising that these rules would not give very good results with a figure having decided angles in it. There was some lack of judgment in selecting a suitable base in dealing with the upper curve, the best method being generally overlooked. The equalising line for the curve *LL* was generally well chosen.

Q. 23. A slider *S* receives an up-and-down motion from a cam on which it rests, the cam consisting of a circular plate *P*, turning about an eccentric axis *C*. Mark successive positions of the end *AA* of the slider corresponding to angular positions of the cam of 30°, 60°, 90°, 120°, 150° and 180° from the given position.

Plot a curve in which the abscissæ represent cam angles to a scale of ¼″ to 30°, and the ordinates show the heights of the slider.

This question was well answered, except that some candidates did not allow for the flat base of the slide, and obtained a result which would have been correct for Q. 4 in Stage 1.

Q. 24. The given moulding is drawn to a linear scale of 0·43. Enlarge the figure so as to get a full-sized drawing of the moulding. What is the ratio of the area of the enlargement to the area of the original figure?

The answers were generally correct in principle, but the accuracy was not very good, candidates not sufficiently realising that where figures are magnified, special care is necessary to ensure a faithful reproduction.

Q. 25. In the plan of an estate, drawn to a scale of 1 inch to 100 yards, three trees A, B, C are marked, and their relative positions measure, in yards,

$$AB = 232_{79\cdot6^\circ}, \quad BC = 358_{6\cdot8^\circ},$$

angles being measured anti-clockwise from the east.

In order to locate two places P and Q on the estate, lying on the north side of BC, the angles subtended by the trees at P and Q are measured with a sextant and are as follows :—

$$APB = 36\cdot2^\circ, \quad BPC = 22\cdot3^\circ, \quad APC = 58\cdot5^\circ.$$
$$BQA = 18\cdot1^\circ, \quad BQC = 78\cdot8^\circ, \quad AQC = 60\cdot7^\circ.$$

Plot the five points to scale, and measure the length and direction of PQ.

The answers were satisfactory and the principles of the construction well understood, but it was easy to make a slip plotting the various angles.

Q. 26. Determine and measure the thrusts in the members A, B, C, D, E and F of the given truss when loaded in the manner shown. Let the scale be $\frac{1}{4}$ inch to 0·1 ton.

Was not popular, though a fair number of the attempts were good. Instead of beginning the force diagram for the joint CD, some first found the reactions at the supports and made one of the end joints the starting point, overlooking the effect of the bending of the beam or lower member. The frame, no doubt, was one of unusual type.

Q. 27. A vertical wall is 80 yards long and 42 feet high. The following table gives the pressures of the wind on it, p pounds per square foot, at various heights h feet above the ground :—

h	4	10	18	25	33	42
p	9	12	16·7	20·3	23·5	26

Draw a diagram showing the relation between p and h, using scales of 1 inch to 10 feet for h, and 1 inch to 10 pounds per square foot for p. Find the mean pressure on the wall in pounds per square foot, and the total wind force on the wall in pounds.

Not very often attempted. The diagram was always set out to scale, but in finding the mean pressure candidates nearly always took the mean of the six given pressures, a method wrong in principle on several accounts, one of which is that the ordinates were not equidistant.

Q. 28. A geometrical model is made by soldering together at O three pieces of wire OA, OB, OC. You are given the plan with OA, OB resting on the horizontal plane, and OC inclined upwards, the height of C being indexed in millimetres.

(a) Draw an elevation of the model on an xy so chosen as to exhibit an edge or a profile view of the plane containing AOC. What is the inclination of this plane to the horizontal?

(b) Draw the plan of the model after it has been turned about OA as axis until OC rests on the horizontal plane. What is now the height of B?

The answers were not so good as they should have been ; candidates are not sufficiently grounded in the general principles of Descriptive Geometry. This question, differing from corresponding questions of previous years, found them therefore unprepared. A number took their xy parallel to OC instead of perpendicular to OA, and gave the inclination of the line OC instead of that of the plane AOC. The second part (b) was also badly answered.

Q. 29. A split wrought-iron collar is shown. SS is a vertical section
plane. Draw a sectional elevation on $x'y'$, taken parallel to SS ,
the portion A in front of the section plane being supposed
removed.

Candidates found the large number of curves somewhat confusing,
though the answers were fairly good, and would have been better if the
whole elevation had first been drawn, and then the superfluous parts erased.

Q. 30. A and B are two branches of a sheet metal pipe of circular
section. Draw an elevation of the pipe on $x'y'$. Also, by
developing A , draw the shape to which the flat piece of metal
forming this branch must be cut.

This question was very generally attempted and was, on the whole, well
done.

Q. 31. The figure is the dimensioned plan of the roof of a house. The
roof planes A and B are inclined to the horizontal at 33°.
Determine and measure—

    (a) The length and inclination of the valley rafter CD , that
         is, of the line whose plan is cd .

    (b) The bevel for cutting the angles of the slates which lie
         along the valley, that is, the true angle between the
         lines whose plans are cd , de .

    N.B.—Employ a scale of $\frac{1}{4}$ inch to 1 foot. The diagram
need not be copied.

This was also a favourite question and was fairly well answered. Some
were evidently puzzled by planes which formed a valley and not a hip, and
could have correctly answered a question on the latter.

Q. 32. Represent by a scale of slope a plane which shall contain the
given line AB and be perpendicular to the given plane. Unit
for heights 0·1″.

This was rarely attempted and more rarely well answered. Better
teaching is required in the fundamental problems of Descriptive Geometry.

Q. 33. Two views of a tusk-tenon joint are shown. Represent the two
parts A and B , separated from each other, in pictorial projection
in a manner similar to that used for the cube, where lines
parallel to oy and oz are drawn horizontally and vertically, to a
scale of full size, and lines parallel to ox are drawn by using the
45° set-square, and to a scale of half size.

    N.B.—The figure need not be copied, dimensions being
taken directly from the diagram.

A favourite question and well answered.

STAGE 3.

Results : 1st Class, 36 ; 2nd Class, 91 ; Failed, 141 ; Total, 268.

Q. 41. A piece of ground is defined by two horizontal sections or
contours, the horizontal scale being $\frac{1}{4}$ inch to 1 yard. Find
the area of each section. The difference in level being 1 yard,
find the volume of material lying between the two sections.

A favourite question and generally well answered. Some good results
were got by means of equalising lines. Others used very laborious
methods in finding the areas of the contours. In finding the mean area a
few used the formula $\frac{1}{3}(A + a + \sqrt{Aa})$ thus considering the ground to form
approximately a frustum of a cone.

Q. 42. The motion which the slider *S* receives from the uniformly rotating cam *C* consists of the upward and downward halves of a simple harmonic vibration, separated by periods of rest, each of the four events occupying one quarter of a revolution of the cam, as defined in the figure. Set out the cam profile to the given dimensions, determining the shapes between *A* and *B*.

Often attempted and with fair results. A mistake sometimes made was to treat the roller as a point and omit the envelope. Occasionally a simple heart shaped cam was drawn as for a uniform reciprocating motion.

Q. 43. Determine and measure the thrusts in the members *A, B, C, D, E,* and *F* of the given truss when loaded in the manner shown. Also draw diagrams of bending moment, shearing force, and pull in the horizontal bottom member of the truss, the linear scale of the figure being $\frac{1}{4}$ inch to 1 foot.

This was often attempted, but the form of the frame being somewhat new to the candidates, the mistake mentioned under Q. 26 was sometimes made, and some candidates, not being able to close their force diagram, added bars to the frame and assumed joints in the beam. Many, however, drew the correct force diagram, but the bending moment, shear, and pull in the beam were not well understood.

Q. 44. A vertical wall is 80 yards long and 42 feet high. The following table gives the pressures of the wind on it, *p* pounds per square foot, at various heights *h* feet above the ground :—

h	4	10	18	25	33	42
p	9	12	16·7	20·3	23·5	26

Draw a diagram showing the relation between *p* and *h*. Find the mean pressure on the wall in pounds per square foot, and the total wind force on the wall in pounds. Find the line of action of this force, and give the moment of the force about the base of the wall.

Employ scales of 1 inch to 10 feet, and 1 inch to 10 pounds per square foot.

Fairly well done, but the mistake noticed in Q. 27 was also met with here. Also when using an equalising line it was sometimes assumed that the centre of area of the trapezoid thus formed coincided with the centre of area of the original diagram.

Q. 45. The diagram shows a radial valve gear, scale $\frac{1}{4}$. The crank *CP* turns uniformly at 12 radians per second, and is pinned at *P* to the rod *PR*, the point *Q* in this rod being guided in the circular path *SS*, centre *T*. For the position of the mechanism shown in the diagram, determine and measure the velocities of the points *R* and *V*.

Not very often attempted. The velocities were generally found correctly and by the method of instantaneous centres, but some forgot that these were vectors and only gave speeds or magnitudes.

Q. 46. The semicircular arch ring has a span of 8 feet and its depth is half brick. Find the centre of gravity of the ring. Taking the only load to be that of the ring itself, draw for this load the link polygon which passes through the points, *A, C, A*.

Another unpopular question. There were some good attempts, but many could only answer the first part of the question.

Q. 47. *OA, OB, OC* are three pieces of wire soldered together at *O*. You are given the plan when *AOB* rests on the ground with *OC* inclined upwards, the height of *C* being indexed in millimetres.

(a) Draw an elevation on a vertical plane so chosen as to exhibit an edge view of the plane containing *AOC*. What is the inclination of this plane to the horizontal ?

(b) Draw the indexed plan of the projection of *OB* on the plane *AOC*, and determine the angle which *OB* makes with this plane.

This question was well answered, but some gave a wrong interpretation to the index defining the height of the projection of *B* on the plane *AOC*.

Q. 48. The figure is the dimensioned roof plan of a house. The roof planes *A* and *B* are inclined to the horizontal at 33°. Determine and measure—

(a) The length and inclination of the valley rafter *CD*, that is, of the line whose plan is *cd* ;

(b) The bevel for cutting the edges of the slates which lie along the valley, that is, the true angle between the lines whose plans are *cd, de* ;

(c) The correct angle of the valley tiles, that is, the dihedral angle between the planes *A* and *B*.

A popular question and well answered, but a few gave the wrong dihedral angle for the valley, their solutions treating it as a hip. Also many took too small a scale.

Q. 49. You are given a sectional plan and elevation of a portion of a screw pile, the blade *BB* of which is helical. Copy the plan, and from it project an outside elevation on *xy*, in place of the sectional elevation shown.

Fairly often attempted, and the attempts were good except that the spreading ends of the screw were not very well projected.

Q. 50. Project the shadows cast on the sink *K*, the waste pipe *W*, the supporting battens *B, B*, and on the walls, the direction of the parallel rays of light being given.

Not very popular, but the answers were good.

Q. 51. Draw a perspective projection of the sink *K*, battens *B, B*, and pipe *W* on the picture plane of which *pp* is the plan, the point of sight *S* being opposite *M*, 5 feet 4 inches away, and 16 inches above the top of the sink, the scale of the figure being $\frac{1}{8}$th.

Also unpopular, but well done, various methods of working being in evidence.

Q. 52. The diagram shows part of the uptake of a marine boiler, consisting of two inclined tubes, horizontal sections of which are rectangular in outline as given in plan. Complete the plan for the portion between *SS* and *xy*. Find the shape of the cross-section of a tube by a plane perpendicular to its axis. Develop the four outer faces of one of the tubes lying between *SS* and *xy*.

Frequently attempted and, on the whole, well answered. Some, however, who got the development right gave the cross-section wrongly as being rectangular.

Honours.

Results : 1st Class, 10 ; 2nd Class, 16 ; Failed, 21 ; Total, 47.

Q. 61. A piece of ground is defined by horizontal sections or contours at vertical intervals of 1 yard, the horizontal scale being ¼ inch to 1 yard. Find the areas of the sections and the volume of material lying between the top and bottom sections.

This question was well answered, but some of the methods for finding the areas were unnecessarily elaborate. The division into eight or ten strips with equalising lines for the end strips gave very accurate results.

Q. 62. The figure shows the gable end of a house, scale 1 cm. to 5 feet. The following table gives the pressures of the wind on it, p pounds per square foot, at various heights h feet above the ground.

h	4	10	18	25	33	42	50
p	9	12	16·7	20·3	23·5	26	27

Draw a diagram showing the relation between p and h. Find the total wind force on the surface in pounds, and the line of action of this force. What is the moment of the force about the base ?

There were a few good answers, but the majority were defective. In the worst of these the mean of the tabulated pressures multiplied by the area of the gable end was given as the total wind force.

Q. 63. The slider S receives the following intermittent motion from the uniformly rotating cam O :—

(a) A period of rest during the quarter turn AB.

(b) The upward half of a simple harmonic vibration during the quarter turn BC.

(c) A second period of rest during the quarter turn CD.

(d) A downward motion during DA consisting of a uniform acceleration from rest followed by an equal retardation back to rest.

Set out the cam profile to the given dimensions, determining the shapes of the parts BC and DA.

This was fairly well answered, the curve for the relative motion of the centre of the roller for (d) being obtained sometimes by calculation of successive displacements and sometimes by the aid of a parabola.

Q. 64. The semicircular arch ring has a span of 8 feet, and its depth is half brick. Draw a linear arch or line of resistance to pass through the three points, A, C, B :—

(a) Taking the only load to be that of the arch ring itself.

(b) Taking additional loads W, W, each equal to ¼ the weight of the ring, applied as shown.

N.B.—In (a), only the half from A to C need be drawn, and in (b) only the half from B to C.

The attempts were comparatively few, but very good.

Q. 65. The diagram shows a radial valve gear, scale ¼. The crank CP
turns uniformly at 12 radians per second, and is pinned at P to
the rod PR, the point Q in this rod being guided in the circular
path SS, centre T. For the position of the mechanism shown in
the diagram, determine and measure the velocities and accelerations of the points R and V.

Where instantaneous centres were used candidates could only find the
velocities of R and V, but when the method of images was employed both
velocities and accelerations were usually determined.

Q. 66. In an ordinary crank and connecting rod engine the inertia force
of the reciprocating parts at any point can be obtained with
close approximation as the sum of the projections on the line of
stroke of two rotation vectors, representing the first two terms
of a Fourier series. The positions of these vectors when the
crank is at OP are shown ; they turn in the same direction as
the crank, the fundamental OF_1 at the same speed, and the
octave OF_2 at double the speed ; also—

$$\frac{\text{magnitude of } OF_1}{\text{magnitude of } OF_2} = \frac{\text{length of connecting rod}}{\text{length of crank}} = \mu, \text{ say.}$$

If OF_1 measures 100 pounds and if $\mu = 4$, draw these vectors in position
when the crank is at OK, and by resolving along QO measure
the inertia force at this instant.

In a symmetrical three-line engine arranged as shown, OF_1 is
100 pounds for each of the outer lines, A, A, and is 200 pounds
for the middle line B. Also $\mu = 4$. Combine (if possible) the
three fundamental vectors into a single resultant vector, and the
three octave vectors into another single resultant. Draw a diagram, set out on a time or crank-angle base, showing the inertia
force throughout a cycle.

N.B.—You need copy only part of the diagram.

This simple graphical method of investigating the inertia forces of a
piston seems little known. The question was attempted by three candidates and there was one complete answer.

Q. 67. OA, OB, OC, are three pieces of wire soldered together at O.
You are given the plan when AOB rests on the ground with
OC inclined upwards, the height of C being indexed in
millimetres.

(a) Find the angle between the planes containing AOC,
BOC.

(b) Determine the indexed plan of a point P which is
situated above the ground, 35 mm. from the plane
AOC, 25 mm. from the line OB, and 55 mm. from
the point O, towards B.

The answers to this question were very good indeed. The principal
difference was one of method, the number of ellipses drawn for the
determination of P varying in different solutions from none to four.

Q. 68. Draw the curve of intersection of the given cone with the helical
surface (of uniform pitch) generated by the revolution of the
horizontal line VH about the axis of the cone, the line
descending to the base during one anti clockwise turn.

The given point P will lie on the required curve. Determine
the tangent to the curve at P. Also draw the normal and
osculating planes at P.

The candidates who attempted this question could easily draw the curve.
One discovered a geometrical construction for the tangent at P based on
the specified motion. A few could draw the normal plane, and one or
two found the osculating plane.

Q. 69. Determine the shadow cast by the split collar on the planes of projection, one of the parallel rays being given, and show the separation of light from shade on the collar.

The answers to this question were satisfactory.

Q. 70. Draw a perspective view of the collar on the picture plane of which pp is the plan, the point of sight being opposite M, 6″ away, and 3″ above the horizontal plane.

The answers here were also satisfactory.

Q. 71. ABC is a sheet metal pipe, the portions A and C, of circular and rectangular sections, being connected by the part B as shown. Draw an elevation of B on $x'y'$. Also, by developing B, set out the shape to which the flat sheet of metal forming it must be cut. Omit all allowances for overlap at the seams.

This was often attempted, with a fair number of good answers. Some, however, did not realise that the surface of B was made up of triangles and parts of oblique cones.

DAY EXAMINATION.

The number of candidates in the Day Examination continues to decrease, being 21½ per cent. less than last year. The quality of the work in both Stages was, on the whole, good, and it compared favourably with the work done in the corresponding Stages of the Evening Examination. The principal defects were the same as those noticed in the Report on the latter, viz., weakness in problems on the tangency of circles and in the more abstract and fundamental portions of Descriptive Geometry, for particulars of which, see the detailed criticisms of the answers to the examination questions, which follow.

STAGE 1.

Results: 1st Class, 44 ; 2nd Class, 36 ; Failed, 31 ; Total, 111.

Q. 1. By the aid of your protractor, and without using the tables, find the value of—

$$3 \cos 20° + 4 \sin 20°.$$

Now verify your answer by calculation from the tables.

This question was well answered. The angle of 20° was generally set off accurately. The principal defect was the employment of too small a scale.

Q. 2. Draw the given figure ₅th size linear, working to the given dimensions, which are in millimetres, and not copying the diagram. Show the construction for determining the centres of the two arcs of 500 mm. radius. Mark all the points where the tangential arcs meet.

The dimensions were well set out, but many were unable to find the centres of the large arcs by construction, and too many omitted to mark the points of contact.

Q. 3. Construct a parallelogram to the following data :
Shorter side = 2·3″, one angle between sides = 68·4°, angle between diagonals = 77°.
Measure the other side.

Not often attempted. The first step of drawing a segment to contain 77° was often not made.

Q. 4. Two plots of land AA and BB are separated by a crooked fence
FFF. Show a straight fence to replace the given one, starting
from P and so drawn that the areas of the plots are unaltered.

Well answered.

Q. 5. Enlarge the given trapezoid so that dimensions parallel to OA
are increased 80 per cent., and dimensions parallel to OB are
increased 30 per cent. What is the percentage increase in the
area of the figure?

The enlarged figure was generally drawn properly, but the percentage
increase was seldom obtained correctly.

Q. 6. Two pieces of sheet material A and B, in the form of equal
isosceles triangles, are hinged or pinned to the drawing board
at O. Four strips of the material, all equal in length to one of
the equal sides of the triangles, are hinged to A and B and to
one another as shown. Find the path or locus of the hinge
point P, when the hinge Q is moved over the given letter L.

N.B.—Only centre lines of the mechanism need be copied.

Fairly well answered, but the candidates generally failed to discover that
the shape of the locus was an exact copy of the original figure.

Q. 7. Two vectors A and B have the following values, angles being
measured anti-clockwise from the East :—

$$A = 29_{11°} , \quad B = 18 \cdot 5_{73} .$$

By adding the vectors in the sequence $A + B$, and again in
the sequence $B + A$, verify that the resultant is the same in
both cases, and measure its magnitude and direction. Determine the easterly and northerly components of the resultant.

Adopt a scale of 1 inch to 10 units.

Well answered. Some obtained the north and east components without
measuring them.

Q. 8. ABC is a piece of bent wire. Find its centre of gravity G by
means of the following construction :—

Bisect AB and BC in D and E. Join DE and divide DE in
G so that $DG : GE = CB : BA$.

Well answered.

Q. 9. A vessel steaming at 15 miles per hour eastwards is timed to pass a
certain pier at a distance of 1 mile, due north, at 12 noon. A
boat leaves the pier 20 minutes before noon, and is rowed at 4
miles per hour. Find the direction in which it must be steered
so as to intercept the vessel at the earliest possible moment. At
what time does the boat reach the steamer?

Seldom attempted and badly answered.

Q. 10. A thin 30°–60° set square ABC, whose long edge or hypotenuse
AB measures 4", is laid on the horizontal plane and is then
turned about AB through an angle of 58° ;

(a) Draw the plan of the set-square ;

(b) Determine and measure the inclinations to the horizontal
of the edges AC and BC ;

(c) Draw an elevation of the set-square on a vertical plane
which makes 45° with AB.

The attempts were disappointing owing to the frequent failure to answer
the part (b).

Q. 11. An eastward path on the plane face of an embankment rises 10 feet vertically in a horizontal distance of 15 feet, and a northward path rises 10 feet in a horizontal distance of 20 feet. Find the direction of the path of steepest ascent, and the inclination, in degrees, of this path to the horizontal.

Not often tried, but most of the attempts were successful.

Q. 12. A right square pyramid rests with a triangular face on the horizontal plane. The plan *abv* of this face is given. Draw the elevation of the pyramid on *xy* and complete the plan of the solid.

Find the shape of the section of the pyramid by the vertical plane *VV*.

An old fault was again apparent in the answers ; some other solid (generally a prism), was often substituted for the pyramid. In many cases the elevation of the solid was incorrectly drawn. On the whole the answers were not very satisfactory.

Q. 13. You are given the development of the frustum of a triangular prism. Draw the plan of the solid when the two outer faces *F, F* have been turned back into position. Project an elevation of the frustum on *xy* as ground line.

Well answered.

Q. 14. Represent the given carpenter's square in pictorial projection in a manner similar to that used for the cube, where lines parallel to *oy* and *oz* are drawn horizontally and vertically, and to a scale of full size, and lines parallel to *ox* are drawn by using the 45° set-square, and to a scale of half size.

N.B.—The figure need not be copied, dimensions being taken directly from the diagram.

A favourite question and well done. Pictorial projection is well understood and is liked by the candidates.

STAGE 2.

Results : 1st Class, 21 ; 2nd Class, 22 ; Failed, 16 ; Total, 59.

Q. 21. By the aid of your protractor, and without using the tables, find the value of—

$$3 \cos 20° + 4 \sin 20° + 5 \tan 20°.$$

Now verify your answer by calculation from the tables.

This question was well answered. Trigonometrical tables are well understood.

Q. 22. *ABCD* is a convex quadrilateral, the diagonals *AC* and *BD* intersecting in *O*. Construct the figure to the given dimensions :—

$AB = 8$ cm., $BC = 6$ cm., $CD = 5·7$ cm., $DA = 4$ cm., $AOB = 120°$.

Measure the diagonal *AC*.

N.B.—A locus may be used if desired.

Very seldom attempted. There were only two or three correct answers.

Q. 23. Two plots of land *AA* and *BB* are separated by a crooked fence *FFF*. Show a straight fence to replace the given one, starting from *P* and so drawn that the areas of the plots are unaltered.

Determine a second straight fence which shall be equally inclined to *XX* and *YY*, and shall again preserve intact the areas of *AA* and *BB*.

The first part of the question was well answered, but few could do the latter part.

Q. 24. Alter the shape of the given figure so that dimensions parallel to
OA are increased 80 per cent., and dimensions parallel to *OB*
are diminished 30 per cent. What is the percentage alteration
in the area of the figure ?

First part well answered. Second part badly done.

Q. 25. Four links *A, A, A, A*, each 2″ long, are hinged together at the
ends, thus forming a jointed rhombus. Two links *B, B*, each
4″ long, are hinged to one another at *O*, and to opposite corners
of the rhombus as shown. A link *D*, 1·3″ long, is hinged to
one of the remaining corners of the rhombus. The links *D* and
B, B, being now pinned to the drawing board at the points
C and *O*, 1·3″ apart, find the locus or path of the hinged point
P, when the mechanism is moved into all possible positions on
the board above its present position.

N.B.—Only centre lines of the mechanism need be drawn.

The attempts were satisfactory.

Q. 26. Three vectors *A, B, C* have the following values, angles being
measured counter clockwise from the East :—

$$A = 29_{110^\circ}, \quad B = 18\cdot5_{72^\circ}, \quad C = 33\cdot3_{141^\circ}.$$

By adding the vectors on the sequence *A + B + C*, and
again in the sequence *C + A + B*, verify that the resultant is
the same in both cases, and measure its magnitude and direction.
Determine the easterly and northerly components of the
resultant.

Adopt a scale of 1 inch to 10 units.

A favourite question, and well answered on the whole.

Q. 27. Find the position of the centre of gravity of a piece of uniform
wire when bent into the form shown.

The answers did not compare favourably with those in Stage 1 to
the corresponding but easier question.

Q. 28. A vessel steaming at 15 miles per hour eastwards is timed to pass
a certain pier at a distance of 1 mile, due north, at 12 noon.
A boat leaves the pier 20 minutes before noon and is rowed at
4 miles per hour. Find the direction in which it must be
steered so as to intercept the vessel at the earliest possible
moment. At what time does the boat reach the steamer ?

What is the latest time at which the boat could start from
the pier so as just to reach the vessel ?

Very few selected this question and scarcely anyone gave a complete
answer. The second part of the question, when attempted, was generally
correctly answered.

Q. 29. A thin 45° set-square *ABC*, longer edge or hypotenuse *AB*=4″,
has the edge *AC* in the vertical plane at right angles to *xy*, and
the edge *CB* in the horizontal plane at 50° to *xy*.

   (*a*) Draw the plan and elevation of the set-square.

   (*b*) Find the angles which *AB* makes with the planes of
projection.

   (*c*) Find the angle which *AB* makes with *xy* (that is with a
line through *A* or *B* taken parallel to *xy*).

The answers to this question, especially to the part (*c*), were not satisfactory.

Q. 30. An eastward path on the plane face of an embankment rises 10 feet vertically in a horizontal distance of 15 feet, and a southward path falls 10 feet vertically in a horizontal distance of 20 feet. Find the direction of the path of steepest ascent, and the inclination, in degrees, of this path to the horizontal.

Represent the plane of the embankment by a scale of slope, the horizontal scale being 1 inch to 10 feet.

The first part of the question was well done, but few could draw the scale of slope properly in answer to the last part of the question.

Q. 31. You are given the development of the frustum of a triangular prism. Draw the plan of the solid when the two outer faces F, F have been turned back into position. Draw also a plan when the frustum stands on its section end.

Not very frequently chosen. Good knowledge was shown in the attempts.

Q. 32. You are given the projections of a cone, of indefinite length, lying on the horizontal plane and enveloping a given sphere S. Draw the projections of the circle of contact of the cone and sphere. Find the shape of the section of the cone by the given vertical plane VV.

Rather unpopular. Some did not understand what was meant by the word "shape," but drew an elevation of the section on the given xy.

Q. 33. Represent the given carpenter's "bevel" in pictorial projection in a manner similar to that used for the cube, where lines parallel to oy and oz are drawn horizontally and vertically and to a scale of full size, and lines parallel to ox are drawn by using the 45° set-square and to a scale of half size.

N.B.—The figure need not to be copied, dimensions being transferred directly from the diagram.

A favourite question and well answered.

Report on the Examination in Machine Construction and Drawing.

STAGE 1.

Results : 1st Class, 1,760 ; 2nd Class, 1,843 ; Failed, 1,850 ; Total, 5,453.

In this Stage the number of candidates was 5,543, showing an increase of nearly 6 per cent. compared with the number in 1906. The quality of the tracing was not very satisfactory, and was inferior to that of last year. The scale drawing was, on the whole, fairly good, and fully equal to the work done in the previous year. The draughtsmanship shows a steady improvement, but there is still far too much slovenly soft pencil work. A certain number of candidates are still ignorant of the proper use of section lines. Quite a number failed through ignoring the instructions and drawing views similar to those on the diagram. A conspicuous fault, noticed also last year, was the lack of knowledge of simple machine parts like bolts, studs and nuts, many otherwise good drawings being disfigured on this account ; candidates were required to add such details from their own knowledge without help from the diagram.

TRACING.

Trace in ink on the tracing paper supplied the two views of the gland shown on Diagram X. Insert the dimensions and print the title as shown.

The lines should be very black, of uniform and moderate width, and as continuous as possible.

A common and serious fault was the use of weak Indian ink, or writing
ink, sometimes even blue ink ; in fact many did not appear to know the purpose for which a tracing is used, viz :—printing. A number of tracings
were done free-hand, all such being cancelled. It was noticeable that
good or bad tracing usually accompanied neat or rough execution of the
drawing example done in pencil to scale.   The circular arcs in the plan of
the gland were seldom well joined.

Example 1.

HYDRAULIC STOP VALVE.

Make full size separate scale drawings of details, fully dimensioned,
as follows :—

    (*a*) Two views of the valve spindle A.   The screw thread may
        be shown conventionally, as in the diagram.
    (*b*) Two views of the nut B.
    (*c*) Two views of the gland C.
    (*d*) Two views of the bush D.
    (*e*) Two views of the seating E.
    (*f*) Three views of the cap F.
    (*g*) Three views of one of the $\frac{3}{4}''$ cap bolts G, with nut.

N.B.—No credit will be given for drawing the parts assembled, as
in the diagram.   Dotted lines, representing hidden parts, are not
required.

Alternative Example 2.

BRACKET.

The form and dimensions of a bracket (for a lathe bed) are exhibited
by two pictorial views.   Draw full size, inserting dimensions :—

    (*a*) An elevation, as seen when looking in the direction of the
        arrow R.   Put in the $\frac{1}{2}''$ setscrew and $\frac{5}{8}''$ stud.
    (*b*) A sectional elevation on a plane parallel to the face H, and
        1″ distant therefrom ; that is, the section plane is taken
        through the axis of the $\frac{1}{2}''$ setscrew and $\frac{3}{8}''$ hole.
    (*c*) A plan.

N.B.—Do not draw the pictorial views.   Dotted lines, representing
hidden parts, are not required.

Both examples proved to be well within the capacity of well-trained
students, the stop valve being the example more frequently chosen.   The
bracket required less drawing, but more power of reading a drawing and of
projecting new views.   In Example 1, many candidates gave only outside
views, these being insufficient to define the forms of some of the details,
for which purpose sections were necessary. Not one per cent. of the
candidates who selected Example 1 could make out the use of the "flat"
part shown in the seating.   The $\frac{3}{4}''$ cap bolt was very badly drawn, the
proportions being often wrong, the nuts shown octagonal, or wrongly
projected, and the bevelled corners being drawn incorrectly.

The most striking feature with regard to Example 2 was the inability of
many candidates to fully make out the shape of the bracket, their drawings
showing it as being symmetrical about a vertical axis in the elevation (a).
Very few were able to project the intersection of the curved surfaces.
In the insertion of the stud and setscrew the candidate too often displayed
his ignorance of machine construction.   Teachers should be careful to
point out to students that in arranging the several views of an example,
care should always be taken that sufficient space is left to allow of the
views being drawn in projection one from another.   It is satisfactory to add
that there were many well-taught classes whose work was excellent, and
the results extremely satisfactory.

Questions, only two to be answered.

*The Sketches in answer to these questions should be drawn freehand
on the squared foolscap paper, the lines on which may be taken as
$\frac{1}{4}$-inch apart.*

The squared paper was generally used and the lines on it taken advantage
of in the execution of the freehand sketches.

Q. 11. Indicate the parts of the stop valve, Example 1, Diagram X, which you would make respectively of brass, cast-iron and wrought iron. Sketch a method of preventing the nut B from turning in the cap F.

This question was a favourite one, and the answering was good, except that wrought iron was frequently given as the material for the spindle.

Q. 12. Explain briefly, with sketches, how you would drill or bore the $\frac{3}{4}''$ hole K, and true up the faces marked K, K, in the bracket of alternative Example 2, Diagram X.

Fairly well answered ; the sketches were often on too small a scale.

Q. 13. You are given the dimensions of a shaft coupling of the ordinary muff or box type. Make dimensioned sketches, half size, consisting of an end view and a longitudinal section, with the shaft ends secured by keys.

Diameter of coupling outside	- - - $4\frac{1}{2}''$
Diameter of bore of coupling	- - - $2''$
Length of coupling	- - - - - $7''$
Width of keys - - - - - -	$\frac{5}{8}''$

The muff coupling was often confused with other types, suggesting mere book knowledge. The keys were very badly shown, and often could have been got neither in nor out. Otherwise the sketches were good and to scale, and properly dimensioned.

Q. 14. Sketch in section, full size, inserting dimensions, a steam engine piston 6'' diameter and $1\frac{1}{2}''$ wide, with three Ramsbottom rings of section $\frac{1}{4}''$ square. The conical hole for the piston-rod is $1\frac{3}{8}''$ diameter at the larger end, and the taper is 1'' per foot.

Often attempted and well done, fully dimensioned and to scale, and with a well-formed piston body. A common fault, however, was to show no clearance for the rings, or to draw the latter without any spring in them.

Q. 15. Describe briefly, with sketches, any method you would consider suitable for joining together the ends of a stranded cable made up of seven copper wires, each of No. 20 guage, for carrying an electric current.

This question was not often taken, but the answers were satisfactory.

STAGE 2.

Results : 1st Class, 692 ; 2nd Class, 1,685 ; Failed, 1,496 ; Total, 3,873.

The tracing was fairly well done, and the average quality of the work was about the same as last year.   The same remark applies equally to the quality of the drawings, though there is still room for much improvement in manual dexterity regarding the use of the drawing implements. The outstanding feature of the work was the many errors made in reading the drawings, and this may be due to the fact that the drawing examples were a little more difficult than those set last year. In the answers to the questions, the freehand sketching was generally poor, and though a fair proportion of the candidates showed accurate knowledge of machine details the proportion is not so large as it should have been considering that the machine parts asked for are so generally to be seen in the workshops, factories, and on the railways of the country.

Example 3, *Diagram* Y.

EQUILIBRIUM ADMISSION VALVE FOR A STEAM ENGINE.

(a) Draw a part sectional elevation of the stuffing-box-cover and the valve seating, looking in the direction indicated by the arrow K. The part of the elevation to the left of the centre line is to be a section along HG, and the part to the right an external elevation of the valve-seating and cover. The valve and the outer casing are to be omitted in this view.

(b) Draw a part-sectional plan. The part above the horizontal centre
line is to be a horizontal section of the valve and seating through
EF, and the part below a plan of the cover.   The outer casing is
again to be omitted.

Scale, ¼ full size.

Neither dotted lines nor dimensions need be shown.

(N.B.—Take the vertical centre line in the direction of the longer
dimension of your drawing paper.)

The smaller proportion of candidates tried this question and many good
drawings were sent in.   In some cases the valve-seating was shown quite
cylindrical so that no steam could get through it.

Alternative Example 4, Diagram Y.

AN ADJUSTABLE BEARING FOR BOLTING TO THE TABLE OF A SMALL BORING
MACHINE FOR THE SUPPORT OF THE BORING BAR.

Draw a sectional elevation through *FG* looking in the direction of
the arrow *H*, and make a complete plan.   Indicate the screw
threads by any conventional method you please.

Scale, ¾ full size.

Neither dotted lines nor dimensions need be shown.

(N.B.—Take the vertical centre line in the direction of the longer
dimension of your drawing paper.)

This was the favourite question, and as it represents a part of a machine
tool some variation of which is very generally found in the machine shops
of the country, so generally, in fact, that a student in Stage 2 might almost
be expected to sketch such an apparatus from memory, the number of errors
made in reading the drawing is greater than would have been thought
possible and seems to show that students do not sufficiently observe the
every-day things of the workshop which pass under their notice.   A common
error was to show the boring bar bracket bolted to the table of the machine
without any possibility of adjustment.   The projection of the plan was, in
general, fairly well done.

Q. 21. Sketch, in good proportion, giving a few leading dimensions, a
muff or box coupling for the connection of two lengths of a
machine shop main shaft 3 inches diameter.

This question was generally attempted though many did not understand exactly what a muff coupling was, and sketched some other form of
coupling.

Q. 22. How would you proceed to mark off and machine the block *Q*,
Alternative Example 4, Diagram *Y*, in order to ensure that the
centre line of the hole for the boring bar shall be exactly
parallel to the sliding surfaces and perpendicular to the direction of vertical sliding ?

This was attempted by few, and not much knowlege of the methods of
the marking-off table was exhibited, though there were some good answers.

Q. 23. The leading screw of a lathe is right-handed and has 4 threads
per inch.   It is required to cut a right-hand screw 8 threads
per inch.   Sketch a suitable train of wheels, and indicate by
the sketch how the wheels are supported. Assume that the
wheel on the mandril has 20 teeth.

The calculation of a correct train of wheels gave little difficulty to the
candidates attempting this question, but few exhibited an accurate knowledge of the details of the common arrangement used for supporting the
train of wheels and making the connection between the mandril and the
leading screw.

Q. 24. Make a sketch of a switch for carrying a continuous current of 100 ampères, showing it in position on a switch-board. The circuit voltage is about 200.

Attempted by few and generally not well done. It was exceptional to find any attempt to calculate the size of the parts to carry the current.

Q. 25. Sketch a gib and cotter connecting rod end, and show clearly how the cotter is prevented from slacking back.

Very generally attempted and fairly well done, but many candidates made the mistake of slotting the end of the rod through so that there was no bearing for the collar to draw up against, thus making an impossible arrangement.

STAGE 3.

Results : 1st Class, 106 ; 2nd Class, 269 ; Failed, 375 ; Total, 750.

The general quality of the work was much the same as in 1906, and there seemed to be about the same proportion of first class work also. More attention should be given to neat and accurate freehand sketching. The questions, Nos. 31 to 35 gave ample opportunities for the exhibition of skill of this kind, but with rare exceptions the sketches were poor, in bad proportion, and slovenly. A good sketch conveys more to the Examiner than a page of vague description. A good many candidates have attempted this stage prematurely, and the drawings sent up in answer to Examples 5 and 6 exhibit a larger proportion of bad draughtsmanship than there should be in this Stage.

Example 5, Diagram Z.

The diagram shows the centre lines and indicates some of the details of a cast-iron lever which can rock about the fixed centre pin A. One end of the lever carries a roller, 3 inches diameter and 1 inch wide, which is always in contact with a cam keyed to the shaft B ; the radial length of the arm carrying the roller is 11⅜ inches. The other end of the lever is provided with an adjusting screw which is always held in contact with the end of a valve spindle as indicated in the diagram. The valve spindle is shown in its central vertical position, and this position is marked 8. The corresponding angular position of the cam-shaft is indicated by the radius marked 8 :—

    (a) Set out the lever, to a scale ¾ full size, in the position corresponding with the central vertical position of the valve spindle, having given that the minimum radial thickness of the cam is ⅜-inch. Measure off and write down on your drawing the angle between the line AC and the centre line from A to the centre of the roller.

    (b) Finish the design of the cam lever complete with the roller in plan and elevation to the data given.

    (c) Find the points on the cam corresponding to positions
        0, 1, 2, 3, 4, 5, 6, 7, 8, 9, 10, 11
of the ends of the valve spindle, it being understood, as indicated on the end view of the shaft B, that these positions correspond to equiangular positions of the shaft.

N.B.—The drawings should be suitably dimensioned.

This question involved the working out of the shape of the cam profile and the design of the cam lever and roller. Some excellent designs were received, though a correct method of obtaining the points on the cam was not often used ; in fact, a small proportion only of the candidates knew the way to go about this part of the question. In a good many cases, the tightening of the nut holding the roller spindle to the end of the cam lever clamped the roller to the lever so that it could not revolve at all, and the design of the details of the lever, though simple in the extreme, indicated that a large number of the candidates had no real knowledge of machine construction.

Alternative Example 6, Diagram Z.

The figure shows a rough sketch of a 5-ton pulley-block for hanging in the loop of a $\frac{1}{8}$inch chain. Having calculated the dimensions of the principal parts of the block, so that the tensile stress shall not exceed 5 tons per square inch, nor the shearing stress 4 tons per square inch :—

(a) Draw the elevation of the block in which the outline of the pulley appears circular and showing the shape of the hook. All omitted details in the sketch to be added in your drawing. Scale, $\frac{1}{4}$ full size.

(b) Draw the sectional elevation of the block made by a vertical plane passing through the long axes of the pin *A*. Scale, $\frac{1}{4}$ full size.

(c) Make a dimensioned plan of the section of the hook at *CD*. Scale, $\frac{1}{4}$ full size.

Write down clearly on your drawing—

(1) The diameter of the pin *A* at the centre.

(2) The dimension *B*, the diameter of the hole in the block *B*, and the extreme horizontal dimension of the block in the direction indicated by the line *F*, and the corresponding nett width.

(3) The dimension *CD*.

(4) The dimension *E*.

This simple example in design was not successfully dealt with by the majority of those attempting it. Drawings were sent in in which no means were shown of holding on the side plates of the block, the design being, in fact, merely a copy of the diagrammatic sketch given, in other cases the nuts holding the side plates clamped the plates and pulley into one rigid whole. In many cases a design was made without any attempt to find by calculation the dimensions of the several parts, and a common error was to make the hook thinner on the inside than on the outside. There was, however, a fair number of good designs well worked out and well drawn.

Q. 31. Sketch a vertical section through any form of sight feed lubricator for introducing oil into the cylinder of a steam engine, and briefly explain the principle of its action.

Many correct sketches were given and the question was fairly well answered.

Q. 32. Make a dimensioned sketch of a foot-step bearing of simple design, proportioning the bearing surfaces so that the vertical shaft supported in the foot-step may carry a load of $\frac{1}{4}$ a ton at, say, a speed of 100 revolutions per minute.

Many answers were given to this question but a large number of candidates made a sketch without mentioning the bearing pressure assumed in estimating the diameter of the shaft.

Q. 33. Describe the moulding of the chain pulley shown on Diagram Z, alternative example 6, sketching clearly the moulding boxes you would employ.

A large number of the candidates failed to notice that by the method they described and illustrated it was impossible to get the pattern out of the mould.

Q. 34. Sketch and dimension a flange coupling for a $3\frac{1}{2}$ inch round shaft. Calculate the number of $\frac{3}{4}$-inch bolts required on an $11\frac{1}{4}$-inch diameter pitch circle so that the torsional resistance of the coupling is equal to the torsional resistance of the shaft, allowing a maximum shearing stress in the shaft of 4 tons per square inch, and an average shearing stress in the bolts of 2 tons per square inch.

The sketches were good and proportionate, but a good many mistakes were made in calculating the number of bolts required, a common error being to measure the torsional strength of the shaft by the product of its area and the shearing strength.

Q. 35. Sketch and briefly describe the trolley pole for collecting current from an overhead trolley wire suitable for use on a tramcar.

Few really good answers were given to this question. The details of the apparatus were rarely drawn, and the question of insulation was not sufficiently considered.

HONOURS.

Results : 1st Class, 4 ; 2nd Class, 6 ; Failed, 85 ; Total, 95.

Example 7.   *Diagram Z.*

On Diagram Z is a diagrammatic indication of a spring governor. It is assumed that the whole of the controlling force is supplied by the spring.

When the governor is at rest, the balls rest against stops in the position shown by dotted lines.

The relation connecting the controlling force F in pounds, exerted by the spring on the two balls, and the radius r, in feet, of the path in which the centres of gravity of the balls rotate is

$$F = 296 \cdot 6 \, r - 12 \cdot 4.$$

The governor spindle is geared to the lay shaft of the engine as indicated.

(a) Determine the velocity ratio of the gearing so that when the lay shaft makes 80 revs. per minute the governor balls revolve at a radius of 4 inches.

(b) Design the governor, showing with other drawings a vertical elevation in section.

(c) Write down the amount in inches by which the spring is compressed into its position in the governor when the governor is at rest.

Many candidates found the velocity ratio correctly, but with some exceptions few made a satisfactory design of the governor. In some cases the designs were absurd, one design, in fact, being arranged so that the governor balls could not revolve, being jointed to the fixed part of the governor. In general the theory of the governor was fairly well understood, but the actual design of the governor details was disappointing and indicated that the bulk of the candidates had not been trained in the first principles of designing, nor had the candidates made a practice of observing machine details themselves.

Alternative Example 8.

Design a hand-worked portable machine for parting off $1\frac{1}{2}$ inch round bar. The machine is to be as light as possible and designed so that it can quickly be clamped to a bar for the purpose of parting it at any assigned place.

There were a few good designs, but the bulk of them were quite impracticable. Many of the students attempting this question had no notion of designing, and some had no exact notion of mechanical drawing either. It cannot be too strongly emphasised that a student of machine construction must observe the details of existing machines and transfer them to his note book, in this way obtaining a knowledge of the fundamental elements from which the most complicated machinery is constituted.

Q. 41. Sketch a section through the speed cones of a lathe provided with a modern arrangement of back gear, and show clearly how the back gear can be thrown in or out without stopping the lathe.

There were many answers to this question and some fairly good sketching, but the ordinary back gear of a lathe which was generally given is really no answer to the question at all. The gear used in modern automatic machinery was the kind required.

Q. 42. Describe a low tension magneto-ignition device suitable for use with gas engines. Sketch the circuits in clearly and show the sparking plug and the way it is insulated.

Attempted by few and, with two or three exceptions, not well done.

Q. 43. Describe and sketch a drop-forging plant, to be worked by hand. What are the particular advantages of drop-forging? Give a short list of articles which may be suitably forged by this method.

Many candidates attempted this, but few gave a really good description of a plant, and fewer still accompanied the description with a good sketch.

Q. 44. Estimate the diameter of a crank shaft where the crank overhangs. Calculate the force exerted on the crank pin by the connecting rod when the crank and the rod are at right angles, taking the following data :—The distance, measured along the crankshaft, from the centre line of the bearing, to the centre line of the cylinder produced is 11". Diameter of cylinder 20". Steam pressure in the cylinder 200 lbs. per sq. inch. Crank radius 1 foot. Length of connecting rod 5 feet. Maximum stress in the shaft 5 tons per square inch.

Some correct answers were received to this question, and the way to go about it was generally understood by those attempting it.

Q. 45. Sketch and describe a slipper attached to the motor bogie of an electric train suitable for picking up the current from a live rail laid in parallel with the running rails of the railway at a distance of about 1 foot outside the track.

Notwithstanding the many miles of track in the country few candidates had observed this particular detail to any purpose.

HONOURS PRACTICAL EXAMINATION.

There were 18 candidates whose work in the first part of the examination justified a further practical examination at South Kensington.

Each candidate was asked to select one from three proposed alternative designs relating respectively to structural steel work, machine tools, and locomotive work. Each question was selected by about equal numbers of candidates. Four candidates did 1st Class work, and six candidates did sufficiently good work to justify the award of a 2nd Class.

Report on the Examination in Building Construction and Drawing.

STAGE 1.

Results : 1st Class, 1,322 ; 2nd Class, 1,035 ; Failed, 567 ; Total, 2,924.

There is a very gratifying improvement in the papers of this Stage this year. With the exception of Questions 3, 11, and 12, which were not well answered, the answers show much more practical knowledge than was the case last year, and on the whole paper the percentage of failures was much lower and of First Classes much higher than has been the case previously, and it is evident that the elementary teaching has greatly improved.

Q. 1. Make a neat tracing in ink of the drawing given, with the writing and figures : the lines should be firm and solid and should finish exactly at the proper points.

This was a compulsory question, and the work generally was satisfactory, although fewer candidates obtained full marks than last year, but in many cases where the candidates did not do justice to themselves (as was evidenced by the inferiority of the tracing to the pencil drawings shown in answers to other questions), this was clearly due to the bad quality of the ink used.   125 candidates obtained full marks and 24 obtained none.

Q. 2. What is the meaning of the following terms : bond (of brickwork), soffit, ground (in joinery), air-brick, trimmer arch, sleepers (for floors), trapped gulley, splayed lining ?   Illustrate your answers by rough sketches.

This was attempted by 1,500 candidates, and was, on the whole, well answered, some of the sketches being very good.   The term " Sleeper (for floors) " was very often confused with "Sleeper wall," and the descriptions and attempted sketches of a "trapped gulley" showed in many cases a lamentable ignorance of elementary drainage.   Full marks were gained by 57 candidates and 10 obtained none.

Q. 3. What is the difference in their appearance and characteristics between chalk lime, grey stone lime, and Portland cement ?

This was attempted by only 439 candidates and was badly answered. The different characteristics of the two kinds of lime and the distinction between these and Portland cement were rarely well explained ; more attention should be paid to this subject.   Only 5 candidates obtained full marks, 33 none at all.

Q. 4. A roof with a pitch of 45° is to be covered with Countess slates laid with a 3 in. lap and centre nailed : draw to a scale of 1½ in. to a foot a section through four consecutive courses and figure the gauge.

Attempted by 1,926 candidates and, on the whole, well answered.   It is evident that more careful attention has been given to the subject of "lap" and "gauge" in roofing, but there were still many bad blunders : in far too many cases the nail was shewn passing through two slates, and not a few candidates distinctly showed the nail head above the top slate ; this is inexcusable.   500 candidates obtained full marks and 232 failed to get any.

Q. 5. Draw to a scale of 3 in. to a foot a cross section through two 2½ in. by 1¼ in. bevelled wood sash bars for a conservatory roof, 12 in. apart centre to centre, and show the glass and putty in position.

This was attempted by 1,438 candidates and was well done on the whole, but it is curious that many answers shewed the bars quite correctly drawn but upside down so that the rebate was above the glass, and the putty underneath.   207 gained full marks and 33 none.

Q. 6. Draw to a scale of 1 in. to a foot the front elevation of a framed and braced batten door 3 ft. wide by 7 ft. high, showing the hidden parts by dotted lines.

This was the favourite question, being answered by 2,496 candidates.   It is a very simple joinery question, and although there were few complete failures, it should have been better answered, many candidates failing to show the requisite detail, and when this was shown, it was frequently done in a very slovenly way.   The complete failures were 38, but only 131 obtained full marks.

Q. 7. The diagram shows the plan of a 14 in. brick wall in English bond at the angle of a square bay.   Draw to a scale of 1 in. to a foot two consecutive courses of the walls as shown, indicating the bond clearly.

⁻ This was a simple question on brickwork bond, and was attempted by 1,591 candidates. English bond was generally drawn correctly, but the position of the closers was often wrongly shown, and at the junctions of the walls vertical straight joints were the rule rather than the exception. It cannot be too strongly insisted on that bond in brickwork can only be taught properly by practical examples. 93 candidates had full marks, 162 had none.

Q. 8. Describe by sketches the use of a bricklayer's line-pins and cord, and give a full size sketch of one line-pin.

This was attempted by 1,555 candidates, and the use of the pins and cord was well indicated, but the full size sketches of the pins were indifferent in very many cases. 74 candidates gained full marks, 33 none.

Q. 9. Sketch neatly on your squared paper to half full size the section of an 8 in. by 3 in. channel iron having a mean thickness of ½ in.

Attempted by 1,208 candidates, many of whom showed perfectly ridiculous and impossible forms, showing that they had not the least notion of what a channel iron is. In all but a few cases the sides of the flanges were shown parallel even when the section was a good one. To 103 papers full marks were awarded, and no marks to 127.

Q. 10. Draw to a scale of 1½ in. to a foot a section through a 6 in. saddle-back Portland stone coping for a 9 in. wall, showing the wall under the coping.

2,327 candidates attempted this question and a large number of very good sketches were shown, no less than 888 obtaining full marks. The projection of the coping beyond the face of the wall was often too large and sometimes it was omitted altogether. It was curious how often the bed of the coping was shown hollowed out, just as if Portland stone was cast in a mould like terra cotta. 68 candidates gained no marks.

Q. 11. Draw to a scale of 1 in. to a foot the elevation of a chimney breast 4 ft. 10½ in. wide with a fireplace opening 30 in. wide and 3 ft. high with relieving arch. Show by dotted lines the arrangement of the flue with wing and gathering-over.

This was attempted by only 804 candidates, and the question was not well answered. The gathering over of the flue was rarely shown properly, and it is clear that a large number of the candidates have had very little instruction in the method of constructing flues. Only 4 gained full marks, 27 had none.

Q. 12. Draw to a scale of 1 in. to a foot the elevation of a stud partition 14 ft. long by 10 ft. high with a 3 ft. by 7 ft. doorway 12 inches from one side. Mark the scantling of the timbers and show a portion of the lathing.

This question also, attempted by 1,209 candidates, was not well answered. Often a trussed and not a stud partition was drawn ; the scantlings of the studs varied greatly ; sometimes the laths were shown running parallel to the studs ; the nogging pieces were often omitted ; and generally there was evidence of a lack of knowledge of the construction of stud partitions. Only 8 were awarded full marks, and 53 gained no marks.

STAGE 2.

Results : 1st Class, 338 ; 2nd Class, 1,122 ; Failed, 924 ; Total, 2,384.

In this Stage there was not a single paper of special excellence, and the papers, as a whole, were marked by mediocrity. Not a few of the candidates were obviously attempting an examination of a standard beyond their abilities and in advance of the instruction they had received. It was noticeable that many fair draughtsmen submitted papers which showed little knowledge of construction, and which suggested that they had not been well taught. Building construction is pre-eminently a practical subject, and instruction in it should aim at inducing those who study it to think practically and to use their powers of observation.

Q. 21. Make a neat tracing in ink of the drawing given, with the writing and figures. The lines should be firm and solid and should finish accurately at the proper points.

The tracing, which was compulsory, was, on the whole, fairly well done, although very unequal merit was shown—89 obtained no marks, but only 20 got full marks. Some good tracings were made by candidates who otherwise answered very badly, and *vice versa.*

As the tracing had to be in ink, those who worked in pencil were disqualified. A curious feature was that many who traced in pencil made an ink copy on their drawing paper, from which their tracing appeared to have been made. The printing and dimensioning have slightly improved, but still lack vigour. Some few of the candidates showed knowledge of the geometrical construction for the determination of the centre of the circular arcs, but detracted from the effect of their tracing by including the construction in pencil thereon instead of using the print for the purpose. Many traced the curves freehand, which is inadmissible, and a few made the whole tracing in this manner. A great number blotted their work by using a flat instead of a bevel ruler, others by charging the pen too heavily with ink, or by leaving ink on the outside of the nibs. In many cases the lines were too thin, and in others were of very unequal thickness.

Q. 22. Make a sketch of a pair of pinchers used in pulling out nails. Explain their action, and show what forces are concerned in the operation.

Attempted by 1,659, of whom 90 obtained no marks, and 21 full marks.

The sketches of the pinchers (or pincers) were poor as a rule, some very bad, shown by single lines and not more than an inch long. The lever acting to grip the nail was generally mentioned, though the subsequent leverage to extract the nail was not so often referred to. The actual forces concerned were rarely calculated. A few good full-sized sketches were given, but in these the claw end was more often bent outwards than inwards, and could not therefore be used.

Q. 23. A window opening of 7 ft. clear width is to be spanned by a flat lintel formed of three separate stones. Draw the elevation of this lintel to a scale of ½ in. to a foot and show clearly the methods of jointing the stones.

Attempted by 1,785, of whom the large number of 420 obtained no marks, and only 17 obtained full marks.

Although this was attempted by so many, there were very few good answers, and the majority confined themselves to one form of jointing. The depth of the lintel and its bearing on the walls was generally insufficient. Many answers showed skewbacks at the corners of the window opening, showing that the principle of the cantilever was not understood. In very many cases the three stones were joined by complicated secret joggles, cramps, dowels and plugs, and in these instances the visible joints were often vertical, which is vicious construction as giving an unnecessary appearance of instability.

Q. 24. A drain inspection chamber 3 ft. by 2 ft. in the clear, and 6 ft. deep to top of footings, has to be constructed in 9 in. brickwork. Calculate the number of bricks required, including the footings, and write out an order for them.

Attempted by 1,145, of whom 375 obtained no marks, and 32 obtained full marks.

This was, on the whole, badly answered, some gave a reasonable total number of bricks, but showed no calculation, although no scribbling paper is allowed and all work of this kind has to be given up. The numbers given, where calculation was shown, varied from 120 to over 5,000, indicating very vague notions as to the co-relation of materials required to

dimensions of work to be executed.   One candidate named 136½ bricks as
the total.   The "orders" were poor, and varied from "Please send me
1,000 bricks," to the whole preamble of a quantity surveyor's bill for
bricklayer.

Q. 25. The diagram shows the plan of a wooden vestibule screen between
an outer and an inner hall : the clear height from floor to ceiling
is 11 ft. 6 in. ; in the centre there is to be a pair of half-glass
doors to swing both ways, with a half-glass screen at each side.
The clear height of doors is to be 8 ft. with a transom and fixed
fanlight over both doors and screen.   Draw a half elevation to a
scale of ½ in. to a foot, and a plan 1½ in. to a foot—through
one hanging style and frame.

Attempted by 1,600, of whom 48 obtained no marks and 74 obtained full
marks.

This question was fairly well answered, as is generally the case with
joinery questions, but the important rounded joint between the hanging
stile and door post was often incorrectly shown, and in many cases the post
was omitted altogether.   Even when the rounded stile was shown it was
often so embedded in the frame that the door could not possibly swing.

Q. 26. The diagram shows portion of the elevation of a building.   Copy
it on your drawing paper and show clearly the following work :
brick quoins at A ; brick lacing courses at BB ; polled flints or
uncoursed rubble at C ; and brick quoins and arch to the window
opening.   Show complete outlines and indicate how the work
should be bonded.

Attempted by 1,422, of whom 109 obtained no marks, and 64 full marks.

This question received some very poor answers ; the quoins to wall end
and window opening were often impracticable, and the filing in of the
polled flints, or rubble, showed very bad draughtsmanship.   The string
courses were, as a rule, shown in stretchers only.   About 10 per cent. of
the answers were distinctly good.

Q. 27. The diagram shows one of the trussed beams of a gantry carrying
a load as indicated.   Calculate the amount and indicate the
nature of the stress in each part.

Attempted by 772, of whom 182 obtained no marks, and 55 full marks.

Having regard to the simple frame and diagram, there should have been
more answers to this question.   Many diagrams showed want of method,
and the "nature" of the stresses was more often correct than the "amount."
A large proportion indicated the nature of the stresses by arrow heads
round the joints, but these were so often wrong that it appears doubtful
whether the mode of using them was properly understood.   Thick or double
lines for the compression members, and single for tension would have been
more definite.

Q. 28. The diagram shows an acute squint at the junction of two 18 inch
brick walls.   Draw the plan of one course in double Flemish
bond, showing the bonding by single lines.   Scale 1 in. to 1 foot.

Attempted by 1,297, of whom 176 obtained no marks, and only 14 obtained
full marks.

The average work was fairly satisfactory, but many marks were lost by
candidates failing to break the vertical joints in the interior of the work.
Those who showed straight "joints" in the facework of course lost heavily ;
they did not appear to know of the simple expedient of "reversing" to test
the work.   Many showed birdsmouthed bricks in the bonding.

Q. 29. A fir beam 12 in. deep and 6 in. broad carries a central load of
36 cwt. over a clear span of 12 ft.   If the beam be reduced to
10 in. deep what load will give the same maximum longitudinal
stresses if placed (a) at the centre, and (b) 2 ft. 1 in. from one of
the supports ?   The weight of the beam may be neglected.   The
method of working must be clearly shown.

Attempted by 428, of whom 155 obtained no marks, and 41 full marks.

Some of the candidates solved this question perfectly, showing a complete grasp of the subject ; others obtained correct solutions by cumbersome methods running into three pages, whereas half a dozen lines suffice. A greater number were able to solve the first part but failed completely with the second part. It was a well marked question, and the marks would have been easily earned if the principles had been clearly taught in the schools. Candidates failed to see that the strength of the two beams varied only as the square of the depth, and in the second case that the load had to be increased until the maximum bending moment was the same as in (a).

Q. 30. The diagram shows the plan of a wooden well staircase with continuous handrail and open cut strings, each step having a rise of 6 in. Draw sections on the lines *AB* and *CD*, in each case showing the portions of the staircase which would be seen in elevation. Describe clearly how you would construct the carriages. Scale 4 ft. to an inch.

Attempted by 622, of whom 142 obtained no marks, and only 2 obtained full marks.

The answers to this question were decidedly bad. Candidates have a very imperfect knowledge of staircase work, and very few knew how to deal with the supports under the winders. Staircase work does not appear to be taught beyond the elementary stage.

Q. 31. Sketch, 8 ft. to an inch, the section through a scaffold with fan guard ; also draw to a scale of 3 in. to a foot the end of a scaffold board showing how it is cut and protected.

Attempted by 499, of whom 42 obtained no marks, and 10 full marks.

This question was badly answered. Very few appeared to know what a fan-guard was, and of those who did few knew how to fix it, although it is common in all town work. The end of the scaffold board was generally correctly drawn.

Q. 32. Draw a full size section through the joint of a flushing pipe with a W.C. flushing cistern.

Attempted by 952, of whom 384 (more than one-third) failed to obtain any marks, and only 5 obtained full marks.

Although many attempted this question, the results were very poor. They knew a wiped joint came in somewhere, but the section shown was often defective, and the remainder of the connection was very vague. Some knew that a brass union was required, but were unable to draw it.

STAGE 3.

Results : 1st Class, 177 ; 2nd Class, 485 ; Failed, 383 ; Total, 1,045.

The general results of the Examination in this Stage closely approximated to those of last year. The failures were slightly more, being 383 as against 337 last year. The first-class candidates were 16·9 per cent. this year, as compared with 19·2 per cent. last year, while the second classes were 46·4 per cent. as against 44·2 per cent. last year. The great fault in the answers was the lack of practical knowledge. This was chiefly shown in the sketches given in answering Questions 44, 49 and 52. In many cases the drawings were excellent.

Q. 41. Describe the general characteristics of the following stones. State where they are found and for what purposes in building you would consider them most suitable : Hopton Wood, Corsehill, Beer, Ham Hill, Ancaster, Red Mansfield. What rough and ready test would you apply to a specimen of stone to ascertain whether it is a sandstone or a limestone ?

This question was attempted by only 83 candidates out of a total of 1,043, and, when selected, was fairly well done, but in many cases the locality and the nature of the stones given were only guessed at. 7 candidates obtained full marks, 2 failed completely.

Q. 42. Describe the preparation of steel rods for ferro-concrete construction as regards their preservation from corrosion. How may wood be treated to render it fire-resisting ?

This was attempted by 216 candidates, and the answers were not very satisfactory ; only a few appeared to know that the present practice is to allow the rods to become slightly rusty and then to coat them with a Portland cement wash, and the majority recommended tarring or painting, which is worse than useless.

Charring the wood, or coating it with sheet iron or asbestos, was the only method suggested by many candidates to make it fire resisting, very few seemed to know anything about cyanite or other liquid treatment. One candidate got full marks, 10 obtained none.

Q. 43. Show by sketches the following defects in timber and state to what they are generally due : heart shake, star shake, cup shake, upset or thunder shake, rind gall, waney edge, wind crack.

Attempted by 680 candidates, but the sketches were poor and slovenly n many cases. Some explanations were not explanations at all, such as 'a thunder shake is caused by thunder, and a wind shake by the wind." A remarkable divergence of opinion existed as to star shakes, about equal numbers stating that these " run from the centre of the tree outwards, but do not reach the outside," and that they "extend from the circumference inwards, being widest at the outer edge," but as these divergent views appear to be taken by two of the chief text books, more credit was given for the latter answer than would otherwise have been the case. Students should be taken by the teachers to a timber yard, where the defects in timber could be practically explained. Full marks were gained by 6 candidates, while 3 got none.

Q. 44. Describe carefully the points to note in inspecting a delivery of plates for a large cast-iron tank. Sketch full size on your squared paper the section of a joint between two plates of such a tank $\frac{5}{8}$ in. thick, flanges $\frac{7}{8}$ in. thick, bolts $\frac{3}{4}$ in. diameter, chipping faces at outer edge of joint, iron rust cement ; and state the composition of the latter.

This was attempted by 222 candidates, very few of whom showed any practical knowledge whatever of the subject.

Flanges were often shewn parallel with and detached from the plates ; the object and position of the chipping faces was unknown ; rivets instead of bolts were shewn in impossible joints, and rust-cement was frequently stated to be composed of iron rust and Portland cement. Five candidates obtained full marks, 18 none at all.

Q. 45. The diagram shows the elevation of an ordinary steel roof truss of 20 ft. clear span. Draw this to a scale of $\frac{1}{4}$ in. to a foot and mark the scantlings ; the sectional area in square inches of the various members may be taken as follows : $a = 1\cdot5$, $b = 0\cdot6$, $c = 1\cdot0$, $d = 0\cdot3$, $e = 0\cdot3$. Draw to a scale of 3 in. to a foot details of the various joints.

This was attempted by 676 candidates, and was badly answered. Although the sectional area—based upon actual calculation—was given for each member, there was rarely any attempt made to find scantlings to match, and in many cases the discrepancies were absurd. The majority had no idea of proportion between width and thickness in tee and angle sections, giving such dimensions as 1½ in. by 1 in. by ½ in., and anything between ¾ in. and 1½ in. for the diameter of the bolt through the end of a ⅝ in. tie rod. On many drawings the rivets look like tin-tacks sprinkled about. One candidate had 36 rivets in the ridge connection, 19 at the junction of strut with rafter, and 20 at the joint at foot of rafter, and many others were nearly as bad. Two candidates obtained full marks, 29 got none.

Q. 46. The diagram shows a section through the base of a rectangular wall 3 ft. thick with a resultant load of 10 tons acting at a point 6 in. from one face. Find the tension and compression at each face of the wall using the formula $P = \dfrac{W}{A} \pm \dfrac{M}{Z}$ where P is the maximum intensity of stress.

Attempted by only 28 candidates, the majority of whom were uncertain how to measure the bending moment M, multiplying the load by its distance from the edge instead of from the centre, and several gave $\dfrac{bd^3}{12}$ instead of $\dfrac{bd^2}{6}$ for the section modulus Z. This formula is of such constant use in calculating walls, arches, roofs, &c., that it ought to have been better known. Eight candidates gave perfectly correct answers and obtained full marks, 5 got none.

Attention must again be called—as in former years—to the amount of ignorance shewn in connection with the questions in Division II. Much more care is required in teaching those subjects.

Q. 47. A building 50 ft. long by 30 ft. wide over all is to have a roof of 60° pitch hipped at each end, and there is to be an overhang of 10 in. at the eaves. Calculate the number of Broseley tiles, laid with a 3 in. lap, required to cover one of the long sides.

This was attempted by 298 candidates. It is an absurdly easy question, but a large number utterly failed to find the correct area of the roof, and the size of a Broseley tile varied from 7 in. by 5 in. to 20 in. by 10 in. A very bad feature was that so many candidates were unable to calculate the exposed surface of a tile with a certain lap. Time after time such statements as this were made explicitly, "A Broseley tile 10″ × 6″ laid with a 3 in. lap will cover 7″ × 6″ square inches = 42″." Attention has frequently been called in the lower stages to the ignorance of what "lap" and "gauge" in roofing mean, and it is clear that this ignorance extends to the higher stages. The number of tiles given in answers to this question varied from 334 to 111,000. 21 candidates got full marks, 48 none.

Q. 48. The drawing shows the ground plan of a semi-detached house with the positions of the various sinks, W.C.'s, &c. Draw *on the drawing* in pencil the lines of the drains as you would lay them, showing traps, inspection chambers, &c., and figuring the sizes of the pipes. The main sewer is in the road in front of the house, but the drains need not be shown further than the front fence.

This practical drainage question was the favourite one in the paper, being attempted by no less than 976 candidates and answered fairly well on the whole, although there were several very bad answers. The manholes were frequently shown too small, in many cases they were too numerous, and their position often had no reference to the drain connections. Several candidates showed 4 in. stoneware drain pipes from the scullery copper, and in two cases the drains were taken through the next house. Equal credit was given whether the rain water was conveyed to the main drain or by a separate system, as the practice varies in different localities. Full marks were gained by 22 candidates, and 42 obtained no marks.

Q. 49. A three-centred arch consisting of stone voussoirs is to be constructed over an opening 12 ft. wide on the ground floor of a lofty building. Draw the elevation of the arch on your drawing paper showing the depth of the voussoirs and the joints, and discuss fully and clearly the various causes which would tend to produce failure in such an arch, and indicate the positions where you would look for signs of failure.

This was attempted by 247 candidates, and although the point of probable fracture was rightly indicated in many instances, at the junction of the two curves on the haunches of the arch, the reason why this was so was rarely stated. In some cases very curious ideas prevailed as to the nature of a three-centred arch. No candidate got full marks, 16 failed altogeth r.

Q. 50. A concrete wall 12 in. thick and 8 ft. high is to be constructed.
Draw a cross section (? in. to a foot) showing how the concrete
is held in place while it is being built up.

Attempted by 801 candidates and, on the whole, well answered, although
in some cases upright boarding was clearly shown on both sides of the wall.
This was a bad blunder. 29 candidates obtained full marks, 25 none.

Q. 51. In a lean-to slated roof of 45° pitch a skylight is to be constructed
8 ft. long horizontally and 5 ft. wide ; the top of the skylight is
to be kept 2 ft. away from the main wall against which the roof
leans ; the depth of the rafters is 5 in. Draw both a vertical
and a horizontal section through the skylight, showing clearly
the trimming of the rafters and the lead flashings round the
light. Scale ½ inch to a foot.

This question was attempted by 802 candidates, and many of the sketches
were excellent. A number of the candidates read the question carelessly
and drew a skylight 8 feet long on the slope, instead of horizontally. The
most frequent mistakes were :—(1) Allowing the water coming from above
the skylight to run over the glass ; (2) not continuing the glass over the
bottom rail. The horizontal section was not drawn nearly so well as the
vertical one. 22 candidates got full marks, and 87 no marks.

Q. 52. The wall of a building 50 ft. high from pavement to parapet, and
having five floors 10 feet apart, but no basement, shows signs of
bulging and is to be supported by a raking shore. Draw the
shore (¼ in. to a foot), name all the parts and figure the scantlings
of the timbers.

This was attempted by 823 candidates, but the answers showed a great
lack of practical knowledge. The needles were often in the wrong positions ;
cleats were omitted above the needles ; the top raker was often shown over
50 feet long instead of as a riding shore ; and in some cases an elaborate
and absolutely impossible system of shoring was shown. In every town in
the kingdom there must be ample opportunities for studying shoring, and
the student should be encouraged to go and sketch the shores from actual
examples. Full marks were awarded to 17 candidates, 50 gained none.

HONOURS.

Results : 1st Class, 8 ; 2nd Class, 25 ; Failed, 247 ; Total, 280.

The Honours papers this year showed a considerable falling off in quality ;
two-thirds of the candidates had no reasonable prospect of passing.

For the Honours Examination candidates ought to have a precise knowledge of their subject. On a merely general knowledge they can obtain
very few marks, and above all things the designs given in connection with
the answers must be practical.

Q. 61. What is meant by "hard" and "soft" waters and how are they
classified ? What is the principal cause of the "furring up" of
hot-water pipes, and of what is the deposited matter generally
composed ?

Attempted by 128, of whom nine obtained no marks and none obtained
full marks. The answers were too general, and when definite statements
were made they were often absurd. "Hard water contains 12 to 15 per
cent. of chalk " was frequently stated with slight variations, and generally
there was confusion between percentage and degrees on Clark's scale. The
deposited matter was commonly given as "iron rust and lime," one gave it
clearly written as "$3A3O_3$."

Q. 62. A bonded warehouse is to be erected on the banks of a tidal river ;
the wall next the stream rising vertically from low water mark,
and the lowest floor being 20 feet above that level. The thickness of the brickwork from top of footings to the floor level is

4 ft. 6 in. Describe fully in their proper order ALL the operations necessary for laying the foundations and building the wall
up to floor level. How would you protect such a wall from
abrasion by barges ?

Attempted by 146, of whom 10 obtained no marks and none full marks.
Beyond the fixing of a cofferdam little was known of the necessary procedure.
Many overlooked the fact that the wall was to rise *vertically* from low
water *mark*. One directed dry cement to be spread over the bottom of the
foundation to keep the water out. Many proposed to protect the wall from
abrasion by driving piles clear of the foundations ; one filled his cofferdam
with concrete ; another covered his wall with sheet iron. One said "a
double row of sheet piling forming an annular space of about 9 inches is
driven." Very few showed any acquaintance with riverside work.

Q. 63. In a large public room—the internal walls of which are of brick—
there are two rows of steel stanchions dividing it into three
bays. The stanchions are encased in concrete and when
finished will appear as circular columns with caps and bases,
and they are to be finished in enamel paint. The walls are to
have an oak dado 7 ft. high, above which they are to be
papered ; the ceiling is entirely of fire-resisting materials.
Write a full specification of the plasterer's work for walls,
columns and ceiling.

Attempted by 109, of whom 1 obtained no marks, and none full marks.
Many of the answers were ordinary plasterers' specifications, with no
provision for the special circumstances of the case.

Q. 64. Describe fully the precautions which you would adopt in constructing the floors and internal partitions of a building where
the transmission of sound is to be prevented as far as possible.

Attempted by 208, of whom 1 obtained no marks, and 1 obtained full
marks. The stock answers were mostly given to this question—" Silicate
of cotton " was to be put under the floor boards and between the studs of
the partitions. Slag wool is not only a more appropriate term, but less
likely to be misunderstood, and there are many other points to note in
preventing the transmission of sound.

Q. 65. The diagram shows the section of a mild steel stanchion 18 ft.
high, carrying a load of 36 tons. Design a suitable base plate
for this stanchion showing clearly the connection between the
two (scale 1½ in. to a foot). State the area of the stone base
which you would consider necessary, and of the concrete
foundation under it on ordinary ground.

Attempted by 162, of whom 39 obtained no marks, and none obtained
full marks. This was in general very badly done. No idea of proportion
existed in the designing of the base plate, and some extremely ridiculous
answers were given.

Q. 66. The diagram shows the section through one of the beams and
part of the floor slab of a ferro-concrete floor. Draw this to a
scale of 1½ in. to a foot and add suitable reinforcement—say
four 1 in. diameter steel rods—with provision for shear.

Attempted by 147, of whom 26 obtained no marks, and none
obtained full marks. Generally the answers seemed to be attempts to
recollect the illustrations shown in books and catalogues, and were not
very successful at that.

Q. 67. An iron tie-rod 1½ in. diameter has an eye at one end. Show by
sketches how the eye is welded up and draw an elevation of the
eye one quarter full size. Figure all dimensions.

Attempted by 46, of whom 7 obtained no marks. Although a simple
question, this was seldom attempted, and of those who did attempt it a
large proportion did not know the difference between forging and welding.

Q. 68. The ground floor windows shown on the diagram are to be
        removed and a bay window built in their place as shown in the
        plan A. Make a working drawing for this bay in plan, section
        and elevation, marking on it the materials and sizes. Scale ½ in.
        to a foot.

Attempted by 197, of whom 5 obtained no marks, and 1 obtained full
marks. Some of these answers were distinctly good, others would be
discreditable to first stage candidates. Many drew the three views without
projecting one from the other.

Q. 69. Draw a section, 1½ in. to a foot, through two adjacent pews in a
        church, showing the seats slightly dished, sloping backs and
        bookboards. All the constructive details are to be given.

Attempted by 177, of whom 10 obtained no marks, and none obtained
full marks. The same remarks apply to the answers to this question as to
the last. The seat was generally shown 15 to 18 in. wide, by 1½ to 2 in.
thick without a joint, and dished out of the solid. A few upright backs
and narrow flat seats were given, and many omitted stall ends and
supporting brackets. Book shelves projecting 6 in. were often shown
without any support below. Hat rails and foot rests or stools were
frequently omitted.

Q. 70. A brick arch carrying a roadway has a clear span of 20 feet and a
        rise of 2 ft. 6 in , and is formed of five half-brick rings. Draw
        this to a scale of ¼ in. to a foot and add the line of thrust for a
        distributed load of 5 cwt. per foot run in addition to the
        structural load which may be represented by brickwork up to a
        level of 1 ft. above the crown. The weight of each voussoir and
        the centre of gravity of the superincumbent load may be
        assumed.

Attempted by 63, of whom 6 obtained no marks, and 1 obtained full
marks. The working was not sufficiently clear and distinct in some cases,
but on the whole the answers to this question were good.

HONOURS PRACTICAL EXAMINATION.

SUBJECT.—A small Cemetery Chapel with vestry attached, to be built of
stone.

There were 47 candidates called up for the practical examination, of
whom 12 obtained less than half marks. The designing was fair on the
whole, but more consistency in architectural details was desirable ; doors
and windows were sometimes shown in different styles. The planning in
many cases was inconvenient, the entrance should have been at the west
end, with a wide processional passage in direct line. One candidate
arranged his plan so that the bearers would have to make three turns
before reaching the support for coffin, which was in many cases placed
north and south instead of east and west. The reading desk was, in some
cases, placed close under the east window, and out of sight of the transepts.
The chief mourners were most conveniently placed in short transepts on
either side, and the general mourners in the nave, but several of the plans
might have been mistaken for an ordinary village chapel. The instructions
omitted any reference to heating, or to lavatory and w.c., but many of the
candidates rightly provided these. The section showed in several instances
an insecure roof, and the entrance door details were mostly poor. The
estimated cost varied from £950 to £9,980. Some of the drawings showed
excellent draughtsmanship and good artistic ability.

Considering the fact that the subject for this practical examination was
announced nearly two months beforehand, the general standard of the
papers was not so high as might have been expected, and scarcely equal to
that of last year.

GENERALLY.

We again found much evidence that the standards of the higher stages of examination are not sufficiently understood. Many candidates presented themselves in stages which were obviously beyond them, and we are inclined to doubt whether teachers are careful to see that students do not enter classes for which they are not prepared. It is against the best interests of a student to admit him to a class in any of the higher stages when he has not mastered the work of the stages below it.

Report on the Examination in Naval Architecture.

STAGE 1.

Results: 1st Class, 129; 2nd Class, 112; Failed, 59; Total, 300.

The number of candidates was 31 less than in 1906. Twenty-three candidates either did not select questions from each of the sections into which the examination paper is divided, or failed to obtain any marks in one or other of the sections. Twelve candidates answered more than the number of questions permitted in the sections. On the whole, the standard of worked papers was a slight improvement on that of last year, but arithmetical errors, in the calculations, were too frequent.

PRACTICAL SHIPBUILDING.

Q. 1. Name the different materials generally used in shipbuilding, stating the purposes for which they are used.

To what tests are mild steel ship plates and angles subjected, in order to satisfactorily pass *either* (a) Lloyds, *or* (b) Admiralty inspection ?

Attempted by about 46 per cent. of the candidates. The first part was generally answered satisfactorily, although a number of candidates gave the different sections of steel bars used for shipbuilding, instead of the *materials* used, the latter being required by the question.

The answers to the second part of the question, relating to the tests of steel plates and angles, were, with few exceptions, generally poor, Lloyds and Admiralty tests being mixed up, and the tests for steel angles being rarely mentioned.

Q. 2. A mild steel plate forming part of the outer bottom of a vessel is $\frac{5}{16}''$ thick, and 4 feet wide. Show the disposition of the rivets in an edge, at a butt joint, and at a frame. State size and pitch of the rivets.

Attempted by about 30 per cent. of the candidates, and the answers were generally very satisfactory.

Q. 3. Show how lap-jointed and butt-jointed steel plates are made water-tight at the laps and butts ; give sketches of the tools used.

Attempted by about 70 per cent. of the candidates, and the answers were generally very good.

Q. 4. Show by a rough sketch, the connections in a double-bottomed ship of the margin plate to the floor plate, bottom plating, frames, &c.

Attempted by about 50 per cent. of the candidates, and the answers were generally very good. A few candidates, however, gave sketches shewing a water-tight longitudinal of a warship.

Q. 5. The frame and reverse angle bars and floor plates of a small
     mercantile vessel being riveted together, describe how they are
     usually got into their correct position on the building blocks and
     secured in place.

Attempted by about 25 per cent. of the candidates, and the answers
were generally satisfactory, but in some cases the answers were not given
in sufficient detail, very general terms being used, such as "the frames are
hoisted into position by a winch" and "secured by means of wood battens."

Q. 6. Describe the process of riveting a bottom plate to the adjacent
     plates and frames, and state the measures adopted for testing
     the watertightness of the rivets and the efficiency of the work.

Attempted by about 25 per cent. of the candidates, and the answers
were generally satisfactory. A few candidates described in detail the
process of "beating up" a rivet.

Q. 7. Describe, with rough sketches, the process of bending and bevelling
     the frame angle bars of a vessel.

Attempted by about 60 per cent. of the candidates, and was fairly well
answered. In some cases the relation between the bending slab and scrieve
board was not clearly given.

Q. 8. Show clearly how a keelson of form 〔⊥〕 can be made watertight,

     where it passes through a bulkhead.

Attempted by about 60 per cent. of the candidates, and the sketches
were generally satisfactory, but the descriptions were incomplete.

Q. 9. What wood is usually employed for the deck planking of ships,
     and why? Show how the butts of the planks are secured, when
     no deck plating is worked on the beams. What form of bolt is
     used for securing the planking?

Attempted by about 68 per cent. of the candidates, and the answers were
generally very good.

Q. 10. Of what material is the stem of a vessel usually made, and how is
      it formed? Show how the stem is connected to the other parts
      of the ship.

Attempted by about 50 per cent. of the candidates; the answers to "what
material the stem is usually made of" were generally very satisfactory,
but, in a very few cases, the material was stated to be "cast iron." About
half of the answers to the other parts of the question were satisfactory, but
the others were poor.

DRAWING.

Q. 11. Enlarge, in pencil, the given drawing, to a scale of twice that upon
      which it is drawn.

Attempted by all the candidates, and was generally very well answered.
Some of the sketches were exceedingly good.

CALCULATIONS.

Q. 12. Explain the difference between "volume" and "weight." A
      floating body has a constant triangular section, with a uniform
      draught of 13 feet, and breadth at the water-line of 28 feet.
      Find the displacement, in tons per foot of length of the body,
      when floating in water of which 1 cubic foot weighs 63$\frac{1}{2}$ lbs.

Attempted by about 15 per cent. of the candidates, and the calculation
was in most cases correctly answered. Not many candidates explained
the difference between "volume" and "weight." A few candidates stated
that "weight" is "displacement in tons."

Q. 13. Find the weight of a hollow mild steel pillar 8′ 7″ long, whose external diameter is 4¾ inches and internal diameter 3⅞ inches. What is the diameter of a solid pillar of the same weight, its length being the same as the hollow one ?

What are the weights of a cubic foot of cast-iron, lead, and copper ?

Attempted by about 50 per cent. of the candidates, and the answers were generally correct. In a number of cases the arithmetical work was untidy, no system or contractions being used, and led to heavy multiplication, and as a consequence the weight of the pillar was given as 234 tons, 20 tons 3 qrs. 13·27 lbs., etc, and the diameter of the solid pillar 11·66 inches. Many candidates obtained the weight of the hollow pillar by assuming it unrolled into the form of a plate the width of which was taken as the mean circumference of the material forming the pillar, but took the thickness of the plate as 1 inch instead of ⅛ inch.

Q. 14. The half-ordinates of the water-plane of a ship are :—·3, 3·5, 8·15, 11·6, 13·7, 14·46, 14·1, 12·8, 10·24, 5·8, and ·6 feet respectively ; the length of the water-plane being 286 feet. Find the area of the water-plane.

Define "centre of gravity" and "centre of buoyancy."

A favourite question of this section of the examination paper ; attempted by about 80 per cent. of the candidates, with generally correct results. Arithmetical errors were too frequent, and a number of the candidates were unable to deduce the common interval, stating it to be 26 feet. The "centre of buoyancy" was not clearly defined by a small number of the candidates, some stating that "centre of buoyancy" was the "centre of gravity" of the immersed portion of the ship, instead of the "centre of gravity" of the water displaced. A few candidates added 0 to each end of the ordinates and proceeded with the calculation, obtaining an incorrect result.

Q. 15. A ship weighing 28,535 tons, floats at a certain water-line in sea water. What is her displacement in cubic feet ?

How much weight would have to be removed from this vessel in order that she may float at the same water-line in fresh water ?

Attempted by about 40 per cent. of the candidates. The answers to the first part of the question were generally correct, but about one-third of the answers to the second part were incorrect, the candidates dividing the difference between the fresh and salt water volumes of displacement by 35 instead of 36.

STAGE 2.

Results : 1st Class, 70 ; 2nd Class, 169 ; Failed, 46 ; Total, 285.

The number of candidates was 45 less than last year.

On the whole the practical part of the examination paper was satisfactorily done, and some very good rough sketches were given.

A satisfactory improvement was shewn in the answers to the "Laying Off" section of the paper, as compared with those of last year's.

The drawing was very satisfactorily done, considering a new departure was made, i.e., the candidates having to set the measurements to scale, from given figured dimensions, similar to what is required in the Drawing Office.

Too many arithmetical errors occur in the calculation section ; with many of the candidates there appears to be an absence of method in laying out the answers to the calculation questions, and in many cases involving the multiplication of different units, etc.

PRACTICAL SHIPBUILDING.

Q. 21. In many large twin-screw merchant ships shaft brackets are not
   fitted. Sketch and describe the method then adopted for
   supporting the after part of the screw shafts.

Attempted by about 16 per cent. of the candidates, and the answers were
generally satisfactory, a few of the sketches were very good.

Q. 22. A new material having been proposed for use in the structure of
   ships, describe what tests you would apply to it to ascertain its
   suitability for the purpose intended.

   To what tests are iron castings for ship work subjected, in
   order to satisfactorily pass *either* (a) Lloyds, *or* (b) Admiralty
   inspection.

Attempted by about 33 per cent. of the candidates. A number of the
candidates, in the answers to the first part of the question, gave tests for
mild or high tensile steel, especially stating the latter to be the new
material. The tests for steel castings were generally given as those
applicable to iron castings.

Q. 23. Sketch a good arrangement of docking blocks, showing how they
   are connected together, and to the floor of the dock. Of what
   materials are the blocks composed ?

   A vessel having been placed in its correct position in a dry
   dock, state where the shores should be placed for supporting the
   vessel when the dock is dry. Show by means of a cross sectional
   sketch of the vessel and dry dock, the arrangement of shores to
   support the vessel.

Attempted by about 50 per cent. of the candidates. The first part of the
question was very well answered, but in the remainder of the question,
although a number of the candidates stated correctly where shores ought
to be placed, they did not shew the longitudinals, framing, etc., in the
cross section.

Q. 24. Sketch an efficient arrangement of butts of bottom plating for a
   ship whose transverse frames are spaced 27″ apart, the plates to
   be used being 18′ long and 42″ wide.

   The plates being $\frac{1}{2}$″ thick, with double riveted landing
   edges, and flush butts with single straps treble riveted ; state
   the size and spacing of the rivets in the edges, butts, and
   frames, and the width of butt strap and lap of edges.

Attempted by about 37 per cent. of the candidates, and generally very
satisfactory answers were given.

Q. 25. Sketch and describe the construction of a bilge keel in a large
   steel ship, and its connections to the bottom plating.

The favourite question of this section of the examination paper
attempted by about 85 per cent. of the candidates. Very good answers
were generally given, but the riveting of the bilge keel to the bottom
plating was omitted in many cases.

Q. 26. What provision is made for mooring a ship when lying alongside
   a wharf or jetty, in the case of ships fitted with bulwarks ?

   Sketch a double-headed bollard, and show in detail how it is
   secured to the deck. Of what material is the bollard usually
   constructed ?

Attempted by about 50 per cent. of the candidates, and the answers
generally were very good.

Q. 27. Show by sketches how the upper deck of a large sailing ship is
   strengthened in wake of the masts.

Attempted by about 30 per cent. of the candidates, and about 75 per cent.
of the answers were satisfactory.

Q. 28. Sketch in detail and describe briefly, an efficient arrangement of engine bearers for a twin screw steamer, naming the type of vessel selected.

Attempted by about 10 per cent. of the candidates, and the answers were generally satisfactory, but in some cases engine bearers of a single screw steamer were given, instead of a twin screw steamer.

LAYING OFF.

Q. 29. What information is required in the mould loft to enable the lines of a ship to be prepared and faired?

Show by sketches the lines of a ship, as they appear on the mould loft floor.

Attempted by about 44 per cent. of the candidates, and the answers were generally satisfactory; some of the sketches were very good.

Q. 30. A ship has a considerable trim by the stern and a list to port. How would you determine the true shape of the plane of flotation?

Attempted by about 14 per cent. of the candidates, but the true shape of the plane of flotation was seldom given; the method of determining the projection only being stated generally.

Q. 31. What is a Scrieve Board? What are the advantages attending its use?

What lines are usually placed upon the scrieve board, and how are they prepared?

The favourite question of this section of the examination paper, attempted by about 64 per cent. of the candidates, and about 75 per cent. of the answers were satisfactory.

DRAWING.

Q. 32. The given sketch represents (not to scale) a boiler bearer, &c., for supporting an ordinary cylindrical boiler. Draw it neatly, in pencil, on a scale of $\frac{1}{4}$" to 1 foot.

Attempted by all the candidates, and was very well done. A number of candidates placed the dimensions on the drawing; there is no need to do this.

CALCULATIONS.

Q. 33. Describe, in detail, how you would proceed to find the area of a plane surface bounded by a given curve, making use of the rule known as "Simpson's second rule."

The areas of the transverse vertical sections of a ship up to the load-water plane are 25, 103, 145·5, 251, 470·5, 485, 290·7. 220, 165·3, and 31 square feet respectively. The length of the ship being 270 feet, calculate :—

(a) the load displacement of the ship in tons, and

(b) the longitudinal position of the centre of buoyancy.

Ten candidates did not attempt this compulsory question. The answers were generally correct. A few candidates stated the rule incorrectly, but worked the calculation correctly, and many did not deduce correctly the common interval from the given length of the vessel.

Q. 34. Define the terms :—"tons per inch," "change of trim," and "moment to change trim one inch."

A ship is 380' long, and floating at a draught of 18' forward and 21' aft, her displacement is 9,000 tons, and the moment to change trim 1" is 645 foot tons. If a weight of 40 tons already on board be shifted forward through 85', what would be the final draughts forward and aft.

Attempted by about 25 per cent. of the candidates, and the answers generally were correct. The "change of trim" was correctly found by a number of the candidates, but many did not divide by two to give the increase of draft forward, and the decrease of draft aft.

Q. 35. A box keelson is formed of $\frac{7}{16}''$ mild steel plates and $3\frac{1}{2}'' \times 3\frac{1}{2}'' \times \frac{7}{16}''$ angles. The top and bottom plates are 24" wide and the depth of the keelson, over all, is 28". Calculate the weight of 376' length of the keelson, including butt-straps, rivets, &c.

Attempted by about 14 per cent. of the candidates. In most cases the work was not laid out in a clear or systematic manner, and as a consequence many arithmetical mistakes were made, which led to the weight of the keelson being variously stated from 15 tons to 5,500 tons.

Q. 36. Define the terms "block coefficient," "midship section coefficient," and "prismatic coefficient." What relation exists between these coefficients ?

A ship whose length is 270' and breadth 42' floats in salt water at a load draught of 19'. What is her displacement in tons if the block coefficient is ·497 ?

Attempted by about 45 per cent. of the candidates, but the relation between the three coefficients was only stated in a few cases, otherwise the answers generally were satisfactory.

STAGE 3.

Results : 1st Class, 35 ; 2nd Class, 100 ; Failed, 94 ; Total, 229.

There was an increase of about 20 per cent. in the number of candidates who sat at the examination in this Stage, as compared with last year, and it is satisfactory to note that there was, on the whole, an improvement in the quality of the work sent in.

Greater attention appears to have been given to the instructions printed at the head of the examination paper, as in a few cases only were more questions attempted in particular sections than were permitted.

The worst feature of the worked papers in this stage was the weakness of the answers to questions set in the "Laying Off" section of the paper. This was referred to in last year's report, and, although there appears to be a slight improvement in this section, the knowledge of candidates generally as regards "laying off" appears to be very poor. Twenty-three of the candidates did not attempt either of the questions in "laying off," and 32 of those who did attempt either or both of the questions failed to obtain any marks ; thus 55 candidates, nearly 25 per cent. of the total number who sat at the examination, failed through not obtaining any marks in the "laying off" section. This is very unsatisfactory, as the "laying off" is a very important part of the work in connection with shipbuilding. Much more attention should be given to this branch of the subject than appears to have been given in the past.

The practical questions were, on the whole, well answered.

The compulsory question was generally well answered ; all the candidates except two attempted the question, and all except nine obtained marks.

PRACTICAL SHIPBUILDING.

Q. 41. Sketch and describe an arrangement of steam and hand steering gear as fitted in a large modern ship, naming the materials of which the different parts are made. Show the method of changing from steam to hand gear, and the method of working by hand as well as steam.

Attempted by about 80 candidates, about 14 of whom gave very good answers, but the remainder only answered parts of the question. A large number of candidates gave simply a sketch of the right and left-handed screw gear, without showing how the rudder was controlled, either by steam or hand gear.

Q. 42. Describe fully the process of water testing a small watertight compartment, such as a ballast-tank, and name the precautions you would take to ensure the test being properly carried out. State what defects are generally met with, how they exhibit themselves, and how they are remedied.

About 120 candidates attempted this question, and the answers were generally satisfactory, except as to details of the precautions to be taken to ensure the test being properly carried out. Retesting after the defects are thought to be made good was seldom referred to.

Q. 43. Sketch and describe the launching arrangements for a large ship, showing the ground and sliding ways, poppets, &c. State the timber employed for the various parts, and the material used for greasing the ways. State the declivity and camber of the launching ways, and the declivity of the keel.

A favourite question, about 135 candidates attempting it. The answers generally were satisfactory, and about 20 per cent. of the answers were very good.

Q. 44. Sketch and describe the construction of a hinged watertight door, and state where they are usually fitted. Explain how the door may be opened from both sides of the bulkhead, and show the method of fitting the india-rubber, clips, hinges, &c.

The most popular question of this section of the paper, about 150 candidates attempting it. The answers were generally satisfactory. The chief difficulty seemed to be as to the particular parts of a ship where these doors are usually fitted.

Q. 45. Sketch an arrangement of upper deck plating for a ship, stating the dimensions of the vessel.

State the dimensions and scantlings of the plates, width of butt-straps and laps of landing edges, and the diameter and spacing of the rivets. How is compensation for loss of strength effected in wake of an opening in the deck?

Attempted by about 90 candidates. About 13 of the answers were good, and the remainder were generally poor and incomplete.

Q. 46. Describe, with sketches, the arrangements adopted in large vessels for taking on board, distilling, storing, and distributing fresh water for drinking, &c., purposes.

What precautions are necessary to prevent the water in the tanks from becoming contaminated?

About 40 candidates attempted this question, and about eight of the answers were very good. The arrangements for distilling water seemed to be the least well-known.

Q. 47. Sketch and describe how the wheels of a paddle steamer are supported, showing the method of building the sponsons, paddle beams, wings, and paddle boxes.

Only 17 candidates attempted this question, but it was fairly well answered by those who attempted it. There were two very good answers.

Q. 48. Sketch and describe the method of constructing a steel lower mast, for a modern ship. Show a section of the mast and the disposition of butts of plates. State the sizes of the plates, angles, rivets, &c., and show the riveting at a butt.

Attempted by about 120 candidates. About 17 of the answers were very good. The method of constructing the mast was only given by about one-third of the candidates; in other respects the question was generally well answered.

Q. 49. Sketch an efficient arrangement of winches, derricks, &c., for rapidly loading and discharging cargo from a hold of a large cargo-ship. Give a detailed sketch of a winch.

About 70 candidates attempted this question, and the answers were generally satisfactory ; 16 of the answers were very good.

LAYING OFF.

Q. 50. In the case of a ship with a double bottom, how are the lines of the inner bottom obtained and faired on the mould loft floor, and the plating arranged ?

Attempted by about 90 candidates, but only about 12 satisfactory answers were given. The answers generally were poor. It is disappointing that a satisfactory answer to this question appears to be so little known.

Q. 51. A steel mast has considerable rake and taper. Find the true form of a doubling plate worked round the heel of the mast, supposing it laid out flat.

About 150 candidates attempted this question and the answers were generally very poor. Many assumed a mast sufficiently short to be a complete cone on the worked paper. About 10 per cent. of the answers were fairly good.

CALCULATIONS.

Q. 52. The given sketch represents part of the fore body of a ship. Calculate the displacement in tons, and the vertical position of the centre of buoyancy of the form represented by the sketch, between the waterlines A and B, 12' apart, and between the sections C and D. The sketch given is on a scale of $\frac{1}{4}$" to 1 foot, and the sections are spaced 18 feet apart. Three waterlines, spaced 3 feet apart, should be introduced between A and B.

Ordinates to be measured to the nearest decimal place.

This was a compulsory question, and all the candidates except two attempted it. The answers were generally very satisfactory. About 75 candidates obtained 40 marks or more. Where mistakes were made, it was generally due to candidates not following the instructions given in the question. Ordinates were frequently stated to two and three places of decimals, and in a few cases feet and inches. Many of the answers for displacement were twice as much as they should be.

Q. 53. Describe the operation known as an "inclining experiment." State the errors that can arise in conducting the experiment, and show how the height of the centre of gravity for any given condition is obtained from the inclining condition.

In the inclining experiment of a vessel of 8,550 tons displacement, the bob of an 11' pendulum moves 9½" when 42 tons of ballast are moved 40 feet across the deck. What is the value of the metacentric height ?

A favourite question of this section of the paper ; attempted by about 150 candidates, but only about 20 attempted the whole of the question. The example given was well answered, but considerable difficulty was experienced with the first part of the question.

Q. 54. State and prove Atwood's formula for statical stability of a ship, stating clearly how to determine the sign of the moment of the correcting layer.

Only 33 candidates attempted this question, and about half of the answers were fairly well done. The last part of the question was frequently omitted.

Q. 55. A transverse watertight bulkhead is worked at a station whose semi-ordinates, commencing from below, are :—5·4, 14·35, 19·3, 20·4, 21·5, 21·57, 21·5, 20·44, 19·3, and 18·5 feet respectively, the common interval being 3 feet.

Find the weight of the bulkhead from the following particulars :—plating lap jointed, and single riveted, $\frac{7}{16}''$ thick for the lower 12 feet, and $\frac{5}{16}''$ thick above. Angle bar stiffeners and boundaries 3″ × 3″ × $\frac{7}{16}''$, the stiffeners being spaced 30″ apart.

About 90 candidates attempted this question, and about 30 per cent. of the answers were correct. The arithmetical work was generally better done, but in many cases the correct areas of the different plates were not obtained ; this was due to wrong rules being used to obtain the thickness of areas. In some cases a zero ordinate was introduced at the bottom of the bulkhead. Many candidates found the area up to the 21·5′ ordinate, and for the remainder of the bulkhead commenced with the ordinate 21·57′, thus omitting the area of bulkhead between the ordinates 21·5′ and 21·57′. To find the weight per foot run of the angle bar stiffeners and boundary angles from the dimensions given, is an elementary question, and it is surprising how many candidates in this stage gave incorrect answers. The percentage taken for the weights of heads and points of rivets varied from 2 to 7.

Q. 56. A stringer plate is 42″ wide and $\frac{11}{16}''$ thick ; sketch the arrangement of rivets in a treble riveted single butt-strap connecting two lengths of the plating, so that the strength of the connection shall be as nearly as possible equal to the strength at a beam. Justify your arrangement by calculation, and state the breaking strength of the stringer at a beam and at a butt.

Attempted by about 55 candidates, and about 25 per cent. of the answers were satisfactory. The remainder were poor and incomplete.

HONOURS.

Results : 1st Class, 5 ; 2nd Class, 7 ; Failed, 60 ; Total, 72.

There were seven fewer candidates sat at the examination in this Stage, in comparison with last year.

There was, on the whole, a slight improvement in the quality of the work sent in, although 30 per cent. of the candidates failed to obtain 25 per cent. of the maximum number of marks allowed—this is no doubt due to the unpreparedness of the candidates with the work stated in the syllabus. Candidates in this Stage should be well prepared ; they should have obtained a First Class in Stage 3 before attempting Honours.

There is still great lack of neatness in the working on many of the papers.

Most of the candidates who attempted the questions requiring curves to be plotted, did not use the squared paper supplied for that purpose, but must have spent considerable time in preparing base line and ordinates, &c., on the plain paper supplied. The advantage of squared paper for plotting curves does not seem to be realised.

The stability questions were generally fairly well answered, but only three candidates attempted Question 68.

The rolling and strength questions were generally much better dealt with than last year.

The questions on propulsion and design were generally badly answered.

Arithmetical errors were again far too frequent.

Q. 61. State the principle by which areas can be found, by using any of Tchebycheff's rules. What advantages and disadvantages does the rule possess as compared with Simpson's rules ?

Prove Tchebycheff's rule for finding the area of a curvilinear figure in the case when 5 ordinates are used, and illustrate the method of using this rule by finding the area of a semicircle of 10′ radius, with 5 ordinates.

This question was attempted by about 23 candidates, and only about seven obtained fairly high marks. One of the candidates gave a proof of Simpson's first rule as an answer to the question.

Q. 62. A vessel of 4,565 tons displacement is 330′ long and floats at a draught of 18′ 9″. While in this condition she is inclined, two pendulums 15′ long being used. The following operations are performed and the respective deflections observed :—

Readings.

	Forward.	Aft.
10 tons moved through 31′ 6″ from port to starboard	4·1″	4·05″
A further 10 tons moved through 31′ 6″ from port to starboard	8·15″	8·05″
Weights restored, ship came to the upright.		
10 tons moved through 31′ 6″ from starboard to port	4·05″	4·15″
A further 10 tons moved through 31′ 6″ from starboard to port	8·1″	8·2″

Estimate the metacentric height at the time of inclining.

Explain the principal precautions you would take while conducting the experiment, and state the necessity for each precaution.

Supposing a double bottom tank 28′ broad by 18′ long and 3′ deep was half full of water during the experiment ; find the metacentric height if there had been no loose water. How would the result be affected if the tank were divided longitudinally by a central watertight bulkhead ?

A favourite question, attempted by about 45 candidates. About half of the answers obtained good marks, but many candidates failed to state correctly the effect of a central divisional bulkhead on the stability of a vessel.

Q. 63. Prove that the line of intersection of consecutive water plane passes through the centre of area of the original water plane. Deduce a formula for the " moment to change trim one inch."

A balsa raft 12′ long is constructed of two logs of timber 15″ diameter and 4′ apart between centres, and is planked over with wood 3″ thick, forming a platform 12 feet by 4 feet. All the wood is of the same density, and the raft floats with the logs half immersed. Calculate its transverse and longitudinal metacentric heights, and the moment to change trim one inch.

Attempted by 37 candidates, and about one-third of the answers merited good marks. Some of the answers to the first part of the question were very poor, and many arithmetical blunders were made in attempting the second part.

Q. 64. The cross curves of stability of a vessel show at 15°, 30°, 45°, 60°, 75° and 90°, the following values of the righting arm, viz.:— ·88, 1·78, 2·57, 2·29, 1·34 and ·12 feet respectively, the displacement being 4,675 tons, and the centre of gravity being assumed in the load-water-plane. The centre of gravity actually is 1·57 feet above the load-water-plane at this displacement.

Determine.—(1) the range of stability ;
(2) the angle of maximum stability ;
(3) the righting moment at this maximum angle.

Attempted by 42 candidates, and generally well answered. Many candidates, however, plotted the stability curve without making the necessary correction due to the actual position of the centre of gravity being 1·57′ above the load-water-plane.

Q. 65. Show that the inclination of the statical curve of stability at zero of inclination is determined by the metacentric height.

Show, by sketches, what is the effect of increasing (a) beam, (b) freeboard, (c) draught, and (d) metacentric height, respectively, on an ordinary curve of stability.

This was the most popular question, being attempted by 51 candidates. About 14 of the answers were good, but the remainder were generally poor. In a statical curve of stability, the main points are—(1) the initial rise of the curve; (2) the maximum righting arm; (3) the range. These three things should have been clearly shown on the sketches representing approximately the curves of stability. Many merely drew curves without indicating any of these points.

Q. 66. Find the size of a cast-steel rudder head or stock, suitable for the rudder of the form shown on the given sketch, the maximum speed of the vessel being 18 knots, and the maximum angle of helm being 40°.

What would be the diameter of the stock supposing the rudder stock to be hollow; the inside diameter being one-half the outside diameter.

Attempted by 37 candidates, and there were about 10 correct answers; the remainder were poor. Many candidates assumed the centre of pressure at ⅔ths the maximum width of rudder from the leading edge, instead of allowing for the form of after edge of rudder. Others divided the area into a semi-circle and a rectangle. The second part of the question was generally badly answered; in some cases the size of the hollow stock was calculated on the basis of the area being the same as for the solid stock.

Q. 67. Describe how by means of launching curves, the shortest length of launching ways, consistent with absence of tipping, is arrived at for a given height of tide. In practice the launching ways are sometimes made less than this length. Explain why this is possible, and what risks have to be accepted.

For a rectangular vessel of 250′ length and 22′ beam, and deep enough not to have the deck submerged when launching, construct the launching curves when the weight is uniformly distributed over the length and her draught after launching is 5′; the ways have a declivity of ¾″ to 1 foot, and the vessel's keel touches water at the commencement of launch.

Only 27 candidates attempted this question. The answers were generally disappointing—only four satisfactory answers were given. Launching curves are becoming more and more important with the great increase in size of ships now building. The question is not a difficult one and it should have been much better answered.

Q. 68. Sketch roughly the form of the locus of pro-metacentres for a ship of ordinary form, when it is heeled continuously through 360° about a longitudinal axis, and examine how the number and character of the positions of equilibrium are affected by a continuous increase in the initial value of the metacentric height.

Point out what conditions must be fulfilled if a lifeboat is to be "self-righting."

Attempted by three candidates only, and very badly answered, shewing that the geometry of the metacentre is little understood.

Q. 69. The drawings and detail weights of a ship being given you, how would you proceed to calculate the bending moment on a wave ? State the standard length and height of wave taken for such calculations.

Give the values of the maximum bending moment, in terms of the length and displacement, in three types of ships with which you are acquainted, naming the types selected.

Attempted by 38 candidates, and about one-half of the answers were good. Many of the answers were in too general terms, and the question was not treated in such detail as is expected from candidates in this Stage. Fairly correct answers were generally given for the values of the maximum bending moment for the various types of ships selected.

Q. 70. Given a structural midship section, explain how you would find the maximum tensile and compressive stresses upon it for a given bending moment.

State how you would take account of the difference between wood and steel, and how the deductions for rivet holes are allowed.

What stresses at keel and upper deck would you regard as acceptable in a new design ?

This was also a popular question, 44 candidates attempting it. About 20 of the answers were good. Many candidates omitted to state what parts of the midship section should be considered as contributing longitudinal strength to the vessel, in estimating the moment of inertia of the section.

Q. 71. Define the terms "slip," "slip ratio," "slip per cent.," and "pitch ratio"? Is it possible to have no slip in a screw steamer? Obtain an expression for "slip" in terms of speed of ship, pitch, and radius of propeller.

Describe the phenomenon known as "cavitation."

Attempted by 10 candidates, and only one gave a fairly good answer ; the rest were poor and incomplete.

Q. 72. Explain how the "effective" and "indicated" horse-power, and weight of engines and boilers required for a ship of new design are estimated.

A vessel 300' long and 2,100 tons displacement, wetted surface 12,300 square feet, requires 4,000 E.H.P. to steam at 20 knots. Assuming that the wave making resistance varies as (speed) ^{4}, find the necessary E.H.P. to drive a similar vessel 600' long at the same speed ?

Attempted by 40 candidates, but only about four good answers were given. The second part of the question was very badly done generally. It is merely an example on the method of deducing the E.H.P. for a new vessel, from the known results of a completed vessel, much smaller but of similar form.

Q. 73. Describe briefly the developments that have taken place in the size, construction, cargo appliances, and economy of working cargo and intermediate steamers, during recent years. Illustrate your remarks by rough sketches where possible.

Attempted by 14 candidates, but only two gave satisfactory answers. This question, with reference to the historical side of Naval Architecture, should have been better known by candidates in Honours,

Q. 74. Describe the usual method of observing both by day and by night, the angles reached by a ship rolling at sea.

How is the curve of extinction plotted, and what can be determined from it in relation to the resistance to rolling of a ship?

State approximately the period of rolling of any two types of ships, naming the types selected.

Attempted by 32 candidates, about one-third obtaining good marks. The deductions that can be made as regards resistance to rolling from a curve of extinction were rarely dealt with. Many candidates were acquainted with the periods of rolling of various types of ships.

Q 75. What are the chief features of ship design and of a sea-way having influence on the rolling motion of a ship? Briefly describe the effect of each feature on the rolling.

Describe the various methods that have been adopted for diminishing the rolling of ships in a sea-way, and discuss their relative values and applicability.

Explain why, on the whole, a small metacentric height is best for steadiness in a sea-way.

Attempted by 40 candidates, but only four gave satisfactory answers. The remainder of the answers were very poor and incomplete. The relative values of the various methods adopted for diminishing the rolling of ships in a sea-way was rarely discussed with success.

Q. 76. State approximate values of the coefficients for hull and machinery weights for two different types of vessels, naming the types selected.

What do you consider are the best dimensions for a steamer designed to carry 200 tons of cargo and 150 passengers over a route the steaming period of which is 20 hours, having given the following data? length of ship to be 12 times its depth ; breadth ⅔rds depth ; draught of water ⅜rds depth ; Admiralty coefficient, 200 ; block coefficient, ·52. The machinery develops 14·5 I.H.P. per ton weight, when burning 1·55 lbs. of coal per I.H.P. per hour, and the speed of the ship 20 knots.

Only seven candidates attempted this question. Two obtained fairly good marks, but the remainder very few marks. The question is based on certain elements of design that should be familar to candidates in Honours, and should have been much better answered.

Honours Practical Examination.

Seventeen candidates who had done sufficiently well in the evening written examination were summoned to South Kensington to sit for the practical examination, and all attended.

The designs were, on the whole, good. The fairing lines were not shewn on the drawings in some cases, and some of the candidates made arithmetical errors in working the displacement sheet.

Report on the Examination in Applied Mechanics.

In Stage 1 the answering this year was satisfactory, and in certain directions showed a distinct improvement as compared with previous years, but in Stages 2 and 3, on the other hand, the answering was distinctly poorer than last year ; this was especially the case in Stage 2. Arithmetic was again a very weak point in all the stages. Candidates frequently use logarithms quite unnecessarily, and, as they are not really familiar with their use, make foolish mistakes ; a simple piece of multiplication is more easily carried out directly than by the use of logarithmic tables. Judging by the fact that obviously ridiculous answers were allowed to stand without any comment on the part of the candidates, it is quite clear that students are rarely taught to check their results by rough calculations. The answers to all the problems in these papers can be quickly checked by rough calculation, and it would well repay a candidate to go rapidly over his calculations again, when obvious errors in decimal place in the final result would at once be detected, though, in most cases, a candidate ought to know perfectly well when his answer is obviously wrong, even without such a rough check. Attention must again be drawn to the fact that candidates evidently have too little drill in the complete working out of practical problems. Even when the candidates use correct formulæ, they get hopelessly muddled in substituting for their symbols the numerical values given in the question. In such a formula, for instance, as that for centrifugal force $\dfrac{W \, V^2}{g \, R}$, for the symbol for V revolutions per minute, revolutions per second, feet per minute, and even miles per hour, are used by candidates ; and for the symbol R one finds a radius of yards, a radius of miles, and even a radius expressed in inches. Such blunders prove conclusively that though a candidate has been taught the formula and has learned it by heart, he has seldom made use of it in any practical problem. In the higher stages many of the most serious blunders arise from a foolish habit of neglecting to work out fully each stage in the problem, and thereby obtaining a numerical answer which can be used in the later stages of the problem. For example, in problems 25 and 45, candidates frequently wrote down a lengthy expression for the weight of the water in the pipe, and then another lengthy expression for the weight of the iron itself ; they then combined these two expressions into one long expression, still not working out the numerical result ; they then used this expression in the formula for the bending moment, and in the same formula inserted another lengthy expression for the moment of inertia of the cross section of the pipe, and, finally, from this complicated expression—stretching right across the paper,—they attempted to work out the final result—the stress in the pipe. Needless to say in hardly a single case was the answer correct, and in many cases the same work was done all over again in order to find the deflection of the pipe, the same lengthy expressions for weight and for moment of inertia being put into the formula for deflection. This method of work not only leads to inaccuracies in the arithmetic and hopeless blunders, but wastes a lot of time quite unnecessarily. If the candidate were in such a case, first, to find the weight of the water in pounds, and also the weight of the pipe, then, secondly, to calculate the value of the moment of inertia of the cross section of the pipe, he would then have only very simple expressions to work out in order to determine, first, the bending moment, and, secondly, the stress in the metal. The quality of the work in all four stages proved conclusively that too little individual attention is given to students by teachers. A student cannot possibly obtain a mastery of such a difficult subject as Applied Mechanics by simply listening to lectures or seeing demonstrations ; he must have a certain amount of individual instruction. Home exercises should form an essential part of the work, and teachers should insist that such exercises must be worked out in full ; this enables teachers to point out to students how they can improve the quality of their work, and shorten and simplify necessary calculations. Attention must again be drawn also to the necessity of systematic experimental work ; the answers in all the stages to the questions dealing with experimental or laboratory work were distinctly unsatisfactory.

STAGE 1.

Results : 1st Class, 638 ; 2nd Class, 637 ; Failed, 560 ; Total, 1,835.

Q. 1 Describe, with the aid of neatly drawn sketches, which should be roughly to scale, only *one* of the following (a), (b), (c), or (d) :—

(a) Any form of micrometer caliper graduated to read accurately to thousandths of an inch.

(b) The making and tempering of a chisel.

(c) A counter shaft carrying fast and loose pulleys, and speed cones.

(d) The cutting of the screw thread on a bolt (say ⅜ inch diameter) by hand-screwing tackle or in a machine.

(a) The description of the micrometer was usually quite good, and showed that this instrument is, on the whole, well understood.

(b) The answers to this section were, as a rule, not satisfactory. Many candidates made no mention of the necessary forging work ; the hardening and tempering processes were more or less fully described, but very few candidates thought it necessary to say anything about grinding the chisel.

(c) The sketches and description of the counter shaft were, on the whole, good and fairly complete.

(d) The answers to this section were disappointing. Not a single answer showed a real knowledge of the use of a die as a cutting tool. Most of the candidates were content with a rough drawing of the outside of a stock, with the dies just showing under the cover plate.

Q. 2. Answer only *one* of the following (a), (b), or (c) :—

Describe how you would determine experimentally,

(a) The moment of inertia of a small flywheel.

(b) The velocity-ratio, and the mechanical efficiency of *either* a differential pulley block *or* a screw-jack.

(c) How the deflection of a beam of rectangular section varies when the span, the load, and the cross sectional dimensions are varied. Write down an expression which represents the results you would expect to obtain.

(a) Not many candidates attempted this section of the question, and those who did gave very scrappy and incomplete descriptions both of the necessary apparatus and of the experiments which would be required.

(b) This was a very favourite question ; about one half of those who attempted it selected the screw-jack and the other half, the differential pulley block. The answers were fairly complete, and showed that the candidates were familiar with this piece of experimental work, but strangely enough only a few knew that the value of the mechanical efficiency varied with the load on the machine.

(c) Very few tried this section, and the answers showed fairly conclusively that the problem of beam deflection is not sufficiently studied in elementary classes.

9897. F 2

Q. 3. The following results were obtained during an experiment to determine the quantity of water which would be discharged through a small circular orifice in the side of a tank. The diameter of the orifice, which had sharp edges, was one inch.

Number of Experiment.	Duration of Experiment.	Actual Discharge.	Head of Water above Centre of Orifice.
	Minutes.	Lbs.	Inches.
1	15	576	1·5
2	15	660	2·0
3	15	733	2·5
4	15	827	3·27
5	15	915	4·01
6	15	1,011	5·0
7	10	737	6·0
8	10	788	7·0

Plot on squared paper a curve to show the relation between the discharge in lbs. per minute, and the head of water above the centre of the orifice.

From your curve determine the discharge in gallons per hour when the head of water was 5½ inches.

A very frequent error was to plot the actual discharge as given in the table, the candidates neglecting to observe that the first six measurements were determined for a longer period than the last two. The last portion of the curve was, therefore, completely distorted, and, as a reading was required from the curve in the region of this distortion, the results were disastrous. It is quite clear from the way in which many candidates drew the curve that they think that every set of experimental results must follow the straight line law.

Q. 4. The rim of a turbine is going at 50 feet per second ; 100 lbs. of fluid enter the rim each second, with a velocity in the direction of the rim's motion of 60 feet per second, leaving with it no velocity in the direction of the wheel's motion. What is the momentum lost per second by the fluid ? This is force. What work is done per second upon the wheel ?

There were comparatively few answers to this problem, and the results were generally poor, probably because the subject of water turbines is almost entirely neglected by students in the elementary stage. In calculating the momentum lost per second, most of the candidates omitted " g," giving as their answer 100 × 60 = 6,000 foot pounds,

Q. 5. An ordinary bell pull, shown in the sketch, is in equilibrium. Determine in any way you please the magnitude of the force Q and the magnitude and direction of the resultant thrust upon the supporting pin A.

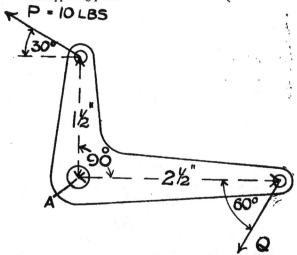

A common mistake was to calculate moments about the pin A, on the assumption that the forces P and Q were perpendicular to the arms of the bell crank. The magnitude of the resultant pressure on the pin was obtained without much trouble, but comparatively few candidates thought it necessary to indicate the direction of this force.

Q. 6. A hydraulic press has a ram 6 inches in diameter ; water is supplied to the press from a single-acting pump, which has a plunger 1 inch in diameter with a stroke of $1\frac{1}{2}$ inches. Neglecting frictional and other losses in the pump and press, find the average rate (in foot-pounds per minute) at which the pump works, if it makes 100 working strokes per minute, while the press is exerting a force of 70 tons.

This was one of the questions in which weakness in arithmetic was most evident. The answers varied from a fraction of a foot-pound up to hundreds of millions of foot-pounds ; many candidates in fact attempted to solve the problem by writing down all the figures given in the question and multiplying them together.

Q. 7. In order to connect together the two halves of a long tie-rod, an eye is forged at the end of one half, and a fork (into which the eye enters) at the end of the other half, and a pin is passed through the two sides of the fork and through the eye. If the total pull in the tie rod is 16 tons, and if the shearing stress in the metal of the bolt is not to exceed 8,000 lbs. per square inch, what diameter would you make the pin ?

The answers to this problem were, as a rule, satisfactory, but many candidates forgot that the pin must shear in two planes. Quite an appreciable number of candidates obtained correctly the necessary cross sectional area of the pin, and then failed completely to determine the correct diameter. This difficulty in determining the diameter of a circle, when its area is known, must be largely due to want of practice in working out problems.

Q. 8. A traction engine travels at 6 miles per hour ; the road wheels are 6 feet in diameter, and are driven through 5 to 1 gearing. Find the angular velocity in radians per second of the fly-wheel on the engine shaft.

This was a favourite question and well answered, though many candidates apparently found the problem of converting from linear to angular velocity, and *vice versâ*, still too much for them ; steady drill in solving such problems is the only cure for this. The answer to the problem given by one candidate was that " the road will go round 44/30 times per second."

Q. 9. A machine weighing 8 tons is dragged slowly along a horizontal floor. If the coefficient of friction between the base of the machine and the floor is 0·35, find in pounds the magnitude of the pull, and the normal pressure on the floor when (*a*) the line of pull is horizontal, (*b*) the line of pull makes an upward angle of 30° with the horizontal.

In this question the first part was well answered, but in the second part very few candidates realised that an upward pull lessened the downward pressure, and, as a result, there was scarcely a single correct solution to the problem.

Q. 10. A windmill is employed to drive a pump which has to lift water from a well and deliver it into an overhead tank. It is found that when the windmill works steadily under the action of a uniform wind for a period of 1 hour, 5,000 gallons of water are raised from the well and delivered into the tank—the average height of lift is 60 feet. What, under these conditions, is the useful horse-power of the windmill ?

This was a very favourite question, and was well answered.

Q. 11. The rim of a cast-iron pulley has a mean radius of 12 inches ; the rim is 6 inches broad, and $\frac{1}{2}$ inch thick, and the pulley revolves at the rate of 150 revolutions per minute ; what is the centrifugal force on the pulley rim per 1 inch length of rim ?

One cubic inch of cast-iron weighs 0·26 lb.

The answers to this question would have been much more successful but for the very serious muddling of units. It was not an uncommon thing to find that a candidate in his answer had multiplied pounds by inches per minute, and had divided the result by feet per second. A large number of candidates determined the centrifugal force for the whole wheel, though the question distinctly stated that it was to be for *one inch* length of the rim only.

Q. 12. An electrical hoist is employed in raising coal from the hold of a ship and delivering it into railway cars, the amount of lift being 125 feet. If the coal is raised at the rate of 2,400 lbs. per minute, what is the useful horse-power ?

Convert this into watts.

If the current is supplied at a voltage of 250, and if the efficiency of the whole arrangement is 50 per cent., how many ampères of current must be supplied to the motor working the hoist ?

This was another favourite question, and the answers were, as a rule, satisfactory, but the necessity of allowing for the efficiency of the motor nearly always seemed to cause trouble.

Q. 13. A strut is built up out of two pieces of T steel, each 6 inches by 3 inches by $\frac{3}{8}$ inch, riveted back to back. If this strut supports a load of 22·3 tons, what is the compressive stress per square inch ?

If a total load of 105 tons would destroy this strut, what is the factor of safety ?

The answers to this question showed that few candidates were able to calculate correctly the cross sectional area of a rolled section. Many candidates seemed to be quite ignorant of the meaning of the term "factor of safety."

Q. 14. In the four bar mechanism shown in the sketch, the bar A is a fixed bar; the bars B and D rotate about the fixed centres OAB and OAD, and they are coupled together at their outer ends by the bar C; the bar B revolves with uniform velocity round its fixed axis OAB at 50 revolutions per minute. Find in any way you please the position of the bar D when the bar B is turned in a clockwise direction through angles of 30°, 60°, and 90° from the position shown in the sketch.

Prepare a table similar to the one shown, and obtain and enter up the results required to complete the table :—

Angle turned through by the bar B.	Angle turned through by the bar D.	Mean Angular Velocity of the bar D in radians per second during each interval.
30° - -		
60° - -		
90° - -		

The lengths of the bars are 15, 30, 25 and 35 inches respectively.

This question was seldom attempted, and still more seldom was it finished. Candidates were able to find the angle turned through by the bar *D*; but were quite unable to deduce from their results the mean angular velocity of the bar *D*.

<h2 align="center">STAGE 2.</h2>

Results : 1st Class, 119 ; 2nd Class, 672 ; Failed, 559 ; Total, 1,350.

Q. 21. Describe, with the aid of neatly drawn sketches, which should be roughly to scale, only *one* of the following, (a), (b), (c), or (d) :—

> (a) Any form of micrometer caliper graduated to read accurately to thousandths of an inch.
>
> (b) An inward-flow water turbine.
>
> (c) A counter-shaft carrying fast and loose pulleys, speed cones, and strap fork arrangements.
>
> (d) The cutting of a screw thread of a bolt (say $\frac{3}{4}$ inch diameter) by hand screwing tackle or in a machine.

· Candidates usually selected one or other of divisions (a), (c), and (d)—all three were about equally popular. On the whole the sketches and the descriptions were complete and satisfactory ; many of the candidates, in fact, gave exceedingly neat sketches—many of the sketches were not only neat in appearance, but were quite fairly drawn to scale. Very few candidates attempted section (b) ; those who did gave very good answers.

Q. 22. Answer only *one* of the following (a), (b), or (c) :—

Describe how you would determine experimentally,

> (a) The moment of inertia of a small flywheel.
>
> (b) The velocity-ratio and the mechanical efficiency of *either* a differential pulley block *or* a screw-jack.
>
> (c) How the deflection of a beam of rectangular section varies when the span, the load, and the cross sectional dimensions are varied.
>
>> Write down an expression which represents the results you would expect to obtain.

Most of the candidates selected section (b), and the work, as a rule, was good. It was a very common error, however, to state that the mechanical efficiency was $= \frac{W}{P}$, or $\frac{\text{Resistance}}{\text{Effort}}$. Candidates too often forgot that it would be necessary to carry out a number of experiments in order to determine how the mechanical efficiency varied as the load on the pulley block, or jack, varied.

Only a few candidates attempted section (a), but there were some very good answers.

The answers to section (c) were not at all satisfactory ; the necessary apparatus was usually fairly well described, but very few candidates knew what kind of results would be obtained from their experiments

Q. 23. The following results were obtained during an experiment to determine the quantity of water which would be discharged through a small circular orifice in the side of a tank. The diameter of the orifice, which had sharp edges, was 1 inch.

Number of Experiment.	Duration of Experiment.	Actual Discharge.	Head of water above Centre of Orifice.
	Minutes.	Lbs.	Inches.
1	15	576	1·5
2	15	660	2·0
3	15	733	2·5
4	15	827	3·27
5	15	915	4·01
6	15	1,011	5·0
7	10	737	6·0
8	10	788	7·0

Plot on squared paper a curve to show the relation between the discharge in lbs. per minute, and the head of water above the centre of the orifice.

From your curve determine the discharge in gallons per hour when the head of water was 5½ inches.

Plot also on squared paper a curve to show the relation between the discharge in lbs. per minute and the square root of the head of water above the centre of the orifice.

From your curve what would you consider the relation to be between quantity of flow and head?

This question was attempted by nearly all the candidates, and on the whole was fairly well done. A number of candidates, however, omitted to divide the total discharge by the time, and they thus plotted the quantity discharged as given in the table, neglecting the important fact that the duration of the experiments was not the same throughout. The plotted curve was, therefore, badly distorted near the end, and the quantity which had to be determined from this curve was therefore quite erroneous.

Q. 24. A bicycle and its rider weigh 200 lbs.; the distance travelled for each turn of the pedal is equal to the circumference of a wheel having a diameter of 80 inches; neglecting frictional and other resistances, how many foot-pounds of work will the cyclist do per revolution of the pedal in ascending a hill with a gradient of 4 in 100.

If the resistance due to friction, air resistance, &c., is 2½ pounds, how many foot-pounds of work per minute is this cyclist doing when he maintains a steady speed of 6 miles per hour up the hill.

In very many cases the answers to this question were exceedingly bad. It was most surprising to find that many candidates should imagine that the work done in propelling a bicycle on the level is found by multiplying together the weight of the machine and rider and the distance through which the bicycle advances in any given time. Such a serious blunder can only be due to absolute want of knowledge of the very elements of mechanics. Many candidates made the mistake of taking the resistance in the second half of the question, due to friction and air resistance, as acting parallel to gravity.

Q. 25. A cast-iron water main, 30 inches in internal diameter and 1½ inches thick, is carried across a stream underneath a road bridge; if the main is unsupported for a length of 16 feet, find (neglecting the weight of the metal) the maximum intensity of tensile stress due to bending. You may assume the pipe to be a beam fixed at the ends.

Refer to the examination tables for the weight of 1 cubic foot of water.

This question was not well answered. Many candidates were able to find correctly the weight of the water in the pipe, but the rest of their work was absolutely incorrect. Incorrect formulæ were used for bending moment and for the moment of inertia of the pipe. In a very large number of cases, however, where the candidate knew all his formulæ quite correctly, the most absurd and foolish blunders were made in arithmetic.

Q. 26. In the epicyclic bevel gear shown in the sketch, the wheels A and B have each 40 teeth, and the wheel C has 20 teeth ; the shafts D and E are in one solid piece, and rotate together at the rate of 60 revolutions per minute about the axis of E ; each wheel is free to rotate on its own spindle, and the wheel A rotates 30 times per minute in a direction opposite to the rotation of the shaft E. Find the speed and direction of rotation of the wheel C.

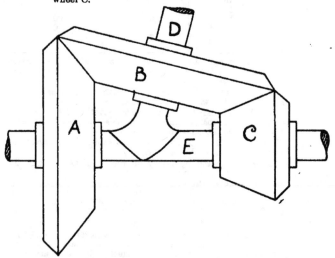

This question was perhaps a little difficult, and, on the whole, it was not well answered. It is quite clear, however, from the reasoning given in many cases, even when the answer obtained was erroneous, that candidates are beginning to study questions of this kind, and that in future years an improvement may be expected in the knowledge of mechanism shown by candidates in Stage 2.

Q. 27. The rim of a turbine is going at 50 feet per second ; 100 lbs. of fluid enter the wheel each second, with a velocity in the direction of the rim's motion of 60 feet per second, leaving it with no velocity in the direction of the wheel's motion. What is the momentum lost per second by the fluid ? What work is done per second upon the wheel ? What work is done per lb. of fluid ?

Though this question was quite a simple one, it was not well answered. A very common blunder was to calculate the momentum lost by multiplying together the mass and the difference between the velocity of the water and the turbine rim, and a great number of candidates failed by leaving out " g " in the calculation for the momentum lost.

Q. 28. A closely coiled helical spring is constructed out of steel wire ¼ inch diameter. The mean diameter of the coil is 3½ inches, and there are 24 turns in the coil. If this spring is subjected to an axial pull of 30 pounds, what is the maximum stress in the metal?

This question was well answered by a considerable percentage of those who attempted it, but it was quite evident that many candidates knew nothing about the theory of the stiffness, or strength of spiral springs, or otherwise it would have been impossible to have such serious blunders as dividing the load on the spring by the cross sectional area of the wire in order to obtain the stress. Only comparatively few candidates attempted the question.

Q. 29. A punching machine needs 4 H.P., a fly-wheel upon the machine fluctuates in speed between 100 and 110 revolutions per minute; a hole is punched every three seconds, and this requires five-sixths of the total energy given to the machine during the three seconds. Find the M and the I of this fly-wheel.

"M" is the kinetic energy of the wheel at one revolution per minute.

This question, though not at all a difficult one, was generally badly answered. Many candidates knew the formula quite perfectly, but evidently want of experience in working out completely examples of similar problems during the time the candidate is preparing for the examination leads to the most serious, and in many cases ridiculous, blunders.

Q. 30. A vertical wall, 12 feet high and 3 feet thick, built of masonry which weighs 150 pounds per cubic foot, is subjected on one face to water pressure. What is the maximum depth of water behind the wall which is permissible, if the resultant force on the base of the wall is not to pass outside the outer edge of the wall.

Refer to the examination tables for the weight of one cubic foot of water.

This question was attempted by a comparatively large number of candidates, but the answers were very unsatisfactory, and showed conclusively a great lack of knowledge of the theory of water pressure. Many candidates stated that the water pressure on such a wall is given by the product of the height of the wall by the weight of a cubic foot of water, and many also imagine that the resultant water pressure acts at a half the height of the wall from its base.

Q. 31. A body of 100 lbs. has a simple vibration, the amplitude or half-travel of which is 1·5 feet, and the time of a complete oscillation ½ second. Calculate the force which acts on the body at the beginning of a swing, and draw a diagram showing the force acting at any point between the beginning and middle of a swing. What is the average force acting during the interval, and what the velocity of the body in its middle position?

Very few candidates attempted this question, and it cannot be said that the work was at all satisfactory. Candidates knew the formula $T = 2\pi \sqrt{\dfrac{\text{Displacement}}{\text{Acceleration}}}$, and started the solution of the problem satisfactorily, but before arriving at any result they got completely mixed up. Many candidates knew that the force curve would be a straight line, but knew very little else about the question.

Q. 32. The rim of a cast-iron pulley has a mean radius of 12 inches, the rim is 6 inches broad, and ½ inch thick, and the pulley revolves at the rate of 150 revolutions per minute; what is the centrifugal force on the pulley rim per 1 inch length of rim?

(1 cubic inch of cast-iron weighs 0·26 lb.)

What is the tensile stress per square inch in the pulley rim under these conditions?

What is the limiting speed of rotation for this pulley if the tenacity of cast-iron is 12·5 tons per square inch?

This question was badly answered. Practically every candidate knew the right formula for the centrifugal force, but beyond that they were unable to proceed, and such serious blunders as employing the figure given for the revolutions per minute as V in the formula for the centrifugal force, or stating that the centrifugal force was ft. lbs. and so on, show clearly that much more drill is wanted in problems of this nature.

Q. 33. In the four-bar mechanism shown in the sketch, the bar A is a fixed bar; the bars B and D rotate about the fixed centres OAB and OAD, and they are coupled together at their outer ends by the bar C; the bar B revolves with uniform velocity round its fixed axis OAB at 50 revolutions per minute. Find in any way you please the positions of the bar D when the bar B has turned in a clockwise direction through angles of 30°, 60°, 90°, 120°, 150°, and 180° from the position shown in the sketch.

Prepare a table similar to the one shown, and obtain and enter up the results required to complete the table :—

Angle turned through by the bar B.	Angle turned through by the bar D.	Mean Angular Velocity of the bar D in Radians per Second during each interval.
Degrees.	Degrees.	
30		
60		
90		
120		
150		
180		

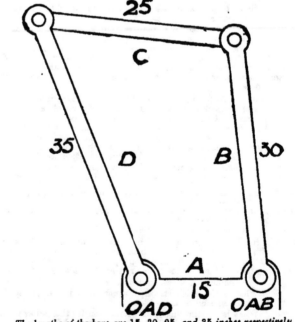

The lengths of the bars are 15, 30, 25, and 35 inches respectively.

Most of the candidates who attempted this question were able to determine accurately enough the angle turned through by the bar D, but very few were able to deduce from their results the mean angular velocities of the bar in radians per second.

STAGE 3.

Results : 1st Class, 9 ; 2nd Class, 131 ; Failed, 128 ; Total 268.

Q. 41. Describe, with the aid of neatly drawn sketches, which should be roughly to scale, only *one* of the following, (*a*), (*b*), (*c*), or (*d*) :—

    (*a*) Any form of micrometer caliper, graduated to read accurately to thousandths of an inch. Show in detail, and explain the principle of, the vernier used with the gauge.

    (*b*) An inward-flow water turbine.

    (*c*) A countershaft carrying fast and loose pulleys, speed cones, with wall brackets and strap fork arrangement.

    (*d*) The operation of "setting out" and turning out of the solid the main driving steel shaft of a punching, shearing, and scrap-shearing machine, which has therefore three eccentric portions.

Most of the candidates selected either division (*a*), or division (*c*), and the answers were good, the sketching being neat and accurate, and the necessary details well brought out. Very few candidates attempted either sections (*b*) or (*d*), and, except in one or two cases, the answers were not satisfactory nor complete.

Q. 42. Answer only *one* of the following, (*a*), (*b*), or (*c*) :—

    (*a*) Describe fully, with the help of sketches of the apparatus, how you would experimentally demonstrate the principles which underlie the balancing of an engine.

    (*b*) Write out a suitable specification for a contract for the supply of a large quantity of Portland cement which is to be employed in connection with the building of a large dock.

        Explain carefully how you would carry out all the tests mentioned in the specification for determining the quality of the cement when delivered.

    (*c*) It is proposed to impound for power purposes the water passing down a small stream ; describe fully a method which could be employed to determine the quantity of water passing down the stream. Explain carefully what degree of accuracy may be expected.

The majority of the candidates selected section (*c*), but only a few gave really satisfactory answers. The method described was usually that of employing a weir, either rectangular or V-shaped, but only occasionally did a candidate give a really satisfactory description of how he would determine the head of water over the weir. Candidate after candidate contented himself with stating "I would then measure the head over the weir." It was quite clear that most of the candidates could never have carried out such a piece of experimental work, or they would never have failed to give a clear description of how they would determine the head of water, and what precautions they would adopt.

The answers given to division (*a*) by those who attempted it were, on the whole, fairly satisfactory. Division (*b*) was attempted by very few candidates, and nearly all of them contented themselves with merely stating that they would determine the tensile strength of the cement.

Q. 43. The following results were obtained during an experiment to determine the quantity of water which would be discharged through a small circular orifice in the side of a tank. The diameter of the orifice, which had sharp edges, was 1 inch :—

Number of Experiment.	Duration of Experiment.	Actual Discharge.	Head of Water above Centre of Orifice.
	Minutes.	Lbs.	Inches.
1	15	576	1·5
2	15	660	2·0
3	15	733	2·5
4	15	827	3·27
5	15	915	4·01
6	15	1,011	5·0
7	10	737	6·0
8	10	788	7·0

Plot on squared paper a curve to show the relation between the discharge in lbs. per minute, and the head of water above the centre of the orifice.

From your curve determine the discharge in gallons per hour when the head of water was 5½ inches.

Plot also on squared paper a curve to show the relation between the discharge in lbs. per minute and the square root of the head of water above the centre of the orifice.

From your curve what would you consider the relation to be between quantity of flow and head ?

Determine for each of the experiments in the above table the "co-efficient of discharge" for this orifice, and plot a curve to show the relation between "co-efficient of discharge" and head of water.

This question was attempted by nearly all the candidates, and the answering was, as a rule, quite satisfactory and complete. A few candidates blundered by neglecting to note that the duration of the experiment was not the same in all cases, and one or two candidates even went the length of giving an elaborate explanation of how it was that under these circumstances the curve was so badly distorted at the end. Many candidates were evidently not quite familiar with what is meant by the term "co-efficient of discharge."

Q. 44. The sketch shows the frame of a tandem bicycle. Calculate and draw bending moment and shear diagrams for this frame, when each of the two riders weighs 150 lbs., 30 lbs. of the weight of each rider being assumed to be borne at the driving axle centres.

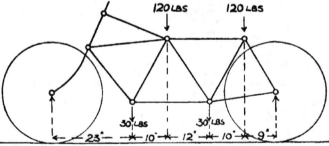

This question was fairly well answered, though a few of the candidates were unable to determine correctly the reactions at the ground.

Q. 45. A cast-iron water-main, 30 inches in internal diameter and 1¼ inches thick, is carried across a stream underneath a road bridge. If the main is unsupported for a length of 16 ft., find the maximum intensity of tensile stress in the metal due to the bending produced by the weight of the water and the weight of the pipe itself.

If $E = 12,000,000$ lbs. per square inch, how much will the pipe sag in the centre of the 16 feet?

Assume the pipe to be a beam fixed at the ends.

One cubic inch of cast iron weighs 0·26 lbs.

Refer to the examination tables for the weight of one cubic foot of water.

The answers to this question, which was attempted by the majority of the candidates, were very unsatisfactory, mainly owing to faulty arithmetic. The candidates knew their formula well, but mixed up feet and inches, and, instead of solving each part of the question independently, went on gradually putting in more and more symbols into their formula, until they became hopelessly bewildered.

Q. 46. The mechanism connecting the pencil and piston of a steam engine indicator is shown in skeleton form in the sketch. The sketch is drawn to scale, but the point G is not in its correct position on the bar EP. Determine the correct position of the point G in order that the pencil P may travel approximately in a vertical line parallel to the path of the piston A. (The travel of the pencil will not be greater than 3½ inches to 4 inches.)

How far does the pencil P move for a 1-inch travel of the piston A?

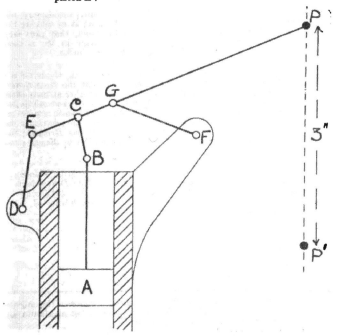

This question was attempted by very few candidates, and was not well answered. There is evidently a lack of training in the principles of mechanisms, and much more attention should be devoted to this subject by teachers.

Q. 47. The rim of a turbine is going at 50 feet per second. 100 lbs. of fluid enter the rim each second, with a velocity in the direction of the rim's motion of 60 feet per second, leaving it with no velocity in the direction of the wheel's motion. What work is done per second upon the wheel? What work is done per lb. of fluid? If the total energy per lb. of fluid is h foot-pounds, and if 12 per cent. is lost in friction, find h.

If the velocity of the water perpendicular to the rim's motion is 10 feet per second, and if the fluid enters the wheel without shock, draw the angles of the guide blade and vane at entrance.

This question was not attempted by many candidates, and was badly answered. It was an astonishing thing to find that candidates in Stage 3 were unable to solve such a simple problem as the calculation of the work done per second upon the wheel of this turbine. The answers given showed conclusively that the subject of Hydraulics must be sadly neglected by most of the teachers.

Q. 48. A piston ring for an 18-inch cylinder is often made about $18\frac{1}{4}$ inches in diameter, a portion cut out and the ring sprung into place. Show that this ring presses most unequally upon the cylinder. What is the correct method of making the ring so that it may press uniformly all round?

The answers to this question were, on the whole, fairly satisfactory, but though candidates were able to give the correct method of making the piston ring so that it may press uniformly all round, they gave very insufficient answers when explaining why a ring, made in the method described in the question, presses unequally upon the cylinder.

Q. 49. In the four-bar mechanism shown in the sketch, the bar A is a fixed bar; the bars B and D rotate about the fixed centres OAB and OAD, and they are coupled together at their outer ends by the bar C; the bar B revolves in clockwise direction with uniform velocity round its fixed axis OAB at 50 revolutions per minute. Find in any way you please the position of the bar D for 12 equidistant positions of the bar B during one complete revolution, and fill in a table similar to the one given below :—

Angle turned through by the bar B.	Angle turned through by the bar D.	Mean Angular Velocity of the bar D in radians per second during each interval.
Degrees.	Degrees.	
0		
30		
60		
&c.		

Plot a curve showing the relation between the angular velocities of B and D. Find the values of the maximum and minimum accelerations of the link D.

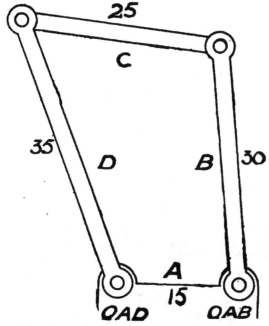

The lengths of the bars are 15, 30, 25 and 35 inches respectively.

This was a favourite question, and was fairly well done. In answering this question, a feature which is too prevalent in the work of candidates was very marked ; the question stated distinctly that the bar *B* revolved clockwise, and yet quite a large number of candidates worked the problem out by revolving the bar *B* counter-clockwise. Candidates should be warned by their teachers to read every question carefully before beginning it. Many errors arise from careless reading of the questions, when there can be no doubt whatever as to the meaning of the particular sentence in the question.

Q. 50. A steel rolled joist rests on two supports which are 12 feet apart ; the depth of the section of the joist is 10 inches, and the moment of inertia of the cross section about the neutral axis is 122 in inch units. From what height must a weight of $\frac{1}{4}$ of a ton fall upon the centre of this beam if the maximum stress produced is not to exceed 20,000 lbs. per square inch ? ($E = 30,000,000$ pounds per square inch.)

This was a favourite question, and was fairly well answered, but again there were very many cases of absurd arithmetical blunders leading to astonishing results, such as that the weight must fall through a height of some thousands of feet.

Q. 51. An upright timber post, 12 inches in diameter, supports a vertical load of 18 tons, the line of action of which is 3 inches from the vertical axis of the post. Determine the maximum and minimum intensities of stress on a normal cross section of the post, and show by a diagram how the intensity of normal stress varies across the section. Prove the formula used by you.

This was also a favourite question, and was well answered as a rule.

Q. 52. A semicircular arched rib, of radius R feet, which is hinged at the springings and also at the crown, carries a uniform load of w tons per foot of horizontal length. Determine, graphically or otherwise, the magnitude of the maximum bending moment on the rib in terms of w and R.

Very few candidates attempted this question, and only some three or four had any real knowledge of the mechanics of an arch.

Q. 53. Give an approximate theory of the strength of a rotating disc. How do the radial and hoop stresses vary at different distances from the the centre.

This question was attempted by very few candidates, and, as a rule, the answering was very unsatisfactory and incomplete.

HONOURS.

Results : 1st Class, 1 ; 2nd Class, 5 ; Failed, 18 ; Total, 24.

Twenty-four candidates entered for this Stage, and, on the whole, the work was fairly satisfactory. Questions 61, 62, 63, 64, 66, and 70 were favourite ones. Most of the answers to Question 61 were very complete and satisfactory ; the section selected was usually either (a) or (c). The sketching was very neat, and fairly accurate to scale in all cases. In Question 62, the majority of the candidates selected section (c), but again, as in Stage 3, there was much weakness shown in the answers, owing to the fact that but little attention was paid to the question of determining the head of water over the weir. The answers given by those who selected sections (a) and (b) were good and complete. The answers to Question 63 were fairly good, but several of the candidates came to grief in drawing the force diagram for the bicycle frame. Only one or two candidates obtained correct results to Question 64. The errors were chiefly due to the fact that the curves drawn were for loss of horse-power per mile, and the length of the pipe for which a loss had to be determined was given in yards. Candidates forgot that there are 1,760 yards in a mile. Question 65 was not attempted by many candidates, and was very badly answered. The answers to this question showed, as was pointed out in dealing with the similar question in Stage 3, that far too little attention is paid to the subject of Hydraulics by most of the teachers. Question 66 was well answered by those who attempted it. Most of the candidates who attempted Question 67 were able to draw the line of resultant pressure in the dam, but were unable to determine the intensity of stress in the masonry. Question 68 was attempted by only one or two candidates, and the answers were by no means satisfactory, the second half of the question in particular being very badly answered. Only one candidate made any attempt to deal with Question 69 ; he gave a very satisfactory answer. In Question 70, most of the candidates determined correctly enough the angle turned through by the bar D, and the mean angular velocity, but came to grief in determining the mean angular acceleration.

Report on the Examination in Steam.

A comparison of the number of candidates this year with the number in 1906 shows a slight decrease, about 4 per cent. of the total, and confined almost entirely to Stage 2. Except in Honours the work done was very satisfactory, and an advance on that of previous years. The sketches of engine and boiler details, in answer to the first two questions of each paper, were particularly good, especially in Stages 2 and 3 and Honours. This, however, cannot be said generally about the sketches of experimental apparatus required in answer to the third question, which were often very weak in detail, though there seems to be a good amount of knowledge acquired in the laboratory. The arithmetic was not so good as the descriptive answering, especially in Stage 1, where difficulty often arose by confusing the Centigrade and Fahrenheit scales of temperature, and by the wrong introduction of the 32 degrees when working in the latter units. Attention may again be called to the fact that many candidates confine their attention almost wholly to what may be called the descriptive questions, ignoring the numerical ones. They are interested in practice but not in principles.

Honours candidates are expected to have a knowledge beyond that found in the text books, and to be interested in the most recent developments of the subject. From this point of view the answers of the 23 Honours candidates were disappointing, no one obtaining a First Class, and only 4 passing in the Second Class.

STAGE 1.

Results : 1st Class, 485 ; 2nd Class, 501 ; Failed, 350 ; Total, 1,336.

Q. 1. Describe, with sketches, one, and only *one*, of the following, (*a*), (*b*), (*c*), (*d*), or (*e*) :—

(*a*) Any form of governor.
(*b*) A large air-pump for a steam engine.
(*c*) The crank axle of a locomotive showing the eccentric sheaves, the direction of the centre of each sheave being shown relatively to the directors of the cranks.
(*d*) An engine used on any kind of motor car.
(*e*) The rotating part of any steam turbine, showing how the vanes are fixed.

The selection was generally (*a*), the sketches being very variable, but on the whole good. When taken, the answers to (*b*) were often excellent, the modern forms of air-pump being well in evidence. The answers to (*c*) were somewhat disappointing. There were some very good sketches of petrol engines. By the few who attempted (*e*), it was often found difficult to make a sketch which exhibited the mechanical construction at all clearly.

Q. 2. Describe with sketches, one, and only *one*, of the following, (*a*), (*b*), (*c*), or (*d*) :—

(*a*) The fire-box of a locomotive, showing how it is stayed. Give larger sketches of a few details.
(*b*) Any important part of any water-tube boiler.
(*c*) Any form of safety valve now in common use.
(*d*) The carburettor of a petrol engine.

(*a*) Not often attempted. Answers good.
(*b*) Rarely attempted. Sketches very superficial.
(*c*) The favourite selection. Good sketches.
(*d*) Rarely taken. A few good answers.

Q. 3. Describe, with sketches, how you would experimentally determine any one, and only *one*, of the following, (*a*), (*b*), (*c*), or (*d*) :—

(*a*) The law connecting pressure, volume and temperature of a quantity of air.
(*b*) The heat required to convert 1 lb. of water at 0° C. into dry saturated steam at, say, 100 pounds per sq. inch.
(*c*) The dryness of steam leaving a boiler.
(*d*) The calorific power of a gas or an oil or petrol.

(*a*) Fairly often attempted, but the answers were bad, and generally obtained from a text book.
(*b*) Seldom taken, and, as in (*a*), there was an absence of laboratory knowledge.
(*c*) Here again there were comparatively few good answers. The candidates generally described some form of separator.
(*d*) Generally selected, and the answers satisfactory.

Q. 4. State the following amounts of energy in foot pounds :—

     (*a*) The kinetic energy of the rim of a fly-wheel whose weight is 3 tons, average velocity 75 feet per second.

     (*b*) The calorific energy of one cubic foot of producer gas 95 Centigrade heat units.

     (*c*) 25 lbs. of water raised from 10° C. to 40° C.

     (*d*) Twenty horse-power during 3 minutes.

     (*e*) Three Board of Trade Units, that is three kilowatt hours.

All the parts of this question were very well answered by a large number of candidates. In working (*b*) and (*c*), some candidates first converted the Centigrade into Fahrenheit degrees, and were lucky if they escaped the 32° trap. Others, to a somewhat surprising degree, introduced the total heat of steam formula in their attempts at (*b*).

Q. 5. Steam enters a cylinder at any initial (absolute) pressure p_1, it is cut off at $\frac{2}{3}$ of the stroke. What is the average pressure during the stroke? It is some fraction of p_1. Assume the hypothetical diagram, no clearance, an expansion law pv constant. Apply your answer to the cases where p_1 is 100, 80 and 60. If the back pressure is 17, what is the mean effective pressure in each case?

     The area of the piston is 300 sq. inches, crank 2 feet; two strokes in a revolution; what is the work done in one revolution in each of the above cases? Tabulate your answers.

Often attempted, and many good answers, though frequently the arithmetic was cumbrous. The formula for mean pressure was often known and the logarithm worked out correctly.

Q. 6. Two strokes in a revolution; area of piston 300 sq. inches; crank 2 feet. What is the volume (neglecting clearance) of steam admitted if the cut-off is at $\frac{2}{3}$th of the stroke? If the initial pressure is 100 or 80 or 60 pounds per square inch, what weight of steam is used in one stroke (assuming no condensation or clearance). What weight is used in one revolution?

p	100	80	60
Volume in cubic feet of one lb. of steam	4·356	5·37	7·03

Fairly often tried. As in Question 5 the answers were generally either quite right, or very weak, particularly in regard to the latter part of the question.

Q. 7. The area of a petrol engine diagram is (using the planimeter which subtracts and adds properly) 4·12 square inches, and its length (parallel to the atmospheric line) is 3·85 inches; what is the average breadth of the figure? If 1 inch represents 70 lb. per square inch, what is the average effective pressure? The piston is 3·5 inches in diameter with a stroke of 4 inches. What is the work done in one cycle? If there are 800 cycles per minute, what is the Horse Power?

A popular question, and for the most part well answered. The breadth of the diagram and the average pressure were generally right, and correct answers to the latter parts of the question were sufficiently numerous to show that there is a fairly general knowledge of the cycle in the internal combustion engine.

Q. 8. A formula for Regnault's total heat H will be found on the tables supplied to you; it is the total heat which must be given to 1 lb. of water at 0° C. to raise its temperature as water to $\theta°$ C., and then to convert it all into steam at $\theta°$ C. What is the heat which must be given to 1 lb. of water at 0° C. to convert it into steam at 150° C. ? What amount of this was required to heat the water before any of it was converted into steam ? What name is given to the remainder, and how much is it ?

Often selected. The total heat was generally found correctly; even those who used the Fahrenheit scale answered fairly well. A considerable number, however, gave 100 C.H.U. instead of 150 C.H.U. as the sensible heat, with the consequent mistake in the value of the latent heat.

Q. 9. Why do we admit air by the fire door as well as from the ashpit through the grate of a boiler furnace.

Knowledge on the subject of this question was very vague, though many attempted it. Very few seemed to have any idea as to the use of admitting air by the fire door under any circumstances.

Q. 10. Sketch and describe any form of steam or gas engine indicator.

Neither popular nor well answered. The sketches were poor, some omitting the spring, and the majority of the link motions being unworkable. Sketches of Bourdon pressure gauges, or of indicator diagrams were too often given as answers to the question.

Q. 11. What is the formula for centrifugal force F pounds in terms of radius r feet, mass m or $w/32.2$, and n revolutions per minute ? Given F, r and m, show how we find n. If F has the following values for the given values of r, and w is 9·66 lb., find n in each case.

r feet.	F pounds.
0·6	87
0·8	120

Rarely attempted. A few gave complete answers, but generally the arithmetic proved too formidable.

Q. 12. Sketch the ports and a simple slide valve in its mid position. In dotted lines show the valve at the beginning of a stroke of the piston. What do we mean by *lap*, *lead* and *advance* of a valve ?

A very popular question and generally well answered. The only common defect was shown in regard to the exhaust lap, many defining it as the lap of the valve over the exhaust port and illustrating it accordingly.

Q. 13. What methods are taken to prevent condensation of steam in the cylinder of an engine ? Why does such condensation tend to take place ?

Fairly often attempted. Many were prepared with an essay on the subject and sometimes the answers were very good.

STAGE 2.

Results : 1st Class, 316 ; 2nd Class, 484 ; Failed, 189 ; Total, 989.

Q. 21. Describe, with sketches, one, and only *one*, of the following, (*a*), (*b*), (*c*), (*d*), or (*e*) :—

    (*a*) Any form of governor.

    (*b*) A large air pump for a steam engine.

    (*c*) The crank axle of a locomotive, showing the eccentric sheaves, the direction of the centre of each sheave being shown relatively to the directions of the cranks.

    (*d*) An engine used on any kind of motor car.

    (*e*) The rotating part of any steam turbine, showing how the vanes are fixed.

The parts (a) or (b) were usually selected, and the sketches were good.

In (c) the sketches were sometimes too diagrammatic.

Those who selected (d) had good practical knowledge, as had the candidates who took (e), but the latter, as noticed in Stage 1, were often unable to make sketches which were clear.

Q. 22. Describe, with sketches, only *one* of the following, (a), (b), (c), or (d) :—

(a) The fire box of a locomotive, showing how it is stayed. Give larger sketches of a few details.

(b) Any important part of any water tube boiler.

(c) Any form of safety valve now in common use.

(d) The carburettor of a petrol engine.

(a) Frequently chosen. Many excellent sketches.

(b) Not often taken. Sketches inclined to be vague.

(c) The favourite of the group. Sketches satisfactory.

(d) Seldom attempted. Sketches good ; the float chamber was generally included.

Q. 23. Describe, with sketches, how you would experimentally determine one (and only *one*) of the following, (a), (b), (c), or (d) :—

(a) The law connecting pressure, volume, and temperature of a quantity of air.

(b) The heat required to convert 1 lb. of water at 0° C. into dry saturated steam at, say, 100 pounds per square inch.

(c) The dryness of steam leaving a boiler.

(d) The calorific power of a gas or an oil or petrol.

(a) Fairly often selected. Boyle's law was generally known, and in some cases the increase of pressure at constant volume was also known. But the answering on the whole was not good. Quite a large number proposed the use of a frictionless piston.

(b) Not very popular nor well answered.

(c) A favourite choice. Answers generally good.

(d) Also very popular and well answered. A decided advance on similar answers last year.

Q. 24. What heat is given to one pound of feed water at 35° C. to convert it into steam, 90 per cent. dry, at 190° C. ? If a steam engine of 132 indicated horse-power uses 2,850 lb. of this steam per hour, how much heat enters the condenser or goes off by radiation or in other ways ?

Nearly always attempted. The answers to the first part of the question were not very good, the common errors being to take $\frac{9}{10}$ths of the total heat, or to subtract the 35° before substituting in the formula for total heat. The second part was better answered.

Q. 25. There is a rule concerning the velocity of a fluid before it enters a turbine wheel and the inclination of the vane and its velocity ; what is the rule ? Give the reason for it.

The comparatively few answers to this question only served to exhibit the prevalent lack of knowledge on the subject.

Q. 26. Taking the hypothetical diagram, no cushioning or clearance, expansion part *pv* constant, the mean pressure in the forward stroke is

$$p_1 (1 + \log_e r)/r.$$

If the back pressure in the cylinder is 17 lb. per sq. inch, and if we look upon friction as equivalent to a back pressure of

14 pounds per sq. inch, what is the *real* work done in a stroke of l feet, the area of the piston being A sq. inches? What is the volume of steam admitted for one stroke? What is the work done per cubic foot of steam if $p_1 = 100$ lb. per sq. inch and $r = 3$?

A favourite question. The principal troubles were arithmetical. In calculating $\log_e r$, many candidates used 2·718 instead of 2·303. Some gave $\frac{Al}{144}$ instead of $\frac{Al}{144r}$ as the volume of the steam admitted. Subject to consequential errors, the last part of the question was well answered.

Q. 27. Describe the method of balancing employed in any motor car engine known to you.

Seldom attempted. The answers generally referred to the balance of the cranks only.

Q. 28. The area of a petrol engine diagram is (using the planimeter which subtracts and adds properly) 4·12 square inches, and its length (parallel to the atmospheric line) is 3·85 inches; what is the average breadth of the figure? If 1 inch represents 70 pounds per square inch, what is the average pressure? The piston is 3·5 inches in diameter with a stroke of 4 inches. What is the work done in one cycle? If there are 800 cycles per minute, what is the horse-power?

Very popular. The answers were always good and usually quite correct. The errors generally arose from a multiplication of the work by 2 or 4, owing to inexact knowledge of the cycle.

Q. 29. Why do we admit air by the fire door as well as from the ashpit through the grate of a boiler furnace?

Fairly often taken. The answers were often incomplete, but some very good attempts were made.

Q. 30. The entropy of 1 lb. of water at θ° C. is

$$\log_e \frac{273+\theta}{273}.$$

What is this if θ is 160°? If this water is converted into dry saturated steam at 160° C., what is the additional entropy?

Frequently attempted, but there were many sources of error. The publication of a temperature-entropy diagram at a popular price (1d.) by the Board of Education will prove very helpful to students in this important branch of the subject. This chart should be in general use during the coming session.

Q. 31. Neglect angularity of the connecting rod. With an ordinary slide valve, lap 1·5 inches, lead 0·5 inches, we desire to cut off at half stroke, what is the half travel and what is the angle of advance? Draw the probable indicator diagram. Take an inside lap of 0·75 inch.

Some gave a geometrical construction for the valve diagram. The majority arrived at the diagram by the method of trial and error, or successive approximations. The indicator diagram was generally consistent with the valve diagram.

Q. 32. What is the cause of condensation in steam engine cylinders? Why is it a great evil? How do we try to prevent it?

Very popular. The answers were good, often very good. Peculiar ideas were occasionally met with, e.g., "We know that Boyle's law (pv = const.) does not prevail even with no expansion, therefore the more expansion we have the further we depart from the law and the more condensation."

Q. 33. A boiler furnace fire is about 12 inches thick. What do we know as to the way in which combustion is going on at various places in the coal and above it, and in the space just on the furnace side of the flues? Does it depend upon the time that has elapsed since the furnace was last fed with coal? If so, say in what state the fire is, to which your description applies.

Not very frequently attempted, and the answers often incomplete. Often the candidates had apparently no knowledge of the chemical processes involved. One candidate remarked that "Sometimes the heat of the lower regions will be used to drive off the gaseous constituents of the coal."

STAGE 3.

Results: 1st Class, 52 ; 2nd Class, 63 ; Failed, 132 ; Total, 247.

Q. 41. Sketch one, and only *one*, of the following, (a), (b), (c), or (d) :—

    (a) A piston rod gland for a steam engine designed for and fitted with metallic packing.

    (b) The cross head of a steam engine showing the provision made for taking up wear and also for lubrication.

    (c) A "sight feed" lubricator fitted on a steam chest.

    (d) Section through the gas valve of a gas engine showing the hit and miss mechanism operated by the governor.

The sketches usually displayed a sound knowledge of constructional details and of the relative proportions of parts. The favourite selections were (a) and (b), but some good sketches of (c) and (d) were made.

Q. 42. Sketch one, and only *one*, of the following, (a), (b), or (c) :—

    (a) A good form of blow-off cock fitted to a boiler.

    (b) The general outline of any form of water-tube boiler, and also show in detail the jointing of a tube with the steam drum.

    (c) A locomotive fire box in general outline ; mark the places where you would put wash-out plugs ; sketch one of the plugs.

The sketches were again satisfactory, often exhibiting, especially in the answers to (b), an extensive knowledge of details, though in some cases vagueness was the characteristic feature. In (a) a steam stop valve was sometimes given.

Q. 43. Describe, with sketches, how you would experimentally determine any one, and only *one*, of the following, (a), (b), (c), or (d) :—

    (a) The law connecting pressure, volume, and temperature of a quantity of air.

    (b) The heat required to convert 1 lb. of water at 0° C. into dry saturated steam at, say, 100 pounds per square inch.

    (c) The dryness of steam leaving a boiler.

    (d) The performance and efficiency of a small direct acting steam pump.

The candidates usually chose either (b) or (c), and many of the answers suggested mere second hand or text-book knowledge. In the answers to (a) it was generally overlooked that the air should be specially dried in order to obtain proper results.

Q. 44. A steam engine of 132 Indicated Horse Power uses 2,850 lb. of steam per hour ; this steam is at 190° C. with a dryness fraction 90 per cent. The feed water is at 35° C. The circulation water of the condenser, 2,660 lb. per minute, is raised 9 degrees centigrade in temperature. How much heat has to be accounted for by radiation, leakage, &c. ?

This was a favourite question, and, on the whole, was well answered. Too many mistakes were, however, made in finding the heat of formation of the moist steam from feed water at the given temperature.

Q. 45. There is a rule concerning the velocity of a fluid before it enters a turbine wheel, and the inclination of the vane and its velocity ; what is the rule ? If the fluid leaves the wheel with no velocity in the direction of the wheel's motion, what is the work done per pound of fluid ?

The candidates were often unable to make their answers clear owing to their insufficient acquaintance with vectors. It was also too common to find the principle of kinetic energy to be wrongly applied to a reaction turbine instead of that of rate of change of momentum, the latter being applicable to reaction and impulse turbines alike. See also the remarks on Q. 64.

Q. 46. Taking the hypothetical diagram, no cushioning or clearance, the expansion part being pv constant ; what is the effective pressure during the stroke ? Prove your answer to be correct. What is the work done per cubic foot of steam ? Take initial pressure 100 pounds per sq. inch ; if the cylinder back pressure is 17, and if we look upon friction as equivalent to a back pressure of 14 lb. per sq. inch, what is the best ratio of cut-off ?

This was a favourite question and it was well answered by many. In the partial answers some knew the rule for the best ratio of cut-off, but were unable to give any reason for it.

Q. 47. Describe how you would arrange four cylinders of a motor car engine so as to get the best balance with a not too varying turning moment on the crank shaft. If the balance is still not perfect, what is the defect due to ?

There were comparatively few attempts and a large proportion of these were worthless, being evidently pure guesses, from the point of view of the cycle of a double acting steam engine instead of that of an ordinary petrol motor. The few who gave the proper arrangement of the cranks and cylinders nearly always discussed the sequence of firing, but no one seemed to know anything of the degree of balance of the inertia forces of the pistons.

Q. 48. Give the ordinary statical theory of the Watt or Hartnell or any other form of governor. If you choose the Watt, it must be a modern loaded governor. Make a numerical illustration to show the range of speed. Why is this theory not sufficiently good ?

This was another favourite question and the answers to the first two parts were satisfactory. But it was rare for anyone to give a valid reason why their theory was defective. Refer to the remarks on Q. 67.

Q. 49. Air is at 1,600° C. and 200 pounds per square inch ; it escapes through an expanding orifice into an atmosphere of pressure 0·2 pound per square inch ; suppose that it enters the vanes of a wheel without shock or friction anywhere, giving all its energy to the wheel, what will be its temperature ?

The answers, though few in number, were fairly good.

Q. 50. What is the entropy of a pound of water-steam at $\theta_1°$C., dryness fraction 0·9 ? If it expands adiabatically to $\theta_2°$C., what is its dryness ? Take as an example $\theta_1 = 160$, $\theta_2 = 40$.

If this steam supplied at θ_1 to a turbine and exhausting at θ_2 is found to be of dryness 0·95 the work done per pound of steam is less than what the Rankine cycle gives ; how much less ? Assume no radiation of heat from the turbine.

Was often attempted, and the candidates could, as a rule, calculate the entropy and the dryness after adiabatic expansion. There was no correct answer to the latter part though it simply required the area of a rectangle (on the temperature-entropy diagram) representing the excess heat rejected. This is the amount by which the area of the Rankine cycle must be diminished. Students should use the new temperature-entropy diagram issued by the Board of Education, and referred to under Q. 30.

Q. 51. A spindle has a heavy wheel fixed at the middle. Give the theory which enables us to find the critical speed ? What occurs if we greatly exceed the critical speed. Neglect the mass of the shaft.

Seldom attempted and only once with any success. Candidates usually gave an investigation of the centrifugal tension in a flywheel rim and got the expression for the limiting speed. There is a simple solution to the question involving only elementary mathematics. Evidently teachers are not alive to the practical importance of problems involving critical speeds of shafts.

Q. 52. Describe, with sketches, a good indicator for gas engines running at about 150 revolutions per minute. Be particular about the shape of the piston and the fastening of the spring.

Not a favourite question. The sketches were not nearly so good as those given in answer to the first two questions, Nos. 41 and 42.

Q. 53. What is the general characteristic of all radial valve gears ? Describe any one form and show how we find, for any position of the gear, the advance and half-travel of the valve.

The answers were fairly good, except that a Stephenson gear was sometimes mistaken for a radial gear.

Q. 54. In the combustion, of, say, C_2H_4, state exactly all the meanings to be extracted from the equation

$$C_2H_4 + 6O = 2H_2O + 2CO_2.$$

How much air is needed for the perfect combustion of one cubic foot of C_2H_4 ?

The answers were seldom as complete as they should have been. It was not uncommon for a candidate to give the proper volume relations and then to attempt to get the cubic feet of air by employing the equation connecting the atomic weights. The symbol 6O being written instead of the usual $3O_2$, was the cause of many of the estimates of the air needed for combustion being often double that required.

HONOURS.

Results : 1st Class, – ; 2nd Class, 4 ; Failed, 19 ; Total, 23.

Q. 61. Sketch one, and only *one*, of the following, (a), (b), (c), or (d) :—

　　(a) A piston rod gland for a steam engine designed for and fitted with metallic packing.
　　(b) The crosshead of a steam engine showing the provision made for taking up wear and also for lubrication.
　　(c) Any form of air pump.
　　(d) Section through the gas valve of a gas engine, showing the hit and miss mechanism operated by the governor.

(a) and (b) were usually chosen. On the whole the sketching may be said to have been well done.

Q. 62. Sketch one, and only *one*, of the following, (*a*), (*b*), or (*c*) :—

    (*a*) A good form of blow-off cock.

    (*b*) The general outline of any form of water-tube boiler, and also show in detail the jointing of a tube with the steam drum.

    (*c*) A locomotive fire-box in general outline ; mark the places where you would put wash-out plugs ; sketch one of the plugs.

(*a*), (*b*), and (*c*) were taken equally often. The sketching was fairly well done.

Q. 63. Describe, with sketches, how you would experimentally determine any one, (and only *one*) of the following, (*a*), (*b*), (*c*), or (*d*) :—

    (*a*) The law connecting pressure, volume and temperature of a quantity of air.

    (*b*) The heat required to convert 1 lb. of water at 0° C. into dry saturated steam at, say 100 lb. per square inch.

    (*c*) The dryness of steam leaving a boiler.

    (*d*) The performance and efficiency of a small steam pump.

(*c*) was taken by almost every candidate. As a rule the answers were good. The throttling calorimetric method was most common. Many candidates do not seem to know that it can only succeed when the steam is fairly dry. There is still a widespread notion that throttling produces a *large* amount of drying of steam, although the calculation is quite easy.

Q. 64. There is a rule concerning the velocity of a fluid before it enters a turbine wheel, and the inclination of the vane and its velocity ; what is the rule ? How do we find the velocity with which the fluid leaves the wheel (take either a reaction or an impulse turbine) ? How do we find the work done per pound of fluid ?

This simple fundamental matter which ought to be known even to elementary students, was not sufficiently well known even to men attempting Honours. The reasons can be given in a few minutes, and the working of some exercises afterwards will make a student feel quite secure in his knowledge. Practically this is the whole known theory of the water or steam turbine. Half the candidates tried this question, but there were only three good answers.

Q. 65. Taking the hypothetical diagram, no cushioning or clearance, the expansion part being *pv* constant ; what is the effective pressure during the stroke ? Prove your answer to be correct. What is the work done per cubic foot of steam ? Take initial pressure 100 pounds per square inch ; if the cylinder back pressure is 17, and if we look upon friction as equivalent to a back pressure of 14 lb. per square inch, what is the best ratio of cut-off ?

A favourite question because the first part has often been set in previous examinations. Even here, however, the proof was not always given, or candidates having gone wrong in the proof gave the right answer which everyone seemed to know. Answers to the end part of the question were, on the whole, good, but not so good.

Q. 66. Describe how you would arrange four cylinders of a motor car engine so as to get the best balance with a not too varying turning moment on the crank shaft. If the balance is still not perfect, what is the defect due to ?

Attempted by few candidates. One answer was good ; the other four answers showed that the balancing of motor-car engines had not been specially considered.

Q. 67. A Hartnell governor on a turbine shaft has a law $F = s\,r - a$ where F pounds is the outward radial force on each ball which would just keep the governor (if motionless) in the position in which each ball is r feet from the axis. What do s and a depend upon ?

When the balls move let there be friction $e\dfrac{d r}{d t}$. Write out the equation of motion radially outwards. Let the method of regulation be such that the torque on the revolving part of the turbine is $c - br$ where b and c are constants. The speed being steady, the resisting torque having been constant, let the torque suddenly alter to another constant value ; write out the differential equation connecting speed and time. State the condition required for stability of motion (that is, no hunting).

Three candidates attempted this question ; one obtained 12 marks out of 56, the others no marks. The question is framed so as to lead a candidate to the solution even if he had never heard of it before.

Q. 68. Steam is flowing from a vessel through an orifice which gets larger outside. What do we know about the changes of pressure and speed of a portion of the steam as it flows ? Take the inside pressure as, say, 200 lb. per square inch and the pressure outside as 2lb per square inch : What is the speed in the throat or narrowest place ? How is it that outside the throat the speed gets greater although the cross section is greater ?

Quite half the candidates attempted this question. It was usual to say that if H, the total heat in a pound of steam at temperature θ° C. and dryness x, is $\theta + x L$, then the loss of H is kinetic energy, so that the speed is known. But this is a very insufficient answer. The Examiner expected candidates to know that there was a rule to find the speed v knowing p, and also that if we choose a small stream whose cross section at any place of pressure p is A, if we make the mathematical statement that the weight of steam flowing through all cross sections per second is the same, we are able to find A for every value of p. The value of A in the throat is a minimum, but v gets greater and greater as p is less.

Q. 69. What is the work done per pound of steam (Rankine cycle), supplied at θ_1° C. and x_1 its dryness fraction ; exhausted at θ_2° C. and dryness fraction x_2. Prove the formula you use. If in a real engine or turbine the exhaust dryness is x_3 ; show that x_3 cannot be less than x_2 ; what is the work done per pound of steam ? Assume no radiation of heat from the engine.

A question frequently attempted, as the first part has often been asked before. But only one candidate answered the second half of the question, although it requires the exercise of only a little common sense.

Q. 70. A fly-wheel has moment of inertia I ; two wheels, one on each side of the first, have moments of inertia i each. Each length of shaft has the same stiffness s. One of the smaller wheels has applied to it a varying torque $a \sin 2\pi ft$, and the other $a \cos 2\pi ft$. Neglect the mass of the shaft. What value of f will cause fracture of the shaft ? Why is this not exact as an illustration of what occurs between two cranks of a steam or gas engine and a fly-wheel midway between them ?

This question was not attempted ; it is easy enough and relates to a subject which has become one of great importance to the designers of all kinds of modern engines. The old method of assuming a mere static application of twisting moment to a crank shaft or of tensile or compressive load to a valve rod leads to sizes which are often much too small for strength.

Q. 71. Describe, with sketches, an indicator which has been used to indicate petrol engines at 2,000 revolutions per minute. What were the results of Prof. Callendar's investigation ?

One candidate received full marks ; the three others who tried the question received less than half marks. Candidates in Honours are supposed to know something of important investigations like this, and not merely elementary text book information.

Q. 72. What is the general characteristic of all radial valve gears ? Describe any one form and show how we find, for any position of the gear, the advance and half travel of the valve.

Attempted by half the candidates. The best of these obtained 37 marks, the other answers were very poor. The subject is one of great importance, and as the question is an easy one the subject is evidently being neglected. It is to be observed that the Examiner does not ask for the octaves in the motion ; it is assumed to be simple harmonic motion. The question is one for elementary students.

Q. 73. In the combustion of, say, C_2H_4, state exactly all the meanings to be extracted from the equation

$$C_2H_4 + 6O = 2H_2O + 2CO_2.$$

How much air is needed for the perfect combustion of one cubic foot of C_2H_4 ?

The equation might have been better understood if instead of $6O$ we had written $3O_2$. A number of candidates said that one cubic foot of C_2H_4 needs six cubic feet of oxygen for perfect combustion. A good number of candidates tried the question but only one obtained as much as 33 marks out of 50. Candidates ought to know that for the study of gas, oil and spirit engines it is essential to have a knowledge of some simple chemical principles.

Q. 74. Assume that in the cylinder the water is at the same temperature as the steam during admission and expansion. Assume the expansion to be adiabatic, the cut-off being quick. The following measurements of p and v are made, $163\cdot3$ pounds per square inch being the pressure of admission—

θ° C.	p	v	u	ϕ_w	ϕ_s
185	163·3	1·433	2·756	·524	1·560
165	101·9	2·313	4·29	·478	1·595

v is in cubic feet, θ° C. is the temperature ; u is cubic feet of each kind of steam per lb.; ϕ_w is the entropy of a pound of water, and ϕ_s is the entropy of a pound of steam of this temperature and pressure.

How much water is there in the cylinder at each of the two points ? How much water was in the cylinder before admission ? Assume the temperature of the water present before admission to be 80° C., and neglect the weight of steam present before admission.

A fair number of students tried this question, two obtained full marks and two others gave fairly good answers which might have obtained full marks if the arithmetic had been correct. We think that all the candidates had the sort of knowledge of the $\theta^\circ \phi$. diagram which would have enabled them to answer the question correctly if they had given to it a little thought.

Report on the Examination in Practical Mathematics.

The number of candidates in this subject continues to increase rapidly, but at a slightly diminishing rate, the percentage increase this year being 36 compared with 44 reported last year and 60 in 1905. This proportionate increase was about the same in all three Stages.

Unfortunately the quality of the work in Stages 1 and 2 was unsatisfactory and distinctly inferior to that of last year, after making due allowance for the fact that some of the examination questions were a little more difficult. There were many large classes quite unprepared to undertake the examination. These were badly grounded in ordinary computations and lost much time and many marks in their answers to the first three questions.

On the other hand the work done in Stage 3 was good and quite equal to that of 1906.

Detailed criticism of questions follows :—

STAGE 1.

Results : 1st Class, 595 ; 2nd Class, 1,182 ; Failed, 1,147 ; Total, 2,924.

Q. 1. The four parts (*a*), (*b*), (*c*), and (*d*) must all be answered to get full marks :—

(*a*) Without using logarithms, compute by contracted methods to four significant figures
$$87\cdot35 \div (0\cdot07568 \times 3\cdot501).$$

(*b*) Write down the logarithms, of 17840, 1·784, 0·0001784, 0·001784.

(*c*) Extract the square root of each of the numbers given in (*b*), using logarithms.

(*d*) Express the sum of money 45 pounds 7 shillings 8 pence in pounds and decimals of a pound.

(*a*) Many could do the contracted multiplication, but fewer could do the contracted division properly. A rather common mistake was to divide the product by 87·35.

(*b*) Usually correctly given.

(*c*) The square roots of the first three numbers were generally correctly found. In the case of the last number a common mistake was to put $\frac{1}{2}$ of $\bar{3}\cdot2514 = \bar{1}\cdot6257$. A certain number gave the logs. of the square roots instead of the square roots themselves. In this case, as in that of others involving the use of logarithms, the connection of a number with its logarithm by the sign $=$ was far too common.

(*d*) Nearly always answered correctly. Various methods were used.

Q. 2. The four parts (*a*), (*b*), (*c*), and (*d*) must all be answered to get full marks :—

(*a*) If
$$V = 2\pi^2 x y^2 \text{ and } A = 4\pi^2 x y,$$
If
$$V = 240 \text{ and } A = 170,$$
find x and y.

(*b*) A sphere of stone is 3 feet in diameter, the weight of the stone per cubic foot is 120 lbs., what is the weight of the sphere ?

(*c*) When x is small we may take $(1 + x)^n$ as being nearly equal to $1 + nx$. What is the percentage error in this, when $x = \cdot01$ and $n = 2$?

(d) Write down algebraically :—x is multiplied by the fourth power of y and this product is subtracted from the square of x multiplied by the cube of y ; the cube root of the square of this difference is divided by the square root of the sum of x and y.

(a) **Badly** answered. The comparatively few who obtained correct answers generally used clumsy methods. A simple division of the equated expressions in order to eliminate π^2 and x appeared to be the last thing thought of. It was of common occurrence for candidates to work out the numerical value of xy^2 from the first equation and xy from the second equation and to stop there. The following mistake was not uncommon

$$240 = 2\pi^2\ xy^2$$
$$170 = 4\pi^2\ xy$$
$$\therefore 70 = 2y$$

(b) A commendable number knew that the volume of a sphere is $\frac{2}{3}$rds that of the circumscribed cylinder, and obtained correct answers. There were, however, many who did not know the correct formula, using expressions such as $4\pi r^3$, $4\pi r^2$, etc. for the volume.

(c) Rather poorly answered. Some used four figure logs. and so arrived at the conclusion that the error was " nil." In the poorer classes there was too much " mathematics " of the following kind :—$1 + 2 \times 0.01 = 3 \times 0.01 = 0.03$; $(1.01)^2\ 2 \times (1.01) = 2.02$; and so on.

(d) Very well answered. The commonest mistakes were to write $y^{1/4}$ for the fourth power of y, and xy for the sum of x and y.

Q. 8. The four parts (a), (b), (c), (d), must all be answered to get full marks :—

(a) A rectangular garden has one side 28 yards longer than the other ; if the smaller side were increased by 40 yards and the greater diminished by 34 yards, the area would remain unaltered ; what are the lengths of the sides.

(b) If $y \propto \sqrt{x}$ and if y is 5 when x is 3, state the true formula connecting x and y. What is y if x is 9?

(c) A circular arc is 4.817 inches long, the radius is 12 inches. What is the angle subtended by the arc at the centre? State it in degrees.

(d) State exactly what we mean by the sine, cosine and tangent of an angle.

(a) A fair number of correct answers were given, but in general the attempts were poor.

(b) Not well answered. The sign $\propto$ is not well understood. The true formula connecting x and y was seldom distinctly given even by those who answered the last part correctly.

(c) The angle was usually found correctly but often by clumsy methods. Very few determined the angle in radian measure as the first step.

(d) Answers very weak. Such answers as :—

$$\text{sine} = \frac{P}{H}; \qquad \cos = \frac{B}{H}$$

etc. or something equivalent were usually given with or without a figure. In the latter case the particular angle referred to was often left doubtful.

Q. 4. Plot x and y on squared paper. What is the average value of y between $x=0$ and $x=50$?

x	5	16	26	35	50	
y	13	22	24	27	31	

A favourite question. The plotting was well done, but the majority got no farther. Of those who found the average value of y, a few obtained good answers by the use of mid-ordinates or of Simpson's rule. Too many, however, gave simply the average of the five tabulated values of x, and of those who drew new ordinates, equally spaced, some gave double weight to the end ordinates, using the faulty rule :—mean ordinates=sum of equally spaced ordinates divided by number of ordinates instead of the rule (half sum of first and last ordinates + remaining ordinates) ÷ number of spaces.

Q. 5. If
$$y = 2 \sin A + 3 \cos A - 3.55$$

take A as 20°, 23°, 26°, &c., finding in each case the value of y. Plot y and A on squared paper. For what value of A is y just 0 ?

Generally well answered. Some weakness was shown in plotting the negative values of y. Very few took values of A intermediate between 23° and 26° so as to ensure a better approximation ; by careful plotting, however, good results could be obtained without this. There was a curious tendency to make use of negative characteristics as in logs ; thus values of y would be tabulated as follows :—

A	20°	23°	26°	
y	1 ·9531	$\overline{1}$ ·9929	0·0232	

| Instead of - - - | —·0469 | —·0071 | | |

Then difficulties of plotting always occurred, showing that negative characteristics are imperfectly understood.

Q. 6. A sliding piece is moving so that at the following times t seconds it has travelled the following distances x feet from a point in its path. Plot x and t. Measure from the curve and tabulate the values of x for the values of t, 1, 1·01, 1·02, &c., at equal intervals, and tabulate the average speed in each hundredth of a second.

t	1·00	1·01	1·018	1·031	1·045	1·052	1·06
x	3·12	3·305	3·420	3·559	3·664	3·700	3·732

The plotting was often well done, but the scales were sometimes too small. Very few got beyond plotting the curve and tabulating the required values of x.

Q. 7. If
$$y = ax^{\frac{3}{2}} - bx^{\frac{5}{2}}$$

if y is 5·82 when x is 0·51, and if y is 32·10 when x is 0.98, find a and b.

Not often attempted and rarely answered well. The advantage of using the factor $x^{\frac{3}{2}}$ was seldom recognised. The raising of 0·98 to the $\frac{3}{2}$ power was beyond the capabilities of most of the candidates.

Q. 8. The area of the horizontal section of a reservoir is A square feet at the height h feet from the lowest point. When h is 30, what is the volume of water ?

h	0	2·5	5	7·5	10	12·5	15	17·5	20	22·5	25	27·5	30
A	0	2510	3860	4670	5160	5490	5810	6210	6890	7680	8270	8620	8780

A fairly popular question. The answering, however, was not good. The incorrect rules referred to under *Q.* 4 were often used. A common mistake was to give the volume as 30 × 8,780 = 263,400 cubic feet.

Q. 9. The following observed values of *x* and *y* are thought possibly to fulfil the law

$$y = a + bx$$

Try if this is so. Find the most probable values of *a* and *b*. What is the probable error of each value of *y*?

x	10	20	30	40	50	60	70	80
y	180	303	492	603	807	919	1131	1200

Rather unpopular. The plotting was satisfactory and good judgment was shown in drawing the average line. Many obtained the values of *a* and *b* from their line, but some used a pair of the given values of *x* and *y* in order to obtain *a* and *b*, making no use of their average line. The "probable error" were not at all understood.

Q. 10. The electrical resistance of a wire is $R \propto l/d^2$ where *l* is length and *d* is diameter; its weight $W \propto ld^2$. Show that the resistance of a wire $R \propto W/d^4$. If a pound of wire of diameter *d* = 0·06 inches has a resistance of 0·25 ohms, what is the resistance of a pound of wire of the same material, the diameter being 0·01 inches?

Q. 11. A dynamo is in two parts whose weights are *x* and *y*. The cost of the machine is

$$z = y + 4x$$

The usefulness of the machine is proportional to

$$v = x^2 + 3xy$$

If *z* is 10, express *v* in terms of *x* alone. Now take various values of *x* (say, from 0·5 to 2) and calculate *v*. Plot *v* and *x* as the co-ordinates of points on squared paper. For what value of *x* is *v* a maximum?

Q. 12. The space *S* in feet passed through by a body in *T* seconds is

$$S = 10 T + 8 T^2.$$

If *T* = 2, find *S*. Now if *T* = 2 + *t*, find the new *S*. The extra space (new *S* − old *S*) divided by *t* is evidently the average velocity in the short interval of time *t*; write out what is its value. Now imagine *t* to be smaller and smaller without limit, what is the velocity?

Q. 13. Because of centrifugal force due to want of balance of a wheel, the stress *y* in a certain shaft when rotating *n* times per second is

$$y = \frac{0·026n^2}{1 - 0·012n^2}$$

What is the critical speed—that is, the speed for which *y* becomes indefinitely great? For speeds 20 per cent. less and more than the critical speed, find the stresses.

Q. 14. A disc varies in thickness so that when running at a certain speed the radial and hoop stresses may be the same and constant everywhere. The thickness x at radius r is .

$$x = x_1\, e^{-ar^2}$$

where e is 2·718.

If a is 0·075 and x_1 is 0·4, find x for various values of r from 0 to 4, and draw a section of the disc.

Questions 11 to 14 were rarely attempted. There were occasional good answers, but as a rule the questions were beyond the powers of the candidates.

STAGE 2.

Results :—1st Class, 152 ; 2nd Class, 769 ; Failed, 502 ; Total, 1,423.

Q. 21. The four parts (a), (b), (c), and (d) must all be answered to get full marks :—

 (a) Without using logarithms, compute by contracted methods, getting four significant figures *correct*,

   87·35 ÷ (0·07568 × 3·501).

 (b) Using logarithms, compute

   97·43 ÷ (0·3524 × 6·321)$^{2·50}$.

 (c) Explain why when we wish to divide numbers we subtract their logarithms.

 (d) The sum of money £45 7s. 8d. is multiplied by 0·3825. What is the answer in pounds.

(a) As in Stage 1 the contracted multiplication was generally well done, but the contracted division was not so well done, the work being inaccurate owing to numerical errors. The carrying figure was often ignored.

(b) Many mistakes were made in working out the log. of the divisor. Many candidates subtracted the log. log. of the divisor from the log. of the dividend and treated the result as the log. of the quotient.

(c) Candidates generally understood the reason but their explanations were somewhat inadequate.

(d) The answers were usually correct.

Q. 22. The four parts (a), (b), (c), and (d) must all be answered to get full marks :—

 (a) A hollow circular cylinder of iron is 10 inches long and weighs 12 lbs.; its internal diameter is 3 inches ; what is its external diameter? A cubic inch of iron weighs 0·28 lb.

 (b) There is a right-angled triangle ABC, the angle ACB is 90°, the angle ABC is 42°. If D is a point in AC ; if $AC = 3\,AD$, find the angle DBC.

 (c) When x is small we may take $(1 + x)^{-n}$ as being nearly equal to $1 - nx$, What is the percentage error in this when $n = 2$ and $x = 0·01$?

 (d) What are the factors of $x^2 + 0·4\,x - 4·37$?

(a) Answered well on the whole, but numerical slips were too frequent. Many candidates made the mistake of inserting the internal diameter instead of radius in a formula otherwise correct. A certain number went wrong by taking the volume as 12 × 0·28 instead of 12 ÷ 0·28 ; the evaluation of the latter was nearly always worked out by long division, very few cancelling the common factor from numerator and denominator.

(b) Not well done. Some candidates are apparently unable to work with the tangent of an angle ; a considerable number gave the angle as $^2/_3$ × 42° or 28°. a mistake scarcely to be expected in Stage 2.

(c) Should have been better answered. Many overlooked the fact that four figure logs. would not give an answer sufficiently correct. The estimation of the error as a percentage was not well answered.

(d) Fairly well done but many candidates failed to get the factors. The method by trial was the one generally adopted. When a quadratic equation was used, the factors were generally given as " $x = 1\cdot9$ and $-2\cdot3$ " instead of $x - 1\cdot9$ and $x + 2\cdot3$.

Q. 23. The three parts (a), (b) and (c) must all be answered to get full marks :—

(a) 100 lb. of bronze contains 85 per cent. of copper and 15 per cent. of tin. With how much copper must it be melted to obtain a bronze containing 92 per cent. of copper?

(b) If $xy^{1\cdot37} = 25$. If $x = 4$, find y.

(c) If $\dfrac{rA}{100a} = \left(1 + \dfrac{r}{100}\right)^{n} - 1$. If $r = 5$, if $A = 20a$. find n.

(a) Badly answered. The large number of unsuccessful attempts seems to indicate that the solution of easy problems involving equations is not much practised.

(b) On the whole not well done. A common mistake was to interpret $xy^{1\cdot37}$ as $(x\,y)^{1\cdot37}$. Candidates whose methods were correct often went wrong in working out the value of log. y, viz., $0\cdot7959 \div 1\cdot37$; some used logs. for this but nearly always failed to get back to the *double* anti-log.

(c) Only fairly well done. A common mistake was to take $\dfrac{5 \times 20a}{100a}$ as 0 instead of 1. In addition, the term -1 was often overlooked or ignored. The result was the equation $(1\cdot05)^{n} = 0$, and of this various solutions were offered.

Q. 24. At the following heights h feet above the ground the wind pressure on a certain occasion was measured as p pounds per square foot on a vertical plane surface.

h	5	15	25	35	50
p	13	22	24	27	31

What is the average value of p between $h = 0$ and $h = 40$? What is the total force due to wind pressure on a vertical wall 40 feet high and 100 feet long (horizontally)?

A very popular question. The majority of the candidates used wrong rules for determining the average pressure, so that although the plotting was well done, full marks were seldom obtained for this easy question.

Q. 25. Find A approximately in degrees, if $2 \sin A + 3 \cos A = 3\cdot55$ There are two answers between $0°$ and $90°$.

Fairly frequently attempted, on the whole the answering was good. The usual method was algebraical, with or without a subsidiary angle. There were also some good graphical solutions.

Q. 26 Electric lamp filaments of length l, diameter d, made of the same material, kept at the same temperature by the application of v volts, the candle power is proportional to ld, and also to $v^2 d^2/l$. There is a 10 candle power lamp whose $l = 3$ and $v = 100$; we wish to make a 20-candle power lamp with $v = 150$; find l for the new lamp.

Not popular, very badly answered. The attempts usually took some such form as the following :—

$$10 = \frac{k \ 100^2 \ d^2}{3} \quad\text{----- (i)}$$

$$20 = \frac{k \ 150^2 \ d^2}{l} \quad\text{----- (ii)}$$

∴ From (i) and (ii), $l = 3·375$.

There were, however, a few correct answers.

Q. 27. A sliding piece is moving so that at the following times t seconds it has travelled the following distances x feet measured along its path. Plot x and t, measure from the curves the value of x at the times 1·00, 1·01, 1·02, 1·03, etc., and tabulate. Find the accelerations approximately at the times 1·01, 1·02, 1·03, 1·04, and 1·05.

t	1·00	1·01	1·018	1·031	1·045	1·052	1·06
x	3·12	3·305	3·420	3·559	3·664	3·700	3 732

Pretty frequently attempted but seldom completely answered. As a rule the points were carefully plotted and a fair curve drawn through them. The required values of x were correctly read off and tabulated, but only a very few were able to make any use of the numbers thus obtained.

Q. 28. L being length in feet and H the height in feet of still water level above the sill of a thin-edged rectangular notch for measuring water, Q being cubic feet per second flowing ; it is known that

$$Q = aLH^{\frac{3}{2}} - bH^{\frac{5}{2}}$$

A notch of length 10 feet was experimented with. When H was 0·51, Q was found to be 5·82, and when H was 0·98, Q was found to be 32·10. What are the values of a and b? What is Q when H is 1·21 ?

Fairly popular. Not very well answered. Few candidates completed the solution without making numerical errors, or mistakes in algebraical signs, or going wrong in some other way.

Q. 29. The area of the horizontal section of a reservoir A square feet at the height h feet from the lowest point is given in the table below. What is the volume when h is 30 ? If the water falls in level from $h = 15·5$ to $h = 14·5$, what is the loss of volume ?

h	0	2·5	4	7	10	12·5	15	17·5	20	23
A	0	2510	3400	4520	5160	5490	5810	6210	6890	7810

Continued	h	25	28	30
	A	8270	8670	8780

Frequently attempted. The great majority of answers were unsatisfactory. The same mistakes were made as noticed under Q. 8. Many candidates who gave the wrong volume, found the loss of volume correctly. A common erroneous answer for the loss of volume was (15·5 × area at 15·5)—(14·5 × area at 14·5).

Q. 30. In a hollow cylindric coil the magnetic field $F \propto nC$, where n is the number of turns and C is the current; $n \propto \dfrac{1}{d}$, where d is the diameter of the wire; $R \propto \dfrac{1}{d^2}$, where R is the resistance of the wire; $t \propto C^2R$, where t is the permanent maximum temperature produced (above that of the room). Show that when we have the same F we have the same t for any size of wire; but if we double F we quadruple t.

[*Note.*—The above rules are not strictly true, because of the varying thickness of insulation.]

Q. 31. Find the area of the parabola
$$y = a + bx + cx^2$$
between the ordinate at $x = a$ and the ordinate at $x = \beta$.

If $a = -h$ and $\beta = h$, what is the answer?

Q. 32. The parabola
$$y = a + bx + cx^2$$
passes through three points, whose co-ordinates are
$$-h,\ y_1\ ;\ 0,\ y_2\ ;\ h,\ y_3.$$
Insert these values, and find a, b, and c in terms of the given quantities y_1, y_2, y_3 and h.

Questions 30, 31 and 32 were rarely attempted. A few complete answers were given in each case.

Q. 33. A machine is in two parts, whose weights are x and y. The cost of the machine is proportional to
$$z = y + 4x.$$
The usefulness of the machine is proportional to
$$v = x^2 + 3xy.$$
If z is 10, what value of x will cause v to be a maximum? For this value of x, what is y?

Not often selected. In nearly all cases the graphical method was adopted and there were some good answers.

Q. 34. A current C is changing according to the law
$$C = 20 + 21t - 14t^2,$$
where t is seconds. The voltage V is such that
$$V = RC + L\frac{dC}{dt},$$
where $R = 0\cdot5$ and $L = 0\cdot01$; find V as a function of the time

Seldom attempted. Good answers were given by the few who had a little knowledge of the calculus. In a few cases the expression $\dfrac{dC}{dt}$ was simplified into $\dfrac{C}{t}$ by cancelling.

Q. 35. The following numbers are authentic; t seconds is the record time of a trotting (in harness) race of m miles:—

m	1	2	3	4	5	10	20	30	50	100
t	119	257	416	598	751	1575	3505	6479	14141	32153

It is found that there is approximately a law $t = am^b$, where a and b are constants. Test if this is so, and find the most probable values of a and b. The average speed in a race is $s = m/t$; express s in terms of m.

Pretty frequently attempted. Many candidates made out the law connecting m and t, and a fair number were able to answer the remainder of the question.

STAGE 3.

Results : 1st Class, 76 ; 2nd Class, 104 ; Failed, 230 ; Total, 410.

Q. 41. The four parts (a), (b), (c), and (d) must all be answered to get full marks :—

    (a) Without using logarithms, compute by contracted methods, getting four significant figures *correct*,

$$87\cdot35 \div (0\cdot07568 \times 0\cdot3501).$$

    (b) Using logarithms compute

$$(0\cdot03524 \times 6\cdot321)^{-0\cdot256} \times 97\cdot43.$$

    (c) Explain why when we wish to divide numbers we substract their logarithms.

    (d) Write down the values of cos 110, sin 213, tan 264, $\sin^{-1}0\cdot3584$, $\cos^{-1}0\cdot6293$.

All the parts of this question were well answered. Only a few, however, used contracted multiplication when evaluating $-0\cdot256 \log (0\cdot03524 \times 6\cdot321)$, this being a case in which the contracted method is specially suited.

Q. 42. The annual cost of giving a certain amount of electric light to a certain town, the voltage being V and the candle power of each lamp C, is found to be

$$A = a + \frac{b}{V}$$

for electric energy and

$$B = \frac{m}{C} + n \frac{V^{\frac{4}{3}}}{C^{\frac{5}{3}}}$$

for lamp renewals.

The following figures are known when C is 10 :—

V	100	200	
A	1500	1200	Find a and b, m and n. If C is 20, what value of V will give minimum total cost ?
B	300	500	

Fairly often attempted. A satisfactory number were able to deal successfully with the numerical work involving fractional indices.

Q. 43. Find A if $2 \sin A + 3 \cos A = 3\cdot55$.

    There are two answers between 0° and 90°, and they must be obtained with no greater inaccuracy than one-fifth of a degree.

A popular question and well answered. Of those who adopted the graphical method the majority very properly enlarged the two portions of the general curve near to the point which gave the required roots, and thus ensured very great accuracy.

Q. 44. The basis of Simpson's rule is that if three successive equidistant ordinates (distant h apart), y_1, y_2, y_3, are drawn to any curve, the three points may be taken as lying on the curve

$$y = a + bx + cx^2.$$

Imagine y_2 to be the axis of y so that $-h$, y_1; 0, y_2, and h, y_3 are the three points. Substitute these values in the equation, and find a and c (b is not needed).

Integrate $a + bx + cx^2$ between the limits h and $-h$ and divide by $2h$; this gives the average value of y. Express it in terms of y_1, y_2, and y_3.

Well answered by a large number of the candidates.

Q. 45. If

$$L = t \frac{dp}{dt} c$$

where L is latent heat (in foot-pounds), t is absolute temperature Centigrade, p is pressure in pounds per square foot, c cubic feet is increase of volume if 1 lb. changes from lower to higher state.

Calculate c at $t = 428$, if the following numbers are given for steam. When $t = 428$, L is 497.2×1393.

t	p
413	7563
418	8698
423	9966
428	11380
433	12940
438	14680
443	16580

Note. $\frac{dp}{dt}$ is to be found as accurately as possible, using all the given numbers, and not using squared paper.

The answers showed a great improvement on those to a similar question set last year. The majority used one or other of several good approximate formulæ, involving successive differences, and there were comparatively few mistakes in the minus signs.

Q. 46. If a crank is at the angle θ from a dead point and $\theta = qt$ where q is angular velocity and t is time in seconds; if x is distance of piston in feet from the end of its stroke; if r is length of crank and l length of connecting rod, then, very nearly

$$x = r(1 - \cos\theta) + \frac{r^2}{4l}(1 - \cos 2\theta).$$

Find the acceleration y of the piston in terms of θ.

If $r = 1$ and $l = 5$, calculate x and y for the following values of θ, 0°, 45°, 90°, 135°, 180°. Plot the values of x and y as co-ordinates of points on squared paper.

There were many good answers, but a common mistake was to write $\frac{d^2x}{d\theta^2}$ instead of $\frac{d^2x}{dt^2}$ for the acceleration. And sometimes y and x were plotted as ordinates on a θ base, instead of the required curve connecting x and y.

Q. 47. If a cubic equation is of the form

$$ax^3 + bx^2 + cx + d = 0,$$

show how we can always reduce it to the form

$$x^3 + px + q = 0.$$

If we have the curve $y = x^3$ and the straight line $y = -px - q$ plotted on a sheet of paper, show that we have the real roots of the equation.

Seldom attempted, and the answers not often satisfactory. The first part was answered fairly well, but few good answers were given to the second part of the question.

Q. 48. Express

$$\frac{x + 19}{x^2 - 2x - 15}$$

as the sum of two simpler fractions and integrate.

A favourite question and very well answered.

Q. 49 Prove the rule for differentiating the product of two functions and deduce from it the rule for integrating by parts.

The reasoning was often very defective. For instance, in the expression $\delta y = u\,\delta v + v\,\delta u + \delta u\,\delta v$ it was common to proceed to the limit before dividing out by δx. Also such expressions as $\int u\,\dfrac{dv}{dx}$ were too frequent.

Q. 50. A closed curve rotates about a straight line in its own plane as an axis and so generates a ring. Prove the rule used for finding the volume of the ring.

Frequently attempted. The answers given were usually quite complete by those who knew Guldinus' rule. Others could only give the expression $\pi\int y^2\,dx$ as the answer.

Q. 51. Prove that in a triangle the ratio of two sides is equal to that of the sines of the opposite angles. Also prove that the area of a triangle is half the product of two sides and the sine of the angle between them.

A favourite question. A common fault was to establish the propositions for an acute angled triangle, without any reference to obtuse or right angled triangles.

Q. 52. If t seconds is the *record* time of a race of y yards; the law $t = cy^n$ seems to be wonderfully true for all races of men and animals excepting men on bicycles; n is the same number in all cases. c has a special value in each case, men walking, running, skating, swimming, or rowing; horses trotting or galloping or pacing.

    (1) For any particular kind of race it is found that when y is increased by 100 per cent., t is increased by 118 per cent ; find n.

    (2) For men running, when $y = 600$, t is 71 ; find c in the above formula. Express s, the average speed of each race, in terms of y.

    (3) Assume that an animal has a certain amount of endurance E which is exhausted at a uniform rate during the race and that $E = E_0 + kt$ where E_0 and k are constants. Calling E/t the rate of fatigue f, express this in terms of s.

Assuming that an animal going at s_0 miles per hour feels no fatigue, or when $s = s_0$, $f = 0$; find f in terms of s.

Not often attempted and badly answered. In (1) the 118 per cent. increase gave trouble, many giving an answer which would have been correct for 18 per cent. In (2), $\dfrac{dy}{dt}$ instead of $\dfrac{y}{t}$ was often used for the *average* speed. Nearly everyone gave up the attempt before reaching the end.

Q. 53. The curve $y = a + be^{cx}$ passes through the three points $x = 0$, $y = 3$; $x = 3$, $y = 4\cdot5$; $x = 7$, $y = 9\cdot5$; find a, b and c. What is $\frac{dy}{dx}$ at the point where $x = 3$? It may save time if it

is known that c lies between the values $0\cdot2$ and $0\cdot3$.

Fairly often attempted, but usually very quickly abandoned. There were only one or two good answers. Sometimes the value of be^{cx} when $x = 0$ was thought to be zero; this gave at once $a = 3$, and the solution then proceeded merrily. The mistake log. $y =$ log. $a + cx$ log. be was sometimes met with.

Q. 54. If compound interest at r per cent. per annum were payable every instant and if at any time t (years) the principal is P, show that

$$\frac{dP}{dt} = \frac{Pr}{100}$$

Express P in terms of r and t.

In what time will P double itself for any value of r?

The answers to this question were fairly satisfactory, a number of complete solutions being given.

GROUP III.—PHYSICS.

BOARD OF EXAMINERS.

VIII. Sound, Light, and Heat
VIII.a. Sound
VIII.b. Light
VIII.c. Heat
IX. Magnetism and Electricity
XXIII. Physiography
(Section 1 only of Stage 1)

Professor H. L. Callendar, M.A., LL.D.,
F.R.S., *Chairman.*
Professor F. T. Trouton, D.Sc., F.R.S.
Professor A. W. Reinold, M.A., F.R.S.
W. Watson, D.Sc., F.R.S.

Report on the Examinations in Sound, Light, and Heat.

EVENING EXAMINATIONS.

STAGE 1.

Results : 1st Class, 130 ; 2nd Class, 147 ; Failed, 119 ; Total, 396.

The answering of this paper must be considered as fairly good on the whole, though not quite up to the average of previous years.

SOUND.

Q. 1. What evidence can you adduce to show that sound is due to vibrations, and that it is transmitted to us through matter.

Candidates in giving the experiment of a bell ringing in vacuum should not omit explaining the very necessary acoustical insulation of the bell.

Q. 2. Explain, from the principle of the conservation of energy, why it is that the voice carries so much further through a tube than in the open air.

This question was one of the least satisfactorily answered. Very few referred properly to the question of energy. Some seemed to think that the enfeebling of the sound depends on the energy getting " used up."

Q. 3. Distinguish between longitudinal and transverse vibrations and give examples of both.

The examples given should be such as can be seen. Thus to give sound waves as an example of longitudinal vibrations is not quite what was expected. A considerable number of candidates believe that the disturbance in a tuning fork is a longitudinal one.

Q. 4. What is the velocity of propagation of sound if the wave length of a note of frequency 100 is 11 feet ? Give reasons for your answer.

In most cases the reasons asked for were well given.

LIGHT.

Q. 5. How are the positions of object and image related in the case of a convex lens ? Distinguish the cases in which the image is real from those in which it is virtual.

A large number of candidates treated this question as if it had been one on mirrors, and some spoke of a point 2 f. from the lens as the " centre of curvature." A few also showed the image as located at the intersection of rays *from different points* in the image, thus getting a real image nearer in than the principal focus.

Q. 6. How would you make experiments to test the manner in which the intensity of the light received at a point varies with its distance from the source ?

Many gave instead of an experiment a deduction from the facts of the conservation of energy and the increase in area with the square of the distance of corresponding illuminated sections.

Q. 7. A horizontal beam of light falls normally on a vertical mirror and is reflected. If the mirror is rotated through 30° about a vertical · axis, show in what direction the beam will now be reflected.

The word " show " seems to have been a cause of trouble. Many gave only a diagram. Diagrams are most desirable for supplementing and shortening written description, but not as a complete substitute for it. Few mentioned that the reflected ray is in the horizontal plane.

Q. 8. Describe the formation of an image by a pin-hole camera. By the help of a diagram show the conditions necessary that the images of two points of light in the object should be just separate.

Very few understood that the image of a point cannot be a point, and spoke of " one ray " only passing through a pin hole, consequently misunderstanding what was meant by the latter part of the question.

HEAT.

Q. 9. What is meant by the coefficient of linear expansion of a solid with a rise in temperature ? Describe any method for measuring it.

It should be noted that heating the bar directly with a Bunsen burner is not a correct method for obtaining a uniform temperature in a bar for purposes of measurement.

Q. 10. Explain the term latent heat of liquefaction. Calculate how many pounds of ice at 0° C. must be added to a thousand pounds of water in order to cool it from 30° C. to 15° C. (The latent heat may be taken as 79.)

Candidates should explain when asked to do so and not reel off a parrot-like definition.

Q. 11. What is meant by the vapour pressure of a liquid ? How is the boiling point affected by change of pressure ?

Many candidates' notions of vapour pressure were vague. The second part involves a short explanation of the meaning of boiling point.

Q. 12. Distinguish between the transference of heat by conduction, convection, and radiation, giving two examples of each.

This question was attempted by nearly all the candidates and was fairly well done by most. The knowledge of radiation was, however, rather meagre.

SOUND.

Stage 2.

Results : 1st Class, 91 ; 2nd Class, 159 ; Failed, 70 ; Total, 320.

Although there were not many exceptionally good papers, the answers were, on the whole, good, rather more than half the candidates obtaining above half marks.

Q. 1. What is meant by the term *temperament* of a musical scale ?

Explain carefully the necessity for temperament, and describe the system ordinarily employed.

Most of those who attempted this question had only a vague idea of the meaning of temperament, and failed to explain clearly the necessity for it

Q. 2. Describe the stroboscopic disc method of measuring the frequency of a tuning fork.

If there are 8 dots in the ring which appears stationary, and the disc makes 52 revolutions per second, what is the pitch of the fork? If the fork is then heated the ring of dots appears to move slowly backwards at the rate of one revolution in ten seconds. What is the change in pitch of the fork due to the heating?

Answers to the first two parts were good, but in a large number of cases a *decrease* of pitch was given as answer to the third part, instead of an *increase*.

Q. 3. What is meant by the interference of sound waves?

Describe an experiment showing the interference of waves, and explain how it may be used to measure the wave-length of the note employed.

The knowledge of the candidates with regard to interference was limited. There was a tendency to give it a very restricted meaning.

Q. 4. Give the laws governing the transverse vibrations of strings. The density of steel wire being 7·7 and that of copper wire 8·9, what must be the ratio of the diameters of two wires, one steel and the other copper, of equal length, so that when stretched by the same force they may give the same note?

These laws were, on the whole, stated very well, and the example was, in most cases, worked out correctly.

Q. 5. What data are necessary for the calculation of the velocity of sound in a gas?

Explain carefully the necessity for the various terms in the expression for the velocity.

The formula for the velocity was usually quoted correctly, but the necessity for the introduction of γ was not well explained. Many candidates made no reference to the effect of temperature.

Q. 6. Describe the construction and operation of a phonograph or gramophone.

This calls for no special comment.

Q. 7. Explain carefully the character of the reflexion of a sound wave at the end of a rod according as the end is fixed or free to move.

Apparently this was beyond most of the candidates, as it was attempted with little success by a small number.

Q. 8. Explain the terms : *stress, strain, coefficient of elasticity.*

Calculate the diameter of a wire 3 metres long which, when stretched by a weight of 10 kilograms is lengthened by 2·5 millimetres, the coefficient of longitudinal elasticity being 10^{12}.

The explanation of terms was poor. In the numerical example, g was omitted by the large majority.

Q. 9. How is it that a tube of given length, such as an organ pipe or bugle, may be made to give different notes according to the way in which it is blown?

Describe how the mode of vibration of the air in a long pipe can be experimentally demonstrated.

The explanations in the first part were not clear. The second part was, however, well done, but a common mistake was to suppose that Koenig's manometric flames would respond at all places *except* the nodes.

STAGE 3.

Results : 1st Class, 3 ; 2nd Class, 12 ; Failed, 30 ; Total, 45.

The chief characteristic of the papers was the extremely disjointed manner in which the various facts were set out in the answers. Very few candidates seem to have spent any time considering how best the results they were describing ought to be grouped so as to make an intelligible and logical answer. The following remarks on the individual questions may be of assistance to teachers :—

Q. 1. Discuss the formation of overtones in the case of tuning forks.

The answers to this question were very poor, not above second stage standard.

Q. 2. Describe the electric method of maintaining the vibrations of a tuning fork. Why does not the attraction oppose the motion of the fork in one direction as much as it assists it in the other ? For what investigations is the method applicable ?

The first part of this question was, in general, well answered. The effect of self-induction was often correctly stated, but the explanations were very brief and wanting in clearness.

Q. 3. Give some account of the determinations which have been made of the velocity of sound in the open air, detailing how the difficulties in connection with the receiver were avoided.

Fairly well answered.

Q. 4. Lord Rayleigh has devised a form of horizontal trumpet for use with lighthouse sirens in which the mouth of the trumpet instead of being circular is lengthened in the vertical direction. This is in order to improve the hearing at sea. Explain the action.

No correct answers were given, the principle of the Rayleigh fog-horn being apparently quite unknown.

Q. 5. Towards the lower end of a vertical tube a transverse grid, made of thin platinum wire, is placed : when the wire is heated by an electric current a note is sounded by the tube. Explain this.

A few fairly complete answers were given. The majority, however, were very poor, many saying that the explanation was the same as in the case of the singing flame, and then proceeding to describe the latter.

Q. 6. It has been noticed that when a reed is supplied with air through tubes of certain lengths it will not " speak." Discuss the cause of this.

Hardly ever attempted, and no really satisfactory answers were given.

Q. 7. Two similar sources of sound are maintained in the same phase at a distance of 40 centimetres apart. If the wave-length is 4 centimetres, describe the nature of the interference produced at points on a line parallel to that joining the sources and at a distance of 2 metres, and explain how you would investigate the effects experimentally.

Fairly well answered, though many candidates assumed that the wave-length was so small compared to the distances involved that the approximations which are usually made in the case of light-waves would hold.

HONOURS.

Result : 1st Class, — ; 2nd Class, — ; Failed, 1 ; Total, 1.

There was only one candidate, who did not do well enough to justify further examination.

126 GROUP III.—PHYSICS.

LIGHT.

STAGE 2.

Results: 1st Class, 63; 2nd Class, 211; Failed, 123; Total, 397.

Candidates generally exhibited considerable familiarity with book knowledge, but many of them showed little acquaintance with apparatus.

Q. 1. Describe one method by which the velocity of light has been directly measured.

Fairly well answered. Many, however, gave an astronomical method of computing the velocity, which was frequently described erroneously.

Q. 2. Describe and explain the use of the sextant. How are the scale and the vernier usually graduated?

Answered well on the whole.

Q. 3. Explain the method of using a diffraction grating, and describe how the spectra produced differ from prismatic spectra.

Many candidates seemed to think that the diffraction grating series of spectra was analogous to the interference bands produced by a biprism.

Q. 4. Draw a curve showing how the angle of refraction of light on entering a transparent substance varies as the angle of incidence increases from 0° to 90°.

Few had any idea of the form of the curve, or appreciated the fact that it becomes parallel to the surface as the critical angle is approached.

Q. 5. Describe the methods which have been employed to observe the infra red spectrum.

When attempted, which was seldom, this question was generally well answered.

Q. 6. Find an expression for the focal length of a lens in terms of the radii of curvature of its surfaces. How is the expression modified if the lens is placed in a medium other than air?

This was not well answered. Candidates should not assume as known the formula for the refraction at a single spherical surface.

Q. 7. Explain how an astronomical telescope may be used for obtaining a magnified image of the sun on a screen. Find the size of the image at a distance of 1 foot from the eye lens, if the focal lengths of the objective and eyepiece are 3 feet and 2 inches respectively, assuming that the sun's angular diameter is half a degree.

There were few correct answers to this question. In many cases it was stated that a virtual image could be received on a screen.

Q. 8. Describe the construction of a spectrometer, and explain how it should be adjusted for measuring refractive indices.

One of the best answered questions. The focussing of the collimator and telescope for parallel rays should be described, not assumed.

Q. 9. The image of a candle reflected in a horizontal glass plate is observed through a slice of tourmaline. Explain carefully how the brightness of the image depends on the angle of reflection and how it varies as the tourmaline is rotated.

Poorly answered on the whole. Candidates seemed unfamiliar with the variation of the intensities of the two polarised components of a reflected beam for various angles of incidence.

STAGE 3.

Results: 1st Class, 6; 2nd Class, 15; Failed, 16; Total, 37.

The results of this examination show nearly the same standard of attainment as last year. The number of candidates was nearly the same, and the proportion of successes and failures very similar. The proportion of failures is still somewhat excessive, and suggests that candidates are allowed to enter without sufficient preparation or ability to master the subject. The following criticisms are suggested with regard to the separate questions.

Q. 1. On what does the resolving power of a spectroscope depend?
Explain how the purity of a spectrum may be estimated.

Many of the candidates were unacquainted with the theory of resolving power, and confused the question of the dispersion with it. The second part was attempted by only a few.

Q. 2. Describe carefully the so-called anomalous dispersion of light, and discuss the theories of the phenomenon which have been proposed.

On the whole, the first part of this question was well answered, and several gave good answers to the second part.

Q. 3. Explain how the angle between the axes of a biaxal crystal may be determined.

This question was attempted by very few, and generally unsucessfully.

Q. 4. Explain how the mechanical pressure of radiation arises, and give a short account of the experimental work which has been done on this subject.

The answers to this question afforded a curious object lesson of the futility of much of the modern teaching commonly known as "cramming." Candidates who had a familiarity with the details of the experimental researches which have been done of recent years on the subject were under the impression that the pressure is produced by normal impact of particles.

Q. 5. Explain carefully how to determine the principal points of a photographic lens.

This was generally attempted by the candidates, but, on the whole, was not well answered.

Q. 6. Describe some form of interferometer, and explain its uses and method of adjustment.

This question was the best answered in the paper. The diagrams were often, however, rather vaguely drawn.

Q. 7. Describe and explain the appearances presented when a thin slice of mica is rotated between crossed nicols.

This question was very generally attempted, but the phenomenon was frequently confused with that of the rotation of polarised light.

HONOURS.

Result: 1st Class, —; 2nd Class, 1; Failed, —; Total, 1.

One candidate did fairly well in both theoretical papers, but showed little knowledge of practical work.

HEAT.

STAGE 2.

Results: 1st Class, 79; 2nd Class, 415; Failed, 173; Total, 667.

The paper, as a whole, was poorly answered. The percentage of failures was rather higher than last year, and there was a much smaller proportion of good papers. Little knowledge was shown of accurate experimental work, and the numerical examples were carelessly done. Many marks were lost by want of practice in elementray physical arithmetic.

Q. 1. Describe a method of measuring the coefficient of linear expansion of a metal between 0° and 100° C.

A metre scale, for which α = ·000011, is tested at 0°C., and found to be shorter than the standard by half a millimetre. What error in metres would be involved in the measurement of a distance of 200 kilometres by this scale at 20°C.?

The methods described were often very rough and quite unsuited for accurate measurement.

Q. 2. Describe carefully the method you would employ to determine the specific heat of metallic copper in small pieces with simple apparatus, and explain how the result is calculated.

The answers seldom went beyond the elementary stage. Few showed any knowledge of the corrections required for water equivalent of the calorimeter, or loss of heat by radiation.

Q. 3. Describe a simple form of constant pressure gas thermometer, and explain how you would use it for measuring temperature.

Many candidates described the constant volume method. Others gave a large bulb with a fine capillary tube and a mercury index. Very few made any allowance for the difference of temperature between the bulb and the air in the overflow reservoir, even when the correct type of instrument was described.

Q. 4. Explain why a gas cools on expansion, and show how to calculate the expansion required to cool a mass of air 1°C. if no heat is supplied.

One third of the candidates made no mention of external work. The second half of the question was seldom attempted with success.

Q. 5. Describe how the latent heat of vaporisation of a liquid has been determined at pressures above and below the atmospheric pressure.

Very little was known of determinations of latent heat at pressures differing from atmospheric ; and even at atmospheric pressure the methods were not well described.

Q. 6. If the vapour pressure of water at 0°C. is 4·6 mm., find the dew point for air of humidity 40 per cent. at 20°C., assuming that the vapour pressure is doubled for each 10°C. rise in temperature.

Most of the candidates found the correct value of the vapour pressure, but assumed a straight line formula for deducing the temperature.

Q. 7. How is the freezing point of a substance affected by change of pressure? Illustrate your answer by reference to phenomena observed in the case of ice.

The general effect of pressure was often given correctly, but many of the candidates were acquainted only with the case of ice.

Q. 8. How is the emissive power of a surface related to its power of absorbing radiant heat? Describe experiments by which the relation may be tested.

The answers were generally qualitative, and the experiments described were of the same character. A few defined emissive and absorptive powers correctly and answered the question well.

Q. 9. If the mechanical equivalent of heat is 777 foot-pounds per British thermal unit, find the value in ergs per gram-calorie if the acceleration of gravity is 981 C.G.S.

Seldom attempted. Many of the mistakes were due to careless work, or to writing down a lot of figures without any order or explanation.

STAGE 3.

Results : 1st Class, 17 ; 2nd Class, 46 ; Failed, 51 ; Total, 114.

It appeared from the answers to some of the questions that too much attention had been paid in many cases to experimental details, and that the candidates had failed to grasp fundamental principles. The questions involving thermodynamics were comparatively easy, but the answers betrayed general weakness. There were few really good papers, and a large proportion of very poor ones, but the standard, on the whole, showed a slight improvement on last year. Many of the candidates, who seemed to possess some knowledge of the subject, were so deficient in power of expression, owing to lack of general education, that they were unable to do themselves justice. The following remarks apply to the several questions.

Q. 1. Describe the general type of deviation of a gas or vapour from Boyle's law, and explain the principles on which it has been sought to obtain an expression to represent more completely the behaviour of substances under changes of temperature and pressure.

This was a very favourite question, but the answers were often too vague. It was not sufficient to say that gases deviated from Boyle's law at temperatures below their critical points, or at high pressures. The type or manner of deviation should have been shown by curves, preferably by plotting pv against p for various temperatures.

Q. 2. Discuss the sudden variations in the thickness of soap films which have been observed in the region of the black spot.

This question was seldom attempted, and few of the candidates showed much knowledge of the subject.

Q. 3. Explain the theory of the method of determining conductivity by observing the distribution of temperature in a bar along which heat is passing, and describe the experimental details necessary for carrying it out.

The majority of the candidates described Forbes' well-known method, but failed to indicate clearly how the quantity of heat transmitted was deduced from the observations.

Q. 4. Explain why in certain saturated vapours compression produces condensation while in others expansion does so.

There were several good answers to this question, but many of the candidates misunderstood it, and none gave the thermodynamical relation between the specific heat of the vapour in the state of saturation and the latent heat.

Q. 5. Describe the phenomena of the freezing of an aqueous solution of a substance such as NaCl. What is a cryohydrate ? Discuss the evidence as to its structure.

Few of the candidates correctly described the case of a solution saturated with NaCl, or showed that the cryohydric point corresponded with the intersection of the solubility and freezing-point curves.

Q. 6. How would you estimate the temperature of a gas flame in air from a knowledge of the composition of the gas ? How would you measure the temperature practically ?

Many of the methods suggested for measuring the temperature of a gas flame, such as the copper ball pyrometer, were most inadequate. Very few realised the difficulty of raising the pyrometer to the actual temperature of the flame, or made any suggestions to correct for radiation loss.

Q. 7. State and explain Carnot's principle, and show how it is employed as the foundation of the absolute scale of temperature.

As a general rule, Carnot's cycle was described, without any clear statement or explanation of the principle. The essential points were obscured in a multitude of unnecessary details.

Honours.

Result : 1st Class, — ; 2nd Class, — ; Failed, 1 ; Total, 1.

One candidate showed some knowledge of practical and descriptive work, but failed entirely in the higher branches of the theory.

Day Examinations.

Stage 1.

Results : 1st Class, 16 ; 2nd Class, 42 ; Failed, 44 ; Total, 102.

The papers were very poorly done on the whole, with the exception of one or two sets, which showed evidence of good teaching.

SOUND.

Q. 1. Explain the terms *pitch* and *wave-length* of a note, and show how to deduce the wave-length if the pitch is given.

The exact definition of pitch was seldom given, and a lack of diagrams prevented wave-length being clearly defined.

Q. 2. How would you show by experiment that the time of vibration of a spring fixed at one end is independent of the amplitude.

Attempted by very few, and apparently not understood.

Q. 3. Enumerate the principal points of difference between waves travelling over the surface of water and sound waves propagated through it.

Also attempted by few. Difference of type usually alone given, differences of velocity and direction being omitted.

LIGHT.

Q. 5. How does the clearness of the image in a pinhole camera depend on the size of the pinhole, and on its distance from the screen ? In what respect is the image inferior to that produced by a lens ?

Candidates again failed to make their meaning clear by omitting to give diagrams.

Q. 6. The shadows of a vertical rod on a wall, at equal distances of 2 feet each from the rod, cast by two gas flames are observed to be equally dark when the flames are at distances of 6 and 4 feet respectively from the rod. Compare the illuminating powers of the flames.

Here many candidates simply wrote down the answer, probably because they did not understand the application of the "inverse square" law.

Q. 7. State the law of the reflection of light. A small object is placed at the centre of curvature of a concave mirror ; find the size and the position of the image.

Many candidates omitted to state that the incident ray, the normal, and the reflected ray were in one plane. A number stated that the incident and reflected rays were in the same plane. This, of course, does not define the direction of the reflected ray.

HEAT.

Q. 9. Explain how the fixed points of a mercury thermomenter are tested.

Well done on the whole. Only a few, however, mentioned the fact that the boiling point varies with change of atmospheric pressure.

Q. 10. Distinguish between real and apparent expansion of a liquid. Draw a curve showing the nature of the apparent expansion of water in a glass bulb from 0° to 100° C.

The curve given was in every case the *real* expansion curve. This was not asked for.

Q. 11. How would you show that the quantity of heat required to raise a pound of water from 10° to 20° C. is nearly equal to that required to raise it from 20° to 30° C. ?

Only attempted by a few. Most of these did not grasp the point of the question.

Q. 12. A glass of hot water is placed on a table. Enumerate and explain the various ways in which it loses heat.

Radiation, convection and conduction were usually given correctly, but the loss by evaporation was given by a small number only.

SOUND.

Stage 2.

Results : 1st Class, 5 ; 2nd Class, 7 ; Failed, 5 ; Total, 17.

The paper was answered fairly on the whole, but the number of candidates was too small to permit any general conclusions of value to be drawn.

Q. 1. Explain carefully what is meant by the statement that the motion of a simple pendulum is a simple harmonic motion if the amplitude is small.

Enumerate and explain the quantities which define a simple harmonic motion.

Poorly done. Harmonic motion was regarded, in some cases, as being any kind of motion which was " backward and forward."

Q. 2. What is meant by the elasticity of a gas ?

Deduce the value of the elasticity from Boyle's law, and explain how the elasticity differs from this value when the gas is rapidly expanded or compressed.

Very well done.

Q. 3. How does the velocity of propagation of a transverse disturbance along a stretched string depend on the mass and tension of the string ? Deduce the time of vibration of a string of given length fixed at both ends.

The method of proof given was obviously not understood. The candidates apparently were writing down equations from memory, without knowing the physical reason of the validity of the equations.

Q. 5. What is meant by the interval between two musical notes ? If the frequency of the note C is 256 and that of E 320, find the frequency of a note at an equal interval from either.

A very easy question which was answered well.

Q. 6. What are the possible modes of vibration of the air in a pipe closed at one end ? Describe how the motion of the air at any point of such a tube may be experimentally demonstrated.

Well done on the whole.

Q. 8. How would you compare the velocities of sound (*a*) in two different gases, (*b*) in the same gas at different temperatures?

Method given usually correct, but very badly described. Little mention of details and necessary precautions was contained in the answers.

132 GROUP III.—PHYSICS.

Q. 9. Describe and explain the phenomena of stationary waves produced by reflection of a train of waves at a fixed obstacle. How may the phenomena be demonstrated in the case of sound waves in air?

Not well done. In a number of cases the diagrams indicated a displacement of the medium at the obstacle at which reflection occurred.

LIGHT.

STAGE 2.

Results : 1st Class, 5 ; 2nd Class, 12 ; Failed, 15 ; Total, 32.

This paper was poorly answered on the whole, but the number of candidates was so small that no conclusions of much value can be drawn.

Q. 1. Define refractive index.
Find the position of the image of an object below the surface of water seen by direct refraction. How does the position of the image appear to change if the refraction is oblique?

Poorly answered in the case of oblique refraction.

Q. 2. Explain, with the aid of a diagram, how a right angled prism is used for erecting an image formed by a convex lens. In what way does the image so erected differ from the object?

The diagrams were seldom clear, and the perversion of the image was usually ignored.

Q. 3. Explain the formation of Newton's rings by transmitted light at normal incidence. Prove that the difference of the squares of the radii of successive rings is constant.

Seldom attempted, and not well answered.

Q. 4. When an object is placed at a distance of 15 cms. from a converging lens the image formed on a screen is found to be twice the size of the object. Find the focal length of the lens.

There was a good deal of confusion of signs in applying the formula.

Q. 5. What is meant by the term complementary colour? Explain how the complementary colour to a given green paper may be determined.

The use of the colour top was not understood.

Q. 6. Describe two methods by which the image seen through a telescope may be erected. What are the advantages or disadvantages of either method?

The advantages of the various possible methods were not understood.

Q. 7. A prism of Iceland spar cut with its refracting edge parallel to the optic axis of the crystal is cemented to a glass prism of equal angle so as to form a plate. Describe and explain the appearances seen by an observer looking through the plate at a source of light.

Seldom attempted. Answers very incomplete.

Q. 8. Describe the observations and explain the argument by which Römer deduced the velocity of light in space.

The actual observations and inferences were not clearly described or understood.

Q. 9. Describe the optical arrangements of a single prism spectroscope, and draw the paths of rays which form the red and blue images of the slit.

The diagrams of rays were usually very poor.

HEAT.

Stage 2.

Results : 1st Class, 13 ; 2nd Class, 46 ; Failed, 39 ; Total, 98.

There was a higher percentage of failures than last year.

A large portion of the subject seems to be neglected altogether. Only a small proportion of the candidates attempted seven questions. Many of the mistakes in the arithmetical work were due to untidiness.

Q. 1. Describe how the fixed points of a mercury thermometer may be tested.

A thermometer of uniform bore reads + 0·5° in melting ice, and 100·8° in steam at normal pressure. What is the temperature when the thermometer indicates 20° C. ?

A large number of correct diagrams of a hypsometer were given without any reasons for its shape. Many candidates found the temperature given by the thermometer when the true temperature was 20° C.

Q. 2. Describe carefully a method of determining the true coefficient of expansion of air at constant pressure, stating the most essential precautions to be observed.

Many inaccurate forms of constant pressure thermometers were given. Only one or two knew how to calculate the result from the measured overflow volume in Regnault's form of apparatus.

Q. 3. What is the characteristic difference between the isothermal curves of a gas and a vapour on the indicator or p. v. diagram? Illustrate your answer by sketching the isothermals for air and steam at 100° C.

Very few knew anything about the question.

Q. 4 Define latent heat of vaporisation.

Steam at 100° C. (Latent Heat 537) is passed into a vessel containing 1 kilogram of ice at 0° C. (Latent Heat 80) until the ice is just melted. Find the weight of water formed.

The temperature (or pressure) at which vaporisation takes place should be stated. No candidate mentioned this.

Q. 5. If the vapour-pressure at the dewpoint is 10 mm., and the density of aqueous vapour is ⅝ths of that of air at the same temperature and pressure, find the weight of water in a cubic litre of air at 20° C. and 760 mm., taking the density of air at 0° and 760 mm. as 1·293 gm. per litre.

Not often attempted, and the answers obtained were not clearly put down.

Q. 6. Explain what is meant by thermal emissivity.

Find approximately the thermal emissivity of a block of iron 1 cm. cube, specific heat ·120, and density 8, if it takes five minutes to cool from 60° to 50° C., in an enclosure at 0° C.

Many candidates took unit mass of the substance instead of unit surface. Few knew the meaning of emissivity.

Q. 7. If the ratio of the specific heat of air at constant pressure to the specific heat at constant volume is 1·40, find the rise of temperature produced in a mass of air at a pressure p, when suddenly compressed by $\frac{1}{11}$rds of its volume at 0° C.

Very few attempts. Of these, most obtained the expression for the temperature but were unable to evaluate it.

Q. 8. Find the external work in kilogram metres done in vaporising 1 gm. of water at 100° C. if the volume of the steam produced is 1675 c.c., and the density of mercury is 13·596 at 0° C.

Seldom attempted for so easy a question.

Q. 9. How is thermal conductivity defined and measured ?

Find the difference of temperature between the two sides of a boiler plate 2 cm. thick, conductivity 0·20 C.G.S., when it is transmitting heat at the rate of 600 kilogram calories per sq. metre per minute.

Most of the candidates gave no account of the *measurement* of conductivity. Only two had any idea of how to measure the heat conducted across any section in Forbes' method.

Report on the Examinations in Magnetism and Electricity.

Evening Examination.

Stage 1.

Results : 1st Class, 870 ; 2nd Class, 583 ; Failed, 566 ; Total, 2,019.

The paper was, on the whole, well done, the number of failures being relatively small. " Voltaic Electricity " was the weakest section.

Some details respecting the answers to the questions are appended :—

Magnetism.

Q. 1. An unmagnetised bar of soft iron is laid on a horizontal table in a north and south direction ; what is its magnetic state ?

How will its magnetic state be altered if the end of the bar which is towards the north is raised until the bar is vertical ?

The majority stated that the polarity would be reversed when the bar was vertical, but few recognized that between the horizontal and vertical positions there was one in which the bar would be unmagnetised. A good many took cognizance only of the horizontal force and thought the bar would be transversely magnetised when vertical. Attempts at diagrams of the lines of force were generally failures.

Q. 2. Explain carefully how you would magnetize a strip of steel, so that one end, marked A, may become a north pole. Give reasons for the various operations you would perform.

Although three or four methods were frequently described, the reasons asked for in the second part of the question were as frequently omitted. In applying the molecular theory of magnetism it should always be clearly stated that the molecules of iron are assumed to be magnets. Many students rotated the molecules without any reference to, or implication of, this fact.

Q. 3. A steel rod when tested is found to have a north pole at each end. What would you expect the magnetic condition of the intermediate portion to be, and how would you test your prediction ?

Generally well done, but the possibility of a number of consequent poles was not often thought of. It was generally assumed that the (single) consequent south pole must be at the centre of the bar. Many suggested breaking the rod as the only test. The fracture test is bad in any case and might disprove the prediction.

Q. 4. Define dip, horizontal component of the earth's field.

If at a place A the vertical component is found to be half the horizontal component, what is the value of the dip ? At what part of the earth's surface would you expect A to be situated ?

Very few candidates attempted this question, when attempted it was generally well done.

Frictional Electricity.

Q. 5. Describe a gold-leaf electroscope.

> When a charged rod of sealing wax is held at a certain distance from an electroscope the leaves diverge ; they fall when the cap of the electroscope is momentarily touched, and diverge again when the sealing wax is removed. Explain these results.

Well done by those who adhered strictly to the old "two fluid" nomenclature. Those who discoursed of potential generally made grievous blunders. The explanations based on changes of potential or Faraday tubes are difficult and should be introduced at this stage to supplement rather than to replace the more elementary explanation. This criticism applies especially to the Faraday tubes ; in a number of cases they were correctly drawn, but there was no suggestion why they should do the things they were assumed to do. On the other hand the potential candidates as often as not ignored the matter of charges entirely.

Q. 6. A point is said to discharge electricity ; describe three experiments in which such discharge takes place.

In the "electric wind" experiment the electricity was thought to blow the candle flame away ; what really occurs was seldom explained. Among the large number who mentioned the lightning conductor there was only one who admitted that lightning is scarcely an experiment.

Q. 7. How did Faraday show that the energy of a charged Leyden jar resides in the dielectric ?

The experiment of the dissected Leyden jar was correctly described by a large number, but discharge on re-assembling the parts was frequently omitted. Most of the answers proved too much, it being stated that the inner coating of the jar after removal by an insulator would not affect an electroscope.

Q. 8. A hollow insulated metal sphere contains two small insulated spheres, one charged with 2 units, and the other with 3 units of positive electricity. What will the consequent charge be on (a) the outside and (b) the inside of the hollow sphere.

Was answered by comparatively few and with less success than any question in the section. A large proportion stated that there would be no charge inside the sphere.

Q. 9. Describe the electrophorus and explain carefully how it acts.

Well answered on the whole.

Voltaic Electricity.

Q. 10. What is meant by local action in a voltaic cell ?

> Why is such action objectionable, and how may it be prevented ?

Confusion with polarisation was the commonest mistake, but it was not often made. Many answers which obtained marks failed to state clearly that local action causes consumption of zinc, even when the main circuit is broken ; and many seemed to think that the impurities, carbon and iron for instance, formed little cells by themselves.

Q. 11. A small compass needle is suspended at the centre of a vertical copper ring through which a current is passed. How is the needle affected by the current (1) when the ring is in the magnetic meridian, and (2) when it is at right angles to the magnetic meridian.

> What are the the forces acting on the needle in each case ?

A large number of ambiguous diagrams. Very few candidates noticed (in the second case) that the current might be strong enough to cause the needle to point south instead of north. Ignorance of mechanics was responsible for much vagueness of expression.

Q. 12. Describe an astatic system for a galvanometer, and explain carefully the reason for using such a system, and how the coils of the galvanometer are arranged with reference to the magnets composing the system.

This question was tried by nearly all, but was not well done. The necessity for fixing the needles in one plane was frequently overlooked, and the reasons for using the combination rarely given with clearness.

Q. 13. How does the heat produced by a current depend upon the strength of the current?

Describe how you would experimentally prove the relation.

Not often tried. Those who knew the formula C^2Rt were often unable to make use of it.

Q. 14. A cell having an E.M.F. of two volts and a resistance of 0·5 ohm is connected up with three lengths of wire having resistances of 1, 2, and 3 ohms respectively, the wires being in series. Find the difference in potential between the ends of the middle wire.

Of those who attempted this question (they were not many) a fair proportion got out the current correctly but could go no further. Others obtained different values of the current in different parts of the circuit.

STAGE 2.

Results : 1st Class, 327 ; 2nd Class, 463 ; Failed, 324 ; Total, 1,114.

The answers to this paper were, on the whole, decidedly better than last year. The proportion of failures was smaller, and that of good papers higher. There were, however, a number of bad mistakes prevalent, and even among the good papers a correct knowledge of the theory in application to practice was often lacking. Those who had studied the subject from the practical side chiefly, were, as usual, very weak on the theory, and often failed in the first two sections of the paper. The following criticisms apply to the separate questions.

Magnetism.

Q. 1. Two magnets are placed in an aluminium frame with their axes horizontal and parallel, one being vertically over the other. The frame is suspended and oscillates in the earth's horizontal field, making 20 and 5 vibrations per minute respectively when similar poles of the magnets are together or opposed. If the moment of the stronger magnet is 300, what is that of the other?

This question was answered correctly by many candidates, but some proceeded on the assumption that the number of oscillations in a certain time was proportional to the magnetic moment.

Q. 2. Describe the effects of variation in temperature on (a) a magnetised piece of steel and (b) a piece of soft iron in a magnetic field.

Beyond the fact that those who attempted this question knew that iron and steel lose their magnetic properties at high temperatures the answers were poor.

Q. 3. How would you compare the moment of a given magnet with that of a given solenoid carrying a given current?

This question was answered unsatisfactorily. Some candidates described a magnetometer method but the lengths of the magnet and solenoid were often ignored, and the "distances" were sometimes measured from the end of the magnet (or solenoid) to the needle and sometimes from the centre. When oscillation methods were described, very little was said with regard to the practical details in the case of the solenoid ; and the moment of inertia was often omitted.

Q. 4. Define a unit magnetic pole.
Describe an experiment to show that two unit poles repel each other with a force which varies inversely as the square of the distance between them.

First part well answered. In the second part most of the candidates stated that the force (on unit pole) at a point on the axis of a magnet produced was inversely proportional to the square of the distance.

Frictional Electricity.

Q. 5. Two copper spheres, each 1 millimetre in diameter, are suspended from the same point by silk fibres 1 metre long, and when equally charged are at a distance of 1 centimetre from centre to centre. Determine the charge on each sphere, the density of copper being 8·9 and the acceleration of gravity 980.

A curious mistake was prevalent in the answers to this question. The candidates often stated that the repulsion between the two charged spheres was equal to $\frac{Q^2}{d^2}$ and that therefore the force acting upon each sphere was equal to $\frac{2Q^2}{d^2}$. Arithmetical mistakes were numerous.

Q. 6. Two Leyden jars, each having a capacity of 1,000 centimetres, are charged in series to a difference of potential of 10 electro static units. Calculate the energy of discharge and state in what units it is expressed.

This question was not well answered although most candidates knew that the energy of the charged condenser was equal to ½ CV², and that the answer was expressed in ergs.

Q. 7. The terminals of a condenser with mica as the dielectric are connected to a quadrant electrometer and the condenser is charged so that the scale deflection is 90. When a second condenser of the same dimensions as the first, but having paraffin wax as the dielectric, is connected in parallel with the first, the deflection falls to 30 divisions. Compare the dielectric constants of mica and paraffin.

Very badly answered. This question, together with Q. 6, points to the fact that candidates are not familiar with the results obtained when condensers are joined up in parallel and series.

Q. 8. Describe a quadrant electrometer, explaining carefully on what factors the sensitiveness of the instrument depends.

The answers were not good. Very few knew anything about the sensitiveness of the instrument.

Voltaic and Technical Electricity.

Q. 9. Describe some form of Wheatstone's bridge, and state clearly how you would determine by means of it the resistance of a coil of wire.

Fairly well answered, although a few joined up battery and galvanometer in series and then found a point on the bridge wire where the galvanometer was not deflected.

Q. 10. It is stated that, in order to separate 1 gram of hydrogen from acidulated water by electrolysis, 96,500 coulombs of electricity must pass; how would you proceed to verify the statement?

Few candidates gained high marks, chiefly owing to the lack of details, such as the correction of the volume of hydrogen formed for temperature, pressure, measurement of current, &c.

Q. 11. Draw up a table giving the practical units in terms of the C.G.S. electromagnetic units for current, quantity, electromotive force, resistance and capacity, detailing the fundamental relations on which the latter system is based.

The relations between the practical units and the C.G.S. units were well known, but the fundamental relations between the C.G.S. units themselves were seldom given.

Q. 12. Describe any one method of comparing capacities.

Not often attempted. Then sometimes treated as a question in electrostatics.

Q. 13. It is required to generate 10 kilos of steam per hour with power developed from a 110-volt circuit. What resistance should the heating coil have in order to do this, supposing loss from radiation negligible?

The numerical value of "J" and the question of units prevented many candidates from arriving at the right answer. The formula, $JH = C^2 R t$ was generally known.

Q. 14. Describe a Ruhmkorff induction coil, showing how the condenser is connected and explaining the function of the condenser.

This question was perhaps as well answered as any on the paper, although the function of the condenser was not very well understood.

Q. 15. Give a diagrammatic sketch of a shunt-wound motor.

How will the speed of such a motor vary under a given load when the resistance in the field circuit is altered?

The sketches were very diagrammatic, and the second part of the question was answered by statements without satisfactory explanations.

Q. 16. Describe the construction of some one form of telephonic receiver. Why would not soft iron do instead of steel for the electro-magnet?

The first part was often incompletely answered, and the second part the candidates knew very little about.

STAGE 3.

Results : 1st Class, 21 ; 2nd Class, 56 ; Failed, 53 ; Total, 130.

The paper was, on the whole, fairly done, the percentage of failures, however, being rather larger than in some previous years.

Subjoined are detailed remarks :—

Q. 1. Describe the phenomenon of electrolytic conduction and explain how our knowledge of ionic velocities has been obtained.

Though many of the answers were good, there was often confusion between the modern view of the mobility of ions and the hypothesis of Grotthüs. The experiments on the direct measurement of ionic velocities were rarely well described.

Q. 2. Describe a method suitable for determining the specific inductive capacity of liquids in rapidly alternating electric fields.

Many of the candidates entirely ignored the alternating character of the electric field, and were content with describing one of the common methods.

Q. 4. Describe carefully how you would determine the permeability of a
magnetic substance in the form of a cylindrical rod one metre
long.

How would you correct your results if you only had a short
rod of the material to experiment with ?

The magnetometer method was generally described, the upper end of the
vertical rod being on a level with the magnetometer, and the question was,
as a rule, well done. Though the necessary corrections for the effect of (a)
the magnetising coil, (b) the action of the lower end of the rod, and (c) the
earth's vertical field, were mentioned, scarcely any of the candidates stated
that the line joining the end of the rod to the magnetometer needle must
be at right angles to the meridian. The second part of the question was
not well done. The correction referred to was for the demagnetising action
of the induced poles and the consequent reduction of the field acting on the
iron ; few candidates saw this.

Q. 5. Describe a method of determining the velocity of the electrons in a
cathode discharge.

In some cases the formulæ used had been learnt by heart and were not
clearly understood. Frequently the deflection of the cathode beam by a
magnetic field was drawn as if the deflection was continued long after the
beam had passed out of the field.

Q. 6. Examine the dimensions of the quantity $\mu\kappa$, where μ denotes
permeability and κ specific inductive capacity. How is the
value of the quantity $\mu\kappa$ practically determined ?

Many candidates knew that the dimensions of $\sqrt{\frac{1}{\mu\kappa}}$ are those of a
velocity, and having investigated the electrostatic dimensions of electric
charge (generally correctly), wrote down the electromagnetic dimensions to
fit in with their knowledge ; this generally led to disaster.

Q. 7. Explain the action of the Wehnelt interrupter. How is the
frequency of the interruptions varied and how measured ?

Most of those who attempted this question were satisfied with a mere
description.

HONOURS.

Results : 1st Class, 1 ; 2nd Class, 1 ; Failed, 6 ; Total, 8.

Only two candidates out of eight did sufficiently well in the first paper
to justify further examination. They both did moderately well in the
second theoretical paper, but one was good and the other weak in the
practical examination.

DAY EXAMINATION.

STAGE 1.

Results : 1st Class, 55 ; 2nd Class, 38 ; Failed, 17 ; Total, 110.

There were only 110 candidates. The general results were good.
Half the candidates obtained the marks required for a First Class, while
only a small percentage failed.

Magnetism.

This section of the paper was generally well done. Not many attempted
the third question about Magnetic Dip. The knowledge of candidates in
this Examination on the subject of the elementary facts of Terrestrial
Magnetism is generally very meagre. The other questions, Nos. 1, 2 and 4
were well done.

Frictional Electricity.

Q. 5. Describe two experiments showing that the charge on a hollow insulated conductor is confined to the outside surface.

In testing the charge on an insulated conductor many of the Candidates connected the conductor directly to the Electroscope and failed to distinguish between the test for charge and the test for potential.

Q. 8. A small metal sphere is suspended by a long dry cotton thread. The sphere having been charged positively is held inside an uncharged metal pot, which rests on the cap of a gold-leaf electroscope, but the sphere is not allowed to touch the pot. After the sphere has been in place for a few seconds the electroscope is momentarily earthed, and then the sphere remaining in place, the leaves of the electroscope are watched. Describe and explain the movements of the gold leaves, starting from the moment when the charged sphere was first introduced.

This question was seldom attempted and was generally not understood. It was assumed that a *dry* cotton thread is a non-conductor of Electricity and the question (now become a very simple one) was answered on this basis.

A dry cotton thread does conduct electricity to a slight extent, and the question had reference to the slow escape of electricity through the thread.

Q. 9. What precautions would you take if you wished to ensure that when glass and silk are rubbed together each is electrified?

How would you prove that, if electrified, their charges are equal and opposite?

Many Candidates carefully insulated the glass, some with ebonite, and some even with wood!

Voltaic Electricity.

This section was well done. Questions 11 and 12 being those least frequently attempted.

Stage 2.

Results: 1st Class, 14; 2nd Class, 45; Failed, 64; Total, 123.

The paper, though apparently an easy one, was answered badly. The standard of excellence was below that of the evening papers in the same Stage. This appears often to be due to defective powers of expression.

Magnetism.

Q. 1. Define the magnetic elements at any place in the earth's surface. The magnetic elements at a given spot are:—declination 30°, dip 60°, horizontal force ·2 c.g.s. Calculate the components of the earth's field in the directions true north, true west, and vertically downwards.

Very few correct answers.

Q. 2. Define magnetic moment, and describe how the magnetic moment of a magnet can be experimentally determined.

In no single instance did the definition of magnetic moment apply to other than an ideal simple magnet with its poles concentrated at points. Few candidates seemed to regard it necessary to specify that the arms of the magnetometer when used in the usual way should be at right angles to the meridian.

Q. 3. What is meant by the critical temperature of iron? By what experiment would you show that iron possessed a critical temperature?

Very vague answers. The usual one being in such terms as "Heat a magnet and bring it near a compass needle from time to time, observing that when a certain temperature has been reached it no longer affects the needle."

Frictional Electricity.

Q. 5. An insulated conductor of irregular shape is charged with electricity. How do the force and the potential vary at points near the surface of the conductor but just inside or just outside respectively?

Done remarkably badly. Almost every student made the potential as well as the electric force vanish inside the conductor.

Q. 6. Two parallel plates of area A are connected to the terminals of a large leyden battery charged to unit difference of potential. How does the strength of the field between the plates vary as the distance between them is increased?

Find the force of attraction between the plates per square centimetre when the distance is 1 millimetre.

Altogether beyond everybody. No instance of even an approximately correct answer. The answer to the second part in every case was that the attraction between the plates is the product of their charges divided by the square of the distance between them. Students should realise that Coulomb's law only has any meaning when applied to charges condensed at points, or on bodies whose linear dimensions are insignificant when compared with the distance between them.

Q. 7. Define electro-static capacity, and show, assuming Coulomb's law, that it is properly measured in terms of units of length as was done by Cavendish.

The second part quite beyond everybody.

Q. 8. One plate of an air condenser is charged and connected to an electroscope, the other plate being earthed. A sheet of sulphur is then introduced between the plates. Describe and explain the effect on the reading of the electroscope produced by the introduction of the sulphur.

A good many answers correct but of little value, there being no idea of specific inductive capacity as a measurable quantity. The general answer being "the induction takes place more effectively through the sulphur" which at best is vague. Candidates seem to think that a given charge is capable of inducing a greater amount of the opposite charge when the induction is through sulphur.

Voltaic and Technical Electricity.

Q. 9. A current of 5 amperes generates heat at the rate of 50 watts in a conductor. Find the resistance of the conductor and the difference of potential between its terminals.

This was answered better than any other question in the paper.

Q. 10. Describe carefully how you would compare the E.M.F. of a storage cell with that of a Leclanche cell, mentioning any precautions which should be taken to obtain a correct measurement.

Done fairly well so far as the first part was concerned. Very few realised that the continued passage of a current through the Leclanche affected its E.M.F.

Q. 11. What is meant by the Peltier effect? Describe an experiment to illustrate this effect.

Fairly well done.

Q. 12. Six wires of equal length and resistance are connected together so as to form the edges of a regular tetrahedron (a pyramid on a triangular base) and a current of 1 ampere is taken in at one corner and out at another. Find the current which passes in each wire.

Fairly well done.

Q. 13. Describe generally the action which takes place in a lead storage cell during charge and discharge.

No correct answer, and very few free from the most obvious absurdities.

Q. 14. A motor running light takes 1 ampere at 100 volts. If its resistance is 20 ohms, how much power is spent in turning the armature and how is it expended ?

Badly done. The general answer is that since the resistance of the motor is 20 ohms and the P.D. 100 volts, the current is 5 amperes, and since the current actually observed is only one ampere, 4 amperes are used in turning the armature. In only two answers was the existence of a back E.M.F. suggested.

Q. 15. Describe a drum wound armature and explain under what conditions such a form of winding is better than the Gramme.

Altogether beyond everybody. The few attempts at drum winding were obviously unworkable.

Q. 16. You are provided with three resistance coils capable of carrying a large current, each having a resistance of 0·1 ohm, and with a voltmeter reading up to 5 volts. Explain how with these instruments you would measure a current of 120 amperes.

A good many candidates got the correct answer to the arrangement of the resistances, but very few could show how to connect the voltmeter and deduce the value of the current from its reading.

Report on the Examinations in Physiography.
Section I. of Stage 1.

EVENING EXAMINATION.

Results : Passed, 70 ; Failed, 101 ; Total, 171.

The standard attained in the answers to this paper was not so good as last year, when the percentage of successes was exceptionally high ; but as the total number of papers was small in both cases the Examiners do not think that any importance can be attached to the falling off.

A.

Q 1. Lubricating oil imported from France is sometimes sold in 4-litre tins and the purchaser generally thinks he is getting a gallon ; what volume does he lose on each tin ? A litre of water weighs 2·2 lbs.

The answer to this question was sometimes obtained simply by assuming the number of pints in a litre. The question, however, was not very often attempted.

Q. 2. Distinguish between solids, liquids, and gases, and give two examples of each.

Well done.

Q. 3. A cyclist when going round a corner fast has to lean over to one side. To which side does he lean and why must he do it ?

The fact that the cyclist has to lean to the inside of the curve, and also that this is due to " inertia," was well known : although no candidate gave a complete answer to the question.

Q. 4. A river flows at 2 miles an hour and a ferryman can row at 4 miles an hour. Draw a diagram showing the direction in which the boat must be rowed in order that it may cross the river at right angles to the stream.

This question was badly answered. Few candidates knew how to apply the parallelogram law to the composition of velocities.

B.

Q. 5. Explain carefully why water pipes which are exposed in the open appear to burst when a thaw sets in after a frost.

The fact that the bursting of pipes is due to the expansion of water on solidification was known, and the question was well answered.

Q. 6. What is meant by conduction of heat ?

Describe an experiment to show whether copper or iron is the better conductor.

The notion was prevalent that the conductivity of a rod of metal depends upon the rate at which heat (as measured by rise of temperature) travels along the bar.

Q. 7. What are the laws of reflection of light ?

Draw a diagram to scale showing how you would place a mirror outside the window so that a person sitting opposite the window may be able to see down the street.

The laws of reflection were stated, but the second part of the question was not well answered.

Q. 8. What experiments would you make to show that the light which reaches our eye from a gas flame is not conveyed by convection or conduction ?

Seldom attempted and badly answered.

C.

Q. 9. Describe experiments, giving a sketch of the apparatus, to show the composition of air.

Very well answered.

Q. 10. What dissolved substances does spring water usually contain ?

Explain how you would prove the presence of any one solid and any one gas dissolved in spring water.

Well answered, although the methods of proving the existence of dissolved gases were not very good.

Q. 11. Give the properties of iron.

Describe carefully how you would prove the composition of iron rust.

Some of the most important properties of iron were often omitted, and in many cases properties common to nearly all solids were given. The composition of iron rust was known.

Q. 12. How do the substances limestone, quicklime, and marble differ in their chemical composition and in their physical properties ?

Not well done. Few knew the chemical compositions of limestone, lime and marble, and the physical properties given were not satisfactory.

DAY EXAMINATION.

Results : Passed, 17 ; Failed, 23 ; Total, 40.

The answers were fairly good on the whole, but the number was too small to permit of a satisfactory comparison with last year.

A.

Q. 1. How would you show that, when a candle burns, the material of
        which it is composed is not destroyed but is converted into other
        forms without loss?

This question was fairly well answered by nearly all the candidates.

Q. 2. What do you understand by "force"? What forces are in action
        in the following cases :—(1) a ball rolling over a smooth
        horizontal surface ; (2) a swinging pendulum ; (3) a ship with
        the wind abeam?

The first part was done well, but the answers to the second part were
complete and unsatisfactory.

Q. 3. It is found that a pound weight may be placed upon a plate of
        thin glass (supported round its edges) without breaking it,
        whereas half-an-ounce dropped from a height of one foot breaks
        the glass. Explain this.

Very badly answered. The principle involved was not understood.

Q. 4. What is the kind of energy possessed by an iron ball in the
        following conditions :—(1) when it is fired from a gun ;
        (2) when it rests on the top of a wall ; (3) when it rests on the
        ground?

Seldom attempted.

B.

Q. 5. Describe a mercury thermometer, and explain how the "fixed
        points" are determined.

The descriptions were not very good, but most candidates knew how to
determine the fixed points.

Q. 6. How would you show that copper is a good conductor of heat, and
        water a bad conductor?

This question was well answered.

Q. 7. Explain by the aid of a diagram how you would hold a glass prism
        in order to see through it a small hole in a piece of cardboard
        illuminated by a gas flame on the other side. What would
        the image of the hole look like?

Q. 8. When you look through a strip of plate glass at a vertical post, the
        part of the post seen through the glass appears to move to
        and fro as you tilt the glass to right and left. Explain this.

These two questions were only occasionally attempted, and were very
badly answered.

C.

Q. 9. How would you show that gunpowder is a mechanical mixture, and
        how would you find its constituents?

Well done.   The separation of gunpowder into nitre, sulphur and carbon
was often well described.

Q. 10. Mention some of the physical properties of hydrogen. Explain
        how (1) heat, (2) electricity, may be employed to produce
        hydrogen.

This question was well answered although the details of the method of
obtaining hydrogen from water by electrolysis were sometimes unsatisfactory.

Q. 11. A small piece of sodium thrown on the surface of water swims about with a hissing noise and disappears. State exactly what happens in this experiment and explain how you would prove your statements.

The fact that hydrogen is generated when sodium acts upon water was known, but the formation of sodium hydrate was not often mentioned.

Q. 12. What is charcoal and how is it made? Mention some of its practical uses. What happens when oxygen gas is passed over red hot charcoal?

The methods of making charcoal were poorly described.

GROUP IV.—CHEMISTRY AND METALLURGY.

BOARD OF EXAMINERS.

X. Inorganic Chemistry
X.*p.*   ,,
    (Practical)"
XI. Organic Chemistry
XI.*p.* ,, ,,
    (Practical)
XIX. Metallurgy
XIX.*p.* ,, (Practical)
XXVI. Elementary Science
of Common Life
	Professor W. A. Tilden, D.Sc., F.R.S.,
	Chairman.
	Professor W. H. Perkin, Junr., Ph.D.,
	F.R.S.
	Professor W. Gowland, Assoc. R.S.M.
	Professor W. P. Wynne, D.Sc., F.R.S.

Report on the Examinations in Chemistry.

EVENING EXAMINATIONS.

INORGANIC CHEMISTRY, THEORETICAL.

STAGE 1.

Results : 1st Class, 739 ; 2nd Class, 671 ; Failed, 636 ; Total, 2,046.

The standard attained was about the same as that of last year, but a few remarks may be useful as to certain characteristics of the Examination. There appears to be some falling off in the practice of expressing definite chemical changes by equations, and teachers should consider whether it is advisable at this early stage to permit students to express the course of a reaction by arrows without accounting for every component of . the interacting materials. Laxity in this direction leads, even at much later stages, to habits of inaccuracy which have a very bad effect on the student's mind. They also lead to the more frequent recurrence of the very common mistake made by beginners which consists in simply dropping any inconvenient atom which does not fit in. Young students should have much practice in writing equations, and the teacher should encourage the habit of summing up the elements on the two sides and proving that they are equal.

Another very prevalent practice to be strongly deprecated is the use of the word " volume " in a particular sense, as in the sentence " 2 volumes of CO_2 weigh 44 grams." It also seems to be taught, though very improperly, that the meaning of the word " equivalent " is that quantity of an element which will combine with or displace *1 gram* of hydrogen. This is shown especially on the present occasion by the answers to Question 10.

Remarks have frequently appeared in previous reports on the desirability of familiarising the young student with the weights and measures of the metric system, a system which is universally employed in scientific writings, and the answers to Question 2 this year show that this familiarity is still lacking. In this question the candidates were asked to explain how they would proceed to fill a gas holder of 50 litres capacity with oxygen. Not five per cent. of the candidates had any idea of the form of a gas holder or of any vessel holding 50 litres. The great majority made the oxygen in a test tube and collected it in a glass cylinder inverted in water.

Question 1, which requires an explanation of how the composition of water *by volume* is ascertained, also shows that a very important fact in connection with this matter is generally neglected. It is not sufficient to show that two volumes of hydrogen combine with one volume of oxygen, or that when water is electrolysed two volumes of hydrogen are liberated for every volume of oxygen. The complete answer to a question as to the volume composition of water requires a knowledge of the fact that steam contains its own volume of hydrogen combined with half its volume of oxygen, and this should be explained and, in fact, demonstrated to the class. The experiment is not difficult, and in view of its fundamental importance is worth a little trouble.

The question "What is an acid?" (Q. 12) received very many unsatisfactory answers. There was a tendency to describe the *oxides* of carbon, sulphur, and nitrogen, and comparatively few seemed to recognise an acid as a salt of hydrogen. Even in cases where the candidates had learnt the definition by rote, after stating that an acid contains replaceable hydrogen they gave the oxides as examples. This seems to show that very few of them have learned to think.

STAGE 2.

Results: 1st Class, 204 ; 2nd Class, 901 ; Failed, 696 ; Total, 1,801.

The standard of work seemed to be about the same as in recent years. Very few papers were thoroughly good throughout, many candidates who gave excellent answers to several questions breaking down in the last two or three. There are also too many who are actually more ignorant than they could have been when presenting themselves in Stage 1, and these give absurd answers. They are unfit for the examination, and should not have been sent in.

The most important deficiencies are manifest in the answers relating to theoretical matters, especially in connection with Questions 21 and 26.

> Q. 21. On passing pure carbon monoxide over heated copper oxide it was found that the loss in weight was 24·360 grams and that the amount of carbon dioxide formed was 67·003 grams. From these data calculate the equivalent of carbon when $O = 16$. What other information would be required to settle the atomic weight?

> Q. 26. Explain why the molecular weight of a substance can be obtained by doubling the vapour density $(H = 1)$. Why is the molecule of chlorine at the ordinary temperature believed to be diatomic?

The equivalent of carbon was very commonly returned as 12·008, and scarcely any candidate gave a clear idea of the further information required to settle the atomic weight after an estimation of the equivalent.

STAGE 3.

Results: 1st Class, 56 ; 2nd Class, 204 ; Failed, 200 ; Total, 460.

The marks obtained by a large section of the candidates seemed to show some improvement on the previous year :—

	1906.	1907.
Above 200	1·3	1·0
Above 100	37	48
Below 100	61	51

There is, however, much to complain of. For example, there were few definite statements of the law of mass action, and hardly any candidate knew how the atomic weight of carbon is fixed (Q. 47). The answers to

Questions 48 and 50 were also both inaccurate and confused. Candidates seem not to discriminate between basic substances, which, like ammonia, unite directly with acids, and the hydroxides like caustic soda, the interaction of which with acids is attended by the production of water. Some even went so far as to refer to the metals as bases.

In Section II., among 62 papers, there was only one decent account of the blast furnace, and with the exception of Q. 52, relating to the well-worn subject of bleaching powder, none of the answers indicated anything more than the most meagre text-book knowledge.

HONOURS.

Results: 1st Class, 4 ; 2nd Class, 10 ; Failed, 13 ; Total, 27.

The four papers recommended for a First Class represented very creditable work, and showed that these candidates had been accustomed to read the current literature of chemistry, and with some degree of intelligence. A smaller number than usual were very bad, and the majority of those who failed should be encouraged to try again.

No question requires very special comment, as all were attempted, and usually with some success. Perhaps the greatest number of failures occurred in connection with the analysis of a mixture of chloride, chlorate, perchlorate, and nitrate, which afforded a comparatively simple analytical problem.

INORGANIC CHEMISTRY, PRACTICAL.

STAGE 1.

Results : 1st Class, 356 ; 2nd Class, 494 ; Failed, 504 ; Total, 1,354.

Many candidates failed to recognise the gas evolved on treating A with strong sulphuric acid, owing to placing too much reliance on the smell, and forgetting that sulphur dioxide does not fume in the air as hydrogen chloride does. The methods employed in Exercise B were satisfactory on the whole, and Exercise C was generally well done. Many candidates, in putting down their results, confused the increase of weight with the weight of the oxide formed.

On the whole, the results may be regarded as satisfactory.

STAGE 2.

Results : 1st Class, 323 ; 2nd Class, 711 ; Failed, 539 ; Total, 1,573.

Both exercises were badly done. The qualitative analysis was required of a mixture containing a carbonate and a sulphate, in each case coloured red by the addition of mercuric oxide. Very few candidates succeeded in detecting all the radicals present, and not more than perhaps one in a hundred even attempted to explain the red colour of the powder. They never seem to consider whether the obvious properties of the substance before them can be accounted for by their analytical results.

For quantitative work they were all supplied with pure bicarbonate of ammonia, in which they were requested to estimate either the CO_2 or NH_3. The majority chose the former and did it badly. Quite a large number attempted to estimate the CO_2 by boiling the salt with standard sodium hydroxide and titrating the solution with standard acid, generally with lamentable results. A few got results approximating to the figures required for the normal carbonate, which apparently they assumed to be the salt supplied.

STAGE 3.

Results : 1st Class, 45 ; 2nd Class, 187 ; Failed, 444 ; Total, 676.

Some difference of procedure occurred in this examination, owing apparently to a misapprehension on the part of the superintendent of the examinations, candidates being supplied with standard dichromate in most laboratories, while in others they had to standardise the solution supplied. It was intended by the Examiners that candidates should prepare solutions for themselves. The volumetric work does not call for comment.

The qualitative work, as usual, was not satisfactory. The calcium, present as phosphate or arsenate, was generally missed, magnesium or aluminium being reported in its place, and the knowledge of some of the candidates may be judged (1) by their going through the phosphate separation with the *aqueous* extract, and (2) by recording the part soluble in water as containing magnesium phosphate or aluminium phosphate in addition to other radicles.

HONOURS.

Results : 1st Class, 2 ; 2nd Class, 6 ; Failed, 9 ; Total, 17.

Seventeen candidates presented themselves, and of these three submitted papers in print or manuscript embodying the results of experiments executed under the direction of their teachers, and one produced two short theoretical papers published in the *Chemical News*.

Students who are preparing to offer themselves for this examination should keep in mind the warning contained in the syllabus that "no candidate can obtain Honours who is not prepared to carry out any observations or experiments commonly practised in the best chemical laboratories." On the present occasion a very simple and straightforward piece of qualitative work and an easy example of quantitative analysis were placed before the candidates, but in neither case were the answers satisfactory, even from the best of them.

The following was the order of work :—

JULY 3RD, 1907.

10 A.M to 5 P.M.

A solution is supplied to you containing potassium and magnesium chlorides together with a small quantity of hydrochloric acid.

Estimate the potassium and magnesium and report your results as grams of K and Mg per litre of solution.

Describe very briefly the process you have employed.

JULY 4TH, 1907.

10 A.M. to 5 P.M.

1. Analyse qualitatively the mixture of inorganic compounds.

The results must be written out clearly, and the evidence on which each conclusion is based plainly set forth.

2. From the base supplied prepare 25 to 30 grams of its acetyl compound, determine its melting point, and place the whole of the specimen in a bottle labelled with your name. The specimens will be collected at the end of the day.

JULY 5TH, 1907.

10 A.M. to 5 P.M.

1. Estimate the percentage of acetyl in the compound prepared by yourself. Standard solutions are provided.

2. From the base prepare a specimen of the chloro-derivative of the corresponding hydrocarbon by way of the diazo-reaction, and determine its boiling point.

Some good results were obtained by direct estimation of the potassium, but this was not what was desired. The methods used and the figures sent in for the magnesium were generally unsatisfactory. No one seemed to be aware of the quick and accurate method of separating magnesium when in the state of chloride by means of mercuric oxide. The qualitative work was in most cases begun and ended without reference to the obvious properties of the substance and, with only about three exceptions, all failed to identify the calomel contained in one mixture or the mercuric oxide in the other.

The production of the acetyl compound of the base (p. toluidine), and the estimation of the acetyl were, as a rule, fairly well done, though several candidates had not been taught to work in a cleanly manner. One candidate even excused the bad colour of his acetyl compound by explaining that it was stained by contact with his fingers ! The untidiness and inaccuracy of this candidate's work and written papers suggest suspicion as to the value of the printed thesis presented by him. The practice of allowing or encouraging students to engage in "research" before they have been trained to habits of order, neatness, and accuracy in common operations is too prevalent at the present time, and is undoubtedly mischievous to the cause of scientific education.

ORGANIC CHEMISTRY, THEORETICAL.

STAGE 1.

Results : 1st Class, 57 ; 2nd Class, 119 ; Failed, 133 ; Total, 309.

The answers of candidates in this Stage reveal the usual degree of inaccuracy, and several points are worthy of attention by the teachers. More care should be given in writing graphic and more or less expanded formulæ so as to indicate clearly the disposition of the valency, as at this stage nothing ought to be assumed.

The answers to Questions 5, 9, and 12, showed that the evidence on which constitutional formulæ are based is not sufficiently explained. This part of the subject is always a little difficult to grasp at first, but the constitution of such simple substances as formic acid, ordinary ether and oxalic and succinic acids should be carefully studied, as such cases represent the application of fundamental principles.

Isomerism was also imperfectly understood in many cases, reference to "propane" and "isopropane" as possible isomerides being too frequent.

STAGE 2.

Results : 1st Class, 53 ; 2nd Class, 119 ; Failed, 111 ; Total, 283.

The general standard appeared to be rather high, but the results are very unequal, and indications are to be found here and there of bad teaching. Methods of preparation proposed were often impracticable. Thus phenylene diamine was represented as obtained from p-dinitrobenzene, resorcinol from m-phenylenediamine, and quinol by the fusion of phenol p-sulphonic acid with caustic soda or potash. There also appears to exist a tendency to neglect the fatty division and to concentrate attention on the aromatic. It should not be forgotten that candidates in this Stage are expected to show that they have advanced and consolidated the knowledge gained in the previous Stage.

STAGE 3.

Results : 1st Class, 4 ; 2nd Class, 9 ; Failed, 21 ; Total, 34.

The papers this year were of unequal character, a few being very well done, while others showed that the respective candidates had not received any instruction in advanced organic chemistry beyond that required in Stage 2.

Questions 41, 42 and 46 see   ,, to be found most difficult.

HONOURS.

See Report on the Examination in Inorganic Chemistry, Theoretical, Honours (page 148).

ORGANIC CHEMISTRY, PRACTICAL.

STAGE 1.

Results : 1st Class, 89 ; 2nd Class, 55 ; Failed, 60 ; Total, 204.

The practical experimental part of the examination was usually well done.

In connection with the written answers, which were fairly satisfactory, it may be pointed out that the detection of methyl alcohol in ethyl alcohol cannot be accomplished by simply oxidising and testing for formic acid. The acetaldehyde formed from the ethyl alcohol must be removed, or its reducing effects lead to an ambiguous result.

The certificates required from the teachers as to the preparation of specimens were supplied with very few exceptions.   This is satisfactory.

STAGE 2.

Results : 1st Class, 45 ; 2nd Class, 76 ; Failed, 87 ; Total, 208.

The written examination was generally done badly.   Even the separation of a mixture of napthalene, aniline and phenol, a very threadbare exercise, failed to produce good answers.   This is all the more remarkable because the practical part of the examination, notwithstanding the accidental introduction of some quantitative work, was fairly satisfactory.   Some very good values were obtained for the equivalent of the acid.

STAGE 3.

Results : 1st Class, 18 ; 2nd Class, 15 ; Failed, 41 ; Total, 74.

The practical work was about equal in quantity to that examined last year.   The estimation of the amide and identification of the corresponding acid was, on the whole, good so far as the quantitative part of the work was concerned.   But the isolation of the acid and its recognition by means of its melting point and behaviour as a pure substance was not undertaken by the majority of the candidates, who rely too much on the ordinary tests learnt from some " table " of acids.

Exercise B was not very successfully attacked, and fusion with potash seems to be an unfamiliar operation.

HONOURS.

See Report on the Examination in Inorganic Chemistry, Practical, Honours (page 149).

DAY EXAMINATIONS.

INORGANIC CHEMISTRY, THEORETICAL.

STAGE 1.

Results : 1st Class, 179 ; 2nd Class, 77 ; Failed, 25 ; Total, 281.

The papers are, on the whole, good, and superior to those of former years. One very prevalent mistake in the answers to Q. 7 seems to show some defective teaching.   Carbonic oxide was represented as being obtained by passing carbon dioxide through a bulb tube containing a small fragment of charcoal heated by a Bunsen flame.   The description was often accompanied by a sketch of the apparatus, showing, apparently, that some teachers indicate the method, but do not carry it out experimentally or explain the necessary conditions. There is also a disposition to avoid the use of symbols and formula, which have hitherto presented no serious difficulty.

STAGE 2.

Results : 1st Class, 7 ; 2nd Class, 76 ; Failed, 84 ; Total, 167.

On the whole, the work appears to be inferior to that of the corresponding stage of the Evening Examination, and may, therefore, be understood to be of very low quality.. The usual mistakes are made, and it is noticeable how commonly the more difficult questions are attacked, while the simpler ones are left untouched, or if attempted are attacked with very little success. For example, Q. 1 was an easy question, on which Stage 2 candidates should have scored well. Nevertheless, from ignorance of the composition of nitrous oxide, or from reckoning phosphoric oxide as a gas, or from want of clearness about molecules and volumes, only a small proportion of the candidates, perhaps 30 per cent. of those who tried the question, obtained full marks.

The answers to Q. 8 on ionic dissociation were also unsatisfactory, and Q. 6, relating to the preparation and properties of certain chromium compounds elicited no correct answer. Q's. 5, 9 and 10, which require a knowledge of quite familiar chemical reactions, also received very imperfect treatment.

INORGANIC CHEMISTRY, PRACTICAL.

STAGE 1.

Results : 1st Class, 38 ; 2nd Class, 23 ; Failed, 15 ; Total, 76.

Fair. The chief defect arises from the habitual use in the quantitative work of too small a quantity for either the sensitiveness of their balances or the skill of the candidates. The few who took five or ten grams of the salt got good figures for the water of crystallisation, but those who weighed out less than a gram, or even less than half a gram, were often wide of the mark.

STAGE 2.

Results : 1st Class, 24 ; 2nd Class, 55 ; Failed, 93 ; Total, 172.

The qualitative work was bad. The quantitative results were somewhat better, but there is much to complain of in the arithmetic, and many candidates did not know how to proceed in the calculation of the equivalent of the metal after measuring the hydrogen evolved.

Report on the Examinations in Metallurgy.

THEORETICAL.

STAGE 1.

Results : 1st Class, 43 ; 2nd Class, 35 ; Failed, 41 ; Total, 119.

The number of papers sent in was 119, a decrease of 26, as compared with last year, and about the same as in 1904. The quality of the answers was hardly equal to that of last year, the percentage of failures being considerably higher.

Greater interest was evidently taken in the Metallurgy covered by the first two sections of the Syllabus, the study of Gold and Silver appearing to have received but little attention.

Candidates showed weakness in their answers to questions in which the principles of a process were required. An account of the operations of a process is not necessarily a statement of the principles involved in these operations; although, on the other hand, the principles cannot well be given without a certain amount of description.

The sketches, as usual, were poor, and this year there were fewer which approached correct representation. Fault is not found with the inability of a candidate to make a good sketch but with the quite erroneous and impossible ideas delineated.

Many candidates had little conception of the magnitude of the various appliances used in metallurgy; neither had they grasped the scale on which the work is conducted. These are matters which are difficult to convey by lectures or text-books, but an idea of the size, together with general proportions of furnaces, and such like, should be given to students wherever possible.

SECTION I.

Q. 2. Describe by the aid of a sketch the method of making and working a pile in which large logs may be converted into charcoal.

Few good answers were given to this simple question. Many described the ordinary method of making charcoal from small logs.

Q. 3. For what purposes are dolomite, ganister and chromite used? State the general properties of each.

This was attempted by many of the candidates, and several good answers were given. Chromite was not generally known.

SECTION II.

Q. 5. Describe and make sketches of two of the chief forms of blast furnace twyers.

This was a favourite question and candidates showed a good knowledge of the common forms of twyers, but the sketches were weak. Some twyers were arranged to supply the water to the interior of the furnace.

Q. 7. What are the chief principles and chemical changes on which the manufacture of steel by the basic Bessemer process is based?

The principles were not, as a rule, well stated. The lining was repeatedly given as the dephosphorising agent.

SECTION III.

Q. 9. State the principles and chemical reactions upon which the operations of smelting and purifying lead are based.

In many answers desilverisation was given as a method of purifying lead.

Q. 10. Give a description, with sketches, of a pan and a settler used in extracting silver by amalgamation. What is the object of using a settler?

Only attempted by four candidates, and not well answered. The purpose of the pan, and therefore the essential features of its construction, did not appear to have been grasped.

Q. 11. Carefully describe the chief parts of a stamp battery.

For such an important milling appliance as the stamp battery, the answers to this question were disappointing and indicated that many had very vague ideas on gold milling.

Q. 12. Describe the operations you would carry out for the extraction of gold from a pyritic ore by the process of chlorination in vats in order to obtain the metal in a marketable form.

This was correctly answered by five candidates. Several erroneously adopted Miller's parting process for the treatment of ores.

Section IV.

Q. 14. Describe and make a sketch of a *modern* reverberatory furnace for smelting copper ores.

The sketches of this furnace were very bad. Many candidates omitted its main features, and also failed to realise how a smelting furnace differs from a calcining furnace, giving hearths of the latter type in answer to this question. Some of the sketches were made with very little thought, no means being shown for charging the material or for tapping the products.

Q. 16. Compare the chief features of the Belgian process and the Silesian process for the extraction of zinc from its ores.

Attempted by sixteen candidates, but not well answered. The forms of furnace used in the two processes did not appear to be generally known.

Stage 2.

Results: 1st Class, 28 ; 2nd Class, 78 ; Failed, 40 ; Total, 146.

The number of candidates taking the examination in this stage was rather greater than last year, 146 papers having been received, as compared with 139 in 1906.

The standard reached by the candidates was, on the whole, not so high. Although the papers of a considerable number afforded satisfactory evidence of careful teaching and obtained good marks, yet it is to be regretted that a few took this stage who, if they could be regarded as being prepared for the examination at all, should have been entered for Stage 1. As regards sketches, there was, in a few cases, a considerable improvement on those of past years, but the majority were not done well. Some candidates again show a complete want of practical acquaintance with the processes they describe, while others evidently know so little chemistry that they are unable to appreciate the fundamental principles underlying ordinary metallurgical processes. In no question was the want of practical knowledge more conspicuous than in the identification of specimens. There were candidates also who were evidently well acquainted with the chemical principles of the various processes, but who drew entirely on their imagination for the description of the plant employed in actual practice.

Section I.

Q. 21. Give the exact meaning of each of the following terms :—Liquation, Segregation, Calcination, Roasting, Ductility, Malleability. Give two characteristic examples of the use of each.

This question was answered fairly well by nearly all the candidates, but very few of them defined the term "Segregation" correctly, the majority not attempting to explain it at all.

Q. 22. What flux would you employ in order to convert one ton of the following gangue in a calcined lead ore into a mono-silicate slag ?

$$Fe_2O_3 \quad \text{-} \quad \text{-} \quad \text{-} \quad 25 \text{ per cent.}$$
$$CaO \quad \text{-} \quad \text{-} \quad \text{-} \quad 20 \quad \text{,,}$$
$$SiO_2 \quad \text{-} \quad \text{-} \quad \text{-} \quad 55 \quad \text{,,}$$

What quantity would be required?

Thirteen candidates only answered this question correctly. In most cases they did not realise that Fe_2O_3 would be converted into FeO in a blast furnace, and applied the formula $2 Fe_2O_3 3 SiO_2$ for the iron monosilicate, instead of $2 FeO SiO_2$. Others lost a few marks through faulty arithmetic, although they adopted the correct method of solution.

Q. 23. Describe a suitable form of thermo-couple pyrometer for the determination of the temperatures of a hot-blast stove.

In a few instances the instrument was well described, but several candidates, especially in one batch of papers, placed only one of the couple wires in the cold junction, the other one being joined to the lead outside it. None of the candidates pointed out the necessity for soldering the couple wires to the galvanometer leads. Several very curious compositions were given for the couple wires, one student recommending a couple made of one wire of bismuth and another of antimony.

Q. 24. Name and describe the six specimens submitted to you.

This question was an obligatory one and was satisfactorily answered by about a third of the candidates. The specimens given for identification were of a perfectly simple character and were quite typical in every way.

Due allowance was made, in every case, for the fact that the examination was held at night and that the lighting was probably not good in some of the examination rooms, but there is certainly no excuse for candidates who describe anthracite as magnetite, blende as galena, blast-furnace slag as blue metal, and blue metal as pig iron. Such mistakes as these occurred, not in isolated cases, but in quite half the number of papers sent in. From the answers given it is apparent that in many institutions students are still not given facilities for recognising ores, metallurgical products and materials. It has been pointed out on several occasions that the actual handling of specimens is of the highest importance in the teaching of metallurgy and that not only should the various institutions be well provided with specimens, but the students themselves should be induced to make collections, and thus to become practically acquainted with various ores and products. There is no better method for this practical teaching, and a little encouragement given in this direction would work wonders in these final examinations.

Section II.

Q. 25. Give an account of a *modern* automatic method for charging a blast furnace smelting iron ores. Make a sketch of the appliances.

In only a few instances was this question well answered ; comparatively few of the candidates, however, described the "cup and cone" as an automatic method for charging a blast furnace, as was the case two years ago. This time the majority of the candidates preferred to describe various forms of bucket elevators, such as might be used for an automatic coal charger for a battery of boilers or a washery.

Q. 26. Give the approximate composition of the pig irons you would select for the manufacture of steel :—

        (1) For the Basic Bessemer process.
        (2) For the Acid Bessemer process.
        (3) For the Basic Open-hearth process.
        (4) For the Acid Open-hearth process.

Give your reasons in each case.

This question was answered quite well in a number of cases. Sulphur, in large quantities, was occasionally given as an essential constituent of cast iron.

Q. 27. State concisely the uses and compositions of the following materials in the manufacture of steel :—(1) Spiegeleisen ; (2) Ferro-Manganese ; (3) Ferro-Silicon.

This question, which was very generally attempted, was on the whole well answered. Some candidates did not realise that "spiegel" was generally used when it is necessary to add a fairly large amount of carbon to the metal, whereas "ferro" is usually reserved for the production of very mild steel.

Q. 28. Describe the manufacture of crucible steel from Swedish bar iron.
What conditions are necessary for the production of sound bars
of the highest quality ?

Many of the answers to this question were good, but several candidates
omitted to describe the process by which the bars are cemented.   Others,
after describing the cementation process, correctly prescribed a plumbago
crucible for the subsequent melting of the steel.

SECTION III.

Q. 29. Describe the English process for the cupellation of argentiferous
lead, and mention the various improvements which have been
made in connection with the " test " and its manipulation.

The candidates who attempted this question generally gave bone-ash as
the material for the " test," instead of marl or cement, or a mixture of
cement and fireclay, while the cooling of modern " tests," by means of
water-coolers, in order to diminish the corrosive action of the litharge, was
hardly ever mentioned.

Q. 30. Describe the construction of a stamp-battery of ten stamps. Make
a sketch showing a vertical transverse section of one of the
stamps and the mortar box.

The first portion of this question was often well done, but the sketch of
a vertical section of one of the stamps and mortar box was very badly
drawn in all but one or two cases.   The shoes were in most instances far
too large and the tappets often placed near the tops of the stems, while the
cams rather resembled tooth-wheels.

Q. 31. Describe the treatment you would recommend for the extraction
of gold from pyritic concentrates containing one per cent. of
copper and 2 ounces of gold per ton. Give the reasons for your
answer.

Generally fairly well done.   Chlorination, which is, of course, the correct
process to use for this ore, was well described in some cases.   The chief
errors were either omitting to give the ore a preliminary roast to remove
sulphur and open it up, or in the subsequent precipitation of the gold after
chlorination.   Some candidates preferred to cyanide the ore without any
preliminary treatment and lost marks accordingly.

Q. 32. Briefly describe the cyanide process for the extraction of gold
from its ores.   Give a list of substances which destroy the
cyanide solution, and point out how they act in each case.

The actual process was quite well known by most of the candidates who
attempted this question, but in only a few instances were the " cyanicides "
correctly stated, and then their actions on the cyanide solution were not
properly understood.   Again this year several of the candidates were not at
all certain of the strengths of cyanide solutions as used in ordinary practice.

SECTION IV.

Q. 33. Make a sketch showing a vertical section through the matte and
slag spout of a modern rectangular water-jacketed blast furnace
for smelting pyritic copper ores. Describe the construction of
the bottom.

Attempted by nine of the candidates, of whom five only obtained more
than half marks.   As a rule an imperfect drawing was given of a vertical
section of the whole of the furnace, instead of that portion containing the
matte and slag spouts only.   In two instances Pilz furnaces were given.

Q. 34. Describe fully the process of refining a charge of blister copper. State the chemical and physical changes which take place during the operation.

This question was attempted by a number of the candidates, many of whom gave quite good answers, but the method of taking samples when the metal is approaching the "tough-pitch" stage was seldom described.

Q. 35. Describe the operations and plant you would employ for the extraction of zinc from zinc blende. What are the chief causes of the losses of zinc in the operation and how may they be minimised?

Some good answers were given, but most of the sketches illustrating the answers were poor and inaccurate. A few of the candidates described the old Silesian form of condenser, while others omitted to calcine the blende before smelting.

Q. 36. How would you prepare the following alloys on a commercial scale?

> (a) Müntz metal.
> (b) Best yellow brass.
> (c) Phosphor bronze.

State their compositions and industrial uses.

In about half-a-dozen cases the compositions of the alloys were correctly given, but most of the methods given for preparing the alloys were hardly those in commercial use. Müntz metal was generally stated to be an alloy of copper, tin and zinc, while best yellow brass was, in several papers, described as a mixture of copper and tin. The figures given for tin and phosphorus in phosphor bronze were often too high; in one or two papers 10 per cent. was stated to be the usual amount of phosphorus present.

STAGE 3.

Results: 1st Class, 11; 2nd Class, 19; Failed, 25; Total, 55.

The number of papers sent in was about the same as last year, and the standard attained by the candidates as a whole was closely similar.

As usual the weakest point in the papers generally was the recognition of the metallurgical materials. Fifteen candidates failed to recognise a single specimen, even such commonly occurring substances as spathic iron ore, fluor spar, and dolomite.

In some of the smaller schools the teaching is either very defective, or imperfectly prepared candidates are sent in from them, and these schools supply a very large proportion of the failures.

SECTION I.

Q. 40. Describe and make a sketch of a chimney stack, about 100 to 120 feet high, suitable for metallurgical work. How would you build it, and what materials would you use in its construction?

Attempted by about half of the candidates. Several of the answers were very good.

Q. 41. Describe and make a sketch of the Delwitz water-gas producer. State how it is worked and the principles and chemical changes on which its operations are based.

Not generally attempted and only two good answers. The chief feature of the process, viz., the use of air under pressure before passing in the steam, was overlooked by most of the candidates, and in nearly all cases the sketch given represented a producer for ordinary producer gas.

Q. 42. Name, and briefly describe, the six specimens submitted to you.

The worst answers for several years. Fifteen papers received no marks, and in twenty-eight others only two specimens were correctly named. Six candidates failed to obtain a first class owing to defective answers to this question.

SECTION II.

Q. 43. Describe and make a sketch of the top of a modern blast furnace in which the charges are fed in with an automatic skip.

Generally attempted and some excellent answers. In others there were very confused notions as to the manner in which the tipping of the skip was effected.

Q. 44. State the physical properties and general characters of the following kinds of iron and steel, and also the uses for which they are suitable :—

———	1.	2.	3.	4.	5.
Carbon—graphitic - -	0·20	1·45	—	—	—
Carbon—combined - -	3·40	1·38	0·15	0·40	1·10
Silicon - - - -	1·00	1·24	0·14	0·07	0·02
Manganese - - -	2·00	0·63	0·10	0·09	0·10
Sulphur - - - -	0·05	0·11	0·04	0·06	0·01
Phosphorus - - -	2·06	0·65	0·14	0·06	0·20

A favourite question and fairly well answered, but too many papers contained very serious errors. Thus No. 2 was said to be suitable for the acid open-hearth process, in spite of the large percentage of phosphorus present.

No. 3. Puddled bar was said to be tin plate steel bar, tyre steel, &c.

No. 5. All the weaker candidates overlooked the high percentage of phosphorus in this steel and attributed to it the properties of crucible tool steel.

Q. 45. State, as fully as possible, the effects of tungsten and of manganese on the physical properties of steel.

Attempted by the majority of the candidates, but, except in about eight papers, the answers were disappointing. The effects of tungsten in self-hardening steels and its use as a constituent of high speed cutting tool steels were known to most, but there was a singular display of ignorance of the properties of manganese steels, and even of the effects of manganese in ordinary Bessemer and open-hearth steels.

SECTION III.

Q. 46. How would you treat an ore of the following composition in order to obtain the metals which can be economically extracted ?

Galena - - - - - -	30
Copper pyrites - - - - -	9
Zinc blende - - - - -	5
Iron pyrites - - - - -	20
Quartz - - - - -	36
	100

Silver, 30 ounces per ton.
Gold, 10 dwts. per ton.

About half the candidates attempted this question and six gave good answers. A greater proportion of the others were better acquainted with the conditions which are necessary respectively for reverberatory and blast furnace smelting than in previous years. Several, however, did not realise that the gold might be contained in the pyrites, or that some of the silver as well as some of the gold would pass into the copper matte.

Q. 47. Give an account of the Diehl process for the cyaniding of gold ores.

Attempted by only ten candidates, but five gave good answers. The others had but little knowledge of the process, and their answers were practically worthless.

Q. 48. State the conditions under which you would recommend respectively : (a) cyanidation ; (b) chlorination, for the extraction of gold from ores.

There were eighteen answers, but only two really good. Ignorance of the conditions which are essential for the success of the cyanide process was a specially characteristic feature of the others.

SECTION IV.

Q. 49. You have to smelt the following ore and produce copper anodes ; state the method you would adopt and describe the plant you would erect. The cost of coke is very high :—

Copper pyrites				9·0
Iron pyrites	-	-	-	58·0
Quartz	-	-	-	22·0
Calc spar	-	-	-	6·0
Zinc blende	-	-	-	5·0
				100·0

Silver, 10 ounces per ton.
Gold, 3 dwts. per ton.

Give your reasons for the operations you would carry out.

This practical question was attempted by sixteen candidates, and it is very satisfactory to note that there were eight good answers, a much larger proportion than in past years to similar questions. In the other answers the weak points were ignorance of pyritic smelting and of the bessemerising of copper mattes, and hence of the best method of treating this ore.

Q. 50. Describe and make a sketch of a Belgian-Silesian or Rhenish furnace with three rows of retorts and using gas as fuel. Give an account of the best method of making the retorts.

In the twelve answers given there was not a single one really very good. The sketches were all bad, and the modern methods of making the retorts by hydraulic pressure were unknown to nearly all the candidates.

Q. 51. How is aluminium prepared on a commercial scale ? Give a concise account of the uses of the metal and of the composition and physical properties of the alloys in the manufacture of which it is employed.

Attempted by about half the candidates and there were several good answers, but too many were either incomplete, or they showed imperfect knowledge of the principles on which the extraction of the metal is based, and hence gave absurd descriptions of both the process and the plant.

HONOURS.

Results : 1st Class, 1 ; 2nd Class, 2 ; Failed, 6 ; Total, 9.

PAPER I.

There were nine candidates, the number last year being 10.   Five were examined in Section II., Iron and Steel ; two in Section III., Gold, Silver, Lead, &c. ; and two in Section IV., Copper, Zinc, Tin, &c.

Three in Section II. and one in Section III. obtained sufficient marks to qualify them for admission to the practical examination and the examination in Paper II.   One of the candidates in Section III. obtained considerably higher marks than those in Section II. ; the latter, in fact, barely exceeded the minimum allowed.

The answers to the easy Question 65 were especially disappointing, as every candidate in this stage ought to be thoroughly conversant with the methods in use in works for preventing unsoundness in steel castings, yet only one obtained more than half marks.

PRACTICAL.

STAGE 1.

Results : 1st Class, 33 ; 2nd Class, 28 ; Failed, 16 ; Total, 77.

The number of papers sent in for this Stage was 77, a decrease of 20 as compared with last year, and being practically the same as in 1904.   The standard of excellence attained by the majority of the candidates was quite equal to that of the last three years.

The candidates were required to perform two of the following tasks, either A and B, or $A A$ and $B B$.

(A) Prepare an alloy of the following composition from the materials supplied :—

Copper	- - -	84 per cent.
Tin	- - -	9 „
Zinc	- - -	7 „

The weight of each metal used and of the alloy obtained must be stated in your paper.

The alloy is to be cast in an *ingot* mould, so that it can be broken to show the fracture.

(B) Extract the lead from the sample of impure litharge supplied.

The weight of the litharge used, and of the lead obtained, must be stated in your paper.

(A A) Prepare, from the materials supplied, an alloy of the following composition :—

Zinc	- - -	70 per cent.
Tin	- - -	20 „
Copper	- - -	10 „

The weight of each metal used, and of the alloy obtained, must be stated in your paper.

The alloy *must* be cast in an *ingot* mould, so that it can be broken to show the fracture.

(B B) Extract the lead from the sample of impure red lead supplied.

The weight of the red lead used and of the lead obtained must be stated in your paper.

In the tasks *A* and *AA* several of the candidates neglected to melt the copper with the tin before adding the zinc ; this is a defect which has been pointed out in previous reports, and it is surprising that it should still continue to occur. The necessity of stirring the alloys with either a small clay or carbon rod should be pointed out to the students, and also the necessity of adding a small percentage of zinc in excess, to compensate for loss by volatilisation. Several of the candidates evidently either had their metal too hot or not covered with carbon when the zinc was added, and therefore lost a large percentage of it. Further, some of the ingots were not well cast, but a little instruction in manipulation on the part of the teacher would soon correct this defect.

Exercises *B* and *BB* were well done by many of the candidates. The errors made were those which have been frequently commented upon in previous reports. Several evidently did not realise that both the red lead and the litharge were impure, and attempted to reduce them with charcoal alone, without the use of a little sodium carbonate and borax. Three candidates returned results which indicated that the red lead supplied contained the correct amount of lead required by theory for Pb_3O_4, while one of them obtained a figure 0·1 per cent. below this percentage, when using the theoretical quantity of carbon in the form of charcoal. In cases like these, and where candidates did not return their samples, as they were requested to do in the instructions, they, of course, failed.

Of both the ingot of alloy and the lead button, a good many candidates sent in creditable samples, but in other cases the ingots and buttons were either extremely dirty or showed excessive loss.

STAGE 2.

Results : 1st Class, 24 ; 2nd Class, 50 ; Failed, 36 ; Total, 110.

The number of papers sent in was 110, a decrease of six on last year ; and the percentage of candidates obtaining First Classes was less than in 1906.

There is still much room for improvement in the style in which the practical questions are answered, especially in the manner of stating the quantities taken and in recording the results.

Candidates had to perform two of the following tasks, *C* and *D*, or *CC* and *DD*.

(*C*) Extract the copper from the pyrites supplied.

The weight of the ore used, and of the copper obtained, must be stated in your paper.

(*D*) Convert the ferric oxide and sand supplied into a monosilicate slag.

The weight of the materials used, and of the product obtained, must be stated in your paper.

(*C C*) Extract the copper from the " course metal " supplied.

The weight of the coarse metal, and of the copper obtained must be stated in your paper.

(*D D*) Convert the ferric oxide and sand supplied into a subsilicate slag.

The weight of the materials used, and of the products obtained must be stated in your paper.

Exercises *C* and *C C* were as a rule carried out fairly well. Several candidates, however, did not obtain good tough copper, the refining not being thoroughly understood. A convenient amount of the material was not always taken ; 20 grams would have proved the most suitable quantity.

Exercises *D* and *D D*. Many candidates failed to realise that in order to obtain a silicate, the iron must be reduced to the ferrous condition, therefore charcoal should form part of the charge of the crucible in which the fusion is made.

STAGE 3.

Results : 1st Class, 16 ; 2nd Class, 28 ; Failed, 21 ; Total, 65.

The number of candidates in this Stage was only 65, whilst last year 81 presented themselves for examination. The improvement in the work done last year was well maintained and a somewhat larger proportion of the candidates obtained high marks.

In most cases the correct methods were followed, so that the failures were, as usual, due to defective manipulation. In the determination of silica in a fireclay, thirteen candidates obtained such erroneous results that no marks could be awarded them.

The assay of the gold ore was only attempted by about one-third of the candidates, but more than half of these obtained good results.

The determination of sulphur in pig iron was generally unsatisfactory, although in ten cases the results were accurate.

Several of the candidates had had quite insufficient training in practical work in the laboratory.

HONOURS.

Results : 1st Class, 1 ; 2nd Class, 2 ; Failed, 0 ; Total, 3.

Only three of the four candidates who had qualified for admission to the practical examination in the Metallurgical Laboratory at South Kensington and the examination in Paper II., presented themselves, and all passed, viz. :—one in the 1st Class in Section III., and two in the 2nd Class in Section II. The practical work in the laboratory was not so well done as last year.

Report on the Examinations in Elementary Science of Common Life.

EVENING EXAMINATION.

Results : 1st Class, 181 ; 2nd Class, 121 ; Failed, 64 ; Total, 366.

The quality of the answers sent in was about the same as last year. This is a subject more easy to teach than to examine by written papers, and while there is abundant evidence that the pupils are receiving interesting information which will be useful to them in their later studies, the papers necessarily exhibit a great deal of childish and inaccurate work, which in some cases amounts to absurdity.

The questions under B (on Section IX. of the Syllabus) were attempted by comparatively few candidates.

DAY EXAMINATION.

Results : 1st Class, 167 ; 2nd Class, 62 ; Failed, 18 ; Total, 247.

The answers were, on the whole, good. There is a very general misunderstanding on the subject of luminous and non-luminous flames (Q. 10), the idea being that more heat is obtained when coal gas is mixed with air before burning than when it gives the ordinary luminous flame. Probably not one in ten referred to the disadvantage of soot and its avoidance in the air-fed flame. Many candidates spend time in drawing sketches, which convey no information, and it would be well if they were taught to supply only the drawings necessary for the elucidation of their descriptions.

GROUP V.—GEOLOGY, MINING, AND PHYSIOGRAPHY.

BOARD OF EXAMINERS.

XII. Geology }
XIII. Mineralogy }
XVIII. Principles of Mining }
XXIII. Physiography }

Professor J. W. Judd, C.B., LL.D., F.R.S., *Chairman.*
Sir J. N. Lockyer, K..C.B., LL.D., F.R.S.
B. H. Brough, A.R.S.M, F.G.S.

Report on the Examination in Geology.

Except in Stage 1, the gratifying increase in the number of candidates in this subject, referred to in last year's report, has been maintained, and this increase in numbers has not been attended with any serious falling off in the quality of the papers. There is still evidence that, in many cases, the teaching is excellent, local illustrations, that could not have been borrowed from text-books, being generally employed, and field work, it is clear, having been organised and encouraged.

STAGE 1.

Results : 1st Class, 58 ; 2nd Class, 70 ; Failed, 44 ; Total, 172.

The results in this Stage are very similar to those of last year, there being, on the whole, an improvement. There is, however, a slight falling off in the number of papers, as was the case last year, this being probably due to the special regulations made with respect to Stage 1.

Q. 1. Name the Class to which you would assign each of the following rocks :—(a) Mica Schist with Garnets, (b) Hornblende Gabbro, (c) Rhyolite, (d) Quartz Diorite, (e) Granulite, (f) Micaceous Sandstone, (g) Augite Andesite, (h) Cannel Coal, (i) Pumiceous Tuff ; (j) Coal-Measure Shale, (k) Tachylyte.

While most of the answers are satisfactory, and show that the teaching has been good so far as it has gone, there are a few cases in which the instruction has evidently been defective. The distinction between minerals and rocks is sometimes quite ignored, and such blunders are made as confusing Tachylyte with Trachyte, Carbonaceous with Carboniferous, and Micaceous Sandstone with Micaceous Schist.

Q. 2. What are the essential minerals present in Diorite and Dolerite respectively? State what you know concerning the composition and characters of each of these minerals.

In this question, also, the mistake of confusing minerals and rocks is made by many candidates, and, in addition, there is a very prevalent want of knowledge as to what is meant by the adjective "essential." Too many of the papers give as *essential* minerals *any* that may be found in the rock, and sometimes mere guesses are evidently made.

Q. 3. Describe the mode of formation of Volcanic Scoriæ and of Pumice, and indicate the chief points of difference between these materials.

This question was generally answered in a very imperfect manner. It is clear that the essential distinction between *glassy* and *stony* materials has not been definitely taught, and instead of confining themselves to the points asked for in the question, long and totally irrelevant matter was introduced with respect to cones, tuff-deposits, &c.

Q. 4. Represent in a diagrammatic section, a series of horizontal Lias shales and limestones affected by an ordinary fault, and covered unconformably by false-bedded sands.

It is to be feared, from the manner in which this question was answered, that practice in drawing geological sections is not included in the teaching of most of the classes at this Stage. Not only were the drawings for the most part very crudely and carelessly executed, but gross mistakes were made (such as representing the sands as lying on an undenuded faulted surface) which would at once have been corrected by any intelligent teacher. Teachers would do well, not only to take care that their own drawings on the blackboard are unimpeachable, but to set their pupils a number of simple exercises, and carefully correct them.

Q. 5. Explain, by the aid of a diagram, the formation of a spring at the base of an escarpment in the Oolites, and state the physical cause on which the formation of springs depends.

It is evident from the way that this question was answered that the subject of the formation of springs had been very imperfectly (in many cases erroneously) taught. The distinction between pervious and impervious strata, and the accumulation of water in the latter was not understood. Instead of this, attempts were made to explain the springs by showing that water would run down an inclined-plane, and in the escarpments, as drawn, this led to obvious difficulties.

Q. 6. What is meant by an "oolitic limestone"? Where in the British Islands do the strata known as "Oolites" occur, and what strata lie respectively below and above them?

The distinction between the structure known as "oolitic" and the geological formation called the "Oolites" was very imperfectly apprehended in many cases, and in some cases oolites were spoken of as little animals. It is clear that the teaching on this subject has been wanting in definiteness.

Q. 7. What is a Volcanic Dyke? How does it differ from an Intrusive Sheet ("Sill") and a Vein? Illustrate your answer by diagrams.

It is possibly due to the circumstance that the geological papers come from mining districts, like Cornwall, that the candidates take "Vein" to mean a mineral vein. The context ought to have indicated that such was not the correct interpretation of the question. The answers were discursive and introduce much irrelevant matter, while the essential points were often missed both in the descriptions and the drawings.

Q. 8. Explain the difference between Contact Metamorphism and Regional Metamorphism, and refer to localities in the British Islands where each of these kinds of Metamorphism is exhibited.

While the subject of *contact* metamorphism was fairly dealt with, the answers concerning *regional* metamorphism were, as a general rule, of a vague and often purely negative character. All metamorphism that is not contact metamorphism, it was inferred, must be regional. Even the induration of rocks by pressure and similar phenomena were referred to by some candidates as examples of regional metamorphism. The distinction between the two classes of phenomena was not made clearer, in many cases, by the examples selected.

STAGE 2.

Results: 1st Class, 54; 2nd Class, 76; Failed, 46; Total, 176.

In this Stage there is a more marked improvement in the character of the answers as compared with those of last year. The candidates have evidently a very considerable amount of knowledge of the subject, but they suffer from the want of power to express their meaning owing to a lack of anything like literary training. It is probably due to the same cause that not a few answers show only a very limited relation to the questions asked. It is to be feared that in many cases, it is not carelessness, but a want of power to grasp the exact meaning of the terms of the question that has led to diffuse and irrelevant answers.

Q. 21. State what you know concerning the varying rates of increase in temperature with depth, in different parts of the earth's crust, giving the extremes and average of the rates observed.

While most of the candidates were acquainted with the mean rate of increase of temperature with depth, there was a great lack of knowledge of the two *extremes*. In this case many candidates went quite outside of terms of the question, and described the *methods* of observation instead of the *results*.

Q. 22. Describe the crystalline form of Augite, and the difference between Augite and Hornblende crystals. To what extent may Augites differ in chemical composition?

Here, too, the failure in many of the answers was due to irrelevancy. Optical properties were given instead of the crystalline form that is asked for, and the normal composition of the minerals was given instead of the variations. In many cases the cleavage angles were remembered but wrongly applied to the faces of the crystals, or were reversed. On the whole the answers to this question were far from satisfactory.

Q. 23. Describe the mineralogical constitution and the structure of the Andesites, indicating the chief varieties of that class of rocks.

This question, on the contrary, was very well answered. The chief error was a want of knowledge of the main varieties, the Augite Andesites on the one hand, and the Hornblende and Mica-andesites on the other. Andesite glass, propylites and porphyrites were much more often referred to.

Q. 24. Draw a diagram showing a "Reversed Fault," and indicate how you would measure its "throw." How are reversed faults related to "Thrusts"?

A great deal of knowledge was shown in the answers to this question. Even when the statements were not quite accurate, the reasoning upon them showed considerable intelligence and powers of observation. While ordinary faults appear to be well understood by the candidates, little knowledge is shown concerning "thrusts."

Q. 25. What are "derived fossils"? Describe the characters by which you would distinguish between derived fossils and those contemporaneous with the beds in which they occur.

As a general rule, this question was fairly understood and well answered, though a few thought "derived" meant pseudomorphous. Besides the physical characters which distinguish derived fossils, some candidates reasoned accurately concerning differences of habitat (*e.g.*, marine forms in fresh-water strata), and the occurrence of ancient types in more modern strata.

Q. 26. Give an account of the Lower-Oolite formations in the South-West of England, stating their chief divisions and naming two fossils from each of these divisions.

This question was selected by only a small minority of the candidates. The answers were by no means good, and the knowledge of fossils was very small.

Q. 27. Explain the difference between "intrusive" and "interbedded" igneous sheets, and indicate the tests by which you would distinguish between them in the field.

This question was well answered, like all those of a general nature. In one centre, "intrusive" and "interbedded" were taken as referring to dykes and sills respectively!

Q. 28. Describe by the aid of diagrams the structures found in spherulitic and perlitic pitchstones, and explain the origin of these
structures.

There was a want of clearness (probably due to lack of powers of
expression) in the description of spherulites and especially of perlites. But
on the other hand a great deal of knowledge was shown concerning adventitious structures found in some rocks of this class.

The economic questions in Series II. are especially well answered, and it
is evident that there is much good teaching in connexion with this subject.

Q. 29 In driving a heading in a coal-mine, the coal-seam is found to be
suddenly cut off by a fault. Describe the observations and
reasoning you would employ in endeavouring to determine the
direction in which the lost seam should be sought.

A very good practical knowledge of the subject is shown by the answers
to this question. It is, unfortunately, rather difficult to follow the
explanations given, owing to the inability of the candidates to make clear
and concise statements. It is manifest, however, that, in spite of imperfect
power of expression, the candidates can reason correctly concerning the
problem referred to them.

Q. 30. Describe a "Mineral Vein," and explain by the aid of diagrams
the nature of "comb-structure" and "horses" in mineral veins.

Very admirably answered by the candidates, who appear to have a
practical knowledge of the subject. It is unfortunate that they have not
had some training in expressing their ideas by drawing.

Q. 31. Explain the several conditions that must be present in order that
Artesian borings may be sunk with success. Show how these
conditions are fulfilled in the case of London and Paris
respectively.

The first part of the question was generally well answered, in spite of
the inability of the candidates to express their meaning in well selected
terms. Some confusion evidently existed in many cases as to the meaning
of "permeable" and "impermeable" strata. But the application to
London was often very far from well done. The water-bearing beds of
the London Basin was imperfectly known in many cases, and the order of
succession of the strata wrongly given. About the conditions in the
Paris Basin there was almost complete ignorance.

STAGE 3.

Results: 1st Class, 12 ; 2nd Class, 23 ; Failed, 14 ; Total, 49.

In his report for 1906 the Examiner had to point out that the candidates
in this Stage showed very exceptional ability. Although the high standard
attained last year has not been reached by the candidates in this stage for
the present year, they are quite up to the average of former years.

Q. 41. Describe the microscopical and chemical characters of the Globigerina Ooze and the Chalk respectively, and point out the
respects in which these substances resemble and differ.

While some of the answers to this question were very good, it was
disappointing to find candidates in this Stage stating that the difference
between these materials is that one consists of silica and the other of
carbonate of lime !

Q. 42. Describe the evidence afforded by the Japan Earthquake of 1891
and by the San Francisco Earthquake of 1906 of actual fractures
having taken place in the Earth's crust.

While there were two or three excellent answers, many candidates wholly
misunderstood the question, and gave *general* accounts of the effects of the
earthquake, altogether ignoring the question of fracture.

Q. 43. If a contoured geological map, with a measured vertical section of the strata shown upon it, were placed before you, describe the manner in which you would proceed to construct a "horizontal" or "longitudinal" section along any line drawn arbitrarily on the map.

It is evident from the answers that most of the candidates had practised the drawing of geological sections. But that this had been done in a somewhat mechanical fashion was shown by the circumstance that, scarcely in any instance, was the important question of the relations of the vertical and the horizontal scale referred to. In arriving at a conclusion as to the dip of the beds, very few of the candidates recognised the help that would be afforded from the vertical section giving the thickness of the several beds, which is one of the data mentioned in the question. Contouring and its use was well understood.

Q. 44. Explain, by the aid of diagrams, different varieties of "perlitic structure," and show how this structure may be produced artificially.

A few candidates confused perlitic structure with spherulitic and proceeded to describe the latter. The differences in perlitic structure, and especially the doubly perlitic varieties, were scarcely ever referred to, and the artificial modes of production were very vaguely dealt with.

Q. 45. Show how the ancestry of the Horse has been elucidated by the successive discovery of extinct mammalian types.

While the modification of the limb-bones was generally fairly well described, there were but few references to the forms of the teeth in the several ancestral forms. In some cases there was much confusion concerning the nomenclature and geological distribution of these forms mentioned.

Q. 46. Give an account of the chief varieties of Augite and Hornblende which are rich in soda, and name the principal rocks in which these varieties are found.

For the most part the answers dealt with varieties, other than the soda-bearing ones, of Augite and Hornblende ; and the conclusion must be arrived at that the important class of rock-forming minerals rich in soda and the interesting rocks containing them had received little attention from the teachers.

HONOURS.

Results : 1st Class, 6 ; 2nd Class, 5 ; Failed, 7 ; Total, 18.

There was an increase in the number of candidates, both in Stage 3 and in Honours in the present year. As the candidates who acquitted themselves so well in Stage 3 last year are probably among those presenting themselves for Honours in the present year, it is not surprising to find a great improvement in this last stage. Some of the papers were excellent, showing not only a large amount of knowledge, but great intelligence and reasoning power.

Report on the Examination in Mineralogy.

There is again a slight increase in the number of papers in this subject, and the proofs of excellent teaching are conspicuous. On the whole, there is an improvement on previous years, the percentage of failures is still small, and the proportion of those obtaining a First Class is greater. As a rule the candidates select questions relating to minerals of the metallic class, rather than the less practical ones relating to crystallography and the optical properties of minerals.

STAGE 1.

Results : 1st Class, 15 ; 2nd Class, 14 ; Failed, 3 ; Total, 32.

There is a falling off in the numbers in this stage which is more than counterbalanced by the increase in Stage 2.

Q. 1. Draw a combination of two forms of the Tetragonal System (Zircon Type), and name two minerals which exhibit the combination you draw.

Very few of the candidates selected this question, but those who attempted it showed a very fair knowledge of the subject. The drawings were quite satisfactory.

Q. 2. Name in order, the minerals constituting the Scale of Hardness, and explain how you would determine in this scale the position of any mineral submitted to you.

Three-fourths of the candidates attempted this question and most of them showed a knowledge of the minerals forming the "Scale of Hardness," though in some cases these were transposed. Scarcely any of the candidates were aware of the use of the file in determining hardness.

Q. 3. How is the fusibility of a mineral tested, and in what way can the degree of fusibility be stated ?

The knowledge of the fusibility scale is much less general among these candidates than that of the hardness scale. Only about one-fifth of them attempted the question, and although some fair answers were given none of them quoted the minerals of the scale of Von Kobell.

Q. 4. Explain what is meant by the statement that Rock salt, Sal-ammoniac and Sylvine (Potassium Chloride) are isomorphous substances. Give two other examples of isomorphism.

More than half the candidates selected this question. The answers showed that the subject had been taught and to some extent understood, for intelligent quotations of examples were made. Want of powers of clear expression, however, caused the definitions given in most cases to be rather unsatisfactory.

Q. 5. State what you know concerning the minerals which consist of carbonate of iron, carbonate of zinc and carbonate of manganese respectively.

There is a great tendency shown to repeat numbers, like those representing specific gravity and hardness (which have evidently been learned by rote), and to omit descriptive terms like those referring to colour, lustre, habit, &c. The confusion between "magnesia" and "manganese" should be guarded against by teachers.

Q. 6. Describe the several forms under which the element carbon occurs as a mineral.

Nearly all the candidates attempted this question, and many of the descriptions of graphite and diamond were good. That "coals" should be classed as "minerals" is not surprising considering the practice of the older books on mineralogy, but very few recognise that only anthracite could be regarded as native carbon : some indeed quote various hydrocarbons as examples of the *element*.

Q. 7. What are the chief anhydrous oxides of iron which occur as minerals ? State briefly the characters of each of these minerals.

Although this question was well answered by more than one-half of the candidates, some showed a great confusion of mind concerning the differences between anhydrous and hydrous oxides.

Q. 8. Name the chief ores of lead, giving their composition and describing their physical characters.

Well answered by more than two-thirds of the candidates, but as in Question 5, the statements of the numbers for hardness and specific gravity, without any reference to other characters, indicate much learning by rote.

Q. 9. Give an account of the different conditions under which gold is found by the miner.

This question was also answered by more than two-thirds of the candidates. While a few gave excellent answers—including a reference to the tellurides—many showed a want of appreciation of the difference between native and combined gold. In some cases there is a want of appreciation of the difference between vein gold and alluvial gold, while nuggets are spoken of as a form distinct from the latter.

Q. 10. Name the three specimens placed before you ; state the chemical composition of each, and the system in which it crystallises. Also make a qualitative blowpipe-analysis of each of the two powdered minerals supplied to you. State your results clearly ; if any chemical symbols or abbreviations are used, write them *distinctly*.

Of the minerals given, Copper Pyrites was generally correctly identified, though the composition was given wrongly. Chalybite was mistaken in many cases, as it had a rather dark colour, for Zinc Blende, while the Orthoclase, in spite of the characteristic form of the crystals, was a source of difficulty in many cases.

The blowpipe work was fairly well done. Nearly all recognised the powders as Strontium Sulphate and Stibnite, though a few who recognised the elements present failed to suggest the right compound.

STAGE 2.

Results : 1st Class, 15 ; 2nd Class, 23 ; Failed, 7 ; Total, 45.

In this Stage the number of candidates is nearly double that of last year, and the character of the papers is even better than in 1906.

SERIES I.

Q. 21. Describe the chief kinds of twinning found in Felspar crystals.

Nearly one-half of the candidates selected this question, and many of them gave entirely satisfactory answers. In a few cases the only knowledge of the subject seems to have been derived from the teaching on microscopical characters (probably given in the Geology Classes) and only simple and lamellar twinning are distinguished more or less imperfectly.

Q. 22. What are the chief liquids employed for separating minerals of different densities ? Explain how you would use one of these liquids to determine the specific gravity of a minute fragment of a mineral.

About one-third of the candidates attempted this question, and in nearly all cases gave good answers. Some, however, were only acquainted with one, or at most two, of the liquids employed.

Q. 23. Explain what is meant by total reflection and the importance of making determinations of this property in a mineral.

Of the few who attempted this, nearly half were quite unacquainted with the relation of the angle of total reflection to the refractive index. The other half gave excellent answers.

Q. 24. Describe and draw some of the chief forms assumed by embryonic crystals (crystallites).

This question was also seldom selected, but several very good answers were given to it.

Q. 25. Give an account of the chief varieties of Garnet, stating the mode of occurrence of each.

Of more than half the candidates answering this question, the majority gave good answers. The varieties and their chief characters were well stated, but it is not generally understood that the account of a mineral is not complete unless its mode of occurrence is stated.

Q. 26. Describe the chief minerals containing manganese which are of economic importance.

The mistake most generally made was that of attempting to name as many manganese minerals as possible without any attempt at discriminating those of economic value. The descriptions were sometimes very meagre.

Q. 27. Give an account of the mineral Cassiterite (Tinstone), describing its crystalline form, its physical properties, and its modes of occurrence.

This question was the one most frequently selected, two-thirds of the candidates giving answers to it. These answers were in nearly all cases good and fairly complete.

Q. 28. Describe the three models placed before you, giving a sketch of each to show which axis you place in an upright position. In each case name a mineral that crystallises in the form shown.

In the case of the models of very common crystals of sulphur, gypsum and left-handed quartz, the system to which each belongs was generally recognised, and the drawings, though poor, showed the correct position of the vertical axis. Most of the candidates rightly named the minerals which exhibit these several forms.

Q. 29. Name the three specimens placed before you ; give the chemical composition of each, and the system in which it crystallises. Also make a qualitative blowpipe-analysis of each of the two powdered minerals supplied to you. Tabulate the results, stating how each was obtained ; if any chemical symbols or abbreviations are used, write them *distinctly*.

The Stibnite specimen given was sometimes taken for Galena or Jamesonite, while the Erubescite was taken for Copper-pyrites, or Peacock Copper or Tetrahedrite. The Topaz was generally correctly identified, but there were mistakes in a few cases in giving the chemical composition of these three minerals. The blowpipe work was not so good as might be expected. Manganese was taken for Nickel, Zinc for Barium, while the Carbon Dioxide was missed. The minerals were seldom named.

SERIES II.

A fair proportion of the candidates selected questions from Series II., and gave fairly good answers.

Q. 30. What are the chief minerals known commercially under the name of Asbestos ? State the composition and chief physical characters of these minerals, and give examples of other "Asbestiform" minerals.

This question was seldom selected, and the few who answered it did so in a very imperfect and unsatisfactory manner. The teaching on this subject appears to be very defective.

Q. 31. State what you know concerning the minerals which contain the metal mercury, and describe the ores which are the source of that metal.

This question was taken by many candidates, and a fair knowledge of the subject was shown in the answers.

Q. 32. Describe the modes of occurrence and the uses of platinum and of the other native metals found associated with it.

The mode of occurrence of these minerals was generally well known, but very few of the candidates were acquainted with the uses of any other members of the group than platinum.

STAGE 3.

Results : 1st Class, 1 ; 2nd Class, 5 ; Failed, 4 ; Total, 10.

In this Stage there is one candidate less than last year. The answers are quite up to the usual standard of excellence, and exhibit evidence of very good teaching.

HONOURS.

Results : 1st Class, 0 ; 2nd Class, 2 ; Failed, 0 ; Total, 2.

Neither of the two candidates show any conspicuous ability, and their theoretical knowledge is greater than their practical acquaintance with minerals.

Report on the Examination in Principles of Mining.

The following Table gives the number of candidates this year and last :—

Year.	Stage 1.	Stage 2.	Stage 3.	Honours.	Total.
1906	951	738	484	128	2,301
1907	967	770	427	. 176	2,340

The comparison shows an increase of 39 candidates, there being a larger number of entries in Stages 1, 2, and Honours, but a falling off in Stage 3.

STAGE 1.

Results : 1st Class, 232 ; 2nd Class, 396 ; Failed, 339 ; Total, 967.

Compared with the previous year the papers in this stage show little change. They are slightly below the average of last year in matter, but show an improvement in neatness and style.

With regard to the questions severally, the following points may be noted :—

BRANCH A.

Q. 1. What are smokeless, bituminous, and hard steam-coals ? Give an example of each.

There are some excellent answers, but whether the general improvement in the answers to this type of question is due to better teaching or to the teacher anticipating that such a question would be asked is open to doubt.

Q. 2. In blasting, when a shot has missed fire what steps should be
   taken ?

This is the favourite question, and, as a rule, is answered very satisfactorily,
some of the answers being exceptionally good.   Blasting is an operation
with which most miners are familiar, but some candidates, naturally enough,
simply say that they " would inform the fireman."   Many candidates
propose to remove the charge, one going so far as to add " taking care that
you are not caught, or you are liable to a fine."   No marks were given for
this question to candidates who would tamper with a shot that had missed
fire.

Q. 3. Describe a method of timbering a longwall face (a) with a strong
   roof, and (b) with a weak roof.   (Sketches required.)

This question is generally attempted, and in many cases well answered.
It is, however, obvious that a great many have had no practical experience
of timbering a longwall face with a weak roof.   The majority would put in
bars or crown-trees, but they make the mistake of placing a second prop
right against the face, which would clearly prevent the coal from being got
down after holing.   The end of the bar nearest to the face should, of course,
be placed in a hole slotted over the coal.

Q. 4. What are "shaft-pillars"?   State how the shape and size of such
   pillars have to be influenced by the depth and inclination of the
   seam.   (Sketch required.)

There are a fair number of good answers to this question, but none of
conspicuous merit.   Candidates seem to be aware that the shaft-pillar is
necessary, but they have no clear idea of the reasons, and are evidently
doubtful as to the influence of the inclination of the seam on the size of the
pillars.   A very general mistake is to state that the pillar should be larger
on the dip than on the rise side.

Q. 5. In what manner should a door in a waggon road be constructed
   so as to open and close without loss of time and without damage
   from the waggon ?   (Sketch required.)

There are some satisfactory answers with good sketches showing the
door hung out of plumb.   Only a very small number, however, answer the
latter part of the question and show a curved flat iron protecting guard on
the door.

Q. 6. How should wire-rope guides or conductors be fixed in a shaft,
   18 feet in diameter and 500 yards deep, in which two cages are
   in use ?   (Sketch required.)

This question is answered very well, but the sketches given are generally
very poor.

Q. 7. Describe a pump suitable for raising water from dip-workings.
   (Sketch required.)

Not only is the question the least frequently attempted, but it is also the
worst answered.   Preposterous arrangements are illustrated, even so
grotesque as the Cornish pump.   Year after year the deficiency in the
knowledge of pumping is most remarkable.

Q. 8. What is the quantity of air per minute passing through an airway
   9 feet 3 inches wide, and 6 feet 6 inches high when the velocity
   of the current is 8¾ feet per second ?

This question is generally attempted, and a decided improvement in the
knowledge of the elementary principles of ventilation is noticeable.   The
mistakes made are usually in the arithmetic, whether vulgar fractions or
decimals are employed.

Q. 9. What do you understand by natural ventilation? State why it is generally found insufficient. (Sketch required.)

This question is generally attempted, and answered fairly well. The well-worn text-book illustrations are given. The common mistake, however, is made that "natural ventilation is produced only when there is a difference of surface level between the two shafts," comparatively few stating that there must be a difference in density between the two air-columns. A few candidates confuse the winter and summer course of the ventilating current, and some who are in doubt ingenuously put in arrows with heads at both ends.

Q. 10. Upon what principle is the Davy-lamp based, and in what ways has the original construction been modified in order to obtain greater security? (Sketches required.)

Although questions on lines similar to this have been asked nearly every year for a considerable period, there is still general confusion as to the correct principles upon which Sir Humphry Davy's invention was based. There are, however, some good sketches of safety lamps, of which the form and construction appear to be well known.

BRANCH B.

Comparatively few candidates entered in Branch B.; some, as in previous years, being coal miners who had inadvertently wandered into this Branch with no knowledge of ore and stone mining. There are a few good papers from classes in tin-mining and in iron ore districts, but, as a rule, the answers in this Branch are disappointing.

Q. 11. What is a mineral vein, and how does it differ from a bed or seam? Give examples of ores met with in beds or seams.

This question is seldom well answered. Coal is often named as an ore, and it is often stated that a bed has no dip.

Q. 13. Explain the construction and use of " stulls " (Sketch required.)

The answers to this question indicate considerable confusion in the minds of the candidates as to its meaning. The term " stull " is in general use among ore-miners for the platform of timber upon which the valueless rock is thrown down in stoping.

Q. 14. What are " open-cast " workings? Give an example, and indicate the advantages of this method of working mineral deposits. (Sketch required.)

The answers generally are poor. Some candidates think that blasting is unnecessary in " open-cast " workings, especially if there is water.

Q. 15. How may a skip be made to discharge its contents without the intervention of any workman? (Sketch required.)

There are some very good answers with excellent sketches.

Q. 16. How should wire-rope guides or conductors be fixed in a vertical shaft, 15 feet by 5 feet and 1,500 feet deep, in which two cages are in use? (Sketch required.)

This question is also answered well, and there are some good sketches.

Q. 17. In what manner are the lifts arranged in a deep-mine pumping engine? (Sketch required.)

An ore-miner ought to be able to answer this question without difficulty. The answers are, however, rarely very good.

Q. 20. Enumerate the various methods by which mines are lighted, and state the advantages and disadvantages of each method. (Sketches required.)

The answers to this question are most disappointing.

STAGE 2.

Results : 1st Class, 121 ; 2nd Class, 462 ; Failed, 187 ; Total, 770.

In this stage the papers afford evidence of careful training on the part of the teachers, and of painstaking work on the part of the candidates. Most of the papers are neat, and there are no absolutely foolish ones. The work as a whole is slightly above last year's standard.

BRANCH A.

Q. 21. Describe fully any deposit of stratified ironstone, or of shale, or of fireclay, with which you are acquainted, giving details as to composition, associated rocks, and geological age. (Sketch required.)

This question is seldom well answered. The candidates do not appear to have even a rudimentary knowledge of geology.

Q. 22. Describe the operation of blasting (a) in coal in a fiery mine, and (b) in hard rock, assuming that the shot-holes have been bored to the requisite distance.

This question is generally well and fully answered. The three essential points : (a) permitted explosive (b) use of clay or non-carbonaceous stemming, and (c) examination to determine the presence of gas, are generally mentioned, but are overlooked by some candidates who give excellent answers in other respects. There are a few preposterous answers. One candidate for example, who incidentally mentions the colliery at which he works, in the course of his answer has the following extraordinary statement : "Fiery mine. If a fuse is the means of igniting the powder, he either opens a lamp or lights the fuse with a lucifer."

Q. 23. Give particulars of the plant that should be provided for sinking a shaft 16 feet in diameter to a depth of 1,000 feet. (Sketches required.)

There are no strikingly good answers to the question. Candidates in general confine themselves to enumerating various items of plant required, the descriptions and illustrations being poor.

Q. 24. Describe the method of working that should be adopted for a seam 500 yards deep, 5½ feet thick, lying nearly horizontal, with a good, hard roof and about 8 inches of holing dirt at the bottom. (Sketch required.)

Some excellent arguments for and against longwall and pillar-and-stall methods of working the particular seam specified are given. The system more favoured is longwall, probably because it is better known and easier to describe. As a matter of fact the seam is suited to either method, and the choice would be determined by the district in which it is situated. In the North of England it would be worked by the pillar-and-stall system, and in the Midlands by longwall.

Q. 25. What precautions would you adopt on a self-acting incline to avoid accidents from mine-waggons running away ? (Sketch required.)

This question is very well answered, and the sketches given, are, as a rule, good.

Q. 26. Describe the best method of signalling in underground haulage-roads. (Sketch required.)

Electric signalling is generally selected for description, but although the majority are aware that in a battery, bell and line wires are employed, they are lamentably ignorant of the method of coupling them together, and the character of the battery remains a mystery. Materials mentioned as the contents include mercury and carbide of calcium, and Leyden jars are also described.

Q. 27. Give a detailed description of a clip for use in underground haulage on an undulating road where the steepest gradient is 1 in 6. (Sketch required.)

Descriptions and illustrations are given of nearly every clip on the market, whether suitable or not for an undulating gradient or for an inclination of 1 in 6.

Q. 28. What diameter of bucket-pump would be required to lift 21,000 gallons of water per hour to a height of 300 feet, allowing 2½ per cent. for slip, and assuming a pump speed of 100 feet per minute ?

This problem is not attempted with the success that might reasonably have been expected. The majority have apparently been misled by the mention of the height of 300 feet. Clear evidence is afforded that the knowledge of the required calculation is not sound.

Q. 29. Give particulars of the methods that should be adopted, and the instruments that should be used to determine the quantity of air passing through a main airway, noting the precautions that should be taken to guard against any errors of observation.

This question is very generally attempted, the answers showing familiarity with the instruments needed, and a fair knowledge of the precautions to be taken when using them. The subject of colliery ventilation seems to be well taught in almost all cases.

Q. 30. Describe a tippler for dealing with waggons holding up to 20 cwt. of coal. How many waggons of this capacity should be dealt with in 9 hours by one tippler ? (Sketch required.)

This question is not well answered as a rule, though there are a few exceedingly good answers. The descriptions given relate chiefly to machine-driven tipplers, but the mechanism for throwing them in and out of gear is imperfectly understood and is badly illustrated. Hazy notions also exist as to the number of waggons that can be dealt with in 9 hours, replies varying from 1 every 3 minutes to 5 per minute. One candidate even gives as many as 12 a minute, a preposterous total of 6,480 in 9 hours.

BRANCH B.

Few candidates entered in this branch, and as usual several of them were coal miners with no knowledge of ore and stone mining, who should have entered in Branch A. They were probably attracted by the greater scope of the question on blasting.

Q. 31. Describe fully any one important deposit of metalliferous minerals, *or* of slate, *or* of rock salt, with which you are acquainted, giving details as to composition, associated rocks, and geological age. (Sketch required.)

The answers show a decided improvement in comparison with answers to questions of similar character in previous years.

Q. 32. Describe the operation of blasting, (a) with gunpowder, and (b) with an explosive of the nitro-glycerine class, assuming that the shot-holes have been bored to the requisite distance.

The answers generally are excellent, the ore-miner being very familiar with the practical use of explosives.

Q. 33. Give particulars of the plant that should be provided for sinking a vertical shaft, 15 feet by 5 feet, to a depth of 1,000 feet. (Sketch required.)

There are some excellent answers. They are certainly better than those of the coal mining candidates. This is probably due to the fact that sinking of shafts or winzes is always going on more or less in ore-mining districts.

Q. 34. Describe the method of working a quartz vein, 8 feet wide, standing nearly vertical between soft walls. (Sketch required.)

This question is generally attempted and answered satisfactorily.

Q. 35. What precautions would you adopt, on a self-acting incline, to avoid accidents from mine-waggons running away ? (Sketch required.)

The descriptions given are very poor, only a drag being mentioned. This is probably due to the fact that self-acting inclines are rarely employed in ore-mining.

Q. 36. Describe the best method of signalling in underground haulage-roads. (Sketch required.)

The answers to this question are not very good. Reference is rarely made to electric signals.

Q. 37. Give a detailed description of a clip for use in underground haulage on an undulating road where the steepest gradient is 1 in 4. (Sketch required.)

This question is practically ignored.

Q. 38. What diameter of bucket-pump would be required to lift 21,000 gallons of water per hour to a height of 300 feet, allowing 2½ per cent. for slip, and assuming a pump speed of 100 feet per minute?

This question is not well answered. The candidates appear barely equal to dealing with the simplest sums.

Q. 39. Describe, with dimensions, an air pump of simple construction that could be made up by a mine carpenter. (Sketch required.)

Some admirable descriptions of the ordinary air pump are given, and the illustrations to some of them are quite worthy of being photographed and reproduced in a text book.

Q. 40. Explain the construction and mode of action of any type of jig. (Sketch required.)

The common Harz jig is generally described quite satisfactorily. The sketches are really excellent. In fact throughout the papers the sketches by the ore miners are far superior to those of the coal miners. Many of the latter failed to get full marks because their drawings were so hopelessly bad.

Stage 3.

Results : 1st Class, 71 ; 2nd Class, 166 ; Failed, 190 ; Total, 427.

The remarkable increase in the number of candidates in this stage noted last year has not been repeated. There has, on the contrary, been a slight falling off in the numbers ; and whilst the general average of the work is higher, there are rather fewer papers of conspicuous merit. As usual, a number of candidates entered who did not realise that the standard of knowledge demanded in this stage is considerably higher than in Stage 2.

The great majority of the candidates select the coal mining Branch A, The methods of putting down deep boreholes (Q. 41) are well described. some good descriptions being given of the Diamond, Calyx, and Mather and Platt systems. Few candidates attempted the question on permitted explosives (Q. 42), but those who did so usually gave good answers. Q. 43 is a favourite one, and there are some good detailed answers of electrically-driven coal-cutting machines of various types. The answers to Q. 44, the most popular question, show a good knowledge of the methods of sinking by piling, and by the freezing, boring, and sinking-drum methods. Q. 45 elicited some good practical descriptions of methods of working. From the answers to Q. 46 it is evident that recent inventions brought before the various Mining Institutes had been carefully noted. Q. 47 is a favourite one, and the answers are generally good. The answers to Q. 48 on earthing electric cables in mines are most disappointing. The ignorance shown of the special rules established under the Coal Mines Regulation Act is surprising in view of the fact that copies of these rules are posted up at all mines where electricity is in application. The problem (Q. 49) on ventilation, the correct answer to which is 45,562 cubic feet per minute, is rarely solved. Curiously enough, it has been in most cases regarded as a simple proportion sum. Candidates are generally aware that the volume of air flowing through an airway varies directly as the area. They forget, however, that it also varies as the square root of the rubbing surface, and, as in this example the length is the same in both cases, the perimeter only has to be taken into account. Q. 50 is not so popular as might have been expected in view of recent discussions in connection with colliery explosions. Some good descriptions of rescue apparatus are given, the Fleuss apparatus being the most usual. More recent inventions, however, receive notice, such as the Shamrock breathing apparatus, the Giersberg, the Draeger, the pneumatogen, the Weg and the pneumatophore.

In the ore and stone mining Branch B., the papers are few and not of such good quality as usual. Q. 52 has elicited some accurate notes on the composition of explosives. Electrically-driven rock-drills (Q. 53) are well described, more particularly the Marvin electric drill. Q. 55 on working vertical mineral veins is not answered with as much detail as was expected. Q. 56 is, however, ably answered, and there are some excellent sketches of Cornish changing-houses.

HONOURS.

Results : 1st Class, 22 ; 2nd Class, 74 ; Failed, 80 ; Total, 176.

The number of candidates in Honours continues to increase in a gratifying manner, showing the growing attention devoted to higher technical education in the coal mining centres. In 1903 and again in 1904 there were 63 candidates. Since then there has been a regular increase. In 1905 there were 74 candidates and in 1906 there were 128. The number of candidates from ore and stone mining districts continues small. As in previous years, many of the failures are to be attributed rather to ill-judged ambition than to faulty teaching. Several of the candidates who wrote fairly satisfactory papers failed by neglecting to bear in mind the instructions printed on the paper of questions that answers must be full and well illustrated and that answers with insufficient sketches will not secure a pass. The examination is of course not intended to be a test of the artistic powers of the candidates ; but closely-written pages of verbose description cannot be accepted as an adequate substitute for a few clear and neatly drawn figures. The papers of several candidates do not contain a single sketch ; and it is only in the Honours Stage that this defect is observed. In this stage, as in the earlier ones, candidates should be encouraged to make rapid free-hand sketches of mining appliances roughly to scale on squared paper. In other respects the answers call for no comment. To each question some excellent answers are given, the most popular being Questions 63, 64, 67, and 68. The answers afford clear evidence not only of extensive practical experience but also of careful study of memoirs read before the Mining Institutes and of the reports of H.M. Inspectors of Mines. It is evident that many candidates having read for their Colliery Manager's Certificate examination find it advantageous to carry their studies further and to present themselves for this examination.

Report on the Examinations in Physiography.

EVENING EXAMINATION.

WHOLE OF STAGE 1.

Results : 1st Class, 87 ; 2nd Class, 81 ; Failed, 52 ; Total, 220.

There is a considerable falling off in the number of candidates in Stage 1 as compared with last year. While the proportion of those obtaining a Second Class is about the same as last year, there is a decrease in the percentage of those obtaining a First Class, this being balanced by a corresponding increase in the proportion of failures. On the whole, therefore, the results in this stage are not quite so good as those of last year. There are very striking divergencies in the quality of the papers sent in from different centres. In some cases it is clear that experiments have been seen, if not actually performed, by the scholars, and their significance pointed out ; in other cases the evidence indicates complete reliance upon text-book teaching.

Q. 21. A flask fitted with a long tube to its neck is filled with water and lumps of ice, so that the water touches a marked point near the bottom of the tube. State and explain what happens when a spirit lamp is applied to the flask and it is slowly warmed.

Although this question was, on the whole, well answered, there were certain mistakes that were prevalent, especially in some sets of papers. There was a confusion of ideas concerning expansion and other temperature phenomena ; and the drawings, which were frequently given, were often quite unsatisfactory. The point most commonly missed in the answer was the contraction due to the melting of the ice.

Q. 22. What gas is given off when sulphuric acid is poured upon iron filings ? State the methods you would employ for collecting and examining the properties of this gas.

This question was very well answered generally. A few made the mistake of stating that oxygen or carbon dioxide is the gas. Very often the only properties mentioned were " colourless, odourless and tasteless." In the present case it was clear that the answers were parrot-like, for if the experiment had been performed the student would know that the gas thus produced was anything but " odourless."

Q. 23. Describe an experiment which shows that matter is indestructible.

The chief mistake made in the answers, which were on the whole very good, was in respect of the necessity for accurate weighing at the beginning and the end of the experiment, and the precaution necessary to prevent loss on the one hand or accession of foreign matter on the other hand.

Q. 24. Show how to find experimentally the position of the centre of gravity of a thin flat piece of wood cut in the form of an equilateral triangle.

This question was generally well answered, the chief mistake being that many candidates stated that three suspensions (instead of two) were necessary.

Q. 25. Explain the fall of the mercury in a barometer as it is carried up a mountain. Why does the mercury rise and fall when the instrument is at the earth's surface ?

Although the principle involved in the first part of this question has been insisted upon in the reports on these examinations in many previous years, teachers do not, even yet, appreciate its great importance. The air being " less dense " or " more rare " on a mountain was again and again given as the cause of the fall of the mercury, and not *the diminution in the height and weight of the column of air above the instrument.* With respect to the second part of the question, much ignorance was shown in some cases. The effect of the presence of water-vapour was often reversed, and changes of temperature were in some cases given as the principal or only cause.

Q. 26. Explain the nature and origin of the land- and sea-breezes.

This subject appears to have been very generally well taught, and nearly all the answers were satisfactory. The only mistake at all common was that of reversing the directions of the two breezes.

Q. 27. How is the depth of the deeper parts of the ocean determined ? Why were the early statements of navigators on this subject untrustworthy ?

Although this question was generally well answered, much ignorance was shown, in not a few cases, as to the impracticability of using a *rope* for sounding, and the reasons of that impracticability.

Q. 28. Describe a Coral-Atoll, a Fringing Reef, an Encircling Reef and a Barrier Reef, stating the nature of the materials of which they are built up.

Very few candidates attempted this question. Of these the majority were unable to discriminate between a Fringing Reef and a Barrier Reef. In no case was any knowledge shown that calcareous algæ, foraminifera, and other organisms take part with corals in building up reefs.

Q. 29. Describe a simple method of determining the true south point by means of observations of the sun.

Many of the candidates were evidently under the belief that the sun always rises due East and sets due West. When a correct method, that of setting up a vertical stick and observing its shadow was given, the necessary precautions were not mentioned. Instead of taking the position in which the shadow of the stick was longest, some said observe at 12 o'clock or take the middle line between that shown at 10 o'clock and 2 o'clock.

Q. 30. Explain Cavendish's method of determining the mean density of the Earth.

This question was attempted by very few candidates. While a general idea of the nature of the experiment was evidently present in the minds of the candidates, the exact mode of procedure, and the nature of the torsion-balance were very imperfectly indicated. The mathematical reasoning was very crudely stated.

Q. 31. What is the shape of the Earth's orbit ? Describe the observations which enable us to determine this.

Many candidates confused the Earth's orbit with the Earth's circumference and some stated that the shape is an " oblate spheroid "! Even when the difference of distance of the sun at various periods of the year was stated, the way in which this is shown by variation in the sun's diameter was not explained.

Q. 32. Describe the behaviour of a compass-needle and a dip-needle if both were placed,

First, in Labrador, and, *secondly,* in Britain.

Of the few candidates who attempted this question a fair proportion gave satisfactory answers. Some were evidently ignorant of the position of Labrador and more were unaware of the abnormally large declination in that district.

STAGE 2.

Results : 1st Class, 123 ; 2nd Class, 106 ; Failed, 88 ; Total, 317.

The standard attained by the candidates in this Stage is almost identical with that of last year's examination, though the proportion of failures is slightly in excess. The number of papers is diminished in about the same proportion as those of Stage 1. Of the instruments referred to in the questions, the only ones with which the candidates indicate any personal knowledge are barometers. Very few, evidently, had seen either sounding apparatus or seismographs, or had looked through a telescope.

Q. 41. Describe the precautions which it is necessary to take in constructing a barometer. Indicate the exact points from which measurements must be taken in determining the height of the mercury column, and state why it is necessary to read the thermometer at the same time as the barometer.

This question was generally well answered, the chief mistake being in explaining why the thermometer has to be read at the same time as the barometer. Most of the candidates refer only to the influence of changes in temperature on the air, and entirely omit any reference to the effect on the mercury in the barometer.

Q. 42. What are isobars and what are the data required for drawing them? Draw a diagram showing the position of isobars during an anti-cyclone with its centre at Derby.

In answering this question the most serious mistake made by the candidates was the omission of any reference to the fact that simultaneous readings are necessary. The maps drawn were often incomplete in not giving any outline of the British Isles, so as to show the position of Derby and the relations of the isobars in space.

Q. 43. What is a facula? State the connection between sun-spots and faculae. In what part of the sun's disc can the latter be best observed?

The answers given to this question in different centres were of very unequal merit. In some cases an almost complete ignorance of the nature of faculae was shown and in other instances they were confounded with prominences. In nearly all cases the knowledge shown was evidently derived from text-books.

Q. 44. Give a rough map of the so-called "isoclinal" lines or lines of equal magnetic inclination in Western Europe. State how they have been determined.

The rarity with which this question was selected probably shows that there had been little teaching on this subject, and this part of the subject, and this conclusion is confirmed by the character of the few answers given. The map asked for was seldom given, and no attempts were made to reason as to the position of the isoclinals from a knowledge of the locality of the magnetic pole.

Q. 45. Describe ocean-currents and give an account of the theories which have been proposed to account for them.

The answers given to this question were generally satisfactory, both the nature of the currents and the theories by which they are explained being well described. A very fair knowledge was shown of the distribution of the currents on the Earth's surface.

Q. 46. What is the cause of twilight? Explain the fact that twilight is of short duration in equatorial regions and becomes longer as we proceed northwards and southwards.

The very unsatisfactory answers given to this question appear to have been the result of reliance upon the statements made in certain text-books. The twilight is stated to be due to refraction, and the varying length in different latitudes is ascribed to variation in the amount of air passed through by the sun's rays or to differences in the density of the atmosphere. It is greatly to be desired that this subject should be more adequately treated in works of this character.

Q. 47. Describe and explain the principle of the method devised by Lord Kelvin for rapidly determining the depth of the ocean.

The valuable sounding apparatus of Lord Kelvin seems not to have been included in the teaching of this subject, and many of the candidates contented themselves with an account of the "Hydra" Sounding Machine, with or without the use of pianoforte wire (an improvement also due to Lord Kelvin). Those who were acquainted with the rapid method gave an excellent account of it and of the chemical and physical principles on which it is based.

Q. 48. How were the earthquakes that destroyed San Francisco, Valparaiso, and Kingston, Jamaica, observed in this country? Describe the nature of the instruments employed in the observations.

Very few candidates selected this question, but there were some very intelligent answers. The point most frequently missed in the descriptions given of seismographs was that the record is produced owing to the pointer remaining at rest while the Earth moves. The statement was often reversed.

Q. 49. What is meant by a shooting star? Explain the cause of its luminosity. When are they most prevalent?

The answers given to this question were of a very satisfactory character. Knowledge was shown not only of the general nature of shooting stars and of the cause of their luminosity, but also of the emanation of showers from radiant points.

Q. 50. Describe the chief features seen on the surface of the planet Mars. State what is known about any changes in the markings which have been observed from time to time.

This question, like the last, was selected by most of the candidates, and the answers were fairly complete. All were acquainted with the seasonal changes in the size of the ice-caps, but only a few described the other corresponding changes in the "canals."

Q. 51. Give an example to illustrate an aberration effect. Describe fully the distinction between "*aberration*" and "*precession.*"

There was evidence in the answers of excellent teaching on both the subjects of aberration and precession, though in a few cases the former was confounded with parallax. The illustrations were well described and correctly applied.

Q. 52. State what is known about the periodicity of sun-spots and prominences.

This question was seldom selected, and the few who attempted to deal with it showed only a very elementary knowledge of the subject. The eleven-year period was just mentioned, but there was an almost complete absence of knowledge of the details of the mutations of spots and prominences and their relations to one another.

STAGE 3.

Results : 1st Class, 3 ; 2nd Class, 9 ; Failed, 14 ; Total, 26.

There was an increase in the number of papers in this Stage, as compared with last year, but the proportion of first class, second class, and failures was nearly the same—the percentage of failures being rather less. The descriptions of deposits in the deep ocean often showed much want of real knowledge—manganese nodules being very constantly described as of meteoric origin. Seldom was there any evidence of special instruction having been given beyond that required for Stage 2. A few candidates exhibited full and fairly exact knowledge of the methods and reasoning by which determinations of the Earth's density have been arrived at ; but a considerable proportion displayed only the most elementary acquaintance with the subject. The same remark applies to the way in which the question on earthquakes was dealt with ; a few had evidently read and understood the accounts which had reached this country of preliminary geological investigations in connection with the recent catastrophies, but the greater number of candidates showed complete ignorance on the subject. The astronomical questions were, as a rule (with several brilliant exceptions), answered in the same incomplete and unsatisfactory manner.

Day Examination.

Results { Stage 1 :—1st Class, 15 ; 2nd Class, 20 ; Failed, 10 ; Total, 45.
{ Stage 2 :—1st Class, 4 ; 2nd Class, 2 ; Failed, 1 ; Total, 7.

As the papers in Stage 2 were only seven in number, and those in Stage 1, forty-five, it would be useless to attempt to draw any general conclusions as to how far the teaching was responsible for the character of the answers given to the several questions. It may be stated, however, that the results are very similar to those of the Evening Examinations.

GROUP VI.—BIOLOGY, PHYSIOLOGY, AND HYGIENE.

BOARD OF EXAMINERS.

XIV. Human Physiology	Professor J. B. Farmer, D.Sc., M.A., F.R.S., F.L.S., *Chairman.*
XV. General Biology	Professor W. A. Herdman, D.Sc., F.R.S.
XVI. Zoology	Professor F. Gotch, M.A., F.R.S.
XVII. Botany	Col. J. L. Notter, M.A., M.D.
XXV. Hygiene	

Report on the Examinations in Human Physiology.

EVENING EXAMINATION.

STAGE 1.

Results : 1st Class, 355 ; 2nd Class, 466 ; Failed, 235 ; Total, 1,056.

There were 1,056 papers in this subject as compared with 1,044 papers in the preceding year. The work as a whole still shows the improvement which has been a feature of the last three years. This is especially evidenced by the small number of hopelessly bad papers and by the more accurate and intelligent answers of the great majority of candidates. It is thus reasonable to suppose that the teaching of those candidates who take this stage has become more efficient, and that attention is being paid to the necessity of making candidates understand the principles and not rely upon text-book accounts learned off by heart. One means of bringing this about which has been repeatedly urged is the use by teachers of simple practical illustrations, which appears to be now far more common than it was a few years ago. The percentage of first class papers is higher than it has been in previous years, amounting to 34 per cent. of the whole, the failures are slightly lower, amounting to 22 per cent. ; the result of the first stage examination is thus quite satisfactory.

The special points which need attention are referred to under each question, but the remarks appended to Questions 4, 5, and 6 show that an intelligent appreciation of physical features is still one of the chief difficulties experienced by the majority of candidates. On the other hand the chemical principles involved in Questions 3 and 8 appeared, as a rule, to be intelligently grasped.

Q. 1. Give a short account of the corpuscles which are seen when a drop of blood is examined under the microscope.

Most of the answers were fairly good but there were few excellent ones, even in otherwise quite good papers. An increasing number of candidates in this stage appear to have seen blood corpuscles under the microscope, which is a very encouraging feature of the teaching development.

Q. 2. Make a diagram to show the course of the blood flow through the mammalian heart. What are the chief structural differences between the right and left side of this organ ?

This calls for no special remark, the great majority of candidates answered the question quite well and many of the diagrammatic drawings were excellent ; candidates should remember to indicate by arrows the direction of the blood flow.

Q. 3. Mention the chief forms in which the chemical elements, carbon, hydrogen, nitrogen and oxygen, enter and leave the body.

As a rule this was answered very well.   The entrance of nitrogen in the inspired air is not strictly speaking an entrance into the body tissues but only into the air of the lung cavities ; it enters the mouth in the same way.

Q. 4. What structures compose the framework of the thorax ? What alterations in their position occur when a deep breath is taken ? Explain the connexion between these alterations and the entry of extra air into the lungs.

This question, involving the intelligent appreciation of certain physical principles, is always difficult for certain sections of candidates. The fact that the lungs suck in air as a consequence of their enlargement must be brought home to the understanding by suitable demonstrative illustrations.

Q. 5. Describe the general differences between any small artery and its corresponding veins, including in your answer (a) the structure of the vessels and (b) the flow of the blood which is contained in them.

This question is concerned with " small " blood vessels, yet many candidates described the differences between large arteries and veins. Thus the existence of valves in veins was mentioned almost universally as an important one, yet valves do not occur in the small veins which lead from a capillary system. The intermittent character of the arterial as contrasted with the continuous character of the venous blood flow was often expressed in unintelligent language ; it depends upon the character of the pressure.

Q. 6. What movements can the head make ? Describe the articulations which enable these movements to occur.

This question was poorly answered by the majority of candidates. The atlanto-occipital articulation is like that of the thumb, a saddle joint, allowing movement in two planes or in any combination of these (nodding and inclination towards shoulders). The atlas and axis allow of rotation.

Q. 7. Describe the general structure and chief functions of the skin. What parts of the skin contain the endings of sensory nerve fibres, and the blood vessels respectively ?

This was generally answered satisfactorily and in a number of cases very well. It should be remembered that it is possible to cut the skin so as to cause pain without bleeding ; the blood vessels are all in the deep dermis, but some sensory nerves lie between the cells of the deep epidermis layers, thus superficial to the blood vessels.

Q. 8. What do you know as to the position, shape, general structure, and functions of the stomach ? Illustrate your answer by an appropriate diagram, showing the relations of the stomach to other organs in the neighbourhood.

This question was satisfactorily answered by the great majority of candidates. The chemical side of the digestive process was given in a way which showed a much better acquaintance with chemical principles than has been the case in former years.

Q. 9. By what nervous structures are motor and sensory nerves brought into connection with the spinal cord ? Is it possible for the muscles to move after the cord has been severed, and if so, under what circumstances ?

Comparatively few candidates answered this question satisfactorily. The points to be brought out by candidates in this stage are : the separation of the nerve roots ; the connection of the sensory ones with cells outside the cord, and the motor ones with cells inside ; the reflex activities.

Q. 10. Make a rough drawing to show the means by which air pulsations can reach the auditory nerves and cause the sensation of hearing.

Fairly well answered by a large number of candidates, and excellently by a few ; calls for no special remark.

STAGE 2.

Results : 1st Class, 111 ; 2nd Class, 485 ; Failed, 198 ; Total, 794.

The number of candidates in this stage was less than in 1906, when there were 879. The failures amounted to 25 per cent., and the number of first class papers to 14 per cent. ; this is not such a good result as that of the previous year, and, as the detailed criticisms given under each question show, many candidates experienced some difficulty in confining themselves to the questions, so that the prominent feature of many papers was the irrelevant character of the answers. It is desirable to impress on those taking this stage, that a large amount of information upon subjects not involved in the questions, is of no value, and betrays either a lack of intelligent appreciation of the subjects asked, or a desire to supply deficiencies of knowledge by stating other facts which the candidate happens to have remembered. It was due chiefly to the widespread character of this defect that the results compare on the whole unfavourably with those of the previous year. There were some exceptionally good papers, and some, so inferior, that it is doubtful if the candidates could have answered even the first stage papers in an adequate manner.

Q. 21. Describe the red corpuscles of human blood, giving their size, number, shape and functions ; state precisely how you would proceed if you wished to examine microscopically your own blood. What is the effect upon the microscopic appearance, of diluting the blood (a) with water, and (b) with strong salt solution ?

The majority of answers were fairly good, but there were very few really satisfactory ones. Units of measurement are now those of the metric system, and the number of corpuscles in a square inch is not ascertained by any measuring instrument. Such answers as that there are 5 millions in the blood are meaningless ; this is the amount in a cubic millimetre.

Q. 22. What is the physiological importance of such nerves as supply the heart and the arteries respectively ? Explain what happens to the circulation if the spinal cord is divided.

This question was beyond most candidates. The old fallacy that the heart stops when the cord is divided was repeated in several instances. The feature of such division is the fall of blood pressure due to the passive dilatation of a large number of the small arteries. Such answers as involve the statement "if the cord is cut above the medulla," show that the candidate does not fully realise what part of the nervous system is termed the spinal cord.

Q. 23. Describe the position, structure and functions of the pancreas. Has this organ any functions which are not directly digestive ?

This question was fairly well done, although the majority of answers do not compare favourably with those in Stage 1 upon the functions of the stomach. Very few candidates realised the peculiarity of the pancreatic digestion of proteids with the production of amido-compounds, such as leucin, tyrosin, etc. The pancreatic internal secretion, and the production of diabetes on its withdrawal after extirpation, was known to very few.

Q. 24. What is the normal temperature in man ? Where are the principal seats for the production and for the discharge of heat ? Explain how it is that in the warm-blooded animal the body temperature can remain constant when the temperature of the surrounding air falls.

The first part of this question was well done by many candidates. The second part was answered by introducing much irrelevant matter. In cold surroundings, radiation loss must increase ; it is made good by (a) increased reflex muscular metabolism and (b) checked loss through evaporation, etc. In prolonged cold there are additional means for making good the excessive radiation loss ; such are, special food to increase production of heat, clothes, hair, etc., for checking the excessive radiation.

Q. 25. Give an account of the uriniferous tubules of the kidney. What is the relation of the blood vessels to the different parts of the tubules ?

This was answered by most candidates satisfactorily, and was the best answered question in the paper. The only prominent defect was the distribution of the renal blood supply, which was rarely completely given.

Q. 26. What varieties of muscle are found in the body ? Illustrate your answer by appropriate drawings.

Fairly well answered. The three main varieties of muscle were generally given. The drawings illustrating the structure were, as a rule, poor, but in a few cases quite satisfactory, and some were extremely good.

Q. 27. Give the composition of atmospheric and of expired air ? The breathing of even an unconscious animal will become rapid and laboured if it breathes air containing CO_2 gas. What is this condition called, and how is it brought about ?

The majority of candidates answered the first part of this question correctly. The second part was treated in many cases by disquisitions of an irrelevant kind. Thus the necessity of oxygen for life was set forth, whereas the question does not refer to oxygen. Excess of CO_2 in the blood arouses the respiratory centres in the medulla, and this condition is the one referred to.

Q. 28. Describe the retina. What structures are concerned in producing the narrowing of the pupil which occurs when the eye is exposed to a bright light ?

Most candidates described the retina correctly, the description being that given in the text-books. The second part was correctly answered by very few. Again there was the introduction of irrelevant matter, including the general structure of the eyeball and sometimes an account of the eyeball muscles. The pupil contraction to light is a most characteristic example of reflex activity, the sensory path being the optic nerves, the motor path the third nerve with its ciliary endings, and the reflex centre in the optic lobes or superior corpora quadragemina.

STAGE 3.

Results : 1st Class, 8 ; 2nd Class, 29 ; Failed, 22 ; Total, 59.

The examination in this stage was for the first time conducted upon a new basis. This involves a separation of the questions into two groups, the first of which deals with the subject-matter as set forth in theoretical text-books, whilst the second deals with such practical aspects of the subject as are indicated in the recently revised syllabus. These practical aspects comprise the examination of two mounted microscopic sections and written accounts of the methods used in elementary physiological chemistry. The examination of the specimens was, as in previous years, compulsory on all candidates, but, in addition, failure in either group, according to the new regulations, prevented any candidate from being awarded a first class in the whole subject.

It is very creditable that under these new regulations 63 per cent. of the candidates should have passed the examination, and although the questions in the second practical group were leniently marked, it is equally creditable that 14 per cent. of the candidates should have obtained a First Class.

Taking all this into consideration, the numbers compare quite favourably with those of 1906, when, out of a total of 58 candidates, 10 obtained First Class, and 27 failed. Attention is drawn to the character of the questions in the second or practical group of the whole series ; these cannot be satisfactorily answered unless the candidate has personally carried out simple chemical experiments in physiological chemistry. The apparatus needed for this purpose is quite simple, the only pieces of apparatus other than those obtainable in any chemical laboratory being a pocket spectroscope for the examination of blood pigments and a ureometer, such, for instance, as Southall's, a cheap form. It is advisable to read carefully the remarks which are appended to the questions in the second group, since these indicate more precisely the special points of such practical work.

Section A.

Q. 41. Describe the structure of an intestinal villus. By what channels are the various digested products absorbed, and in what form do they reach the circulating blood?

Q. 42. What is the sympathetic chain of ganglia. Describe its situation and the chief paths by which it innervates the head and the abdominal viscera respectively. How is it related to the spinal cord?

Q. 43. From what part of the central nervous system do the vagus nerves arise? Give any facts which show the extent to which these nerves are concerned in regulating the movements of the heart and those of respiration?

In regard to Question 41, no special remarks appear to be necessary, as it was satisfactorily answered by most candidates. The answers to Question 42 varied very greatly in merit ; the chief difficulty appeared to be the paths by which the sympathetic innervates the head and the abdominal viscera. The former is reached by the cervical sympathetic, the latter by the splanchnic, hypogastric and pelvic nerves. The relation of these to the cord was unknown to all but a very few candidates. The sympathetic nerve fibres are the axons of sympathetic ganglion cells, and the cord sends distinct fine medullated fibres to these cells, the axons being branches of cells within the cord itself.

Question 43 was, as a rule, answered much better than the preceding one, although the functional significance of the afferent impulses ascending the vagus nerves from the lungs was not fully realised by any candidate. These impulses starting from the expanding lung tend to cut short the discharge of the inspiratory centre which produces this expansion. In the same way, if there is forced expiration compressing the lungs other ascending impulses cut short the discharge of the expiratory centre which has produced this forcible compression.

Section B.

Q. 44. Identify and describe with appropriate drawings the microscopic specimens labelled A and B.

The two specimens were : A, a section through the tongue and subjacent mixed salivary glands, showing the surface epithelium and the characteristic tongue muscle fibres ; B, a section through a foetal finger, showing the cartilages which in this condition are the precursors of the true bones, the calcification of these cartilages with the characteristic arrangement of the cartilage cells, and the surface epidermis with small hairs here and there. In regard to the description of both these specimens, attention is drawn to the uselessness of elaborate descriptions of tissues which are not displayed in the actual specimens. If the organ from which the section is made is not recognised, then the candidate should describe such tissues, muscle, epithelium cartilage, etc., as are seen. In some cases this description was followed by such statements as that the whole specimen is therefore a section through the trachea, which it in no way resembled, and acting on this hypothesis, candidates described the trachea in detail.

Q. 45. A solution coloured red is said to be obtained from blood. How would you proceed to study it and make sure whether or no it contains oxyhæmoglobin ?

The answers to this question were, as a rule, unsatisfactory. The vast majority of those who answered it brought forward various methods for showing that the solution was blood ; such. for instance, as determining the presence of proteids, examining microscopically for blood corpuscles and obtaining crytals of hæmin. But the question asked is the proof of the presence or absence of one thing, namely oxyhæmoglobin. There is only one simple proof of this, the occurrence of the characteristic absorption bands when the solution is examined spectroscopically, and the replacement of these by the hæmoglobin band, when the solution is gently warmed with reducing agents; the most convenient reducing agent is ammonium sulphide.

Q. 46. By what methods would you demonstrate the action of your salivary ferment and the influence upon this activity of various favourable or unfavourable conditions ?

One of the essential preliminary points in reference to methods of demonstrating the action of the salivary ferment is the preparation of a suitable solution of starch. This was not appreciated by candidates. The solution to be used must be quite weak ($\frac{1}{4}$ per cent.), otherwise the change would take a very long time, and as long as any starch remains in the solution unchanged, the blue coloration with iodine will mask any other effect. In such a solution, if kept cold and tested from time to time, after addition of the saliva, the various stages through dextrine to maltose may be readily demonstrated. If kept at body temperature the process is so accelerated that the dextrine stage can only be ascertained by arresting the whole ferment process ; this is done by boiling a part of the solution. The retardation of the process with acid, and the destruction of the ferment by boiling were generally referred to, but except in a few instances the methods used would not in practice have furnished a convincing demonstration. Finally, the presence of the end product, maltose, could only be ascertained practically if a very small quantity of copper sulphate, previously diluted, were used ; this is because the amount of starch being small, that of maltose is also small, and in order to perform Trommer's or Fehling's test, the copper sulphate must not be in excess of the reducing sugar present. Of the two tests Trommer's is the best ; since Fehling's solution, unless freshly prepared, is liable to change, reducing substances being set free in it. In using Fehling's test solution it is therefore always necessary to boil the solution first and ascertain whether it reduces without any reducing sugar being present. Maltose in sufficient quantity gives characteristic yellow crystals of maltasozone under appropriate conditions.

HONOURS.

Results : 1st Class, — ; 2nd Class — ; Failed, 4 ; Total, 4.

Of the four candidates who presented themselves for this part of the examination only one did sufficiently well in the theoretical part to justify a further practical examination. The examination calls for no special remark, the practical part being along the lines of previous years and dealing with the methods employed in histology, physiological chemistry, and experimental work upon muscle and nerve.

DAY EXAMINATION.

STAGE 1.

Results : 1st Class, 101 ; 2nd Class, 93 ; Failed, 34 ; Total, 228.

The number of candidates was considerably larger than in 1906, being 228 as compared with 161. The character of the work was very good and shows a great improvement on that of the preceding year. Thus, whereas last year there were 19 per cent. of failures, this year there were only 15 per cent. below pass standard and 44 per cent. reached the First Class level.

Q. 1. Describe the appearances successively presented when blood is received into a glass vessel and allowed to stand. If the clot formed is kept and then cut open, what difference in colour between the external and internal portions is observed ?

This was generally well done by most candidates, especially the first part. It calls for no special remarks.

Q. 2. Describe the general structure, position and use of the valves in the left side of the mammalian heart. Illustrate your answer by drawings.

The question was well done by most candidates, some of the drawings being particularly good.

Q. 3. What substances are contained in white of egg ? What happens if the fresh material is (a) heated to 100° C., (b) heated to dryness so as to burn, and (c) treated with acid pepsin ?

The bulk of candidates answered this question satisfactorily ; there were, however, several inadequate answers in connexion with (b). It would be well for teachers to show the effect of heating white of egg in a capsule until it chars and incinerates, giving rise to the characteristic burnt-feather smell, which is indicative of an organic nitrogenous substance.

Q. 4. Give a short account of the position, general structure and functions of the intestinal villi. By what channels do the absorbed constituents of the digested food reach the systemic circulating blood ?

This question was satisfactorily answered by almost all the candidates ; it calls for no special remark.

Q. 5. What is the average number of respirations and of heart beats per minute in the case of man ? In what respects does the expired air differ from that which has been inspired.

There were some bad answers to this question ; in these, candidates confused nitrogen with hydrogen, and placed the latter gas as a normal constituent of air. Many of the answers were, however, quite good, and the composition of expired air was accurately stated by quite a large proportion of candidates.

Q. 6. Describe, by means of appropriate drawings, the shape of the long bones present in the arm and in the leg. To what extent can these bones move in relation to one another ?

Fairly well answered, but, as a rule, the drawings were not good.

Q. 7. What do you know as to the position, general structure and function of the pancreas ?

Quite good ; calls for no special remark.

Q. 8. Describe, in general terms, the structural and functional differences between any muscle and its tendons ? Why does exercise make us warm ?

Not so satisfactorily answered as the preceding questions, especially as regards the function of muscle and of tendon. Candidates write more intelligently on chemical than on mechanical aspects of the body functions. Such functions as that " muscles give shape and beauty " cannot be termed physiological. Muscle is the one tissue which has a distinctly mechanical function, and associated with this is the function of heat production.

Q. 9. Draw a diagram to show the formation of a real image when a convex lens is placed in front of a lighted candle. Where is such an image formed in the case of the eye ?

The answers to this question afford another example of the difficulty which the candidates have in realising physical aspects of physiological structures. For this illustrative demonstrations are most desirable ; the image of a candle flame ought to be thrown on a screen so as to show the principles of refraction through a lens. The old error of confusing " refraction " with " reflection " was still prominent, and teachers should endeavour to enforce the distinction between these two phenomena.

Q. 10. What does the spinal cord look like to the eye when observed without any magnifying glass ? Why is it necessary for the reflex movement of a limb.

There were very few satisfactory answers to this question ; it would appear that this part of the subject is not adequately studied even in a general way.

STAGE 2.

Results : 1st Class, 22 ; 2nd Class, 49 ; Failed, 11 ; Total, 82.

The number of candidates was much less than in 1906, when there were 134 : it is possible that the weaker class of candidates was that chiefly diminished, and that this accounts for the excellence of the results. At any rate the examination as a whole is much the best in its results of any Second Stage examination during the last eight years, and the large proportion of First-class Papers, 27 per cent., is as striking as is the small proportion of failures, only 13 per cent. There were a large number of really good answers, intelligently and clearly expressed, and correct as to the details set forth ; the only general criticism is as to the style of most of the answers—they lacked conciseness.

Q. 21. Describe the microscopic characters and the chemical composition of lymph. Where does lymph come from ? By what channels does it flow and what agencies are concerned in the production of this flow ?

Generally attempted and produced some very good answers.

Q. 22. Describe the structure of an arteriole. What changes may take place in the size of arterioles and how may they be brought about ? Explain the effect of this alteration in size upon the arterial, capillary and venous blood pressure respectively ?

Satisfactorily answered by the great majority of candidates, the answers showing a very great improvement on those which in previous years have been written in this stage upon this subject.

Q. 23. Enumerate the principal varieties of carbohydrate, and state the chief conditions under which the higher forms can be changed into the lower. How would you ascertain the presence of a reducing sugar ?

Attempted by very few candidates. Probably the last part was not known ; teachers should show candidates the tests for starch and for the sugars ; cane sugar does not reduce cupric hydrate in alkaline solution ; dextrine does, and is thus termed a " reducing sugar." The copper test is very simple and quite demonstrative.

Q. 24. What gases can be obtained from blood ? From what sources are these gases derived ? State what happens to the blood if an atmosphere containing carbonic oxide gas is breathed ?

Comparatively few good answers. This was largely due to the widely prevalent confusion of carbonic oxide gas with carbonic acid gas. Carbonic oxide (CO) is a definite and poisonous compound, and is present in some little amount in ordinary lighting gas. It forms the dangerous element when such ordinary household gas is inspired, because it unites with hæmoglobin and prevents this from taking in oxygen. It may be very easily demonstrated ; a weak solution of blood is put in a vessel and gas from a gas pipe is led through it for 15 minutes by means of an india-rubber tube. The solution becomes cherry red and will not change colour like the ordinary blood when treated by any reducing agent (ammonium sulphide, &c.), nor will it take up oxygen.

Q. 25. Describe the structure of the liver and the manner in which this organ is supplied with blood. State shortly the chief functions of this important organ.

The majority of answers were quite satisfactory, and a number of these were excellent.

Q. 26. Give an account of the agents concerned in the production of the body heat. In what ways is this heat discharged from the body? How is it that the mammalian temperature remains approximately constant when the temperature of the surrounding air varies?

Well done on the whole. Many candidates appear not to realise that whilst the discharge of heat is varied, the muscular production is also varied involuntarily, being increased reflexly through the excitation of the skin sensory nerves by external cold. This is proved by the increased discharge of carbonic acid gas in the expired air, this increase being absent if the muscles are paralysed or the reflex centres enfeebled by anæsthetics, sleep, &c. Hence the necessity for extra precautions during sleep to check the heat discharge from the skin, coverings, &c.

Q. 27. Describe the structure of a medullated nerve fibre and of the nerve cell which is connected with it. Where are the nerve cells situated which are respectively connected with the sensory and with the motor nerves of any single limb?

A surprising number of good answers, several being excellent and illustrated by appropriate, careful and accurate drawings.

Q. 28. By what mechanism can the eye be accommodated for near and distant vision? Explain what is the precise meaning of the term "accommodation," and illustrate your answer by appropriate drawings.

Very few good answers. The remarks made in connection with the refraction phenomena, on question 10 of the first stage, are applicable also to this question of the second stage. In order to appreciate the formation of a real image by means of a biconvex lens, it is necessary to take such a lens and practically study such formation. By interposing screens between the object and the lens and between the lens and the paper on which the image is thrown, it is easy to convince oneself of the passage of the refracted (i.e., bent) rays. As a matter of fact there was no really satisfactory answer to the second part of this question.

Report on the Examination in General Biology.

A good deal of correct detail was given by the candidates, but in many cases the impression was conveyed that the writer was not describing what he had actually seen. The drawings were for the most part poor, and were too often mere reproductions of text-book diagrams. Those that attempted to represent an actual object were frequently vague and unsatisfactory. Practice in drawing is evidently required.

SECTION I. OF STAGE 1.

Results : Passed, 105 ; Failed, 25 ; Total, 130.

Q. 1. Write an account of the life history of the cabbage white butterfly, making a simple drawing of each stage that you mention. When and where would you expect to find (a) the eggs, and (b) the pupa ?

On the whole this question was well done. Nearly all candidates took it, and most gave satisfactory answers. The drawings were poor.

Q 2. Where do you find the eggs of Chironomus, and what do they look like ? Give a series of figures showing the stages this insect passes through in its history from the egg to the fly.

Moderately well done, not so well as the last question. The drawings were often too indefinite.

Q. 3. Make one or more drawings of the interior of the mouth of the frog so as to show the arrangement of the teeth and the shape and mode of attachment of the tongue.

Drawings too diagrammatic and unlike the object. Vomerine teeth frequently omitted. Comparatively few took the question.

Q. 4. Draw three-different stages in the life of a tadpole, pointing out how they differ from one another and from a frog.

Most candidates took this question and it was fairly well answered. Some showed want of judgment in choosing the stages.

Q. 5. Describe fully (with illustrations) the feather of a bird ; distinguish between any different kinds of feathers that you know, and explain the uses of feathers to a bird.

A favourite question, and well done on the whole ; but the answers suggested book-work rather than practical acquaintance with the objects.

Q. 6. Describe the external characters in which the rabbit differs from the frog and a bird ; point out how the rabbit differs from (a) the cat, and (b) the sheep, in its feet and its teeth. State, if possible, the uses of any peculiarities you mention.

Want of arrangement of the facts and of a sense of their relative importance is very noticeable. There seems to be an impression that the sheep has no teeth at all in the upper jaw.

Q. 7. Describe, as fully as you can, the fruit of a dandelion. Sketch it, and say what is the use of the different parts.

Many candidates confused the *fruit* of the dandelion with the *seed*. The structure of the pappus, as seen in real specimens, was often not appreciated.

Q. 8. Show, by drawings, what happens when the winter bud of a tree grows out to form the young shoot in the spring.

This question was often well done, but the drawings were generally poor.

Q. 9. Describe, as fully as you can, how pollination is effected in any plant you have studied.

The primrose was generally selected, but the mistakes as to the facts of pollination seemed to show that the candidates had for the most part derived their information from sources other than that of the plant itself.

Q. 10. Explain, as well as you can, why it is that the seeds of some plants are enabled to be spread or scattered by birds, whilst other seeds cannot be dispersed in this way. Give some examples to illustrate your answer.

Very well done by some, and very badly by others who entirely missed the point of the question.

Q 11. When you pull up a seedling plant carefully from the soil, you see that particles of soil stick to some portions of the roots and not to the whole surface. Why is this?

Most candidates seemed to know something of root hairs, but it was disappointing to find so much ignorance on the subject of their distribution on the root. Very few attempted to explain *why* the soil clings to the root hairs.

Q. 12. Describe and sketch the specimen provided, and explain as far as you can the use of the various parts.

The seed (kidney bean) was on the whole well done. The term "embryo" was often used wrongly, as though it did not include the cotyledons.

WHOLE OF STAGE 1.

Results : 1st Class, 12 ; 2nd Class, 27 ; Failed, 18 ; Total, 57.

Q. 21. Give briefly what you consider to be the leading characters of vertebrate animals, as exemplified by the frog.

There were a considerable number of poor answers with mistakes on fundamental points, such as that vertebrate animals "breathe by means of lungs and suckle their young."

Q. 22. Show, with illustrations, how the skull of the frog is arranged to form a brain-case, protect the sense organs, and bound the mouth cavity.

Very few candidates attempted this question—probably because it is outside the run of ordinary text-book work and, although involving only facts with which they ought to be familiar, required a little thought.

Q. 23. Describe the lungs of the frog ; show how air is made to enter and is removed from the lungs.

There were some absurd answers showing a want of any real knowledge of the structures—such as that "the lungs of the frog at first resemble gills."

Q. 24. Describe the processes and organs involved, in the frog, between the sight of a particle of food and the distribution of the products of its digestion to the tissues.

The answers to this were very unequal, some being very poor while others were satisfactory.

Q. 25. Give the leading distinctions between a higher animal such as the frog, and an ordinary green plant. To what extent do these distinctions disappear in lower organisms?

Fairly done on the whole. The principal facts seem generally known. Some extraordinary statements occur—such as "animal obtains food from air by means of lungs"—which indicate want of thought.

Q. 26. Describe the heart of a sheep and trace the course of the blood through its cavities. In what respects does this heart differ from that of the frog?

A number omitted this question. Some answers contained fundamental errors—such as making the pulmonary artery emerge from the right auricle and, in other cases, making the caval veins enter the right ventricle.

Q. 27. Describe a fern-prothallium. If you wished to obtain a lot of prothallia how would you proceed to grow them?

On the whole this was well answered.

Q. 28. If you cut off the stem of such a plant as a vine to the ground in the spring a quantity of water continues to flow out from the surface. Why is this, and what conditions affect the rate of flow?

Very poorly done. A great deal of confusion between root pressure and transpiration was shown, and some answers were perfectly absurd. So striking a phenomenon, and one so easy to demonstrate, ought to be better understood.

Q. 29. What are the chief uses of green leaves to a plant? How would you demonstrate by experiment any *one* of the functions you mention?

On the whole rather well done.

Q. 30. How would you demonstrate (1) the presence of starch in the leaves, and (2) the conditions under which the leaves can become freed from their starch?

The iodine experiment had evidently been generally seen, but not performed by the candidates themselves. Many omitted to mention the need for the removal of the alcohol before adding the iodine. Very few suggested the exclusion of carbon dioxide in the second part of the question.

Q. 31. What can you learn from a " water culture" as to the source from which a plant obtains the nitrogen it requires? Describe carefully how you would set up a water culture.

The answers were very meagre. Many candidates confined themselves to the statement that nitrogen is not obtained from the atmosphere.

Q. 32. Describe the specimen provided, and explain, as far as you can, the use of the various parts.

The castor oil bean was very often badly described. The endosperm was frequently mistaken for cotyledons.

STAGE 2.

Results : 1st Class, 13 ; 2nd Class, 33 ; Failed, 31 ; Total, 77.

Q. 41. Give an account, with figures, of the early stages in the development of the vertebrate nervous system, and show which regions in the brains of a frog are formed from each of the primary vesicles.

Many omitted this question, and some who took it obtained very few marks. The developmental figures were generally very poor. The first part of the question was answered better than the last part. The thamencephalon seems liable to be omitted.

Q. 42. Describe the alimentary canal of the crayfish, and point out the more important features in which it differs from that of the frog.

Nearly everyone wrote on this question, and most gave satisfactory answers, a few getting practically full marks.

Q. 43. Explain what is meant by a "segmented" body. Which organs show segmentation in the earthworm?

This was also a favourite question, and was fairly well answered.

Q. 44. Describe one of the abdominal segments in the crayfish, including the appendages, and show what modifications in the structure of the appendages are found in the mandible, the second maxilla and the great claw respectively.

Many omitted this question, and the answers were very unequal. The drawings were poor, and often quite unlike the hard structures they were intended to represent.

Q. 45. Explain the reasons which lead you to believe that the wood is concerned with the passage of sap in a tree.

The answers were rather meagre, and the matter did not seem to be familiarised by experiment to the candidates.

Q. 46. In what respects do the reproductive organs of selaginella (a) resemble, (b) differ from, those of a fern?

The answers were suggestive of "cram" and text-books. Very few shewed any real acquaintance with the actual objects.

Q. 47. In what ways may reserve materials of food be stored in the seed ? State the chief stages they pass through when germination takes place.

A fairly good elementary knowledge was shown as to the first part of the question, but the germination changes were ignored.

Q. 48. Describe fully the fruit of *two only* of the following plants, and explain how the seed is dispersed :—Pea, meadow-geranium, clematis, willow, burdock.

On the whole this was well done; the burdock, however, proved a stumbling-block to many.

Report on the Examination in Zoology.

There were candidates in all stages, including Honours ; and the standard of work throughout was satisfactory. A fair proportion obtained the marks necessary for a pass in each stage.

In criticising detail, one is struck by the feebleness in many cases of the drawings and diagrams given in the papers, and occasionally by the reluctance or inability of the candidate to make an illustrative figure where it might have been used with advantage. Characters and comparisons derived from the outsides of animals were in most cases more completely and satisfactorily given than those involving internal structure. This sometimes extended to the omission of rather fundamental points.

Even in the higher stages there was occasional evidence that the candidates were not writing from their personal observations. There is a tendency to write too profusely ; conciseness and precision should be inculcated.

STAGE 1.

Results : 1st Class, 33 ; 2nd Class, 28 ; Failed, 4 ; Total, 65.

Q. 1. State briefly the more important points in which the frog differs from a fish and from a bird respectively in mode of life and in external characters.

The knowledge shown and the general arrangement in the answers were both good. This question was generally answered, and generally answered well. Some obtained full marks.

Q. 2. What is an exoskeleton ? Indicate the chief differences in respect of exoskeleton between the following animals :—cray-fish, earthworm, pond-mussel, dog-fish, frog, and bird.

The definitions of an exoskeleton were unsatisfactory ; very few candidates appreciated its importance in connection with muscles, some did not realise its essential relations to the soft parts, and several seemed to think that the term was applicable to the outside of any animal irrespective of hardness or rigidity.

Q. 3. How does the skull of the frog differ from (*a*) that of the bird, and (*b*) that of a mammal in respect of teeth, jaws, and articulation with the vertebral column ?

As a rule this question was well done by those few who took it. The differentiation of the mammalian teeth was generally overlooked.

9897. N 2

Q. 4. Give a classification of the vertebrata with a few leading characters of each group you mention.

The answers to this question were generally satisfactory, but there was a tendency to omit either the structural differences of the heart in the groups, or the peculiarities of the skull articulation ; most candidates gave one or the other, but very few gave both. There was little if any allusion to the characters of the coloured blood corpuscles ; and the mammalian diaphragm was often forgotten.

Q. 5. Define the group Insecta. How would you distinguish an insect from a spider and an earth worm respectively ? Mention any characters in which all three animals agree.

In defining Insecta the exoskeleton was frequently omitted, otherwise the answers were good. The functions of the dorsal pores of the earth-worm were not correctly given by anyone. The character of the appendages in the spider was sometimes given erroneously.

Q. 6. Give a short account of the life-history of the pond-mussel.

A large number of candidates apparently do not understand what is meant by " life-history." The adult structure was given by many without reference to, or at any rate largely to the exclusion of, the phenomena of the immature animal. Some gave internal anatomy, some mode of life, without any reference to the development. There were many inaccuracies regarding the mode of nutrition of the parasitic Glochidium.

Q. 7. How does a fish differ in external appearance, in internal skeleton, and in method of locomotion, from a frog, and from a bird ?

This was well done on the whole ; but there was no reference to the characteristic shapes of the vertebræ.

Q. 8. Refer the following animals to their classes :—herring, pigeon, rabbit, frog, dog-fish, cat, tortoise, whale, ape, lizard, bat, crocodile.

Accurate, on the whole, and some obtained full marks ; but there were some extraordinary mistakes—for example, the tortoise was not infrequently classed as an " Arthropod " or a " Crustacean " ; the lizard and the crocodile were also sometimes placed erroneously.

Q. 9. How do molluscs differ from arthropods ? Give a classification of the Mollusca.

Many candidates were content with a mere bald statement of the chief Molluscan subdivisions, and gave no diagnostic features. Mollusc was frequently mis-spelt " mullusc."

Q. 10. Refer the following to their classes and state where you would expect to find each : — snail, cuttlefish, oyster, cockroach, scorpion, dragon-fly.

Generally accurate, but a few curious mistakes frequently occurred :— the cuttlefish was put amongst Fishes, and the scorpion and dragon-fly were classed as Vertebrates by some.

Q. 11. How do the following animals breathe :—cray-fish, cockroach, pond-mussel ?

The function of the mantle of the mussel was generally overlooked, and comparatively few realised the essential differences in the methods of respiration.

Q. 12. Give an account of the structure and life-history of Vorticella, and compare that type with Amœba and Hydra respectively.

The facts were usually correctly enough stated, but the comparisons of the specialised *Vorticella* with the generalised *Amœba* and with the multicellular *Hydra* were feeble,

STAGE 2.

Results : 1st Class, 8; 2nd Class, 23; Failed, 14   Total, 45.

Q. 21. Draw diagrams showing the mode of suspension of the jaws in the cod, the frog, and the rabbit, and explain how these are related to the conditions seen in the dogfish.

This question was attempted by very few ; and while one of those who took it gave a very complete answer, the others had very incorrect ideas of the disposition of the parts concerned.

Q. 22. Describe fully the pectoral girdle in the pigeon, and compare it with that of the frog and that of the rabbit.

Some did this very well ; but the pectoral girdle of the frog was not satisfactorily dealt with by most.

Q. 23. Give a concise account of the life-history and the social habits of the honey-bee.

Evidently a favourite question, and done well by nearly all.

Q. 24. What are the general characters of Cœlenterata, and how do these distinguish that group from the Protozoa on the one hand and the Cœlomata on the other ?

The facts asked for were well known, but many candidates showed lack of power of arrangement, and did not marshall their facts so as to bring out the contrasts between the three groups.

Q. 25. Compare and contrast the Arthropoda, the Mollusca, and the Chordata in respect of segmentation, nervous system, and respiration.

The segmentation of the Chordata was not satisfactorily brought out as a rule. Few candidates realised the metameric arrangement of the spinal column or of the spinal nerves or of the trunk musculature of the lower forms. The external segmentation of the Arthropoda was emphasised, but the internal arrangements were often disregarded.

Q. 26. Compare the skull and teeth of the sheep, the cat, and rabbit, and refer these animals to their orders.

This question was well answered. There was, however, some tendency to put down dental formulæ in an unintelligent manner. A frequent mistake was the statement that sheep have no teeth in the upper jaw.

Q. 27. Describe the external characters and mode of locomotion (a) of the starfish, or (b) of Daphnia.

This question was answered well and was generally well illustrated. There was some weakness in regard to the appendages of Daphnia.

Q. 28. Give an account of the life-history (a) of Obelia, or (b) of Anodon.

In the answers there were a good many errors respecting the origin and behaviour of the Medusa stage of *Obelia* ; and also in dealing with the structure and parasitic habit of the Glochidium stage of Anodon.

STAGE 3.

Results : 1st Class, 3 ; 2nd Class, 3 ; Failed, — ; Total, 6.

Q. 31. Describe fully the microscopic object provided, and refer the animal to its group, giving your reasons for the identification.

The object was a transverse section of a sea-anemone. Several candidates failed to recognise it.

Q. 32. Refer Daphnia, Lepas, Gammarus, and Cancer to their groups. Contrast them with one another, and also state characters they possess in common.

Classification correct enough, but the comparison was poorly done.

Q. 33. State the circumstances under which you would expect to find the following :—Vorticella, Cordylophora, Bugula, Dytiscus, Chironomus, Chiton, Sepia, and Amphioxus.

Fairly well answered. Some had evidently not personally collected the animals in question.

Q. 34. Describe the heart and chief blood-vessels in the leading types of Vertebrata, and contrast the conditions seen in Perca, Columba, and Lepus.

Correct enough so far as the answers went. There were usually some omissions.

Q. 35. Compare the respiratory organs of Amphioxus with those of Ascidia and of Raia—how do all these differ from the respiratory organs of Mya and of Cancer ?

Only moderately answered. There was some want of appreciation of the fundamental differences involved.

Q. 36. Give an account of the vertebrate renal organs with special reference to the conditions found in the frog, the rabbit, and the dogfish.

Not well done by the few candidates who attempted the question.

Q. 37. Give a classification of the Mollusca ; place Mya, Chiton, Helix, Buccinum, and Sepia in their proper groups, and discuss the modifications of the nervous system found in these types.

Only taken by three candidates, and not very well done.

Q. 38. Give a full account of the mouth-organs of the cockroach and of the odontophore of Buccinum, explaining the action of the parts in each case.

The cockroach was done better than the Buccinum. The latter part of the question was very feebly answered—if attempted at all.

HONOURS.

Results : 1st Class, 1 ; 2nd Class, 1 ; Failed, - ; Total, 2.

Q. 41. Describe fully Antedon, or Lepas ; refer it to its group, and state where it is found.

Not taken by the candidates.

Q. 42. Describe in detail the life-history of Ascidia and discuss its significance.

Not taken.

Q. 43. Write an account of—

> The formation of coral reefs and islands,
> or Parasitism.

Parasitism treated well, coral reefs not so well.

Q. 44. Classify *either* the Mollusca or the Fishes, giving illustrative genera of each group. .

Mollusca satisfactorily done, Fishes less well.

Q. 45. Describe four of the following larvæ, and state what adult animals they respectively belong to :—Planula, Pluteus, Nauplius, Trochophore, Veliger, Zoea, Pilidium.

Fairly well answered.

Q. 46. Give an account *either* of the surface life of the sea around the coast of England, or of the characters of the Australian land fauna.

Australian fauna taken and only moderately well done.

Report on the Examinations in Botany.

Evening Examination.

Stage 1.

Results : 1st Class, 194 ; 2nd Class, 291 ; Failed, 142 ; Total, 627.

The work, on the whole, was very satisfactory and shewed evidence of good and careful teaching. Many candidates shewed a creditable grasp of principles, but more care must be devoted to observation and drawing of actual specimens.

Q. 1. Describe the specimen placed before you. Sketch it, and name the parts. (You are expected to dissect it sufficiently to enable you to identify and describe its principal features.)

The specimen set was *Pyrus Japonica*. It was generally well done, although many were puzzled by the stipules.

Q. 2. What is meant by sympodial branching ? Explain your answer by means of diagrams, and describe one example of a sympodium that you may have studied.

This was often well done, though the sketches were frequently careless.

Q. 3. What functions other than the absorption of water do roots perform ? Illustrate your answer by descriptions of any examples you may select.

The answers were uneven. Some were very good, and shewed a familiar acquaintance with the functions of roots, whilst others practically knew nothing beyond the statement conveyed in the question.

Q. 4. Describe fully what structures you would expect to find in a cross-section of a 3 year old branch of such a tree as a willow. Illustrate your answer by sketches.

Nearly always very badly done. It is quite surprising that such an object should be so unfamiliar. The hand lens seems not to be intelligently used on such objects although nearly all the chief points of structure can be made out by its aid. Most knew nothing beyond blackboard demonstrations.

Q. 5. What is the use of starch to a plant ? Where is it found, and what structures does it show ?

Very few seem to have realized that starch is an insoluble reserve of food. The knowledge of its structure was very superficial.

Q. 6. Describe and explain as far as you can the appearance of a potato that has sprouted (1) in a dark cellar (2) on the surface of the soil.

Often very well done.

Q. 7. What are the principal modes in which seeds are dispersed ? Describe the mode of dispersal in gorse (*Ulex*), violet, willow, blackberry.

The answers were disappointing as a whole. Many wild guesses were made, but a few candidates who had evidently examined the objects for themselves secured high marks.

Q. 8. Describe the structure of a bulb, *e.g.*, that of a daffodil, and explain how such a bulb is formed.

Some good answers were sent in, but most candidates are ignorant of the real morphological nature of the bulb.

Q. 9. Many plants when wounded allow a milky juice to exude. What is this juice, and what do you know of its occurrence in plants?

Very few attempted this question successfully—a surprising result considering how commonly latex occurs.

Q. 10. What is meant by a biennial? How does it differ from (a) an annual, (b) a perennial? Give two examples of each of these three classes of plants.

Generally well answered.

Q. 11. In what respects does a flower of the Deadnettle (a) resemble (b) differ from, that of a Borage or a Forget-me-not?

Very unevenly done. More training in drawing useful comparisons is needed.

STAGE 2.

Results : 1st Class, 89 ; 2nd Class, 274 ; Failed, 76 ; Total, 439.

The general standard reached by Stage 2 candidates is rather low, and the quality of the work relatively much poorer than that of Stage 1. The teaching up to this stage is evidently beyond many of those responsible for the candidates.

Q. 21. Refer the specimen placed before you to its Natural Order, giving your reasons ; describe it, taking the organs (when present) in the following order :—

Root,	Flower,	Gynæcium,
Stem,	Calyx,	Fruit,
Leaf,	Corolla,	Seed.
Bracts,	Andrœcium,	

The specimen set was *Rosmarinus officinalis.* It was generally fairly well done, though there was much carelessness shewn in details.

Q. 22. What is meant by an albuminous and an exalbuminous seed respectively? Describe carefully any albuminous seed of a *dicotyledon* which you may have studied.

A very large proportion of utterly worthless answers were sent in. Many candidates still seem to be unaware of the occurrence of examples amongst *dicotyledons*, and often instanced wheat or maize!

Q. 23. How would you show that plants respond to the stimulus of gravity? What conditions must be present in order that they may be able to respond, and what experiments would you perform to illustrate your statement.

Comparatively few students showed acquaintance with any form of klinostat, and on the whole the answers were decidedly poor.

Q. 24. Explain why it is that in the early summer it is easy to detach the bark from a willow twig, and why it is more difficult to do this in the late summer.

This question which required a little independent thought was very badly done. Scarcely anyone connected the difference with the way in which new tissue is formed in the stem.

Q. 25. Describe the gynæcium, and also the fruit, of the Primulaceæ, and compare them with the corresponding structures of the Caryophyllaceæ.

The answers were not good. Very few seemed to point beyond black-board illustration. Candidates in this stage are expected to have some knowledge of the range of form met with in, at any rate, common British representatives of the orders prescribed for special study.

Q. 26. What is a sporangium ? In what respect does a sporangium differ from a seed ?

The answers were very confused, and the homologies were often either left untouched or entirely misunderstood.

Q. 27. Write a short account of the life-history of the moss, and explain the use of the peristome in these plants.

This was often well done, but the use of the peristome was often not understood.

Q. 28. Describe the changes which occur in the female cone of a pine from the time of pollination up to the dispersal of the seeds. Illustrate your answer by sketches.

Often very well done.

Q. 29. Give a short account of the structure of a lichen. In what kinds of localities do lichens chiefly occur ?

A fair knowledge was shewn, and some really excellent answers were sent in.

Q. 30. How would you determine experimentally the source from which green plants obtain the carbon they require? Sketch the apparatus you would employ.

Generally badly done. Many of the suggested experiments were quite imaginary and would not work in practice. But a few good answers were returned.

Q. 31. Describe, with illustrative sketches, the ways in which roots branch.

Generally very badly done. Great confusion was shewn between roots and stems in respect to their modes of branching.

STAGE 3.

Results : 1st Class, 8 ; 2nd Class, 25 ; Failed, 19 ; Total, 52.

Some of the candidates attempting this stage had clearly never really gone through any advanced course of training, and the general average was somewhat low.

Q. 41. Describe the specimen provided. Dissect it so as to enable you to see its various parts, and make sketches so as to fully illustrate its structure, so far as it can be seen with the aid of a simple lens.

A considerable amount of "cram" was shown. Much absolutely irrelevant matter was introduced and the order, which was *not* asked for, was commonly given as Saxifragaceæ. The specimen set was *Staphylea pinnata*.

Q. 42. Give a short account of the existing Lycopodineæ. What light has a study of fossils thrown on the affinities of the genera composing the group ?

Sometimes really well done, and these candidates showed evidence of having really seen many of the things they wrote about.

Q. 43. Under what circumstances may alcohol be formed in green plants ? How would you identify its presence, and what do you regard as the meaning of its occurrence ?

No real knowledge on this subject was shown at all. The whole physiology of respiration was commonly misunderstood.

Q. 44. The Rosaceæ are often said to be closely related to the Leguminosæ. On what evidence does this statement rest ?

This question was very badly done indeed, although it was often attempted. Hardly anyone seemed to know anything of the Leguminosæ, except as exemplified by the pea or bean !

Q. 45. Give some account of mycorrhiza, and discuss its significance in the economy of the plant.

Often rather well done.

Q. 46. Give an account of *either* the Truffle fungi, *or* of the Erysipheæ.

Very seldom attempted. Many confused the Truffle with forms like *Scleroderma*.

Q. 47. Write a short essay on parasites and the evolution of the parasitic habit in plants.

The answers were rather rambling and little grasp of the matter was shewn.

Q. 48. Give an account of the experimental evidence on which our knowledge as to the relation of light to photosynthesis is based.

A few good answers, but the majority of those who attempted the question had none but the most elementary knowledge.

HONOURS.

Results : 1st Class, — ; 2nd Class, 3 ; Failed, 10 ; Total 13.

The majority of candidates presenting themselves for this examination were quite inadequately prepared. But on the other hand, a few of those who were successful sent in good answers, showing considerable knowledge and independant thought.

On the whole the work compares well with that of recent years.

HONOURS PRACTICAL EXAMINATION.

Four candidates presented themselves. One of them was a decided failure, and shewed no evidence of really advanced knowledge of the subject.

Those who passed exhibited an imperfect acquaintance with the principles of chemistry and physics, which prevented their acquitting themselves well in the physiological part of the examination.

The candidates were tested by an examination partly consisting of practical work and partly *viva voce*.

DAY EXAMINATION.

STAGE 1.

Results : 1st Class, 39 ; 2nd Class, 34 ; Failed, 21 ; Total, 94.

The answers to the questions in Stage 1 call for no special comment. These are, on the whole, more mediocre than those of last year. The detailed criticisms of the answers are given below.

Q. 1. Describe the specimen placed before you. Sketch it, and name the parts. (You are expected to dissect it sufficiently to enable you to identify and describe its principal features).

The specimen set was *Papaver nudicaule*. The descriptions were uneven, and candidates often lost marks because they failed to examine the structure, especially of the gynæcium, sufficiently. The sketches were, however, sometimes remarkably good. Many candidates made a guess at the natural order, although it was not asked for, and generally were unsuccessful in the attempt.

Q. 2. What are the "veins" of a leaf? What are their uses? How would you experimentally test your statements?

The answers were uneven, some being very good. A not uncommon mistake was that the veins were stated to carry starch. Of course, starch cannot move at all from cell to cell.

Q. 3. Mention three examples of plants with creeping stems, and explain the mode of arrangement of the leaves in each case. Illustrate your answer by sketches.

The answers to this question were unexpectedly bad. Hardly anyone gave the leaf arrangement correctly, and no one explained the twisting that the leaves of such stems so often exhibit.

Q. 4. Describe and compare the gynæcium of the buttercup and pea.

This question was generally well done, sometimes indeed the answers were really excellent.

Q. 5. Explain exactly what is meant by endosperm and perisperm. How are they respectively formed?

Very seldom attempted, and very little knowledge as to perisperm was shewn.

Q. 6. What are lenticels? How would you ascertain the nature of the functions they discharge?

The general nature of lenticels was often fairly well understood. The suggestions as to experiments were often very crude.

Q. 7. Give two examples of irritability as shewn by plants. Describe carefully what may be observed when the irritable organ is stimulated.

This question was often fairly well answered. The stamens of Barberry and the leaf of Dionaea were often quoted, but it was clear that the latter had been seen by very few. Scarcely any one mentioned the "trigger hairs" on the surface of the leaf, which receive the stimulus.

Q. 8. Write a short account, illustrating your answer by sketches, of the mode of scattering the seeds to be seen in any four *capsular* fruits you may choose.

The answers were very uneven. Candidates for the most part showed only a very superficial knowledge of the structure of any one example, and often the actual mode of opening was almost entirely passed over. The Poppy was often described, but scarcely any one seemed to know that the pores are closed in wet weather, or how this is effected.

Q. 9. Show, by means of a sketch, the way in which the roots of a seedling plant are arranged. Explain, as far as you can, the reason for the arrangement you describe.

This question was very badly answered indeed, considering the ease with which seedlings can be made to grow with their roots just behind the glass of a glass-fronted box when it is tilted so as to cause the roots to press slightly against it. The answers were often rambling, and quite off the point. The drawings also were bad, and showed great ignorance of the whole matter.

Q. 10. Give a short account of the mode of pollination as seen in any two flowers you may select.

This question was generally well answered, though the details were sometimes inaccurately given.

Q. 11. In what ways do the solanaceæ (1) resemble, (2) differ from, the scrophulariaceæ?

The answers were meagre, and especially the salient points of resemblance were often very scantily given. Even the gamopetalous corolla was often left without mention.

STAGE 2.

Results : 1st Class, 13 ; 2nd Class, 27 ; Failed, 10 ; Total, 50.

As the same merits and defects characterised the work sent in by both training college and other students, the two may be suitably considered together.

There is evidence that the more advanced teaching, required in Stage 2, is improving in quality. The general level of excellence attained to by the candidates is higher than in previous years, and in a considerable number of instances candidates might, with very little more training, have gained a First Class.

A specially encouraging feature of their work of this year lies in the evidence afforded by the answers, that the physiological side of the science is receiving more genuine attention, and that the method of experiment is being more widely adopted.

Q. 21. Refer the specimen placed before you to its natural order, giving your reasons ; describe it, taking the organs (when present) in the following order :—

Root,	Flower,	Gynæcium,
Stem,	Calyx,	Fruit,
Leaf,	Corolla,	Seed.
Bracts,	Androecium,	

The specimen set was *Spiræa Japonica*. Many candidates made wild guesses at the natural order, Primulaceæ, Polygonaceæ, Ericaceæ, &c., being amongst the suggestions !

On the whole the actual description was generally good, but under the heading " Flower " what is wanted is a statement as to the symmetry, and not a mere repetition of what has been already given under other headings.

Q. 22. In what way does the structure of the stem of a pine differ from that of a dicotyledon ?

This was seldom well done. The answers were obviously in many cases taken from notes of lectures, without any knowledge of the actual things. A few good answers, however, were given.

Q. 23. Describe the structure of the flower and fruit of any member of the Gramineæ you choose, and explain how its flower is pollinated.

Sometimes this question was extremely well answered, but most candidates who attempted it lost marks because either they had never really examined a grass flower, or had become confused as to the different parts. Some elected to describe the maize, but *really* described, more or less imperfectly, the flower of a Brome.

Q. 24. Give an account, with illustrative sketches, of the various modes of reproduction exhibited by Aspidium.

This was generally well done, but the vegetative reproduction was not understood by some candidates. The adventitious buds that occur on the persistent leaf bases should be more widely known.

Q. 25. In what way do the muscinæ (1) resemble, (2) differ from the vascular cryptogams ?

The answers were often diffuse, and the points of importance were not properly brought out.

Q. 26. How would you investigate the questions as to the path through which the water passes between the root and leaves of a plant ?

On the whole the answers were fairly good, though the experiments were often rather imperfectly described. Irrelevant matter concerning root pressure and osmosis was often introduced.

Q. 27. Write a short account of the structure of the vegetable cell.

This question was very generally attempted, and though the answers were not very full, they were generally correct in the principal features.

Q. 28. Describe any three parasitic flowering plants known to you, and point out any features in them which are specially related to a parasitic habit.

This question was seldom taken. A few good answers were returned, but most of them showed very little acquaintance with the examples quoted.

Q. 29. Write a life-history of Puccinia, and illustrate the principal features by means of sketches.

The answers were generally good, although some candidates are hazy in their ideas of the teleutospores and the sporidia that spring from them.

Q. 30. Compare and contrast the flowers of the Liliaceæ and Iridaceæ.

This question was often fairly well done and some good drawings were given, showing that those candidates had really mastered the structures they were comparing.

Q. 31. Explain, by means of sketches, the changes which an ovule undergoes during its transformation into a seed.

This was a favourite question, but it was generally poorly answered.

Report on the Examinations in Hygiene.

Evening Examination.

Stage 1.

Results: 1st Class, 443 ; 2nd Class, 634 ; Failed, 118 ; Total, 1,195.

The number of students who entered this year for the Evening Examination in Hygiene, in Stage 1, is considerably below that of last year, and far below the numbers who took this examination in former years (1893-1900).

The following table shows the number of papers examined and the results of the examination for the years 1904-1907.

Year.	Number of Papers Examined.	1st Class.	Per Cent.	2nd Class.	Per Cent.	Fail.	Per Cent.
1904	1,028	357	34·7	565	55·0	106	10·3
1905	1,378	478	34·7	788	57·2	112	8·1
1906	1,295	475	36·7	722	55·7	98	7·6
1907	1,195	443	37·0	634	53·1	118	9·9

There seems to be a better organised system of instruction, and the answers to the several questions show intelligence on the part of the students ; they are not given so frequently in a set form, so common in former years, but appear more often in the words of the students themselves. The worked papers in Stage 1 show a distinct advance this year, more especially in the elementary human physiology section, which was answered very well by a large number of students,

It may be noted here that the scope of the examination in this Stage is planned to test the student's knowledge of ordinary domestic hygiene and of those rules of sanitary science which will enable them to observe the conditions necessary to secure a healthy home and surroundings.

For the first time in these examinations a paper on Sanitary Engineering and Construction was given, and a candidate was at liberty to select to be examined in Elementary Human Physiology (Section A), or in Sanitary Engineering or Construction (Section B), but could not choose questions from both of these subjects. In Stages 1 and 2, few candidates attempted Section B, but in Stage 3 more did so, and as a rule answered the questions very creditably.

The following remarks have reference to the four questions in Section A and Section B, as well as to those in Hygiene.

Section A.—Elementary Human Physiology.

Q. (a). Write a short account of the forms and relative positions of the bones which make the upper limb.

Fairly frequently taken, but many candidates failed to understand what was meant by upper limb, and wandered into accounts of the whole scapular girdle.

Q. (b). Give an account of the structure of the spinal cord, so far as it can be made out with the naked eye. Explain the meaning of reflex action and state what structures are concerned in a reflex act.

Not a very popular question. Few candidates gave a good account of the naked eye appearances of the spinal cord. Many described the spinal column and vertebræ, generally failing to appreciate what was asked. The explanation of a reflex act was nearly always good.

Q. (c). Give a brief description of the kidney and explain its functions.

Quite a favourite question, usually extremely well done.

Q. (d). Write a short account of the structures and uses of the lungs.

This was another popular question and excellently answered.

Section B.—Sanitary Engineering and Construction.

Q. (a). Give the construction of the system of pulleys which, in your opinion, is most practically useful.

Very few candidates attempted this question, and those who did answered it indifferently.

Q. (b). Write a short account of the nature, characteristics, peculiarities and uses of the following materials : — Mortar, cements, concrete, asphalt.

A few took this question and did it well.

Q. (c). Name the different kinds of bricks used in building. What are the relative advantages of each from a hygienic point of view.

Very few attempted this question.

Q. (d). What rules should be followed in the preparation of footings for brick walls ? Describe and illustrate by means of drawing a suitable footing for a deep wall built on clay.

When attempted, this question was intelligently handled. It was the best attempted question in the series.

HYGIENE.

Q. 1. How is water likely to be contaminated in (*a*) a well, (*b*) a cistern ? Explain how, in each case, the contamination can be prevented.

Most candidates answered this question, and, on the whole, the replies showed good teaching and intelligence.

Q. 2. What is the composition of inspired and expired air ? By what standard is respiratory impurity expressed ? Describe a simple experiment to indicate the effect of respiration on air.

This was one of the best answered questions in the paper, the second part being usually very well done.

Q. 3. What general properties characterise the carbo-hydrates ? Explain the purposes they serve in the body.

When attempted, this question was well answered ; some replies displayed an excellent knowledge of sugars.

Q. 4. Explain the changes which meat undergoes in cooking, and indicate the essential differences between the processes of stewing and boiling.

This question did not lend itself to the display of much ability, but, notwithstanding this, it was usually intelligently answered.

Q. 5. Name three soils with which you are familiar, and state what precautions should be taken in erecting healthy dwellings upon each of them.

On the whole, this was an unsatisfactory question, and not so well answered. It produced very commonplace replies.

Q. 6. Describe a good form of dust or ashpit, and explain some good methods for the disposal of house refuse in town and country.

This is a practical question of great importance, and it is satisfactory to note that the large majority of the students tried this question and answered it very well.

Q. 7. Describe and illustrate by means of a diagram a good form of water-closet. Explain its proper connection with any form of drainage.

This also was a favourite question and extremely well done, as a rule.

Q. 8. What materials are in common use for clothing ? Mention the advantages or disadvantages of each, and indicate the more important points to be borne in mind in the construction of clothing.

This was a very popular question, and in most cases very intelligently and carefully answered.

Q. 9. How is the disease called tuberculosis spread ? Explain the principles which should be observed to prevent the spread of tuberculosis.

Considering its practical bearing, this question was not so frequently attempted as one expected. Many of the replies were good, but the greater number showed an inability to grasp the fact that hand feeding and cow's milk play a dominant part in the dissemination of this disease. Too many candidates harped upon the influence of filth and dirt as a cause of tubercle. The teaching on this subject could, with advantage, be improved.

STAGE 2.

Results: 1st Class, 214; 2nd Class, 755; Failed, 73; Total, 1,042.

This Stage also shows a decrease in the number of papers sent in. The results of the examinations in this stage for the last four years are given in the following table:

Year.	Number of Papers Examined.	1st. Class.	Per cent.	2nd. Class.	Per cent.	Failed.	Per cent.
1904	1,114	246	22·1	726	65·2	142	12·7
1905	1,250	280	22·4	863	69·0	107	8·6
1906	1,178	262	22·2	791	67·2	125	10·6
1907	1,042	214	20·5	755	72·5	73	7·0

Generally it may be said that the papers in this Stage were equal to the average of the last few years. Those who obtained a First Class gave evidence of a more organised system of teaching. On the whole, there are fewer failures; and a higher percentage obtain a Second Class. It cannot be said there is much advance over last year. At the same time there is internal evidence in the papers that the students take an intelligent interest in the subject, and the fewer number of failures must be regarded as satisfactory.

SECTION A.—ELEMENTARY HUMAN PHYSIOLOGY.

Q. (a). Describe the structure and functions of the skin. To what other organs is it most closely allied, so far as its functions are concerned?

The majority of the candidates answered this question very well.

Q. (b). Explain the differences between an artery, vein, and capillary. Describe how these differences affect the circulation of the blood.

This was another favourite question and was usually very well done.

Q. (c). Describe the liver and the circulation of the blood through it. Where is it placed in the body and what are its functions?

Many candidates tried this question and for the most part submitted good answers.

Q. (d). Give a short account of the structural arrangement of the eye.

This was not a popular question. Comparatively few candidates attempted it. A few good answers were received, but on the whole the question was not well answered.

SECTION B.—SANITARY ENGINEERING AND CONSTRUCTION.

Q. (a). Give an example of simple electrical action. Explain how an electric current can be conveyed from one point to another, indicating the precautions and why.

Very few candidates attempted this question, but in the few cases it was tried the answers were distinctly good.

Q. (b). What are the points to be looked for in the selection of good drain-pipes? Compare the advantages and disadvantages of cast-iron and stoneware drain-pipes, and sketch reliable forms of joints for each kind of pipe.

Only a very few attempted this question. It was not taken up except in one or two cases, and the answers were indifferent and not too well done.

Q. (c). Describe a good form of floor surface for a school-room, and explain the disadvantages of surfaces formed of (1) wood blocks, (2) boarding, (3) cement.

The same comment applies to this question as to the previous one.

Q. (d). In the selection of timber for building purposes, it is desirable that it be sound and well-seasoned ; in this connection describe any processes known to you for preserving timber. Explain "dry rot" and "wet rot," and how can each be prevented.

Of the few who took up this section nearly all tried this question and gave excellent replies. It was perhaps the best answered question in the series.

HYGIENE.

Q. 21. Define the term "hard water" and "soft water." State the geological formations which yield hard water and those which yield soft water. What are the principal characteristics of river water and water derived from shallow wells.

This was a simple question, and appealed to nearly all the candidates. On the whole, the replies were very satisfactory. The answers showed evidence of careful instruction by the teachers.

Q. 22. What is the composition of the atmosphere when fairly pure ? Why does the air vary in density and volume at different elevations and temperatures ? Explain what bearing these have on ventilation.

This question was attempted by nearly everyone, but the answers were very unequal. Many broke down when they attempted to apply the working of physical laws and the practical attainment of ventilation.

Q. 23. How do we obtain energy from food ? Which yields most energy, an ounce of butter, an ounce of bread, or an ounce of cheese ? Explain what is meant by a "standard" diet.

Nearly all the candidates tried this question, some of the answers being really very good. On the other hand, there were many who could quote figures but failed to give a lucid explanation of how the body converts food into energy. Considering the difficulty of the subject, the question was very well answered.

Q. 24. What are the common parasites most likely to be introduced into our bodies by means of food ? Give a short account of any one of them.

This was an unsatisfactory question, and the answers difficult to judge. The majority of the candidates gave disquisitions on bacteria, failing to understand the meaning of parasite.

Q. 25. Compare the various subsoils used as building sites as to their fitness from a health point of view.

Like a somewhat corresponding question in Stage 1, the answers to this one were commonplace, but on the whole good.

Q. 26. Describe the construction of a hot-water service for bath and other purposes in a large house. Describe how the circulation of water is obtained, and state the precautions that should be taken to prevent damage by frost.

Some of the replies to this question were very good, and evidently written by candidates having a practical knowledge of plumbing work. Few attempted to answer without displaying most creditable familiarity with practical details.

O

Q. 27. Describe the various methods of testing house drains, giving the advantages and disadvantages of each method.

This was not so favourite a question as one expected. When attempted the answers were generally good and accurate.

Q. 28. It is proposed to convey the sewage of a town by a outfall sewer to discharge into a tidal estuary. State what conditions should be observed in order to prevent pollution of the foreshore.

The replies to this question were often discursive, but nearly all showed an intelligent grasp of the subject. Taken as a whole, this question was far better answered than might have been expected.

Q. 29. What are the distinctions between an antiseptic and disinfectant ? Give examples of each. Describe how an infected schoolroom may be disinfected.

This was a most popular question. The replies showed the existence of sound views on a very important practical question. Many still are taught to place reliance on sulphur dioxide as a disinfecting agent for rooms, but a conspicuous number showed a familiarity with formaldehyde, and with the value of ordinary soap, water, and a scrubbing brush.

STAGE 3.

Results : 1st Class, 23 ; 2nd Class, 72 ; Failed, 38 ; Total, 133.

The following table shows the results of this year's examination, compared with the last three years.

Years.	Number of Papers Examined.	1st Class.	Per cent.	2nd Class.	Per cent.	Failed.	Per cent.
1904	111	13	11·7	48	43·3	50	45·0
1905	143	15	10·5	90	63·0	38	26·5
1906	204	20	9·8	66	32·4	118	57·8
1907	133	23	17·3	72	54·1	38	28·6

From the above table it is noticeable that the numbers entering for this part of the examination vary greatly from year to year. This year, although the number of papers sent in were much fewer than last year, there has been a very decided advance on last year's work. The results are better than any of the previous years noted. Section B.—Sanitary Engineering and Construction was taken up by 26 candidates, nearly all of whom showed practical knowledge of the work. The papers were of a higher order than previous years. By the introduction of a paper on Sanitary Engineering as an alternative to that on Human Physiology, it is possible that the examination has attracted another class of students. The results this year must be regarded as very satisfactory.

SECTION A.—ELEMENTARY HUMAN PHYSIOLOGY.

Q. (a). Describe the structure and functions of the skin. To what other organs is it most closely allied, so far as its functions are concerned ?

This question was a favourite one and, as a rule, was fairly well answered, but there were fewer sketches than in former years, and these were not so well done. Too much stress was laid on the fact that the skin excreted the waste products of the body in large quantities.

Q. (b). Explain the differences between an artery, vein, and capillary. Describe how these differences affect the circulation of the blood.

Nearly every student who took up the subject of Human Physiology attempted this question. The answers were, on the whole, satisfactory. The least satisfactory feature of many of the answers were those relating to the last part of the question.

Q. (c). Describe the liver and the circulation of the blood through it. Where is it placed in the body, and what are its functions?

Those who attempted this question gave a fairly correct account of the structure of the liver and the circulation of the blood through it. The last part of the question was done excellently in some instances.

Q. (d). Give a short account of the structural arrangement of the eye.

Very well answered by those who attempted it, and excellently by some candidates. The sketches were well done and correct. The answers call for no special remarks.

SECTION B.—SANITARY ENGINEERING AND CONSTRUCTION.

Q. (a). Give an example of simple electrical action. Explain how an electric current can be conveyed from one point to another, indicating the precautions to be observed and why.

Only two students attempted this question. It was particularly well answered by one.

Q. (b). What are the points to be looked for in the selection of good drain-pipes? Compare the advantages and disadvantages of cast-iron and stoneware drain-pipes, and sketch reliable forms of joints for each kind of pipe.

This was a very favourite question. The large majority of the answers were excellent and clearly showed that the candidates had a sound practical knowledge of the subject.

Q. (c). Describe a good form of floor surface for a school-room, and explain the disadvantages of surfaces formed of (1) wood blocks, (2) boarding, (3) cement.

Comparatively few attempted this question, but those who did realised the difficulty of the problem involved, and gave fairly good answers to the question.

Q. (d). In the selection of timber for building purposes, it is desirable that it be sound and well seasoned; in this connection describe any processes known to you for preserving timber. Explain "dry rot" and "wet rot," and how can each be prevented?

Those who attempted this question evidently had, in the large majority of cases, some practical experience, and their replies were excellent.

HYGIENE.

Q. 41. What are the advantages and disadvantages of continuous and intermittent sand filtration for the purification of water on a large scale? What evidence is there that the depth of the filter bed plays an important part in bacterial purification? Describe the best way of filling a filter bed and controlling the rate of filtration.

This question was attempted by a little over one-half of the candidates. The first part was not well done. A number of students failed to realise the difference between continuous and intermittent filtration. While they showed a knowledge of controlling the rate of flow, many were not clear as to how a filter bed is filled with water, and how necessary it is to prevent channelling of the filter surface.

Q. 42. What are the respective advantages, disadvantages, and dangers, if any, attendant upon the use for warming rooms of (a) open fire grates, (b) slow combustion stoves, (c) closed coke stoves, and (d) gas stoves? How may these disadvantages and dangers be best overcome?

This was a very favourite question and was, on the whole, well answered. The necessity of providing flues for gas stoves was in some cases overlooked.

Q. 43. What changes are produced in the air of dwelling rooms by the use of artificial lights? Discuss the relative merits, as illuminants, of (a) electricity, (b) incandescent coal gas, and (c) acetylene, considered from a hygienic point of view.

This also was a favourite question. On the whole, it was only fairly well answered. Some of the candidates had a very confused idea of incandescent gas-light, and others were not clear as to the effect of illuminants on the air in living rooms. Such errors as "the nitrogen in air is changed," "gas dries the air," "organic matter is increased by the use of gas," &c., is not expected from students who come up for this examination.

Q. 44. Explain the characteristics of a proteid, hydrocarbon or fat, and a carbo-hydrate. What part do these elementary principles play in the human economy, and how much of each class is needed daily by an adult doing ordinary work?

This was a very favourite question. As is generally the case, it was well answered. There were fewer errors than in any other question on the paper.

Q. 45. Describe and compare the various subsoils of sites for dwellings. State which are porous and which are impervious. What other considerations affect the choice of a site for a dwelling?

Nearly every candidate attempted this question. Very few gave a satisfactory answer. No distinction was made, except in three or four instances, between the upper or surface soil and a deeper or subsoil layer, nor the fact that the latter is due to the breaking up of the underlying primitive rocks. Recognising the origin of all soils from the disintegration of rocks, it is of importance to have some idea of earlier formations. As a rule the answers were very commonplace and of an extremely elementary character.

Q. 46. Of what materials, of what size, and with what fall should a house drain for a middle-class dwelling, inhabited by ten people, be constructed? State the means you would adopt to prevent leakage, to secure a proper flow of sewage, and to prevent the access of sewer gases into the house.

This was a favourite question, and, on the whole, not so well answered as one would expect. Some of the candidates did not read the question carefully, and described a system of drainage altogether too large and too elaborate for a middle-class dwelling with a limited number of people. Others described the soil-pipe as the house drain. Some very good answers were given, but the large majority failed to give either a complete or satisfactory reply.

Honours.

Results : 1st Class, 1 ; 2nd Class, 3 ; Failed, 20 ; Total, 24.

The following table shows the results of this examination compared with the last three years :

Years.	Number of Papers Examined.	1st. Class.	Per cent.	2nd. Class.	Per cent.	Fail.	Per cent.
1904	20	2	10·0	6	30·0	12	60·0
1905	17	2	11·8	4	23·5	11	64·7
1906	22	nil.	nil.	5	22·7	17	77·3
1907	24	1	4·2	3	12·5	20	83·3

During the last three years a practical examination has been held for the Honours candidates in the chemical laboratory at South Kensington, and the combined marks of the paper and practical examination determine the results of the examination. It has been found in some cases that the candidates, while writing a good paper, are not able to obtain sufficient marks in the practical work to qualify for First Class Honours. The practical examination this year, however, showed that more attention and study had been given to this part of the examination, and the candidates summoned up to attend it were more or less familiar with the technique of chemical analysis. There is a decided improvement this year in this respect over last year, and as the knowledge required for First Class Honours becomes generally known, further advance will be made. All students who aspire to obtaining First Class Honours should endeavour to obtain a course of laboratory training in the methods of analysis as applied to public health work. Candidates should not rely altogether on their notes, but make themselves familiar with the methods of analysis by practical work in a laboratory.

Five students who had obtained qualifying marks in their paper were summoned to attend at South Kensington for the practical examination. One failed to enter an appearance.

This examination is only meant for advanced students, and therefore the standard is proportionately high.

Taken as a whole the examination papers were, as a rule, well written, and the general mass of students appeared better prepared in some subjects than last year. The large majority failed in their answers to the last two questions on the paper. They were not familiar with the simplest knowledge of statistical methods, or in the legal enactments intended to provide against the sale of unsound foods. These questions should not have presented any difficulty to students who were prepared to enter for this examination.

Q. 61. What is the effect of heat upon a gas, a liquid, and a solid respectively ? As illustrative of this question explain what will happen to a given volume of water at a temperature of 45° F. and 35° F. respectively, if slowly cooled down to those temperatures from 60° F.

Twenty-three students attempted this question. Of these only five gave anything like a complete answer. On the whole the question was not well answered.

Q. 62. Distinguish between *fissures* and *faults*. Assuming that a certain area has been proposed as a gathering ground for the water supply of a town, how far would your opinion as to its suitability be modified in the event of your learning that the underlying tract was traversed by "faults."

Sixteen students attempted this question. Three gave excellent answers, the others were, many of them, sketchy. As a rule the students seemed to understand the question, but some failed to attempt an answer to the last part.

Q. 63. Define the terms isobars, cyclones, V-shaped depressions, anticyclones, wedges of high pressure, cols, and straight isobars. State briefly the general weather characteristics usually associated with each of these systems.

This was a favourite question. Twenty-one candidates attempted it. As a rule it was only fairly well answered in the majority of cases. One candidate obtained full marks ; but very many were quite unaware of the type of weather associated with these systems.

Q. 64. It has been said that the recent diminution of small-pox is due rather to improved sanitary conditions than to compulsory vaccination. Discuss critically this statement.

All the candidates attempted this question, and with varying success. The answers were more in the form of statements, and few gave any figures in support of the facts they brought forward. The answers, while in many cases true, were very commonplace.

Q. 65. State the precautions necessary to ensure the accuracy in statistics. Explain the law of error and how it is applied.

Sixteen candidates attempted this question. Only three gave anything like a correct answer. Six failed completely in their attempt. The question is not a difficult one, and should have occasioned no trouble to a student who had been properly prepared.

Q. 66. Give the substance of the several legal enactments intended to provide against the sale of unsound or unwholesome foods.

Eighteen students tried this question, and the same remarks apply as to the preceding one. Four candidates failed almost completely. This question obtained the least number of marks from any candidate working the paper. The question is not a hard one, and every candidate should know the legal enactments intended to provide against the sale of unwholesome foods.

HONOURS PRACTICAL EXAMINATION.

Q. 1. Examine the sample of water marked A.

(1) Qualitatively (including physical characters).

(2) Quantitatively, as to

(a) Hardness, total and removable, expressed as centigrammes of lime (CaO) per litre.

(b) Chlorine, in parts per 100,000.

(c) Oxygen required to oxidise the organic matter (Tidy's process, 15 minutes exposure) expressed as parts per 100,000.

The free ammonia is 0·046 part per 100,000.

The albuminoid ammonia is 0·002 part per 100,000.

Nitrites are absent.

Report on the fitness or otherwise of the water for drinking purposes, giving your reasons.

The qualitative examination was not so well done as it should have been. Candidates relied too much on their notes. The hardness and chlorine were accurately estimated by two candidates, and the other two did the experiment fairly well.

Only one candidate made a really successful examination of the oxygen absorbed. The others were not familiar with the experiment.

The report was perhaps the best part of the work. Two candidates submitted a well reasoned report on the analysis made and the figures given them.

Q. 2. Examine the sample of water marked B for lead, and estimate the quantity present. Give your results in parts per 100,000, and in grains per gallon.

The estimation of lead was done by all the candidates. They varied in their results, but did the experiment correctly. Want of practice appears to be the chief drawback. They are not familiar enough with the technique necessary to make a good analysis.

Q. 3. Name and give a brief account of the appearance of, life history, and the symptoms which the parasites shown under the microscopes A, B and C produce in the human being.

All the candidates attempted this question. Only two gave a really satisfactory answer, and one of these failed to describe the life history of the parasite. The question was not well answered.

DAY EXAMINATION.

STAGE 1.

Results : 1st Class, 84 ; 2nd Class, 128 ; Failed, 6 ; Total, 218.

The following table shows the number of papers examined and the results, compared with the last three years.

Year.	Number of papers examined.	1st Class.	Per Cent.	2nd Class.	Per Cent.	Fail.	Per Cent.
1904	423	145	34·3	251	59·3	27	6·4
1905	271	104	38·4	131	48·3	36	13·3
1906	231	89	38·5	136	58·9	6	2·6
1907	218	84	38·5	128	58·7	6	2·8

These results are, on the whole, satisfactory. The numbers who obtain a First Class are fairly constant for the last three years. The most marked improvement is in the decrease of the numbers who fail. From the examination of these papers they are thought to be, on the whole, superior to those submitted at the Evening Examinations.

Very few tried the Sanitary Engineering and Construction paper.

There appears to be more careful teaching, and the instruction given seems to be more systematic.

Section A.—Elementary Human Physiology.

Q. (a) Describe the heart and explain how the blood is circulated in the
body.

This was a very popular question and exceedingly well done. Very many
candidates illustrated their answers by drawings and showed that they
thoroughly understood the question and knew how to answer it.

Q. (b) In what parts of the alimentary tract and by what agencies are
bread, lean meat, and fat digested and absorbed?

Comparatively few attempted this question, but those who did so gave
fairly good and accurate replies.

Q. (c) Describe the structure of the lung. What are its uses?

This was a very favourite question, the answers being very good. Some
of the replies were astonishingly clear and accurate. The candidates seem
to have been well instructed.

Q. (d) Describe the human foot, and show its adaptation to the act of
walking.

Very few students tried this question. Those who did gave fairly correct
replies to it.

Section B.—Sanitary Engineering and Construction.

Q. (a) Explain the practical application of the three kinds of lever.

Only one or two students attempted this question. The replies were
fairly good, but somewhat short.

Q. (b) What is the object and construction of a lightning conductor?
Give the reasons for the construction.

No candidate tried this question.

Q. (c) Describe any two methods of preventing walls from getting damp.

Very few students attempted this question. Those who did gave fairly
correct replies.

Q. (d) Give a list of the materials used for cisterns for the storage of
water in houses, mentioning the advantages of each and the
defects each is liable to.

This was a favourite question with those who took up this part. It was
well and correctly answered. Only a very few, however, attempted it.

Hygiene.

Q. 1. Mention the chief causes concerned in the natural ventilation of a
room. Explain their effect.

A large number attempted this question, but the answers were for the
most part unsatisfactory. The students in the great majority of their
replies gave ventilating devices, such as Tobin's tubes, Sherringham valves,
&c., instead of discussing the causes concerned in natural ventilation : the
mistake may have been due to careless reading of the question.

Q. 2. Name the common sources of water used for domestic purposes, and explain how each may be liable to pollution.

This was a very popular question and brought forth a large number of good answers. In many instances, to the first part of the question the replies were excellent, but fell off rather when they come to deal with the sources of pollution. On the whole it may be said that it was well and correctly answered.

Q. 3. What do you understand by the terms *hard* and *soft* water ? How may water be softened ?

This, too, was a very favourite question and was, on the whole, exceedingly well answered. Nearly every student gave an intelligent and clear answer to the question ; some few, entering more fully into details, gave replies of exceptional excellence.

Q. 4. Why is common salt a necessary article of food ? Whence is it obtained ? What important mineral salts are contained in food?

Those who attempted this question gave fairly good replies ; but their answers were somewhat short.

Q. 5. How would you boil (a) an egg ; (b) a potato ? Explain the changes which occur in each as the result of boiling.

Few students who attempted this question seemed to understand the drift of it. They did not explain or grasp the nature of the physical change which egg constituents undergo when boiled. So also in the case of a potato few realised the loss of salts from this tuber by soakage into the water, when boiled, especially if the peel is removed beforehand.

Q. 6. How does the aspect of a building affect the health and comfort of the inmates ?

This is a simple question—it was well answered and presented no difficulty to those who tried it.

Q. 7. Describe two ways of heating a room, and explain what effect they have on ventilation.

The first part of this question was well answered ; the replies to the second part were very commonplace, and it cannot be said that they were remarkably good.

Q. 8. What are the effects of bodily exercise on the respiration, circulation, and digestive apparatus ?

This was a favourite question. As a rule it was very well answered ; indeed some of the replies were of exceptional excellence. It also, perhaps, showed that the teaching had been more systematic this year. This subject evidently interested a large number of students.

Q. 9. Where is a stoppage in a drain most likely to occur, and from what causes ? Of what materials and in what sizes are drains generally made ? How are drains ventilated?

This question appears to have been of too practical a nature for the candidates. Very few knew where a drain gets blocked up or why. They were also weak on the ventilation of drains, and did not realise the importance of ventilating in sections.

Q. 10. A person's clothing has caught fire ; describe exactly what you would do to put it out (a) supposing it happened to yourself ; (b) supposing it happened to your sister. What should be done to the burnt parts until either the doctor comes or the person is taken to hospital ?

This is a class of question which invariably brings out correct answers. First-aid teaching is evidently well done and apparently popular with pupils, as this question was usually selected.

STAGE 2.

Results : 1st Class, 46 ; 2nd Class, 138 ; Failed, 12 ; Total, 196.

The following table shows the number of papers and the results of the examination this year compared with the last three years.

Year.	Number of papers examined.	1st Class.	Per Cent.	2nd Class.	Per Cent.	Fail.	Per Cent.
1904	266	62	23·3	171	64·3	33	12·4
1905	261	39	14·9	197	75·5	25	9·6
1906	273	48	17·5	188	69·0	37	13·5
1907	196	46	23·5	138	70·4	12	6·1

The above table shows that the results of this year's examination are far better than they have been for the last two years. Some series of papers were exceptionally good : the teaching appears much more uniform and systematic. The questions on Human Physiology were, as a rule, exceedingly well answered : there has been some improvement in this subject, very marked over last year.

Only three students took up Section B.—Sanitary Engineering and Construction.

SECTION A.—ELEMENTARY AND HUMAN PHYSIOLOGY.

Q. (a) What are the boundaries and position of the contents of the chest or thorax ?

This was not a favourite question, but those who tried it, as a rule, gave correct answers. In some cases these were exceptionally good.

Q. (b) Give a short account of the teeth, more particularly with reference to their number, names and structure.

This was a very favourite question. A very large number of students attempted it. As a rule the great majority of the answers were excellent. Many illustrated their answers by excellent drawings. The subject had been well taught.

Q. (c) Explain the structure of the skin. How do its parts differ one from the other, and what are the chief uses of each part ?

More than half the candidates attempted this question. The answers were very good and in many cases the illustrations given were excellently done and correct.

Q. (d) Describe the position of the liver in the body. What are its functions ?

A large number of the candidates attempted this question and some excellent answers were given. In point of fact some of the answers were surprisingly good. The subject appears to have been carefully taught.

SECTION B.—SANITARY ENGINEERING AND CONSTRUCTION.

Q. (a) Describe two methods of forming (1) sound-proof floors, (2) fire-resisting floors.

Only three students attempted this question. Two gave fairly good replies.

Q. (b) What are the constituents of Portland cement ? From what does it derive its hydraulic property and to what is its setting due ?

This question was not tried by any student.

Q. (c) What do you understand by the electrolysis of metals used in plumbers' work? Describe the causes of such action and methods of preventing it.

One candidate attempted this question and with very satisfactory results. He evidently had practical knowledge of the work.

Q. (d) State briefly the composition and process of manufacture of stone-lime mortar, of lime and hair mortar, and of pressed bricks.

Two candidates attempted this question and gave fairly good replies.

HYGIENE.

Q. 21. How may pure water, which is supplied through pipes from a storage reservoir, become fouled in distribution?

The general run of answers to this question was good, and in not a few cases the replies showed a comprehensive grasp of the practical points raised by the question. Very few referred to the danger attending domestic filters as a source of contamination.

Q. 22. Explain the terms "shallow well," "deep well," "Artesian well." Discuss the suitability of waters derived from these for drinking and trade purposes.

This was a very favourite question, and the replies given were fairly good. A very large number in the text and by illustrations assumed that deep wells and Artesian wells are the same, and that both wells produced the same class of waters. Many candidates seemed to have only a vague idea of what an Artesian well is.

Q. 23. What do you understand by overcrowding on space and in buildings? Explain what effect these conditions have on health.

This was not a favourite question. A large number of students considered the question as only applicable to living rooms, and seemed to think that an increase in the carbon dioxide in the air space was the chief condition that affected health. Few mentioned the effect density of population has on the health of a community or what the evils of overcrowding in a densely populated district are. On the whole, the question was not well answered.

Q. 24. What are the common causes of dampness in houses, and what are the means adopted to prevent it?

Nearly every student attempted this question and with varying success. A large number considered that dampness in a house is due only to the soil or an absence of a damp-proof course. No mention was made by many students of other causes, such as badly-fitting shoots, insufficient rain-water pipes or these being choked, roofing badly laid or imperfect gutters, badly constructed chimney-stacks, &c.

Q. 25. What are the dangers attaching to the storage of food in houses? Explain the precautions you would take to prevent meat, milk and butter from going bad in your own home during hot weather.

As a rule, this question was exceptionally well answered. It is satisfactory to find that this important part of domestic hygiene has been well and correctly taught.

Q. 26. Describe a system for heating a house by means of hot water, and explain what effect it has on the air of rooms.

A large number attempted this question, but comparatively few gave correct answers. Some regarded the system of heating a house by hot water or steam as the same as an ordinary hot water supply and connected the system with the kitchen range.

On the whole, the question was indifferently answered by the large majority of the students who tried it.

Q. 27. What is the value of exercise in the training and development of
       the body ? What forms of exercise are the best adapted for this
       purpose ? Give your reasons.

This was a favourite question and, on the whole, very well answered.
Some replies were exceptionally good. The subject has received more
careful study, especially in connection with schools, than one would expect.

Q. 28. Discuss the respective merits of brick, of stoneware, and of iron
       drains. What precautions are desirable when a drain is to
       be laid at a great depth below the surface of the ground ?

About one-third of the students attempted this question. A few good
answers were given, but the large majority failed to give a very satisfactory
reply. The last part of the question was better answered, as a rule, than
the first part.

Q. 29. What do you understand to be the difference between an anti-
       septic and a disinfectant ? Give an example of each, and
       explain how and why a disinfectant should always be available
       in the house of a person suffering with consumption.

As is nearly always the case, this was a favourite class of question, and
some exceedingly good answers were given. Perchloride of mercury was
nearly always given as an example of a true disinfectant—and quite
rightly, for so it is ; but there are other far less dangerous and more
efficient disinfectants which can be used to disinfect tubercular sputum
and which are not open, on account of its highly poisonous qualities, to
the same objection for ordinary use.

Report on the Examinations in Agricultural Science and
Rural Economy.

Examiners :—A. D. HALL, M.A., and Professor W. SOMERVILLE, D.Sc.

The Examiners are convinced that the teaching of the Principles of
Agriculture is, on the whole, intelligent and sound, though naturally some
of the teachers are doing better work than others. The fact that Classes
under the Board of Education have, in many cases, to compete with
University Extension and County Council lectures probably accounts for
the absence in growth of the numbers of candidates in the Board's examinations ; but it is evident, from the results just reported on, that the
teaching of this subject must be exerting no inconsiderable influence on
the prosperity of English Agriculture.

While the teachers appear to keep themselves informed of the experimental results accumulated at Rothamsted, they do not seem to give so
much attention as they might to manurial and other field demonstrations
frequently conducted in their own districts. The desirability of more fully
utilising local object lessons for the illustration of class-room instruction
might with advantage be brought to the notice of teachers taking a section
of Subject xxiv.

It is also evident that teachers are not so fully aware as is desirable of
the numerous leaflets on Agricultural and Horticultural Science prepared
and issued by the Board of Agriculture and Fisheries ; these may be
obtained free of charge on application to the Secretary of that Board,
4, Whitehall Place, S.W., and every teacher might, with great advantage,
take steps to procure for his pupils those leaflets that bear upon the work
of the class.

EVENING EXAMINATION.

STAGE 1.

Results : 1st Class, 19 ; 2nd Class, 10 ; Failed, 13 ; Total, 42.

The Examiners are forced to repeat the remarks that have so often been made with regard to the answers in this stage—that the chief defects are due to the lack of experiment in the teaching. The course in this subject was devised to secure some training in experimental method and personal observation on the part of the pupil, and the questions are made to cover a wide range in order that the teacher may have the opportunity of taking up a part of the Syllabus practically and thoroughly. It is not necessary, neither is it desirable, that the teaching should cover the whole of the Syllabus, but the part selected must be treated experimentally. The sketches continue to be very poor.

Q. 1. Make drawings of various seeds to show the different ways in which they store food for the future plant. Has the size of a seed anything to do with the depth at which it should be sown ?

On the whole only indifferently answered.

Q. 2. Give some examples of roots which are used by the plant, (1) as store-houses of food, (2) to pull the plant deeper into the ground. Which of the following are stems and which roots—a potato, a turnip, a carrot, a tulip bulb, a bit of couch grass, an artichoke ? Give your reasons.

The first part of the question was generally correctly answered, but candidates had not had their attention called to the dandelion, crocus, and similar plants with contractile roots.

Q. 3. Suppose you place marks, one-tenth of an inch apart, extending backwards from the tip of the root of a young bean, show by a drawing how the marks would look a week later, and explain the cause of the result.

Some good answers were submitted, but the drawings were very poor.

Q. 4. Describe distinct experiments to show under what conditions the leaf of a plant (1) removes carbonic acid from, (2) adds it to, the atmosphere.

Very rarely were real experiments described ; instead, something fictitious and impossible was set down.

Q. 5. Why do the leaves of the English oak fall every year ? Why do the leaves not fall from a branch that has died in the course of the summer ?

Frequently attempted, and generally successfully, as regards the first half of the question.

Q. 7. Describe the appearance of the two grasses, Cocksfoot and Perennial Ryegrass. Can you name a grass that may be found in flower all the year round ?

It was satisfactory to find that the two grasses were generally known, even though the descriptions were poor.

Q. 6. What is the difference between the bud at the end of a Sycamore shoot, and that at the end of a Willow shoot ? Which has the greater number of scales ?

Q. 8. What do you mean by heartwood and sapwood, and how does the difference arise ? Mention one tree in which the distinction between heartwood and sapwood is very plain, and another in which it is hardly visible.

Q. 9. What is a knot in wood ? How can knots be prevented naturally and artificially ?

These questions were generally avoided and the answers rarely showed any observation. No. 9, however, was better answered than the other two.

Q. 10. What is humus ? If it is of value in soil, why is a peat bog not fertile ?

Q. 11. Describe various experiments to prove that the plant draws certain substances from the soil.

Q. 12. Of what substances is soil composed and how does it come into being ? Describe the processes which are always at work making soil ?

The answers to these questions showed evidence of sound teaching, though with regard to the constituents of the soil there was a tendency to go into detail beyond the scope of students in this stage, *e.g.*, to enumerate things like phosphoric acid, potash, magnesia, &c. The burning of plants to ash, and a simple water culture or two, are sufficient to show the student that the plant draws certain soluble salts, including nitrates, from the soil ; more he does not need at this stage.

STAGE 2.

Results : 1st Class, 28 ; 2nd Class, 91 ; Failed, 29 ; Total, 148.

SECTION A.—TILLAGE AND CROPS.

The answers this year showed a distinct improvement, especially in the questions involving a consideration of the labour and cost of farm operations. Throughout, the teaching of practical agriculture seems to be progressing on very sound lines : it is to be noted that the average marks obtained by candidates have risen and that a large proportion were nearly up to the first class standard.

Q. 1. What do you understand by the natural fertility of a soil? Suppose you have a 30-ton crop of mangolds got by liberal manuring, how much of this would you expect to be due to the natural fertility of the soil ?

This question was designed to ascertain to what extent teachers of Agriculture are encouraging their pupils to take note of the field demonstrations now so common throughout the country. The answers, on the whole, were satisfactory.

Q. 2. What conditions of soil and situation are favourable to irrigation in this country ? What would you regard as suitable and unsuitable water for use in the process ?

Candidates are recommended to avoid questions dealing with matters of which they have no personal experience.

Q. 3. What effect have the operations of ploughing, harrowing, rolling, and hoeing on the amount and distribution of soil moisture ? Explain what is meant by a soil mulch.

This proved a popular question, and elicited useful answers.

Q. 4. Describe the appearance of the weed called Charlock, Yellow Weed, or Wild Mustard (*Sinapis arvensis*), and explain how it can be got rid of.

This question was generally attempted, but many candidates seemed to think that spraying was the one way of dealing with the weed.

Q. 5. What do you understand by the unit system of valuing artificial manures? Give examples from two common manures.

Candidates had evidently been well taught in the important section of manurial valuation.

Q. 6. Starting with a wheat stubble on a medium loam, how would you prepare it for a swede crop? What are the chief difficulties met with in getting a good "plant" of swedes, and how are they to be met?

Fair answers on the whole, though candidates hardly realised how carefully the cultivation must be directed to conserve soil moisture if a plant of swedes is to be obtained in the drier parts of the country.

Q. 7. If you have to cut and make 40 acres of old land hay, draw up a table of the labour that will be required—men, horses, and time—for each operation, assuming that the hay is stacked in the field.

Well answered where attempted.

Q. 8. Suppose you are farming some light land, and want to make as much farmyard manure as possible, none of which, however, can be spared for the arable land ; suggest a rotation that will give you a large amount of straw, and explain how you will maintain the fertility of the soil.

This question was very generally attempted, but without much success, since candidates were evidently not acquainted with such rotations as those in vogue in Wiltshire, where corn crops are frequent, and the fertility is maintained by folding fallow and catch crops on the land. Candidates often failed to read the question carefully, since they wrote of manuring with farmyard manure, though expressly told that none could be spared for the arable land. Both here and in the Day Examination, Lucerne was often included among catch crops.

Q. 9. What are the nature and origin of "wireworm"? Under what conditions is it most troublesome, and how can its attacks best be met?

It was curious to find that some of the candidates evidently had not known a wireworm when they had seen it.

Q. 10. What different varieties of red clover exist, and for what purposes is each used?

Seedmen's catalogues form very good adjuncts to the text-books !

Section B.—Horticulture.

The general average of the answers was high. Without discussing the questions in detail the answers suggest that a little attention in teaching might be given to the classification of garden crops, e.g., it was evident that candidates had rarely considered the distinction between broccoli and cauliflower from any general standpoint, or again, in the Day Examination, recognised any differences in beans beyond that some were tall and others dwarf. Questions dealing with pests and diseases were again indifferently answered.

Section C.—Animal Husbandry.

Several very good sets of answers were sent up in this section.

Q. 1. Describe the appearance ("points") of a typical animal belonging either to the Polled Angus or Red Polled breed of cattle. Indicate the home of the breed you select, and the purposes for which it is chiefly employed.

This question was almost always attempted, and was generally well done ; but several candidates maintained that the Polled Angus is red in colour, which seems to show that the teacher was at fault.

Q. 2. Sketch the ground plan and a cross-section, giving dimensions in figures, of a double shippon or cow-house, suitable for a dairy herd of 28 shorthorn cows.

Where attempted, this question was usually answered almost perfectly, and the sketches were creditable.

Q. 3. Give a description of the duties of the stockman in charge of fattening cattle. How many can one man give proper attention to, and what rules must he observe in order to get the best results?

Some excellent answers were submitted.

Q. 4. Given a farm of 200 acres of light loam, consisting of 40 acres of good permanent pasture and 160 acres of tillage land worked on the Norfolk four-course shift, what live stock would you recommend, assuming that cattle breeding and feeding is the main object? Show the steps by which you arrive at your answer.

This question was not often attacked : as the class matures the teacher should discuss such questions and show how a rough estimate can be made of the labour and stock required on a given farm.

Q. 5. Describe the daily feeding and attendance required by a farm horse at work. What do you estimate the food and attendance to cost?

Q. 6. Explain the management of any breed of sheep with which you are familiar. At what age are the wethers (male tegs) sold, and how are they prepared for market?

These two questions were well answered.

Q. 7. What is the most suitable artificial food to be given to bullocks fattening upon grass towards the end of the summer? What quantities would you supply daily? On what grounds would you decide whether to sell the beasts off the grass, or to bring them into the yards for further fattening?

Candidates hardly recognised the poor quality and scouring tendency of the late growth of grass.

Q. 8. Discuss the advantages or otherwise in preparing food for stock (1) of slicing roots, (2) of chopping straw instead of first letting the cattle pick it over and using the residue as litter, (3) of steaming or otherwise cooking the food, (4) of mixing the food and leaving it in a heap for a few hours before feeding.

Frequently attempted and often well answered.

Q. 9. Discuss the returns from 100 gallons of milk (1) sold as new milk, (2) made into butter, (3) made into cheese.

Teachers might give a little more attention to the discussion of questions such as this. Such a problem as is involved in the question often confronts the farmer.

Q. 10. Name three breeds of poultry that are recognised as good winter layers. What treatment would you recommend to secure a supply of eggs in the winter months?

As was to be expected, a popular question and generally well answered.

SECTION D.—CHEMISTRY OF PLANT AND SOIL.

In this section the answers show an improvement, the defects arise in the main from a lack of preliminary chemical knowledge.

Q. 1. A plant is said to contain carbohydrates, fats, proteids, amides and essential oils. Explain the relationships, if any, and the composition of these bodies.

It is important that the student should be given at the outset a clear idea of the nature of these bodies, fundamental in agricultural chemistry.

Q. 2. What is meant by the "fixation of nitrogen"? Give some examples in which the fixation of nitrogen is brought about by living organisms.

It was curious to find how many candidates misinterpreted so classical a term as the "fixation of nitrogen," yet the distinction between elementary and compound nitrogen should be early impressed upon the agricultural student.

Q. 3. What substances are dissolved by rainwater (1) in passing through the air, (2) in percolating through the soil?

Rainwater gets but little carbonic acid from the air, until it comes in contact with soil gases rich in carbonic acid.

Q. 4. How do stones upon the surface of a soil affect (1) its temperature, (2) the amount of moisture it contains? Are there any disadvantages attached to removing the stones? How is it that on arable land there are many more stones on the surface than a few inches down, while on old grass land adjoining there may be no stones on the surface at all?

Often attempted and generally correctly answered.

Q. 5. What do you understand by specific heat? What are the thermal characteristics of a soil of low specific heat? Which substance has most influence on the specific heat of soil?

The question was largely avoided and was seldom well answered.

Q. 6. What is meant by the "weathering" of rocks and stones? Name the agents that induce weathering.

Every candidate, without exception, attempted this question, and the information supplied was usually sound. This is eminently satisfactory, as the subject is essentially "fundamental."

Q. 7. What are the principal effects of bare-fallowing? Under what circumstances would you recommend the practice?

Good answers were submitted, and considerable acquaintance was shown with the results obtained at Rothamsted.

Q. 8. Compare the amount of phosphoric acid in the soil with that removed by a crop of swedes, expressing the results in lb. per acre in each case. In the light of these figures explain why a crop may be greatly benefited by a dressing of superphosphate.

A question seldom attempted, though one perfect answer was submitted.

Q. 9. Name the elements that are essential to the growth of all crop-plants. In the experiments at Rothamsted very little increase of crop has been got where superphosphate of lime and ammonia salts were used separately, whereas a large increase has been obtained when both have been used together. Explain this result.

Some excellent answers were sent in to this question. These displayed a sound conception of the Law of Minimum.

Q. 10. Which of the three cereals—wheat, barley, oats—has the deepest roots? Which shows the least response to dressings of manure? What circumstances influence the root-range of farm-crops?

Very well answered on the whole.

SECTION E.—CHEMISTRY OF MANURES AND CROPS.

Here again an imperfect knowledge of chemistry was responsible for the worst mistakes.

Q. 1. Give various equations to explain the actions that go on (1) at once, (2) slowly and after some time, when quicklime is applied to the soil.

(1) Refers to slaking and carbonating, (2) to the slow action upon the clay, which results in the solution of potash. The first and easier half of the question elicited some good answers.

Q. 2. What risk of loss by washing out is there when sulphate of ammonia, superphosphate, and sulphate of potash respectively are applied to the soil? Explain the chemical reactions by which any of the three are retained in an insoluble condition.

Too often candidates argued that as the substances were soluble they must be in danger of washing through the soil.

Q. 3. What differences in chemical composition would you expect between farmyard manure (1) fresh from the yards, (2) after storage for three months in a tight heap, (3) after it had been repeatedly turned and stored for a long time?

Fairly answered as regards the nitrogenous material, but too little attention is paid to the oxidation of the non-nitrogenous carbon compounds of the straw.

Q. 4. Compare the effects of nitrate of soda as a nitrogenous manure with those of sulphate of ammonia, indicating the crops and soils for which one or the other is most suitable.

Fairly answered, though the general opinion that sulphate of ammonia is the better manure in wet seasons can hardly be justified.

Q. 5. If nitrate of soda is 12l. per ton, calculate the value of the unit of nitrogen, and from that calculate the value of a unit of phosphoric acid in bone meal, containing 3 per cent. of nitrogen and 20 per cent. of phosphoric acid, at 5l. 5s. per ton. From these unit values calculate the value of a guano containing 9 per cent. of ammonia and 34 per cent. of phosphate of lime.

Q. 8. How much superphosphate of lime, containing 30 per cent. of "soluble phosphate," would you require to use in order to supply 60 lb. of phosphoric acid? Under what circumstances would you recommend basic slag as a substitute for superphosphate?

These answers, involving calculations, showed an improvement on previous years.

Q. 6. What amount of nitrogen would you expect to be removed from an acre of land by the growth of a 4-quarter crop of wheat? How much nitrogen is supplied in a dressing of 2 cwt. of nitrate of soda per acre. What percentage of the nitrogen so applied would you expect the crop to take up, and what would be the fate of the remainder?

Candidates are expected to know the approximate amount of the chief manurial constituents contained in an average crop, and to show some acquaintance with Rothamsted results.

Q. 7. Much land has been laid down to grass in this country during the past 30 years. Would you expect that such land, if again brought under the plough, would grow better or worse crops of grain than it did originally? Give reasons for your answer.

Very intelligently attempted by many candidates.

Q. 9. What are the main differences in the character of manure furnished by (a) cows and (b) horses? How do you recommend that farmyard manure in an open dungstead should be treated so as to produce the best results?

The difference was generally understood, and suggestions as to treatment were generally sound.

Q. 10. Why is the potato crop said to be exhausting? What would you consider to be a suitable mixture of artificial manures for use on a moderate loam in the case of (a) a potato crop, where 12 tons per acre of farmyard manure is employed, (b) a rye-grass crop, where no farmyard manure is used?

The potato crop may be regarded as "exhausting" in that it is the only root crop, containing a large amount of plant food as compared with cereal crops, which is sold off the farm.

SECTION F.—CHEMISTRY OF ANIMALS AND FOODS.

Only two candidates presented themselves, but both had been well prepared.

HONOURS.

Results: 1st Class, 1; 2nd Class, 3; Failed, 2; Total, 6.

AGRICULTURE.—The two candidates who passed Part I. also worked a satisfactory subsidiary paper corresponding to Part II. They attended a *viva voce* examination held by Dr. Somerville on a farm. The candidates were perfectly familiar with agricultural routine, identified all the commoner grasses and clovers, and had an intimate acquaintance with weeds and parasitic diseases. Both candidates were recommended for a pass.

HORTICULTURE.—Two candidates wrote very good answers and attended for a *viva voce* examination and a subsidiary paper. Both candidates proved to be practically acquainted with gardening, were skilful in the routine operations of Horticulture, and were able to identify various diseased and abnormal specimens presented to them. Both candidates were recommende 1 for a pass, one in the First Class.

DAY EXAMINATION.

STAGE 2.

Results: 1st Class, 31; 2nd Class, 63; Failed, 6; Total, 100.

SECTION A.—TILLAGE AND CROPS.

Again generally sound sets of answers, showing evidence of good teaching.

Q. 1. What do you understand by a waterlogged soil, and by a "water-table"? Give an account of the results of putting drains into such a soil.

Almost invariably attempted and generally well answered.

Q. 2. What is meant by the warping of land, and where is it practised? Give a short account of the process.

A question like this should be left alone by candidates who have never seen the process or its results.

Q. 3. In the case of the turnip crop how long will it take a man (a) to hoe ("single") and (b) to top-and-tail an acre; and how long will it take a man and horse (a) to ridge ("stitch") (b) to sow and (c) to horse-hoe ("scuffle") an acre?

Produced very unequal answers.

Q. 4. How many tons of farmyard manure would you expect to get from the consumption as food and litter of 100 tons of straw ? What are the advantages and disadvantages of moss-litter as compared with straw as litter for stock ?

Not enough consideration seems to have been given to the question of the amount of manure normally made on a farm.

Q. 5. Give a rotation suitable for a strong clay farm, where the crops are chiefly marketed. Show what change you would recommend if the farmer resolved to make dairying his principal object.

Candidates hardly appreciated the point of the question, but described the rotation with which they happened to be familiar. Speaking generally, the teaching seems to be a little behind the times with regard to the many special-purpose rotations now in vogue.

Q. 6. Discuss the relative advantages and disadvantages of growing roots (turnips or mangolds) on the flat or on ridges. Do you consider it more advisable to apply the farmyard manure for the root crop in the spring or in the autumn, and why ?

Well answered.

Q. 7. Give a mixture of seeds suitable for a two years' ley on light land, stating quantities per acre and cost.

The general principles on which seed-mixtures should be prepared seemed to be well understood.

Q. 8. What varieties of thistle are usually met with on grass and arable land ? How should they be dealt with ?

The answers to this question were weak, yet it has been well dealt with in a recent leaflet issued by the Board of Agriculture. Students should have their attention directed to the Journal and the leaflets issued by the Board of Agriculture.

Q. 9. What is meant by the germinating capacity of seeds and how can it be tested in a simple manner ? What percentage of rye grass, clover, swede, and mangold seeds, respectively, ought to germinate ?

Candidates were too often mistaken in their estimates of the average germinating percentage of the seeds specified, many not knowing that mangold " seed " germinates more than 100 per cent.

Q. 10. Describe the method, that is now widely practised, of sprouting potatoes before they are planted. What is gained by this practice ; (1) with early potatoes ; (2) with main crops ?

Fairly answered.

SECTION B.—HORTICULTURE.

The remarks made on the Evening Examination apply equally to the Day Examination.

SECTION C.—ANIMAL HUSBANDRY.

Only a small number of candidates, but of generally good quality. It was noticeable that very few of them knew (Q. 10) that a cow may and ought to bring up more than one calf.

SECTIONS D, E, F.

While the general average of the answers was high, the compulsory questions set to test the candidates' knowledge of chemistry were indifferently answered, and in some cases omitted entirely, resulting in the disqualification of the candidate.

SECTION D.—CHEMISTRY OF PLANT AND SOIL.

Q. 1. What is the chemical composition of clay and by what reaction does it retain ammonium salts applied to the soil? How is it that clay soils are generally rich in potash?

Fairly answered.

Q. 2. Discuss the origin of the red sticky clay soil generally found upon the surface of a limestone or chalk formation.

Rarely attempted.

Q. 3. Describe the progress of the nutrition and development of the wheat plant from the time of its flowering to harvest. When does the plant cease to take any nutriment from the soil and from the air respectively?

The answers to this question were disappointing; students did not seem to have been taught how the plant accumulates material in the stem, &c., and subsequently transfers it to the grain, during which latter period it derives little nutriment from the air and practically none from the soil.

Q. 4. Give some examples of enzymes (unorganised ferments) in plants, and explain their function.

Rarely attempted.

Q. 5. Within what limits will the percentage of water vary in swedes, mangolds, potatoes and meadow hay? What loss of weight would you expect in the last-mentioned crop between the times of cutting and stacking?

The latter part of this question might be easily and simply illustrated in any class that meets during summer, but this presumably is seldom the case. The answers were not satisfactory.

Q. 6. What chemical elements are commonly met with in the ash of farm crops? Which of these are essential, and which are supplied in manures?

Attempted by all candidates, and usually with excellent results.

Q. 7. What change must sulphate of ammonia undergo before it can nourish a crop? Indicate the conditions that favour the change.

Supplied some excellent answers.

Q. 8. Other things being equal, is a dark or a light-coloured soil the warmer? Give reasons for your answer. Explain as fully as you can why a few branches laid over seedling plants will often prevent damage by frost.

The answers generally showed sound teaching.

Q. 9. Discuss the action of worms in soil.

Attempted by every candidate, and, on the whole, very satisfactorily.

Q. 10. What are the conditions (1) chemical, (2) physical, which lead to the formation of peat or a peaty soil? Show how your statements bear upon the methods employed for reclaiming peaty land.

The answers were generally sound, though they did not always show an appreciation of the sharp distinction to be made between aerobic and anaerobic decay of organic matter.

SECTION E.—CHEMISTRY OF MANURES AND CROPS.

Q. 1. What substances applied to the soil as manures, or for ameliorating purposes, contain lime? Which of them serve to, and which do not, increase the amount of what is commonly called "lime" in the soil?

Answers better, generally showing an appreciation of the fact that lime is wanted in the soil as a base, not as a calcium compound.

Q. 2. What substances have been proposed for employment as "fixers" of ammonia in cattle stalls? Give the reaction in each case. For what reasons has their employment not been satisfactory.

Answers generally sound.

Q. 3. What kind and quantities of plant-food are carried to the land in the rain and snow? What proportion of the total requirement of a crop of wheat would such plant food satisfy.

Answers rather vague as to quantities.

Q. 4. What are the principal effects of lime when applied to land that is being reclaimed from natural hill-pasture? It has been noticed that the first dressing of lime produces more striking effects than a second; give reasons for this result.

The effects of lime on accumulated humus generally well understood.

Q. 5. Compare the relative composition of the solid and liquid portions of farmyard manure.

Students ought to be impressed with the fact that the digestible nitrogenous matter of the food reappears in the liquid manure as urea, etc., in an active form, whereas the fæces only contain the solid undigested and therefore slow acting residues of the food.

Q. 6. A farmer sells a 40-ton crop of mangolds, and is bound by covenant to replace the fertility thus removed. How much farmyard manure, or what mixture of artificial manures, would be a fair equivalent?

Candidates did not always understand this question, but described a suitable manure for the mangold crop.

Q. 7. What is the function of phosphoric acid in the nutrition of the plant? For what crops and under what circumstances are phosphatic manures most likely to be valuable?

Not often attempted, but some good answers were supplied.

Q. 8. Discuss the reasons for the great increase in fertility brought about on certain poor clay lands under grass by a single application of basic slag.

It was disappointing to find that few candidates realised that the improved fertility is closely associated with the accumulation of nitrogen by the clovers, &c., stimulated to luxuriant growth by the phosphoric acid and lime of the basic slag.

Q. 9. What is the difference in the character and composition of steamed bones, boiled bones, and natural bones? In the case of the boiled and unboiled bones, which would decay the more slowly, and why?

Generally attempted. Most candidates were alive to the retarding influence exerted by fat on the decay of the bones.

Q. 10. Show by the unit system of valuation what would be a reasonable price per ton of sulphate of ammonia when nitrate of soda is selling at 12l. per ton.

Invariably attempted, and in most cases, successfully.

SECTION F.—CHEMISTRY OF ANIMALS AND FOODS.

Q. 1. What is the chemical composition of starch and what changes does it undergo during digestion? How does cellulose differ from starch in its composition and in its properties? Is cellulose digested by animals?

Fairly answered, though no mention was made of the part played by bacteria in the intestines of herbivorous animals.

Q. 2. What acid is produced when milk turns sour? From what constituent of the milk does it arise, and how does it bring about the curdling of the milk?

Fairly answered.

Q. 3. The usual analysis of a feeding stuff states the percentage of fat, albuminoids, carbohydrates, fibre, ash and sand. What do these terms represent? What other information is necessary in order to arrive at an estimate of the food value of the material?

The answers to this question were rather disappointing; students should be made to appreciate the fact that fat in an analysis represents the matter soluble in ether, albuminoids the nitrogen × 6·25, assumptions often involving considerable errors. Again, it is the digestible constituents that alone are of value to the animal.

Q. 4. Meat meal is used both as a food for poultry and as a manure for crops, explain how it supplies nourishment in each case. Why cannot starch serve this double purpose?

A simple question, though requiring intelligent treatment. Always well answered where attempted.

Q. 5. Linseed cake containing 30 per cent. albuminoids, 8 per cent. oil, and 36 per cent. carbohydrates is offered at 9*l*. per ton; what should be the price of another sample of linseed cake containing 26 per cent. albuminoids, 12 per cent. oil, and 32 per cent. carbohydrates? Show how you arrive at your answer?

All answers were good, and most were excellent.

Q. 6. What amount of water does a two-year-old shorthorn steer require daily? Assuming that its food consists of a stone of hay and half a stone of cake daily, what weight of swedes would it have to consume in order to get a sufficient quantity of water?

Very intelligently treated by the few candidates who attempted it.

Q. 7. In feeding animals, what is the value of mixing with the food a little spice or other condiments? What substances are commonly used in this way? Do they increase the digestibility of the food? Has malt any special properties in this way, or any food value greater than that of the barley from which it was made?

Well answered.

Q. 8. What is the average increase in weight per diem of a fattening bullock? How much dry food (approximate composition to be stated) is necessary to obtain this increase? What will be the approximate composition of the increase (1) in the early stages, (2) when nearly fat?

Seldom attempted, but the few answers were excellent.

Q. 9. How does butter fat differ from most other fats? Is this fat derived directly from fat in the food or can it be made by the cow out of other materials in the food?

Too often candidates supposed that butter fat is the only complex glyceride.

Q. 10. What is the approximate composition, as regards fat, of the mixed milk of a shorthorn dairy herd? How does the fat vary (a) with the stage in the period of lactation, (b) with the season of the year, (c) with the time of day?

Without exception, all the answers were perfect or nearly so. This result, it may be assumed, reflects the great interest being taken in dairy farming, and in the State regulations affecting the industry.

SCIENCE EXAMINATIONS, 1907.

SUMMARIES OF THE RESULTS.

Details of Successes and Failures in each Stage of each Subject at the Evening Science Examinations, 1907.

SUBJECT.	Honours 1st Class	Honours 2nd Class	Honours Failures	Honours Total	Stage 3. 1st Class	Stage 3. 2nd Class	Stage 3. Failures	Stage 3. Total	Stage 2. 1st Class	Stage 2. 2nd Class	Stage 2. Failures	Stage 2. Total	Stage 1. 1st Class	Stage 1. 2nd Class	Stage 1. Failures	Stage 1. Total
I. Practical Plane and Solid Geometry	10	16	21	47	36	91	141	268	264	431	298	993	574	602	752	1,928
II. Machine Construction and Drawing	4	6	85	95	106	269	375	750	692	1,685	1,496	3,873	1,760	1,843	1,850	5,453
III. Building Construction and Drawing																
IV. Naval Architecture	8	25	247	280	177	485	383	1,045	338	1,122	924	2,384	1,322	1,035	567	2,924
V. Mathematics	5	7	60	72	35	100	94	229	70	169	46	285	129	112	59	300
Vp. Practical Mathematics	—	—	—	—	—	—	—	—	See below.				595	1,182	1,147	2,924
VIa. Theoretical Mechanics (Solids)					76	104	230	410	152	769	502	1,423	141	193	117	451
VIa. „ (Fluids)	—	2	1	3	18	75	39	132	157	338	192	687	73	84	28	185
VIb. Applied Mechanics	1	5	18	24	12	40	20	72	108	173	52	333	638	637	560	1,835
VII. Sound, Light, and Heat					9	131	128	268	119	672	559	1,350	130	147	119	396
VIIIa. Sound	—	1	—	1	3	12	30	45	91	159	70	320	—	—	—	—
VIIIb. Light	—	1	—	1	6	15	16	37	63	211	123	397	—	—	—	—
VIIIc. Heat					17	46	51	114	79	415	173	667	—	—	—	—
IX. Magnetism and Electricity	1	1	6	8	21	56	53	130	327	463	324	1,114	870	583	566	2,019
X. Inorganic Chemistry	4	10	13	27	56	204	200	460	204	901	696	1,801	739	671	636	2,046
Xp. „ (Practical)	2	6	9	17	45	187	444	676	323	711	539	1,573	356	494	504	1,354
XI. Organic Chemistry	†	See	X.	—	4	9	21	34	53	119	111	283	57	119	133	309
XIp. „ (Practical)	†	See	Xp.	—	18	15	41	74	45	76	87	208	89	55	60	204
XII. Geology	6	5	7	18	12	23	14	49	54	76	46	176	58	70	44	172
XIII. Mineralogy	—	2	—	2	1	5	4	10	15	23	7	45	15	14	3	32
XIV. Human Physiology					8	29	22	59	111	485	198	794	355	466	235	1,056
XV. General Biology					—	—	—	—	13	33	31	77	12	27	18	57
XV. „ Stage I., Section I.	—	—	4	4									*106	—	25	130
XVI. Zoology				2	3	3	—	6	8	23	14	45	33	28	4	65
XVII. Botany	1	3	10	13	8	25	19	52	89	274	76	439	194	291	142	627
XVIII. Principles of Mining	22	74	80	176	71	166	190	427	121	462	187	770	232	396	339	967
XIX. Metallurgy	1	2	6	9	11	19	25	55	28	78	40	146	43	35	41	119
XIXp. „ (Practical)					16	28	21	65	24	50	36	110	33	28	16	77
XX. Navigation	1	1	—	1					8	22	9	39	3	15	4	22
XXI. Nautical and Spherical Astronomy									4	12	1	17				
XXII. Steam	—	4	19	23	52	63	132	247	316	484	189	989	485	501	350	1,336

SUBJECT															
XXIII. Physiography, except Stage I., Section I.	—	—	—	—	—	9	14	26	123	106	88	317	87	81	52	220
XXIII. Physiography, Stage I., Section I.	—	—	—	—	—	—	—	—	—	—	—	—	*70	—	101	171
XXIV. Agricultural Science and Rural Economy †	1	3	2	6	—	—	—	—	28	91	29	148	19	10	13	42
XXV. Hygiene	1	3	20	24	23	72	38	133	214	755	73	1,042	443	634	118	1,195
XXVI. Elementary Science of Common Life	—	—	—	—	—	—	—	—	—	—	—	—	181	121	64	366
TOTAL	67	177	610	854	847	2,281	2,745	5,873	4,241	11,388	7,216	22,845	9,842	10,476	8,667	28,985

* Passes. † Honours in Subjects X. and XI. and in Subjects Xp. and XIp. are combined.

SUBJECT.	Stages.	1st Class.	2nd Class.	Failures.	Total.
V. Mathematics	1	515	1,245	1,113	2,873
	2	472	898	530	1,900
	3	225	511	215	951
	4	4	3	6	13
Hons. Div. I.	5	5	52	53	110
	6	81	211	132	424
	7	25	52	26	103
Hons. Div. II.		—	6	2	8
		—	—	1	1
TOTAL		1,327	2,978	2,078	6,383

Total Number of Candidates in all Subjects . . . . 64,940.

Total Number of Successes in all Subjects . { 1st Class . 16,324 } 43,624.
{ 2nd Class . 27,300 }

N.B.—These figures include the exercises received from the Isle of Man and Channel Islands, but not those from Malta, Cape Colony, Natal, and New Zealand.

236

Details of Successes and Failures in each Stage of each Subject at the Day Science Examinations, 1907.

SUBJECT.	STAGE 2.				STAGE 1.			
	1st Class.	2nd Class.	Failures.	Total.	1st Class.	2nd Class.	Failures.	Total.
I. Practical Plane and Solid Geometry	21	22	16	59	44	36	31	111
V. Mathematics	—	—	—	See below.	—	—	—	—
VIa. Theoretical Mechanics (Solids)	15	29	19	63	18	53	46	117
VIb. Theoretical Mechanics (Fluids)	8	4	—	12	39	32	22	93
VIII. Sound, Light, and Heat	—	—	—	—	16	42	44	102
VIIIa. Sound	5	7	5	17	—	—	—	—
VIIIb. Light	5	12	15	32	—	—	—	—
VIIIc. Heat	13	46	39	98	—	—	—	—
IX. Magnetism and Electricity	14	45	64	123	55	38	17	110
X. Inorganic Chemistry	7	76	84	167	179	77	25	281
Xp. ,, ,, (Practical)	24	55	93	172	38	23	15	76
XIV. Human Physiology	22	49	11	82	101	93	34	228
XVII. Botany	13	27	10	50	39	34	21	94
XXIII. Physiography, except Stage I., Section I.	4	2	1	7	15	20	10	45
XXIII. Physiography, Stage 1, Section I.	—	—	—	—	*17	—	23	40
XXIV. Agricultural Science and Rural Economy	31	63	6	100	—	—	—	—
XXV. Hygiene	46	138	12	196	84	128	6	218
XXVI. Elementary Science of Common Life	—	—	—	—	167	62	18	247
Total	228	575	375	1,178	812	638	312	1,762

* Passes.

SUBJECT.	Stage.	1st Class.	2nd Class.	Failures.	Total.
V. Mathematics	1	195	287	101	583
	2	70	401	133	604
	3	26	47	21	94
	4	2	—	—	2
	5	6	12	10	28
	6	1	1	2	4
	7	—	1	—	1
Total	—	300	749	267	1,316

Total Number of Candidates in all Subjects - - - - 4,256.

Total Number of Successes in all Subjects { 1st Class - - 1,340 } 3,302.
{ 2nd Class - - 1,962 }

COMPETITIONS FOR ROYAL EXHIBITIONS, NATIONAL
SCHOLARSHIPS, AND FREE STUDENTSHIPS, 1907.

Competitions for Royal Exhibitions, National Scholarships, and Free Studentships, 1907.

NAMES OF SUCCESSFUL CANDIDATES.

Name.	Age.	Occupation.	Address.	Award.
Frew, William F. -	18	Student - -	Plymouth - -	
Morgan, George E. -	20	Engine Fitter's Apprentice.	Portsmouth - -	
Grigg, Ernest - -	19	Shipwright's Apprentice.	Southsea - -	
Steed, Ernest A. -	19	Engine Fitter's Apprentice.	Devonport - -	Royal Exhibitions.
Curtis, William E. -	17	Student - -	London - - -	
Carter, Harry - -	19	Student - -	Triangle, Halifax -	
Turner, Henry W. -	20	Engine Fitter's Apprentice.	Portsmouth - -	
Judge, Arthur W. -	19	Engine Fitter's Apprentice.	Portsmouth - -	
Regnauld, Alfred -	21	Engineer's Apprentice.	London - -	
Rogers, Frederick R.	20	Engine Fitter's Apprentice.	Devonport - -	National Scholarships for Mechanics (Group A).
Bartlett, Colin - -	21	Shipwright's Apprentice.	Plymouth - -	
Marks, Fred H. G.	20	Shipwright's Apprentice.	Plymouth - -	
*Thomas, Joe H. -	17	Student - -	Ovenden, Halifax -	
Symns, Samuel Ll. -	23	Student - -	London - - -	
Bumpus, Frank A. -	21	Engine Fitter -	Birmingham - -	Free Studentships for Mechanics (Group A).
†Frost, Reginald G. M.	19	Shipwright's Apprentice.	Plymouth - -	
†Stedman, Ernest W.	18	Engine Fitter's Apprentice.	Sheerness - -	
Tarrant, Arthur G. -	19	Student - -	London - -	
Hill, John - -	19	Laboratory Assistant.	Glasgow - -	National Scholarships for Physics (Group B).
Macpherson, John -	22	Student - -	Manchester - -	
Holmes, Arthur -	17	Student - -	Gateshead - -	
White, William -	16	Student - -	Glasgow - -	
Simmons, William C.	19	Student - -	Southampton -	Free Studentship for Physics (Group B).
Illingworth, Stewart R.	21	Demonstrator -	Shipley - -	
Griffiths, Hugh -	15	Student - -	Middlesbrough -	National Scholarships for Chemistry (Group C).
Eggington, Alfred T.	19	Student - -	Ibstock, Leicester -	
Caruth, Alexander	27	Teacher - -	Birkenhead - -	
Burridge, Leonard W.	18	Student - -	London - -	
Knott, Frank A. -	17	Student - -	London - - -	Free Studentship for Chemistry (Group C).
Bateson, Ernest -	24	Teacher - -	Bradford, Yorks -	National Scholarships for Biology (Group D).
Sharpe, Joseph -	27	Weaver - -	Burnley - - -	
Rushton, Wilfred -	25	Weaver - -	Burnley - - -	
Cunnington, Cecil H.	18	Student - -	London - - -	National Scholarships for Geology (Group E).
Eastwood, Tom -	18	Weaver - -	Burnley - - -	
Wayland, Edward J.	19	Clerk - -	London - - -	

* Extra National Scholarship transferred from Group C.
† Extra Free Studentships transferred from Groups D and E.

239

COMPETITION FOR WHITWORTH SCHOLARSHIPS
AND EXHIBITIONS, 1907.

Competition for Whitworth Scholarships and Exhibitions, 1907.

NAMES OF SUCCESSFUL CANDIDATES.

Name.	Age	Occupation.	Address.	Value of Scholarships and Exhibitions awarded.
I. SCHOLARSHIPS (tenable for 3 years).				
Rowse, Arthur A. -	22	Engineer - - - -	London - - -	£125 a year each.
Perryman, Nelson J. -	18	Engine Fitter's Apprentice	Portsmouth - -	
Hudson, George - -	19	Engine Fitter's Apprentice	Portsmouth - -	
Warren, James - -	19	Engine Fitter's Apprentice	Portsmouth - -	
II. EXHIBITIONS (tenable for 1 year).				£
Judge, Arthur W. -	19	Engine Fitter's Apprentice	Portsmouth - -	50
Hyde, James H. -	20	Engineer's Apprentice -	Leytonstone - -	50
Steed, Ernest A. -	19	Engine Fitter's Apprentice	Devonport - -	50
Begg, Alfred J. -	20	Assistant Artificer - -	Plumstead - -	50
Dewhurst, Maurice R. -	21	Engineer's Pupil - -	London - - -	50
Given, Ralph D. -	25	Draughtsman - - -	Edinburgh - -	50
Bumpus, Frank A.	21	Engine Fitter - - -	Birmingham - -	50
Iliffe, Reginald J.	25	Draughtsman - - -	Liverpool - -	50
Symns, Samuel Ll.	23	Student (late Engineer's Apprentice)	London - - -	50
Morris, Frederick	18	Engine Fitter's Apprentice	Portsmouth - -	50
Johnson, William P. -	24	Student (late Draughtsman)	Kelsall Hill, Chester	50
Johnstone, Thomas W.	19	Engine Fitter's Apprentice	Neyland - - -	50
Neal, James H. -	21	Engine Fitter's Apprentice	Devonport - -	50
Mawson, Hubert -	23	Student (late Engine Fitter)	Hunslet, Leeds -	50
Stedman, Ernest W. -	18	Engine Fitter's Apprentice	Sheerness - -	50
Morrison, Francis -	22	Engineer - - - -	Aberdeen- - -	50
Milner, Richard G. -	22	Draughtsman - - -	Plumstead - -	50
Hutchison, Alexander -	22	Engineer's Apprentice -	Glasgow - - -	50
Middleton, Horace J. -	23	Engineer - - - -	Forest Gate - -	50
Phillips, Arthur T. -	19	Engineer's Apprentice -	Barking, Essex -	50
Macgregor, William -	25	Draughtsman - - -	Greenock - -	50
McCarthy, Michael J. C.	20	Engine Fitter's Apprentice	Sheerness - -	50
Wright, Harry T. -	22	Student (late Draughtsman)	London - - -	50
McFadyen, Alexander-	24	Demonstrator in Engineering.	Lasswade, Midlothian	50
Rendell, Frederick G. -	20	Boiler Maker's Apprentice	Portsmouth - -	50
Blight, John H. -	18	Engine Fitter's Apprentice	Devonport - -	50
Mann, Frederick C. D.	22	Engineer - - - -	Hayes, Kent -	50
Collyer, John E. -	18	Engineer's Apprentice -	South Woolwich -	50
Baker, Bernard - -	19	Engine Fitter - - -	Southsea - - -	50
Brown, Leonard C.	24	Draughtsman - - -	Wolverton - -	50

www.ingramcontent.com/pod-product-compliance
Lightning Source LLC
LaVergne TN
LVHW012207040326
832903LV00003B/179